James Gray & Billy Gray

STALLCUP'S®

Generator, Transformer, Motor, and Compressor

based on the NEC® and related standards

2023

www.grayboyinc.com

Written by James Gray Stallcup
Design, illustrations, layout & cover by Billy Gray Stallcup

Copyright© 2023 by GRAYBOY, Inc.

Published by GRAYBOY, Inc.
PO Box 821757
North Richland Hills, Texas 76182
Phone: 817-454-5068

Notice Concerning Liability: Publication of this work is for the purpose of circulating information and opinion among those concerned for fire and electrical safety and related subjects. While every effort has been made to achieve a work of high quality, neither the authors or contributors to this work guarantee the accuracy or completeness of or assume any liability in connection with the information and opinions contained in this work. GRAYBOY and the authors and contributors shall in no event be liable for any personal injury, property, or other damages of any nature whatsoever, whether special, indirect, consequential, or compensatory, directly or indirectly resulting from the publication, use of or reliance upon this work.

This work is published with the understanding that GRAYBOY and the authors and contributors to this work are supplying information and opinion but are not attempting to render engineering or other professional services. If such services are required, the assistance of an appropriate professional should be sought.

National Electrical Code® and NEC® are registered trademarks of the National Fire Protection Association, Inc.
STALLCUP'S® is a registered trademark of GRAYBOY, Inc.

ISBN: 978-1-62270-355-5

Printed in the United States of America
01   02   03   04   05   06   07   5   4   3   2   1

Introduction

This book is intended for all who are interested and work in a daily capacity with these subjects. It is also designed to help the student in his search for learning. For this reason, the book is profusely illustrated to help visualize for the reader the points referenced in the text while joining theory and practice into a closer relationship.

For user friendly and easy study, Stallcup's *Generator, Transformer, Motor, and Compressor* has been divided into three parts and they are as follows:

Part I: Generators

Part II: Transformers

Part III: Motors

Review questions have been provided at the end of each chapter. To purchase the answers to the review questions, please go to the GRAYBOY website at www.grayboyinc.com.

Note: Students and users of this workbook may find a problem that is not worked properly. Not often, but if and when they do, they will show their skills and ability to work the problem correctly from the knowledge obtained in viewing this workbook.

Table of Contents

Part One

Generators

From the small standby unit to the largest hydroelectric plant, today's world demands speed, light, and power. The generator is the device that converts mechanical energy into electrical energy and supplies power where needed. The generator can be designed and installed to provide the starting point for power to an electrical service, as well as the backup power when things go wrong.

Engine-driven generators that are fueled by diesel, gasoline, or natural gas commonly produce and provide alternative emergency or standby power when normal power systems fail. Gas-turbine generators are also used to create such power.

A facility with engine-driven generators provides the necessary power for human safety as well as the protection of property, while maintaining continuous operation of specific types of equipment.

The design requirements for selecting an on-site generator differ depending upon the generator's use.

> **For example,** generators can be utilized as emergency systems, standby power systems, or other power sources when used in health care facilities.

A portable generator can provide power for construction, remodeling, maintenance, or making repairs on equipment.

Part I covers the theory of generators, the various types, and the rules and regulations of the *National Electrical Code*® pertaining to their design and installation.

Magnetism and Electromagnetism

Magnetism is one of the fundamental forces involved in the use of electricity. Therefore, it is imperative that electricians, technicians, and maintenance personnel obtain a good understanding and knowledge of the subject.

THEORY OF MAGNETS

A magnet is an object that attracts magnetic substances such as iron or steel, by producing an external magnetic field that reacts with a magnetic substance. A permanent magnet maintains an almost constant magnetic field without the application of any magnetizing force. As an example, for many years, some magnetized substances show practically no loss of magnetic strength and therefore maintain such strength.

MAGNETIC FIELDS

A magnetic field is assumed to consist of invisible lines of force that leave the north pole of a magnet and enter the south pole. The direction of this force is used only to establish rules and references for such operation.

This action is indicated, for example, by the fact that a north pole will repel another north pole and be attracted by a south pole and vice versa.

NATURAL MAGNETS

A natural magnet is called a lodestone, or "leading stone." The natural magnet gets its name from being used by early navigators to determine direction.

When a lodestone is freely suspended, one end always points in a northerly direction. Because of this action, one of the lodestones is called the "north-seeking" and the other the "south-seeking" end. The terms are better known as the north and south poles. The reason that a freely suspended magnet assumes a north-south position is that the earth is a large magnet and its magnetic field exists over its entire surface.

For example, the magnetic lines of force leave the earth at a point near the south pole and enters near the north pole. Therefore, since the north pole of a magnet is attracted to the south pole of another magnet and repels another north pole, one can understand that the magnetic pole near the geographic north pole of the earth is actually a south pole, and that the pole near the geographic south pole of the earth is actually a north pole. (See Figure 1-1)

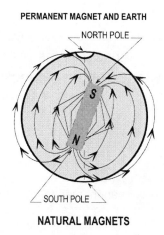

PERMANENT MAGNET AND EARTH

NATURAL MAGNETS

Figure 1-1. The above illustrates the magnetic field of a magnet and its relationship to the earth's magnetic field.

PERMANENT MAGNETS

Certain metallic alloys such as hard steel have the ability to retain magnetism and are able to do so due to the fact they are difficult to magnetize. Hard steel is more difficult to magnetize than soft iron because of the internal friction among the atoms. If such a substance is placed in a strong magnetic field and struck with a hammer, the atoms become aligned with the field. When the substance is removed from the magnetic field, it retains its magnetism and becomes a permanent magnet.

ELECTROMAGNETS

A bar magnet can be pushed into a coil of wire (solenoid) and current flows in a certain direction as the magnet moves into the coil. However, as soon as the magnet stops moving,

the current flow stops. When the magnet is withdrawn, the current reverses and the current flows in the opposite direction. The current induced in the coil is caused by the field of the magnet as it cuts across the turns of wire in the coil.

> **Theory Tip:** If a piece of soft iron is placed in the magnetic field of a permanent magnet, it takes on the same characteristics as the permanent magnet and becomes magnetized. **(See Figure 1-2)**

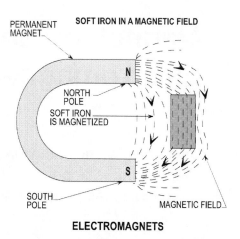

SOFT IRON IN A MAGNETIC FIELD

ELECTROMAGNETS

Figure 1-2. The above illustrates a permanent magnet, magnetizing a piece of soft iron that is placed in its magnetic field.

Figure 1-3(a) illustrates that the north pole of the coil is adjacent to the north pole of the bar magnet and opposes the insertion of the magnet into the coil. However, the instant that the magnet begins to move out of the coil, current induced in the coil changes to the opposite direction. This is due to the field of the coil being reversed.

Note, the south pole of the coil field is now adjacent to the north pole of the bar magnet and opposes the withdrawal of the magnet as shown in Figure 1-3(b).

MAGNETIC FIELD

The field of force existing between the poles of a magnet is called a magnetic field. The lines of force of this field may be demonstrated by placing a stiff paper over a magnet and sprinkling iron filings on the paper.

See Figure 1-4 for a detailed illustration of the lines of force for magnetic circuits. A magnetic force, known as magnetic flux, travels from north to south in invisible lines.

For example, if a soft iron bar is placed across the poles of a magnet, almost all the magnetic lines of force (flux) go through the bar, and the bar becomes magnetized. (See Figure 1-2)

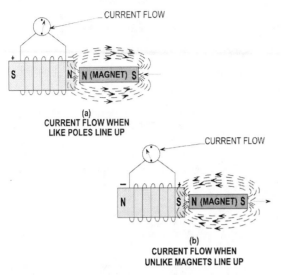

CURRENT FLOW

(a)
**CURRENT FLOW WHEN
LIKE POLES LINE UP**

CURRENT FLOW

(b)
**CURRENT FLOW WHEN
UNLIKE MAGNETS LINE UP**

ELECTROMAGNETS

Figure 1-3(a) and (b). The current flows in a magnet when magnets are induced by a changing magnetic field.

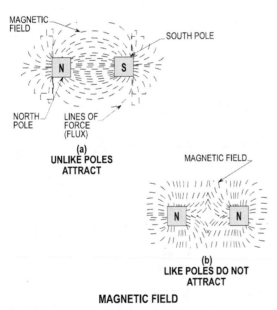

(a)
**UNLIKE POLES
ATTRACT**

(b)
**LIKE POLES DO NOT
ATTRACT**

MAGNETIC FIELD

Figure 1-4. The magnetic lines of force between the poles of a magnet are called a magnetic field.

ELECTROMAGNETICS

An electric current flowing through a conductor creates a magnetic field around the conductor. When a wire is grasped in the left hand with the thumb pointing from negative to positive poles, the magnetic field around the conductor is in the direction that the fingers are pointing.

Note, this can be easily demonstrated by the use of the left-hand rule, which is based on the true direction of current flow. (See Figure 1-5)

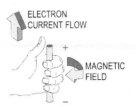

ELECTROMAGNETICS

Figure 1-5. When a wire is grasped in the left hand, the thumb points from negative to positive poles, one finger points in the direction of the magnetic field and the index finger in the direction of movement.

When a current-carrying conductor is formed into a loop, the loop takes on the properties of a magnet.

For example, one side of the loop will be a north pole and the other side will be a south pole.

Where a soft-iron core is placed in the loop, the magnetic lines of force will magnetize the iron core and it becomes a magnet. When a wire is formed into a coil and connected to a source of power, the fields of the separate turns join and travel through the entire coil. (See Figure 1-6)

Theory Tip: When a coil is grasped in the left hand with the fingers pointing in the direction of current flow, that is, from negative to positive, the thumb will point toward the north pole of the coil.

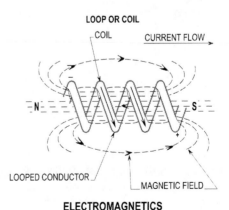

ELECTROMAGNETICS

Figure 1-6. When a conductor is formed into a coil and connected to a source of power, the magnetic fields of each separate turn add and travel through the entire coil.

ELECTROMAGNETIC INDUCTION

The transfer of electric energy from one circuit to another without the aid of electric connections is known as induction. When electric energy is transferred by means of a magnetic field, it is known as electromagnetic induction.

Electromagnetic induction occurs whenever there is a relative movement between a conductor and a magnetic field, that is, when the conductor is cutting across magnetic lines of force and is not moving parallel to them.

Note, this relative movement may be accomplished in two ways (1) by using a stationary conductor and a moving field and (2) by using a moving conductor with a stationary field. A moving field may be created by a moving magnet or by changing the value of the current in an electromagnet. **(See Figure 1-7)**

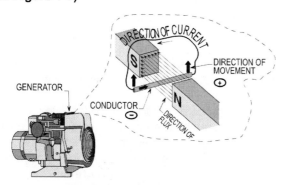

ELECTROMAGNETIC INDUCTION

Figure 1-7. The above illustrates the transfer of electric energy by means of a magnetic field and conductor. This process is called electromagnetic induction.

GENERATOR ACTION

Figure 1-8 illustrates the basic principle action of a generator. As the conductor moves through the field, a voltage is induced in it.

Note, the same action occurs if the conductor is stationary and the magnetic field is moved. The direction of the induced voltage depends on the direction of the field and can be verified by applying the left-hand rule for generators. **(See Figure 1-9)**

Theory Tip: When using the left-hand rule for generators, extend the thumb, forefinger, and middle finger of the left-hand so that they are at right angles to one another. Then turn the hand so that the index finger points in the direction of the magnetic field and the thumb points in the direction of the conductor movement. The middle finger will then be pointing in the direction of the induced voltage and flow of current.

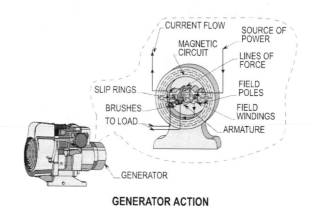

GENERATOR ACTION

Figure 1-8. The above illustrates the basic action that takes place in generators to produce electricity.

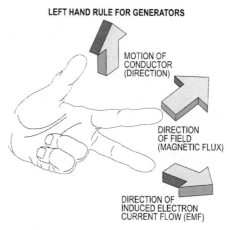

GENERATOR ACTION

Figure 1-9. The above illustration represents the left hand rule for generators.

TYPES OF POWER

All electric power supplied by generators or batteries may be divided into two general groups as follows:

(1) Alternating-current (AC) unit

(2) Direct-current (DC) unit

ALTERNATING-CURRENT (AC) POWER

Alternating-current power sources feed electricity directly to the electrical network to which the lights, motors, appliances, and other equipment are connected. Generators are usually used between the power source and the line instead of batteries. However, in most cases, a battery is used for engine-starting purposes only.

Generators and batteries with additional equipment can be utilized to produce the following voltage levels.

(1) 1000 volts or less
 • Single-phase
   120 volts, two-wire
   120/240 volts, three-wire
   240 volts, two-wire
 • Three-phase
   240 volts, three-wire
   120/208 volts, four-wire
   120/240 volts, four-wire
   480 volts, three-wire
   277/480 volts, four-wire
   600 volts, three-wire

(2) Over 1000 volts
 • Three-phase
   2,400 volts
   4,160 volts
   12,470 volts
   13,200 volts or 13,800 volts

See Figures 1-10(a) and **(b)** for a detailed illustration of the different voltages supplying electrical systems.

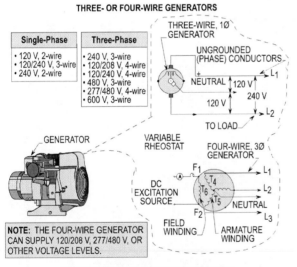

THREE- OR FOUR-WIRE GENERATORS

ALTERNATING-CURRENT (AC) POWER

Figure 1-10(a). The above illustrates the most popular voltages used at 1000 volts or less.

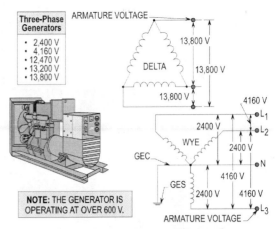

ALTERNATING-CURRENT (AC) POWER

Figure 1-10(b). The above illustrates the most popular voltages used to supply loads requiring voltages rated over 1000 volts.

DIRECT-CURRENT (DC) POWER

Direct-current power sources feed electricity directly to the line to which the lights, motors, appliances, and other equipment are connected. There are limitations to direct-current power sources.

> **For example,** they will only operate ordinary light bulbs, motors, and appliances that are designed for direct current, and motors of the universal type. Direct-current power may also feed fluorescent bulbs, but only if they are installed with a special converter. Because, direct-current power sources cannot operate any equipment designed for alternating current, they are not usable as a standby for most emergency systems. **(See Figure 1-11)**

> **Generator Tip:** Direct-current power sources are normally used to supply special types of equipment including accessories, etc.

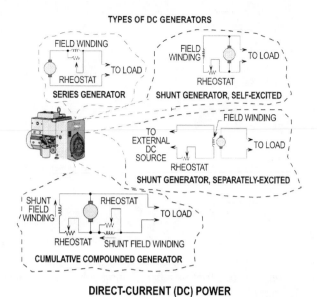

Figure 1-11. The above illustrates the different types of direct-current generators. For more details, see **Chapter 2**.

Chapter 1: Magnetism and Electromagnetism

Section   Answer

1. A magnet is an object that _____ magnetic substances such as iron or   _____ _____
   steel by producing an external magnetic field that reacts with a magnetic
   substance.
   (a) attracts   (b) repels
   (c) forces   (d) none of the above   .

2. A magnetic field is assumed to consist of invisible lines of force that leave   _____ _____
   the _____ pole of a magnet and enter the south pole.
   (a) polar   (b) south
   (c) north   (d) none of the above

3. The field of force existing between the poles of a magnet is called a(n)_____   _____ _____
   field.
   (a) invisible   (b) magnetic
   (c) core   (d) pole

4. The transfer of electric energy from one circuit to another without the aid of   _____ _____
   electric connections is known as _____.
   (a) magnetism   (b) electromagnetism
   (c) induction   (d) none of the above

5. When electric energy is transferred by means of a magnetic field, it is known   _____ _____
   as _____ induction.
   (a) electromagnetic   (b) magnetic
   (c) invisible   (d) none of the above

6. Low voltage is considered 1000 volts or less while high voltage is considered   _____ _____
   over _____ volts.
   (a) 500   (b) 750
   (c) 600   (d) 1000

7. The voltage to ground on 4160 volt is considered _____ volts.   _____ _____
   (a) 240   (b) 480
   (c) 1000   (d) 2400

8. The voltage on 13,800 volt corner ground is considered _____ volts.   _____ _____
   (a) 8000   (b) 12,470
   (c) 13,200   (d) 13,800

9. Unlike poles attract while like does do not _____.   _____ _____
   (a) attract   (b) pull
   (c) both (a) and (b)

10. A permanent magnet will set up a magnetic field in a piece of soft _____.   _____ _____
    (a) rock   (b) PVC
    (c) iron   (d) clad

2

Generator Principles

The conversion of mechanical to electrical energy occurs in the generator by the rotation of a magnetic field that intersects the windings and induces a voltage. In generators, the growth and collapse of the magnetic field is accomplished by physically moving or revolving the fixed field, called the primary winding, past the conductors (secondary winding). Naturally, the stronger the field, the higher the voltage and the weaker the field, the lower the generated voltage. The contents of this chapter deals with the basic operation of generators.

BASIC OPERATION OF GENERATORS

The basic AC generator consists of a loop of wire that is free to rotate in a magnetic field. The loop of wire is called the armature, and the magnetic field is called the field. The armature is turned by an element called the prime mover. The prime mover can be water, steam, or wind turbines, an engine, or an electric motor depending on the application and use.

Note, the terms *armature* and *field* are electrical terms. Electrically, the armature windings are those windings that are connected to the load. The field windings are those windings that are used to create the magnetic field. The rotor always rotates and the stator is always stationary.

The armature loop is connected to slip rings. Such slip rings have an electrical conducting brush that slips over the surface of the ring as the armature rotates through the field. **(See Figure 2-1)**

As the armature rotates in the field, a voltage is generated that can be utilized to supply a transformer and a switchgear that can be used to step the voltage up or down. Loads are then supplied by the switchgear voltage or the transformer voltage. **(See Figure 2-2)**

Note, AC generators are usually referred to as alternators. Alternators generate most of the electrical power used in modern-day electrical systems.

THE ARMATURE OF AN AC GENERATOR MAKING A COMPLETE TURN THROUGH THE MAGNETIC FIELD

- When the armature reaches position 2, the armature (loop of wire) is moving perpendicular to the magnetic field; therefore, it is cutting the maximum number of lines per second.

- As the loop rotates past position 2, the voltage drops off since the loops are not perpendicular to the magnetic field, therefore cutting few lines of flux.

- As the armature reaches position 3, its motion is again parallel to the field and the output voltage is once more zero, the same as position one.

- As the armature rotates from position 3 to 4, the voltage again reaches a maximum value.

- When the armature completes its turn past position 4, the voltage drops to zero again. No lines of flux are cut.

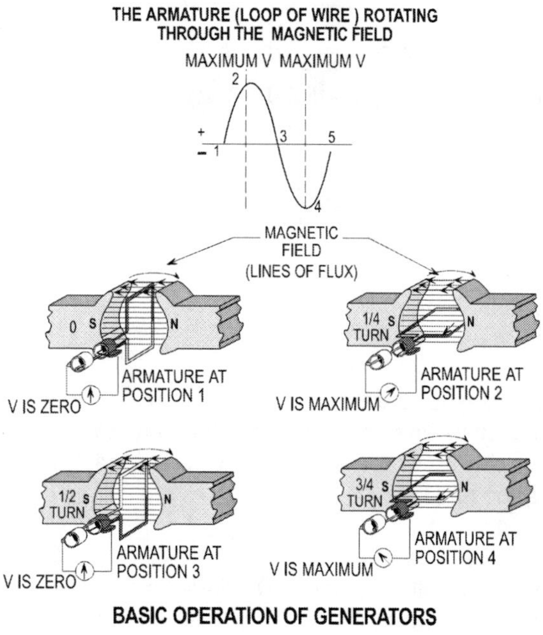

THE ARMATURE (LOOP OF WIRE) ROTATING THROUGH THE MAGNETIC FIELD

MAXIMUM V   MAXIMUM V

MAGNETIC FIELD (LINES OF FLUX)

0 TURN — ARMATURE AT POSITION 1 — V IS ZERO

1/4 TURN — ARMATURE AT POSITION 2 — V IS MAXIMUM

1/2 TURN — ARMATURE AT POSITION 3 — V IS ZERO

3/4 TURN — ARMATURE AT POSITION 4 — V IS MAXIMUM

BASIC OPERATION OF GENERATORS

Figure 2-1. The above illustrates an armature rotating through the flux of a magnetic field and completing a full turn with an entire output of voltage.

BASIC OPERATION OF DIRECT-CURRENT (DC) GENERATORS

By replacing the slip rings on a basic AC generator with two semicylindrical segments called a commutator and connecting two stationary brushes on opposite sides of the commentator, a basic DC generator is obtained. The brushes are so mounted that each brush contacts each segment of the commutator, which revolve simultaneously with the loop.

Note, the rotating parts of a DC generator, the coil and two piece commutator, are called an armature.

The switching action of the commutator segments makes the output of the DC generator produce direct current, with no part of the output current going in reverse direction as would occur in an AC generator. At the instant each brush contacts two segments of the commutator, a direct short circuit is produced. If an electromotive force (EMF) were generated, a high current would flow in the short circuit, which would cause an arc and thus could damage the commutator. To prevent this from happening, the brushes must be placed in the exact position where the short will occur when the generated EMF is zero. In a DC generator, this position is called the neutral plane. **(See Figure 2-3)**

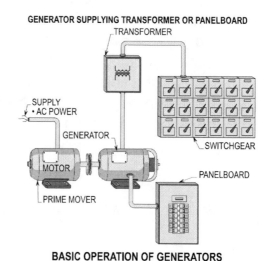

GENERATOR SUPPLYING TRANSFORMER OR PANELBOARD

TRANSFORMER

SUPPLY • AC POWER

GENERATOR

MOTOR

PRIME MOVER

SWITCHGEAR

PANELBOARD

BASIC OPERATION OF GENERATORS

Figure 2-2. The above illustrates a generator driven by a motor and such generator is supplying a transformer and panelboard. **Note,** the transformer can be used to step up or step down the voltage to serve the switchgear.

BRUSHES

Brushes ride on the surface of the commutator and form the electrical contact between the armature coil and the external circuit. Brushes are made of high-grade carbon and are held in place by brush holders. The brushes are insulated from the frame and are free to slide up and down in their holders so that they can follow the surface of the commutator. The pressure of the brushes may be varied and their position on the commutator as well may be adjusted for neutral plane position.

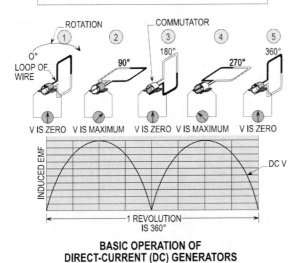

THE LOOP OF A DC GENERATOR MAKING ONE REVOLUTION THROUGH THE MAGNETIC FIELD

- When the loop is in position 1, (0°) the voltage is zero. No lines of flux are cut.

- After the loop has rotated 90° from position 1 and is passing through position 2, the black coil side is moving downward and the white side is moving upward. Both sides are cutting a maximum number of flux lines, and the voltage is maximum.

- As the loop moves through an angle of 180° in position 3, the coil sides are again cutting no flux lines. The generated EMF or voltage is zero.

- As the loop moves through an angle of 270°, as in position 4, the coil sides are cutting a maximum number of flux lines. The generated voltage is at a negative maximum.

- The next 90° turn of the loop completes a 360° revolution and the generated voltage falls to zero.

BASIC OPERATION OF DIRECT-CURRENT (DC) GENERATORS

Figure 2-3. The above illustrates a loop of wire rotating through the flux field of a magnetic field and completing one revolution of 360 degrees.

COMMUTATOR

A commutator is a mechanical rectifier that is nothing more than a slip ring split into segments. The ends of the rotating armature coil are attached to each segment of the commutator.

Figure 2-3 shows the commutator cutting through the magnetic field, with current flowing in one direction toward the commutator.

Note, the current is flowing from the unshaded side of the armature to the shaded side and the cross-hatched brush is touching the shaded section of the commutator while the other brush is touching the unshaded section of the commutator.

By this operation, current flows out of the exciter armature through the cross-hatched brush to the main generator field winding and returns through the other brush to complete the circuit.

As the armature continues to turn through 180 degrees, current flows in the opposite direction in the armature. The current is now flowing from the shaded section of the armature to the unshaded side, and the unshaded section of the commutator is now touching the cross-hatched brush. It is by this action of the commutator that DC voltage/current is produced.

COMMUTATION

As an armature revolves in a DC generator, the armature coil cuts through the magnetic lines of force (magnetic flux) and a voltage is induced in them that appears at the brushes. As the commutator segments (to which the coils are connected) pass the brushes, current is drawn from the segments. This is due to voltage being induced when the coil passes the field poles. Coils that are in the interpole spaces are shorted momentarily, and the connection to the coils are reversed to allow DC current flow. **(See Figure 2-4)**

ARMATURE REACTION

There is an EMF generated in a moving armature that opposes the magnetic field used to produce the electrical output. The neutral plane of the armature is perpendicular to the lines of force, or flux field, when there is no current in the armature.

The effect of armature reaction can be minimized or overcome by shifting the brush assembly as follows:

(1) By using chamfered poles,

(2) By using commutating poles,

(3) By using pole face windings, or

(4) By any combinations of the above

Basically, the procedure for eliminating such shift in the neutral plane is actually nullifying the change.

For example, the entire brush assembly can be adjusted to bring the brushes in line with the shifted neutral plane. Because the neutral plane shifts with the load, this means shifting the brushes every time the load changes. **Note,** this method is not practical.

A more practical method is that the poles be slightly chamfered. In other words, the radial distance between the pole face and the armature is increased slightly at the edges of the poles.

The effect of this procedure produces an increase in the air gap at the edges of the poles, which offsets to some extent the tendency of the field to shift due to the armature reaction. **(See Figure 2-5)**

Another method is to place the commutating poles in the interpolar spaces; such poles are smaller and narrower than the main field poles, and their winding is in series with the armature. They are so connected that their field opposes the field created by the armature reaction.

The final method is to design the faces of the main field pole so they are slotted longitudinally with the windings placed in the slots. These windings are then connected so that their field opposes the field created by the armature.

See Figure 2-6 for a detailed illustration of using interpoles and windings to correct armature reaction.

PURPOSE OF ARMATURE
• To produce electricity, the armature must be mounted between *field coils*, so that the magnetic force (flux) generated by the electromagnet will be cut by the rotating armature.
PURPOSE OF BRUSHES
• *Brushes* make sliding contact so that they may contact the commutator and carry generated electricity to the load.
PURPOSE OF COMMUTATOR
• The commutator acts as a reversing switch as the armature rotates in the different fields.
PURPOSE OF SWITCHING ACTION
• As a result of the switching action, the current output is a series of maximums and minimums with current flowing in only *one direction*.

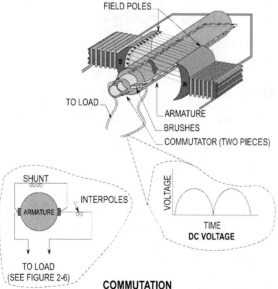

COMMUTATION

Figure 2-4. The above illustrates the main purpose and use of the armature brushes, the commutator, and their relationships in a generator to produce DC voltage.

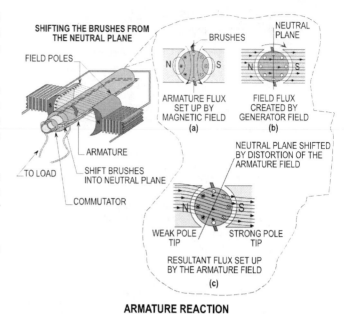

ARMATURE REACTION

Figure 2-5. The above illustrates the problems of armature reaction; by shifting the position of the brushes so that they are in the neutral plane when the generator is producing its normal load current, the generator operates properly under a fairly constant load.

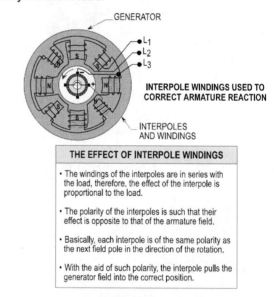

INTERPOLE WINDINGS USED TO CORRECT ARMATURE REACTION

THE EFFECT OF INTERPOLE WINDINGS
• The windings of the interpoles are in series with the load, therefore, the effect of the interpole is proportional to the load.
• The polarity of the interpoles is such that their effect is opposite to that of the armature field.
• Basically, each interpole is of the same polarity as the next field pole in the direction of the rotation.
• With the aid of such polarity, the interpole pulls the generator field into the correct position.

ARMATURE REACTION

Figure 2-6. The above illustrates the use of interpoles and windings to correct the problems due to the armature reaction of generators.

GENERATED VOLTAGE

The voltage output of generators can be generated for single-phase or three-phase use. The frequency of the generated power is directly related to the speed of the generator, which in turn, is directly related to the prime mover speed.

The voltage output will have a sine-wave pattern in the field poles that turn at a constant speed. The sinusoidal voltage is sinusoid because the field flux that intersects the windings produces a voltage that grows and collapses with each rotation of the field poles. **(See Figure 2-7)**

SINGLE-PHASE OUTPUT

Single-phase output is obtained by having one set of armature windings in the stator. A two-pole, single-phase generator consists of a north pole and a south pole with conductors that are part of a continuous armature conductor (winding) that fills the slots in the stator.

Note, the stator slots are separated mechanically and electrically by 180 degrees. When the flux from the north pole intersects the A(1) side of the conductor in **Figure 2-7**, the flux returning to the south pole intersects the A(2) side of the conductor, resulting in generation of a peak voltage between A(1) and A(2). When the north and south poles are perpendicular to the plane of the A(1) and A(2) conductors, no lines of force are intersecting the conductors and the voltage difference between A(1) and A(2) is zero. One complete revolution of the rotor through 360 degrees is considered one cycle.

See Figure 2-7 for a detailed illustration of a two-pole generator producing a single-phase output.

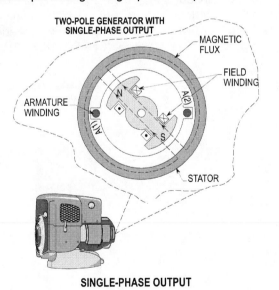

Figure 2-7. The above illustrates a single-phase generator that is used to supply single-phase power of 120/240 volts.

THREE-PHASE OUTPUT

Three-phase output can be produced in a rotating field having two or four poles as shown in **Figure 2-8**. As illustrated, the rotating field is equipped with one north and one south pole.

Note, there are three sets of conductors, A(1) and A(2), B(1) and B(2), and C(1) and C(2). Each set of conductors is located 120 degrees apart, with each group of conductors generating a single-phase voltage. Since the groups are spaced 120 degrees apart, the single-phase voltage of each group is electrically spaced 120 degrees from the other two. The total output of the three single-phase voltages produces a three-phase output.

A four pole generator requires two north poles and two south poles on the rotor, with a three-group set of conductors on the stator.

See Figure 2-8 for a detailed illustration of a two-pole and four-pole generator producing a three-phase output.

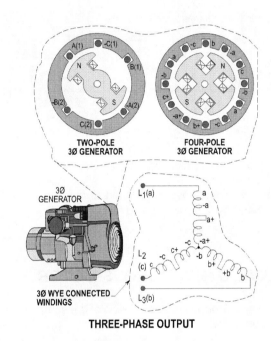

Figure 2-8. The above illustrates two- and four-pole generators with the windings of the four-pole generator connected in a wye configuration.

THE DIFFERENCE BETWEEN A GENERATOR AND MOTOR

In comparing a generator with a motor, there are similarities that must be pointed out and discussed.

For example, a generator is a machine that converts the mechanical power of a prime mover into electrical energy, expressed in kilowatts (kW). In comparison, a motor is a machine that converts electrical energy into mechanical energy and delivers this energy in the form of horsepower to the shaft of a driven load.

TYPICAL SYNCHRONOUS GENERATOR

A typical synchronous generator consists of field windings supplied by DC voltage that are mounted on a rotor and rotated inside of a stationary winding called the armature. The generator shaft is turned by a mechanical prime mover. As the generator shaft turns, the magnetic field is rotated, causing flux to intersect the armature winding and induce an EMF. The rotation of the field causes the induced EMF to increase and decrease, which produces a voltage at the terminals of the armature winding. By connecting the terminals of the armature winding to an electrical load, an alternating current will flow. **(See Figure 2-9)**

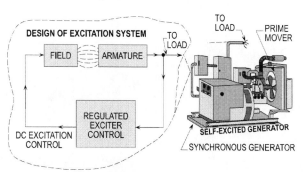

TYPICAL SYNCHRONOUS GENERATOR

Figure 2-9. The above illustration shows an excitation diagram and synchronous generator.

TYPICAL SYNCHRONOUS MOTOR

A typical synchronous motor consists of the same elements as the generator.

For example, a rotating magnetic field stator is mounted inside of a stationary armature winding with an additional motor that has an induction winding that is used for starting and it is mounted on the surface of the rotor. During motor start-up, no direct current is applied to the field winding rotor; instead, an alternating current is supplied to the terminals of the armature winding, which creates a magnetic field in the winding. Because this field is served by an alternating current, it travels around the armature winding at the same frequency as the supplying current. The rotating armature field induces a current in the winding on the surface of the rotor which develops a torque that causes the rotor to turn and the motor to start as an induction motor. When the speed is near the synchronous speed of the motor, direct current is then applied to the rotating field and the motor is brought up to synchronous speed. **(See Page 15-14)**

GENERATOR EXCITERS

The value of the AC voltage generated by a synchronous machine is controlled by varying the current in the DC field windings, while frequency is controlled by the speed of rotation.

Power input is controlled by the torque applied to the generator shaft by the driving engine. It is by this procedure that the synchronous generator controls the power in which it generates.

Synchronous generators normally use a brushless exciter, which is nothing more than a small AC generator mounted on the main shaft. The AC voltage generated is rectified by a three-phase rotating rectifier assembly, also on the shaft. This DC voltage is applied to the main generator field, which is also mounted on the main shaft. A voltage regulator controls the exciter field current, which controls the field voltage. In this manner, a well-controlled generator output can be obtained. **(See Figure 2-10)**

DC EXCITERS

This type of exciter operates on the principle of an AC voltage being induced in a coil that is rotating in a magnetic field. A commutator added to the output connection makes this device a DC generator. The process by which AC voltage is induced and by which the AC voltage is then converted to DC voltage is called rectification. **(See Figure 2-10)**

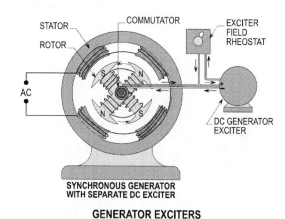

**SYNCHRONOUS GENERATOR
WITH SEPARATE DC EXCITER**

GENERATOR EXCITERS

Figure 2-10. The above illustrates a synchronous generator with a DC exciter.

IN COMPARISON

In selecting a generator for various applications, synchronous generators are normally applied instead of induction generators because induction generators operate at a fixed power factor. As a result of this characteristic, induction generators must always operate in parallel with synchronous machines or capacitors to correct power factor. However, a synchronous generator is capable of correcting power factor while delivering a constant frequency with an over-adjustment of the field current and power.

TYPICAL INDUCTION GENERATOR

A typical induction generator is essentially the same as that of an induction motor in that they both have a squirrel-cage rotor and wound stator. When this machine is driven above its designed synchronous speed, it becomes a generator. When operated at less than synchronous speed, it functions as a motor. Because induction generators do not have an exciter, they must operate in parallel with the utility. This outside power source provides the reactive power for generator operation.

Note, its frequency is automatically locked in with the utilities.

An induction generator is also a popular choice for use when designing and installing cogeneration systems, which operate in parallel with the utility.

ADVANTAGES

An induction generator offers several advantages over a synchronous generator and they are as follows:

(1) Voltage and frequency are controlled by utilities.

(2) Regulations are not required.

(3) Construction of generator allows high reliability and requires little maintenance.

(4) Only a minimum of protective relays and controls are necessary.

DISADVANTAGES

The major disadvantage of an induction generator is that it is difficult to operate alone as a standby or emergency generator. **(See Figure 2-11)**

TYPES OF ENGINES

Fuel availability determines the type of the engine-generator set to be used. If a certain type fuel is already in use at the site, a generator set using the same fuel is usually selected and utilized.

If the generator set is located in an area where public utilities are not available, liquid petroleum gas or diesel fuel are normally the types of fuel sources used.

ADVANTAGES OF AN INDUCTION GENERATOR
• Utilities control voltage and frequency.
• Regulators are not needed.
• Provides high reliability and needs very little maintenance.
• Relays and controls are easy to service and maintain.

DISADVANTAGES OF AN INDUCTION GENERATOR
• It is hard to use as an emergency or standby unit.

TYPICAL INDUCTION GENERATOR

Figure 2-11. The above lists the advantages and disadvantages of an induction generator.

GASOLINE ENGINES

Gasoline engines are economical up to about 100 kW. Initial costs are comparatively low, and they have reliable starting ability.

DIESEL ENGINES

Diesel engines are very popular due to their reliability, ruggedness, low maintenance, economical operation, and the low initial cost for larger units. For industrial and commercial applications, diesel engines are built in sizes up to about 2000 kW. For the needs of a prime power installation, they come in sizes up to 20,000 horsepower or greater.

GASEOUS FUEL ENGINES

Gaseous fuel engines are comparable to diesel engines, except that the normal gas supply is subject to interruption in the event the supply line is damaged. To compensate for this problem, an on-site propane gas tank is usually used to provide an alternate fuel supply should the normal supply be lost.

GAS TURBINE ENGINES

Gas turbine engine sets have had success as on-site power sources for heavy loads ranging from about 500 kW or greater. They are small in weight, and due to their lack of vibration, they can be installed on floors or on roofs.

Gas turbine engines have the ability to burn a wide variety of fuels, either liquid or gas. If needed, they come as dual-fuel sets, such as natural gas and diesel, or natural gas and liquid petroleum gas.

See **Figure 2-12** for a detailed illustration of the various kinds of engine-generator sets.

For the same reason above, synchronous motors are selected over induction motors for applications where constant speed is necessary. Induction motors will decrease in speed as a mechanical load is applied and this decrease in speed causes a decrease of counter electromotive force, which allows more current to be supplied by the source. Because of a separate DC supply, a synchronous motor always runs at synchronous speed, even if the load is increased.

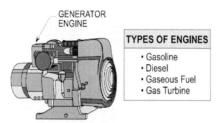

TYPES OF ENGINES

Figure 2-12. The above illustrates the types of engines that are most used, based on the types of fuel used.

SINGLE-PHASE GENERATORS

A single-phase generator consists of a rotating magnet called the field, which is inside a stationary winding called an armature. The rotating magnet is generally an electromagnet that is wound on a cylindrically shaped shaft called the rotor. The rotor is elongated on one end and to this end a coupling is attached to connect the generator to a prime mover. The stator core is contained in the generator frame and the bearings are mounted on end plates, which are called bearing brackets. The armature winding exits the generator frame through insulated terminals known as bushings. These terminals are attached to the generator frame in a compartment called a terminal box. The power leads from the load are connected in the box to the terminal loads of the armature. **(See Figure 2-13)**

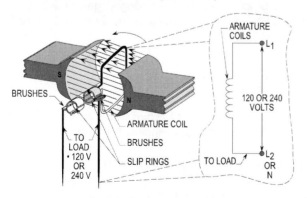

SINGLE-PHASE GENERATOR

Figure 2-13. The above illustrates a single-phase generator supplying either 120 volts or 240 volts to specific loads.

THREE-PHASE GENERATORS

A three-phase generator has three separate windings that are placed in the slots of the stator core. The windings are arranged so three voltages are produced that are 120 electrical degrees apart. In a two-pole generator, each phase winding is divided into two parallel groups, and in a four-pole generator, each phase is divided into four parallel phase groups. These phase groups are connected to the main and neutral leads by parallel rings. These rings are located at the stator winding and positioned at the collector end for proper continuity. **(See Figure 2-14)**

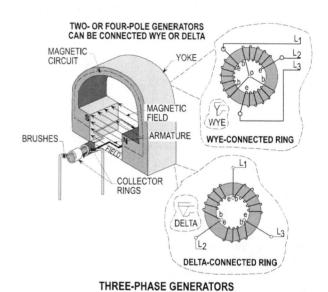

THREE-PHASE GENERATORS

Figure 2-14. Windings are shown connected in wye and delta configurations on rings to demonstrate how easily they can be connected.

OPERATION

Three-phase generators are much more efficient than comparably sized single-phase generators.

For example, as the magnetic field rotates across the armature winding, an electromotive force is induced in the armature winding. The rotation of the field causes this induced electromotive force to increase and decrease at the terminals of the armature winding. As the rotor spins, three sets of AC voltages are generated in the stator windings as the rotor turns through the magnetic field. These voltages are equal in amplitude, but they are shifted in phase by 120 electrical degrees from each other. When the terminals of the armature winding are connected to complete a circuit through a load, such as the primary winding of a three-phase transformer, an alternating current will flow and supply the load.

COMPONENTS OF AN AC GENERATOR

The following components are considered major elements of an AC generator that electrical personnel must understand:

(1) Stator,

(2) Rotor,

(3) Cooling system,

(4) Exciters, and

(5) Commutator.

STATOR

The following items are the most pertinent elements to consider about the stator components of an AC generator:

(1) Mechanical components, bearings, shafts, etc.

(2) Wye-connected windings, and

(3) Delta-connected windings.

MECHANICAL COMPONENTS

The most important mechanical components of an AC generator are as follows:

(1) The frame,

(2) The core,

(3) Termination box, and

(4) The winding (coils).

FRAME

The stator frame, called the housing, is fabricated from steel plates and bars electrically welded into a rigid box section. A short piece of ductwork is provided on the bottom of the frame through which ventilating air can be discharged. Holes drilled and tapped around the edges of the duct provides a means for attaching the necessary ductwork. Port holes with a removable glass serve as windows for the inspection of the end windings during operation.

CORE

The stator core is basically built up of low-loss segmental silicon steel laminations and assembled on bars that span the entire length of the core. Both sides of the laminations are treated with an insulating material to prevent short-circuiting the laminations. Vent spacers are built-in with the laminations at intervals to provide radial passages through the core for the ventilating air.

Adequate pressure is applied at intervals during the stacking operation to produce a tight core. Heavy end plates and nonmagnetic finger plates are used at the ends of the core to maintain adequate pressure at all times.

TERMINATION BOX

This component, of the generator frame, is located either on the bottom or the top of the frame. Contained in the termination box are the six lead bushings. These bushings are designed to serve two purposes. They provide a gastight penetration in the generator frame for the three line leads and the three neutral leads that make up both ends of the three phases of the stator winding. Secondly, such bushings are used to insulate the high-voltage leads from the generator frame, which is at ground potential. **(See Figure 2-15)** For trouble shooting, see **Table A-8**.

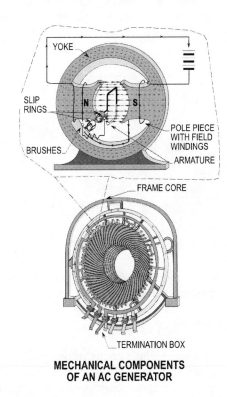

MECHANICAL COMPONENTS OF AN AC GENERATOR

Figure 2-15. The above illustration shows the main components that are necessary to operate an AC generator.

WYE-CONNECTED SYSTEMS

Generator stator windings are typically connected in a wye configuration. Line leads numbered T_1, T_2, and T_3 are the line leads connected to the phase conductors and T_4, T_5, and T_6 are the grounded (neutral) leads tied together and usually connected to ground. **(See Figure 2-16)**

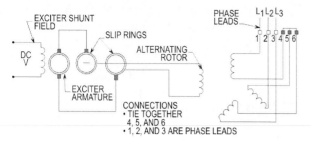

WYE-CONNECTED GENERATOR

Figure 2-16. The above illustrates a generator that has its windings connected in a wye configuration.

DELTA-CONNECTED SYSTEMS

The delta connection is made by connecting terminals 1 to 6, 2 to 4, and 3 to 5. Phase leads are then connected to terminals 1, 2, and 3 accordingly. The generator windings when connected in a delta configuration reduces the line-to-line voltage. However, the available line current is increased. **(See Figure 2-17)**

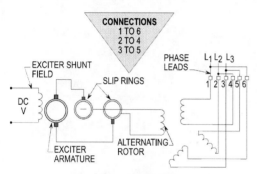

DELTA-CONNECTED SYSTEMS

Figure 2-17. The above illustrates a generator that has its windings connected in a delta configuration.

TYPES OF ROTORS

To impose the magnetic field on the rotor, poles are utilized that consist of stacked magnetic iron laminations (to reduce eddy currents) with copper conductors wrapped around the iron. These poles are excited by a direct current. Poles built in this manner reduce the problem created by eddy currents. The rotor poles must be arranged in pairs with a minimum arrangement of one pair of poles. The pairs are located 180 electrical degrees apart. As the north pole of the magnetic field of the rotor intersects one phase group of the stator winding, the south pole of the rotor intersecting the diametrically opposite portion of the same phase winding. The construction of the rotor is primarily determined by the speed of operation.

To accomplish this purpose, two basic rotor constructions for generators are available. They are salient poles, which have projecting poles with concentrated windings and cylindrical poles, which are equipped with distributed windings.

The rotor selected is based on the characteristics of the generator.

> **For example,** large, low-speed generators usually are designed with salient pole rotors. However, generators operating at 1800 rpm (four-pole) or 3600 rpm (two-pole) use cylindrical rotors.

SALIENT POLE ROTORS

Salient pole rotors can be built with either laminated poles or solid poles. The constructions of such poles are as follows:

LAMINATED POLES

This type of construction is more efficient because the magnetic lines of flux travel through the laminated core in a perpendicular direction to the field winding. This reduces iron losses and provides a more efficient magnetic coupling to the laminated core of the stator winding.

SOLID POLES

This type of construction is utilized where the rating of the generator requires less concentrated flux density.

CYLINDRICAL POLES

This type of construction is utilized in high-speed generators. These rotors generally carry higher field ratings and are more rigid. The surface of these rotor bodies is grooved to reduce surface currents and to increase heat transfer to the cooling medium of air or hydrogen. Radial slots for the field windings are machined in the rotor body and the field coils are imbedded in slots. **[See Figures 2-18(a) and (b)** for the types of rotors]

COOLING SYSTEMS

The types of cooling systems normally used for AC generators are air-cooled, air-to-water heat exchanger, and gas-to-water heat exchanger. Each type is explained as follows:

AIR-COOLED

A natural, air-cooled generator uses outside air, at ambient temperature, as a cooling medium. Such air is circulated through the stator and rotor by propeller-type blowers on both ends of the rotor. The warm air exiting the stator and rotor is exhausted back outside the generator in a complete cycle. In other words, air passes through only one time. **(See Figure 2-19)**

> **Generator Tip:** This type of cooling system sometimes requires air filters on the intake to minimize the contaminants that can get into the generator. Such filters can get dirty and can thus restrict air flow. To prevent this problem, proper maintenance must be provided.

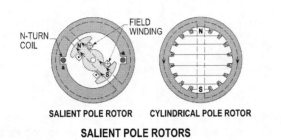

SALIENT POLE ROTORS

Figure 2-18(a). The above illustrates the difference between a salient pole rotor and cylindrical pole rotor.

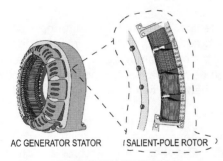

SALIENT POLE ROTORS

Figure 2-18(b). The above is a detailed illustration of an AC generator with a salient pole rotor.

AIR-TO-AIR HEAT EXCHANGER

A generator with an air-to-air heat exchanger is different from the natural cooled type: the heat exchanger constantly recirculates the same air through the stator and rotor.

Note, such circulation keeps the generator windings cleaner than a system that does not recirculate the same air.

> **Generator Tip:** This type of air circulation eliminates the need for a filter system, but does require additional secondary air-cooling equipment.

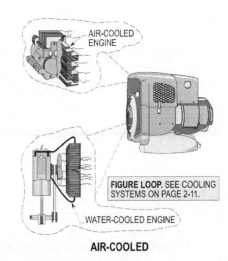

AIR-COOLED

Figure 2-19. The above shows a generator engine cooled by either air or water.

AIR-TO-WATER HEAT EXCHANGER

A generator with an air-to-water heat exchanger is different from the air-to-air heat exchanger type. The warmer air coming out of the stator and rotor is circulated across a cooler that consists of a number of copper tubes with circular fins around the outside diameter of the tubes. Water circulated through the tubes removes the heat from the air being passed over the outside of the tubes.

Note, a source of cooling water must be pumped through these coolers.

> **Generator Tip:** This type of air circulation reduces the problem of contaminants getting into the generator, because the same air is being recirculated through the generator constantly.

GAS-TO-WATER HEAT EXCHANGER

This system has many advantages over other types because it uses hydrogen as a cooling means.

For example, hydrogen has lower density and better thermal conductivity to reduce windage loss as well as increasing heat transfer output per unit volume.

> **Generator Tip:** The benefit of having a closed gas system is that it reduces dirt and moisture combination in the machine and achieves quieter operation.

OTHER EXCITERS

The commutator illustrated in **Figure 2-3** requires a great deal of maintenance and has been replaced primarily by the following devices:

STATIC EXCITATION

Static excitation uses power from the main generator output, which is fed back to the voltage regulator through an excitation transformer to produce the DC field current for the field windings on the generator rotor. The direct current is then connected to the field windings of the generator's rotor through collector rings. A closed-loop feedback circuit allows the voltage regulator to monitor and regulate the output of the generator.

BRUSHLESS EXCITATION

The brushless excitation method eliminates the inherent inefficiencies of slip rings and brushes. The exciter in the brushless excitation system consists of an alternating current generator with a rotating armature and a stationary magnetic field. The alternating current generated in the rotating armature is converted to direct current by a rectifier, which is mounted on the same shaft as the armature.

Note, the brushless exciter uses a permanent magnet generator as a pilot exciter to supply power to the voltage regulator. **(See Figure 2-20)**

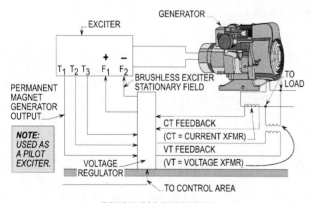

BRUSHLESS EXCITATION

Figure 2-20. The above illustrates a generator with a voltage regulator and a brushless excitation system.

REGULATOR

The function of a regulator is to use the feedback signals from the voltage potential transformers (PTS) and current transformers (CTS – connected in series) to keep the generator voltage at the desired usable level. Its function also protects from sudden load swings or voltage spikes by tripping and taking the generator off the line, if it becomes necessary. **(See Figure 2-21)**

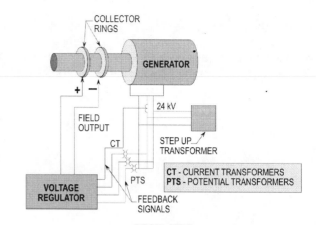

Figure 2-21. The above illustrates a voltage regulator receiving signals and using such signals to regulate the desired voltage level.

MANUAL SYNCHRONIZATION OF GENERATORS

A simple device, capable of monitoring instantaneous voltage between generators and recognizing a voltage difference, is a neon lamp. A common circuit arrangement that uses three neon lamps to monitor and indicate voltage differences between two three-phase generators is often used.

The circuit in generator 1 is supplying current to the load and generator 2 is about to be synchronized and connected in parallel with generator 1. The three neon lamps are connected across the open contacts of the tie breaker to monitor and indicate voltage differences between the respective phases for the two generators. When the lamps indicate that the generators are matched or synchronized, the tie breaker is closed and the generators are connected in parallel.

When the neon lamps are continuously dark, the generators are usually in exact and continuous synchronization. **(See Figure 2-22)**

For installations where the voltages of the generators are greater than 480 volts, step-down potential transformers must be used to reduce the voltage to the neon lamps to a safe level.

Note, when transformers are utilized for this purpose, care must be exercised to properly connect the secondary leads of the potential transformers before energizing the generators.

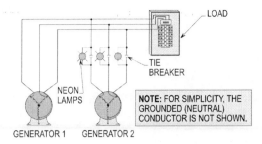

MANUAL SYNCHRONIZATION OF GENERATORS

Figure 2-22. The above shows the procedure for manually synchronizing two generators supplying a load.

AUTOMATIC SYNCHRONIZATION OF GENERATORS

The difference between automatic and manual synchronization is that automatic synchronization uses some form of logic circuitry to automatically monitor, adjust, and connect the generators. The logic circuitry automatically controls the generator to speed it up or to slow it down and to regulate the generator field current to increase or decrease the voltage.

Note, a special interlock circuit is used for the tie circuit breaker to prevent it from closing until synchronization has been established.

Automatic synchronization is mainly used for permanent installations where the phase rotation of the generator's lines is known to be correct. Just like (similar) the manual process of synchronization, the automatic process controls adjust the parameters of the generator that is to be connected in parallel with the generator that is already on-line. **(See Figure 2-23)**

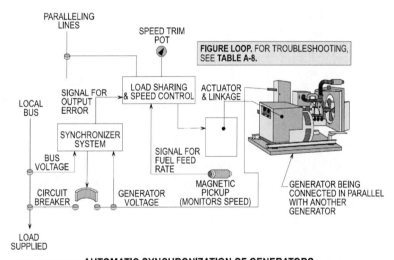

AUTOMATIC SYNCHRONIZATION OF GENERATORS

Figure 2-23. The above illustrates the procedure for automatic synchronization of two generators supplying a load.

Chapter 2: Generator Principles

	Section	Answer

1. A prime mover can be _____.
   - (a) water
   - (b) steam
   - (c) wind turbine
   - (d) all of the above

2. A commutator is a mechanical _____ that is nothing more than a slip ring split into segments.
   - (a) brush
   - (b) rectifier
   - (c) armature
   - (d) magnet

3. As an armature revolves in a DC generator, the armature coil cuts through the _____ lines of force and a voltage is induced in them that appears at the brushes.
   - (a) magnetic
   - (b) invisible
   - (c) mechanical
   - (d) electromagnetic

4. The effect of armature reaction can be minimized or overcome by shifting the brush assembly as follows:
   - (a) by using chamfered poles
   - (b) by using commutating poles
   - (c) by using pole face windings
   - (d) by any combination of the above

5. Single-phase output is obtained by having one set of armature windings in the _____.
   - (a) armature
   - (b) rectifier
   - (c) stator
   - (d) brushes

6. A two-pole, single-phase generator consists of a north pole and a south pole with conductors that are part of a continuous _____ conductor (winding) that fills the slots in the stator.
   - (a) armature
   - (b) rectifier
   - (c) stator
   - (d) brush

7. Three-phase output can be produced in a rotating field having two or _____ poles.
   - (a) three
   - (b) four
   - (c) five
   - (d) six

8. A typical synchronous generator consists of field windings supplied by DC voltage that are mounted on a rotor and rotated inside of a stationary winding called the _____.
   - (a) stator
   - (b) magnet
   - (c) rectifier
   - (d) armature

9. The value of the AC voltage generated by a synchronous machine is controlled by varying the current in the _____ field windings.
   - (a) magnetic
   - (b) AC
   - (c) DC
   - (d) armature

10. DC exciters operate on the principle of a(n) _____ voltage being induced in a coil that is rotating in a magnetic field.
     (a) magnetic   (b) AC
     (c) DC   (d) armature

11. Gasoline engines are economical up to about _____ kW.
     (a) 50   (b) 75
     (c) 100   (d) 150

12. For industrial and commercial applications, diesel engines are built in sizes up to about _____ kW.
     (a) 1000   (b) 2000
     (c) 3000   (d) 5000

13. A single-phase generator consists of a(n)_____ magnet called the field.
     (a) rotating   (b) stationary
     (c) electro   (d) stator

14. A three-phase generator has three separate windings that are placed in the slots of the stator _____.
     (a) winding   (b) armature
     (c) rectifier   (d) core

15. The stator _____, called the housing, is fabricated from steel plates and bars electrically welded into a rigid box section.
     (a) coils   (b) core
     (c) frame   (d) termination box

16. The stator _____ is basically built up of low-loss segmental silicon steel laminations and assembled on bars that span the entire length of the core.
     (a) coils   (b) core
     (c) frame   (d) termination box

17. Generator stator windings are typically connected in a _____ configuration.
     (a) wye   (b) delta
     (c) single-phase   (d) three-phase

18. Salient pole rotors can be built with _____ poles.
     (a) laminated   (b) solid
     (c) all of the above   (d) none of the above

19. A gas-to-water heat exchanger uses _____ as a cooling means.
     (a) air   (b) water
     (c) hydrogen   (d) none of the above

20. _____ synchronization is mainly used for permanent installations where the phase rotation of the generator's lines is known to be correct.
     (a) Automatic   (b) Manual
     (c) Logic   (d) Regulator

3

Generators and the *National Electrical Code*®

In addition to the requirements of **Article 445**, generators shall comply with the requirements of other Sections of the *National Electrical Code*® (NEC®), most notably are **Articles 215, 225, 230, 250, 700, 701, 702,** and **705**.

Articles 215, 225, and **230** deal with generators when they are used to supply service equipment and feeders. **Article 250** addresses the special grounding techniques based on where the generator is installed and used. **Article 700** contains the rules for generators that are utilized when supplying power to emergency systems. **Articles 701** and **702** pertain to generators that serve legally required and optional standby systems. **Article 705** is used when generators are connected in parallel with the utility power sources to serve as an interconnected electric power production source.

LOCATION OF GENERATORS
445.10

One of the first requirements is that the generator be suitable for the location where it is installed. Basically, standard-type generators are designed to operate indoors in dry places. The requirements of **430.14** shall be met to help protect the operation of generators. If generators are installed in hazardous locations or used to supply special equipment, the requirements of **Articles 500 through 503, 505, 510 through 517, 520, 525, 530, 665,** and **695** shall also be complied with.

Note: For more information on the location of generator exhaust, review NFPA 37, "Standard For The Installation And Use OF Standard Combustion Engines and Gas Turbines".

NAMEPLATE MARKINGS
445.11

To aid designers and electrical personnel every generator shall have a nameplate that contains the following information:

- The manufacturer's name and rating frequency,

- Number of phases (if of alternating current) and power factor,

- The subtransient and transient impedances,

- The rating in kilowatts and kilowatt amperes,

- The normal volts and amperes corresponding to the rating,

- The rated revolutions per minute,

- Insulation system class, ambient temperature or temperature rise, and time rating.

Such information shall be used when designing, installing, and maintaining generators in residential, commercial, and industrial applications.

Note: Nameplates or manufacturer's instructions shall provide the following information for all stationary generators and portable generators rated more than 15 kW.

Subtransient, transient, synchronous, and zero sequence reactances

- Power rating category

- Insulation system class

- Indication if the generator is protected against overload by inherent design, an overcurrent protective relay, circuit breaker, or fue

- Maximum short-circuit current for inverter-based generators, in lieu of the synchronous, subtransient, and transient reactances

Marking shall be provided by the manufacturer to indicate whether or not the generator neutral is bonded to its frame. Where the bonding is modified in the field, additional marking shall be required to indicate whether the neutral is bonded to the frame.

OVERCURRENT PROTECTION FOR GENERATORS
445.12

Constant-voltage generators, except for AC generators and exciters, are protected from overload by inherent design, circuit breakers, fuses, protective relays, or overcurrent protective means suitable for the condition of use. (AC generators are exempt from the need of overcurrent protection.) This is due to impedance that limits the short-circuit current to a value that is not damaging to their

windings. All generator exciters are usually separately excited. In most installations, DC as well as AC units are normally operated without overcurrent protection. **(See Figure 3-1)**

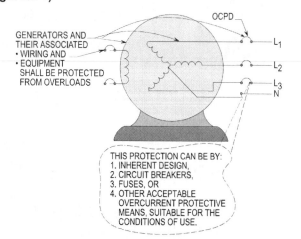

OVERCURRENT PROTECTION FOR GENERATORS
NEC 445.12

Figure 3-1. Generators and their elements shall be protected from overloads, short circuits, and ground faults.

CONSTANT-VOLTAGE GENERATORS
445.12(A)

The basic rule requires DC generators to have overcurrent protection. However, AC generators may be so designed that on a high overload the voltage of the generator falls off, thereby reducing the overload current to a safe value. For this reason, the NEC does not always require overload protection for all AC generators.

There are installations where overload protection can be omitted. In some cases, it is considered better to risk damage to the exciter rather than have the generator shut down through operation of an exciter overcurrent protection device. **(See Figure 3-2)**

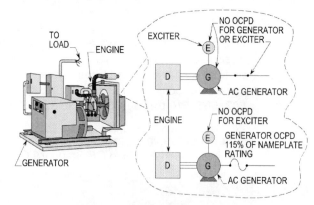

CONSTANT-VOLTAGE GENERATORS
NEC 445.12(A)

Figure 3-2. The above illustrates when overcurrent protection is required for generators.

Generator Tip: Generators that produce a constant voltage (most commonly used generators are of this type) are required to be protected from overloads. This may be accomplished by using overcurrent protective devices such as fuses, circuit breakers, etc. or by inherent design.

TWO-WIRE GENERATORS
445.12(B)

Two-wire DC generators shall be permitted to have overcurrent protection in one wire, if the overcurrent protection device is activated by the entire current and not the current in the shunt coil. However, the overcurrent device shall not, under any circumstances, open the shunt coil.

Generator Tip: The NEC does not permit an overcurrent protection device in the generator's positive lead only, because an overcurrent device in the positive lead would not always be actuated by the entire current generated. **Note,** an overcurrent protection device is not permitted for the shunt field. If the shunt field circuit were to open and the field was at full strength, a dangerous high voltage would be induced, which might damage the generator. **(See Figure 3-3)**

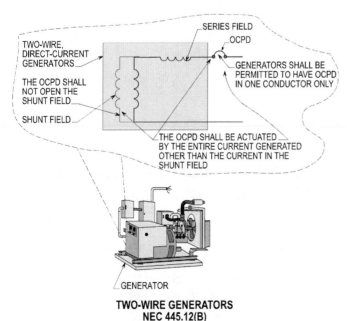

TWO-WIRE GENERATORS
NEC 445.12(B)

Figure 3-3. The above illustrates overcurrent protection for two-wire DC generators.

GENERATORS OPERATING
AT 65 VOLTS OR LESS
445.12(C)

A generator operating at 65 volts or less, and driven by an individual motor, shall be considered adequately protected by the motor overcurrent protection device, where such overcurrent protection device will operate when the generators are delivering not more than 150 percent of the generator's full-load current. **(See Figure 3-4)**

Generator Tip: If the fuse(s) or circuit breaker protecting the motor is set to operate when the generator is 50 percent or less overloaded, no protection is required in the generator leads. However, if the generator voltage is above 65 volts, it is the intent of the NEC to require separate overcurrent protection for the generator.

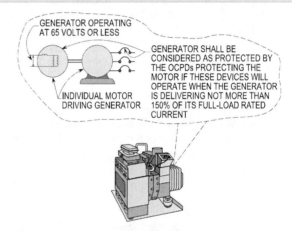

GENERATORS OPERATING AT 65 VOLTS OR LESS
NEC 445.12(C)

Figure 3-4. The above illustrates the protection of generators operating at 65 volts or less.

BALANCER SETS
445.12(D)

Balancer sets consist of two smaller DC generators used with a larger two-wire generator. The two balancer generators are connected in series across the two-wire main generator lines. A neutral tap (point) is brought out from the midpoint connection between the two balancer generators.

Note, each of the two balancer generators carries about one-half of any unbalanced load condition.

With such an arrangement, where there is a heavy unbalance in the load, the balancer generators may become overloaded, while there is no overload on the main generator. The balancer generators shall be equipped with an overload device that will actuate the main generator disconnect if the balancer generators should become overloaded. **(See Figure 3-5)**

Generator Tip: Balancer sets shall be equipped with overload devices that disconnects the three-wire system in case of an excessive unbalanced condition. Three-wire direct current generators shall be provided with overcurrent protection devices, one in each armature lead arranged to disconnect the three-wire circuit in case of heavy overloads or extreme unbalanced current conditions.

THREE-WIRE, DC GENERATORS
445.12(E)

As in two-wire generators, the overcurrent protection device protecting a three-wire generator shall be capable of taking the full generator current. When equalizer leads are provided, the overcurrent protection device, if not properly installed in the circuit, might take only a part of the generator current. To help solve this problem, three-wire DC generators operating in parallel are equipped with two equalizer leads. The overcurrent protection devices shall be so placed in the circuit that they will take the full generator current without tripping open the circuit.

A two-pole breaker placed ahead of the junction of the main and equalizer leads can provide such protection. However, a four-pole circuit breaker with two poles for the main leads and two poles for the equalizer leads can also be used, provided such circuit breaker is actuated by the full current flow of the generator. **(See Figure 3-6)**

Generator Tip: These generators which are either shunt wound or compound wound shall be provided with overcurrent protection devices in each armature lead. Such devices shall sense the entire armature current and be multipole devices that open all the poles in the event of an overcurrent condition.

EXCEPTION TO (A) THROUGH (E)
445.12(A) THROUGH (E), Ex.

There are cases where a generator fails and it is less of a hazard than disconnecting it when an overcurrent condition occurs. In such instances, the AHJ may permit the generator to be connected to a supervision panel with an annunciator or alarm, instead of requiring overcurrent protection.

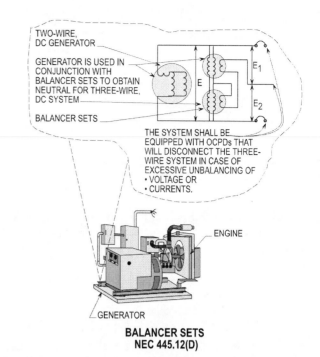

BALANCER SETS
NEC 445.12(D)

Figure 3-5. The above illustrates balancer sets used with a generator to disconnect the system if an excessive unbalanced current condition should occur.

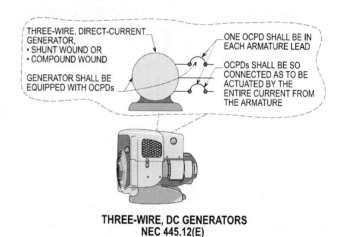

THREE-WIRE, DC GENERATORS
NEC 445.12(E)

Figure 3-6. The above illustrates the overcurrent protection requirements for three-wire DC generators.

AMPACITY OF CONDUCTORS FROM GENERATORS
445.13

Ungrounded (phase) conductors from a generator shall be sized at no less than 115 percent of the nameplate current value. Grounded (neutral) conductors can be calculated and sized according to **220.61** and **215.2(A)(1), Ex. 3** and **215.2(B)**. (**Table 310.16**, or the over 2000 volt Tables.) Ungrounded (phase) conductors shall be capable of carrying ground-fault currents and shall be sized in accordance with **250.30(A)**. [Also, see **310.15(E)**]

For example, a generator with 100 amp output shall have conductors with an ampacity of at least 115 amps respectively (100 A x 115% = 115 A). For the definition of a neutral conductor and neutral point, see **Article 100. (See Figure 3-7)**

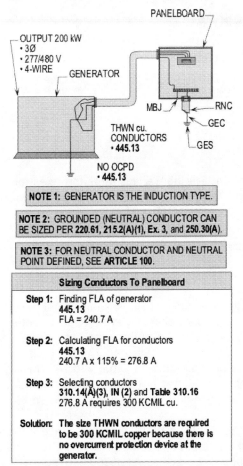

AMPACITY OF CONDUCTORS FROM GENERATORS
NEC 445.13

Figure 3-7. The above illustrates the procedure for sizing conductors from a generator to a load using 115 percent multiplier.

PREVENTING OVERLOAD CONDITIONS 445.13, Ex.

The conductors shall be protected at 100 percent of the rated generated current (100 amps). However, to do so, the design or operation of the generator shall be such as to prevent overloading. Therefore, an ampacity of 100 percent loading is all that is permitted.

For example, a generator with 100 amp output shall have conductors with an ampacity of at least 100 amps (100 A x 100% = 100 A) and the load limited to this value. **(See Figure 3-8)**

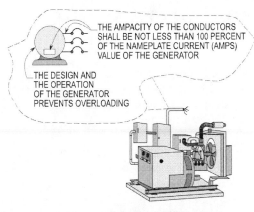

PREVENTING OVERLOAD CONDITIONS
NEC 445.13, Ex.

Figure 3-8. The above illustrates the procedure for sizing the conductors from a generator to a load using the 100 percent multiplier.

PROTECTION OF LIVE PARTS 445.14

Live parts of generators operated at more than 50 volts-to-ground shall not be exposed to accidental contact where accessible to unqualified persons. The basic rule is that live parts of generators shall not be exposed to accidental contact. Such live parts are as follows:

(1) Brushes,

(2) Collector rings, and

(3) Other live parts.

See Figure 3-9 for a detailed illustration pertaining to this rule.

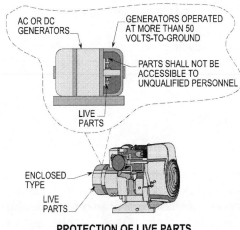

PROTECTION OF LIVE PARTS
NEC 445.14

Figure 3-9. The above illustrates the requirements for generators with exposed parts.

GUARDS FOR ATTENDANTS
445.15

If generators operate at more than 150 volts-to-ground, no live parts shall be permitted to be exposed to contact by unqualified personnel. Section **430.233** requires insulating mats or platforms around motors.

Note, these protective items are also required for generators when the generator voltage is greater than 150 volts-to-ground. **(See Figure 3-10)**

> **Generator Tip:** Generators and controllers shall be guarded against accidental contact only by location as specified in **430.232** and **430.233**, and because adjustments or other maintenance may be necessary during the operation of the apparatus, suitable insulating mats or platforms are to be provided so that a qualified person cannot readily touch live parts unless standing on the mats or platforms.

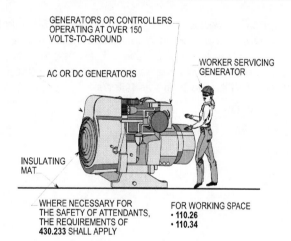

GUARDS FOR ATTENDANTS
NEC 445.15

Figure 3-10. Insulating mats or platforms shall be provided for attendants servicing a generator when the voltage is greater than 150 volts-to-ground.

BUSHINGS
445.16

Where wires pass though an opening in an enclosure, conduit box, or barrier, a bushing shall be used to protect the conductors from the edges of an opening having sharp edges. The bushings shall have smooth, well-rounded surfaces where they may be in contact with the conductors. If used where oils, grease, or other contaminants may be present, the bushing shall be made of a material that will not be deleteriously affected. **(See Figure 3-11)**

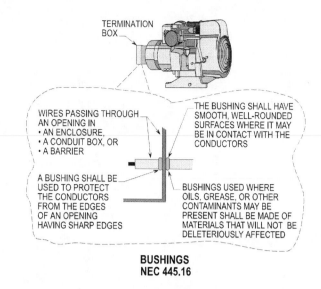

BUSHINGS
NEC 445.16

Figure 3-11. The above illustrates the rules for installing bushings to protect conductors passing through the openings of enclosures.

GENERATOR TERMINAL HOUSINGS
445.17

Generator terminal housings shall comply with **430.12**. Where a horsepower rating is required to determine the required minimum size of the generator terminal housing, the full-load current of the generator shall be compared with comparable motors in **Table 430.247 through Table 430.250**. The higher horsepower rating shall be used whenever the generator selection is between two ratings.

> **For example,** a 460 volt, three-phase generator with an output of 345 amps shall be rated at 361 amps with a horsepower of 300 per **Table 430.250**.

DISCONNECTING MEANS AND EMERGENCY SHUTDOWN
445.18(A) AND 445.19

A disconnecting means shall be required for generators to disconnect the generator and all protective devices and control apparatus.

Note, the disconnecting means shall be capable of being locked (lockable) in the open position. **(See Figure 3-12)**

A disconnecting means with a permanent locking means for the generator shall not be required if the driving means for the generator can be readily shut down and there is no other generator or other source of voltage in parallel with it per **445.18(A)** and **(B)** and **110.25**.

Note, For cord and plug-connected generators, see **445.18(A) in the NEC.**

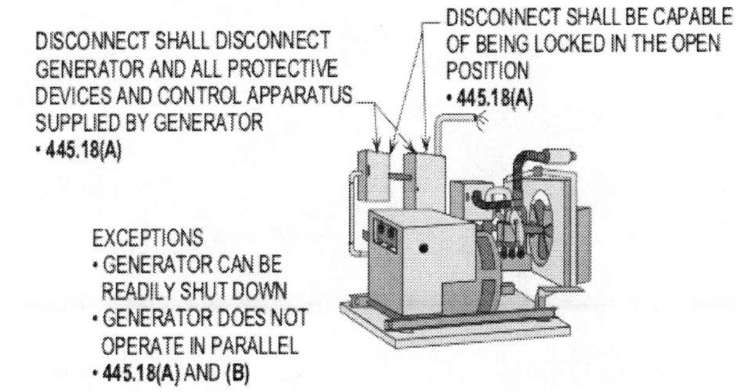

DISCONNECT SHALL DISCONNECT GENERATOR AND ALL PROTECTIVE DEVICES AND CONTROL APPARATUS SUPPLIED BY GENERATOR
• 445.18(A)

DISCONNECT SHALL BE CAPABLE OF BEING LOCKED IN THE OPEN POSITION
• 445.18(A)

EXCEPTIONS
• GENERATOR CAN BE READILY SHUT DOWN
• GENERATOR DOES NOT OPERATE IN PARALLEL
• 445.18(A) AND (B)

**DISCONNECTING MEANS REQUIRED FOR GENERATORS
NEC 445.18(A) AND (B)**

Figure 3-12. A disconnecting means shall be required to disconnect all protective devices and control apparatus from generator.

EMERGENCY SHUTDOWN OF PRIME MOVER
445.19(A)(1) AND (A)(2)

Generators shall have provisions to shut down the prime mover. The means of shutdown shall comply with all of the following:

(1) Be equipped with provisions to disable all prime mover start control circuits to render the prime mover incapable of starting

(2) Initiate a shutdown mechanism that requires a mechanical reset.

The provisions to shut down the prime mover shall be permitted to satisfy the requirements of **445.18(A)** where it is capable of being locked in the open position per **110.25**.

GENERATORS SUPPLYING MULTIPLE LOADS
700.10(B)(6)(a) thru (6)(b)

A single generator supplying more than one load, or multiple generators operating in parallel, shall be permitted to supply either of the following:

(1) A vertical switchboard with separate sections

(2) Individual enclosures with overcurrent protection tapped from a single feeder for load separation and distribution if a generator(s) is provided with overcurrent protection meeting the requirements of **NEC Article 240**.

See **Figures 3-13(a)** and **(b)** as well as **Figures 4-6(a) through (6)(c)** for a detailed illustration pertaining to generator supplying multiple loads.

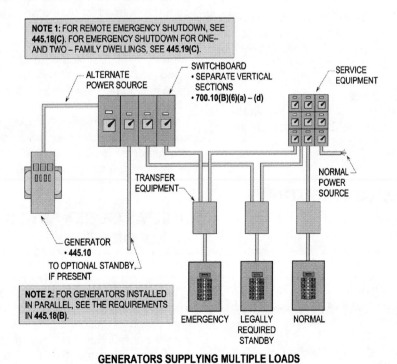

NOTE 1: FOR REMOTE EMERGENCY SHUTDOWN, SEE 445.18(C). FOR EMERGENCY SHUTDOWN FOR ONE- AND TWO – FAMILY DWELLINGS, SEE 445.19(C).

ALTERNATE POWER SOURCE

SWITCHBOARD
• SEPARATE VERTICAL SECTIONS
• 700.10(B)(6)(a) – (d)

SERVICE EQUIPMENT

TRANSFER EQUIPMENT

NORMAL POWER SOURCE

GENERATOR
• 445.10

TO OPTIONAL STANDBY, IF PRESENT

NOTE 2: FOR GENERATORS INSTALLED IN PARALLEL, SEE THE REQUIREMENTS IN 445.18(B).

EMERGENCY   LEGALLY REQUIRED STANDBY   NORMAL

**GENERATORS SUPPLYING MULTIPLE LOADS
NEC 700.10(B)(6)(a)**

Figure 3-13(a). A single generator source supplying power to a vertical switchboard with separate sections.

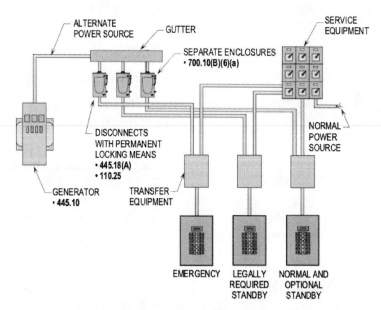

GENERATORS SUPPLYING MULTIPLE LOADS
NEC 700.10(B)(6)(a)

Figure 3-13(b). A single generator source supplying separate enclosures.

GROUND-FAULT CIRCUIT-INTERRUPTER PROTECTION FOR RECEPTACLES ON 15 kW OR SMALLER PORTABLE GENERATORS 445.20(A) AND (B)

All 125-volt, single-phase, 15- and 20-ampere receptacle outlets that are a part of a 15-kW or smaller portable generator either shall have ground-fault circuit-interrupter protection for personnel integral to the generator or receptacle or shall not be available for use when the 125/250 volt locking-type receptacle is in use. If the generator does not have a 125/250-volt locking-type receptacle, this requirement of GFCI protection shall apply. **(See Figure 3-14)**

UNBONDED (FLOATING NEUTRAL) GENERATORS 445.20(A)

Unbonded generators with both 125-volt and 125/250-volt receptacle outlets shall have listed GFCI protection for personnel interal to the generator or receptacle on all 125-volt, 15- and 25-ampere receptacle outlets.

In the **Ex.** to **445.20(A)**, GFCI protection shall not be required where the 125-volt receptacle outlet(s) is interlocked such that it is not available for use when any 125/250-volt receptacle(s) is in use.

BONDED NEUTRAL GENERATORS 445.20(B)

Bonded generators shall be provided with GFCI protection on all 125-volt, 15- and 20-ampere receptacle outlets. The **Informational Note** to **445.20(B)** refers you to **590.6(A)(3)** for GFCI requirements for 15-kW or smaller portable generators used for temporary electric power and lighting. The **Exception** to **445.20(A)** and **(B)** notes that if the generator was manufactured or remanufactured prior to January 1, 2015, listed cord sets or devices incorporating listed GFCI protection for personnel identified for portable use shall be permitted **(See Figure 3-15)**

Note: Receptacle outlets that are a part of a 15kW or smaller portable generator shall have listed ground-fault circuit-interrupter protection (GFCI) for personnel integral to the generator or receptacle as indicited in either 4**45.20(A) or (B)**

PORTABLE GENERATORS 15 KW OR LESS 702.12(B) AND 590.6(A)(3)

Where a portable generator, rated 15-kW or less, is installed using a flanged inlet or other cord- and plug-type connection, a disconnecting means shall not be required where ungrounded conductors serve or pass through a building or structure. **(See Figure 3-15)**

Note: For generators greater than 15 kW, see **702.12(A)**.

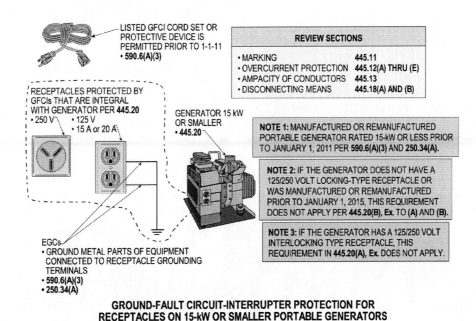

GROUND-FAULT CIRCUIT-INTERRUPTER PROTECTION FOR RECEPTACLES ON 15-kW OR SMALLER PORTABLE GENERATORS NEC 445.20(A) AND (B)

Figure 3-14. The requirements for GFCI protection for receptacles on 15kW or smaller portable generators are illustrated above.

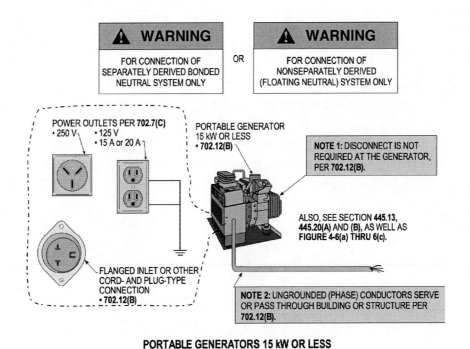

PORTABLE GENERATORS 15 kW OR LESS NEC 445.20(A) AND (B) AND 702.12(B)

Figure 3-15. A disconnecting means shall not be required where ungrounded (phase) conductors serve or pass through a building structure where a portable generator, rated 15kW or less, is installed using a flanged inlet or other cord- and plug-type connection. Note: For generators greater than 15 kW and permanently installed, see **250.35(A)** and **(B)** as well as **702.12(A)**.

GENERATORS INSTALLED IN PARALLEL
445.18(B)

Where a generator is instaled in parallel with other generators, the provisions of **445.18** shall be capable of isolating the generator outuput terminals from the paralleling equipment. The disconnecting means shall not be required to be located at the generator. **(See Figure 3-15)**

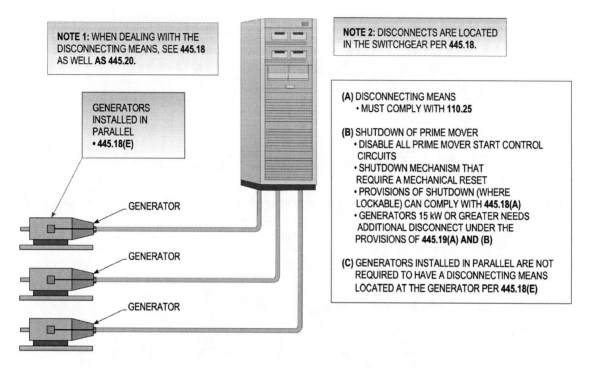

NOTE 1: WHEN DEALING WIITH THE DISCONNECTING MEANS, SEE **445.18** AS WELL **AS 445.20.**

GENERATORS INSTALLED IN PARALLEL
• **445.18(E)**

GENERATOR

GENERATOR

GENERATOR

NOTE 2: DISCONNECTS ARE LOCATED IN THE SWITCHGEAR PER **445.18.**

(A) DISCONNECTING MEANS
   • MUST COMPLY WITH **110.25**

(B) SHUTDOWN OF PRIME MOVER
   • DISABLE ALL PRIME MOVER START CONTROL CIRCUITS
   • SHUTDOWN MECHANISM THAT REQUIRE A MECHANICAL RESET
   • PROVISIONS OF SHUTDOWN (WHERE LOCKABLE) CAN COMPLY WITH **445.18(A)**
   • GENERATORS 15 kW OR GREATER NEEDS ADDITIONAL DISCONNECT UNDER THE PROVISIONS OF **445.19(A) AND (B)**

(C) GENERATORS INSTALLED IN PARALLEL ARE NOT REQUIRED TO HAVE A DISCONNECTING MEANS LOCATED AT THE GENERATOR PER **445.18(E)**

DISCONNECTING MEANS AND SHUTDOWN PRIME MOVER
NEC 445.19(A), (B), AND (C)

Figure 3-16. The illustration above is a clarification for the requirements for generator disconnecting means and the disconnecting of the prime mover. A remote shutdown means, in the event of an emergency, shall be provided. Section **445.18(B)** clarifies that where generators are installed in parallel it is not necessary to provide a disconnecting means at the generator location.

Name   Date

Chapter 3: Generators and the *National Electrical Code*®

Section   Answer

1. Each generator shall be provided with a nameplate that contains: _____ _____
   (a) the manufacturer's name   (b) number of phase
   (c) the rated revolutions per minute (d) all of the above

2. Two-wire, DC generators shall be permitted to have overcurrent protection   _____ _____
   in _____ conductor(s) only if the overcurrent device is activated by the entire
   current generated other than the current in the shunt field.
   (a) 1   (b) 2
   (c) 3   (d) 4

3. A generator operating at _____ volts or less, and driven by an individual   _____ _____
   motor, shall be considered adequately protected by the motor overcurrent
   protection device, where such overcurrent protection device will operate when
   the generators are delivering not more than 150 percent of the generator's
   full-load current.
   (a) 50   (b) 65
   (c) 100   (d) 250

4. Ungrounded (phase) conductors from a generator shall be sized at not less   _____ _____
   than _____ percent of the nameplate current value.
   (a) 80   (b) 100
   (c) 115   (d) 125

5. Where the design and operation of the generator prevent overloading, the   _____ _____
   ampacity of the conductors shall not be less than _____ percent of the
   nameplate current rating of the generator.
   (a) 80   (b) 100
   (c) 115   (d) 125

6. Live parts of generators operated at more than _____ volts-to-ground shall not   _____ _____
   be exposed to accidental contact where accessible to unqualified persons.
   (a) 50   (b) 120
   (c) 150   (d) 277

7. If generators operate at more than _____ volts-to-ground, no live parts shall   _____ _____
   be permitted to be exposed to contact by unqualified personnel.
   (a) 50   (b) 120
   (c) 150   (d) 277

8. Where wires pass through an opening in an enclosure, a _____ shall be used   _____ _____
   to protect the conductors from the edges of an opening having sharp edges.
   (a) sleeve   (b) connector
   (c) filling compound   (d) bushing

9. The disconnecting means for a generator shall be capable of being locked in   _____ _____
   the _____ position
   (a) closed   (b) open
   (c) rotating   (d) none of the above

_____ _____ **10.** A single generator supplying more than one load, or multiple generators operating in parallel, shall be permitted to supply either of the following:
       (a) A vertical switchboard with separate sections
       (b) Individual enclosure with overcurrent protection tapped from a single feeder for load separation and distribution
       (c) Neither (a) nor (b)
       (d) Both (a) and (b)

4

Emergency System Generators

This chapter covers systems that are legally required to be installed and supply loads essential to safety and life, such as emergency lighting, essential refrigeration and ventilation, and signaling systems. Emergency systems are also installed in places of assembly, such as theaters, schools, stadiums, or locations where large numbers of people may gather. Such systems must be designed to assure safe evacuation by providing electric power for adequate emergency lighting, proper fire detection, reliable operation of fire pumps, dependable alarm signals, communications, etc.

GENERATOR SET
700.12(B)(1) THRU (B)(5)

A generator is supplied by a prime mover acceptable to the AHJ and sized as covered in **700.4(A) thru (C)**. The generator shall have automatic starting of the prime mover when the normal source of power fails, and shall have a transfer switch for all electrical equipment supplied by the emergency circuit. To prevent immediate retransfer in cases of short-time restoring of the normal source of power, a time-delay feature allowing for a 15-minute setting shall be provided.

Internal combustion engines used as the prime movers shall have an on-site fuel supply that will function at full demand for not less than 2 hours of operation. Fuel transfer pumps shall be connected to the emergency power system where power is needed for the operation of the fuel transfer pumps to deliver fuel to a generator set day tank.

Note: Section **700.4(A)** deals with "rating", **700.4(B)** deals with "capacity" and **700.4(C)** deals with "selective load pickup, load shedding, and peak load shaving".

Prime movers are not to rely solely on public utility gas systems for the fuel supply. Automatic transferring means shall be provided for transferring from one fuel supply to another when a dual fuel supply is used.

> **Generator Tip:** When acceptable to the AHJ, other than on-site fuels shall be permitted to be used when there is a low probability of the failure of the on-site fuel delivery system and the power from the outside electrical utility company occurring at the same time.

If a storage battery is used for control or signal power or as a means of starting prime movers, it shall be suitable for that type of service and equipped with an automatic charging means independent of the generator set. A battery charger shall be connected to the emergency system where the battery charger is required for the operation of the generator set. Dampers shall be connected to the emergency system where power is required for the operation of dampers used to ventilate the generator set.

Note, monthly check of batteries should be done.

When an emergency generator requires more than 10 seconds to develop power, an auxiliary power supply shall be permitted to energize the emergency system until the regular generator is capable of picking up the load. For documentation requirements, see **700.5(E). (See Figure 4-1)**

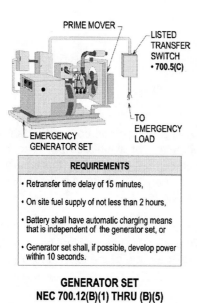

GENERATOR SET
NEC 700.12(B)(1) THRU (B)(5)

Figure 4-1. The above illustration lists the rules for a generator set under certain conditions of use.

PURPOSE AND SCOPE OF EMERGENCY GENERATORS 700.1

The same types of emergency systems might not be suitable for all applications. The conditions must be evaluated as to whether the emergency system will be needed for a long period of time or a short period of time, and how much capacity the emergency system must have to supply the emergency demands.

In the case of interruption of service to a hospital, whether from within or without, the emergency system might be required to provide a large amount of power for a long period of time. Such a situation requires a complete evaluation of the possible needs, the type of system, and its capacity to serve loads and comply with the requirements of the NEC.

> **Generator Tip:** Emergency systems are usually installed in places of assembly to provide illumination in the event of a normal power outage so that there will be a means of safe exit and panic control in those buildings that may be occupied by a large number of people. Such places of assembly are hotels, theaters, sports arenas, health care facilities, and similar institutions.

Emergency systems may supply power for ventilation that may be essential for sustaining life, for fire protection and alarm systems, elevators, fire pumps, safety communications, or industrial processes where interruption of current can cause serious life, safety, or health hazard problems. For maintenance requirements, see **700.3(C)** as well as **700.3(F). (See Figure 4-2)**

Note, meter-mounted transfer switch shall not be permitted to be reconditioned.

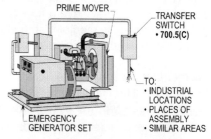

PURPOSE OF EMERGENCY GENERATORS
NEC 700.1 AND 700.2, IN

Figure 4-2. A generator set can be used to supply emergency loads such as places of assembly, special types of equipment, industrial related loads, and similar loads and equipment.

SIZING GENERATORS
700.4(A) THRU (C)

The capacity of the emergency system shall be sized adequately to handle the requirements of all the equipment to be operated simultaneously without overloading the generator. The equipment shall be designed and fully capable of handling the available fault current at its terminals. For local shielding requirements, see **700.4(B)** **(See Figure 4-3)**

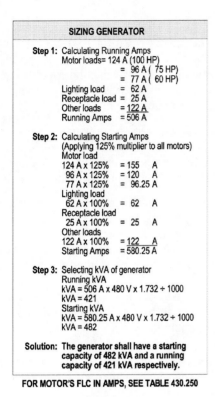

```
              SIZING GENERATOR

Step 1:  Calculating Running Amps
         Motor loads = 124 A (100 HP)
                     =  96 A ( 75 HP)
                     =  77 A ( 60 HP)
         Lighting load    = 62 A
         Receptacle load  = 25 A
         Other loads      = 122 A
         Running Amps     = 506 A

Step 2:  Calculating Starting Amps
         (Applying 125% multiplier to all motors)
         Motor load
         124 A x 125%  = 155    A
          96 A x 125%  = 120    A
          77 A x 125%  =  96.25 A
         Lighting load
          62 A x 100%  =  62    A
         Receptacle load
          25 A x 100%  =  25    A
         Other loads
         122 A x 100%  = 122    A
         Starting Amps = 580.25 A

Step 3:  Selecting kVA of generator
         Running kVA
         kVA = 506 A x 480 V x 1.732 ÷ 1000
         kVA = 421
         Starting kVA
         kVA = 580.25 A x 480 V x 1.732 ÷ 1000
         kVA = 482

Solution: The generator shall have a starting
          capacity of 482 kVA and a running
          capacity of 421 kVA respectively.
```

FOR MOTOR'S FLC IN AMPS, SEE TABLE 430.250

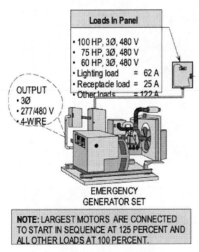

```
        Loads In Panel

• 100 HP, 3Ø, 480 V
•  75 HP, 3Ø, 480 V
•  60 HP, 3Ø, 480 V
• Lighting load   = 62 A
• Receptacle load = 25 A
• Other loads     = 122 A
```

OUTPUT
• 3Ø
• 277/480 V
• 4-WIRE

EMERGENCY
GENERATOR SET

NOTE: LARGEST MOTORS ARE CONNECTED TO START IN SEQUENCE AT 125 PERCENT AND ALL OTHER LOADS AT 100 PERCENT.

SIZING GENERATORS
NEC 700.4(A) THRU (C)

Figure 4-3. Sizing an emergency generator set to supply loads at an industrial process area.

TRANSFER SWITCH AND EQUIPMENT
700.5(A) THRU (E)

The transfer switch (600 volts or less) and equipment shall be automatically operated, be listed for emergency system use, and be approved by the AHJ. When installing the transfer equipment, it shall be so designed and installed so that accidental interconnection of the normal and the emergency source will not occur with the operation of the transfer equipment. Automatic transfer switches shall be electrically operated and mechanically held. Transfer equipment may supply only emergency loads. For documentation, see **700.5(E)**. **(See Figure 4-4)**

> **Generator Tip:** A means for isolating the transfer switch shall be permitted. If isolation switches are installed, inadvertent parallel operations are to be avoided.

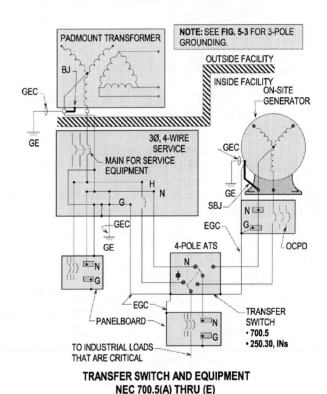

NOTE: SEE FIG. 5-3 FOR 3-POLE GROUNDING.

PADMOUNT TRANSFORMER

OUTSIDE FACILITY

INSIDE FACILITY

ON-SITE GENERATOR

BJ

GEC

GE

3Ø, 4-WIRE SERVICE

MAIN FOR SERVICE EQUIPMENT

GEC

GE

SBJ

H

N

G

N

G

GEC

EGC

GE

4-POLE ATS

N

OCPD

N

G

EGC

PANELBOARD

N

G

TRANSFER SWITCH
• 700.5
• 250.30, INs

TO INDUSTRIAL LOADS THAT ARE CRITICAL

TRANSFER SWITCH AND EQUIPMENT
NEC 700.5(A) THRU (E)

Figure 4-4. A four-pole transfer switch can be used to supply critical loads in different facilities.

WIRING IDENTIFICATION
700.10(A)

All boxes and enclosures that contain emergency circuits shall be marked so that they will be readily identified as being a part of the emergency circuit or system.

WIRING SYSTEMS
700.10(B)

Emergency source wiring, including its source of disconnecting overcurrent protection devices supplying the emergency load, shall be kept entirely separate from all other wiring and equipment, raceways, cables, and cabinets that contain other than emergency wiring. Wiring of two or more emergency circuits supplied from the same source shall be permitted in the same raceway, cable, box, or cabinet. These systems shall be located and designed to avoid damage due to vandalism, flooding, icing, and other adverse conditions. **(See Figure 4-5)**

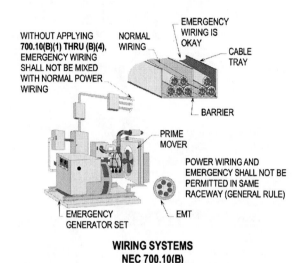

**WIRING SYSTEMS
NEC 700.10(B)**

Figure 4-5. Emergency wiring and normal power shall not be permitted to occupy the same raceway, cable tray, cable, etc.

WIRING SYSTEMS
700.10(B)(1) THRU (B)(5)

The emergency wiring system shall be permitted to be mixed with other power under any of the following conditions.

- In transfer equipment enclosures, the transfer equipment shall supply only emergency loads.

- In exit or emergency luminaires, a supply from two sources shall be permitted.

- In a common junction box attached to exit or emergency luminaires, a supply from two sources shall be permitted in a listed load control relay supplying exit or emergency luminaires.

- In a common junction box attached to unit equipment, that contains only the branch circuit supplying the unit equipment and the emergency circuit supplied by the unit equipment shall be permitted.

- Wiring from an emergency source to supply any combination of emergency, legally required, or optional loads in accordance with (a), (b), (c) or (d):

(a) From separate vertical switchboard sections, with or without a common bus, or from individual disconnects mounted in separate enclosures.

(b) The common bus or separate sections of the switchboard or the individual enclosures shall be permitted to be supplied by single or multiple feeders without overcurrent protection at the source.

Exception to **700.10(B)(5)(b):** Overcurrent protection shall be permitted at the source or for the equipment, provided the overcurrent protection is selectively coordinated with the downstream overcurrent protection.

(c) Legally required and optional standby circuits shall not originate from the same vertical switchboard section, panelboard enclosoure, or individual disconnect enclosure as emergency circuits.

(d) It shall be permissible to utilize single or multiple feeders to supply distribution equipment between an emergency source and the point where the combination of emergency, legally required, or optional loads are separated.

Note, wiring of two or more emergency circuits from the same source shall be permitted in the same raceway, cable, box, or cabinet.

See Figures 4-6(a), (b), and **(c)** for a detailed illustration pertaining to emergency wiring systems mixed with other power.

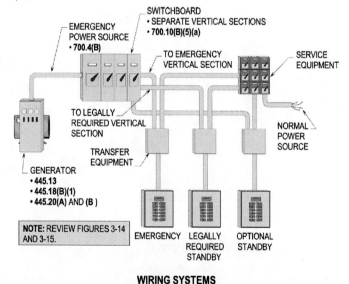

**WIRING SYSTEMS
700.10(B)(5)(a)**

Figure 4-6(a). Emergency source supplying a switchboard with vertical sections used to separate wiring.

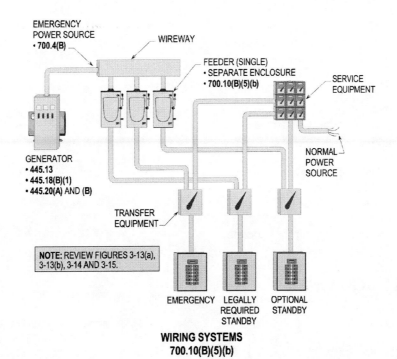

Figure 4-6(b). Emergency source supplying separate enclosures used to separate wiring.

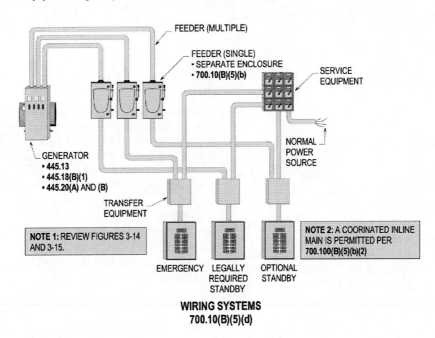

Figure 4-6(c). Multiple feeder sources from emergency generator supplying single separate enclosures used to separate wiring.

FEEDER WIRING PROTECTION 700.10(D)(1)

Emergency systems shall meet the additional requirements in **700.10(D)(1)** through **(D)(4)** in assembly occupancies for not less than 1000 persons or in buildings above 75 ft (23 m) in height with any of the following occupancy classes: assembly, educational, residential, detention and correctional, business, and mercantile.

Feeder wiring shall meet one of the follllowing conditions:

- Be installed in spaces or areas that are fully protected by an approved automatic fire suppression system.

- Be a listed electrical circuit protective system with a minimum 2-hour fire rating.

Note, UL guide information for electrical circuit protection systems (FHIT) contains information on proper installation requirements to maintain the fire rating.

- Be protected by a listed thermal barrier system for electrical system components with a maximum 2-hour fire rating.

- Be protected by a listed fire-rated assembly that has a minimum fire rating of 2 hours and contains only emergency wiring circuits.

- Be encased in not less than 2 in. (50 mm) of concrete.

FEEDER-CIRCUIT EQUIPMENT
700.10(D)(2)

Equipment for feeders (including transfer switches, transformers, and panelboards) shall be located either in spaces fully protected by approved automatic fire suppression systems (including sprinklers, carbon dioxide systems) or in spaces with a 2-hour fire resistance rating.

GENERATOR CONTROL WIRING
700.10(D)(4)

Control conductors installed between the transfer equipment and the emergency generator shall be kept entirely independent of all other wiring and shall meet the conditions of **700.10(B)(1). (See Figure 4-7)**

Note: The integrity of the generator control wiring shall be continuously monitored. Loss of integrity of the remote start circuit(s) shall initiate visual and audible annunciation of generator malfunction at the generator local and remote annunciator(s) and start the generator(s).

COORDINATION
700.32 AND 701.27

Emergency system(s) overcurrent devices shall be selectively coordinated with all supply side overcurrent protective devices.

Selective coordination shall not be required between two overcurrent devices located in series if no loads are connected in parallel with the downstream device.

Note, for a similar requirement, see **701.27** (legally required standby systems).

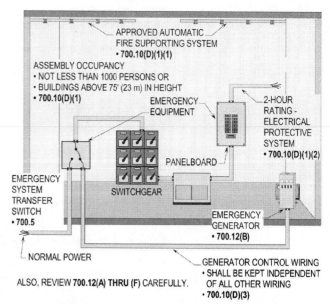

FEEDER WIRING AND GENERATOR CONTROL WIRING
700.10(D)(1) THRU (D)(3)

Figure 4-7. Generator control wiring installed between the transfer equipment and the emergency generator shall be kept entirely independent of all other wiring.

GROUNDING
700.7(B)

A warning sign shall be installed at the normal power service equipment where removal of a grounding or bonding connection in normal power source equipment interrupts the grounding electrode conductor connection to the alternate power source(s) grounded conductor. The warning sign shall include the following:

WARNING!
SHOCK HAZARD EXISTS IF GROUNING ELECTRODE CONDUCTOR OR BONDING JUMPER CONNECTION IN THIS EQUIPMENT IS REMOVED WHILE ALTERNATE SOURCE(S) IS ENERGIZED.
(See Figure 4-8)

Note, for the different methods used to ground a generator, see pages 6-5 through 6-10 in Chapter 6 of this book.

DISCONNECT FOR OUTDOOR GENERATOR SETS
700.12(D)(5), 701.12(D)(5), AND 702.12

Where an outdoor housed generator set is equipped with a readily accessible disconnecting means located within sight of the building or structure supplied, an additional disconnecting means shall not be required where ungrounded (phase) conductors serve or pass through the building or structure. The disconnecting means shall meet the requirements of **225.36. (See Figure 4-9)**

DISCONNECT FOR OUTDOOR GENERATOR SETS
700.12(D)(5)

The generator set disconnecting means shall not be required to be located within sight of the buliding or structure served for installations under single management, where conditions of maintenance and supervision ensure that only qualfied persons will monitor and service the installation and where documented safe switching procedures are established and maintained for disconnection. **(See Figure 4-10)**

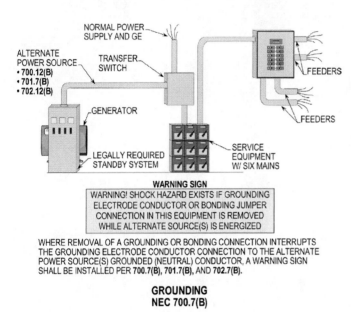

Figure 4-8. This illustration shows the warning sign requirements for emergency systems where a grounding or bonding connection is removed at the normal power source equipment.

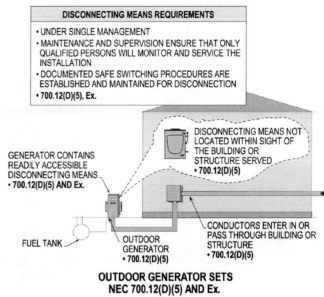

Figure 4-10. This illustration shows the disconnecting means requirements for outdoor generator sets under single management.

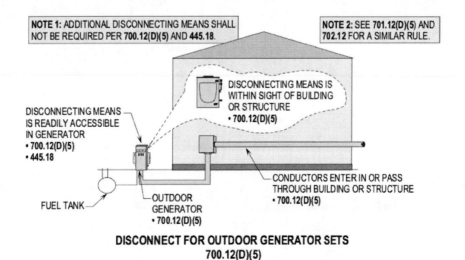

Figure 4-9. If a disconnecting means is located at an outdoor generator as described in **700.12(D)(5)**, an additional disconnecting means at the buliding is not requred. Also, review the **Ex.** to **700.12(D)(5)**.

Chapter 4: Emergency System Generators

Section   Answer

1. To prevent immediate retransfer in cases of short-time restoring of the normal source of power, a time-delay feature allowing for a _____ minute setting shall be provided for emergency system generators.
   (a) 10   (b) 30
   (c) 20   (d) none of the above

2. Internal combustion engines used as the prime movers for emergency system generators shall have an on-site fuel supply that will function at full demand for not less than _____ hours of operation.
   (a) 1   (b) 1-1/2
   (c) 2   (d) 2-1/2

3. When an emergency generator requires more than _____ seconds to develop power, an auxiliary power supply shall be permitted to energize the emergency system until the regular generator is capable of picking up the load.
   (a) 10   (b) 15
   (c) 20   (d) 30

4. An emergency system shall have adequate capacity and rating for all loads to be operated _____.
   (a) automatically   (b) manually
   (c) simultaneously   (d) nonsimultaneously

5. Feeder wiring for emergency system generators shall be permitted to be a listed electrical circuit protective system with a minimum _____ hour fire rating.
   (a) 1   (b) 2
   (c) 3   (d) 4

6. Feeder wiring for emergency system generators shall be permitted to be encased in not less than _____ in. of concrete.
   (a) 1   (b) 2
   (c) 3   (d) 6

7. Feeder wiring for emergency system generators shall be permitted to be protected by a listed thermal barrier system for electrical system components with a minimum _____ hour fire rating
   (a) 1   (b) 2
   (c) 3   (d) 4

8. Equipment for feeders shall be located either in spaces fully protected by _____ automatic fire suppression systems or in spaces with a 1-hour fire resistance rating.
   (a) identified   (b) labeled
   (c) listed   (d) approved

9. Generator control wiring installed between the transfer equipment and the emergency generator shall be kept entirely _____ of all other wiring.
   (a) labeled   (b) approved
   (c) independent   (d) none of the above

————————— ————————— **10.** Emergency systems shall meet the additional requirements in **700.10(D)(1)** and **700.10(D)(2)** in assembly occupancies for not less than _____ persons.

      (a) 100   (b) 250

      (c) 500   (d) 1000

5

Legally Required and Optional Standby Systems

This chapter covers legally required standby systems that are classified by municipal, state, federal, and/or other codes, or by any governmental agency having jurisdiction.

In the event that there is a failure of the normal power source, these systems are intended to supply power automatically to special selected loads that are not classified as emergency systems.

Legally required standby power systems also supply such loads as heating and refrigeration systems, communications systems, ventilation and smoke removal systems, sewage disposal, lighting, and industrial processes that, when stopped during a power outage, could create hazards or hamper rescue or firefighting operations.

This chapter also covers optional standby systems intended to protect private business or property where life safety does not depend on the performance of the system. Optional standby systems are not those systems that are classified as emergency or legally required standby systems. These systems serve as an alternate power source for industrial and commercial buildings, farms, and residences by supplying such loads as heating and refrigeration systems, data processing and communications systems, and industrial processes that, when stopped during any power outage, could cause discomfort, serious interruption of the process, or damage to the product or process.

PART III – LEGALLY REQUIRED STANDBY SYSTEMS
GENERAL REQUIREMENTS
701.12

In selecting a legally required standby generator, consideration shall be given to the type of service to be rendered, whether of short-time duration or long-time duration.

Consideration shall also be given to the location or design, or both, of all equipment to minimize the hazards that might cause complete failure due to floods, fires, icing, and vandalism.

> **Generator Tip:** The assignment of the degree of reliability of a recognized legally required standby supply system depends on the careful evaluation of the variables at each particular installation.

GENERATOR SET
701.12(D)(1) THRU (D)(3)

A generator set driven by a prime mover shall be sized by **701.4** and be acceptable to the AHJ. A means shall be provided for automatically starting the prime mover upon failure of the normal service and to automatically transfer all electrical circuits. A time-delay feature permitting a 15-minute setting shall be provided to avoid retransfer in case of a short-time reestablishment of the normal source.

Where internal combustion engines are used as the prime mover, an on-site fuel supply shall be provided with a fuel supply of not less than 2 hours full-demand operation. Fuel transfer pumps shall be connected to the legally required standby power system where power is needed for the operation of the fuel transfer pumps to deliver fuel to a generator set day tank.

Prime movers are not to solely depend upon a public utility gas system for their fuel supply or municipal water supply for their cooling systems. Automatically transferring of one fuel supply to another where dual fuel supplies are used shall be provided.

> **Generator Tip:** Where acceptable to the AHJ, the use of other than on-site fuels shall be permitted where there is a low probability of a simultaneous failure of both the off-site fuel delivery system and power from the outside electrical utility company.

Where a storage battery is used for control or signal power, or as the means of starting the prime mover, it shall be suitable for the purpose and be equipped with an automatic charging means independent of the generator set. **(See Figure 5-1)**

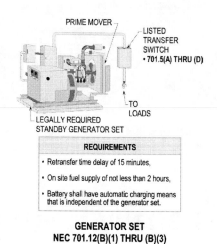

REQUIREMENTS
• Retransfer time delay of 15 minutes,
• On site fuel supply of not less than 2 hours,
• Battery shall have automatic charging means that is independent of the generator set.

GENERATOR SET
NEC 701.12(B)(1) THRU (B)(3)

Figure 5-1. This illustration sows the rules for a generator set under certain conditions of use. **Note:** For maintenance reirements, see **701.3(C)**.

PURPOSE OF LEGALLY REQUIRED STANDBY SYSTEM
701.1 AND ARTICLE 100

Legally required standby systems are those required by municipal, state, federal, or by other codes, or any governmental agency having jurisdiction, the intent of which is to supply power to selected loads other than those classified as emergency systems. In the event that the normal power source fails, this system shall provide the necessary power.

LEGALLY REQUIRED STANDBY SYSTEMS – WHERE USED
701.1, IN's 1 THRU 5

Typical installations of legally required standby systems are intended for operation to serve loads such as heating, refrigerator systems, communications systems, ventilation and smoke removal systems, sewage disposal, and industrial processes, which, if the normal operation of the normal power supply fails, could create hazards or hinder rescue or firefighting operations. **(See Figure 5-2)**

SIZING GENERATORS
701.4(A) THRU (D)

A legally required standby system shall have adequate capacity and rating for supplying all equipment intended to be operated at the same time.

The alternate power source shall be permitted to supply legally required standby and optional standby loads when these loads are automatically picked up for load shedding so as to ensure power to the legally required standby circuits. **(See Figure 4-3)**

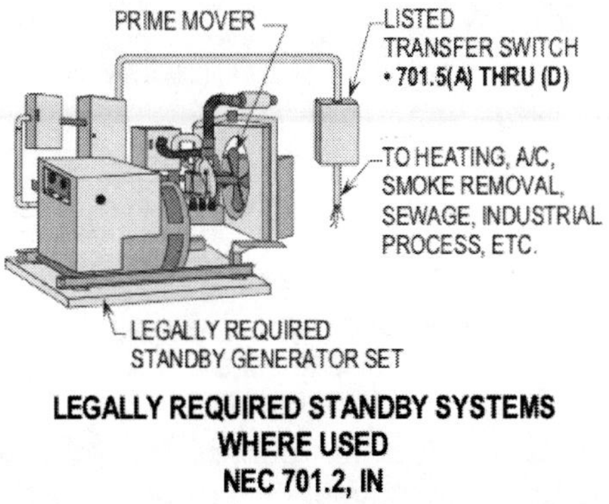

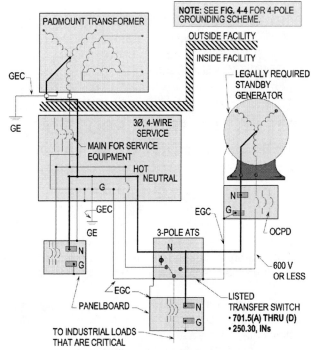

Figure 5-2. This illustration shows the loads that are served by a legally required standby system.

TRANSFER SWITCHES AND EQUIPMENT
701.5(A) THRU (D)

Automatic transfer equipment shall be listed for legally required standby use. The automatic transfer equipment shall be so designed so that no accidental connection of the normal and alternate sources of supply occurs at the same time in the operation of any transfer equipment. The AHJ shall approve the transfer equipment, per **110.3(B)**. Isolation equipment shall be permitted to be used to isolate the transfer equipment. However, if isolation equipment is used, any inadvertent parallel operation shall be avoided. Automatic transfer switches (ATS) shall be electrically operated and mechanically held. **(See Figure 5-3)**

WIRING LEGALLY REQUIRED STANDBY SYSTEMS
701.10(A) AND (B)

Legally required standby system wiring shall be permitted to occupy the same raceways, cables, boxes, and cabinets with other general wiring systems. This is a big advantage over emergency wiring systems, which are not permitted this privilege. **(See Figure 5-4)**

OVERCURRENT PROTECTION DEVICES – ACCESIBILITY
701.30

Only authorized persons shall be permitted to have access to overcurrent protection devices of legally required standby circuits. This will prevent tampering or interference with the operation of the overcurrent protection devices and circuits.

Generator Tip: The alternate power source that supplies legally required standby systems shall not be required to have ground-fault protection of equipment with automatic disconnecting means per **701.31**. For selectively coordinated of supply side overcurrent protection devices, see **700.32**.

Figure 5-3. A three-pole transfer switch shall be permitted to be used to supply critical loads in different facilities.

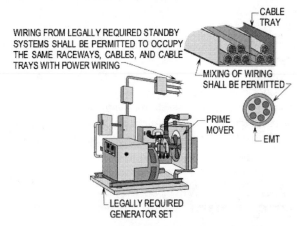

Figure 5-4. Legally required standby wiring shall be permitted to occupy the same raceway, cable tray, and cable as power wiring.

GROUNDING
701.7(B)

A warning sign shall be installed at the normal power source equipment where removal of a grounding or bonding connection in normal power source equipment interrupts the grounding electrode conductor connection to the alternate power source(s) grounding (neutral) conductor. The sign shall state the following:

WARNING:
SHOCK HAZARD EXISTS IF GROUNDING ELECTRODE CONDUCTOR OR BONDING JUMPER CONNECTION IN THE EQUIPMENT IS REMOVED WHILE ALTERNATE SOURCE(S) IS ENERGIZED.

PART I – OPTIONAL STANDBY SYSTEMS AND THE PURPOSE OF OPTIONAL STANDBY GENERATOR SYSTEMS
702.1 AND ARTICLE 100

Optional standby systems are intended only for the protection of business or property and do not include places where life safety is dependent on the performance of the system. They may be operated manually or automatically.

With brownouts and blackouts over the country, many individuals and especially ranches, farms, and dairy operations may have a standby source of power to eliminate losses and unscheduled outages from the loss of power.

OPTIONAL STANDBY SYSTEMS – WHERE USED
702.1, IN

Optional standby systems are typically installed to provide an alternate source of electrical power for facilities such as industrial and commercial buildings, farms, ranches, and residences, heating or refrigeration systems, data processing and communications systems, and industrial processes, which, if stopped during a power outage, could cause interruption to the process or damage to the product, etc. **(See Figure 5-5)**

SIZING OPTIONAL STANDBY GENERATORS
702.4(A) AND (B)

The following shall be considered for sizing generators:
• Available short-circuit current
• System capacity

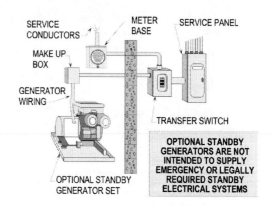

**OPTIONAL STANDBY SYSTEMS
WHERE USED
NEC 702.1. IN**

Figure 5-5. Optional standby generators shall be permitted to be used to supply any loads except those supplied by emergency and legally required standby generator sets.

AVAILABLE SHORT-CIRCUIT CURRENT
702.4(A)(1) AND (A)(2)

Optional standby system equipment shall be suitable for the maximum available short-circuit current at its terminals.

SYSTEM CAPACITY
702.4(A)(2)

The calculations of load on the standby source shall be made in accordance with **Article 220** or by another approved method.

MANUAL TRANSFER EQUIPMENT
702.4(B)

Where manual transfer equipment is used, an optional standby system shall have adequate capacity and rating for the supply of all equipment intended to be operated at one time. The user of the optional standby system shall be permitted to select the load connected to the system.

AUTOMATIC TRANSFER EQUIPMENT
702.4(A)(2)(a) AND (b)

Where automatic transfer equipment is used, an optional standby system shall comply with the following:
• Full load
• Load management

FULL LOAD
702.4(A)(2)(a)

The standby source shall be capable of supplying the full load that is transferred by the automatic transfer equipment.

LOAD MANAGEMENT
702.4(A)(2)(b)

Where a system is employed that will automatically manage the connectged load, the standby source shall have a capacity sufficient to supply the maximum load that will be connected by the load management system. **[See Figure 5-6(a)** and **(b)]**

TRANSFER SWITCHES AND EQUIPMENT
702.5(A) THRU (D)

Transfer equipment shall be suitable for its intended use, and designed and installed so as to prevent an accidental connection with the normal or alternate sources of power. The AHJ shall give approval of such transfer equipment. **(See Figure 5-7)**

WIRING OPTIONAL STANDBY SYSTEMS
702.10

The wiring from the optional standby equipment shall be permitted to be in the same raceways, cables, boxes, and cabinets as other general wiring. This is a big advantage over emergency systems, which do not allow such privileges. **(See Figure 5-8)**

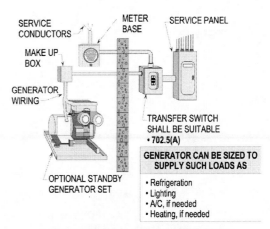

SIZING OPTIONAL STANDBY GENERATORS NEC 702.4(A)(1) AND (2)

Figure 5-6(a). Optional standby generators shall be permitted to be used to supply specific loads and not the entire load supplied by the electrical system.

GROUNDING
702.7(B)

A warning sign shall be installed at the normal power source equipment where removal of a grounding or bonding connection in normal power source equipment interrupts the grounding electrode conductor connection to the alternate power source(s) grounded (neutral) conductor. The sign shall state the following:

WARNING:
SHOCK HAZARD EXISTS IF GROUNDING ELECTRODE CONDUCTOR OR BONDING JUMPER CONNECTION IN THE EQUIPMENT IS REMOVED WHILE ALTERNATE SOURCE(S) IS ENERGIZED. **[See Figure 5-9(a) and (b)]**

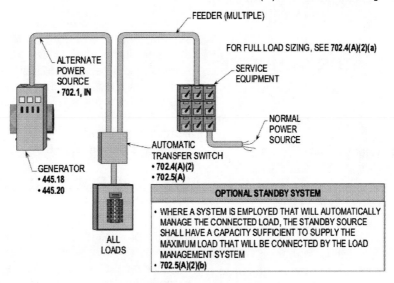

SIZING OPTIONAL STANDBY GENERATORS NEC 702.4(A)(1) AND (A)(2)

Figure 5-6(b). This requirement clarifies the installation of manual transfer and automatic transfer applications for optional standby systems.

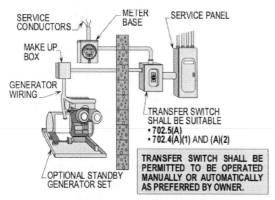

**TRANSFER SWITCHES AND EQUIPMENT
NEC 702.5(A) THRU (D)**

Figure 5-7. Transfer switches used to transfer the generator power to the premise can be accomplished by a manual or automatic means.

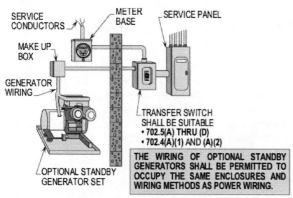

**WIRING OPTIONAL STANDBY SYSTEMS
NEC 702.10**

Figure 5-8. The wiring of optional standby systems shall be permitted to be run with the power wiring of the facility.

PORTABLE GENERATOR GOUNDING 702.11

The following shall be considered for portable generator grounding:
- Separately derived system
- Nonseperately derived system

SEPARATELY DERIVED SYSTEM 702.11(A)

Where a portable optional standby source is used as a separately derived system, it shall be grounded to a grounding electrode in accordance with **250.30**.

NONSEPARATELY DERIVED SYSTEM 702.11(B)

Where a portable optional standby source is used as a nonseparately derived system, the equipment grounding conductor shall be bonded to the system grounding electrode.

For detailed illustrations describing these grounding requirements, see **Figures 6-15, 6-16** and **6-17** in Chapter 6 of this book. Also, review **250.35(A)** and **(B)** below.

GROUNDING OF PERMANENTLY INSTALLED GENERATORS 250.35(A) AND (B)

A conductor that provides an effective ground-fault current path shall be installed with the supply conductors from a permanently installed generator(s) to the first disconnected means as follows:

SEPARATELY DERIVED SYSTEM 250.35(A)

Where the generator is installed as a separately derived system, the requirements in **250.30** shall apply.

NONSEPARATELY DERIVED SYSTEM 250.35(B)

A supply-side bonding jumper shall be installed between the generator equipment grounding terminal and the equipment grounding terminal, bar, or bus of the disconnecting mean(s) if the generator is installed as a nonseparately derived system, and overcurrent protection is not integral with the generator assembly. The supply-side bonding jumper shall be sized per **250.102(C)(1)** based on the size of the conductors supplied by the generator. (**See Figure 5-9** for a description of the above requirements.)

Note, for the different methods used to ground a generator, see **pages 6-5 through 6-9** in Chapter 6.

SIGN FOR POWER INLET 702.7(C)

Where a power inlet is used for a temporary connection to a portable generator, a warning sign shall be placed near the inlet to indicate the type of derived system that the system is capable of, based on the wiring of the transfer equipment. The sign shall display one of the following warnings:

WARNING:
FOR CONNECTION OF A SEPARATELY DERIVED
(BONDED NEUTRAL) SYSTEM ONLY
or
WARNING:
FOR CONNECTION OF A NONSEPARATELY DERIVED
(FLOATING NEUTRAL) SYSTEM ONLY
[See Figure 5-9(b)]

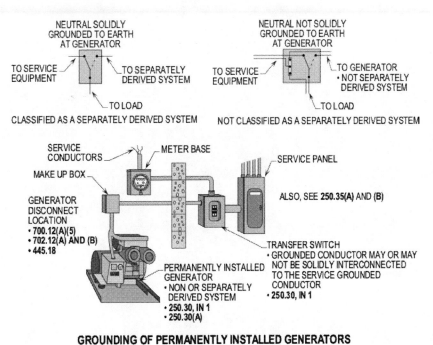

GROUNDING OF PERMANENTLY INSTALLED GENERATORS
NEC 250.35(A) AND (B)

Figure 5-9(a). A separately derived system shall be grounded where transfer equipment is provided that includes switching the grounded (neutral) conductor, and where the grounded (neutral) conductor is not solidly interconnected to the service supplied grounded (neutral) conductor, it shall not be considered a separately derived system.

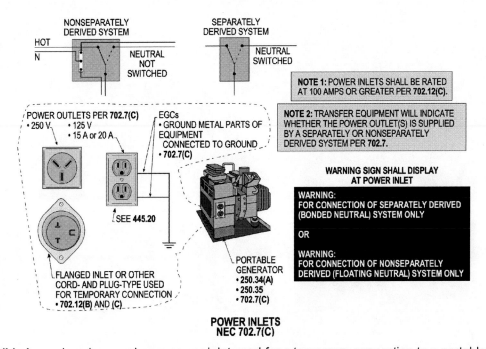

POWER INLETS
NEC 702.7(C)

Figure 5-9(b). A warning sign requires a power inlet used for a temporary connection to a portable generator.

Chapter 5: Legally Required and Optional Standby Systems

	Section	Answer

1. Where a legally required standby is used, a time-delay feature permitting a _____minute setting shall be provided to avoid retransfer in case of a short-time reestablishment of the normal source.
   - (a) 10
   - (b) 15
   - (c) 20
   - (d) 30

2. Where internal combustion engines are used as the prime mover for legally required standby systems, an on-site fuel supply shall be provided with a fuel supply of not less than _____ hours full-demand operation.
   - (a) 1
   - (b) 1-1/2
   - (c) 2
   - (d) 2-1/2

3. Where a system is employed that will _____ manage the connected load, the optional standby source shall have a capacity sufficient to supply the maximum load that will be connected by the load management system.
   - (a) automatically
   - (b) manually
   - (c) simultaneously
   - (d) nonsimultaneously

4. Where an optional standby system is used, transfer equipment shall be _____ for its intended use.
   - (a) identified
   - (b) listed
   - (c) approved
   - (d) suitable

5. Where a portable optional standby source is used as a nonseparately derived system, the equipment grounding conductor shall be bonded to the _____ grounding electrode.
   - (a) system
   - (b) bonding
   - (c) copper
   - (d) aluminum

6. A locking type power inlet for temporary connection of generator with cord and plug eliminates requirements for _____ protection of 125 volt outlets.
   - (a) GFCI
   - (b) AFCI
   - (c) GFPE
   - (d) none of the above

7. The code calls for a grounding warning sign to be placed at the service equipment when the generator is _____ as a non-separately derived system.
   - (a) serviced
   - (b) classified
   - (c) fed
   - (d) none of the above

8. A _____ that is permanently installed is required to comply with certain rules in the NEC.
   - (a) transformer
   - (b) feeder
   - (c) generator
   - (d) none of the above

9. Calculations for a standby power source must comply with Article _____ of the NEC.
   - (a) 90
   - (b) 100
   - (c) 110
   - (d) 220

_____ _____ **10.** Overcurrent protection devices for legally required standby systems must be _____ the user.

        (a) accessible to   (b) unaccessible to

        (c) near   (d) none of the above

6

Generators Supplying Essential Loads for Hospitals

This chapter covers essential electrical loads that are designed to be supplied by all types of alternate power sources, all distribution systems, and ancillary equipment that have been designed to ensure electrical power continuity to designated areas and functions of a health care facility when the normal power source is disrupted. It shall also be designed to minimize the disruption of power in the internal wiring system.

Note, the essential electrical systems used in hospitals are the emergency system and the equipment system, respectively.

TRANSFER SWITCHES
517.31(B) AND 517.42(B)

Feeders or branch circuits that conform to **Article 700** and are intended to supply power from an alternate source to a limited number of designated functions that are vital for the protection of life and for the patient's safety, shall operate within 10 seconds of the interruption of the normal power source per **517.32(B)**.

Note, for a list of definitions pertaining to hospitals see **Article 100** in the **NEC.**

LIFE SAFETY BRANCH
Article 100

The life safety branch is a subsystem of the emergency system consisting of feeders and branch circuits that meet the requirements of **Article 700**. The intent is to provide adequate power needs to ensure safety to the patients and other personnel. These circuits shall automatically be connected to the alternate power sources upon interruption of the normal supply of power.

CRITICAL BRANCH
Article 100

The critical branch is a subsystem of the emergency system consisting of feeders and branch circuits supplying energy to task illumination, special power circuits, and receptacles that are selected to serve those areas where proper functioning is essential to patient care. Such circuits shall be connected to an alternate power source by means of one or more transfer switches that are energized from the temporary power source when the normal power source is interrupted.

EQUIPMENT BRANCH
517.44(A) AND (B)

The equipment branch consists of feeders or branch circuits arranged for delayed automatic or manual connection to the power source. This ordinarily serves the three-phase power loads as defined in **Article 100**.

This equipment branch is used to supply power to major pieces of electrical equipment that are essential for either hospital operations or patient care. **(See Figure 6-1)** Review these requirements in the NEC carefully.

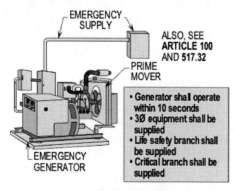

EQUIPMENT SYSTEM
NEC 517.44(A) AND (B)

Figure 6-1. The equipment system shall supply certain types of critical loads in hospitals.

TRANSFER SWITCHES
517.31(B)

Each branch of the essential electrical system shall be served by at least one transfer switch. This is illustrated in **Figures 517.31(B)(1)** and **(B)(2)** in the NEC, which should be carefully reviewed. One transfer switch shall be permitted to serve more than one branch of the essential system, up to 150 kVA, as illustrated in **Figure 517.31(B)(2)**. The exact number of transfer switches for a facility shall be based on a good engineering design that considers load, switch design, switch reliability, and dependability. **(See Figure 6-2)**

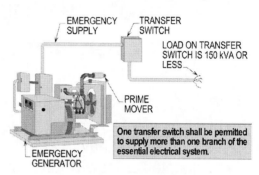

TRANSFER SWITCHES
NEC 517.31(B)

Figure 6-2. The number of transfer switches required is based on the type, number, and amount of loads served.

OPTIONAL LOADS
517.31(B)(1) AND (B)(2)

Loads supplied by generating equipment not specifically listed in **517.31(D)**, **517.32**, **517.33**, and **517.34** shall be served by their own transfer switch. Such loads shall not be:

(1) transferred if the transfer will overload the generating equipment and

(2) automatically shed upon generating equipment overloading conditions.

See **Figure 6-3** for details of such rules.

WIRING REQUIREMENTS
517.31(C)(1) THRU (C)(3)

Certain rules shall be applied to wiring that is routed to locations where the life safety and critical branches of the emergency system are used. Such wiring shall be separated from other wiring. However, in some cases, junction boxes, luminaires, and transfer switch wiring shall be permitted to be mixed. **(See Figure 6-4)**

These systems shall be limited to circuits that are essential to maintaining life and safety. There are two parts of this emergency system:

(1) Life safety branch and

(2) Critical branch.

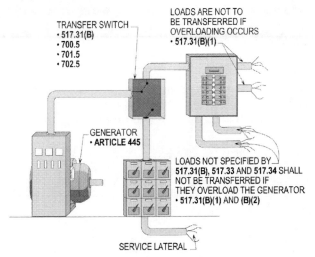

OPTIONAL LOADS
NEC 517.31(B)(1) AND (B)(2)

Figure 6-3. Transfer switches shall not be overloaded when transferring from the normal power to the emergency power.

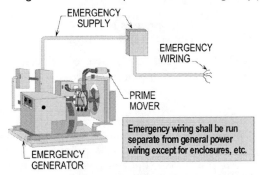

WIRING REQUIREMENTS
NEC 517.31(C)(1) THRU (C)(3)

Figure 6-4. This illustration shows that general wiring shall not be run in raceways, etc. with emergency wiring.

SEPARATION FROM OTHER CIRCUITS 517.31(C)(1) THROUGH (C)(3)

The life safety and critical branches of the emergency system shall not be permitted to be installed in a common raceway, enclosure, or box with any other wiring systems, except in one of the following conditions:

(1) In transfer equipment enclosures,

(2) In the exit or emergency luminaires that are supplied by two sources,

(3) In a common junction box attached to exit or emergency luminaires such as in "(2)" above, and

(4) Wiring of two or more emergency circuits supplied from the same branch and same transfer switch.

Note, the wiring of the equipment system shall be permitted to share raceways, etc. with other wiring systems that are not part of the emergency system.

See Figure 6-5 for the rules of installing the wiring (separately) of the life safety and critical branches per **517.31(C)(1)**. (Review these requirements carefully.)

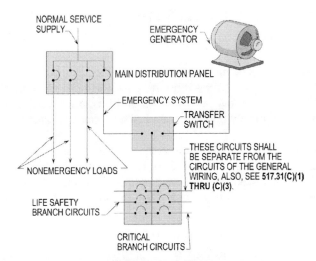

SEPARATION FROM OTHER CIRCUITS
NEC 517.31(C)(1) THRU (C)(3)

Figure 6-5. This illustration shows the requirements for installing the wiring of the life safety and critical branches.

ISOLATION AND PROTECTION 517.31(C)(2) AND (C)(3)

Isolated power systems that are installed in anesthetizing locations or in special environments shall be supplied by an individual, dedicated circuit supplying no other loads. For mechanical protection, the wiring of an emergency system shall be installed in nonflexible metal raceways, Type MI cable, or Schedule 80 RNC.

517.31(C)(3)(1) THROUGH (5)

Cords of appliances and other pieces of equipment connected to the emergency system are exempt from such rules. The secondary circuits of communications or signaling systems that are supplied by transformers do not have to be enclosed in metal raceways, except as required by **Chapters 7** and **8**.

Schedule 80 (PVC), rigid nonmetallic conduit, and Schedule 40 PVC encased in at least 2 in. (50 mm) of concrete or electrical metallic tubing shall be permitted, except for branch circuits that serve patient care areas.

Listed flexible metal raceways and listed cable assemblies shall be permitted to be used as a wiring method if they are installed in listed prefabricated medical headwalls, listed office furnishings, or where necessary for flexible connections to equipment.

Note, review **(1) thru (5)** to **517.31(C)(3)** very carefully before installing the above wiring methods in such areas.

CAPACITY OF SYSTEMS
517.31(D)

Essential electrical systems shall be sufficient to supply any demand placed on them. In the past, this normally meant that they were over-engineered and provided more than enough capacity under any and all conditions of use.

These feeders, in the past, were usually calculated by the rules of **Articles 215** and **220**. However, the 1996 edition of the NEC permits the use of demand calculations to be used for sizing the generator set or sets if based on the following criteria:

   (1) Prudent demand factors and historical data, or

   (2) Connected load, or

   (3) Feeder calculation procedures described in **Article 220**, or

   (4) Any combination of the above.

Note: Section 700.4 shall not apply to alternate power sources.

See Figure 6-6 for a detailed illustration of the rules for calculating such loads.

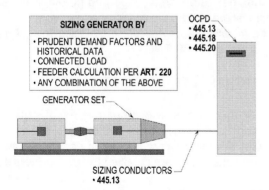

**CAPACITY OF SYSTEMS
NEC 517.31(D)**

Figure 6-6. Emergency generators shall be permitted to be sized by demand factors, historical data, or calculations per **Articlue 220** of the NEC.

SOURCES OF POWER
517.30(A), (B), AND (C)

Basically, essential systems are required to have a minimum of two sources of power available. One may be the normal source and the other may be the alternate source(s) for use when the normal power is interrupted, or may be a generator set(s) driven by a prime mover and located on the facility. Where the normal power consists of a generating unit(s) on the premises, the alternate source may be another generating set(s) or an external utility source. Extreme care shall be exercised in the location of equipment to protect it from damage, floods, etc. **(See Figure 6-7)**

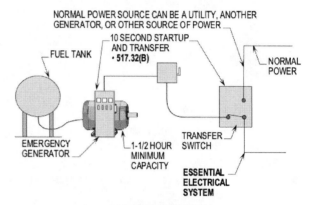

**SOURCES OF POWER
NEC 517.30(A), (B), AND (C)**

Figure 6-7. This illustration shows the power sources permitted to be used for the normal power supply.

Generator Tip: Facilities whose normal source of power is obtained from two or more central stations experience electrical service reliability that is greater than that of facilities whose normal supply of power are served from only a single source. Such a source of electrical power consists of power supplied from two or more electrical generators or two or more electrical services supplied from separate utility distribution networks that have local power in the input sources and that are arranged so as to provide mechanical and electrical separation. This is so that a fault between the facilities and the generating source will not be likely to cause the interruption of more than one of the service feeder facilities.

GENERATOR GROUNDING FOR 480 V TO 1000 V SYSTEMS
250.36(A) THROUGH (G)

When a high-impedance grounded neutral system is utilized for a 480 volt to 1000 volt system in compliance with **250.36(A) through (G)**, the grounding connections shall be made by the rules and regulations of this section, as follows:

High-Impedance Grounded Neutral Systems

- The grounding impedance (usually a resistor) shall be installed between the system neutral point and the grounding electrode conductor. The neutral point may be that of a wye transformer connection, or a neutral point may be derived from a 480 volt delta system by the use of a zigzag grounding autotransformer.

- The grounded system conductor from the neutral point to the grounding impedance shall be fully insulated for it to operate at a substantial voltage above ground.

- The system shall not be connected to ground except through the grounding impedance.

- The neutral conductor from the neutral point to the grounding impedance shall be permitted to be installed in a separate raceway.

- The equipment bonding jumper (the connection between the system equipment grounding conductors and the grounding impedance) shall be an unspliced conductor run from the first system disconnect or overcurrent device of the system to the grounded side of the grounding impedance.

- The grounding electrode conductor shall not be connected at any point from the grounded side of the impedance to the equipment ground bus or terminal at the service equipment or the first disconnecting means.

- Where the grounding electrode conductor connection is made at the grounding impedance, the equipment bonding jumper shall be sized per **250.66**, based on the size of the service entrance conductors for a service or the derived phase conductors for a separately derived system. If the grounding electrode conductor is connected at the first system disconnecting means or overcurrent device, the equipment bonding jumper shall be sized the same as the grounded system conductor in **250.36(B)**.

See Figure 6-8 for the grounding methods most often used to ground industrial electrical power sources.

GENERATOR GROUNDING OF 1000 VOLTS OR MORE 250.187(A) THROUGH (D)

All high-voltage electrical systems utilizing an impedance-grounded neutral technique shall comply with the following:

High-Impedance Grounded Neutral Systems

- The grounding impedance shall be inserted into the grounding conductor between the grounding electrode and the neutral point of the supply transformer or generator.

- The neutral of this type of system shall be identified and insulated with the same insulation as the phase conductors.

- The system neutral conductor shall be permitted to be connected to the neutral grounding impedance.

- In this kind of system, equipment grounding conductors shall be permitted to be connected to the ground bus and grounding electrode conductor, and brought to the system ground. It shall be permitted to be bare.

See Figure 6-8 for a detailed illustration of high-impedance grounding.

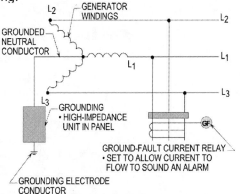

NEC LOOP HIGH-IMPEDANCE GROUNDING	
LOCATION	250.36(A)
CONDUCTOR INSULATION AND AMPACITY	250.36(B)
SYSTEM GROUNDING CONNECTION	250.36(C)
CONDUCTOR RATING	250.36(D)
EQUIPMENT BONDING JUMPER	250.36(E)
GEC CONNECTION LOCATION	250.36(F)
EQUIPMENT BONDING JUMPER SIZE	250.36(G)

GENERATOR GROUNDING
FOR 480 V TO 1000 V SYSTEMS
NEC 250.36(A) THRU (G)

Figure 6-8. The above illustrates the rules for high-impedance grounding of generators rated 1000 volts or less. **Note**, the same rules apply per **250.187** for grounding generators of 1000 volts or greater.

SEPARATELY DERIVED SYSTEMS 250.30 AND IN 1 AND IN 2

Separately derived systems, as covered in **250.20(B)** or **(B)**, shall be grounded as specified in **250.30(A)**. Where an alternate source such as an on-site generator is provided with transfer equipment that includes a grounded conductor that is not solidly interconnected to the service-supplied grounded conductor, the alternate source (derived system) shall be grounded in accordance with **250.30(A)**.

IN 1

An alternate ac power source such as an on-site generator is not a separately derived system if the grounded conductor is solidly interconnected to a service-supplied system grounded conductor. An example of such situations is where alternate source transfer equipment does not include a switching action in the grounded (neutral) conductor and allows it to remain solidly connected to the service-supplied grounded conductor when the alternate source is operational and supplying the load served.

IN 2

For systems that are not separately derived and are not required to be grounded as specified in **250.30**, see **445.13** for minimum size of conductors that carry fault current. **(See Figure 6-9)**

PERMANENTLY INSTALLED GENERATORS 250.35

A conductor that provides an effective ground-fault current path shall be installed with the supply conductors from a permanently installed generator(s) to the first disconnecting mean(s) as follows:

SEPARATELY DERIVED SYSTEM 250.35(A)

Where the generator is installed as a separately derived system, the requirements in **250.30** shall apply.

NONSEPARATELY DERIVED SYSTEM 250.35(B)

A supply-side bonding jumper shall be installed between the generator equipment grounding terminal and the equipment grounding terminal, bar, or bus of the disconnecting mean(s) where the generator is installed as a nonseparately derived system, and overcurrent protection is not integral with the generator assembly. The supply-side bonding jumper shall be sized per **250.102(C)** based on the size of the conductors supplied by the generator. **(See Figure 6-10)**

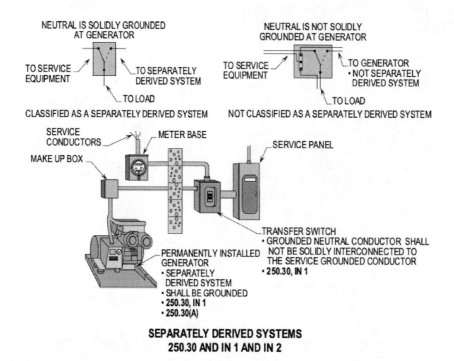

Figure 6-9. This section clarifies that a separately derived systems, such as a generator, shall be grounded where transfer equipment is provided that includes switching the grounded (neutral) conductor and where the grounded (neutral) conductor is not solidly interconnected to the service-supplied grounded conductor.

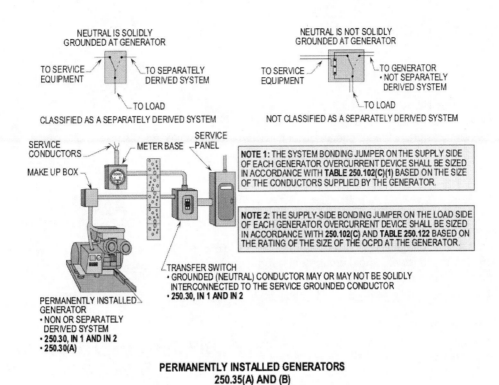

NOTE 1: THE SYSTEM BONDING JUMPER ON THE SUPPLY SIDE OF EACH GENERATOR OVERCURRENT DEVICE SHALL BE SIZED IN ACCORDANCE WITH **TABLE 250.102(C)(1)** BASED ON THE SIZE OF THE CONDUCTORS SUPPLIED BY THE GENERATOR.

NOTE 2: THE SUPPLY-SIDE BONDING JUMPER ON THE LOAD SIDE OF EACH GENERATOR OVERCURRENT DEVICE SHALL BE SIZED IN ACCORDANCE WITH **250.102(C)** AND **TABLE 250.122** BASED ON THE RATING OF THE SIZE OF THE OCPD AT THE GENERATOR.

PERMANENTLY INSTALLED GENERATORS
250.35(A) AND (B)

Figure 6-10. This section addresses the installation of supply-side bonding jumpers (based on ungrounded conductors) and equipment grounding conductor(s) (based on OCPD) for permanently installed generators that may or may not be separately derived systems.

METHODS OF GROUNDING
250.130(A) AND (B)

The decision to ground or not to ground a generator is a choice that designers will have to make at one time or another during their careers. By definition, an ungrounded system is a system that has no intentional connection to ground. A grounded system is a system that has an intentional connection to ground.

A generator that has no intentional connection to ground is known in the industry as an ungrounded system. However, it is connected to ground through the stray capacitance of the ungrounded (phase) conductors. If a ground fault does not occur, the neutral of an ungrounded system operates close to ground potential. The neutral voltage is held at such potential by the balanced stray capacitance between each ungrounded (phase) conductor and ground. **(See Figure 6-11)**

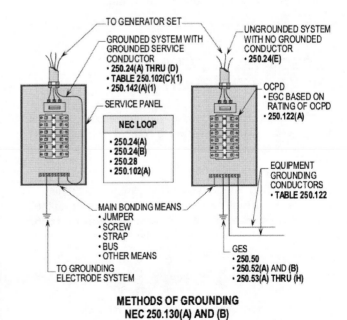

METHODS OF GROUNDING
NEC 250.130(A) AND (B)

Figure 6-11. This illustration shows the grounding of electrical equipment supplied from a grounded or ungrounded generator set.

PURPOSE OF GENERATOR GROUNDING
250.4(A)(1) THROUGH (A)(5)

One of the most important, but usually the most misunderstood and controversial elements of an industrial electrical power system design, is the subject of grounding. The term *grounding* is often used to describe circuit and system and equipment grounding, although each has different objectives.

Electrical systems and circuit conductors are grounded to limit voltage due to lightning, line surges, or unintentional contact with other "higher" voltage lines. System grounding ensures longer insulation life for electrical equipment such as motors, generators, and transformers by suppressing overvoltages associated with different types of faults.

System grounding also stabilizes the voltage-to-ground under normal operation and improves protection of the electrical system by providing fast and selective operation of protective devices in the event of ground faults.

Equipment grounding consists of a network of grounding conductors used to ground nonelectrical conductive material that encloses or is adjacent to energized conductors. Similar to circuit and system grounding, equipment grounding also limits the voltage-to-ground and provides fast and selective operation of overcurrent protection devices in the event of ground faults. The two major objectives of generator grounding are as follows:

(1) To improve personnel safety and

(2) To improve protection of equipment.

PERSONNEL SAFETY
250.4(A)(1) THROUGH (A)(5)

An equipment grounding system improves personnel safety and protects personnel from electrical shock and other hazards as follows:

- Reducing electric shock hazards,

- Providing adequate current-carrying capability to carry the high currents produced by a ground fault without creating a fire or explosive hazard to the electrical equipment or its elements,

- Providing a low-impedance return path for ground-fault current necessary for the operation of the overcurrent protection devices, and

- Limiting voltage on the system to line-to-ground magnitudes.

See Figure 6-12 for the rules pertaining to personnel safety grounding and bonding.

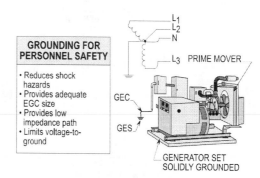

GROUNDING FOR PERSONNEL SAFETY
- Reduces shock hazards
- Provides adequate EGC size
- Provides low impedance path
- Limits voltage-to-ground

**PERSONNEL SAFETY
NEC 250.4(A)(1) THRU (A)(5)**

Figure 6-12. This illustration shows the importance of grounding electrical systems for personnel safety.

EQUIPMENT PROTECTION
210.20(C), TABLE 240.3, AND 250.4

Proper system grounding improves the protection of equipment by:

- Providing a low-impedance return path for ground fault current necessary for the operation of the overcurrent protection devices,

- Improving differential relay protection of motors, generators, and transformers,

- Limiting voltage on the system to line-to-ground magnitudes,

- Minimizing transient overvoltages to acceptable levels,

- Allowing the use of grounded-neutral type arresters, and

- Reducing electrical arc/flashes or blast hazards.

See Figure 6-13 for the benefits of grounding and bonding equipment for safety.

METHODS OF HIGH-IMPEDANCE GROUNDING

The following grounding methods are normally used for grounding generators:

- Solidly grounded generators,

- Resistance-grounded generators, and

- Reactance-grounded generators.

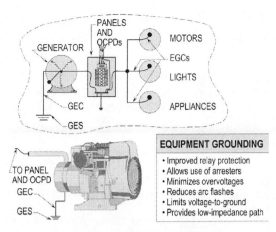

EQUIPMENT PROTECTION
NEC 210.20(C), TABLE 240.3, AND 250.4

Figure 6-13. This illustration shows the benefits of grounding the noncurrent-carrying metal parts of equipment.

SOLIDLY GROUNDED GENERATORS

A solidly grounded system has an intentional and direct connection to ground normally through the middle wire or neutral point of a generator's winding.

Note, there is no intentional impedance added in the path from the neutral-to-ground.

In solidly grounded systems, line-to-ground fault currents can be very high and they may exceed three-phase fault currents. Solidly grounding generators are sometimes used in industrial facilities; however, it is not always the preferred grounding scheme for generators by most designers. **(See Figure 6-14)**

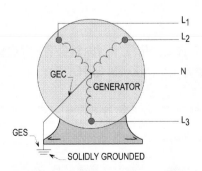

SOLIDLY GROUNDED GENERATORS

Figure 6-14. A solidly grounded generator allows the maximum current available to flow and trip the overcurrent protection devices.

RESISTANCE-GROUNDED GENERATORS

In resistance-grounded systems the neutral is connected to ground through a resistor. There are two types of resistance-grounded systems:

(1) Low-resistance grounding and

(2) High-resistance grounding.

LOW-RESISTANCE GROUNDING

Low-resistance grounding is accomplished by inserting a resistance between a generator grounded (neutral) conductor and ground. When a line-to-ground fault occurs, the voltage across the resistor equals the normal line-to-neutral voltage of the system and the ground-fault current equals the line-to-neutral voltage divided by the size of the grounding resistor. **(See Figure 6-15)**

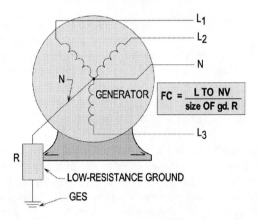

Figure 6-15. Low-resistance-grounded generators allow the designer to regulate the amount of fault-to-ground current flowing in the system.

> **Note:** Finding fault current
> FC = fault current
> L to NV = line-to-neutral voltage
> V of gd.R = Size of the grounding resistor
>
> Formula: $FC = \dfrac{L \text{ to } NV}{V \text{ of gd. } R}$

HIGH-RESISTANCE GROUNDING

This grounding scheme is accomplished by sizing a resistor to provide a resistive fault current slightly greater than or equal to three times the normal current flowing in the stray line-to-ground capacitance per ungrounded phase. **(See Figure 6-16)**

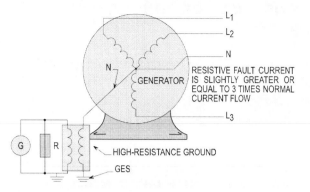

HIGH-RESISTANCE GROUNDING

Figure 6-16. The above illustrates the characteristics of high-resistance-grounded generator systems.

REACTANCE-GROUNDED GENERATORS

This grounding scheme is one in which a reactor is connected between the system grounded (neutral) conductor and ground. Reactance grounding of generators is only used to limit ground-fault current to a value no greater than the generator three-phase fault-current level. Therefore, it is used in very few applications. When selecting the grounding technique, verify the size of the generator and its use.

> **For example,** is the generator small or large and fed from a utility transformer or a separately derived system? Is such generator used as the sole supply? The size of the generator and the way it is supplied or used usually determines its grounding scheme. **(See Figure 6-17)**

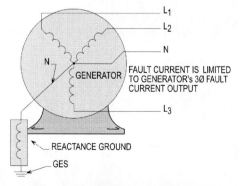

REACTANCE-GROUNDED GENERATORS

Figure 6-17. This illustration shows the use of reactance-grounded systems to ground generators.

PORTABLE GENERATORS
250.34(A)

The frame of a portable generator shall not be required to be connected to a grounding electrode as derived in **250.52** if it supplies only the equipment on the generator or cord-and-plug-connected equipment connected to receptacles mounted on the generator, provided all the following conditions are complied with:

- An equipment grounding conductor is installed to bond the receptacles to the frame of the generator.

- The equipment grounding conductor in the cord is installed to bond the exposed noncurrent-carrying metal parts of the equipment to the frame of the generator.

See Figure 6-18 for a detailed illustration when applying these requirements.

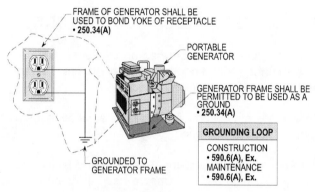

PORTABLE GENERATORS
NEC 250.34(A)

Figure 6-18. The frame of a portable generator shall not be required to be connected to a grounding electrode as defined in **250.52** if it supplies only the equipment on the generator or cord-and-plug connected equipment to receptacles mounted on the generator.

TRANSFER SWITCH IS NOT PROVIDED
702.5(A), Ex. AND 215.10, Ex. 3

Transfer equipment shall be required for all standby systems subject to the provisions of **Article 702** and for which an electric-utility supply is either the normal or standby source.

Temporary connection of a portable generator without transfer equipment shall be permitted where conditions of maintenance and supervision ensure that only qualified persons service the installation and where the normal supply is physically isolated by a lockable disconnect means or by disconnection of the normal supply conductors.
(See Figure 6-19)

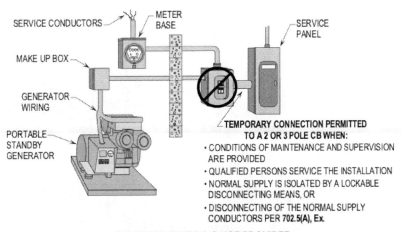

TEMPORARY CONNECTION PERMITTED
TO A 2 OR 3 POLE CB WHEN:
• CONDITIONS OF MAINTENANCE AND SUPERVISION ARE PROVIDED
• QUALIFIED PERSONS SERVICE THE INSTALLATION
• NORMAL SUPPLY IS ISOLATED BY A LOCKABLE DISCONNECTING MEANS, OR
• DISCONNECTING OF THE NORMAL SUPPLY CONDUCTORS PER 702.5(A), Ex.

TRANSFER SWITCH IS NOT PROVIDED
702.5(A), Ex. AND 215.10, Ex. 3

Figure 6-19. The requirements for conditions where a transfer switch is not required.

PORTABLE GENERATOR GROUNDING FOR SEPARATELY DERIVED SYSTEMS 702.11(A) AND 250.30, IN 1

In installations, where the generator operates as a separately derived system and the transfer switch interrupts all conductors, including the grounded circuit conductor, the generator shall comply with the normal grounding electrode requirements outlined in **250.30**.

Note, this rule consummates the intent that an independent connection to the premises grounding electrode system in the standby panelboard be provided. (See **250.30, IN 1**) **(See Figure 6-20)**

PORTABLE GENERATOR GROUNDING FOR NONSEPARATELY DERIVED SYSTEMS 702.11(B) AND 250.30, IN 2

The grounding requirements for portable, optional type generators that are nonseparately derived systems and where the transfer switch only interupts the ungrounded (phase) conductors are covered in this section of the NEC. In this installation, the equipment grounding (bonding) conductor shall be bonded to the grounding electrode system. **(See 250.30, IN 2) (See Figure 6-21)**

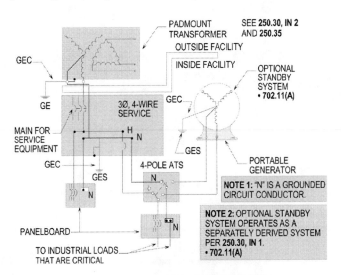

PORTABLE GENERATOR GROUNDING FOR SEPARATELY DERIVED SYSTEMS
702.11(A) AND 250.30, IN 1

Figure 6-20. This illustration shows the grounding of a portable generator used as a separately derived system.

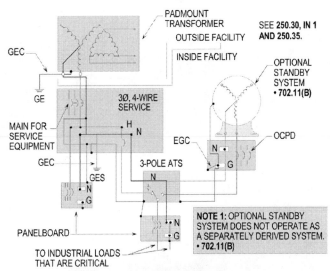

PORTABLE GENERATOR GROUNDING FOR NONSEPARATELY DERIVED SYSTEMS
702.11(B) AND 250.30, IN 2

Figure 6-21. This illustration shows the grounding of a portable generator used as a nonseparately derived system.

Chapter 6: Generators Supplying Essential Loads for Hospitals

Section   Answer

1. The branches of the emergency system shall be installed and connected to
   the alternate power source so that all functions for the emergency system shall
   be automatically restored to operation within _____ seconds after interruption
   of the normal source.
   (a) 5   (b) 10
   (c) 15   (d) 30

2. Each branch of the emergency system and each equipment system shall have
   _____ or more transfer switches.
   (a) 1   (b) 2
   (c) 3   (d) 4

3. One transfer switch for an emergency system shall be permitted to serve one
   or more branches or systems in a facility with a maximum demand on the
   essential electrical system of _____ kVA.
   (a) 100   (b) 120
   (c) 150   (d) 200

4. If the generator is installed as a nonseparately derived system, and overcurrent
   protection is not integral with the generator assembly, a _____ bonding jumper
   shall be installed between the generator equipment grounding terminal bar and
   the equipment grounding terminal, bar, or bus of the disconnecting means.
   (a) system   (b) equipment
   (c) attached   (d) supply-side

5. Low-resistance grounding is accomplished by inserting a(n) _____ between
   a generator neutral and ground.
   (a) resistance   (b) inductance
   (c) capacitance   (d) reactance

6. High-resistance grounding is accomplished by sizing a(n) _____ to provide a
   resistive fault-current slightly greater than or equal to three times the normal
   current flowing in the stray line-to-ground capacitance per ungrounded phase.
   (a) capacitor   (b) inductor
   (c) resistor   (d) reactor

7. Temporary connection of a portable generator without transfer equipment shall
   be permitted where conditions of maintenance and supervision ensure that
   only _____ persons service the installation.
   (a) approved   (b) qualified
   (c) identified   (d) nonqualified

8. The life safety branch and _____ branch of the emergency system shall be
   kept entirely independent of all other wiring and equipment.
   (a) emergency   (b) common
   (c) transfer   (d) critical

_____ _____ **9.** Where encased in not less than _____ in. of concrete, Schedule 40 PVC conduit shall be permitted to be installed for the wiring of the emergency system.
                         (a) 1   (b) 2
                         (c) 3   (d) 6

_____ _____ **10.** Proper system grounding improves the protection of equipment by:
                         (a) Improving differential relay protection of motors, generators, and transformers
                         (b) Limiting voltage on the system to line-to-ground magnitudes
                         (c) Reducing electrical arc/flashes or blast hazards
                         (d) All of the above

Part Two

Transformers

A vital part of maintaining an uninterrupted electrical service is the transformer. In a period of great industrial activity there are likely to be unusual power demands. New types of industrial machinery, and high-energy efficient motors and equipment that create new uses for electricity are likely to impose greater loads, thereby making transformers even more vital to meeting customer needs. Dependable operation of transformers is therefore becoming increasingly necessary.

Transformers are used for the transmission of electrical power from the generating plant and ultimately to the consumer. A step-down transformer is used for electrical energy in the form of alternating current (AC) at a high voltage and stepped down to a lower voltage. A step-up transformer is used for electrical energy in the form of alternating current (AC) at a low voltage and stepped up to a higher voltage. The *National Electrical Safety Code* (NESC) provides the requirements for utility owned transformers, while privately owned transformers not only adhere to the NESC, but, in some cases to the *National Electrical Code®*.

Part II reviews the basic theory, operation, construction, and troubleshooting procedures that are necessary for a full understanding of the performance of a transformer.

7

Transformer
Theory

Transformer windings are connected in either series or parallel to obtain the different voltages required for supplying various loads. Basic voltages are 120 volt, single-phase; 120/240 volt, single-phase; 120/208 volt, three-phase; and 277/480 volt, three-phase. Higher voltages are available for other applications. These voltages are usually 2400/4160 volts, three-phase; 12,470 volt, three-phase; and 13,800 volts, respectively.

To obtain the different voltage levels for a transformer and to supply the various loads, the windings are connected in either series or parallel. These windings or loads must be balanced between phases and from each phase-to-neutral to prevent possible overloads. Transformer windings are generally connected in a wye or in an open or closed delta-connected system. The primary and secondary sides of the transformer may have combination connections in order to obtain different voltage configurations.

TRANSFORMER PRINCIPLES

The amperage of a single-phase transformer is found by dividing the kVA rating of the transformer by the primary or secondary voltage. This calculation determines the amount of current that a transformer will deliver, under normal operating conditions, when supplying various loads.

> **For example:** What is the amperage for a 20 kVA transformer with a 240 volt, single-phase secondary output?
>
> **Step 1:** Finding amperage of Secondary
> A = (20 kVA x 1000) ÷ 240 V
> A = 83 amps
>
> **Solution: The transformer amperage is 83 amps for the secondary output.**

> **For example:** What is the amperage for a 20 kVA transformer with a 480 volt, single-phase secondary output?
>
> **Step 1:** Finding amperage of Secondary
> A = (20 kVA x 1000) ÷ 480 V
> A = 42 amps
>
> **Solution: The transformer amperage is 42 amps for the secondary output.**

The voltage, current, and impedance are determined by the number of turns on the primary and secondary windings of a transformer. Based upon the number of turns on the primary and secondary windings of a transformer, the following characteristics of the voltage, current, and impedance shall apply:

Number of turns are the same

(1) Input voltage and output voltage are the same

(2) Impedance remains constant

(3) Input current and output current are the same

Fewer turns on the primary than the secondary

(1) Voltage is stepped up

(2) Current is stepped down

Fewer turns on the secondary than the primary

(1) Voltage is stepped down

(2) Current is stepped up

See Figure 7-1 for applying the number of turns on the primary and secondary of a transformer.

The transformer voltage, amperage, and turns ratio are determined by the ratio of the number of turns on the primary windings to the number of turns on the secondary windings. The transformer kVA or volt-amp rating is the same value for the primary and secondary outputs. **(See Figure 7-2)**

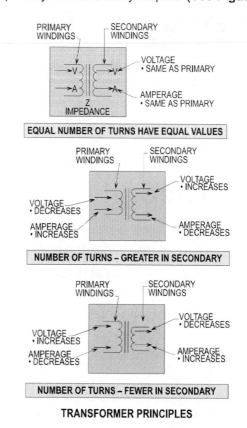

TRANSFORMER PRINCIPLES

Figure 7-1. The output voltage and amperage is determined by the number of turns on the primary and the secondary of a transformer.

WINDINGS

Depending on the job to be performed, a transformer winding can be connected in a number of ways. Depending on the desired voltage, two or more transformer windings can also be connected together in a number of ways. The most commonly used transformer connections are delta and wye. When applying voltage configurations for these connections, high-voltage systems are connected in series and low-voltages systems are connected in parallel.

SINGLE-PHASE OUTPUT

When the secondary of a transformer supplies 120/240 volt, single-phase loads, there will be 120 volts between either one of the phase lines and the neutral. When the secondary of a transformer supplies 120/240 volt, single-phase loads, there will be 240 volts between both the phase lines.

Lighting, receptacle, and appliance loads are supplied

from the 120 volt lines. Water heaters, air conditioning, and electrical heating are supplied from the 240 volt lines.

Note, these transformers may be connected for 120 volt or 240 volt, single-phase systems.

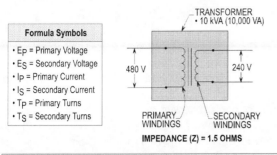

APPLYING FORMULA TO FIND VOLTAGE, AMPERAGE, AND TURNS		
Finding Voltage	**Finding Amperage**	**Finding No. of Turns**
Primary Voltage	**Primary Amperage**	**Primary Turns**
$E_P = \dfrac{E_S \times I_S}{I_P}$	$I_P = \dfrac{E_S \times I_S}{E_P}$	$T_P = \dfrac{E_P \times T_S}{E_S}$
$E_P = \dfrac{240\,V \times 52.5\,A}{26.25}$	$I_P = \dfrac{240\,V \times 52.5\,A}{480\,V}$	$T_P = \dfrac{480\,V \times 800\,T}{240\,V}$
$E_P = \dfrac{12,600\,VA}{26.25}$	$I_P = \dfrac{12,600\,VA}{480\,V}$	$T_P = \dfrac{384,00}{240\,V}$
$E_P = 480\,V$	$I_P = 26.25\,A$	$T_P = 1600$
Secondary Voltage	**Secondary Amperage**	**Secondary Turns**
$E_S = \dfrac{E_P \times I_P}{I_S}$	$I_S = \dfrac{E_P \times I_P}{E_S}$	$T_S = \dfrac{E_S \times T_P}{E_P}$
$E_S = \dfrac{480\,V \times 26.25\,A}{52.5\,A}$	$I_S = \dfrac{480\,V \times 26.25\,A}{240\,V}$	$T_S = \dfrac{240\,V \times 1600\,T}{480\,V}$
$E_S = \dfrac{12,600\,VA}{52.5\,A}$	$I_S = \dfrac{12,600\,VA}{240\,V}$	$T_S = \dfrac{384,000\,VA}{480\,V}$
$E_S = 240\,V$	$I_S = 52.5\,A$	$T_S = 800\,T$

TRANSFORMER PRINCIPLES

Figure 7-2. The voltage, amperage, and number of turns in transformer windings are determined by applying the proper formula.

WYE-CONNECTED TRANSFORMERS

The voltage between phase-to-phase and phase-to-neutral will always be the same on a wye-connected, three-phase, four-wire transformer. The voltage of the power conductors (phase-to-phase) will always be more than the voltage between any one of the phase conductors and the neutral.

For example, if the voltage between the power conductors of any two phases for a 120/208 volt, three-phase, four-wire transformer is 208 volts, the voltage from any phase power conductor to ground will be 120 volts. The voltage between any two phase conductors for a wye-connected transformer is derived by multiplying the voltage-to-ground by the square root of 3 (1.732). The voltage from any phase conductor to ground for a wye-connected transformer is derived by dividing the phase-to-phase voltage by the square root of 3 (1.732). **(See Figure 7-3)**

When all three ungrounded power conductors and neutrals are connected to form a wye-connected secondary, the transformer's output produces a three-phase voltage. When connecting only two ungrounded power conductors plus a neutral to a wye-connected supply, the voltage obtained will be a single-phase system.

The ungrounded phase-to-phase voltage for a wye-connected transformer is the same, but the coil voltage is equal to the square root of 3 (1.732) divided into the phase-to-phase voltage. Each phase leg is connected through the winding to a common connection where they all meet to form a wye-connected secondary. **(See Figure 7-4)**

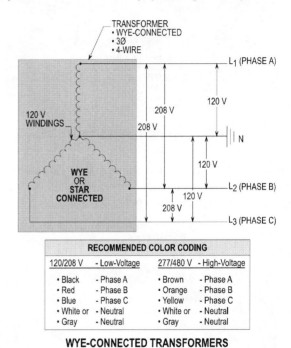

WYE-CONNECTED TRANSFORMERS

Figure 7-3. Phase-to-phase voltage for a wye-connected transformer is found by multiplying the phase-to-neutral voltage by square root of 3 (1.732). Phase-to-neutral voltage is found by dividing the phase-to-phase voltage by the square root of 3 (1.732). (The above is a 1000 volt system or less.)

BALANCED CURRENT FLOW

The winding voltage in a wye-connected system is not the same as the phase-to-phase voltage. The winding voltage is multiplied by the square root of 3 (1.732) to find the phase-to-phase voltage or by dividing the phase-to-phase voltage by 1.732 to find the winding's voltage. The flow of current in the windings of a wye system is the same as the line current. **(See Figure 7-5)**

The windings in a wye system will develop more heat than delta-connected windings because they are pulling the same current as the line. The windings of a delta-connected system only pulls 58 percent of the line current.

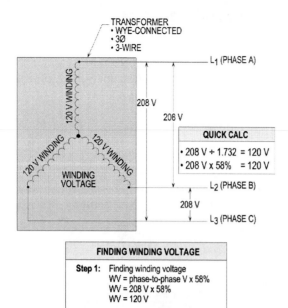

Figure 7-4. The winding voltage in a wye-connected transformer system can be found by dividing the phase-to-phase voltage by the square root of 3 (1.732).

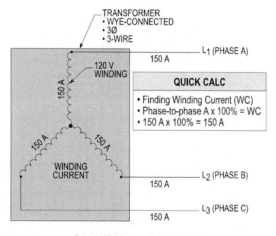

Figure 7-5. The flow of current in a wye-connected system is the same in the windings as the line current.

UNBALANCED CURRENT FLOW

The grounded (neutral) conductor of a three-wire, 120/208 volt feeder is required to be the same size as the ungrounded (phase) conductors for a feeder derived from a four-wire, 120/208 volt system. The reason is that the grounded (neutral) conductor of a three-wire circuit consisting of two ungrounded (phase) conductors and the grounded (neutral) conductor to a four-wire, three-phase system

carries approximately the same amount of current as the ungrounded (phase) conductors. Therefore, per **220.61**, a reduction in ampacity is not allowed.

NEUTRAL CURRENT FLOW

A 120/208 volt or 277/480 volt wye-connected system is different from a 120/240 volt, single-phase or 120/240 volt delta-connected system when determining the flow of current in the grounded (neutral) conductor. To find the amount of current flow in the grounded (neutral) conductor of a 120/208 volt or 277/480 volt wye-connected system, use the formula in **Figure 7-6** and replace the values as necessary to calculate another neutral value.

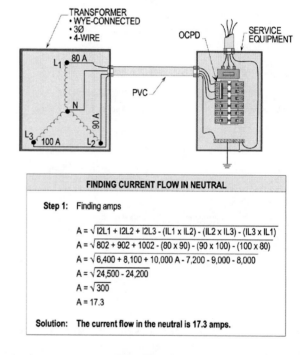

Figure 7-6. This illustration shows the procedure for finding the current in amps for the neutral of a three-phase, four-wire wye-connected system.

DELTA-CONNECTED TRANSFORMERS

A delta-connected system is a good installation when used for short-distance distribution systems. This type of system is most commonly used for neighborhood and small commercial loads close to the supplying substation. In a delta-connected system only one voltage is available between any two lines. The coil voltage in a delta-connected system is the same as the phase-to-phase voltage. The windings of a delta-connected transformer may be connected by one of the following:

(1) Open connected delta systems or

(2) Closed connected delta systems.

A triangle is used to show a delta-connected system. A wire from each connection point of the triangle represents a three-phase, three-wire delta system. Between any two wires the voltage is the same. **(See Figure 7-7)**

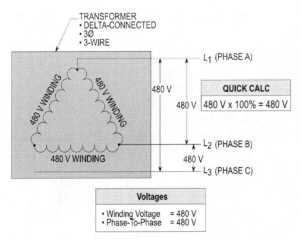

DELTA-CONNECTED TRANSFORMERS

Figure 7-7. Between any two conductors the voltage is 480 volts. The winding voltage is also 480 volts.

OPEN DELTA-CONNECTED WINDINGS

Only two transformers are used when connecting the windings of an open delta-connected system. One transformer is always larger than the other due to 120 volt loading.

CLOSED DELTA-CONNECTED WINDINGS

Three transformers are used when connecting the windings of a closed delta-connected system. Depending on the three-phase and single-phase loads served when using a closed delta-connected system, one transformer may be larger than the other two.

BALANCED CURRENT FLOW

The winding voltage and phase-to-phase voltage are the same in a delta-connected system. The winding current and line current are not the same in a delta-connected system. In a delta-connected system the flow of current has two paths to follow at each closed end where the phase conductors terminate. The amount of current in a delta-connected winding is 58 percent of the line current measured on each phase. The multiplier (58 percent) is found by dividing 1 by the square root of 3 ($1 \div \sqrt{3}$ (1.732) = 58%).

For example, if the current of each phase is 150 amps, the coil current would be 87 amps (150 A x 58% = 87 A). **(See Figure 7-8)**

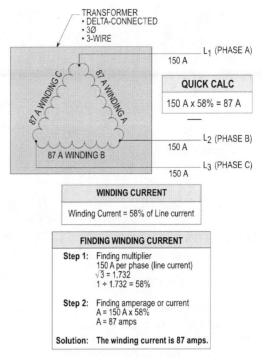

BALANCED CURRENT FLOW

Figure 7-8. The winding current of a balanced delta-connected system is found by multiplying the phase (line) amperage by 58 percent.

UNBALANCED CURRENT FLOW

When the current flow in a delta-connected system is unbalanced, the current flow in L_1 is found by the square root of the other winding currents ($B^2 + C^2 + BC$). The current flow in L_2 and L_3 is found by substituting the appropriate winding current values. **(See Figure 7-9)**

NEUTRAL CURRENT FLOW

The unbalanced current in a four-wire, three-phase delta-connected system is carried by the neutral between phases A and C. This portion of a delta-connected system has only 120 volt ungrounded (phase) conductors.

Note, 120 volts is derived from tapping one of the 240 volt windings. From the tap to each outside phase conductor (phases A and C) 120 volts is derived. The current flow in phase B must travel through one 240 volt and one 120 volt winding to reach the tap, which is connected to ground. The 208 volts (phase B to ground) is derived by measuring the voltage-to-ground (120 V + 240 V = 360 V) and dividing by $\sqrt{3}$ (360 V ÷ 1.732 = 208 V). **(See Figure 7-10)**

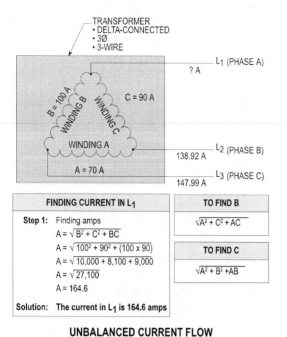

FINDING CURRENT IN L₁

Step 1: Finding amps

$A = \sqrt{B^2 + C^2 + BC}$

$A = \sqrt{100^2 + 90^2 + (100 \times 90)}$

$A = \sqrt{10,000 + 8,100 + 9,000}$

$A = \sqrt{27,100}$

$A = 164.6$

Solution: The current in L₁ is 164.6 amps

TO FIND B

$\sqrt{A^2 + C^2 + AC}$

TO FIND C

$\sqrt{A^2 + B^2 + AB}$

UNBALANCED CURRENT FLOW

Figure 7-9. As illustrated, the current flow of an unbalanced delta-connected system in L_1 is found by the square root of the other winding currents ($B^2 + C^2 + BC$). The current flow in L_2 and L_3 is found by substituting the appropriate winding current values.

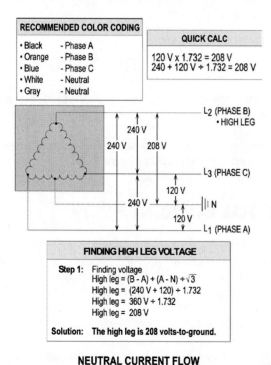

RECOMMENDED COLOR CODING

- Black - Phase A
- Orange - Phase B
- Blue - Phase C
- White - Neutral
- Gray - Neutral

QUICK CALC

120 V x 1.732 = 208 V
240 + 120 V ÷ 1.732 = 208 V

FINDING HIGH LEG VOLTAGE

Step 1: Finding voltage
High leg = (B - A) + (A - N) ÷ √3
High leg = (240 V + 120) ÷ 1.732
High leg = 360 V ÷ 1.732
High leg = 208 V

Solution: The high leg is 208 volts-to-ground.

NEUTRAL CURRENT FLOW

Figure 7-10. This illustration shows that only two 120 volt circuits and one 208 volt circuit-to-ground are produced in a four-wire, three-phase, delta-connected system.

BALANCING LOADS ON TRANSFORMER WINDINGS

The loads connected to single-phase and three-phase transformers must be balanced as evenly as possible. Branch-circuit loads in panelboards shall be divided as evenly as possible on phases A, B, and C to assure that transformer windings are not overloaded.

SINGLE-PHASE LOAD BALANCING

Single-phase, three-wire transformer systems have a secondary voltage of 120/240 volts. One of the windings can be overloaded if loads are not distributed as evenly as possible on each 120 volt winding. Where a 240 volt winding is center-tapped and connected to ground, there will be two 120 volt windings for a transformer. The 30 kVA, single-phase transformer is balanced for each 120 volt winding. Dividing by 2 (30 kVA ÷ 2 = 15 kVA) will derive a capacity of each 120 volt winding. Each balanced 120 volt winding can be loaded to 15 kVA or less. Proper balancing of the 30 kVA transformer prevents the winding from overheating. **(See Figure 7-11)**

> **For example,** the 30 kVA transformer has a 120/240 volt secondary to serve loads of 24 kVA at 240 volts and two 3 kVA loads at 120 volts. Each 120 volt winding must be divided as evenly as possible to balance the single-phase load. The 240 volt loads must be balanced using the same procedure. To prevent overheating of windings, the loads must be properly balanced. The load is unbalanced if the two 120 volt, 3 kVA loads are connected to one 120 volt winding instead of one load to each winding.

THREE-PHASE LOAD BALANCING

Three-phase, four-wire transformer systems usually have a secondary voltage of 120/208 volts or 277/480 volts. When balancing the load, each phase of a three-phase transformer must be considered as a single-phase transformer.

> **For example,** a 40 kVA transformer has a 120/208 volt secondary to serve five loads of 12 kVA, 8 kVA, 6 kVA, 5 kVA, and 3 kVA at 120 volts, single-phase. Each 120 volt phase of the 40 kVA transformer can be loaded up to 13.3 kVA (40 kVA ÷ 3 = 13.3 kVA). **(See Figure 7-12)**

DERATING FOR HIGH ALTITUDE

High-altitude operation of distribution transformers can also be a problem. Dry-type transformers are air cooled and require a flow of fresh air in and around the transformer windings to maintain normal operating temperatures. At very high altitudes, the air becomes thinner and transformer cooling is not as efficient as at lower latitudes. The NEMA standard is based on normal operation at an altitude of 3300 ft above sea level. So, for every additional 330 ft the transformer load capacity must be derated by $3/10$ of one percent (.3%) for safe and reliable loading. **(See Figure 7-13)**

For derating the load capacity of motors installed in high altitudes, see title head "TEMPERATURE RISE" on **page 19-2**.

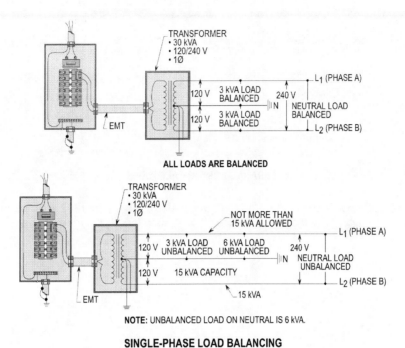

ALL LOADS ARE BALANCED

NOTE: UNBALANCED LOAD ON NEUTRAL IS 6 kVA.

SINGLE-PHASE LOAD BALANCING

Figure 7-11. To prevent overheating, single-phase transformer loads must be balanced (as close as possible) phase-to-ground and phase-to-phase.

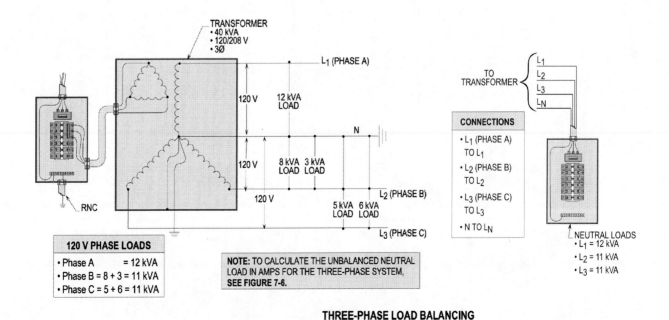

THREE-PHASE LOAD BALANCING

Figure 7-12. Each 120 volt phase of the 40 kVA transformer must not exceed 13.3 kVA (40 ÷ 3 = 13.3 kVA). A neutral load of 13.3 kVA or less is permitted, which will not overload windings.

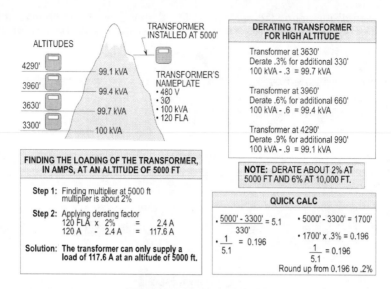

DERATING FOR HIGH ALTITUDE

Figure 7-13. This illustration shows the rule-of-thumb method for determining the FLC in amps for transformers installed in high altitudes. **Note:** For reducing the load in amps for motors installed in altitudes above 3,300 ft, see page 19-2 in this book.

Chapter 7: Transformer Theory

Section   Answer

1. When the secondary of a transformer supplies 120/240 volt, single-phase _____ _____
   loads, there will be _____ volts between either one of the phase lines and the
   neutral.
   (a) 120   (b) 240
   (c) 277   (d) 480

2. When the secondary of a transformer supplies 120/240 volt, single-phase _____ _____
   loads, there will be _____ volts between both the phase lines.
   (a) 120   (b) 240
   (c) 277   (d) 480

3. The windings of a delta-connected system only pulls _____ percent of the line _____ _____
   current.
   (a) 33   (b) 42
   (c) 58   (d) 67

4. The ungrounded phase-to-phase voltage for a wye-connected transformer is _____ _____
   the same but the _____ voltage is equal to the square root of 3 divided into
   the phase-to-phase voltage.
   (a) coil   (b) winding
   (c) primary   (d) secondary

5. The grounded (neutral) conductor of a three-wire, 120/208 volt feeder is _____ _____
   required to be the same size as the _____ conductors for a feeder derived
   from a four-wire, 120/208 volt system.
   (a) grounded   (b) equipment
   (c) bonding   (d) ungrounded

6. _____ transformer(s) are used when connecting the windings of a open delta- _____ _____
   connected system.
   (a) One   (b) Two
   (c) Three   (d) Four

7. _____ transformer(s) are used when connecting the windings of a closed _____ _____
   delta-connected system.
   (a) One   (b) Two
   (c) Three   (d) Four

8. The winding voltage and phase-to-phase voltage are the same in a _____ _____
   _____-connected system.
   (a) delta   (b) wye
   (c) all of the above   (d) none of the above

9. Single-phase, three-wire transformers have a secondary voltage of _____ _____ _____
   volts.
   (a) 120/208   (b) 120/240
   (c) 277/480   (d) 600

Section   Answer

_____ _____ **10.** Three-phase, four-wire transformer systems usually have a secondary voltage
                             of _____ volts.
                             (a) 120/208   (b) 277/480
                             (c) Both (a) and (b)   (d) none of the above

8

Installing Transformers

Transformers and transformer vaults shall be designed, installed, and protected per **Article 450** in the *National Electrical Code*®. Based upon design and type, a transformer installation can be located either inside of a building or outside, sometimes exposed to adverse weather conditions.

Transformers are installed to provide a level of safety for nonqualified personnel as well as for qualified personnel.

Note, a provision of accessibility shall also be designed into the installation.

Other safety factors include ventilation of transformer vaults and the compliance of minimum fire-resistant standards for the walls, doors, and roof that are associated with a transformer installation.

MARKING
450.11

Transformers shall be provided with a marking on the nameplate giving the following information:
- **(1)** Name of manufacturer,
- **(2)** Rated kVA,
- **(3)** Frequency,
- **(4)** Primary and secondary voltage,
- **(5)** Impedance for transformers rated 25 kVA and higher,
- **(6)** Clearances for transformers with ventilating openings,
- **(7)** Amount and kind of insulating liquid, and
- **(8)** Dry-type transformers, temperature class for the insulation system.

GUARDING
450.8

Transformers shall be permitted to be isolated in a room or accessible only to qualified personnel to prevent accidental contact with live parts. To safeguard live parts from possible damage, the transformer shall be elevated. The following are acceptable means of safeguarding live parts as required in **110.27(A)** and **110.34(E)**:

(1) Transformers shall be permitted to be isolated in a room or accessible only to qualified personnel,

(2) Permanent partitions or screens shall be permitted to be installed, and

(3) Transformers shall be elevated at least 8 ft (2.5 m) above the floor to prevent unauthorized personnel from contact.

> **Transformer Tip:** Signs indicating the voltage of live exposed parts of transformers, or other suitable markings, shall be used in areas where transformers are located.

VENTILATION OF TRANSFORMERS
450.9

Transformers shall be located and installed in rooms or areas that are not subject to exceedingly high temperatures to prevent overheating and possible damage to windings. Transformers with ventilation openings shall be installed so that the ventilating openings are not blocked by walls or other obstructions that could block air flow.

ACCESSIBILITY OF TRANSFORMERS
450.13

Transformers shall be located where readily accessible to qualified personnel for inspection and maintenance. Where it is necessary to use a ladder, lift, or bucket truck to get to a transformer, it shall not be considered readily accessible. See definition of *readily accessible* in **Article 100**. **(See Figure 8-2)**

HUNG FROM WALL OR CEILING
450.13(A)

Dry-type transformers not over 1000 volts and located on open walls or steel columns shall not be required to be readily accessible. It is permissible to gain access to this type of installation using a portable ladder or bucket lift. **(See Figure 8-2)**

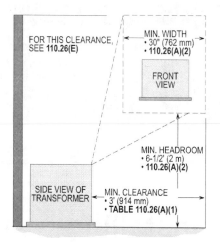

ACCESSIBILITY OF TRANSFORMERS
NEC 450.13

Figure 8-1. The general rule of **450.13** requires transformers to be readily accessible for maintenance, repair, and service. See AHJ for this requirement.

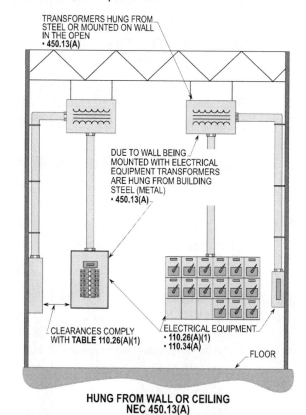

HUNG FROM WALL OR CEILING
NEC 450.13(A)

Figure 8-2. Transformers hung from a wall or ceiling shall not be required to be readily accessible.

MOUNTED IN CEILING
450.13(B)

Dry-type transformers not over 1000 volts and 50 kVA shall be permitted to be installed in hollow spaces of buildings. The transformers cannot be permanently closed in and there shall be some access to the transformers, but they do not have to be readily accessible per **Article 100**. It was not clear in the 1993 or previous editions of the NEC whether dry-type transformers not exceeding 1000 volts, nominal, and rated 50 kVA or less were permitted to be installed in the space above suspended ceilings with removable panels, even if the transformer was accessible and provided with proper working clearances.

Note, the space where the transformer is installed shall comply with the ventilation requirements of **450.9** and be designed by the rules of **450.21(A)** and **(B)**. If such ceiling space is used as a return air space for air conditioning, **300.22(C)** shall be reviewed and the provisions of this section shall also be complied with. **(See Figure 8-3)**

> **Transformer Tip:** The two exceptions to the general rule are for dry-type transformers. These exceptions do not apply to oil- or askarel-filled transformers due to the damage of possible oil spillage or the threat of fire because of a rupture occurring in the case.

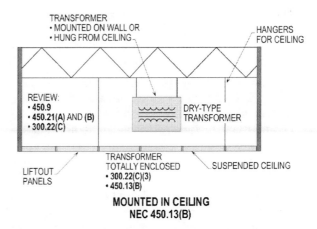

MOUNTED IN CEILING
NEC 450.13(B)

Figure 8-3. Transformers mounted in a ceiling shall not be required to be readily accessible.

DRY-TYPE TRANSFORMERS INSTALLED INDOORS
450.21

The rules for installing dry-type transformers indoors can be summed up as follows:

• Dry-type transformers greater than 112-1/2 kVA and having Class 155 or higher insulation systems shall have a fire-resistant, heat-insulating barrier placed between transformers and combustible material, or, if no barrier, shall be separated at least 6 ft (1.83 m) horizontally and 12 ft (3.7 m) vertically from the combustible material per **450.21(B), Ex. 1**. **(See Figure 8-5)**

DISCONNECTING MEANS
450.14

A disconnecting means shall be located either in sight or in a remote location for transformers other than Class 2 or Class 3 transformers. The disconnecting means shall be lockable and the location field marked on the transformer where located in a remote location. **(See Figure 8-4)** **(See NEC 110.25)**

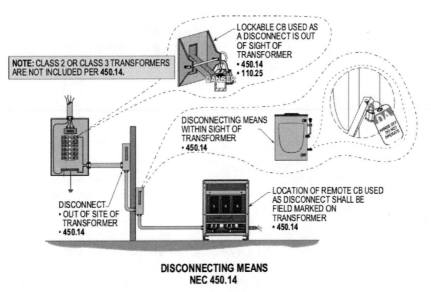

DISCONNECTING MEANS
NEC 450.14

Figure 8-4. This illustration shows the requirements of the disconnecting means for transformers other than class 2 or class 3 transformers.

- Dry-type transformers greater than 112-1/2 kVA and having Class 155 or higher insulation systems shall be installed in a fire-resistant transformer room per **450.21(B), Ex. 2. (See Figure 8-6)**

- Dry-type transformers rated 112-1/2 kVA or less and 1000 volts or less shall have a fire-resistant, heat-insulating barrier between transformers and combustible material, or, without a barrier, shall be separated at least 12 in. (300 mm) from the combustible material where the voltage is 1000 volts or less per **450.21(A). (See Figure 8-7)**

- Dry-type transformers rated 112-1/2 kVA or less and 1000 volts or less shall not be required to have a 12 in. (300 mm) separation or barrier if they are completely enclosed, except for vent openings. **(See Figure 8-8)**

- All indoor dry-type transformers of over 35,000 volts shall be installed in a vault. Vault requirements shall fully comply with **Part III** to **Article 450. (See Figure 8-9)**

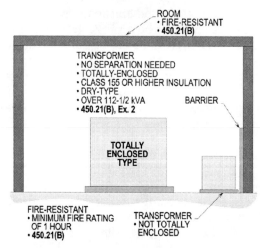

DRY-TYPE TRANSFORMERS INSTALLED INDOORS
OVER 112-1/2 kVA
NEC 450.21(B), Ex. 2

Figure 8-6. Dry-type transformers greater than 112-1/2 kVA and having Class 155 or higher insulation systems shall be installed in a fire-resistant transformer room.

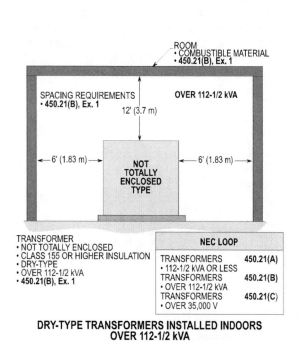

DRY-TYPE TRANSFORMERS INSTALLED INDOORS
OVER 112-1/2 kVA
NEC 450.21(B), Ex. 1

Figure 8-5. Dry-type transformers greater than 112-1/2 kVA and having Class 155 or higher insulation systems shall have a fire-resistant, heat-insulating barrier placed between transformers and combustible material, or, if no barrier, shall be separated at lease 6 ft (1.83 m) horizontally and 12 ft (3.7 m) vertically from the combustible material.

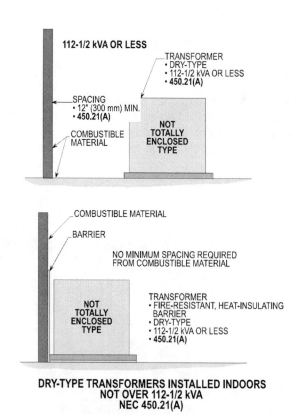

DRY-TYPE TRANSFORMERS INSTALLED INDOORS
NOT OVER 112-1/2 kVA
NEC 450.21(A)

Figure 8-7. Dry-type transformers rated 112-1/2 kVA or less and 1000 volts or less shall have a fire-resistant, heat insulating barrier between transformers and combustible material, or, without a barrier, shall be separated at least 12 in. (300 mm) from the combustible material where the voltage is 1000 volts or less.

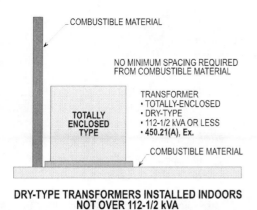

DRY-TYPE TRANSFORMERS INSTALLED INDOORS
NOT OVER 112-1/2 kVA
NEC 450.21(A), Ex.

Figure 8-8. Dry-type transformers rated 112-1/2 kVA or less and 1000 volts or less shall not be required to have a 12 in. (300 mm) separation or barrier if they are completely enclosed except for vent openings.

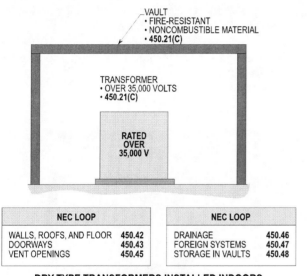

DRY-TYPE TRANSFORMERS INSTALLED INDOORS
OVER 35,000 VOLTS
NEC 450.21(C)

Figure 8-9. All indoor dry-type transformers over 35,000 volts shall be installed in a vault.

DRY-TYPE TRANSFORMERS INSTALLED OUTDOORS
450.22

Dry-type transformers installed outdoors shall have weatherproof enclosures. See the definition in **Article 100** for the difference between "weatherproof" and "watertight."

LESS FLAMMABLE LIQUID-INSULATED TRANSFORMERS
450.23

Transformers using a "listed" high fire point liquid shall be permitted to be installed indoors, but only in "noncombustible" areas of "noncombustible" buildings. The NEC sets the minimum fire point at 300°C (572°F). This is the minimum temperature at which the liquid ignites. Such transformers shall be permitted to be installed indoors, for voltages up to 35,000. Higher voltages require a vault if they are installed indoors. This is due to the safety required because of the higher voltage and associated equipment. **(See Figure 8-10)**

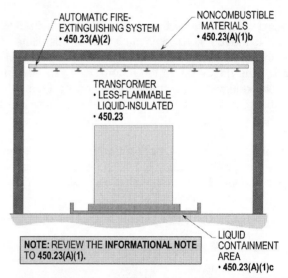

LESS FLAMMABLE LIQUID-INSULATED TRANSFORMERS
NEC 450.23

Figure 8-10. Transformers using a "listed" high fire point liquid shall be permitted to be installed indoors, but only in "noncombustible" areas of "noncombustible" buildings. The NEC sets the minimum fire point at 300°C (572°F).

NONFLAMMABLE FLUID-INSULATED TRANSFORMERS
450.24

Transformers using a "dielectric" nonflammable liquid shall be permitted to be installed indoors in any location, for voltages up to 35,000. Higher voltages require a vault, when installed indoors due to the safety required for the higher voltage and associated equipment.

For the purpose of this section, a nonflammable dielectric fluid is one that does not have a flash point or fire point, and is not flammable in air.

ASKAREL-INSULATED TRANSFORMERS INSTALLED INDOORS
450.25

Askarel is a liquid that does not burn; therefore, it is safer than oil for use as a transformer liquid. However, arcing in askarel produces greater gases that are nonexplosive.

Askarel-insulated transformers of over 25 kVA shall be furnished with a relief vent such as a chimney to relieve the pressure built up by gases that may be generated within the transformer.

In rooms that are well ventilated, the vent may be discharged directly to the room. In rooms that are poorly ventilated, the vent shall be piped to a flue or chimney that is capable of carrying the gases out of the room. Or, as an alternative to such ventilating, the transformer can be fitted with a gas absorber placed inside the case. When there is a gas absorber, the vent may also be discharged to the room.

Askarel transformers of more than 35,000 volts shall be installed in a vault because the oil and higher voltage are a hazard to unqualified personnel. **(See Figure 8-11)**

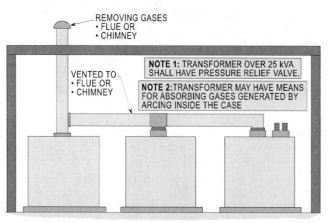

ASKAREL-INSULATED TRANSFORMERS
INSTALLED INDOORS
NEC 450.25

Figure 8-11. Askarel-insulated transformers of over 25 kVA shall be furnished with a relief vent such as a chimney to relieve the pressure built up by gases that may be generated within the transformer.

OIL-INSULATED TRANSFORMERS INSTALLED INDOORS
450.26

The rules for installing oil-insulated transformers indoors can be summed up as follows:

- Indoor, oil-filled transformers greater than 1000 volts shall be installed in a vault, with the following exceptions, where, regardless of voltage, a vault is not required:

  (a) Electric furnace transformers with a total rating of 75 kVA or less shall be permitted to be located in a fire-resistant room.

  (b) Oil-filled transformers shall be permitted to be installed in a building without a vault, provided the building is accessible to qualified personnel only and is used solely for providing electric service to other buildings.

- If suitable provisions are taken to prevent a possible oil fire from igniting other materials, oil-filled transformers of 1000 volts or less shall be permitted to be installed without a vault. When installed without a vault, the total kVA ratings of all transformers allowed in a room or section of a building is limited to 10 kVA for nonfire-resistant buildings and to 75 kVA for fire-resistant buildings.

See Figure 8-12 for installation rules when applying **Ex.'s 1 thru 6** to **450.26**.

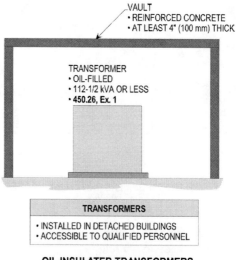

OIL-INSULATED TRANSFORMERS
INSTALLED INDOORS
NEC 450.26, Ex.'s 1 THRU 6

Figure 8-12. Oil-insulated transformers rated at 112-1/2 kVA or less that are installed in detached buildings and accessible only to qualified personnel shall be installed in a vault with reinforced concrete at least 4 in. (100 mm) thick.

OIL-INSULATED TRANSFORMERS INSTALLED OUTDOORS
450.27

When oil-filled transformers are installed on or adjacent to combustible buildings or material, the building or material shall be safeguarded from possible fire originating in a transformer. Fire-resistant barriers, water-spray systems, and enclosures for the transformers are approved safeguards if, where used, they are installed by the rules of the NEC. **[See Figures 8-13(a) and (b)]**

Also, review **450.27, Items 1 thru 4** very carefully when designing and installing oil-insulated transformers outdoors.

MODIFICATION OF TRANSFORMERS 450.28

When modifications are applied to a transformer in an existing installation, the following rules and regulations shall be adhered to:

(1) The type of insulating liquid installed shall be marked on the transformer.

(2) Any modifications shall comply with applicable requirements for the modified transformer.

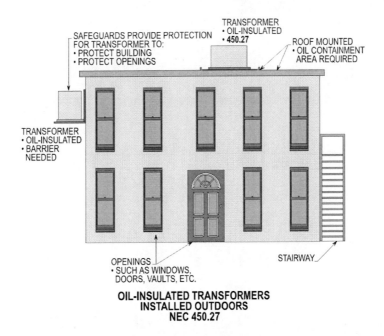

Figure 8-13(a). When oil-filled transformers are installed on or adjacent to combustible buildings or materials, the building or material shall be safeguarded from possible fire originating in a transformer.

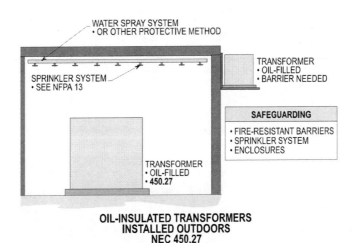

Figure 8-13(b). Fire-resistant barriers, water-spray systems, and enclosures for the transformers are approved safeguards if, where used, they are installed by the rules of the NEC.

Chapter 8: Installing Transformers

Section   Answer

1. Transformers shall be provided with a marking on the nameplate that gives   _____ _____
   the following information:
   (a) name of manufacturer   (b) frequency
   (c) amount and kind of   (d) all of the above
       insulating liquid

2. Transformers shall be elevated at least _____ ft above the floor to prevent   _____ _____
   unauthorized personnel from contact. (50 to 300 V)
   (a) 6   (b) 8
   (c) 10   (d) 12

3. Dry-type transformers shall be located where _____ to qualified personnel for   _____ _____
   inspection and maintenance.
   (a) identified   (b) accessible
   (c) readily accessible   (d) none of the above

4. Dry-type transformers not over 1000 volts and _____ kVA shall be permitted   _____ _____
   to be installed in hollow spaces of buildings.
   (a) 25   (b) 50
   (c) 75   (d) 100

5. Dry-type transformers installed indoors and rated 112-1/2 kVA or less shall have   _____ _____
   a separation of at least _____ in. from combustible material unless separated
   from the combustible material by a fire-resistant, heat-insulated barrier.
   (a) 2   (b) 6
   (c) 12   (d) 18

6. All indoor dry-type transformers of over _____ volts shall be installed in a vault.   _____ _____
   (a) 25,000   (b) 30,000
   (c) 35,000   (d) 50,000

7. Less flammable liquid-insulated transformers shall be permitted to be installed   _____ _____
   indoors, for voltages up to _____.
   (a) 35,000   (b) 50,000
   (c) 75,000   (d) 80,000

8. Askarel-insulated transformers of over _____ kVA shall be furnished with a   _____ _____
   relief vent to relieve the pressure built up by gases that may be generated
   within the transformer.
   (a) 10   (b) 15
   (c) 20   (d) 25

9. An oil-insulated transformer of _____ kVA or less shall be permitted to supply   _____ _____
   a voltage of 1000 volts or less that is an integral part of charged particle
   accelerating equipment.
   (a) 50   (b) 75
   (c) 80   (d) 90

_____ _____   **10.** Where the nominal voltage does not exceed 1000 for an oil-insulated transformer, a vault shall not be required if suitable arrangements are made to prevent a transformer oil fire from igniting other materials and the total capacity does not exceed _____ kVA in a section of the building.

(a) 10   (b) 20
(c) 25   (d) 50

9

Transformer Vaults

Vaults are used to house dry-type transformers that are rated over 35 kV or transformers filled with combustible material used as an aid in cooling their windings.

Vaults shall be designed and built with specific rules and regulations.

Wherever possible, transformer vaults shall be located at an outside wall of the building. This rule is intended to allow ventilation direct to the outside without the use of ducts, flues, etc. per **450.45**.

WALLS, ROOFS, AND FLOORS
450.42

The rules for construction of vaults are set forth in this section. Floor, walls, and roof shall be of fire-resistant material such as concrete and capable of withstanding heat from a fire within for at least three hours. A 6 in. (150 mm) thickness is specified for the walls and roof. The floor, when laid and in contact with the earth, shall be at least 4 in. (100 mm) thick. Walls, roofs, and floors shall have at least a three-hour fire rating. **(See Figure 9-1)**

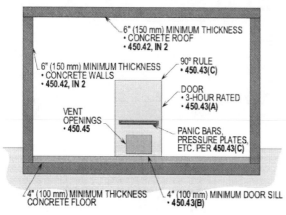

WALLS, ROOFS, AND FLOORS
NEC 450.42

Figure 9-1. Floors, walls, and roofs shall be of fire-resistant material such as concrete and capable of withstanding heat from a fire within for at least three hours. A 6 in. (150 mm) thickness is specified for the walls and roof. The floor, when laid and in contact with the earth, shall be at least 4 in. (100 mm) thick.

DOORWAYS
450.43(A) THRU (C)

The door to a transformer vault shall be built according to the standards of the *National Fire Protection Association,* which requires a three-hour fire rating. The door sill shall be at least 4 in. (100 mm) high. This is to prevent any oil that may accumulate on the floor from running out of the transformer room and moving to other areas. Doors shall be kept locked at all times to prevent access of unqualified persons to the vault.

Transformer Tip: Personnel doors shall swing out at least 90° and be equipped with panic bars, pressure plates, or other devices that open under simple pressure per **450.43(C)** and be listed as Fire Exit Hardware.

VENTILATION OPENINGS
450.45(A) THRU (F)

Where ventilation is direct to the outside, without the use of ducts or flues, the vent opening shall have an area of at least 3 sq. in. (1900 mm²) for each kVA of transformer capacity, but never less than 1 sq. ft (0.1 m²) in area. The vent opening shall be fitted with a screen or grating and an automatic closing damper. If ducts are used in the vent system, the ducts shall have sufficient capacity to maintain a suitable vault temperature. **(See Figure 9-2)**

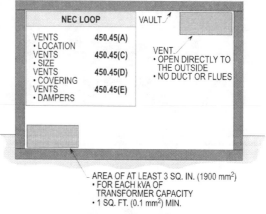

VENTILATION OPENINGS
NEC 450.45

Figure 9-2. Where ventilation is direct to the outside, without the use of ducts or flues, the vent opening shall have an area of at least 3 sq. in. (1900 mm²) for each kVA of transformer capacity, but never less than 1 sq. ft (0.1 m²) in area.

DRAINAGE
450.46

Drains shall be provided for vaults containing more than 100 kVA transformer capacity to drain off oil that might accumulate on the floor due to a leak in a transformer caused by an accident. This rule is designed to prevent a fire hazard from occurring.

WATER PIPES AND ACCESSORIES
450.47

Piping for fire protection within the vault or piping to water-cooled transformers shall be premitted to be present in a vault. No other piping or duct system shall enter or pass through. Valves or other fittings of a foreign piping or duct system shall not be permitted in a vault containing transformers. **(See Figure 9-3)**

STORAGE IN VAULTS
450.48

No storage of any kind shall be permitted to be in a vault other than the transformers and equipment necessary for their operation. This typically means that transformer vaults are not to be used as warehouses or storage areas but are to contain transformers and accessories only. The reasons that the vault is to be kept clear are the high voltage and safety measures needed for personnel servicing such equipment. Also, consideration shall be given to foreign materials being a threat of fire under certain conditions. **(See Figure 9-4)**

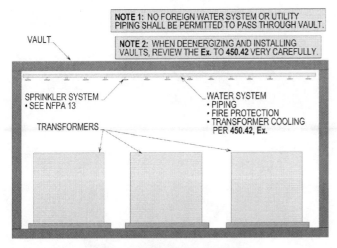

NOTE 1: NO FOREIGN WATER SYSTEM OR UTILITY PIPING SHALL BE PERMITTED TO PASS THROUGH VAULT.

NOTE 2: WHEN DEENERGIZING AND INSTALLING VAULTS, REVIEW THE **Ex.** TO **450.42** VERY CAREFULLY.

VAULT

SPRINKLER SYSTEM
• SEE NFPA 13

WATER SYSTEM
• PIPING
• FIRE PROTECTION
• TRANSFORMER COOLING PER **450.42, Ex.**

TRANSFORMERS

**WATER PIPES AND ACCESORIES
NEC 450.47**

Figure 9-3. Piping for fire protection within the vault or piping to water-cooled transformers shall be permitted to be present in a transformer vault. No other piping or duct system shall enter or pass through.

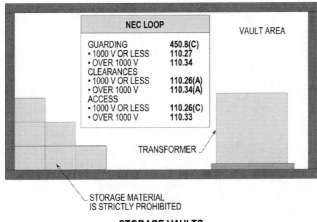

NEC LOOP	
GUARDING	450.8(C)
• 1000 V OR LESS	110.27
• OVER 1000 V	110.34
CLEARANCES	
• 1000 V OR LESS	110.26(A)
• OVER 1000 V	110.34(A)
ACCESS	
• 1000 V OR LESS	110.26(C)
• OVER 1000 V	110.33

VAULT AREA

TRANSFORMER

STORAGE MATERIAL IS STRICTLY PROHIBITED

**STORAGE VAULTS
NEC 450.48**

Figure 9-4. No storage material of any kind shall be placed in a vault other than the transformers and the equipment necessary for their operation.

Chapter 9: Transformer Vaults

Section   Answer

1. Floor, walls, and roof of a transformer vault shall be made of fire-resistant material such as concrete and shall be capable of withstanding heat from a fire within for at least _____ hours.
   (a) 2   (b) 3
   (c) 4   (d) 6

2. The walls and roof of a transformer vault shall have a thickness of at least _____ in.
   (a) 2   (b) 3
   (c) 4   (d) 6

3. The floor of a transformer vault, when laid and in contact with the earth, shall be at least _____ in. thick.
   (a) 2   (b) 3
   (c) 4   (d) 6

4. The door sill of a transformer vault shall be at least _____ in. high.
   (a) 2   (b) 3
   (c) 4   (d) 6

5. Personnel doors of transformer vaults shall swing out and be equipped with _____ that are normally latched but open under simple pressure.
   (a) panic bars   (b) pressure plates
   (c) listed fire exit hardware (d) (a), (b), and (c)

6. Where ventilation is directed to the outside for a transformer vault, without the use of ducts or flues, the vent opening shall have an area of at least _____ sq. in. for each kVA of transformer capacity.
   (a) 1   (b) 3
   (c) 5   (d) 6

7. Doors to transformer vaults shall be kept locked at all times to prevent access of _____ persons to the vault.
   (a) unqualified   (b) qualified
   (c) authorized   (d) identified

8. Which of the following shall be permitted to be installed in a transformer vault.
   (a) duct system   (b) storage
   (c) valves for foreign piping or duct (d) piping for fire protection

9. Vent openings for a transformer vault shall be fitted with a screen or grating and a(n) _____ closing damper.
   (a) automatic   (b) manual
   (c) listed   (d) identified

10. The door to a transformer vault shall be built with a minimum _____ hour fire rating.
    (a) 2   (b) 3
    (c) 4   (d) 6

Sizing Transformers and Connections

The total volt-amps of all loads in a building shall be used to size a transformer. Depending on the load requirements of a building, single-phase and three-phase voltage may be used to supply the building. The windings are connected in the configurations necessary to supply voltage load requirements of the facility. Many times, in this chapter, the transformer secondary conductors are referred to as tap conductors. Even though they are also called secondary conductors.

SIZING WYE-CONNECTED SECONDARIES

The size transformers required to supply a wye-connected secondary system can be found by applying the following:

(1) Adding the total single-phase and three-phase loads together for an individual transformer.

(2) Dividing the load in VA by 1/3 (.33) to derive three transformers.

The kVA rating of three transformers, if they are separately connected together, will add up to one individual transformer. Using this method, a single transformer rating can be sized and selected from the total volt-amps. One transformer with three windings is sized by adding the total VA of all the loads together and selecting the transformers kVA rating based on this value per Table 12A from the Troubleshooting Tables in the back of this book. **(See Figure 10-1)**

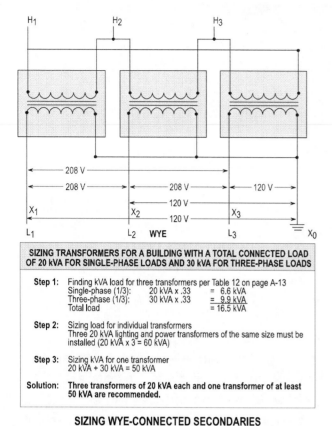

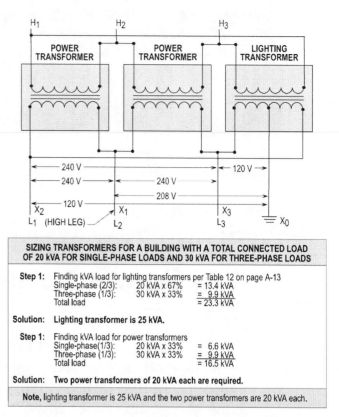

Figure 10-1. Sizing wye-connected transformers with single-phase and three-phase loads.

Figure 10-2. Sizing closed delta-connected transformers with single-phase and three-phase loads.

SIZING CLOSED DELTA-CONNECTED SECONDARIES

The size transformer required to supply a closed delta-connected secondary system can be found by multiplying the following:

- Multiply the single-phase load in VA by 67 percent.

- Multiply the three-phase load in VA by 33 percent.

- Add the kVA load of (a) and (b) together to derive the two lighting and power transformers.

- Multiply the single-phase and three-phase loads in VA by 33 percent.

- Use this total in kVA to derive the two power transformers.

See Figure 10-2 for the rules and regulations for sizing the transformer used in a closed delta-connected system.

SIZING OPEN DELTA-CONNECTED SECONDARIES

Open delta-connected secondary systems can be determined by calculating the single-phase load at 100 percent and the three-phase load at 58 percent, and using this total value to size the transformer. By adding these two loads together, the size of a mid-tap transformer can be determined. A power transformer can be sized by calculating the three-phase load at 58 percent, which is the reciprocal of the square root of 3 (1 ÷ 1.732 = 58%). This reduced total is then used to size the power transformer, which will be smaller in rating than the lighting and power transformer. **(See Figure 10-3)**

SIZING AUTOTRANSFORMERS

Autotransformers are used to boost or buck voltage by multiplying the nameplate kVA by 1000 and then dividing by the secondary voltage. Autotransformers shall be equipped with kVA, amperage, and secondary voltage rating having enough capacity to supply the load served.

For more information on autotransformers, see **210.9, 215.11, 450.4,** and **450.5**.

For example: What is the secondary amps for an autotransformer rated 2.5 kVA with a secondary voltage of 24 volts? The supply voltage is boosted from a 208 to 230 volt, single-phase system.

Step 1: Finding secondary amps
Sec. A = (kVA x 1000) ÷ secondary V
Sec. A = (2.5 kVA x 1000) ÷ 24 V
Sec. A = 104

Solution: The secondary amperage is 104 amps.

For example: By multiplying the output volts by the secondary amps, then dividing by 1000, the kVA of the autotransformer can be sized.

Step 1: Finding secondary kVA
kVA = (output V x secondary A) ÷ 1000
kVA = (230 V x 104 A) ÷ 1000
kVA = 23.9

Solution: The kVA of the load is 23.9 kVA.

Note, the size of the autotransformer shall be capable of handling a load of 23.9 kVA.

For example: What is the required rating for an autotransformer with a 24 volt secondary voltage serving a 230 volt motor with a connected load of 12,000 volt-amps?

Step 1: Finding amps
A = load served ÷ supply V
A = 12,000 VA ÷ 230 V
A = 52

Step 2: Sizing VA (Round Up kVA)
AXFMR = A x secondary V
AXFMR = 52 A x 24 V
AXFMR = 1248 VA

Solution: The autotransformer shall supply a load of 1.25 kVA.
(1248 ÷ 1000 = 1.25 kVA)

Transformer Tip: The autotransformer shall have a rating of at least 1248 VA with a transformation voltage of 24 volts, and supply a load of 12,000 VA.

See Figure 10-4 for a detailed procedure for sizing an autotransformer to supply a motor circuit in a commercial or industrial application.

Note, the supply voltage used is too low for the motor to operate properly. The autotransformer is to be used to boost the voltage from 185 volts to 208 volts.

See Figure 10-5 for a detailed procedure for sizing an autotransformer to supply a motor circuit in a commercial or industrial application.

Note, the supply voltage is too high for the motor to operate properly. The voltage can be reduced by a buck-type autotransformer if the supply voltage is too high. The autotransformer is used to reduce the voltage from 269 volts to 240 volts.

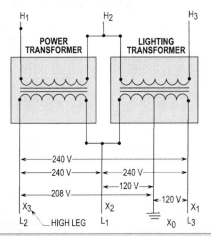

SIZING OPEN DELTA-CONNECTED SECONDARIES

Figure 10-3. Sizing open delta-connected transformers with single-phase and three-phase loads.

SIZING CONNECTIONS FROM THE SECONDARY OF TRANSFORMERS 240.21(B) AND (C)

Overcurrent protection devices of circuits shall be located at the point where the service to those circuits originates. However, it shall be permitted to make connections from the secondary side of transformers. Such conductors shall be designed and installed by the rules and regulations of **240.21(B)** and **(C)**. Sizing connections, not over 25 ft (7.5 m) long, shall be designed and installed per **240.21(B)(3)** and **(C)(5)**. Transformer secondary conductors of separately derived systems for industrial locations shall be sized per **240.21(C)(2), (C)(3), and (C)(6)**. Outside transformer

connections shall be sized per **240.21(C)(4)** and **240.92(D)**. Overcurrent protection shall be provided by **450.3(B)** and **Table 430.3(B)**. **(See Figure 10-6)**

Note: For supervised industrial locations, see **240.92(C)** and **(E)**.

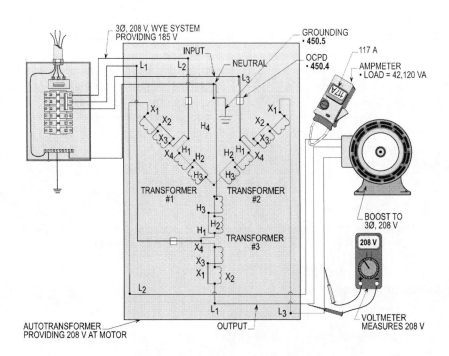

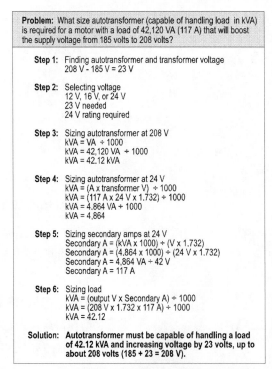

SIZING AUTOTRANSFORMERS

Figure 10-4. Sizing and selecting an autotransformer to boost the supply voltage to the motor.

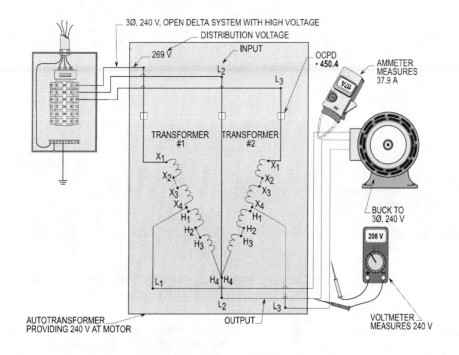

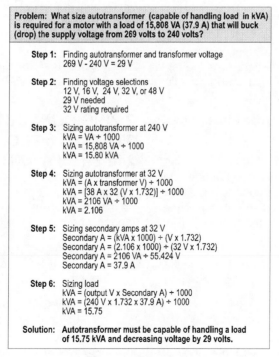

SIZING AUTOTRANSFORMERS

Figure 10-5. Sizing and selecting an autotransformer to buck the supply voltage to the motor.

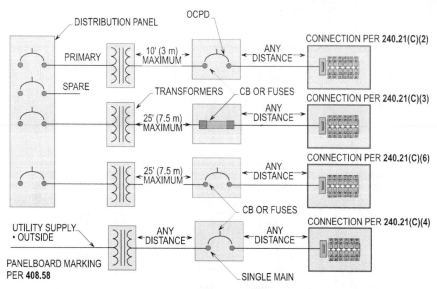

SIZING CONNECTIONS FROM THE SECONDARY OF TRANSFORMERS
NEC 240.21(B) AND (C)

Figure 10-6. The illustration above shows the four most used transformer connections that are utilized to supply electrical systems with transformer secondary conductors. [For industrial installations, see **240.21(C)(3)** and **240.92(C)** and **(E)**.]

SIZING CONNECTIONS NOT OVER 10 FT (3 m) LONG 240.21(C)(2)

Conductors shall be permitted to be connected, without overcurrent protection at the connection, to a feeder or transformer secondary where all of the following conditions are met:

- Connecting conductors do not exceed 10 ft (3 m) in length.

- Connecting conductors shall have a current rating not less than the combined calculated loads of the circuits supplied by connecting conductors. Their ampacity shall not be less than the rating of the overcurrent protection device at the termination of the connecting conductors.

- Connecting conductors shall not extend beyond the switchboard, panelboard, disconnecting means, or control devices they supply.

- Connecting conductors shall be enclosed in a raceway that will extend from the connection to the enclosure of an enclosed switchboard, panelboard, or control devices, or to the back of an open switchboard.

- The rating of the overcurrent device protecting the primary of the transformer, multiplied by the primary to the secondary voltage ratio, shall not exceed 10 times the ampacity of the secondary conductor for field installations where the secondary conductors leave the enclosure or vault.

Overcurrent protection for panelboards shall comply with the provisions outlined in **408.36**, including **Ex. 1** and **Ex. 2**, whichever applies. The maximum number of overcurrent devices shall be permitted to be determined per **408.54** and **408.55(A), Ex. 1**.

See Figure 10-7 for the proper procedure for making a connection using the 10 ft (3 m) rule.

SIZING CONNECTIONS NOT OVER 25 FT (7.5 m) LONG 240.21(B)(3) AND (C)(5)

Conductors supplying a transformer shall be permitted to be tapped, without overcurrent protection at the tap from a feeder, where all of the following conditions are met:

- Tap conductors supplying the primary shall have an ampacity at least 1/3 of the rating of the feeder being tapped.

- Connecting conductors supplying the secondary shall have an ampacity at least 1/3 of the rating of the feeder being connected, based on the primary-to-secondary voltage ratio.

- The total length of one primary plus one secondary conductor shall not be over 25 ft (7.5 m).

- The primary and secondary conductors shall be protected from physical damage.

- Secondary conductors shall terminate in a single circuit breaker or set of fuses, sized to protect the secondary.

See **Figure 10-8** for the proper procedure for making a tap and connection using the 25 ft (7.5 m) rule.

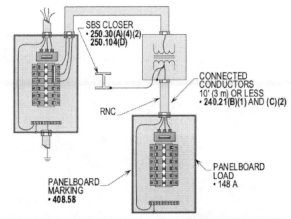

SIZING THWN cu. CONDUCTORS	SIZING OCPD
Step 1: Calculating minimum size connection 240.21(C)(2)(1) Calculated load is 148 A	**Step 1:** Calculating OCPD 240.4(E), 240.21(C)(2)(1), and 240.4(B) 1/0 AWG cu. = 150 A OCPD rated at 150 A protects conductors from overload
Step 2: Sizing conductors Table 310.16 1/0 AWG THWN cu. = 150 A	
Step 3: Verifying size 240.21(C)(2)(1) 150 A is greater than 148 A	**Solution:** The size overcurrent protection device is permitted to be 150 amps.
Solution: The size THWN copper conductors are 1/0 AWG rated at 150 amps.	

**SIZING CONNECTIONS NOT OVER 10 FT (3 m) LONG
NEC 240.21(C)(2)**

Figure 10-7. This illustration shows the procedure for sizing a 10 ft (3 m) connection from the secondary of a transformer.

INDUSTRIAL INSTALLATION SECONDARY CONDUCTORS NOT OVER 25 FT (7.5 m) LONG 240.21(C)(3)

Conductors shall be permitted to be connected to a transformer secondary of a separately derived system for industrial locations, without overcurrent protection at the connection, where all of the following conditions are met:

- Secondary conductors shall not exceed 25 ft (7.5 m) in length.

- Ampacity of connected conductors shall be equivalent to current rating of the transformer, and the overcurrent protection devices shall not exceed the ampacity of the connected conductors.

- All overcurrent devices are grouped.

- Connected conductors shall be protected from physical damage.

See **Figures 10-9** and **10-15** for the procedure to be applied when a 25 ft (7.5 m) connection rule is installed from the secondary side of a transformer.

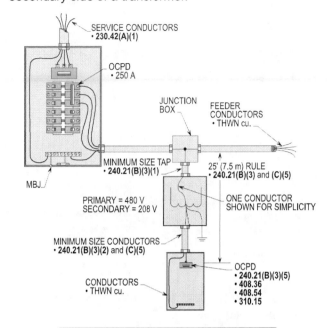

SIZING PRIMARY TAPPED CONDUCTORS	
Step 1:	Calculating primary tap 240.21(B)(3)(1) 1/3 of 250 A = 83 A
Step 2:	Selecting conductors Table 310.16 83 A requires 4 AWG cu.
Solution:	The size THWN copper conductors are 4 AWG.
SIZING SECONDARY CONNECTING CONDUCTORS	
Step 1:	Calculating secondary connection 240.21(B)(3)(2) (480 V ÷ 208 V) x (1/3 x 250 A) = 192 A
Step 2:	Selecting conductors Table 310.16 192 A requires 3/0 AWG
Solution:	The size THWN copper conductors are 3/0 AWG.
SIZING SECONDARY CONNECTING OCPD	
Step 1:	Selecting OCPD in secondary 240.4(E), 240.21(B)(3)(2), 240.21(C)(5), and 240.6(A) 200 A (3/0 AWG) requires 200 A
Solution:	The size overcurrent protection device is 200 amps.

SIZING CONNECTIONS NOT OVER 25 FT (7.5 m) LONG

Figure 10-8. The primary tap for this connection rule shall be at least 1/3 of the overcurrent protection device protecting the larger feeder conductors. The secondary connecting conductors shall be at least 1/3 of the overcurrent protection device protecting the feeder conductors based on the primary-secondary transformer ratio.

Note: When feeding through a transformer to supply a panelboard, see **408.36(B)**.

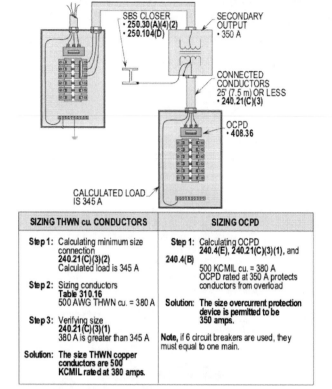

SIZING THWN cu. CONDUCTORS	SIZING OCPD
Step 1: Calculating minimum size connection 240.21(C)(3)(2) Calculated load is 345 A	**Step 1:** Calculating OCPD 240.4(E), 240.21(C)(3)(1), and 240.4(B)
Step 2: Sizing conductors Table 310.16 500 AWG THWN cu. = 380 A	500 KCMIL cu. = 380 A OCPD rated at 350 A protects conductors from overload
Step 3: Verifying size 240.21(C)(3)(1) 380 A is greater than 345 A	**Solution:** The size overcurrent protection device is permitted to be 350 amps.
Solution: The size THWN copper conductors are 500 KCMIL rated at 380 amps.	**Note,** if 6 circuit breakers are used, they must equal to one main.

INDUSTRIAL INSTALLATION
SECONDARY CONDUCTORS NOT OVER 25 FT (7.5 m) LONG
NEC 240.21(C)(3)

Figure 10-9. The above illustration shows the procedure for sizing a 25 ft (7.5 m) connection from the secondary of a transformer installed in an industrial plant.

OUTSIDE SECONDARY CONDUCTORS 240.21(C)(4)

Outside conductors shall be permitted to be connected to a feeder or be connected at the transformer secondary without overcurrent protection at the connection. However, all of the following conditions shall be complied with:

- The connected conductors are suitably protected from physical damage.

- The conductors terminate at a single circuit breaker or a single set of fuses that will limit the load to the ampacity of the conductors. This single overcurrent protection device can supply any number of additional overcurrent devices of its load side.

- The overcurrent protection device for the conductors is an integral part of a disconnecting means or shall be located immediately adjacent thereto.

- The disconnecting means for the conductors are installed at a readily accessible location either outside of a building or structure or inside, nearest the point of entrance of the conductors.

See Figure 10-10 for the rules pertaining to outside transformer connections from the secondary side of transformers.

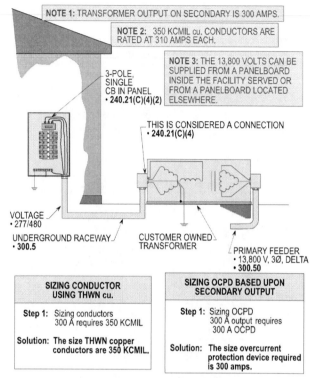

SIZING CONDUCTOR USING THWN cu.	SIZING OCPD BASED UPON SECONDARY OUTPUT
Step 1: Sizing conductors 300 A requires 350 KCMIL	**Step 1:** Sizing OCPD 300 A output requires 300 A OCPD
Solution: The size THWN copper conductors are 350 KCMIL.	**Solution:** The size overcurrent protection device required is 300 amps.

SECONDARY CONDUCTORS
NEC 240.21(C)(4)

Figure 10-10. This illustration shows the rules for sizing the conductors and overcurrent protection device for a feeder connection from a transformer located outside.

TRANSFORMER SECONDARY CONDUCTORS IN LENGTHS OF OVER 10 FT (3 m) TO 25 FT (7.5 m) 240.21(C)(6)

Conductors over 10 ft (3 m) and up to 25 ft (7.5 m) in length shall be permitted to be connected to the secondary side of a transformer. When applying this section, the 25 ft (7.5 m) secondary connection shall be terminated in a single overcurrent protection device (circuit breakers or fuses) to limit the load and to also comply with the 1/3 rule when multiplied by the secondary-to-primary voltage ratio. The secondary conductors shall be protected from physical damage and abuse. **(See Figure 10-11)**

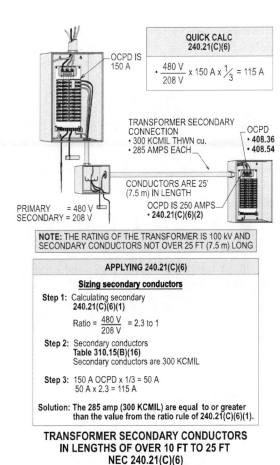

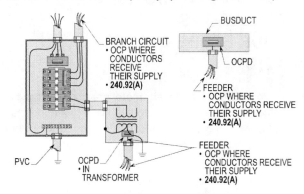

SUPERVISED INDUSTRIAL INSTALLATIONS FEEDER AND BRANCH-CIRCUIT CONDUCTORS NEC 240.92(A)

Figure 10-11. This illustration shows the rules for making a 25 ft (7.5 m) secondary conductor connection in other than industrial locations. (usually a commercial tap)

SUPERVISED INDUSTRIAL INSTALLATIONS – FEEDER AND BRANCH-CIRCUIT CONDUCTORS 240.92(A)

Feeder and branch-circuit conductors shall be protected at the point where the conductors receive their supply. However, this permits a variation of requirements for transformer secondary conductors taken from separately derived systems and outside feeder taps. **(See Figure 10-12)**

SUPERVISED INDUSTRIAL INSTALLATIONS AND CONNECTIONS UP TO 100 FT (30 m) 240.92(C)(1)(1) AND (C)(1)(2)

Unprotected lengths of secondary conductors shall be permitted at up to 100 ft (30 m) if the transformer primary

overcurrent device is sized at a value (reflected to the secondary by the transformer phase voltage ratio) of not more than 150 percent of the secondary conductor ampacity. **(See Figure 10-13)**

Additionally, the conductors shall be protected by a differential relay with a trip setting equal to or less than the conductor ampacity.

Note, a differential relay provides superior short-circuit protection at a trip open value that is almost always well below the conductor ampacity. **(See Figure 10-13)**

Figure 10-12. This illustration shows feeder and branch-circuit conductors protected at the point where the conductors receive their supply. [Also, see **240.21(C)(4)** for a similar rule.]

SHORT-CIRCUIT AND GROUND-FAULT PROTECTION 240.92(C)(1)(3)

Conductors up to 100 ft (30 m) in length shall be permitted if calculations are made under engineering supervision and it is determined that the secondary conductors will be protected within recognized time-versus-current limits for all short circuits and ground fault conditions that could occur. **(See Figure 10-13)**

OVERLOAD PROTECTION 240.92(C)(2)

To provide overload protection, the secondary conductors shall be permitted to be terminated in a single overcurrent protection device or in lugs of the bus, if not more than six overcurrent protection devices with a combined rating are installed that do not exceed the ampacity of the conductors. Another method of protection is to provide overload current relaying with the ability (design into) to trip either the primary overcurrent protection devices or the those downstream overcurrent protection devices so that the load current does not exceed the conductor's ampacity. **(See Figure 10-14)**

Transformer Tip: In some cases, the short circuit and ground fault protective arrangements may provide overload protection. If engineering calculations prove this to be the case, separate overload protection is not really needed.

SUPERVISED INDUSTRIAL INSTALLATIONS OUTSIDE FEEDER TAPS 240.92(D)

Section **240.92(D)** permits alternate means of protecting transformer secondary conductors in supervised industrial installations where the transformer is located outside.

The secondary conductors shall be protected against (1) overloads, with the additional stipulation that (2) they are suitably protected against physical damage. **(See Figure 10-15)**

Transformer Tip: Such protection shall be permitted to be provided by six or less overcurrent protection devices where the total rating does not exceed the ampacity of the conductors routed per **240.92(D). U**p to six overcurrent protection devices can be used instead of just one overcurrent protection device at the feeder termination.

Note: For 100 ft transformer secondary conductor taps, see **240.92(C)** and for any length, see **240.92(E).**

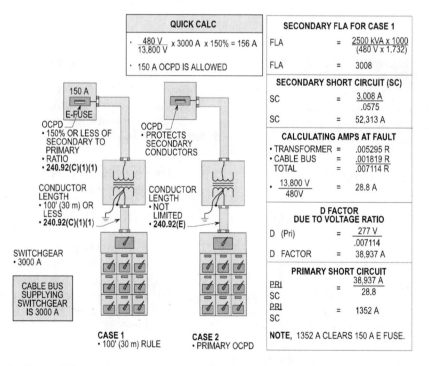

Consider a 2500 kVA transformer with a 13.8 kV to 480/277 ratio and 500 mVA available short-circuit current on the primary.

For 100 circuit feet of 3000 amp cable bus, and a three-phase bolted fault at the end of the bus (worst case), about 38,937 amps will flow from the system or 1352 amps on the primary, which will clear a typical 150 E fuse (which meets the maximum 150 percent requirement) within 42 seconds.

This time vs. current value is well within the rating of the secondary conductors. (Cable bus has a resistance of .001819 and the transformer has a resistance of .005295.)

SUPERVISED INDUSTRIAL INSTALLATIONS
ENGINEERING SUPERVISION
NEC 240.92(C)(1)(1) THRU (C)(1)(3)

Figure 10-13. This illustration shows methods of providing short-circuit and ground-fault protection for transformers and transformer secondary conductors not exceeding 100 ft.

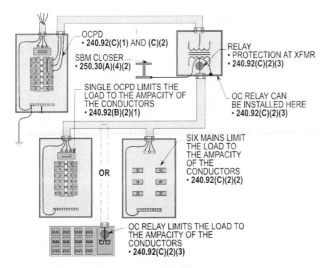

OVERLOAD PROTECTION
NEC 240.92(C)(2)

Figure 10-14. This illustration shows methods of providing overload protection.

Note, relays are capable of opening the OCPD on the primary side of the transformer if a ground-fault or short-circuit should occur or an overload condition develop.

TAP RULE SECTIONS

Supply Side Service Taps
• 230.82
Taps From Feeder Circuits (Load Side)
•240.21(B)
Taps From Transformers (Considered Supply side)
• 240.21(C)
• 240.92(C)
• 240.92(E)
Taps For Motor Circuits
• 430.28

Note, there is no OCPD ahead of conductors for supply side but there is an OCPD ahead of conductors on load side.

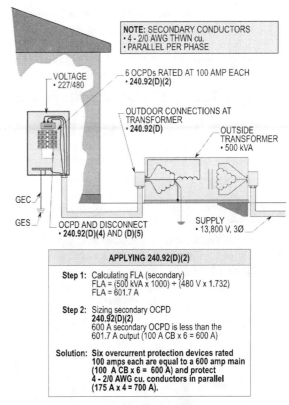

APPLYING 240.92(D)(2)

Step 1: Calculating FLA (secondary)
FLA = (500 kVA x 1000) ÷ (480 V x 1.732)
FLA = 601.7 A

Step 2: Sizing secondary OCPD
240.92(D)(2)
600 A secondary OCPD is less than the
601.7 A output (100 A CB x 6 = 600 A)

Solution: Six overcurrent protection devices rated
100 amps each are equal to a 600 amp main
(100 A CB x 6 = 600 A) and protect
4 - 2/0 AWG cu. conductors in parallel
(175 A x 4 = 700 A).

SUPERVISED INDUSTRIAL INSTALLATIONS
OUTSIDE FEEDER TAPS
NEC 240.92(D)

Figure 10-15. This illustration shows an alternate means permitted for protecting conductors tapped to a transformer located outside.

REACTOR FUNCTION

A reactor is a device used for introducing inductive reactance into a circuit. Its purpose is to limit the current that is allowed to flow through the circuit, particulary under the short-circuit and ground-fault conditions to protect equipment from excessive heat and destructive mechanical forces. It is therefore, connected in series with the equipment or feeders that it is designed to protect.

PRINCIPLE OF OPERATION

A reactor usually consists of a coil wire. The current flowing through the coil produces a magnetic field that cuts the turns of the coil and sets up a counter voltage. With normal current flowing, the counter voltage is relatively small. With large short-circuit current flowing, however, the counter voltage becomes relatively large and bucks the applied voltage. The resultant voltage, which will push current into the fault, is small and the fault current (by Ohm's Law Formula) will also be small. The isolation of the fault from the system is obtained by means of circuit breakers (CB's). Since reactors limit short-circuit currents, lower capacity may be installed.

When reactance is placed in series with the euqipment under fault conditions, the voltage applie to the fault is reduced, but the voltage on the remainder of the circuit or system is maintained while the fault is being cleared.

ADVANTAGES OF REACTORS

Protective reactors are used to reduce the flow of short circuit current at the fault point so as to protect the apparatus from excessive mechanical stresses and from over heating and thus protect the system as a whole.

Note, whenever a capacitive load is connected to the transmission line or feeder, a shunt reactor is connected which injects lagging reactive VARs to the power system. As a result the power factor is improved for the user. **(See Figure 10-16.)**

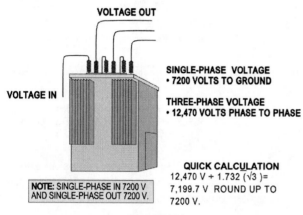

VOLTAGE OUT

VOLTAGE IN

SINGLE-PHASE VOLTAGE
• 7200 VOLTS TO GROUND

THREE-PHASE VOLTAGE
• 12,470 VOLTS PHASE TO PHASE

QUICK CALCULATION
12,470 V ÷ 1.732 ($\sqrt{3}$)=
7,199.7 V ROUND UP TO
7200 V.

NOTE: SINGLE-PHASE IN 7200 V AND SINGLE-PHASE OUT 7200 V.

REACTOR

Figure 10-16. A reactor, also known as a line reactor, is a coil wired in series between two points in a power system to minimize inrush current, voltage notching effects, and voltage spikes.

Chapter 10: Sizing Transformers and Connections

Section   Answer

1. The size transformer required to supply a closed delta-connected secondary system can be found by multiplying the single-phase load in VA by _____ percent.
   (a) 33   (b) 50
   (c) 58   (d) 67

2. The size transformer required to supply a closed delta-connected secondary system can be found by multiplying the three-phase load in VA by _____ percent.
   (a) 33   (b) 50
   (c) 58   (d) 67

3. Open delta-connected secondary systems can be determined by calculating the single-phase load at 100 percent and the three-phase load at _____ percent.
   (a) 33   (b) 50
   (c) 58   (d) 67

4. Tap conductors not over 10 ft (7.5 m) long supplying the primary shall have an ampacity at least _____ of the rating of the feeder OCPD.
   (a) 1/4   (b) 1/3
   (c) 1/2   (d) 3/4

5. Unprotected lengths of secondary conductors for supervised industrial installations shall be permitted at up to _____ ft, if the transformer primary overcurrent device is sized at a value (reflected to the secondary by the transformer phase voltage ratio) of not more than 150 percent of the secondary conductor ampacity.
   (a) 10   (b) 25
   (c) 75   (d) 100

6. To provide overload protection, the secondary conductors for supervised industrial installations shall be permitted to be terminated in a single overcurrent protection device or in lugs of the bus, if not more than _____ overcurrent protection devices with a combined rating are installed that do not exceed the ampacity of the conductors.
   (a) 2   (b) 3
   (c) 6   (d) 8

7. The rating of the overcurrent device protecting the primary of the transformer, multiplied by the primary to the secondary voltage ratio, shall not exceed _____ times the ampacity of the secondary conductor for field installations where the secondary conductors (not over 10 ft long) leave the enclosure or vault.
   (a) 6   (b) 10
   (c) 12   (d) 25

8. Transformer secondary conductors can extend _____ ft.
   (a) 100   (b) 125
   (c) 150   (d) 175

9. Conductors up to _____ ft in length shall be permitted if calculations are made under engineering supervision and it is determined that the secondary conductors for supervised industrial installations will be protected within recognized time versus current limits for all short circuit and ground fault conditions that could occur.
   (a) 10   (b) 25
   (c) 75   (d) 100

10. The size transformer required to supply a closed delta-connected secondary system can be found by multiplying the single-phase and three-phase loads in VA by _____ percent.
   (a) 33   (b) 50
   (c) 58   (d) 67

11. Transformer secondary conductors in lengths of over 10 ft and up to _____ ft in length shall be permitted to be connected to the secondary side of a transformer that is not installed in an industrial site.
   (a) 10   (b) 12
   (c) 15   (d) 25

12. What size wye-connected transformers are required for a building with a total connected load of 25 kVA for single-phase loads and 40 kVA for three-phase loads?

13. What size closed delta-connected transformers are required for a building with a total connected load of 25 kVA for single-phase loads and 40 kVA for three-phase loads?

14. What size open delta-connected transformer (lighting and power) is required for a building with a total connected load of 25 kVA for single-phase loads and 40 kVA for three-phase loads?

15. What are the secondary amps for an autotransformer rated 2 kVA with a secondary voltage of 24 volts?

16. What is the size and rating of an autotransformer with a 24 volt secondary voltage serving a 230 volt motor with a connected load of 10,000 volt-amps?

17. What size THWN copper conductors and overcurrent protection device are required for a 10 ft transformer secondary connection with a pre-calculated load of 168 amps?

18. What size primary and secondary THWN copper conductors and secondary overcurrent protection device is required for a 25 ft connection from a feeder with a 200 amp overcurrent protection device having a 480 volt primary and 208 volt secondary?

19. What size connected THWN copper conductors and overcurrent protection device is required for a separately derived system installed in an industrial location with a pre-calculated load of 312 amps? Note, the load on the secondary side never exceeds 248 amps.

20. What size connected THWN copper conductors and overcurrent protection device are required for an outside transformer with an output on the secondary of 280 amps? Note, the load on the secondary side never exceeds 224 amps.

11

Protecting Transformers

Transformers must be sized with enough capacity to supply power to loads served and allow loads with high inrush currents to start and run. In addition, they must be protected by properly sized overcurrent protection devices and be equipped with conductors having allowable ampacity ratings to supply the loads. Overcurrent protection devices and conductors must be designed and installed in such a manner to safely protect the windings of such power sources from dangerous short circuits, ground faults, and overloads.

The overcurrent protection devices and conductors are sometimes required to be adjusted in size in order to protect the transformer windings or the conductors from overload conditions

Note 1: When selecting the actual size circuit breaker or fuse for the protection of electrical systems rated over 1000 volts, see one of the ANSI C Standards.

For example, for fuses rated at 100 amps or less, see ANSI C 37.46 and for over 100 amps, see ANSI C 37.46 and ANSI C 37.40. When circuit breakers are used to protect high-voltage systems, see ANSI C 37.06. However, there may be protection designs that require reference to other ANSI C Standards, and the designer must be prepared to refer to such standards. However, OCPDs are selected from **Table 240.6(A).**

Note 2: When performing maintenance on transformers, review Chapter 21 and Annex L in NFPA 70B and apply the requirements in NFPA 70E for selecting PPE and safety related work practices.

CALCULATING PRIMARY AND SECONDARY CURRENT

The transformer's primary amp rating shall be equivalent to the amps of the connected load when installing a feeder to supply the primary of a transformer to step up or step down the voltage. To determine the FLA of a transformer, the kVA of the transformer must be divided by the voltage times 1.732 if the supply is three-phase. **[See Figures 11-1(a) and (b)]**

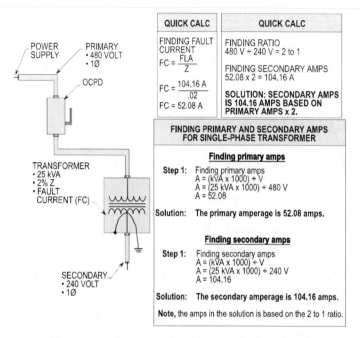

CALCULATING PRIMARY AND SECONDARY CURRENTS

Figure 11-1(a). Finding amps for a single-phase transformer.

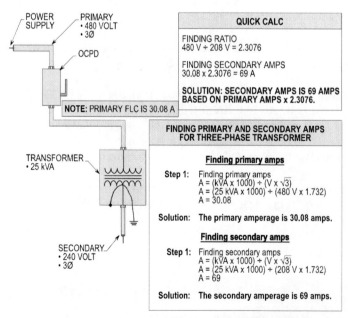

CALCULATING PRIMARY AND SECONDARY CURRENTS

Figure 11-1(b). Finding amps for a three-phase transformer.

FINDING AMPERAGE

The kVA or amp rating for the primary or secondary of a transformer can be determined for a single-phase system by applying the following formulas:

kVA = (volts x amps) ÷ 1000
amps = (kVA x 1000) ÷ volts

The following formula must be applied to determine the ratio of a transformer having a 480 volt primary and 240 volt secondary:

primary ÷ secondary
480 V ÷ 240 V
2:1 ratio

The amp rating for the primary or secondary can be determined for a three-phase system by applying the following formula:

kVA = (volts x 1.732) x (amps ÷ 1000)
amps = (kVA x 1000) ÷ (volts x 1732)

CALCULATING FAULT CURRENTS

When determining the fault current of a transformer, the interrupting-current rating of the overcurrent protection device shall be determined for the amount of fault-current to be delivered at the terminals of the transformer when a short circuit develops at that point. The current-limiting characteristic of a transformer at its terminals is called impedance. The impedance of a transformer (always expressed as a percentage) is used for sizing the interrupting capacity rating of fuses and circuit breakers used to protect the primary of a transformer.

For example: What is the interrupting capacity or fault-current rating of a 25 kVA transformer with a 1.5 percent impedance supplied by a 120/240 volt, single-phase secondary?

Step 1: Finding FLA
FLA = (kVA x 1000) ÷ V
FLA = (25 kVA x 1000) ÷ 240 V
FLA = 104 A

Step 2: Finding interrupting capacity
Fault current = FLA ÷ impedance
Fault current = 104 A ÷ .015
Fault current = 6933 A

Solution: The fault current is 6933 amps.

Note, the greater the impedance rating is, the lower the fault current will be, in amps.

OVERCURRENT PROTECTION 450.3(A) AND (B)

There are two sets of rules when providing overcurrent protection of transformers: rules for transformers rated over 1000 volts **[450.3(A)]** and transformers of 1000 volts or less **[450.3(B)]**. The overcurrent protection device may be placed in the primary only or in the primary and secondary side of the transformer.

PRIMARY ONLY – OVER 1000 VOLTS 450.3(A) AND TABLE 450.3(A)

The term *primary* is often inferred in the field as being the high side, and the term *secondary* as the low side of the transformer. This is really not the proper terminology. The primary is the input side of the transformer and the secondary is the output side. Thus, voltage has nothing to do with "high" or "low."

Each transformer shall be protected by an overcurrent device in the primary side. If the overcurrent protection device is fuses, they shall be rated not greater than 250 percent (2.5 times) of the rated primary current of the transformer. When circuit breakers are used, they shall be set not greater than 300 percent (3 times) of the rated primary current. **(See Figure 11-2)**

This overcurrent protection device shall be permitted to be mounted in the vault or at the transformer, if approved for such purpose. It shall also be permitted to be mounted in the panelboard and be designed to protect the windings and circuit conductors supplying the transformer.

If not installed in a vault, the overcurrent proteciton device shall be permitted to be installed outdoors on a pole, with a disconnecting means installed in the vault to disconnect supply conductors.

APPLYING ITEM 1 TABLE 450.3(A), ITEM 1

Where 250 percent (2.5 times) of the rated primary current of the transformer does not correspond to a standard rating of a fuse, the next higher standard rating **[240.6(A)** and **Table 240.6(A)]** shall be permitted.

PRIMARY AND SECONDARY OVER 1000 VOLTS 450.3(A) AND TABLE 450.3(A)

A transformer over 1000 volts, nominal, having an overcurrent protection device on the secondary side rated to open not greater than the values listed in **Table 450.3(A)**, or a transformer equipped with a coordinated thermal overload protection by the manufacturer, shall not be required to have individual protection in the primary. However, a feeder overcurrent protection device rated or set to open at not greater than the values listed in **Table 450.3(A)** shall be provided.

SUPERVISED LOCATIONS
450.3(A) AND TABLE 450.3(A)

Overcurrent protection shall be permitted to be placed in the primary and secondary side of high-voltage transformers if the overcurrent protection devices are designed and installed according to the provisions listed in **Table 450.3(A)**.

Where the facility has trained engineers and maintenance personnel, the overcurrent protection device for the secondary shall be be sized at not more than 250 percent of the FLC for voltage of 1000 volts or less. With higher voltage on the secondary side of the transformer, the percentages for sizing the overcurrent protection devices shall be selected from **Table 450.3(A)** based on the particular voltage level. **[See Figures 11-3(a) and (b)]**

See Figure 11-4 for certain design conditions that permit the primary overcurrent protection device to be used to protect the primary and secondary sides of two-wire to two-wire connected transformers and three-wire to three-wire delta-connected transformers per **240.4(F)** and **240.21(C)(1)**.

NONSUPERVISED LOCATIONS
450.3(A) AND TABLE 450.3(A)

Overcurrent protection for a nonsupervised location shall be permitted to be placed in the primary and secondary side of high-voltage transformers if the overcurrent protection devices are designed and installed according to the provisions listed in **Table 450.3(A)**.

If the secondary voltage is 1000 volts or less, the overcurrent protection device and conductors on the secondary side shall be sized at 125 percent of the FLC rating. Overcurrent protection devices sized at 125 percent of the FLC protect the conductors and windings of the transformer from dangerous overload conditions. With higher voltage (over 1000 volts) on the secondary side of the transformer, the percentages for sizing the overcurrent protection devices shall be selected from **Table 450.3(A)** (any location) based on the particular voltage level. **(See Figure 11-5)**

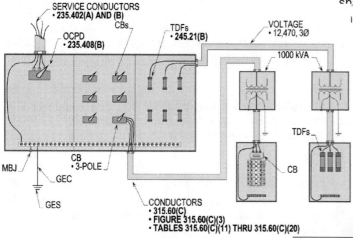

NOTE: FOR SIMPLICITY, **TABLE 240.6(A)** IS USED TO SIZE OCPDS. SEE "FOR EXAMPLE" AT THE BEGINNING OF CHAPTER 11.

FINDING INDIVIDUAL OCPD FOR THE PRIMARY SIDE OF THE TRANSFORMER		
	Sizing OCPD using CBs	**Sizing OCPD using TDFs**
Step 1:	Finding FLA of primary 450.3(A) FLA = (kVA x 1000) ÷ (V x √3) FLA = (1000 x 1000) ÷ (12,470 V x 1.732) FLA = 46.3 A	**Step 1:** Calculating FLA for TDFs 450.3(A) and Table 450.3(A) 46.3 A x 250% = 115.8 A
Step 2:	Calculating FLA for OCPD 450.3(A) and Table 450.3(A) 46.3 A x 300% = 138.9 A	**Step 2:** Selecting TDFs Table 450.3(A), Item 1 and Table 240.6(A) 115.8 A permits 125 A
		Solution: The size time delay fuses are 125 amps.
Step 3:	Selecting OCPD Table 450.3(A), Item 1 and Table 240.6(A) 138.9 A requires 150 A	**Note 1,** supervised location with any impedance 138.9 A requires 150 A per Table 450.3(A).
Solution:	The size circuit breaker is 150 amps.	**Note 2,** for simplicity, overcurrent protection devices are selected from Table 240.6(A).

INDIVIDUAL PROTECTION
NEC 450.3(A) AND TABLE 450.3(A)

Figure 11-2. If the overcurrent protection devices is fuses, they shall be rated not greater than 250 percent (2.5 times) of the rated primary current of the transformer. When circuit breakers are used, they must be set not greater than 300 percent (3 times) of the rated primary current.

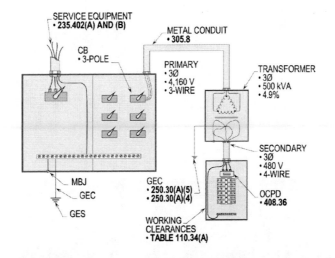

SIZING OCPD FOR PRIMARY SIDE	SIZING OCPD FOR SECONDARY SIDE
Step 1: Finding FLA of transformer FLA = (kVA x 1000) ÷ (V x √3) FLA = (500 x 1000) ÷ (4160 V x 1.732) FLA = 69.4 A	**Step 1:** Finding FLA of transformer FLA = (kVA x 1000) ÷ (V x √3) FLA = (500 x 1000) ÷ (480 V x 1.732) FLA = 601.7 A
Step 2: Calculating FLA for OCPD 450.3(A) and Table 450.3(A) FLA = 69.4 A x 600% FLA = 416.4 A	**Step 2:** Calculating FLA for OCPD 450.3(A) and Table 450.3(A) FLA = 601.7 A x 250% FLA = 1504.3 A
Step 3: Selecting OCPD Table 450.3(A), Item 3 and Table 240.6(A) 416.4 A permits 400 A	**Step 3** Selecting OCPD Table 450.3(A), Item 3 and Table 240.6(A) 1504.3 A permits 1500 A
Solution: **The size overcurrent protection device for the primary side is 400 amps.**	**Solution:** **The size overcurrent protection device for the secondary side is 1500 amps.**
Note 1, transformer's impedance is less than 6%. **Note 2,** for simplicity, **Table 240.6(A)** was used to select the overcurrent protection devices.	**Note,** if the secondary voltage is 4160, the overcurrent protection device using a circuit breaker shall be sized at 300 percent and a fuse shall be sized at 250 percent of the transformer FLC.

SUPERVISED LOCATIONS
NEC 450.3(A) AND TABLE 450.3(A)

Figure 11-3(a). Sizing the primary and secondary side of a transformer in a supervised location. **Note:** When actually sizing OCPDs for high-voltage systems, review the "For Example" on page 11-1 in thie Chapter.

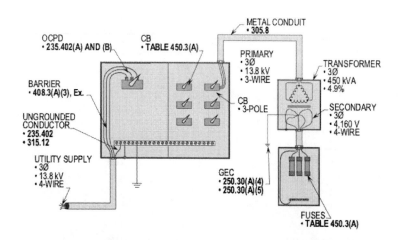

SUPERVISED LOCATION
NEC 450.3(A) AND TABLE 450.3(A)

Figure 11-3(b). Sizing the primary and secondary side of a transformer in a supervised location.

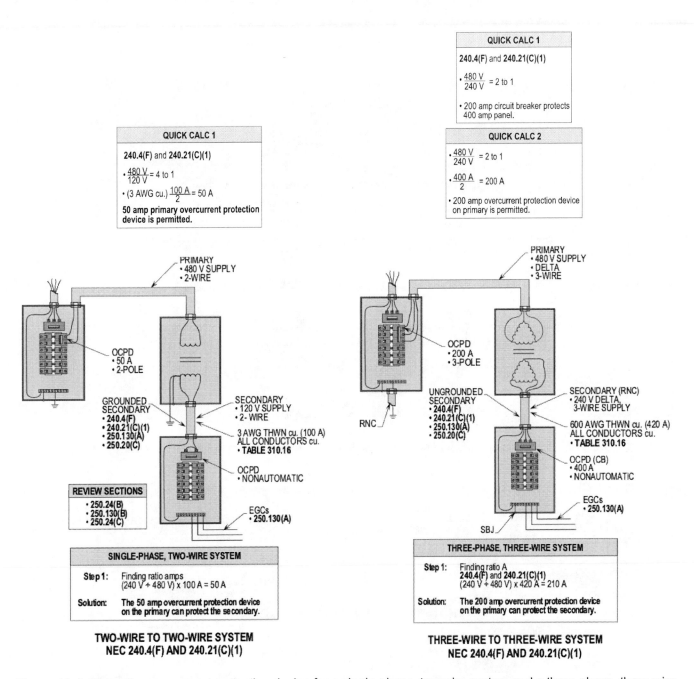

Figure 11-4. Sizing the overcurrent protection device for a single-phase, two-wire system and a three-phase, three-wire system. **Note:** When sizing and selecting OCPDs for low-voltage systems, see **Table 240.6(A)** in the **NEC**.

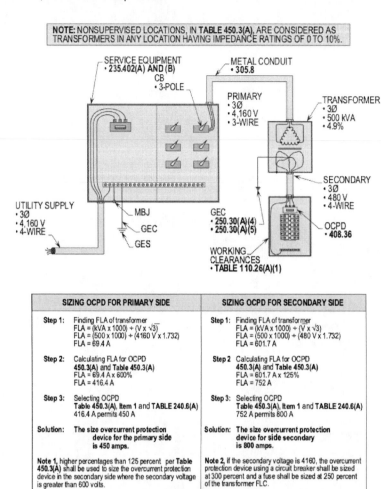

NOTE: NONSUPERVISED LOCATIONS, IN **TABLE 450.3(A)**, ARE CONSIDERED AS TRANSFORMERS IN ANY LOCATION HAVING IMPEDANCE RATINGS OF 0 TO 10%.

SIZING OCPD FOR PRIMARY SIDE	SIZING OCPD FOR SECONDARY SIDE
Step 1: Finding FLA of transformer FLA = (kVA x 1000) ÷ (V x √3) FLA = (500 x 1000) ÷ (4160 V x 1.732) FLA = 69.4 A	**Step 1:** Finding FLA of transformer FLA = (kVA x 1000) ÷ (V x √3) FLA = (500 x 1000) ÷ (480 V x 1.732) FLA = 601.7 A
Step 2: Calculating FLA for OCPD 450.3(A) and Table 450.3(A) FLA = 69.4 A x 600% FLA = 416.4 A	**Step 2** Calculating FLA for OCPD 450.3(A) and Table 450.3(A) FLA = 601.7 A x 125% FLA = 752 A
Step 3: Selecting OCPD Table 450.3(A), Item 1 and TABLE 240.6(A) 416.4 A permits 450 A	**Step 3:** Selecting OCPD Table 450.3(A), Item 1 and TABLE 240.6(A) 752 A permits 800 A
Solution: The size overcurrent protection device for the primary side is 450 amps.	**Solution:** The size overcurrent protection device for side secondary is 800 amps.
Note 1, higher percentages than 125 percent per **Table 450.3(A)** shall be used to size the overcurrent protection device in the secondary side where the secondary voltage is greater than 600 volts.	**Note 2,** if the secondary voltage is 4160, the overcurrent protection device using a circuit breaker shall be sized at 300 percent and a fuse shall be sized at 250 percent of the transformer FLC.

NONSUPERVISED LOCATIONS
(ANY LOCATION)
NEC 450.3(A) AND TABLE 450.3(A)

Figure 11-5. Sizing the primary and secondary side of a transformer in a nonsupervised (any) location.

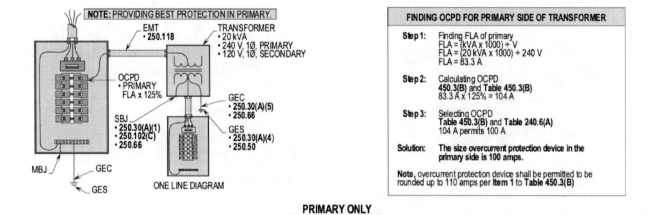

FINDING OCPD FOR PRIMARY SIDE OF TRANSFORMER
Step 1: Finding FLA of primary FLA = (kVA x 1000) ÷ V FLA = (20 kVA x 1000) ÷ 240 V FLA = 83.3 A
Step 2: Calculating OCPD 450.3(B) and Table 450.3(B) 83.3 A x 125% = 104 A
Step 3: Selecting OCPD Table 450.3(B) and Table 240.6(A) 104 A permits 100 A
Solution: The size overcurrent protection device in the primary side is 100 amps.
Note, overcurrent protection device shall be permitted to be rounded up to 110 amps per **Item 1** to **Table 450.3(B)**

PRIMARY ONLY
1000 VOLTS OR LESS
NEC 450.3(B) AND TABLE 450.3(B)

Figure 11-6. A transformer of 1000 volts or less, nominal, having an individual overcurrent protection device on the primary side shall be sized at not more than 125 percent of the transformer's full-load current rating.

PRIMARY ONLY
1000 VOLTS OR LESS
450.3(B) AND TABLE 450.3(B)

A transformer 1000 volts or less, nominal, having an individual overcurrent protection device on the primary side shall be sized at not more than 125 percent of the transformer's full-load current rating.

Note, with the overcurrent protection device and conductors sized at 125 percent or less of the transformer's FLC, the supply conductors and transformer windings shall be considered protected from overload conditions. It appears that individual protection in the primary is not recognized per **450.3(B)** and **Table 450.3(B)**. **(See Figure 11-6)**

PRIMARY
9 AMPS OR MORE
450.3(B) AND TABLE 450.3(B)

Where the rated primary current of a transformer is 9 amps or more and 125 percent of this current does not correspond to a standard rating of a fuse or circuit breaker, the next size shall be permitted to be used per **240.6(A)** and **Table 240.6(A)**. **(See Figure 11-7)**

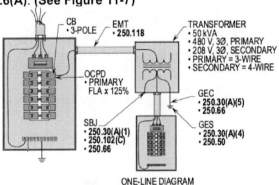

ONE-LINE DIAGRAM

FINDING OCPD FOR PRIMARY SIDE OF TRANSFORMER

Sizing primary OCPD (First Level) per Table 450.3(B)

Step 1: Finding FLA of primary
FLA = (kVA x 1000) ÷ (V x √3)
FLA = (50 kVA x 1000) ÷ (480 V x 1.732)
FLA = 60.2 A

Step 2: Calculating OCPD
450.3(B) and Table 450.3(B)
60.2 A x 125% = 75.3 A

Step 3: Selecting OCPD
Table 450.3(B), Item 1 and Table 240.6(A)
75.3 A permits 80 A

Solution: The size overcurrent protection device in the primary side is 80 amps.

PRIMARY 9 AMPS OR MORE
NEC 450.3(B) AND TABLE 450.3(B)

Figure 11-7. Where the rated primary current of a transformer is 9 amps or more and 125 percent of this current does not correspond to a standard rating of a fuse or circuit breaker, the next size shall be permitted to be used per **240.6(A)** and **Item 1** to **Table 450.3(B)**.

PRIMARY
2 AMPS OR MORE BUT LESS THAN 9 AMPS
450.3(B) AND TABLE 450.3(B)

Where the rated primary current of a transformer is less than 9 amps but more than 2 amps, an overcurrent protection device rated or set at no more than 167 percent of the primary current shall be used. **(See Figure 11-8)**

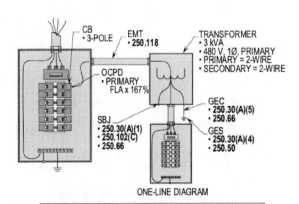

ONE-LINE DIAGRAM

FINDING OCPD FOR PRIMARY SIDE OF TRANSFORMER

Sizing primary OCPD (second level) per Table 450.3(B)

Step 1: Finding FLA of primary
FLA = kVA x (1000) ÷ V
FLA = 3 kVA x (1000 ÷ 480 V)
FLA = 6.25 A

Step 2: Calculating OCPD
450.3(B) and Table 450.3(B)
6.25 A x 167% = 10.4 A

Step 3: Selecting OCPD
450.3(B) and Table 240.6(A)
10.4 A permits 10 A

Solution: The size overcurrent protection device in the primary side is 10 amps.

PRIMARY 2 AMPS OR MORE BUT LESS THAN 9 AMPS
NEC 450.3(B) AND TABLE 450.3(B)

Figure 11-8. Where the rated primary current of a transformer is less than 9 amps but 2 amps or more, an overcurrent protection device rated or set at no more than 167 percent of the primary current shall be used.

PRIMARY
LESS THAN 2 AMPS
450.3(B) AND TABLE 450.3(B)

When the rated primary current of a transformer is less than 2 amps, an overcurrent protection device rated or set at not more than 300 percent shall be used. **(See Figure 11-9)**

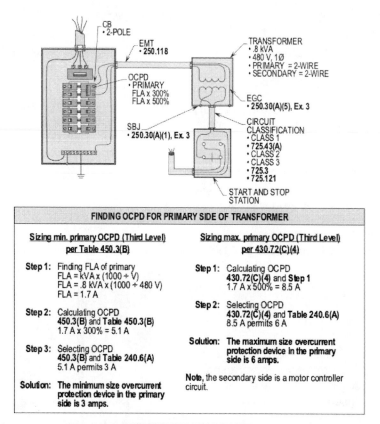

PRIMARY LESS THAN 2 AMPS
NEC 450.3(B), 430.72(C)(4), and TABLE 450.3(B)

Figure 11-9. When the rated primary current of a transformer is less than 2 amps, an overcurrent protection device rated or set at not more than 300 percent shall be used, unless **430.72(C)(4)** is applied.

PRIMARY AND SECONDARY 1000 VOLTS OR LESS 450.3(B) AND TABLE 450.3(B)

Combination protection shall be permitted to be provided for both the primary and secondary sides of a transformer. A current value of 250 percent of the rated primary current of the transformer shall be used if 125 percent of the rated primary current of the transformer is not sufficient to allow loads with high inrush currents to start and operate. However, the secondary overcurrent protection device shall be sized at 125 percent of the rated secondary full-load current of the transformer. Where the rated secondary current of a transformer is less than 9 amps, an overcurrent device rated or set at no more than 167 percent of secondary current shall be used. **(See Figure 11-10)**

9 AMPS OR MORE TABLE 450.3(B), ITEM 1

Where the rated secondary current of a transformer is 9 amps or more and 125 percent of this current does not correspond to a standard rating of a fuse or circuit breaker, the next size shall be permitted to be used per **240.6(A)**.

CALCULATING OVERCURRENT PROTECTION DEVICES FOR AUTOTRANSFORMERS 450.4

Autotransformers rated at 1000 volts or less shall be protected by an overcurrent protection device installed on their primary side. The size of the overcurrent protection device is found by multiplying the full-load current rating of the autotransformer times the percentage.

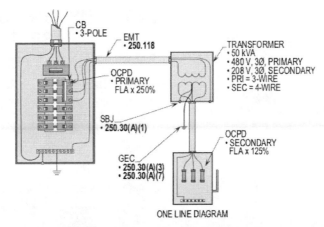

FINDING OCPD FOR PRIMARY AND SECONDARY SIDE OF TRANSFORMER

Sizing OCPD in primary

Step 1: Finding FLA of primary
FLA = (kVA x 1000) ÷ (V x √3)
FLA = (50 x 1000) ÷ (480 V x 1.732)
FLA = 60.2 A

Step 2: Calculating OCPD
450.3(B) and Table 450.3(B)
60.2 A x 250% = 150.5 A

Step 3: Selecting OCPD
450.3(B) and Table 240.6(A)
150.5 A allows 150 A

Solution: **The minimum size overcurrent protection device in the primary side is 150 amps.**

Note, the size of the overcurrent protection device in primary shall not exceed the 250% x FLA of the primary.

Sizing OCPD in secondary

Step 1: Finding FLA of primary
FLA = (kVA x 1000) ÷ (V x √3)
FLA = (50 x 1000) ÷ (208 V x 1.732)
FLA = 138.9 A

Step 2: Calculating OCPD
450.3(B) and Table 450.3(B)
138.9 A x 125% = 173.6 A

Step 3: Selecting OCPD
450.3(B), Item 1 and Table 240.6(A)
173.6 A allows 175 A

Solution: **The maximum size overcurrent protection device in the primary side is 175 amps.**

Note, Table 450.3(B), Item 1 permits the next higher size overcurrent protection device to be used.

**PRIMARY AND SECONDARY
1000 VOLTS OR LESS
NEC 450.3(B) AND TABLE 450.3(B)**

Figure 11-10. Sizing overcurrent protection device for the primary and secondary side of a transformer rated 1000 volts or less.

OVERCURRENT PROTECTION 9 AMPS OR MORE 450.4(A)

When sizing the overcurrent protection device for an autotransformer rated 9 amps or more, the full-load input current rating of the autotransformer shall be multiplied by 125 percent and the next size device shall be permitted to be used.

OVERCURRENT PROTECTION LESS THAN 9 AMPS 450.4(A), Ex.

When sizing the overcurrent protection device for an autotransformer rated less than 9 amps, the full-load input current rating of the autotransformer shall be multiplied by 167 percent and the next lower size device shall be permitted to be used.

GROUNDING AUTOTRANSFORMERS 450.5

Autotransformers are connected to three-phase, three-wire ungrounded systems to derive a three-phase, four-wire grounded system. Three autotransformers connected in a star (wye) configuration to a three-phase ungrounded system converts to a three-phase, four-wire grounded system.

Autotransformers are installed today because many electrical systems are not grounded. Existing ungrounded delta systems are grounded with autotransformers to derive a neutral. Three-phase zigzag transformers are generally installed for this purpose.

THREE-WIRE CIRCUIT TO THREE-PHASE, FOUR-WIRE CIRCUIT
450.5(A)

Grounding autotransformers are connected to derive a neutral from a three-phase, three-wire ungrounded system to a three-phase, four-wire grounded system. The following conditions shall apply:

- Proper connections shall be made.
- Overcurrent protection shall be provided.
- Transformer fault sensing shall be installed.
- Rating shall be adequately sized.

CONNECTIONS
450.5(A)(1)

Transformers shall be directly connected to the ungrounded (phase) conductors with no switches or overcurrent protection devices installed between the connection and the autotransformer.

OVERCURRENT PROTECTION
450.5(A)(2)

An overcurrent protection sensing device shall be designed to trip at 125 percent of its continuous current per phase or neutral rating. The next higher standard rating shall be permitted to be installed where the input current is 9 amps or more and calculated at 125 percent. Input current of 2 amps or less shall not exceed 167 percent. **(See Figure 11-11)**

TRANSFORMER FAULT SENSING
450.5(A)(3)

A main switch or common-trip overcurrent protection device for a three-phase, four-wire system shall be provided with fault sensing systems to guard against single-phasing or internal faults.

RATING
450.5(A)(4)

Autotransformers shall be designed with a continuous neutral current rating sufficient to handle the maximum possible unbalanced neutral load current that could flow in the four-wire system.

DETECTING GROUNDS ON THREE-PHASE, THREE-WIRE SYSTEMS
450.5(B)

The following conditions shall apply when autotransformers are used to detect grounds on three-phase, three-wire systems:

- Proper rating.
- Overcurrent protection sized adequately.
- Ground reference for damping transitory over voltages.

RATING
450.5(B)(1)

Autotransformers shall have a continuous neutral current rating sufficient for the specified ground fault current that could develop in the system.

OVERCURRENT PROTECTION
450.5(B)(2)

The overcurrent protection device shall open simultaneously with a common trip all ungrounded (phase) conductors and be set to trip at not more than 125 percent of the rated phase current of the transformer.

Note, 42 percent of the overcurrent protection device's rating may be used if connected in the autotransformer's neutral connection. When dealing with high-impedance grounded systems per **250.36**, review the **Ex.** to **450.5(B)(2)** and **110.9. (See Figure 11-12)**

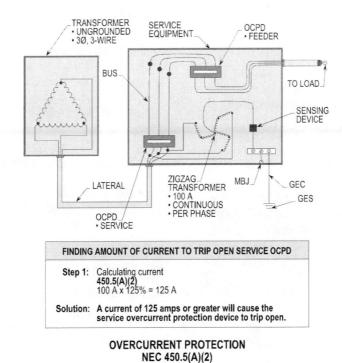

OVERCURRENT PROTECTION
NEC 450.5(A)(2)

Figure 11-11. An overcurrent protection sensing device shall be designed to trip at 125 percent of its continuous current per phase or neutral rating.

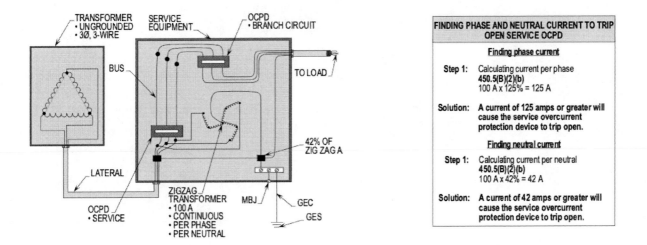

OVERCURRENT PROTECTION
NEC 450.5(B)(2)(b)

Figure 11-12. The overcurrent protection device shall open simultaneously with a common trip of all ungrounded (phase) conductors and be set to trip at not more than 125 percent of the rated phase current of the transformer. OVERCURRENT

SOURCE MARKING
450.11(B)

A transformer shall be permitted to be supplied at the marked secondary voltage, provided that the installation is in accordance with the manufacturer's instructions.

Design Tip: Reverse-connecting is the connecting of secondary output windings with the power supplyand using the primary input winding to supply the load. Dry-type transformers can be reverse-connected and still supply the same kVA. Single-phase transformers rated at 1 kVA and larger and three-phase transformers rated at 15 kVA and larger can be reverse-connected without losing any kVA capacity. The kVA rating is limmited to this value because the turns ration is the same as the voltage ratio.

Single-phase transformers rated below 1 kVA have a turns ration that compensates for the low voltage winding. The compensation becomes greater as the kVA ratig becomes smaller. When the transformer is reverse-connected, the voltage is less at full load than at no load. Before connecting a transformer for a backfed (reverse) operation, always consult with the manufacturer for installation instructions.

Note: The X_0 on the 208 V side shall not be connected to ground. In other words, this connection (X_0) shall not be connected to earch ground. The 480 V should be corner grounded or operate ungrounded as outlined in **250.26(4)** and **220.21(B) and (C)** in the NEC. **(See Figure 11-13.)**

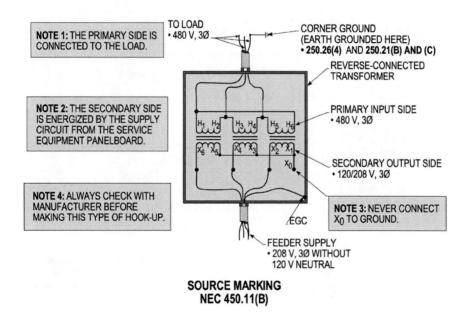

NOTE 1: THE PRIMARY SIDE IS CONNECTED TO THE LOAD.

NOTE 2: THE SECONDARY SIDE IS ENERGIZED BY THE SUPPLY CIRCUIT FROM THE SERVICE EQUIPMENT PANELBOARD.

NOTE 4: ALWAYS CHECK WITH MANUFACTURER BEFORE MAKING THIS TYPE OF HOOK-UP.

TO LOAD
• 480 V, 3Ø

CORNER GROUND
(EARTH GROUNDED HERE)
• **250.26(4)** AND **250.21(B) AND (C)**

REVERSE-CONNECTED TRANSFORMER

PRIMARY INPUT SIDE
• 480 V, 3Ø

SECONDARY OUTPUT SIDE
• 120/208 V, 3Ø

NOTE 3: NEVER CONNECT X_0 TO GROUND.

EGC

FEEDER SUPPLY
• 208 V, 3Ø WITHOUT 120 V NEUTRAL

**SOURCE MARKING
NEC 450.11(B)**

Figure 11-13. This illustration shows the sourcemarking requirements for a transformer.

Chapter 11: Protecting Transformers

1. When circuit breakers are used to protect a transformer over 600 volts they shall be set not greater than _____ percent of the rated primary current.
   (a) 250   (b) 300
   (c) 400   (d) 600

2. Where _____ percent of the rated primary of the transformer does not correspond to a standard rating of a fuse, the next higher standard rating shall be permitted.
   (a) 250   (b) 300
   (c) 400   (d) 600

3. Transformers located in supervised locations shall have the overcurrent protection device for the secondary sized at not more than _____ percent of the FLC for voltages, 1000 volts or less.
   (a) 150   (b) 200
   (c) 250   (d) 300

4. If the secondary voltage is 1000 volts or less for transformers located in nonsupervised locations, the overcurrent protection device and conductors on the secondary side shall be sized at _____ percent of the FLC rating.
   (a) 100   (b) 125
   (c) 175   (d) 225

5. A transformer rated 1000 volts or less having a primary overcurrent protection device only (rounding down) on the primary side shall be sized at not more than _____ percent of the transformer's full-load current rating.
   (a) 100   (b) 125
   (c) 175   (d) 225

6. Where the rated primary current of a transformer is less than 9 amps but more than 2 amps, an overcurrent protection device rated or set at not more than _____ percent of the primary current shall be permitted.
   (a) 125   (b) 133
   (c) 167   (d) 200

7. When the rated primary current of a transformer is less than 2 amps, an overcurrent protection device rated or set at not more than _____ percent shall be used.
   (a) 133   (b) 167
   (c) 250   (d) 300

8. Transformers rated 1000 volts or less may have a current value of _____ percent of the rated primary current if 125 percent of the rated primary current of the transformer is not sufficient to allow loads with high inrush current to start and operate.
   (a) 133   (b) 167
   (c) 250   (d) 300

9. When sizing the overcurrent protection device for an autotransformer rated 9 amps or more, the full-load input current rating of the autotransformer shall be multiplied by _____ percent and the next size standard device shall be permitted to be selected.
   (a) 125   (b) 167
   (c) 250   (d) 300

10. When sizing the overcurrent protection device for an autotransformer rated 9 amps or less, the full-load input current rating of the autotransformer shall be multiplied by _____ percent and the next size standard device shall be permitted to be selected.
    (a) 125   (b) 167
    (c) 250   (d) 300

11. What is the primary and secondary amperage for a 20 kVA, single-phase transformer with a 480 volt primary and 240 volt secondary?

12. What is the primary and secondary amperage for a 20 kVA, three-phase transformer with a 480 volt primary and 240 volt secondary?

13. What is the interrupting capacity (IC) rating of a 20 kVA transformer with a 1.5 percent impedance supplied by a 120/240 volt, single-phase secondary?

14. What size overcurrent protection device using a circuit breaker is required on the primary side for a 1500 kVA, 12,470 volt, single-phase secondary?

15. What size overcurrent protection device is required for the primary and secondary side of a 400 kVA, three-phase transformer with a 4160 volt primary and 480 volt secondary installed in a supervised location? [impedance (Z) is less than 6 percent].

16. What size overcurrent protection device is required for the primary and secondary side of a 500 kVA, three-phase transformer with a 13,800 volt primary and 4160 volt secondary installed in a supervised location? [impedance (Z) is less than 6 percent].

17. What size overcurrent protection device is required for a two-wire to two-wire, 480 volt primary and a 240 volt secondary transformer with 3 AWG THWN copper conductors on the secondary side?

18. What size overcurrent protection device is required for a three-wire to three-wire delta, 480 volt primary and a 240 volt secondary transformer with 500 KCMIL THWN copper conductors on the secondary side?

19. What size overcurrent protection device is required for the primary and secondary side of a 400 kVA, three-phase transformer with a 4160 volt primary and 480 volt secondary installed in a nonsupervised location? [impedance (Z) is less than 6 percent].

20. What size overcurrent protection device is required for the primary side (only) of 25 kVA, single-phase transformer with a 240 volt primary and 120 volt secondary?

21. What size overcurrent protection device is required for the primary side (only) of .7 kVA, single-phase transformer with a 480 volt primary?

22. What size overcurrent protection device is required for the primary and secondary side of 40 kVA three-phase transformer with a 480 volt primary and 208 volt secondary?

    _____ _____

23. What is the amount of current needed to trip open an overcurrent protection sensing device for a zigzag transformer with a 150 amp continuous load?

    _____ _____

24. The _____% times the transformer's full load current in amps determines the size of the primary's overcurrent protection device.

    _____ _____

    (a) 125   (b) 150
    (c) 175   (d) 250

25. If primary protection of _____% is provided in the transformer's primary only then secondary protection is not required.

    _____ _____

    (a) 125   (b) 250
    (c) 300   (d) 600

12

Secondary Ties

In large industrial plants and facilities, a "network" distribution system is usually utilized for supplying power loads. Three-phase banks of transformers are located at various points throughout the plant or facility. There are normally two high-tension primary circuits feeding such transformers. A double-throw switch that is located at each transformer bank allows either primary circuit to serve any bank of transformers. The primary circuit conductors are sized with enough capacity so that either circuit is capable of carrying the entire load if a fault develops in the other circuit. Secondary voltage is usually three-phase systems rated 1000 volts or less. The transformer secondaries are connected together in a network system, and all transformers are used to feed all the loads involved that can be all at once or as necessary.

TIE CIRCUITS
450.6

Secondary ties shall be protected at both ends, and such protection shall be permitted to be fuses based on the current-carrying capacity of the conductors per **450.6(A)** or the ties protected by a limiter installed at each end per **450.6(A)(3)**. A limiter protects the elements against a short circuit; however, it does not provide overload protection. Usually, limiters, rather than fuses, are used for protection of the ties due to the fact they are very current limiting and will protect the circuit elements from damage during short-circuit conditions.

There is normally a load center connected to the tie at the points where a transformer bank connects to the tie. The transformer is protected by a circuit breaker in the secondary leads between the transformer and the load center. Circuit breaker setting shall be permitted to be up to 250 percent (2.5 times) of the transformer's secondary current rating per **450.6(B)**.

A reverse power relay shall be provided per **450.6(B)** that opens the circuit in case the transformer should fail for any reason. A reverse power relay is provided to prevent current from being fed to an out-of-service transformer from the other transformers of the network. Where the secondary voltage is greater than 150 volts to ground, to ensure adequate protection, ties shall be provided with a switch at each end per **450.6(A)(5)**.

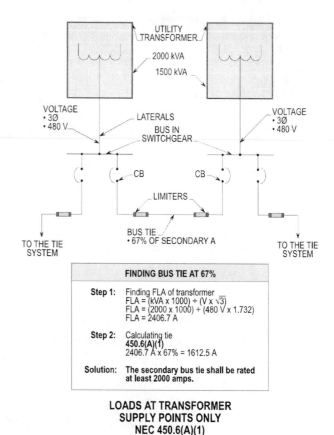

**LOADS AT TRANSFORMER
SUPPLY POINTS ONLY
NEC 450.6(A)(1)**

Figure 12-1. The ampacity of the ties connecting conductors shall not be less than 67 percent of the rated secondary current of the largest transformer in the tie circuit.

LOADS AT TRANSFORMER SUPPLY POINTS ONLY
450.6(A)(1)

Where transformers are tied together in parallel and connected by tie conductors that do not have overcurrent protection as per **Article 240,** the ampacity of the ties connecting conductors shall not be less than 67 percent of the rated secondary current of the largest transformer in the tie circuit. **(See Figure 12-1)**

This rule applies where the loads are at the transformer supply points per **450.6(A)(1)**.

The paralleling of transformers is common, but great care should be exercised to ensure that the transformers are similar in all conditions of use. If they are not, one transformer will try to carry more of the load than the other transformer load. If the transformers are of the same capacity and similar characteristics, they each, in theory, will carry 50 percent of the total load. The 67 percent allows for differences in transformer sizes and thus allows for adjusting situations.

LOADS CONNECTED BETWEEN TRANSFORMER SUPPLY POINTS
450.6(A)(2)

Where the load is connected to the tie at any point between the transformer supply points, and overcurrent protection is not provided by the provisions listed in **Article 240,** the rated ampacity of the tie shall not be not less than 100 percent of the rated secondary current of the largest transformer connected to the secondary tie system except as provided in **450.6(A)(4)**. **(See Figure 12-2)**

This rule applies mainly where the loads are connected between the transformer supply points per **450.6(A)(2)**.

TIE CIRCUIT PROTECTION
450.6(A)(3)

Sections **450.6(A)(1)** and **(A)(2)** state that both ends of each tie connection shall be provided with a protective device that opens at a certain temperature of the tie conductor. This prevents damage to the tie conductor and its insulation, and such installations shall consist of:

- A limiter is a fusible-link cable connector. The limiter is selected and designed for the insulation, conductor material, etc., on the tie conductors.

- A circuit breaker, actuated by devices having characteristics that are comparable to the above, can be used if designed and sized properly.

The above applies where the tie circuit protection is provided per **450.6(A)(3),** and the tie conductor shall fully comply with all rules and regulations in such sections.

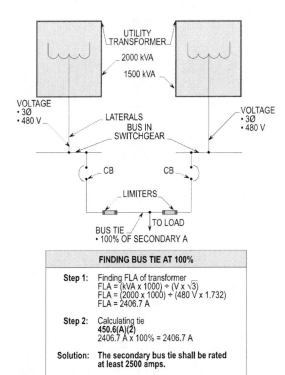

FINDING BUS TIE AT 100%

Step 1: Finding FLA of transformer
FLA = (kVA x 1000) ÷ (V x √3)
FLA = (2000 x 1000) ÷ (480 V x 1.732)
FLA = 2406.7 A

Step 2: Calculating tie
450.6(A)(2)
2406.7 A x 100% = 2406.7 A

Solution: The secondary bus tie shall be rated at least 2500 amps.

Note, the 2500 amps is the next standard size.

LOADS CONNECTED BETWEEN TRANSFORMER SUPPLY POINTS NEC 450.6(A)(2)

Figure 12-2. The rated ampacity of the tie shall not be less than 100 percent of the rated secondary current of the largest transformer connected to the secondary tie system except as provided in **450.6(A)(4).**

INTERCONNECTION OF PHASE CONDUCTORS BETWEEN TRANSFORMER SUPPLY POINTS 450.6(A)(4)

Where the tie consists of more than one conductor per phase, the conductors of each phase shall be interconnected in order to create a load supply point. The protection required in **450.6(A)(3)** is to be provided in each tie conductor at this point, except as follows:

- Section **450.6(A)(4)(b)** permits the loads to be connected to the individual conductor(s) of each phase and without the protection listed in **450.6(A)(3)** if, at load connection points, the tie conductors of each phase have a combined capacity of not less than 133 percent of the rated secondary current of the largest transformer connected to the secondary tie system. The total load of such taps shall not exceed the rated secondary current of the largest transformer, and the loads shall be equally divided on each phase and on the individual conductors of each phase as closely as possible. **(See Figure 12-3)**

The use of multiple conductors on each phase and the requirement that loads do not have to tap the multiple conductors of the same phase might possibly set up unbalanced current flow in the multiple conductors on the same phase.

The requirement that the combined capacity of the multiple conductors on the same phase is rated at 133 percent of the secondary current of the largest transformer is satisfied. Limiters are necessary at the tap or connections to the transformers that are tied together to properly protect the elements of the circuit.

The above applies where the interconnection of phase conductors between the transformer supply points occurs, per **450.6(A)(4)(a). Note:** See **450.6(A)(4)(b)** when the interconnection is not as outlined above.

TIE CIRCUIT CONTROL 450.6(A)(5)

If the operating voltage of secondary ties exceeds 150 volts to ground, there shall be a switch ahead of the limiters and tie conductors that is capable of deenergizing the tie conductors and the limiters. This switch shall comply with the following:

- The current rating of the switch shall not be less than the current rating of the conductors connected to such switch.

- The switch shall be capable of opening its rated current.

- The switch shall not open under the magnetic forces caused by short-circuit currents.

The above applies where the tie circuit control is located as mentioned in **450.6(A)(5).**

Note: Review **450.6(A)(1) thru (A)(5)** very carefully before designing and installing secondary ties.

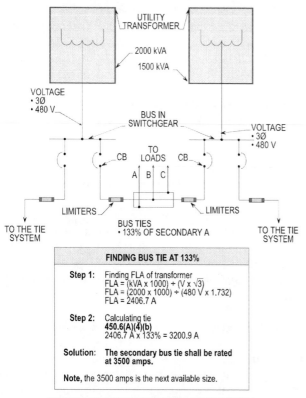

FINDING BUS TIE AT 133%	
Step 1:	Finding FLA of transformer FLA = (kVA x 1000) ÷ (V x √3) FLA = (2000 x 1000) ÷ (480 V x 1.732) FLA = 2406.7 A
Step 2:	Calculating tie **450.6(A)(4)(b)** 2406.7 A x 133% = 3200.9 A
Solution:	The secondary bus tie shall be rated at 3500 amps.
Note, the 3500 amps is the next available size.	

**INTERCONNECTION OF PHASE CONDUCTORS
BETWEEN TRANSFORMER SUPPLY POINTS
NEC 450.6(A)(4)(a)**

Figure 12-3. Section **450.6(A)(4)(a)** permits the loads to be connected to the individual conductor(s) of each phase and without the protection listed in **450.6(A)(3)** if, at load connection points, the tie conductors of each phase have a combined capacity of not less than 133 percent of the rated secondary current of the largest transformer connected to the secondary tie system.

OVERCURRENT PROTECTION FOR SECONDARY CONNECTIONS 450.6(B)

When secondary ties from transformers are used, an overcurrent device in the secondary of each transformer that is rated or set at not greater than 250 percent (2.5 times) of the rated secondary current of the transformer shall be provided. In addition, there shall be a circuit breaker actuated by a reverse-current relay; the breaker shall be set at not greater than the rated secondary current of the transformer. Such overcurrent protection protects against overloads and short-circuit conditions, and the reverse-current relay and circuit breaker shall be designed to handle any reversal of current flow into the transformer. **(See Figure 12-4)**

The above applies where overcurrent protection for secondary connections is installed to protect the system as required by **450.6(B)**.

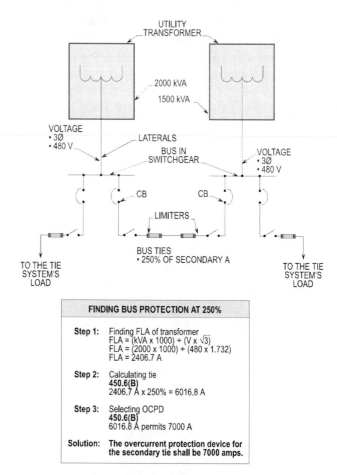

FINDING BUS PROTECTION AT 250%	
Step 1:	Finding FLA of transformer FLA = (kVA x 1000) ÷ (V x √3) FLA = (2000 x 1000) ÷ (480 x 1.732) FLA = 2406.7 A
Step 2:	Calculating tie **450.6(B)** 2406.7 A x 250% = 6016.8 A
Step 3:	Selecting OCPD **450.6(B)** 6016.8 A permits 7000 A
Solution:	The overcurrent protection device for the secondary tie shall be 7000 amps.

**OVERCURRENT PROTECTION FOR
SECONDARY CONNECTIONS
NEC 450.6(B)**

Figure 12-4. When secondary ties from transformers are used, an overcurrent device in the secondary of each transformer that is rated or set at not greater than 250 percent (2.5 times) of the rated secondary current of the transformer shall be provided.

RADIAL SUPPLY SYSTEMS

Radial low-voltage and high-voltage systems are systems provided with high voltage from the power company to the plant's transformer. Service equipment for low-voltage systems and the service equipment for high-voltage systems are installed as needed.

RADIAL LOW-VOLTAGE SYSTEMS

Radial low-voltage systems are installed with lower voltage feeders that are run to switchboards and load centers in the plant. This type of installation is costly because larger conductors and conduits are installed and the elements and components of the load centers require lower voltage with higher current ratings. **(See Figure 12-5)**

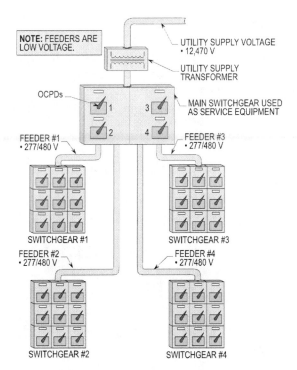

Figure 12-5. An installation of a radial low-voltage system with wiring methods and components.

RADIAL HIGH-VOLTAGE SYSTEMS

Radial high-voltage systems can be installed to transformers at each distribution point, and the voltage stepped down to the desired operating level. This type of installation is less costly due to the feeders requiring smaller conduits, conductors, and equipment. This type of installation raises the voltage on a feeder and lowers the current ratings for all the elements and components for the feeder. **(See Figure 12-6)**

LOOP SUPPLY SYSTEMS

The distribution loop supply system is superior to radial low-voltage and high-voltage systems. Distribution loop supply systems are formed in a loop or circle by a pair of circuit breakers that are connected to the power company's supply loop. These circuit breakers are installed between each transformer and load center connected to the loop. Protection is provided by the circuit breakers for any section of the feeders connected to the loop and also provides isolation in case of a fault or disorderly shutdown.

A distribution loop supply system would alleviate problems if trouble developed between two switchgear. The circuit breakers would remove the damaged load center.

For example, if trouble were to develop between switchgear 3 and switchgear 4, the circuit breakers would remove the damaged load center. All other switchgears connected to the loop would continue to be in service. If switchgear 4 were damaged in some way to create a fault condition, this fault condition would be cleared by one of the circuit breakers installed from the service or in the loop system that would disconnect switchgear 4. **(See Figure 12-7)**

Note, switchgear is considered a load center.

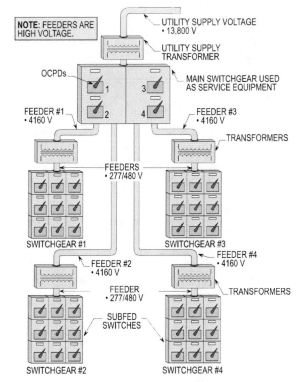

RADIAL HIGH-VOLTAGE SYSTEMS

Figure 12-6. An installation of a radial high-voltage system with wiring methods and components.

BUS-TIE LOOPS

Bus-tie distribution loop supply systems are installed to eliminate a complete shutdown of a feeder section that has been damaged. The transformer, service equipment, or any of the elements could have this type of damage to the feeder system. The bus-tie loop feeder, in addition, has a second loop called the bus-tie loop feeder that is connected between the transformers forming the loop.

Circuit breakers protect these secondary connections installed at each switchgear (load center) location. A continuous circle (bus-tie loop system) is formed from these loops at each switchgear from 1 through 4 and back to 1.

This continuous loop provides power to the service of the section if a fault or trouble develops at the transformer. **(See Figure 12-8)**

BUS-TIE CONDUCTORS

Bus-tie conductors or secondary conductors are low-voltage (600 volts or less) secondary loop connections. Bus-ties are used to connect two power sources to the secondaries of two transformers. Overcurrent devices are set at 150 percent to limit the maximum current of the capacity of the conductor where loads are connected at the supply points. If protection is not provided for conductors rated at 150 percent or less, the current of the bus-tie shall be at least 67 percent of the full-load current rating of the largest transformer. **(See Figure 12-9)**

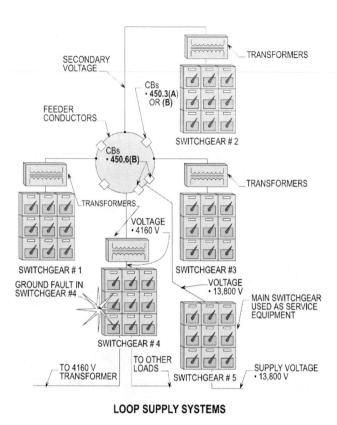

Figure 12-7. An installation of a distribution loop supply system.

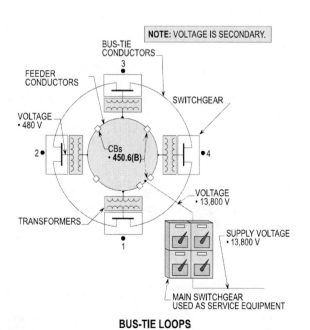

Figure 12-8. An installation of bus-tie conductors used in a loop system with components and equipment.

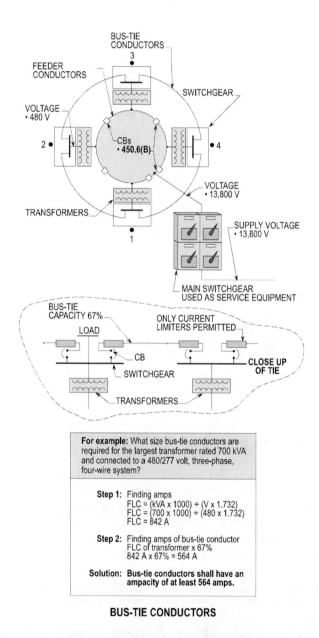

Figure 12-9. An installation of bus-tie conductors calculated at 67 percent and minimum amps selected.

The current-carrying capacity of the bus-tie conductor shall be 100 percent of the full-load current rating of the largest transformer for loads connected from the secondary bus-tie and not the transformer location. **(See Figure 12-10)**

The secondary tie can consist of a number of conductors, parallel per phase, with loads connected to individual conductors between the locations of the transformers. The combined total rating of the conductors between stations shall be at least 133 percent of the full-load secondary current of the largest transformer, provided the loads are not tapped to every one of the tie conductors. **(See Figure 12-11)**

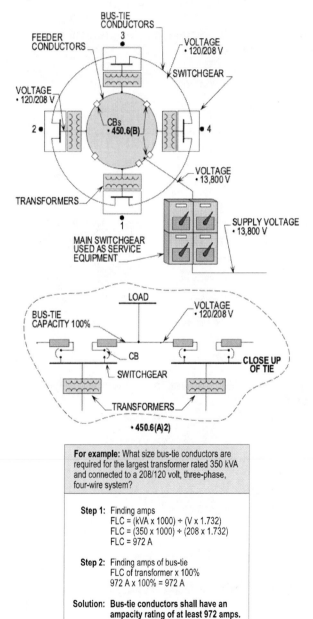

BUS-TIE CONDUCTORS

Figure 12-10. An installation of bus-tie conductors calculated at 100 percent.

When loads are tapped, they shall be equally divided on each phase and on the individual conductors of each phase, as close as possible. **(See Figure 12-12)**

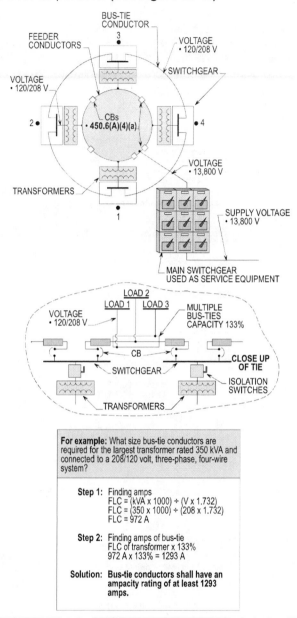

BUS-TIE CONDUCTORS

Figure 12-11. An installation of bus-tie conductors calculated at 133 percent per **450.6(A)(4)(b)**.

BUS-TIE PROTECTION

To protect conductors from short-circuit conditions, current limiters or automatic circuit breakers shall be installed at both ends of each tie. Current limiters can be used when the operating voltage is above 150 volts-to-ground. A switch shall be provided at either end of the tie and equal to the conductor's ampacity. In addition, an overcurrent protection device shall be installed in the secondary circuit of each transformer and set at 250 percent or less of the rated full-load current to protect the bus-tie conductors. **(See Figure 12-13)**

If reverse current exceeding the full-load current of a transformer tries to flow into the unit, a reverse-current relay shall be installed to actuate a circuit breaker. The secondary windings of the transformer are disconnected from the circuit breaker actuated by the reverse-current relay due to faults or current feedback.

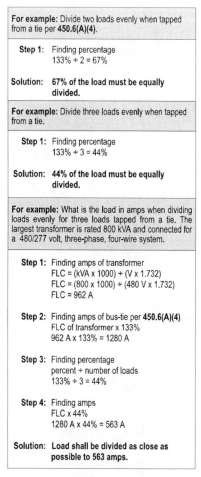

For example: Divide two loads evenly when tapped from a tie per **450.6(A)(4)**.

Step 1: Finding percentage
133% ÷ 2 = 67%

Solution: **67% of the load must be equally divided.**

For example: Divide three loads evenly when tapped from a tie.

Step 1: Finding percentage
133% ÷ 3 = 44%

Solution: **44% of the load must be equally divided.**

For example: What is the load in amps when dividing loads evenly for three loads tapped from a tie. The largest transformer is rated 800 kVA and connected for a 480/277 volt, three-phase, four-wire system.

Step 1: Finding amps of transformer
FLC = (kVA x 1000) ÷ (V x 1.732)
FLC = (800 x 1000) ÷ (480 V x 1.732)
FLC = 962 A

Step 2: Finding amps of bus-tie per **450.6(A)(4)**
FLC of transformer x 133%
962 A x 133% = 1280 A

Step 3: Finding percentage
percent ÷ number of loads
133% ÷ 3 = 44%

Step 4: Finding amps
FLC x 44%
1280 A x 44% = 563 A

Solution: **Load shall be divided as close as possible to 563 amps.**

BUS-TIE CONDUCTORS

Figure 12-12. An installation of loads divided evenly on ties to prevent unbalanced loading.

NETWORK POWER SYSTEMS

A simple network power system consists of two power sources fed into a loop and connected to transformers. Transformers 1 and 3 are connected to power source PS1. Transformers 2 and 4 are connected to power source PS2. In case one of the transformers develops trouble, switches are installed to provide a disconnecting means. **(See Figure 12-14)**

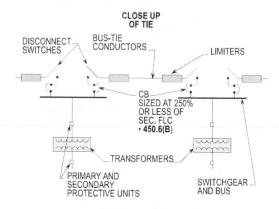

BUS-TIE PROTECTION

Figure 12-13. An installation for protection of bus-tie conductors per **450.6(B)**.

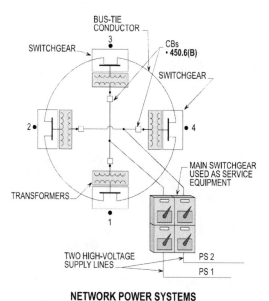

NETWORK POWER SYSTEMS

Figure 12-14. An installation of a simple network power system.

Chapter 12: Secondary Ties

Section   Answer

1. Where transformers are tied together in parallel and connected by tie conductors that do not have overcurrent protection, the ampacity of the ties connecting conductors shall not be less than _____ percent of the rated secondary current of the largest transformer in the tie circuit.
   (a) 33   (b) 50
   (c) 67   (d) 75

2. Where the load is connected to the tie at any point between the transformer supply points, and overcurrent protection is not provided, the rated ampacity of the tie shall not be less than _____ percent of the rated secondary current of the largest transformer connected to the secondary tie system.
   (a) 100   (b) 115
   (c) 125   (d) 150

3. If the operating voltage of secondary ties exceeds _____ volts-to-ground, there shall be a switch ahead of the limiters and tie conductors that is capable of deenergizing the tie conductors and the limiters.
   (a) 50   (b) 120
   (c) 150   (d) 240

4. When secondary ties from transformers are used, an overcurrent device in the secondary of each transformer that is rated or set at not greater than _____ percent of the rated secondary current of the transformer shall be provided.
   (a) 125   (b) 250
   (c) 300   (d) 400

5. Bus-tie distribution _____ supply systems are installed to eliminate a complete shutdown of a feeder section that has been damaged.
   (a) radial   (b) feeder
   (c) branch   (d) loop

6. Where loads are connected between transformer supply points, the tie ampacity shall not be less than _____%.
   (a) 50   (b) 75
   (c) 80   (d) 100

7. Loads connected at transformer's supply points only shall be not less than _____%.
   (a) 50   (b) 55
   (c) 75   (d) 100

8. Where the secondary voltage is greater than _____ volts to ground, to ensure adequate protection,.
   (a) 150   (b) ties
   (c) all of the above   (d) none of the above

9. In tie circuits, the overcurrent protection device (CB) shall be permitted to be up _____%
   (a) 250   (b) 300
   (c) 400   (d) 600

_____ _____ **10.** A radial low-voltage system is usually supplied by _____ transformer(s).
                                       (a) one   (b) two
                                         (c) three   (d) four

13

Windings and Components

Transformer windings are connected for either additive or subtractive polarity and connected in a delta or wye configuration to supply either single-phase or three-phase voltage to service equipment or other electrical equipment. Windings must be connected for the proper polarity for the current to flow through the windings in the proper direction.

TESTING WINDINGS

When testing transformer windings for a delta- or wye-connected configuration to supply single-phase or three-phase voltages to the service equipment or other electrical equipment, the following polarity checks must be made to verify if they are connected in:

(1) additive polarity or

(2) subtractive polarity.

ADDITIVE POLARITY

The induced voltage in the primary and secondary windings will be in opposite directions for transformer windings connected in additive polarity. Additive connected transformer windings are wound in the same direction. However, a subtractive transformer can be used as an additive transformer by reversing the flow of current through the windings.

Note, the overcurrent protection device will trip or the transformer will not operate properly if one of the windings is accidently connected in subtractive polarity. **(See Figure 13-1)**

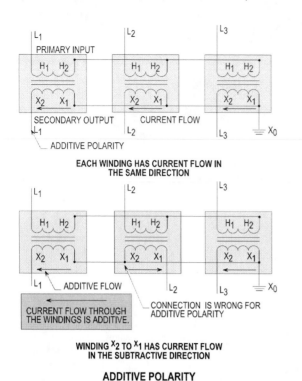

Figure 13-1. Transformer windings connected for additive polarity with one connection subtractive.

SUBTRACTIVE POLARITY

The induced voltage and current in the primary and secondary windings will be in the same direction for transformer windings connected in subtractive polarity. A subtractive transformer can be used as an additive transformer by reversing the flow of current through its windings. The overcurrent protection device will trip or the transformer will not operate properly if one of the windings is accidentally connected in additive polarity. **(See Figure 13-2)**

TESTING FOR POLARITY

Transformer windings are identified as either additive or subtractive polarity by measuring the primary and secondary voltage. The voltage would be equal to the primary and secondary added together for transformer windings that are additive connected.

Note, the primary voltage is always greater than the voltage measured.

The voltage would be equal to the primary minus the secondary for transformer windings connected in subtractive polarity. The primary voltage is always more than the voltage measured between primary and secondary. **(See Figure 13-3)**

Transformer Note: This is under the assumption that the primary voltage is higher than the secondary. **Warning:** A lower voltage may have to be applied to measure the voltage safely if the voltage is high. **(See Figure 13-3)**

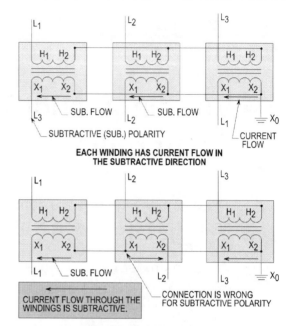

Figure 13-2. Transformer windings connected for subtractive polarity with one connection additive.

POLARITY CONNECTIONS AND IDENTIFYING TERMINALS

The letter H and accompanying numbers are used for identification of high voltage or input terminals that are located at the left of the primary side of the transformer windings. The letter X and accompanying numbers are used for identification of low voltage or output terminals. The primary or secondary side of a transformer can be used as input or output terminals under certain conditions.

If the windings are connected with additive polarity, the X terminal and number are located at the left of the secondary side of the transformer. If the windings are connected with subtractive polarity, H_1 on the primary side will line up with X_1 on the secondary side of the transformer. If the transformer windings are connected in additive polarity, the current flows in the opposite direction. However, if the transformer windings are connected in subtractive polarity, the current flows in the same direction. **(See Figure 13-4)**

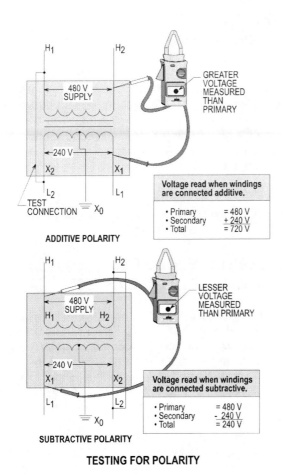

ADDITIVE POLARITY

Voltage read when windings are connected additive.

- Primary = 480 V
- Secondary + 240 V
- Total = 720 V

SUBTRACTIVE POLARITY

Voltage read when windings are connected subtractive.

- Primary = 480 V
- Secondary − 240 V
- Total = 240 V

TESTING FOR POLARITY

Figure 13-3. A simple test for polarity is to connect two adjacent terminals of the high- and low-voltage windings together and apply a moderate voltage to either winding. If the voltage reading is greater than the primary voltage, the windings are connected additive. If the voltage reading is less than the primary voltage, the connection is subtractive.

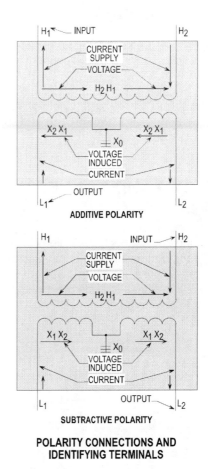

ADDITIVE POLARITY

SUBTRACTIVE POLARITY

POLARITY CONNECTIONS AND IDENTIFYING TERMINALS

Figure 13-4. If the transformer windings are connected in additive polarity, the two windings are in the opposite direction. If the transformer windings are connected in subtractive polarity, the two windings are in the same direction.

TESTING VOLTAGE OF WINDINGS

When testing the voltage of windings for single-phase and three-phase transformers, the following two measurements are used to determine the voltage level:

(1) Phase-to-phase and

(2) Phase-to-ground.

PHASE-TO-PHASE VOLTAGE

The voltage is measured between the phases to determine the voltage for a single-phase or three-phase transformer.

For example, a 120/240 volt, single-phase transformer measured phase-to-phase is 240 volts. **(See Figure 13-5)**

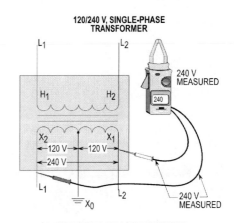

PHASE-TO-PHASE VOLTAGE

Figure 13-5. Measuring the voltage from phase-to-phase to determine the voltage.

PHASE-TO-GROUND VOLTAGE

The voltage is measured between the phase-to-ground to determine the voltage for a single-phase or three-phase transformer.

For example, a 120/240 volt, single-phase transformer measured phase-to-ground is 120 volts. **(See Figure 13-6)**

IDENTIFYING AND CONNECTING WINDINGS

When identifying and connecting windings based upon the installation, transformers may be connected in a number of different ways. There are several ways of connecting a single-phase or three-phase transformer to the power supply and the loads to be served.

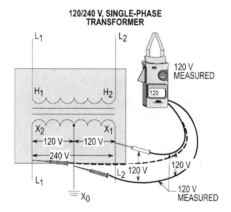

PHASE-TO-GROUND VOLTAGE

Figure 13-6. Measuring the voltage from phase-to-ground to determine the voltage level.

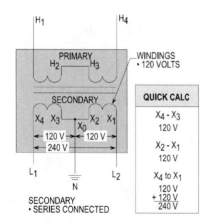

120/240 VOLT, SINGLE-PHASE TRANSFORMERS

Figure 13-7. Connecting the secondary terminals of a transformer to derive a single-phase, 120/240 volt system.

120/240 VOLT, SINGLE-PHASE TRANSFORMERS

When connecting the secondary terminals of a 120/240 volt single-phase transformer, the first transformer winding is connected to X_3 and the second winding is connected to X_2, making the neutral connection X_0. The connection between the first winding X_3 to the second winding X_2 will series the two 120 volt windings to derive 240 volts from L_1 to L_2. To obtain the neutral, a jumper from X_3 to X_2 is tapped and connected to ground.

Note, 120 volts is derived from the connections between L_1 to X_0 and L_2 to X_0. **(See Figure 13-7)**

THREE-PHASE, CLOSED DELTA-CONNECTED SYSTEM

When connecting the secondary terminals of a three-phase closed delta-connected system transformer, the first transformer winding X_6 is connected in series with a jumper to X_1 of the third transformer, the first transformer winding X_5 is connected in series with a jumper to X_4 of the second transformer, and the second transformer winding X_3 is connected in series with a jumper to X_2 of the third transformer.

The neutral connection can be tapped from the center of any 240 volt winding. 120 volts-to-ground is derived from the outside lines of the tap that is connected to ground. 208 volts-to-ground (high leg) is derived from the current that must travel through one full winding and one-half of the other winding to ground. The windings of a 120/240 volt, four-wire closed delta-connected transformer are rated at 240 volts each with the high leg rated at 208 volts. **(See Figure 13-8)**

THREE-PHASE, OPEN DELTA-CONNECTED SYSTEM

When connecting the secondary terminals of a three-phase open delta-connected system transformer, the first transformer winding X_3 is connected in series with a jumper to X_2 of the second transformer. 120 volts-to-ground is derived from either one of the 240 volt windings that are tapped. 240 volts is derived from phase-to-phase voltage that is connected from L_1 to L_2, L_1 to L_3, and L_2 to L_3. 208 volts-to-ground is derived from the high leg. **(See Figure 13-9)**

THREE-PHASE, WYE-CONNECTED SYSTEM

When connecting the secondary terminals of a three-phase, wye-connected system transformer, the first winding X_5 is connected in series with a jumper to X_3 of the second transformer and to X_1 of the third transformer, making the neutral connection. The connections in a wye (system) transformer, X_6, X_4, and X_2, will be Phases 1, 2, and 3. The neutral conductor connected to ground is X_0.

120 volts-to-ground is derived from L_1 to X_0, L_2 to X_0, and L_3 to X_0. 208 volts is derived from L_1 to L_2, L_1 to L_3, and L_2 to L_3. **(See Figure 13-10)**

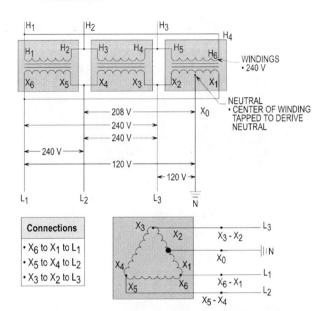

THREE-PHASE, CLOSED DELTA-CONNECTED SYSTEM

Figure 13-8. Connecting the secondary terminals of a transformer to derive a three-phase, closed delta-connected system.

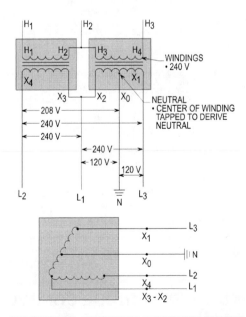

THREE-PHASE, OPEN DELTA-CONNECTED SYSTEM

Figure 13-9. Connecting the secondary terminals of a transformer to derive a three-phase, open delta-connected system.

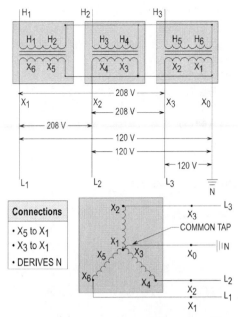

THREE-PHASE, WYE-CONNECTED SYSTEM

Figure 13-10. Connecting the secondary terminals of a transformer to derive a three-phase, wye-connected system. Each winding is rated at 120 volts for a 120/208 volt, three-phase, wye-connected system.

THREE-PHASE, CORNER GROUNDED DELTA-CONNECTED SYSTEM

When tapping any one of the ungrounded (phase) conductors of a corner grounded delta-connected system, the grounded (neutral) conductor is derived. The phase-to-phase voltage would be 480 volts if the voltage of the windings is 480 volts. The voltage-to-ground from the grounded (phase) conductor is 0 volts.

A color of white or gray identification shall be used for the grounded (phase) conductor per **200.7**. The grounded (phase) conductor shall never be fused per **230.90(B)**, except for motor circuits per **430.36**. Where the grounded (phase) conductor enters into a panelboard or switchgear it shall be connected to ground at the service equipment location only. **(See Figure 13-11)**

SEPARATELY DERIVED AC SYSTEMS 250.30

Low-voltage and high-voltage feeders are sometimes installed from floor to floor in a high-rise building, with transformers installed on each floor to reduce the voltage to 120/240, 120/208, or 277/480 volts for general-use lighting and receptacle loads in large building applications. When designing and installing the bonding and grounding of a transformer system, the secondary of a separately derived

system is divided into three parts. Such grounding since the 1978 National Electrical Code can be installed either at the transformer or at the load served, which is connected and supplied from the secondary side per **240.21(B)** and **(C)**. The following three parts shall be designed and installed for a separately derived system per **250.30(A)(1), (A)(2), (A)(3),** and **(A)(7):**
(See Figure 13-12)

(1) System bonding jumper,

(2) Grounding electrode conductor, and

(3) Grounding electrode.

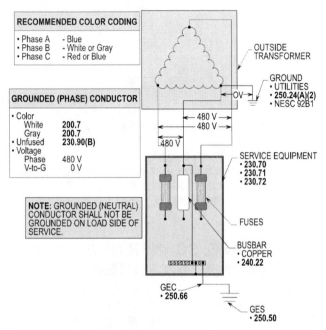

THREE-PHASE, CORNER GROUNDED DELTA-CONNECTED SYSTEM

Figure 13-11. Voltage relationships and secondary terminal connections of a three-phase, corner grounded delta-connected system.

SYSTEM BONDING JUMPER 250.30(A)(1)

The system bonding jumper (unspliced) shall be designed and installed based on the derived ungrounded (phase) conductors supplying the panelboard, switch, or other equipment connected from the secondary side of the transformer and sized per **250.28(B)** and **250.102(C)(1).** The system bonding jumper shall be sized per **250.66** and **Table 250.102(C)(1)** from the ungrounded (phase) conductors up to 1100 KCMIL for copper and 1750 KCMIL for aluminum. The system bonding jumper shall be sized at least 12-1/2 percent (.125) of the area of the largest ungrounded (phase) conductor where the service conductors are installed larger than 1100 KCMIL copper or 1750 KCMIL aluminum. The system bonding jumper shall be installed and connected at any single point on the separately derived system from

the source to the first system disconnecting means or overcurrent protection device. If the grounded (phase) conductors are larger than 1100 KCMIL for copper and 1750 KCMIL for aluminum, the system bonding jumper will normally be larger than the grounding electrode conductor.

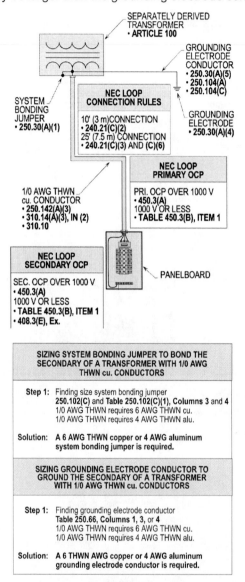

SEPARATELY DERIVED AC SYSTEMS
NEC 250.30

Figure 13-12. The system bonding jumper and grounding electrode conductor is designed and installed based on the derived ungrounded (phase) conductors supplying the panelboard, switch, or other equipment connected from the secondary side of the transformer.

GROUNDING ELECTRODE CONDUCTOR 250.30(A)(5)

The grounding electrode conductor shall be designed and installed based on the derived ungrounded (phase) conductors supplying the panelboard, switch, or other equipment connected from the secondary of the transformer and shall be sized per **Table 250.66**. The grounding electrode conductor shall be installed and connected at any point on the separately derived system from the source to the first system disconnecting means or overcurrent protection device. When the KCMIL rating is greater than 1100 KCMIL for copper and 1750 KCMIL for aluminum, the grounding electrode conductor will usually be smaller than the bonding jumper.

A common continuous grounding electrode conductor shall be permitted to be extended from the grounding electrode system and run through the building and the connection made at an accessible location near the separately derived system required to be grounded per **250.30(A)(6)** and **250.64(B)**.

GROUNDING ELECTRODE
250.30(A)(4)

The grounding electrode shall be as near as possible and preferably in the same area as the grounding electrode conductor connection to the system. From the following choices, one shall be selected and installed in the order that they are listed: **(See Figure 13-13)**

- Nearest grounded metal water pipe within 5 ft (1.5 m) from the point of entrance into the building per **250.52(A)(1)** or

- Nearest grounded structural building steel per **250.52(A)(2)**.

Note, metal water pipes located in the area shall be bonded to the grounded (neutral) conductor per **250.104(D)(1)**.

OTHER ELECTRODES
250.30(A)(4), Ex.

Any of the electrodes identified in **250.52(A)(1) through (8)** shall be permitted to be used where the electrodes specified by **250.30(A)(4)** are not available.

The grounding electrode conductor shall not be required to be installed larger than 3/0 AWG copper or 250 KCMIL for aluminum when connecting to the nearest building steel or nearest metal water pipe system. The grounding electrode conductor shall not be required to be installed larger than 6 AWG copper or 4 AWG aluminum when connecting to a driven rod or other made electrodes.

SIZING GROUNDING ELECTRODE
CONDUCTOR
250.30(A)(4) AND TABLE 250.66

The procedure for selecting the grounding electrode conductor to ground a separately derived system to the building steel is determined by the size of the ungrounded (phase) conductors in the feeder (connected conductors) between the panelboard and transformer.

Note: For supply-side bonding jumpers (S-SBJs), see **Section 250.102(C)(1)** in the NEC.

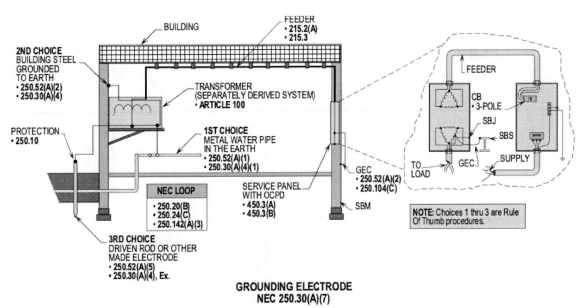

Figure 13-13. The grounding electrode conductor shall be as near as possible and preferably in the same area as the grounding electrode conductor connection to the system.

For example: What size copper grounding electrode conductor is required to bond and ground the secondary of a separately derived system to the structural building steel when supplied by 500 KCMIL copper conductors?

Step 1: Finding the GEC
250.30(A)(5) and **Table 250.66**
500 KCMIL cu. = 1/0 AWG cu.

Solution: The size grounding electrode conductor is 1/0 AWG copper.

For example: What size copper copper grounding electrode is required to bond and ground the secondary of a separately derived systems to a metal water pipe supplied by 250 KCMIL copper conductors?

Step 1: Finding size GEC
250.30(A)(3) and **Table 250.66**
250 KCMIL cu. = 2 AWG cu.

Solution: The size grounding electrode conductor is 2 AWG copper.

The procedure for selecting the grounding electrode conductor to ground a separately derived system to a metal water pipe is determined by the size of the connected conductors from the secondary of the transformer. **(See Figure 13-14)**

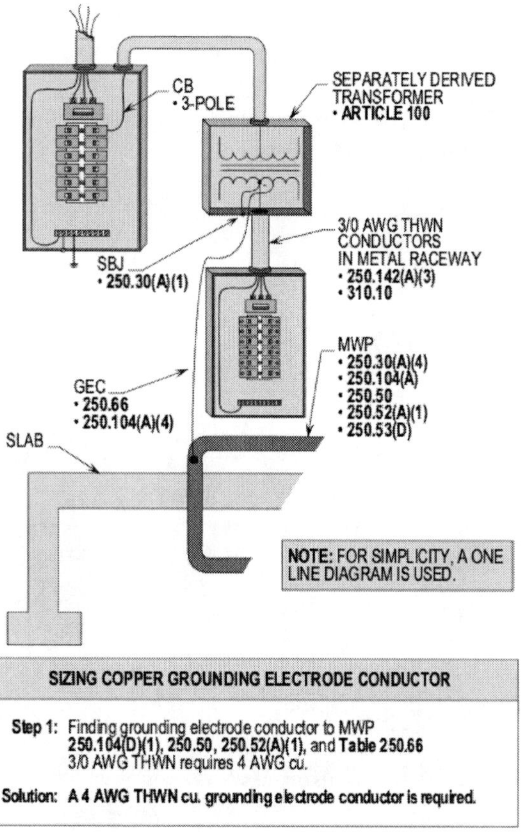

SIZING COPPER GROUNDING ELECTRODE CONDUCTOR

Step 1: Finding grounding electrode conductor to MWP
250.104(D)(1), 250.50, 250.52(A)(1), and Table 250.66
3/0 AWG THWN requires 4 AWG cu.

Solution: A 4 AWG THWN cu. grounding electrode conductor is required.

**SIZING GROUNDING ELECTRODE CONDUCTOR
NEC 250.30(A)(5) AND TABLE 250.66**

Figure 13-14. The procedure for selecting the grounding electrode conductor to ground a separately derived system to the metal water pipe shall be determined by the size of the transformer's secondary conductors.

In cases where there are no other electrodes available, a separately derived system can be grounded with a driven rod or plate per **250.52** and **250.53**. A driven rod with a resistance of 25 ohms or less is considered low enough to allow the grounded system to operate safely and function properly. The grounding electrode conductor shall not be required to be larger than 6 AWG copper or 4 AWG aluminum where connected to electrodes such as driven rods.

For example: What is the current flow in a 6 AWG copper grounding electrode conductor connecting the common grounded terminal bar in a separately derived system to a driven rod? (The supply voltage is a 120/208 volt, three-phase system.)

Step 1: Finding amperage
250.53(A)(2), Ex.
$I = 120 \text{ V} \div 25 \text{ R}$
$I = 4.8 \text{ A}$

Solution: The normal current flow is about 4.8 amps.

TROUBLESHOOTING TRANSFORMER WINDINGS

The winding of a transformer can be tested by taking resistance readings with an ohmmeter.

To check the X_1 winding, touch the case of the transformer with one lead of the ohmmeter and with the other lead touch the lead terminal of X_1. If a low resistance is measured, the winding is defective. X_2 and X_3 windings can be tested using the same procedure. **(See Figure 13-15)**

Note, primary windings can be tested using the same procedures.

CONNECTING SECONDARY WINDINGS IN A WYE CONFIGURATION

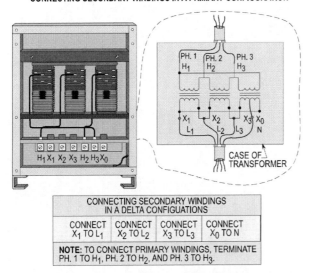

CONNECTING SECONDARY WINDING WYE			
CONNECT X_1 TO L_1	CONNECT X_2 TO L_2	CONNECT X_3 TO L_3	CONNECT X_0 TO N
NOTE: TO CONNECT PRIMARY WINDINGS, TERMINATE PH. 1 TO H_1, PH. 2 TO H_2, AND PH. 3 TO H_3.			

CONNECTING SECONDARY WINDINGS IN A PRIMARY CONFIGURATION

CONNECTING SECONDARY WINDINGS IN A DELTA CONFIGUATIONS			
CONNECT X_1 TO L_1	CONNECT X_2 TO L_2	CONNECT X_3 TO L_3	CONNECT X_0 TO N
NOTE: TO CONNECT PRIMARY WINDINGS, TERMINATE PH. 1 TO H_1, PH. 2 TO H_2, AND PH. 3 TO H_3.			

TROUBLESHOOTING TRANSFORMER WINDINGS

Figure 13-15. If a low resistance is read from one or all of the secondary windings to ground, measuring from the transformer's case to each individual winding, a ground is usually present.

Note, for further information on procedures for troubleshooting dry-type transformers, see Table 10 in Annex A at the back of this book.

Chapter 13: Windings and Components

Section   Answer

1. The induced voltage in the primary and secondary windings will be in opposite
   directions for transformer windings connected in _____ polarity.   _____   _____
   (a) additive   (b) subtractive
   (c) reduced   (d) reversed

2. The induced voltage and current in the primary and secondary windings will   _____   _____
   be in the same direction for transformer windings connected in _____ polarity.
   (a) additive   (b) subtractive
   (c) reduced   (d) reversed

3. The letter _____ and accompanying numbers are used for identification of high   _____   _____
   voltage or input terminals.
   (a) E   (b) V
   (c) H   (d) X

4. The letter _____ and accompanying numbers are used for identification of low   _____   _____
   voltage or output terminals.
   (a) E   (b) V
   (c) H   (d) X

5. When connecting the secondary terminals of a 120/240 volt single-phase   _____   _____
   transformer, the first transformer is connected to X_3 and the second winding
   connected to _____, making the neutral connection X_0.
   (a) X_1 (b) X_2
   (c) X_4 (d) X_5

6. When connecting the secondary terminals of a three-phase, wye-connected   _____   _____
   system transformer, the first winding _____ is connected in series with a jumper
   to X_3 of the second transformer and to X_1 of the third transformer, making the
   neutral connection.
   (a) X_1 (b) X_2
   (c) X_4 (d) X_5

7. The supply-side bonding jumper shall be sized at least _____ percent of the area _____   _____
   of the largest ungrounded (phase) conductors where the service conductors
   are installed larger than 1100 KCMIL copper or 1750 KCMIL aluminum.
   (a) 12-1/2   (b) 15-1/2
   (c) 22-1/2   (d) 33-1/2

8. The grounding electrode conductor for a separately derived system shall not   _____   _____
   be required to be installed larger than _____ AWG copper when connecting
   to the nearest building steel.
   (a) 1/0   (b) 2/0
   (c) 3/0   (d) 4/0

9. The grounding electrode conductor shall not be required to be installed larger   _____   _____
   than _____ AWG copper when connecting to a driven rod.
   (a) 8   (b) 6
   (c) 4   (d) 2

10. The procedure for selecting the grounding electrode conductor to ground a separately derived system to the building steel is determined by the size of the _____ conductors in the feeder.
    (a) bonding   (b) grounded
    (c) grounding   (d) ungrounded

11. The bonding jumper in a separately derived system is called a _____ bonding jumper.
    (a) main   (b) system
    (c) primary   (d) secondary

12. The system bonding jumper can be connected at the _____ or the first disconnecting means of a separately derived system.
    (a) source   (b) service-point
    (c) none of the above   (d) all of the above

13. Transformer windings can be connected subtractive or additive _____.
    (a) wye   (b) polarity
    (c) delta   (d) all of the above

14. Transformers, under certain conditions, can be _____ fed.
    (a) reverse   (b) back
    (c) all of the above   (d) none of the above

15. A disconnecting means must be provided in the _____ side of a transformer. (general rule)
    (a) primary   (b) supply
    (c) all of the above   (d) none of the above

16. Transformers rated 112-1/2 kVA or less, installed indoors, must have a separation of at least _____ inches from combustible material. (general rule)
    (a) 3   (b) 6
    (c) 10   (d) 12

17. Transformers rated over _____ volts must be installed in a vault.
    (a) 15,000   (b) 25,000
    (c) 30,000   (d) 35,000

18. Vault doors shall have at least a _____ hour rating
    (a) 1   (b) 2
    (c) 2-1/2   (d) 3

19. Vault door sills or curbs shall have a height of at least _____ in.
    (a) 1   (b) 2
    (c) 3   (d) 4

20. What size supply-side bonding jumper is required to bond the secondary of a transformer with 2/0 AWG THWN copper conductors?

21. What size grounding electrode conductor is required to ground the secondary of a transformer with 2/0 AWG THWN copper conductors? (Use building steel)

22. What is the voltage when additive polarity is used?

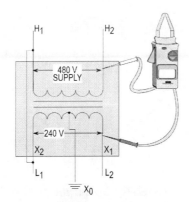

ADDITIVE POLARITY

23. What is the voltage when subtractive polarity is used?

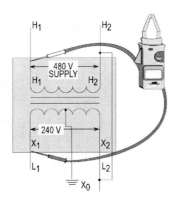

SUBTRACTIVE POLARITY

24. What is the voltage from phase-to-phase?

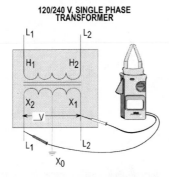

PHASE-TO-PHASE VOLTAGE

_____ _____   **25.** What is the voltage from phase-to-ground?

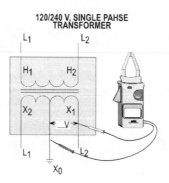

PHASE-TO-GROUND VOLTAGE

14

Motor Theory

For the operation of a motor, electricity and magnetism play a major role in producing power to the field windings called poles. These windings induce magnetic lines of force from north to south poles. The rotor is connected in the motor to the load so that the rotor can drive the load. Circulating currents induced in the conducting material of the rotor as it cuts through the magnetic flux lines of the magnetic field are called eddy currents and must be circulated properly.

Note, the foundation of motor operation is the attracting of unlike poles and the repelling of the like poles.

REGULAR MAGNETS

The earth is a permanent magnet with the north and south poles connected by an invisible field of magnetic force. If a piece of soft iron is placed within the field of a magnet, it becomes energized. The piece of soft iron is magnetized by the field of the permanent magnet. The piece of soft iron, when placed in the field of the permanent magnet, does not have to touch the permanent magnet to become magnetized, and it takes on the same characteristics as the permanent magnet. This type of action is called induction and is essential for motor operation. **(See Figure 14-1)**

The poles of two permanent magnets either attract or repel each other. Like poles repel each other, while unlike poles attract. By suspending a permanent magnet from a string, the suspended permanent magnet will rotate by attracting or repelling each end of a second magnet. This type of action illustrates one of the major principles used in the operation of electric motors. The attracting and repelling action by the field poles causes the rotor to rotate through the magnetic field and drive its connected load. **(See Figure 14-2)**

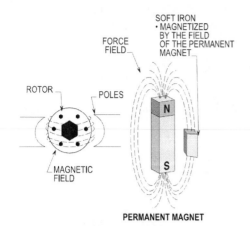

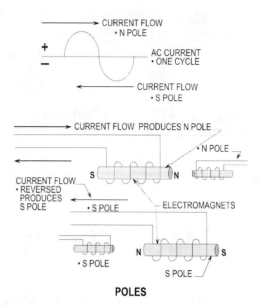

Figure 14-1. A permanent magnet becomes energized when a piece of soft iron is placed in the force field.

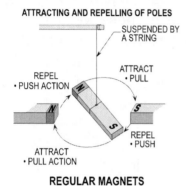

Figure 14-2. The poles of two permanent magnets either attract each other for unlike poles or repel each other for like poles.

Figure 14-3. Reverse current flow causes the alternating current to change the poles of an electromagnet from a north pole to a south pole. (**Note**, see **Figure 14-6**.)

ELECTROMAGNETS

A single insulated conductor wound around a soft iron core will produce an electromagnet that is much stronger than a permanent magnet. The strength of a magnetic field around a straight conductor carrying a current is relatively weak. A strong magnetic field is produced by the number of turns in the winding (coil). A weak magnetic field is produced by fewer number of turns in the coil.

POLES

The polarity of the poles in an electromagnet is changed by reversing the current flow. By reversing the current flow in an electromagnet in one direction, the magnet produces a south pole at one end, and it produces a north pole when current flow is in the opposite direction. Alternating current changes the poles of an electromagnet from north to south due to the flow of current changing direction. (**See Figure 14-3**)

BASIC INDUCTION MOTORS

A basic induction motor consists of a fixed section called a stator and a rotating section called a rotor. A stator is cut into thin sections of soft iron or steel (laminations) and assembled in a sandwich-like manner to reduce eddy current losses. Circulating currents induced in the conducting material of the rotor when it cuts through the magnetic flux lines of the magnetic field are called eddy currents.

A heating effect is produced when eddy currents flow in a solid piece of metal. Eddy currents will only flow in sections of metal that are sandwiched or cut. Therefore, the heating effect is decreased by this process.

A stator that is equipped with two or more field poles with insulated wire wound around them and connected together will create two or more electromagnets. When applying 60 hertz (cycles) of alternating current to electromagnets, the magnetic poles of the electromagnet reverse their polarity 120 times per second. This occurs every time the current reverses direction and alternates. (**See Figure 14-4**)

FIELD POLES

Induction motors operate on the following types of systems:

(1) Single-phase,

(2) Two-phase, or

(3) Three-phase voltage.

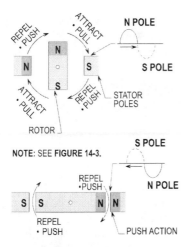

NOTE: SEE FIGURE 14-3.

BASIC INDUCTION MOTORS

Figure 14-4. Eddy currents are reduced by a rotor being sandwiched together and laminated.

Single-phase AC motors operate by the rotating magnetic field being produced by splitting the phases and shifting the AC power applied to the stator field poles. A means of starting must be provided for the rotor in a single-phase motor. The magnetic field alternates at such a fast rate (60 times a second) that the rotor cannot follow the alternating field. The rotor must start and turn fast enough to catch the rotating field. By using your hand or by using a starting winding, a rotor can be caused to rotate, and it will try to catch the magnetic field.

The current changes in the stator poles from north to south as the current alternates from positive to negative in a single-phase, 120 volt motor.

The phase displacement of different voltages is used when installing polyphase AC motors. The voltage in polyphase AC motors is one of the following:

(1) In-phase currents that rise and fall simultaneously.

(2) Out-of-phase currents 180 degrees out-of-phase have one current that rises past zero as the other falls past zero. Currents 90 degrees out-of-phase have one current reaching a peak while the other is at zero.

See Figure 14-5 for the rotating magnetic field of the stator using two voltages 90 degrees out-of-phase.

Figure 14-5 shows the relationship of single-phase voltage and current. Phase A current flow is at the 0 degree position when at maximum and Phase B current flow is at zero. Phase A windings in the stator will be at maximum value, as will be its magnetic field. Phase B windings will produce a magnetic field that will be at zero.

Note, Phase A and Phase B currents are of equal values at the 45 degree position.

Phase A current is at zero while Phase B is at maximum at the 90 degree position. Phase B windings produce a magnetic field that is at maximum value while Phase A windings are at zero. Phase A and Phase B currents flowing at the 45 and 225 degree position are equal. The rotor continues to turn with the rotating magnetic field until it completes 360 degrees. By placing the two poles (windings) at right angles to each other in the stator, the rotating magnetic field can be accomplished with voltages that are 90 degrees out-of-phase.

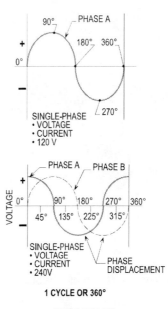

FIELD POLES

Figure 14-5. Relationship of single-phase currents that are 90° out-of-phase.

ROTOR

The rotor is made of slotted sections that are cut and sandwiched together to reduce eddy current losses. The rotor is embedded with copper or aluminum bars and welded together by a ring. The flow of current travels a path provided by the ring through the bars of the rotor. Insulation between the bars and rotor is not required since the voltage induced into these bars is low.

The rotor may be placed between two or more stator poles. A power source of 60 hertz AC is applied to the stator poles. The stator poles build up a magnetic field and collapse for each alternation. The poles of the stator change from south-to-north or north-to-south from these alternations. The rotor has a push-and-pull action through the rotating magnetic field of the stator poles. **(See Figure 14-6)**

Current is induced into the bars of the rotating rotor from the expanding and collapsing fields of the stator poles. This is accomplished by the rotor cutting the magnetic lines of force produced by the stator poles or field windings.

Motor Theory Tip: The magnetic field of the stator field poles is opposite to the magnetic field in the rotor.

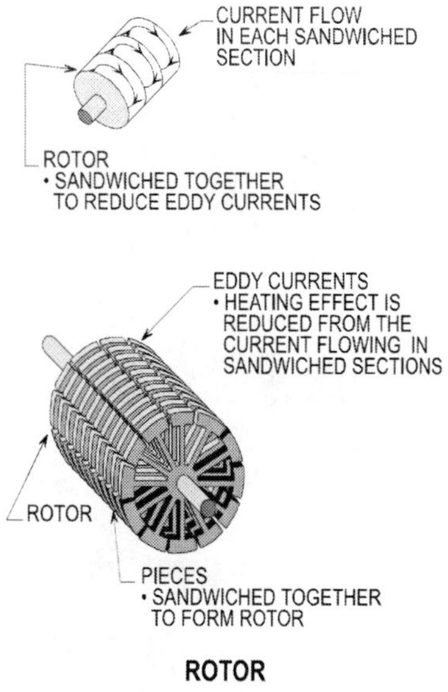

Figure 14-6. The operation of a basic induction motor.

DESIGNS OF MOTORS

The following designs of motors are to be considered when designing speed regulation, starting torque, and full-voltage starting current:

    (1) Class B,

    (2) Class C,

    (3) Class D, or

    (4) Class E per 2002 NEC.

CLASS B MOTORS

A speed regulation based on 2 to 5 percent slip is used when designing and installing Class B motors. Class B motors are designed to drive loads such as blowers, fans, and centrifugal pumps.

A Class B motor has a starting torque of about 150 percent times the full-load torque rating of the motor. The full-voltage starting current is approximately 600 percent to 725 percent of the full load running current of the motor.

Class B motors have a normal starting torque and normal starting current. Class B motors are used on loads that are started and reversed infrequently. Class B motors are the most used motors in the electrical industry. They are almost equal to motors marked with a code letter B.

CLASS C MOTORS

A speed regulation based on 2 to 5 percent slip is used when designing Class C motors. Class C motors are designed to drive hard-to-start loads such as compressors, conveyors, reciprocating pumps, and crushers.

A Class C motor has a starting torque of about 225 percent of the full-load torque rating of the motor. The full-voltage starting current is approximately 600 to 650 percent of the running current of the motor. Class C motors have high starting torque and normal starting current. They are capable of starting loads that are hard to start and then accelerate up to their running speed.

CLASS D MOTORS

A speed regulation based on 5 to 13 percent slip is used when designing Class D motors. Class D motors are known as high-slip motors. Class D motors are designed to drive very hard-to-start loads that are started and reversed frequently such as cranes, hoists, elevators, cyclical loads, and punch presses.

A Class D motor has a starting torque of about 275 percent of the full-load torque rating of the motor. The full-voltage starting current is approximately 525 to 625 percent of the running current of the motor. Class D motors have high starting torque and low starting current.

CLASS E MOTORS

Due to a new law and the Energy Conservation Act, it is very clear that the need to install high energy efficiency motors will become more urgent. In fact, it is essential that electrical personnel learn as much as possible about high energy efficiency motors, for in the near future, such motors will be the only type available.

For example, Tables **430.251(A)** and **(B)** only recognize design letter motors. See **Table 430.7(B)** for code letter motors.

Note, high-efficiency motors per 2005 NEC are NEMA Design B.

THE LAW

In October 1992, the Energy Policy Act was accepted. The law required that standard efficiency motors no longer be built after October 1997. After this date, only high-efficiency motors were to be manufactured. The motor industry seems to apply the term *premium efficiency* (PE) to identify high-efficiency motors.

The law basically requires all NEMA induction design motors of 200 HP or less that are single-speed to comply with this rule. This law applies to motors as follows:

(1) Mainly Design A and B, continuous rated, and operating at 230/460 volt, 60 hertz

(2) General purpose T-frame with the following characteristics:

    (a) Single speed,

    (b) Foot-mounted,

    (c) Polyphase,

    (d) Squirrel-cage,

    (e) Induction motors, and

    (f) 200 HP or less with exceptions.

HIGH-EFFICIENCY MOTORS

To improve motor efficiency, the manufacturer must reduce motor losses. There are three categories of motor losses:

(1) I^2R losses,

(2) mechanical losses, and

(3) core losses.

I^2R LOSSES

I^2R losses account for 20 to 30 percent of the total loss of the motor. The I^2R losses of the windings depend on the current and the winding resistance. There are many conditions that will affect resistance and current.

For example, Such conditions as temperature, load, excitation, and magnetic influences will affect the resistance in the windings. Since the current that a motor draws is primarily a function of the load, steps must be taken to improve the motor's power factor. This can be done by reducing the reactive component of the total motor current.

Note, the way to reduce I^2R is to reduce the resistance of the windings. This is done by improving the motor's stator resistance by increasing both the size and number of conductors.

Rotor losses may be minimized by increasing the size of the conductor bars and using low-loss laminated steel.

For larger motors, copper bars can be utilized in rotors for best efficiency. For maximum efficiency, copper rotor bars are custom-fitted, brazed, formed, and designed and fitted into the rotor slots.

By reducing the air gap between the stator and rotor, winding losses can be reduced. This diminishes the reactive element of the motor's total current. In general, the needed excitation current is reduced, which improves the overall power factor. Due to the better-designed steel core, the magnetic field does not have to be as large to provide the same amount of motor performance.

Note, there is less current needed to produce the magnetic field.

MECHANICAL LOSSES

Mechanical losses are produced in motor operation from friction and windage that takes place within the motor. Windage losses are losses created by moving parts of the motor.

For example, windage losses can be developed by the fan blade if it is not designed to help alleviate such unwanted friction. Another component of the motor that creates friction losses are the bearings. To help diminish bearing losses, high quality bearings are used, and due to such close tolerance operation, the air gap variation between the stator and rotor greatly reduces these types of losses.

CORE LOSSES

Core losses are caused by two elements:

(1) Hysteresis and

(2) Eddy currents.

The hysteresis loss is the element of the core loss in a magnetic circuit that can be reduced by using high quality steel to build the core.

Eddy current losses are reduced by laminating the core with thin sheets of steel that are insulated from each other. Thin sheets of steel are sandwiched together which will reduce eddy current problems even further. Eddy currents are circulating currents in the core of the stator poles. These currents are caused by varying magnetic fields in the core. Due to the I^2R losses in the resistance of the core material, unwanted heat is produced.

Note, these currents do no useful work, they just create heating effects in the motor.

Motor Theory Tip: Stray load losses are dependent on the loading of the motor, and they increase as the load is applied. These losses are due to the location of the conductors in the motor, skin effect, poor laminations, etc.

See Figure 14-7 for a detailed illustration of a high-efficiency motor.

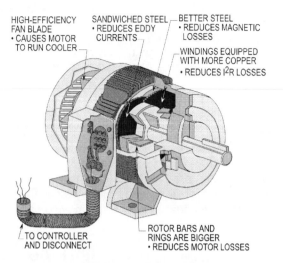

HIGH-EFFICIENCY FAN BLADE
• CAUSES MOTOR TO RUN COOLER

SANDWICHED STEEL
• REDUCES EDDY CURRENTS

BETTER STEEL
• REDUCES MAGNETIC LOSSES

WINDINGS EQUIPPED WITH MORE COPPER
• REDUCES I²R LOSSES

TO CONTROLLER AND DISCONNECT

ROTOR BARS AND RINGS ARE BIGGER
• REDUCES MOTOR LOSSES

HIGH-EFFICIENCY MOTORS

Figure 14-7. The above is an illustration of a high-efficiency motor with elements that are designed to provide better efficiency.

MOTOR FACTS

The following items must be taken into consideration when designing and selecting a motor:

(1) Operating voltage,

(2) Operating current,

(3) Operating torque,

(4) Operating slip,

(5) Power factor, and

(6) Frequency.

OPERATING VOLTAGE AND CURRENT

Single-phase voltage of 120 volts is like one person riding a bicycle. Only one stroke is produced that will peak and produce power from the one person riding the bicycle. Single-phase voltage of 208 or 240 volts is like two people riding a bicycle. Two power-producing strokes are provided by one rider, leaving a power-producing stroke (peak) and the other rider, entering the peak and producing power to drive the bicycle. This type of example shows that a 208 or 230 volt, single-phase motor is more efficient than a 120 volt, single-phase motor.

Three-phase voltage is compared to three riders on a bicycle. Three power-producing strokes are provided by the first rider, leaving the peak stroke and the second rider entering at the peak. The third rider enters the peak as the second rider leaves the peak stroke. This type of example

shows that a three-phase motor will produce more power because there are three different phases that are peaking and providing a smooth and continuous power to drive the rotor and load at its operating speed. **(See Figure 14-8)**

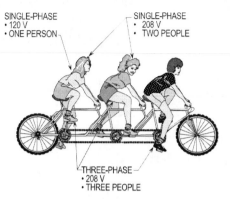

SINGLE-PHASE
• 120 V
• ONE PERSON

SINGLE-PHASE
• 208 V
• TWO PEOPLE

THREE-PHASE
• 208 V
• THREE PEOPLE

OPERATING VOLTAGE AND CURRENT

Figure 14-8. Single-phase and three-phase voltages and currents operate in comparison to riders on a bicycle.

The three phases of voltage and current supply one of the three separate pairs of poles. The first phase (peak stroke) delivers the greatest power. The second phase enters the peak as the first phase leaves the peak, delivering its greatest stroke of power. The third peak phase enters the peak as the second phase leaves the peak, and the process repeats itself. **(See Figure 14-9)**

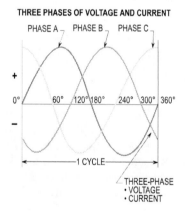

THREE PHASES OF VOLTAGE AND CURRENT

PHASE A   PHASE B   PHASE C

0°   60°   120° 180°   240° 300° 360°

1 CYCLE

THREE-PHASE
• VOLTAGE
• CURRENT

OPERATING VOLTAGE AND CURRENT

Figure 14-9. The three phases (A, B, and C) of voltages supply one of the three separate pairs of poles.

Refer to **Figure 14-10** and notice that between poles A and D, the greatest power stroke and magnetic field is produced for Phase 1. Between poles B and E, the greatest power stroke is produced for Phase 2. Between poles C and F, the greatest power stroke is produced for Phase 3. The voltage and current of the three phases are displaced 120 degrees on the stator of the motor. **(See Figure 14-10)**

POWER STROKES FOR PHASES 1, 2, AND 3

PHASE 1 OPERATION

MOTOR
• 3Ø

PHASE 2 OPERATION

POLES
• A and D
• B and E
• C and F

PHASE 3 OPERATION

OPERATING VOLTAGE AND CURRENT

Figure 14-10. Between poles A and D, the greatest power stroke and magnetic field is produced for Phase 1. Between poles B and E, the greatest power stroke is produced for Phase 2. Between poles C and F, the greatest power stroke is produced for Phase 3.

OPERATING TORQUE AND SLIP

Good starting torque and slip is provided for the motor by dual bars installed in the rotor. The outer bars that are close to the surface have a high-resistance winding and the inner bars have a low-resistance winding. Good starting is provided by the outer bars. More current is allowed to flow at the running speed of the motor from the inner bars. **(See Figure 14-11)**

The percentage of slip desired for each motor is designed by placement of these bars shown in **Figure 14-11**. The magnetic lines of force cutting across these bars embedded in the rotor produce the slip of the motor. Voltage is induced in the rotor only when these copper bars cut the magnetic lines of force created by the alternations of current in the stator field.

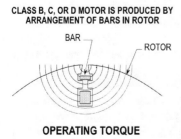

CLASS B, C, OR D MOTOR IS PRODUCED BY
ARRANGEMENT OF BARS IN ROTOR

BAR   ROTOR

OPERATING TORQUE

Figure 14-11. Different classes of motors with different torque ratings can be produced by the bars in the rotor.

Note, the rotor will never rotate at the same speed as the rotating magnetic field. This difference in rotating speed is the slip of the motor. **(See Figure 14-12)**

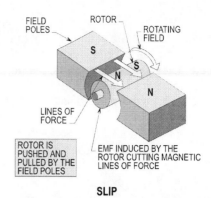

FIELD POLES   ROTOR   ROTATING FIELD

LINES OF FORCE

ROTOR IS PUSHED AND PULLED BY THE FIELD POLES

EMF INDUCED BY THE ROTOR CUTTING MAGNETIC LINES OF FORCE

SLIP

Figure 14-12. The rotor will never rotate at the same speed as the alternations of the current and rotating field.

The greater the slip a rotor has, resulting from a driven load, the more lines of force are cut during rotation and the slower the rotor will turn. The actual running speed of a motor is designed to have 5 percent slip, which will allow the rotor to rotate at less than the synchronous speed created by the alternating current. **(See Figure 14-13)**

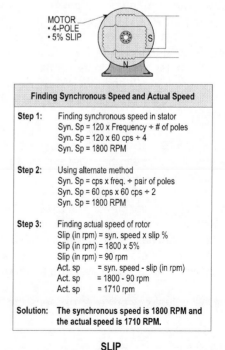

MOTOR
• 4-POLE
• 5% SLIP

Finding Synchronous Speed and Actual Speed	
Step 1:	Finding synchronous speed in stator Syn. Sp = 120 x Frequency ÷ # of poles Syn. Sp = 120 x 60 cps ÷ 4 Syn. Sp = 1800 RPM
Step 2:	Using alternate method Syn. Sp = cps x freq. ÷ pair of poles Syn. Sp = 60 cps x 60 cps ÷ 2 Syn. Sp = 1800 RPM
Step 3:	Finding actual speed of rotor Slip (in rpm) = syn. speed x slip % Slip (in rpm) = 1800 x 5% Slip (in rpm) = 90 rpm Act. sp = syn. speed - slip (in rpm) Act. sp = 1800 - 90 rpm Act. sp = 1710 rpm
Solution:	**The synchronous speed is 1800 RPM and the actual speed is 1710 RPM.**

SLIP

Figure 14-13. Finding the synchronous and actual speed of a motor due to its slip characteristics.

The rotor has 100 percent slip when the rotor is at rest and no lines of magnetic force are cut. However, the rotor begins to turn with the stator field when power is applied to the stator poles.

The rotor current tries to reach the peak of the alternation of current, creating the magnetic lines of force between the stator field poles. As the rotor turns, the percentage of slip begins to decrease (usually 2 to 5 percent) until the designed amount of slip is reached as the motor drives the load. **(See Figure 14-14)**

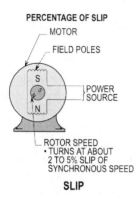

Figure 14-14. In an induction motor, the rotor speed usually turns at about 2 to 5 percent slip.

POWER FACTOR

The ratio of the actual power used in a circuit to the apparent power drawn from the line is the power factor. The true power used to produce heat or work is the actual power. Actual power is also known as true, real, or useful power. A wattmeter is used to measure the actual power in watts and kW. A voltmeter and ammeter is used to measure the apparent power in VA and kVA. When measuring the voltage and current waveforms, they may be in-phase or out-of-phase.

Note, the degree (0 - 90°) of shift indicates power factor. When the actual and apparent power are the same value, the power factor is 100 percent.

Less actual power is consumed for circuits with motors and transformers having windings producing magnetic fields. These circuits have a power factor that is less than 100 percent. The inductance of the windings causes the inequality between the actual power and apparent power.

Note, that the actual power never exceeds the apparent power.

Fewer lines of force are cut when the rotor turns at a faster speed through the field. The voltage and magnetic lines of force in the rotor become weaker and causes the rotor to slow down.

REACTIVE POWER

When the kVA exceeds the kW, a reactive power exists. The operating current consists of true current (in-phase) and reactive current. The current drawn by an inductive load is used to develop magnetic fields required for operation; this is reactive current. **(See Figure 14-15)**

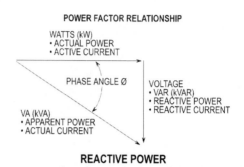

Figure 14-15. The above illustration shows the right angle relationship of terms used to demonstrate power factor.

APPARENT POWER

By multiplying the volts times amps, the apparent power can be found. Apparent power can be equal to or greater than actual power. When apparent power and actual power are equal, their ratio is 1 to 1, 1.0, or 100 percent.

For example, if the apparent power is 2000 watts and the power consumed is 800 watts, the ratio is .4 or 40 percent (PF = 800 W ÷ 2000 W = .4). A 40 percent power factor is low. A phase angle of 66 degrees is equal to cosine Ø of 40. See the trigonometric in **Figure 14-16.**

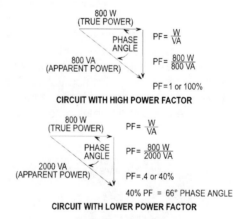

Figure 14-16. Circuits with watts (or kW) closer to the VA (or kVA) rating of the apparent power have a higher power factor. Circuits with watts (or kW) less than the VA (or kVA) rating of the apparent power have a lower power factor. See trigonometric charts on **page 15-5** to match power factor to the phase angle, starting with 50 percent power factor.

ACTUAL POWER

By multiplying the volts times amps in a pure resistance circuit, the actual power can be found.

For example: What are the watts for a 240 volt, single-phase load rated at 20 amps?

> **Step 1:** Finding W
> W = V x A
> W = 240 V x 20 A
> W = 4800
>
> **Solution: The actual power for the load is 4800 watts.**

By multiplying the volts times amps times cosine Ø (PF), the actual power can be found.

For example: What are the watts for a 240 volt, single-phase load rated at 20 amps and a power factor of 70 percent?

> **Step 1:** Finding W
> W = V x A x PF
> W = 240 V x 20 A x 70%
> W = 3360
>
> **Solution: The actual power for the load is 3360 watts.**

By multiplying the volts times amps times cosine Ø (PF) for a three-phase circuit, the actual power can be found.

For example: What are the watts for a 480 volt, three-phase motor with an FLC of 40 amps having a power factor of 80 percent?

> **Step 1:** Finding W
> W = V x $\sqrt{3}$ x A x PF
> W = 480 V x 1.732 x 40 x 80%
> W = 26,592
>
> **Solution: The actual power for the motor is 26,592 watts.**

OPERATING 230 V MOTORS ON 208 V SUPPLY CIRCUIT

Slight changes in voltage, torque, slip, and current occur where 230 V, three-phase, 60 Hz motors operate on 208 V, three-phase, 60 Hz supply circuits.

For example, the full-load current for a motor operating 10 percent plus above rated voltage is 7 percent below normal. **(See Figure 14-17)**

NEMA standards allow motor terminal voltage to vary 10 percent below or above rated voltage.

For example, a 230 volt motor can operate between 207 volts (230 V x 10% = 230 V - 23 V = 207 V) and 253 volts (230 V x 110% = 253 V).

CHARACTERISTIC	+10%	-10%
TORQUE	UP 21%	DOWN 19%
FULL-LOAD SPEED	UP 1%	DOWN 2%
POWER FACTOR	DOWN 4%	UP 3%
FULL-LOAD CURRENT	DOWN 7%	UP 11%
TEMPERATURE	DOWN 10%	UP 17%
MAXIMUM OVERLOAD	UP 21%	DOWN 19%
EFFICIENCY	UP 1%	DOWN 2%

NOTE: FOR MORE FACTS, SEE FIGURE 16-13.

OPERATING 230 V MOTORS ON 208 V SUPPLY CIRCUIT

Figure 14-17. Characteristic of induction motors operating 10 percent above or 10 percent below supply voltage.

TORQUE

The torque of a motor varies with the square of the voltage. The starting torque and maximum running torque of motors running on 208 volts are determined by squaring voltage (208 V) and dividing by the voltage of the motor (230 V) squared.

For example, a motor with a starting torque of 150 lb ft has a starting torque of 123 lb ft [(208 V/230 V)^2 = .82 x 150 lb ft = 123 lb ft)].

SLIP

The slip of induction motors varies inversely with the square of the voltage. The slip of a 230 volt motor operating on a 208 volt supply is 1.22 times the slip of the 230 volt rating on the motor's nameplate [(230 V/208 V)^2 = 1.22].

For example, if the synchronous speed is 1800 RPM and the actual speed is 1725 RPM, the slip is 75 RPM (1800 RPM − 1725 RPM = 75 RPM). The new slip of RPM for a 230 volt motor operating on 230 volts is 91.5 RPM [(230 V/208 V)² = 1.22 x 75 RPM = 91.5 RPM].

CURRENT

Motors are more efficient at a higher voltage because they draw less current and run slightly cooler. Motors operating at a lower voltage pull more current and are less efficient. Motors rated at 230 volts and operating on a 208 volt supply draw approximately 11 percent more current than when operating at 230 volts.

For example, a 230 volt motor operating at 30 amps on 208 volts draws approximately 33.3 amps (30 A x 111% = 33.3 amps).

MEASURING OPERATING AMPS

The operating amps of a motor must not exceed the nameplate rating of the motor for the motor to have normal operating life. The amp rating is taken with an ampmeter for an accurate measurement. **(See Figure 14-18)**

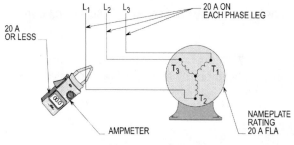

MEASURING OPERATING AMPS

Figure 14-18. An amp reading of 20 amps or less indicates the motor should have a normal life of twenty years or less. (See NEMA 1, Motors and Generators)

MEASURING OPERATING VOLTAGE

Two measurements are required to determine the operating voltage of a motor. The first measurement is for the system voltage to the motor. This voltage reading can be 10 percent above or 10 percent below the operating voltage. **(See Figure 14-19)** The second measurement is for the unbalanced voltage from each phase-to-ground, and you must average the measurements to obtain a percentage. The percentage must not exceed 1 percent. **(See Figure 14-20)**

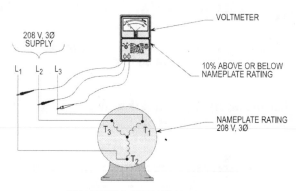

MEASURING OPERATING VOLTAGE

Figure 14-19. The operating voltage can read within 10 percent above or below the operating voltage listed on the nameplate of the motor.

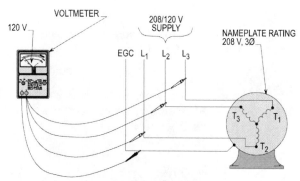

MEASURING OPERATING VOLTAGE

Figure 14-20. Unbalanced voltage (if measured) must not exceed 1 percent, or the running current of the nameplate must be derated to compensate for the percentage that exceeds 1 percent.

Chapter 14: Motor Theory

Section   Answer

1. A single insulated conductor wound around a soft iron core will produce a(n) _____ _____
   _____ that is much stronger than a permanent magnet.
     (a) regular magnet   (b) electromagnet
     (c) magnetic field   (d) eddy current

2. Alternating current changes the _____ of an electromagnet from north to south _____ _____
   due to the flow of current changing direction.
     (a) stator   (b) rotor
     (c) poles   (d) core

3. A basic induction motor consists of a fixed section called a(n) _____ and a _____ _____
   rotating section called a rotor.
     (a) stator   (b) pole
     (c) core   (d) electromagnet

4. Circulating currents induced in the conducting material of the rotor when it cuts _____ _____
   through the magnetic flux lines of the magnetic field are called _____ currents.
     (a) magnetic   (b) electromagnetic
     (c) alternating   (d) eddy

5. When applying 60 hertz (cycles) of alternating current to electromagnets, the _____ _____
   magnetic poles of the electromagnet reverse the polarity _____ times per
   second.
     (a) 60   (b) 90
     (c) 120   (d) 180

6. The _____ is made of slotted sections that are cut and sandwiched together _____ _____
   to reduce eddy current loses.
     (a) stator   (b) rotor
     (c) poles   (d) core

7. A speed regulation based on 2 to _____ percent slip is used when designing _____ _____
   and installing Class B motors.
     (a) 3   (b) 5
     (c) 8   (d) 13

8. A Class B motor has a starting torque of about _____ percent times the full- _____ _____
   load torque rating of the motor.
     (a) 100   (b) 125
     (c) 150   (d) 175

9. A Class C motor has a starting torque of about _____ percent of the full-load _____ _____
   torque rating of the motor.
     (a) 225   (b) 250
     (c) 300   (d) 400

10. A speed regulation based on 5 to _____ percent slip is used when designing _____ _____
    with Class D motors.
      (a) 3   (b) 5
      (c) 8   (d) 13

11. I²R losses account for 20 to _____ percent of the total loss of the motor.
    (a) 30   (b) 40
    (c) 50   (d) 60

12. Eddy current losses are reduced by laminating the _____ with thin sheets of steel that are insulated from each other.
    (a) stator   (b) core
    (c) poles   (d) rotor

13. The rotor has _____ percent slip when it is at rest and no lines of magnetic force are cut.
    (a) 30   (b) 50
    (c) 75   (d) 100

14. The ratio of the actual power used in a circuit to the apparent power drawn from the line is the _____.
    (a) operating torque and slip   (b) power factor
    (c) reactive power   (d) reactance power

15. When the kVA exceeds the kW, a(n) _____ power exists.
    (a) apparent   (b) actual
    (c) reactive   (d) reactance

16. By multiplying the volts times amps, the _____ power can be found.
    (a) apparent   (b) actual
    (c) reactive   (d) reactance

17. By multiplying the volts times amps in a pure resistance circuit, the _____ power can be found.
    (a) apparent   (b) actual
    (c) reactive   (d) reactance

18. The _____ of a motor varies with the square of the voltage.
    (a) power factor   (b) slip
    (c) rotor   (d) torque

19. The _____ of induction motors varies inversely with the square of the voltage.
    (a) power factor   (b) slip
    (c) rotor   (d) torque

20. Motors rated at 230 volts and operating on a 208 volt supply draw approximately _____ percent more current than when operating at 230 volts.
    (a) 2   (b) 5
    (c) 11   (d) 13

21. What are the synchronous speed and actual speed for a four-pole motor with 5 percent slip?

22. What are the watts (actual power) for a 240 volt, single-phase water heater with a 30 amp heating element?

23. What are the watts for a 240 volt, single-phase motor with a 30 amp FLC having a power factor of 70 percent?

24. What are the watts for a 480 volt, three-phase motor with an FLC of 50   _____ _____
amps having a power factor of 80 percent? (use 831 volt for the three-phase
calculation)

25. A code letter _____ has a kVA per horsepower (HP) rating of 3.15 to 3.54 kVA   _____ _____
per horsepower.
    (a) A   (b) B
    (c) C   (d) D

Part Three

Motors

No day passes without the discovery of new ways to use the most efficient and most important device ever invented, the electric motor. Without it, the wheels of industry would grind to a halt and millions of time and labor saving devices would be rendered useless.

AC electrical motors are designed and selected by finding the three currents that make up the circuits that supply the power to the motors. The first current found is the full-load amps (FLA) from **Table 430.248** for single-phase and **Table 430.250** for three-phase. The second current determined is the nameplate amps found on the motor. And the third current is the locked-rotor current (LRC), in amps, from **Table 430.7(B)** for motors with code letters and **Tables 430.251(A)** and **(B)** for motors with design letters.

AC electrical motors are designed and installed in a wide variety of sizes, types, and styles, ranging from tiny fractional horsepower units to very large machines of 20,000 HP and larger. These types of motors can be either of single-phase or three-phase construction based on the horsepower and voltage.

Part III covers motor theory, types of motors, and the regulations of the *National Electrical Code*® that pertain to the design and installation of these motors.

15

Types of Motors

Alternating current is used in the United States to power the majority of motors installed. These motors are usually connected by journeyman electricians and maintained by maintenance personnel. These motors are designed to operate on a single or dual voltage, based on the connections of the windings of the stator. These motors are equipped with either single-phase or three-phase windings.

Of all the different types of motors, the squirrel-cage induction motor is designed to have fewer parts, is less expensive, and requires less maintenance than wound rotor, synchronous, or direct-current motors. (See **Table 430.52(C)(1)** of the *National Electrical Code*® for a listing of the different types of motors.)

SINGLE-PHASE MOTORS

The most common type of single-phase motors can operate from a single-phase lighting or power circuit. The following are the most commonly used single-phase motors:

(1) Split-phase,
(2) Capacitor-start,
(3) Capacitor start-and-run,
(4) Permanent split-capacitor,
(5) Shaded-pole, and
(6) Universal.

SPLIT-PHASE MOTORS

The split-phase motor is an AC motor of fractional horsepower size and is used to operate such devices as washing machines, oil burners, and small pumps. The motor consists of the following four main parts:

(1) A rotor (rotating part),

(2) Stator (a stationary part),

(3) Brackets (fastened to the frame of the stator by means of screws or bolts), and

(4) A centrifugal switch (located inside the motor).

Two windings are provided on the stator for a split-phase motor. These two windings consist of the main (running) winding and the auxiliary (starting) winding. The torque needed to start turning the load is produced from the starting windings, which are placed about 30 degrees from the running windings.

A centrifugal switch (starting switch) is placed in series with the starting winding, and the starting winding is connected in parallel with the running winding. The centrifugal switch contacts are closed when the rotor is at rest. The contacts open when the motor starts and begins to accelerate up to its running speed. The starting winding is taken out of the circuit by the centrifugal switch at about 75 to 80 percent of the motor's running speed. The split-phase motor operates as a single-phase induction motor when the starting winding is disconnected from the circuit. **(See Figure 15-1)**

Split-phase motors have a high resistance in the starting windings, which produces a high inrush current when starting. Starting windings consist of small wire and have many turns, which have a greater resistance than the running winding. Running (field) windings consist of larger size wire with fewer turns and thus a lower resistance. **(See Figure 15-2)**

WITH CAPACITORS

The capacitor is used as the starting device in some motors. These are called capacitor-start motors. The capacitor motor operates on alternating current and is made in sizes ranging from 1/20 HP to 10 HP. It is mainly used to operate such machines as refrigerators, compressors, etc. A so-called capacitor motor is a split-phase motor with the addition of a capacitor that is connected in series with the starting or auxiliary winding. The capacitor is usually mounted on top of the motor, but it may be mounted in other external positions or inside the motor housing. The added capacitor provides higher starting torque with lower starting current than the regular split-phase motor. **(See Figure 15-3)**

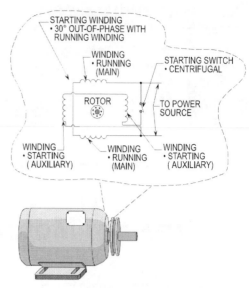

SPLIT-PHASE MOTORS

Figure 15-1. The starting windings of a split-phase motor help start the motor and are disconnected from the circuit at about 75 to 80 percent of its running speed.

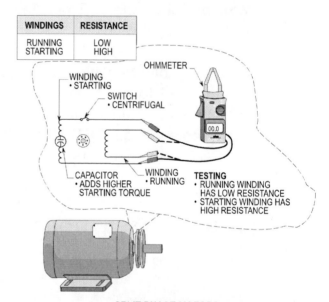

SPLIT-PHASE MOTORS

Figure 15-2. The running windings and starting windings are measured using an ohmmeter. Running windings have less resistance than starting windings.

STARTING WINDINGS

There are three separate windings in the split-phase motor. The following are the three types of windings:

(1) Squirrel-cage winding (located in the rotor),

(2) Stator run winding (located at the bottom of the stator poles and known as the running or main winding), and

(3) Starting or auxiliary winding.

At the start, the current flowing through both the running and starting windings, which are connected in parallel, causes a magnetic field to form inside the motor. This magnetic field rotates and induces a voltage in the rotor winding, which in turn causes another magnetic field. These magnetic fields combine in such a manner as to cause rotation of the rotor. The starting winding is necessary at the start to produce the rotating field. After the motor is running, the starting winding is no longer needed and is cut out of the circuit by means of the centrifugal switch.

Use these methods to check the starting winding if the motor fails to start:

(1) Turn the shaft of the motor by hand. If it starts, the trouble is in the starter winding circuit.

(2) Disassemble the motor and check the starting winding for an open circuit.

(3) Use a test light or an ohmmeter to determine whether the winding is complete. **(See Figure 15-4 and Table 1 in the Annex)**

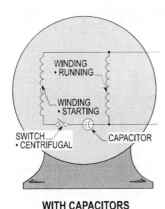

WITH CAPACITORS

Figure 15-3. Connections of a capacitor-start motor.

REVERSING DIRECTION

The flow of current in a split-phase motor is changed by reversing the flow of current through the running or starting windings. The rotor will rotate in a counterclockwise direction when the flow of current in the starting winding and the running winding are in the same direction. The rotor will rotate in a clockwise direction when the flow of current in the starting winding and running winding are in the opposite direction. **(See Figure 15-5)**

IDENTIFICATION OF LEADS

While older motors are usually tagged M_1 and M_2 for the running winding, S_3 and S_4 for starting winding, or R_1 and R_2 for the running winding, new motor types dictate a different color coding of the starting and running windings. These newer motors follow a typical color coding of red for T_1, black for T_2, yellow for T_3, and blue for T_4.

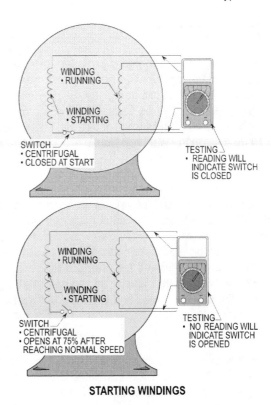

STARTING WINDINGS

Figure 15-4. This split-phase motor is started by a centrifugal switch that closes and opens the starting winding.

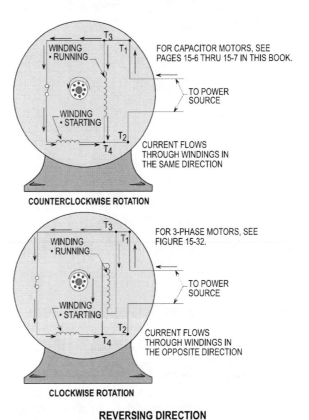

COUNTERCLOCKWISE ROTATION

CLOCKWISE ROTATION

REVERSING DIRECTION

Figure 15-5. The rotation of the split-phase motor is reversed by changing the flow of current through the running winding, as shown above.

THERMAL PROTECTION

An additional switch is sometimes provided for split-phase motors to protect them from overheating. Overheating can be caused by lack of ventilation or by high temperatures. Ventilation problems can be caused by the motor's inlets and outlets being covered with lint or dirt. High temperatures can also develop in the windings from a stuck bearing in the motor or on the driven load.

Overcurrent protection devices (bimetal disks or strip composed of dissimilar metals) are connected in series with the running winding. The amount of current flow and temperature rise of the windings is moderated by the overload protector. The overload protector will open the circuit if the current flow and temperature rise exceed the predetermined (set) value. The overload can be designed to connect the power supply and start the motor when the running winding temperature decreases. **(See Figure 15-6)**

Motor Theory Tip: A motor will shut down and not restart until the problem is corrected. The overload protector provides protection against this.

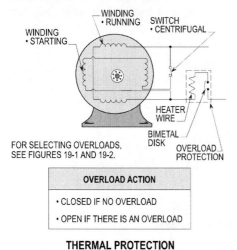

FOR SELECTING OVERLOADS, SEE FIGURES 19-1 AND 19-2.

OVERLOAD ACTION
• CLOSED IF NO OVERLOAD
• OPEN IF THERE IS AN OVERLOAD

THERMAL PROTECTION

Figure 15-6. Overload protection is provided for the running winding by the bimetal disk or strip.

CAPACITOR-START MOTORS

A capacitor-start motor creates a greater starting torque when a capacitor is connected in series with the starting winding and the centrifugal switch. The capacitor causes the current in the starting winding to lead, by almost 90 degrees, the current in the running winding. This condition produces a revolving magnetic field in the stator, which in turn induces a current in the rotor winding. As a result, the magnetic field acts in such a manner as to produce rotation of the motor.

ELECTROLYTIC CAPACITORS

Many capacitor motors employ the electrolytic capacitor. This type of capacitor consists of two sheets of aluminum foil that are separated by one or more layers of gauze. The gauze has previously been saturated with a chemical solution called an electrolyte. The electrolyte forms a film that acts as the insulating medium of the electrolytic capacitor. These layers are rolled together and fitted into an aluminum container. Electrolytic capacitors should not be kept in a circuit for more than a few seconds at a time because they are designed for only intermittent operation. **(See Figure 15-7)**

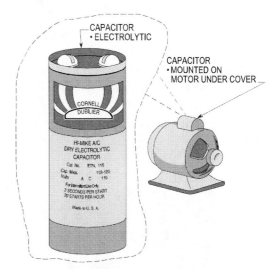

ELECTROLYTIC CAPACITORS

Figure 15-7. The above is an illustration of an electrolytic capacitor.

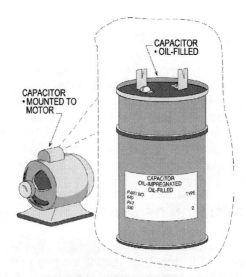

OIL-FILLED CAPACITORS

Figure 15-8. The above is an illustration of an oil-filled capacitor.

OIL-FILLED CAPACITORS

Some capacitors are made with paper that has been impregnated with oil and then inserted in a container that is filled with oil. This is done to increase the insulating quality of the paper and to help keep the capacitor from overheating. **(See Figure 15-8)**

SELECTING CAPACITORS

The capacitor acts essentially as a storage unit; that is, it has the capacity to store and release electricity when needed.

All capacitors have this quality, and all are electrically the same. They differ only in mechanical construction as detailed previously.

USING CHARTS

To correct an existing power factor when the existing power factor for a motor is known and the power factor is low, you may find the size kVAR capacitor needed by using the manufacturer's capacitor chart in **Figure 15-9.**

CAPACITOR CALCULATING CHART																	
%	80	81	82	83	84	85	86	87	88	89	90	91	92	93	94	95	96
50	0.982	1.003	1.034	1.060	1.086	1.112	1.139	1.165	1.192	1.220	1.248	1.276	1.306	1.337	1.369	1.403	1.442
51	.937	.962	.989	1.015	1.041	1.067	1.094	1.120	1.147	1.175	1.203	1.231	1.261	1.292	1.324	1.358	1.395
52	.893	.919	.945	.971	.997	1.023	1.050	1.076	1.103	1.131	1.159	1.187	1.217	1.248	1.280	1.314	1.351
53	.850	.876	.902	.928	.954	.980	1.007	1.033	1.060	1.088	1.116	1.144	1.174	1.205	1.237	1.271	1.308
54	.809	.835	.861	.837	.913	.939	.966	.992	1.019	1.047	1.075	1.103	1.133	1.164	1.196	1.230	1.267
55	.769	.795	.821	.847	.873	.899	.926	.952	.979	1.007	1.035	1.063	1.090	1.124	1.156	1.190	1.228
56	.730	.756	.782	.808	.834	.860	.887	.913	.940	.968	.996	1.024	1.051	1.085	1.117	1.151	1.189
57	.692	.718	.744	.770	.796	.822	.849	.875	.902	.930	.958	.986	1.013	1.047	1.079	1.113	1.151
58	.655	.681	.707	.733	.759	.785	.812	.838	.865	.893	.921	.949	.976	1.010	1.042	1.076	1.114
59	.618	.644	.670	.696	.722	.748	.755	.801	.828	.856	.884	.912	.939	.973	1.005	1.039	1.077
60	.584	.610	.636	.662	.688	.714	.741	.767	.794	.822	.850	.878	.905	.939	.971	1.005	1.143
61	.549	.575	.061	.627	.653	.679	.706	.732	.759	.787	.815	.843	.870	.904	.936	.970	1.008
62	.515	.541	.567	.593	.619	.645	.672	.698	.725	.753	.781	.809	.836	.870	.904	.936	.974
63	.483	.509	.535	.561	.587	.613	.640	.666	.693	.721	.749	.777	.804	.838	.870	.902	.942
64	.450	.476	.502	.528	.544	.580	.607	.633	.660	.688	.716	.744	.771	.805	.837	.871	.909
65	.419	.445	.471	.497	.523	.549	.576	.602	.629	.657	.685	.713	.740	.744	.806	.840	**.878**
66	.398	.414	.440	.466	.492	.518	.545	.571	.598	.626	.654	.682	.709	.743	.775	.809	.847
67	.358	.384	.410	.436	.462	.488	.515	.541	.568	.596	.624	.652	.679	.713	.745	.779	.817
68	.329	.355	.381	.417	.433	.459	.486	.512	.539	.567	.595	.623	.650	.684	.716	.750	.788
69	.299	.325	.351	.377	.403	.429	.456	.482	.509	.537	.565	.593	.620	.654	.686	.720	.758
70	.270	.296	.322	.348	.374	.400	.427	.453	.480	.508	.536	.564	.591	.625	.657	.691	.729
71	.242	.268	.294	.320	.346	.372	.399	.425	.452	.480	.508	.536	.563	.597	.629	.633	.701
72	.213	.239	.265	.291	.317	.343	.370	.396	.423	.451	.479	.507	.534	.568	.600	.634	.672
73	.186	.212	.238	.264	.290	.316	.343	.369	.396	.424	.452	.480	.507	.541	.573	.607	.645
74	.159	.185	.211	.237	.263	.289	.316	.342	.369	.397	.425	.453	.480	.514	.546	.580	.618
75	.132	.158	.184	.210	.236	.262	.289	.315	.342	.370	.398	.426	.453	.487	.519	.553	.591
76	.105	.131	.157	.183	.209	.235	.262	.288	.315	.343	.371	.399	.426	.460	.492	.526	.564
77	.079	.105	.131	.157	.183	.209	.236	.262	.289	.317	.345	.373	.400	.434	.466	.500	.538
78	.053	.079	.105	.131	.157	.183	.210	.236	.263	.291	.319	.347	.374	.408	.440	.474	.512
79	.026	.052	.078	.104	.130	.156	.183	.209	.236	.264	.292	.320	.347	.381	.413	.447	.485
80	.000	.026	.052	.078	.104	.130	.157	.183	.210	.238	.266	.294	.321	.355	.387	.421	.459

USING CHART TO DETERMINE kVAR	USING FORMULA TO DETERMINE MICROFARADS
For example: A power factor of 65% is present in an existing circuit to a motor. How many kVAR will it take to correct the power factor to 96%? (The motor is 100 HP, 208 V, three-phase)	Smaller capacitor rated in microfarads (µf) is determined by applying the following formula.

USING CHART TO DETERMINE kVAR

Step 1: Finding existing VA
VA = V x √3 x A
VA = 208 V x 1.732 x 273 A (360 V x 273 A)
VA = 98,280

Step 2: Applying existing PF; Finding Watts
W = VA x PF
W = 98,280 x 65%
W = 63,882

Step 3: Applying multiplier in chart to find kVAR
kvar = 63,882 W ÷ 1000 x .878
kvar = 56.09

Solution: **It will take 56.09 kVAR to correct the power factor.**

USING FORMULA TO DETERMINE MICROFARADS

$$\mu f = \frac{159,300}{hertz} \times \frac{amps}{volts}$$

For example: The microfarads of a 15 HP, 208-volt, three-phase motor pulling 46.2 amps can be found by the following procedures.

Step 1: $\mu f = \dfrac{159,300}{hertz} \times \dfrac{amps}{volts}$

$\mu f = \dfrac{159,300}{60} \times \dfrac{46.2\ A}{208\ V \times 1.732}$

$\mu f = 340$

Solution: **340 µf**

Note: See **page 20-13** for a similar calculation.

USING CHARTS

Figure 15-9. The kVAR is selected from the capacitor calculating chart based on the existing power factor of the motor, and the existing VA is multiplied by this value to correct power factor problems. The procedure for determining microfarads for a smaller capacitor is also shown. (Also, see **Figure 20-18** in this book.)

REVERSING DIRECTION

Reversing the direction of a capacitor-start motor can be achieved by reversing the flow of current through the running or starting winding or the cpapcitor. If the flow of current in the starting winding and running winding are the same, the rotor will rotate in a counterclockwise direction. If the current flow of the starting and running winding is in opposite directions, the rotor will rotate in a clockwise direction. **(See Figure 15-10)**

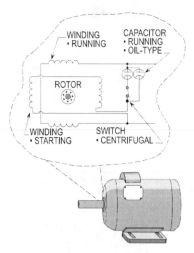

CAPACITOR START-AND-RUN MOTORS

Figure 15-11. Starting torque can be increased by providing a properly sized capacitor.

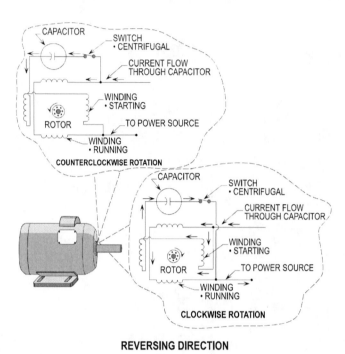

Figure 15-10. The rotation of a rotor is determined by the direction of current flow through the capacitor and windings in the motor. (For motor without capacitors, see page 15-3 in this book.)

CAPACITOR START-AND-RUN MOTORS

In capacitor start-and-run motors, the capacitor is utilized during starting and remains in operation during running. The capacitor start-and-run motor is quiet and smooth-running. It is similar to the capacitor-start motor, except that the starting winding and capacitor are connected in the circuit at all times. The capacitor is connected in series with the starting winding and is connected in parallel with the running winding.

A high starting torque is provided with a capacitor start motor. When the motor reaches its running speed, the centrifugal switch opens the circuit and drops out the starting capacitor. The running capacitor is left in the running circuit to provide a higher running torque and improve the running power factor while the motor is in operation. **(See Figure 15-11)**

REVERSING DIRECTION

To reverse the rotation of a capacitor start-and-run motor, the terminal cover must be removed and the leads of the starting or running winding must be reversed. Reversing switches may also be used. **(See Figure 15-10)**

PERMANENT SPLIT-CAPACITOR MOTORS

Permanent split-capacitor motors are similar in all respects to the capacitor-start motor except that they do not contain a centrifugal switch.

By checking the resistance of the starting and running winding, the windings of a permanent split-capacitor motor can be identified. **(See Figure 15-2)** These motors are commonly called *single-value motors.* The low value of the capacitor results in a motor of medium starting torque. Consequently, this motor can only be used for oil burners, voltage regulators, fans, etc. **(See Figure 15-12)**

REVERSING DIRECTION

Permanent split-capacitor motors may be reversed by reversing the terminal leads or by using a reversing switch. However, most permanent split-capacitor motors are used in equipment, such as fans and blower motors, that requires a reversing switch. **(See Figure 15-13)**

SHADED-POLE MOTORS

The trailing edge of each pole for a shaded-pole motor is wound with a shaded coil. Torque is provided to start and run

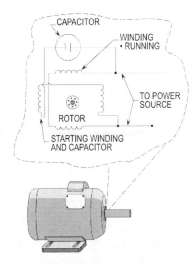

PERMANENT SPLIT-CAPACITOR MOTORS

Figure 15-12. A centrifugal switch is not required for permanent split-capacitor motors. The capacitor is never moved from the circuit.

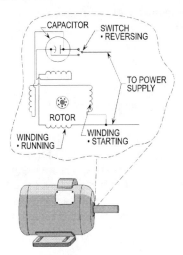

REVERSING DIRECTION

Figure 15-13. A reversing switch is used to reverse a permanent split-capacitor motor.

the load when the shaded coil produces a slip. Equipment that requires a high starting torque cannot be operated with shaded-pole motors. Shaded-pole motors provide a very low starting torque. Each field pole is cut with a slot containing the shaded coil. The coil forms a closed circuit (loop) with the running windings wound around each field pole. **(See Figure 15-14)**

A magnetic field is set up between the poles and the rotor when power is applied to the running windings. An out-of-phase condition is created with the flux lines when the shaded coil cuts through a portion of the magnetic field. A two-phase magnetic field is then created, and the phase shifting provides the torque needed to start and rotate the driven equipment. **(See Figure 15-15)**

Additional starting torque is provided for shaded pole motors by using a high-resistance rotor. A higher slip and poor speed regulation is created by using a high-resistance rotor. Shaded pole motors are available for 115 volt, 230 volt, and dual-voltage operation.

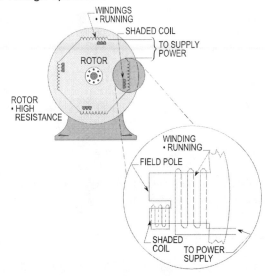

SHADED-POLE MOTORS

Figure 15-14. The shaded coil of a shaded-pole motor forms a closed (loop) circuit with the running windings.

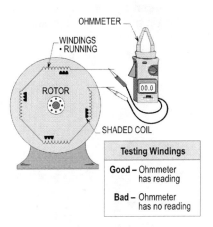

SHADED-POLE MOTORS

Figure 15-15. The resistance of the winding in a shaded pole motor is measured by an ohmmeter.

REVERSING DIRECTION

Shaded-pole motors can be reversed:

(1) by placing the rotor in the motor housing in the opposite direction.

(2) by two sets of field windings used with each shaded coil.

(3) by a switch that can open or close the circuit to the correct windings for the direction of rotation. The rotor will always rotate toward the shaded coil. **(See Figure 15-16)**

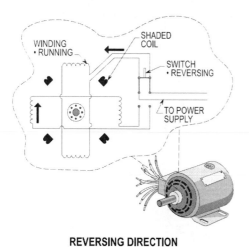

REVERSING DIRECTION

Figure 15-16. Two sets of field (running) windings are used to reverse shaded-pole motors.

REGULATING SPEEDS

A shaded-pole motor can have different speeds that are provided by tapping a coil.

For example, a coil can be used to provide three speeds: low (L), medium (M), and high (H). Low speed is produced by tapping all the windings. Medium speed is produced by tapping half of the windings. High speed is produced by tapping none of the windings. **(See Figure 15-17)**

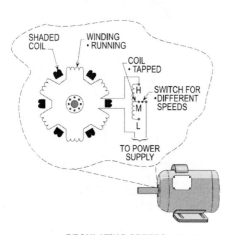

REGULATING SPEEDS

Figure 15-17. Different speeds for shaded-pole motors are obtained from a tapped coil.

A multiple (six) winding provides two motor speeds with the windings located in separate slots. The same size wire is used for five of the windings, while smaller wire with more turns is used for the sixth winding. When all six windings are used in the motor, the motor has a low-speed operation. When only five of the windings are used, the motor has a high-speed operation. **(See Figure 15-18)**

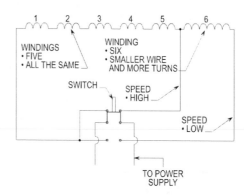

REGULATING SPEEDS

Figure 15-18. When all six windings are used in the motor, the motor has a low-speed operation. When only five of the windings are used in the motor, the motor has a high-speed operation.

UNIVERSAL MOTORS

A universal motor is one that can be operated on either direct current or single-phase alternating current at approximately the same speed. All windings are series-connected, and the motor has high starting torque and a variable speed characteristic. They are usually designed and built in sizes varying from 1/150 to 3/4 HP but are obtainable in much larger sizes for special applications.

Universal motors are equipped with field windings and an armature with brushes and a commutator. The commutator keeps the armature turning through the magnetic field of the field windings. It also changes the flow of current in relation to the field windings and armature so there is a push-and-pull action. This push-and-pull action is created by the north and south poles of the field windings and armature. **(See Figures 15-19 and 15-20)**

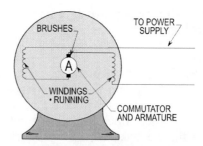

UNIVERSAL MOTORS

Figure 15-19. Universal motors are equipped with field windings and an armature with brushes and a commutator.

The north pole of the field windings pulls the south pole of the armature (loop) into the main strength of the magnetic field (field force). The commutator and brushes reverse the current flow through the armature, creating a north pole in the loop. The north pole of the field winding then repels the north pole of the armature. This push-and-pull action rotates the armature through the magnetic field of the field windings, establishing motor operation.

When the universal motor operates on AC voltage, the current is constantly changing direction in the field windings. Both the armature and field windings have their current reversed simultaneously. Therefore, the motor operates similar to an inductive motor. The field windings of a universal motor are connected in series with the brushes and armature. **(See Figure 15-20)**

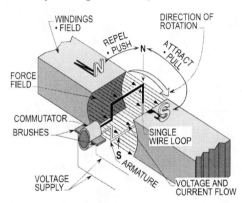

UNIVERSAL MOTORS

Figure 15-20. The above illustrates a simple universal motor with all of its parts.

REVERSING DIRECTION

Changing the flow of current through the armature by interchanging the leads on the terminals or using a reversing switch will reverse the rotation of the motor.

REGULATING SPEED

Resistance determines the speed of a motor. The higher the resistance, the lower the speed. By using a variable resistor, the speed of a universal motor can be controlled.

To obtain three speeds, one of the field windings must be tapped. For slow speed, tap all of the winding. For medium speed, half of the winding, and for fast speed, the entire winding is bypassed. **(See Figure 15-21)**

REPULSION MOTORS

Repulsion motors are divided into three distinct classifications. The following are the types of repulsion motors:

   (1) Standard repulsion,

   (2) Repulsion-start induction, and

   (3) Repulsion-induction.

These classifications are often confused because of the similarity of the names. But each is different and has its own characteristics and applications. However, one feature common to all is that each has a rotor containing a winding that is connected to a commutator. These motors generally operate from a single-phase lighting or power circuit, depending on the size of the motor.

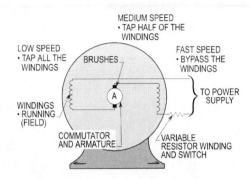

Figure 15-21. The above illustrates that high resistance in a circuit is used for slower motor speeds and low resistance in a circuit is used for higher motor speeds. Resistance is produced by using a variable resistor.

STANDARD REPULSION MOTORS

The standard repulsion motor is a single-phase motor, often called an inductive series motor. It starts and runs on the induction principle and is a varying-speed type of motor. This motor is a brush-riding type and does not have any centrifugal mechanism. It starts and runs on the repulsion principle. **(See Figure 15-22)**

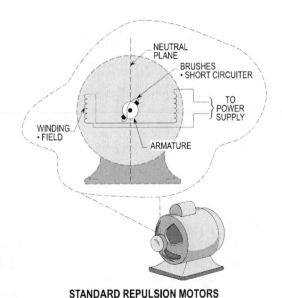

STANDARD REPULSION MOTORS

Figure 15-22. A standard repulsion motor has field windings and a wound rotor with brushes and a commutator.

REPULSION-START INDUCTION MOTORS

The repulsion-start induction motor and the standard repulsion motor's starting procedures are the same, but at a predetermined speed, a special device is actuated that short circuits all the commutator windings. From this point on, the motor operates as a single-phase induction motor. This device is typically called a *short circuiter*.

Since an induction motor functions on the magnetic induction principle, where fields of both the stator and armature rotate in the same direction, the higher the speed at which the *short circuiter* operates, the less line current is drawn by the motor. **(See Figure 15-23)**

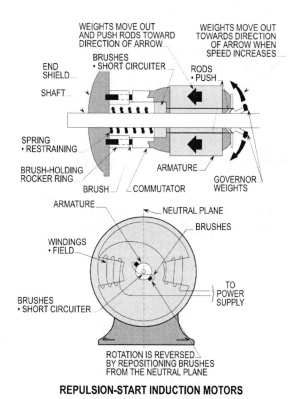

REPULSION-START INDUCTION MOTORS

Figure 15-23. A repulsion-start induction motor develops a centrifugal force which operates the short circuiter and brush-lifting mechanisms to cause a normal induction motor operation.

REPULSION-INDUCTION MOTORS

As in the standard and repulsion-start induction motor, the repulsion-inductor motor has the same starting principle, but no mechanism is included in its construction. It instead combines a repulsion and squirrel-cage winding in its armature. Both windings are always in operation while the armature rotates. **(See Figure 15-24)**

All starting torque is provided by the repulsion winding. However, once the armature begins its rotation, the voltage induced in the squirrel-cage winding produces some torque within its winding.

The characteristics of the repulsion-induction motor are very similar to that of the standard type. Direction of rotation and setting of the neutral are the same. In fact, it is sometimes difficult to differentiate between the two. An easy way to determine the difference is to remove the load, start the motor, and then remove the brushes. If the motor continues to run, it is a repulsion-induction type motor.

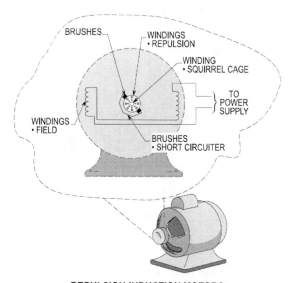

REPULSION-INDUCTION MOTORS

Figure 15-24. A repulsion-induction motor has a squirrel-cage rotor with a wound armature and a commutator with short circuiter brushes.

REVERSING ROTATION

A repulsion motor is reversed by shifting the brush holder to either side of the neutral position. Its speed can be decreased by moving the brush holder further away from the neutral position. **(See Figure 15-25)**

THREE-PHASE MOTORS

Three-phase motors vary from fractional horsepower sizes to several thousand horsepower ratings. These motors have a fairly constant speed characteristic and are made in designs giving a variety of torque characteristics. They are made for practically every standard voltage and frequency and are almost always dual-voltage motors.

The operating principles of a two-phase motor apply to the three-phase motor. For the three-phase motor, however, the generated magnetic fields are 120 degrees out-of-phase with each other. An additional starting winding is not required for three-phase motors to start and run. An induction motor will always have a peak phase of current. This is due to alternating current reversing its direction of flow. In other words, when the alternating current of one phase reverses its direction of flow, a peak current will be developed on one phase and as current reverses direction again, a second phase will peak, etc. Three-phase motors provide a smooth and continuous source of power once they are started and driving their load. Three-phase motors are used to drive machine tools, pumps, elevators, fans, hoists, and many other machines. **(See Figure 15-26)**

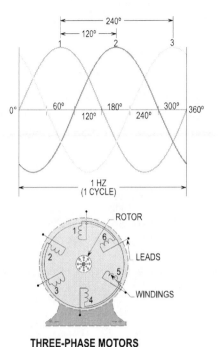

THREE-PHASE MOTORS

Figure 15-26. Voltage from 2 to 1 is 120° behind 1 and voltage from 3 to 1 is 240° behind 1.

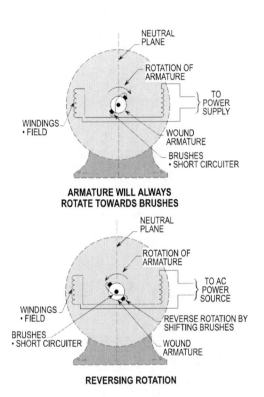

ARMATURE WILL ALWAYS ROTATE TOWARDS BRUSHES

REVERSING ROTATION

Figure 15-25. The armature of a repulsion motor always rotates toward the position of the short circuiter brushes from the neutral plane.

SQUIRREL-CAGE INDUCTION MOTORS

A squirrel-cage motor is an induction motor and is so called because of its construction. The rotating (stator) magnetic field induces voltages in the rotor which in turn cause the rotor to turn. The rotor consists of an iron core mounted on a concentric shaft. Copper or brass bars run the entire length of this core and are set into slots on the core. At each end of the core, end rings are welded to the copper or brass bars so that a complete short circuit exists within the rotor. The entire assembly resembles the type of cage within which squirrels, etc. are placed to run through various tests. In effect, the rotor acts as the secondary winding of the transformer while the stator acts as the primary winding. **(See Figure 15-27)**

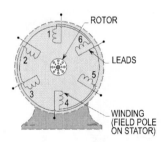

SQUIRREL-CAGE INDUCTION MOTORS

Figure 15-27. The above illustrates a stator (field poles) and a rotor equipped in a squirrel-cage motor.

CONNECTING LEADS

All three-phase motors are wound with a number of coils that are placed in slots in the stator. These coils are connected to produce three separate windings called phases, and each must have the same number of coils. The number of coils in each must be one-third the total number of coils in the stator. Therefore, if a three-phase motor has 36 coils, each phase will have 12 coils. These phases are listed as phase 1, phase 2, and phase 3.

All three-phase motors have their phases arranged in either a wye, which is sometimes called a star connection (⅄), or a delta, which is sometimes called a triangle connection (Δ). Either of these connections are connected so that only three leads come from the stator, making the line connections very simple.

SIX-LEAD MOTORS

The windings of a motor can be designed with six leads to connect the windings to the three-phase supply. A six-lead motor used for a delta connection has the winding leads connected so that 1 and 2 close one end of the delta (triangle), 5 and 6 close one end of the delta, and 3 and 4 close one end of the delta to form a closed-delta connection of the motor windings. **(See Figure 15-28)**

The six leads can be wye-connected with one lead for each winding being connected to form the wye or star connection. The three remaining leads are connected to the three-phase supply lines L_1, L_2, and L_3. **(See Figure 15-29)**

Note, delta-connected windings in a motor will most always run cooler than windings connected in a wye configuration.

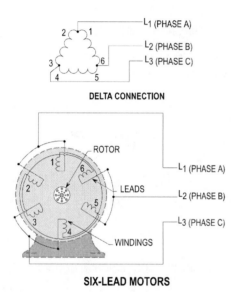

DELTA CONNECTION

SIX-LEAD MOTORS

Figure 15-28. The above illustrates a six-lead squirrel-cage induction motor with internal windings connected for delta operation.

NINE-LEAD MOTORS

The windings of a motor can be designed with nine leads to connect the windings to the three-phase supply. The nine leads are connected to the internal windings for delta operation. A closed delta is formed by connecting six internal windings together. The three windings are marked 1-4-9, 2-5-7, and 3-6-8. A nine-lead motor is used to operate as a closed-delta system with the windings connected for single- or dual-voltage operation. **(See Figure 15-30)**

The nine leads can be wye-connected with three leads of its windings, which are connected to form a wye with three remaining leads (7-8-9). The three remaining windings are

numbered 1-4, 2-5, and 3-6. The windings are connected to operate on low or high voltage. Windings are connected in parallel for low voltage and in series for high voltage. This type of connection applies for either wye- or delta-connected windings. **(See Figure 15-31)**

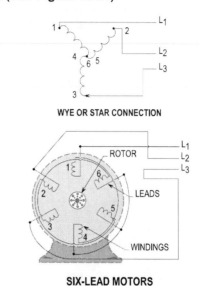

WYE OR STAR CONNECTION

SIX-LEAD MOTORS

Figure 15-29. The above illustrates a six-lead squirrel-cage induction motor with internal windings connected for wye operation.

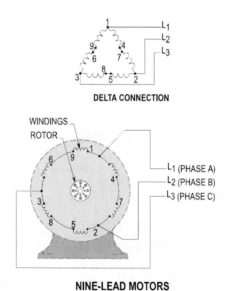

DELTA CONNECTION

NINE-LEAD MOTORS

Figure 15-30. The above illustrates a nine-lead squirrel-cage induction motor with internal windings connected for delta operation.

REVERSING DIRECTION

By interchanging any two of the three-phase leads, the rotation can be reversed for any three-phase squirrel-cage induction motor. Using windings 1, 2, and 3 as a reference, the 3 winding will follow the 2 winding rather than the 1 winding. The rotating field will rotate in the opposite direction when reversing the polarity through the windings, carrying the rotor with it. **(See Figure 15-32)**

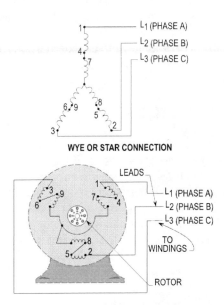

WYE OR STAR CONNECTION

NINE-LEAD MOTORS

Figure 15-31. The above illustrates a nine-lead squirrel-cage induction motor with internal windings connected for wye operation. (For single-phase motors, see **Figure 15-3**.)

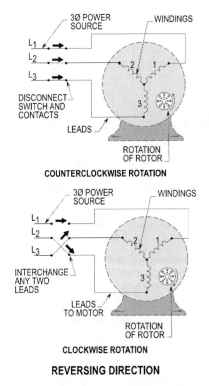

COUNTERCLOCKWISE ROTATION

CLOCKWISE ROTATION

REVERSING DIRECTION

Figure 15-32. By interchanging any two leads of a three-phase squirrel-cage induction motor, the rotation is reversed.

REGULATING SPEED

The speed of a squirrel-cage motor depends upon the following four conditions:

    (1) Load,

    (2) Applied voltage,

    (3) Frequency, and

    (4) Number of poles within the stator.

In the squirrel-cage motor, we are interested in the amount, in which the rotor speed lags the speed of the rotating field. This difference in speed, called slip, is entirely dependent on the load. The greater the load, the greater the amount of slip, and the slower the speed of the rotor. However, this slip is such a small fraction of the synchronous speed that the squirrel-cage motor is used widely as a constant-speed type.

Because of their constant-speed characteristics, squirrel-cage motors are more often used in items such as larger types of fans, conveyor-belt applications, presses, etc.

SYNCHRONOUS MOTORS

Synchronous motors are available in a wide range of sizes and types that are designed to run at synchronous speeds. The following are two types of synchronous motors that are available:

    (1) Nonexcited

    (2) Direct-current excited

A DC source of excitation is required. The torque required to turn the rotor for a synchronous motor is produced when the DC current of the rotor field locks in with the magnetic field of the stator AC current. **(See Figure 15-33)**

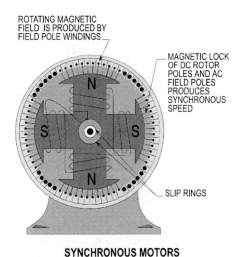

SYNCHRONOUS MOTORS

Figure 15-33. The torque required to turn the rotor of a synchronous motor is produced when the DC current of the rotor field locks in with the magnetic field of the stator AC current. **(See Figure 16-4)**

Synchronous motors are made in sizes varying from approximately 20 HP to hundreds of horsepower and are used wherever it is necessary or desirable to obtain constant speed. In many cases, synchronous motors are used to improve the power factor of the electrical system in a plant or factory. Many small synchronous motors are also made for clocks, but they are constructed differently from the larger ones.

STARTING METHOD

The synchronous motor does not start by itself; some kind of starting action must be supplied to bring the rotor up to synchronous speed.

WITH MOTORS

One type of starting method uses another motor – either DC or induction – with a high starting torque. This auxiliary motor brings the synchronous motor almost up to full speed and is automatically disconnected. The synchronous motor comes up to full speed under its own power when DC excitation is applied.

WITH DAMPER WINDINGS

Another method of starting may be provided by adding a common winding to the rotor DC winding. The added winding is an induction type or squirrel-cage construction. The voltage induced in this winding by the rotating stator field produces poles of opposite polarity in the rotor. Opposite poles attracting the rotating magnetic field in the stator provide the necessary starting torque. At some point slightly below synchronous speed, the rotor DC voltage is fed into the rotor, and the motor reaches full operating speed.

WOUND-ROTOR MOTORS

Wound-rotor motors are classified as three-phase induction motors and have two sets of leads. One set is the main leads to the motor windings (stator or field poles), and the other set is the secondary leads to the rotor. The secondary leads are connected to the rotor through the slip rings, while the other ends of the leads are connected through a controller and a bank of resistors.

Wound-rotor motors operate on the same principle as the squirrel-cage induction motor. The major difference is in construction. Where the squirrel-cage motor has copper or brass bars that are permanently short circuited, the wound rotor has insulated windings in their place. These windings are not permanently short circuited.

PRINCIPLES OF STARTING

The starting principle of the wound-rotor motor is identical to that of the squirrel-cage motor, but the wound-rotor is not permanently short circuited; instead, the currents produced in the rotor are fed into slip rings mounted on the end of the rotor. These currents, in turn, are coupled through slip ring brushes (carbon or graphite) into an external control device that is either a variable resistor or a variac – usually the latter.

SPEED REGULATION

Because of the external control, the starting torque, current, operating speed, and acceleration of the motor up to full-load speed can be varied. However, even though it is possible to control the wound-rotor motor's operation, a big disadvantage results. Any loss in motor speed results in a loss of efficiency. Therefore, the wound-rotor motor is used mostly on heavy equipment that requires a high starting torque and smooth acceleration up to full-rated load, or is used where variable speed is essential.

REVERSING DIRECTION

Reversing direction of three-phase motors may be done very simply. The entire procedure consists of disconnecting any two of the three stator leads from the line, interchanging them, and then reconnecting them to the line.

Note, the stator leads are changed to achieve a reversal in rotation.

See Figure 15-34 for a detailed illustration of the parts that make up a wound-rotor motor.

NEMA TYPE ENCLOSURES

Underwriters Laboratories (UL) has defined the requirements for protective enclosures according to the hazardous conditions, and the National Electrical Manufacturers Association (NEMA) has standardized enclosures from these requirements. (See NEMA 250)

The correct selection and installation of an enclosure for a particular application can contribute considerably to the length of life of a motor.

When selecting and installing a motor enclosure, it is always necessary to consider carefully the conditions under which the motor must operate.

Note, there are many applications where a general-purpose enclosure does not afford protection. (See **Table 110.28** in the NEC and NEMA 250.)

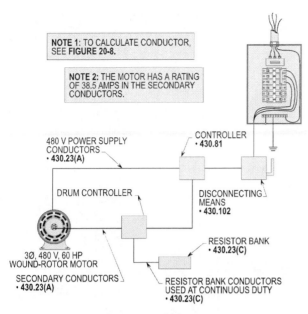

NOTE 1: TO CALCULATE CONDUCTOR, SEE **FIGURE 20-8.**

NOTE 2: THE MOTOR HAS A RATING OF 38.5 AMPS IN THE SECONDARY CONDUCTORS.

CONTROLLER • 430.81

480 V POWER SUPPLY CONDUCTORS • 430.23(A)

DRUM CONTROLLER

DISCONNECTING MEANS • 430.102

RESISTOR BANK • 430.23(C)

3Ø, 480 V, 60 HP WOUND-ROTOR MOTOR

SECONDARY CONDUCTORS • 430.23(A)

RESISTOR BANK CONDUCTORS USED AT CONTINUOUS DUTY • 430.23(C)

WOUND-ROTOR MOTORS

Figure 15-34. The above illustrates the parts of a wound-rotor motor. (One line diagram for simplicity)

NEMA TYPE 1 ENCLOSURES

This enclosure is suitable for general purpose applications indoors where it is not exposed to unusual service conditions. A NEMA 1 enclosure serves as protection against limited falling dirt; dust; and light, indirect splashing water.

NEMA TYPE 2 ENCLOSURES

This enclosure is intended to provide suitable protection against specified weather hazards. A NEMA 2 enclosure is intended for indoor use, primarily to provide a degree of protection against limited amounts of falling water and dirt.

NEMA TYPE 3 ENCLOSURES

This enclosure protects against interference in operation of the contained equipment due to rain and resists damage from exposure to weather. A NEMA 3 enclosure is intended for outdoor use, primarily to provide a degree of protection against rain, sleet, windblown dust, and damage from external ice formation.

NEMA TYPE 3R ENCLOSURES

This enclosure is intended for outdoor use, primarily to provide a degree of protection against rain, sleet, and damage from external ice formation; it must have a drain hole.

NEMA TYPE 3S ENCLOSURES

This enclosure is intended for outdoor use, primarily to provide a degree of protection against rain, sleet, and windblown dust, and to provide for operation of external mechanisms when ice-laden.

NEMA TYPE 4 ENCLOSURES

This enclosure is intended for indoor or outdoor use, primarily to provide a degree of protection against windblown dust and rain, splashing water, hose-directed water, and damage from external ice formation.

NEMA TYPE 4X ENCLOSURES

This enclosure is intended for indoor or outdoor use, primarily to provide a degree of protection against corrosion, windblown dust and rain, splashing water, hose-directed water, and damage from external ice formation.

NEMA TYPE 5 ENCLOSURES

This enclosure is intended for indoor use, primarily to provide a degree of protection against settling airborne dust; falling dirt; and dripping, noncorrosive liquids.

NEMA TYPE 6 ENCLOSURES

This enclosure is intended for indoor or outdoor use, primarily to provide a degree of protection against hose-directed water, the entry of water during occasional temporary submersion at a limited depth, and damage from external ice formation.

NEMA TYPE 6P ENCLOSURES

This enclosure is intended for indoor or outdoor use, primarily to provide a degree of protection against hose-directed water, the entry of water during prolonged submersion at a limited depth, and damage from external ice formation.

NEMA TYPE 7 ENCLOSURES

This enclosure is intended for indoor use in locations that are classified as Class I, Groups A, B, C, or D, as defined in the NEC.

NEMA TYPE 8 ENCLOSURES

This enclosure is for indoor or outdoor use in locations that are classified as Class I, Groups A, B, C, or D, as defined in the NEC.

NEMA TYPE 9 ENCLOSURES

This enclosure is intended for indoor use in locations that are classified as Class II, Groups E, F, and G, as defined in the NEC.

NEMA TYPE 10 ENCLOSURES

This enclosure is constructed to meet the applicable requirements of the Mine Safety and Health Administration.

NEMA TYPE 12 ENCLOSURES

This enclosure is intended for indoor use, primarily to provide a degree of protection against circulating dust; falling dirt; and dripping, noncorrosive liquids.

NEMA TYPE 12K ENCLOSURES

This enclosure, with knockouts, is intended for indoor use, primarily to provide a degree of protection against circulating dust; falling dirt; and dripping, noncorrosive liquids.

NEMA TYPE 13 ENCLOSURES

This enclosure is intended for indoor use, primarily to provide a degree of protection against dust, spraying of water, oil, and noncorrosive coolant.

For more information about enclosures, see the NEMA Standards Publication No. 250, *Enclosures for Electrical Equipment (1000 Volts Maximum)* or other third party certification standards for specific requirements for product construction, testing and performance, such as Underwriters Laboratories Inc.©, Standard UL 50, *Standard for Enclosures for Electrical Equipment* and UL 886 *Outlet Boxes and Fittings for Use in Hazardous (Classified) Locations.*

Note, for enclosures that can be used for motors installed indoors or outdoors, see **Table 110.28** in the NEC and NEMA 250.

Chapter 15: Types of Motors

Section   Answer

1. The torque needed to start turning the load for a split-phase motor is produced
   from the starting windings, which are placed about _____ from the running
   windings.
   (a) 10°   (b) 25°
   (c) 30°   (d) 40°

2. A capacitor motor operates on alternating current and is made in sizes ranging
   from 1/20 HP to _____ HP.
   (a) 1   (b) 3
   (c) 5   (d) 10

3. Older motors are usually tagged _____ and _____ for the running winding.
   (a) M_1, M_2 (b) S_3, S_4
   (c) R_1, R_2 (d) T_1, T_2

4. Older motors are usually tagged _____ and _____ for the starting winding.
   (a) M_1, M_2 (b) S_3, S_4
   (c) R_1, R_2 (d) T_1, T_2

5. Older motors are usually tagged _____ and _____ for the running winding.
   (a) M_1, M_2 (b) S_3, S_4
   (c) R_1, R_2 (d) T_1, T_2

6. Newer motors are typically color coded _____ for T_1.
   (a) black   (b) blue
   (c) red   (d) yellow

7. Newer motors are typically color coded _____ for T_2.
   (a) black   (b) blue
   (c) red   (d) yellow

8. Newer motors are typically color coded _____ for T_3.
   (a) black   (b) blue
   (c) red   (d) yellow

9. Newer motors are typically color coded _____ for T_4.
   (a) black   (b) blue
   (c) red   (d) yellow

10. A capacitor-start motor creates a greater starting torque when a capacitor is
    connected in series with the _____ winding and the centrifugal switch.
    (a) starting   (b) running
    (c) thermal   (d) field

11. In capacitor-start motors, the capacitor causes the current in the starting winding
    to lead, by almost _____, the current in the running winding.
    (a) 30°   (b) 60°
    (c) 75°   (d) 90°

_____ _____ **12.** By checking the _____ of the starting and running winding, the windings of a permanent split capacitor motor can be identified.
    (a) voltage   (b) amperage
    (c) resistance   (d) power

_____ _____ **13.** Shaded-pole motors provide a very low starting _____ .
    (a) slip   (b) torque
    (c) voltage   (d) amperage

_____ _____ **14.** A shaded-pole motor can have different speeds, which are provided by tapping a _____ .
    (a) coil   (b) winding
    (c) rotor   (d) stator

_____ _____ **15.** Universal motors are usually designed and built in sizes varying from 1/150 HP to _____ HP.
    (a) 1/2   (b) 3/4
    (c) 5   (d) 10

_____ _____ **16.** Universal motors are equipped with _____ windings, and an armature with brushes and a commutator.
    (a) starting   (b) running
    (c) thermal   (d) field

_____ _____ **17.** Changing the flow of current through the _____ by interchanging the lead on the terminals will reverse the rotation of an universal motor.
    (a) stator   (b) rotor
    (c) armature   (d) coil

_____ _____ **18.** A standard repulsion motor is a single-phase motor, often called a(n) _____ series motor.
    (a) resistive   (b) reactive
    (c) capacitive   (d) inductive

_____ _____ **19.** A repulsion motor is reversed by shifting the _____ to either side of the neutral position.
    (a) brush holder   (b) armature
    (c) stator   (d) rotor

_____ _____ **20.** All three-phase squirrel-cage motors are wound with a number of _____ which are placed in slots in the stator.
    (a) windings   (b) coils
    (c) brushes   (d) wires

_____ _____ **21.** A six lead motor used for a delta connection has the winding leads connected so that _____ close one end of the delta, _____ close one of the delta, and _____ close one end of the delta to form a closed-delta connection of the motor windings.
    (a) 1 and 3, 2 and 4, 5 and 6   (b) 1 and 6, 2 and 5, 3 and 4
    (c) 1 and 2, 3 and 4, 5 and 6   (d) 1 and 4, 2 and 5, 3 and 6

_____ _____ **22.** Wound-rotor motors are classified as three-phase induction motors and have _____ sets of leads.
    (a) 2   (b) 3
    (c) 6   (d) 9

23. A NEMA _____ enclosure serves as protection against limited falling dirt, dust, and light indirect splashing water.
    (a) 1   (b) 3
    (c) 4   (d) 5

24. A NEMA _____ enclosure is intended for outdoor use, primarily to provide a degree of protection against rain, sleet, windblown dust, and damage from external ice formation.
    (a) 1   (b) 3
    (c) 4   (d) 5

25. A NEMA _____ enclosure is intended for indoor use, primarily to provide a degree of protection against settling airborne dust, falling dirt, and dripping noncorrosive liquids.
    (a) 1   (b) 3
    (c) 4   (d) 5

16

Design Letters and Code Letters

Motor circuits shall be designed to provide protection for motor windings and components when motors are starting, running, and driving loads. Motor windings are protected by overcurrent protection devices that are selected according to the type of motor that is used, based on the amount of starting current required. Overcurrent protection devices shall be sized by percentages based on the type of motor, starting method, design, or code letter. Starting methods shall be selected based on the amount of current required to start and run the motor or the amount that is to be reduced by utilizing a starting method.

This chapter adresses these motors and their many different characteristics and why it is sometimes desirable to choose one over the other, based on the requirements of the driven load or equipment.

TYPES OF MOTORS
TABLE 430.52(C)(1)

The following are five types of motors to be considered when sizing overcurrent protection devices to allow motors to start and run:

(1) Single-phase AC squirrel-cage,

(2) Three-phase AC squirrel-cage,

(3) Wound-rotor,

(4) Synchronous, and

(5) DC.

SINGLE-PHASE AC SQUIRREL-CAGE MOTORS

Squirrel-cage motors are known in the electrical industry as induction motors. An induction motor operates on the same principles as the primary and secondary windings of a transformer. When power energizes the field windings, they serve as the primary by inducing voltage into the rotor that serves as the secondary windings. Squirrel-cage motors have two windings on the stator: one winding is the run winding, and the other is the starting winding. This additional starting winding on the stator is required for split-phase, single-phase, induction motors to have the capacity to start and run. The starting winding has a higher resistance to ground than the running winding, which creates a phase displacement between the two windings. It is this phase displacement between the two windings that gives split-phase motors the power to start.

The phase displacement is about 18 to 30 degrees in angular phase displacement, which provides enough starting torque (twist or force) to start the motor. The motor operates on the running winding when the rotor starts turning and has established a running speed at about 75 to 80 percent of the motor's synchronous speed. The starting winding is disconnected by a centrifugal switch that is installed in the circuit of the starting winding. **(See Figure 16-1)**

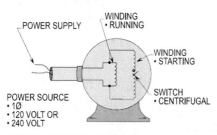

SINGLE-PHASE AC SQUIRREL-CAGE MOTORS

Figure 16-1. The above is an example of a single-phase AC squirrel-cage motor that is listed in **Table 430.52(C)(1)** and **Table 430.248. (See Figure 15-1)**

THREE-PHASE AC SQUIRREL-CAGE MOTORS

Three-phase AC squirrel-cage motors have three separate windings per pole on the stator that generates magnetic fields that are 120 degrees out-of-phase with each other. An additional starting winding is not required for three-phase motors to start and run. An induction motor will always have a peak phase of current. This is due to alternating current reversing its direction of flow. In other words, when alternating current of one phase reverses its direction of flow, a peak current will be developed on one phase and, as current reverses direction again, a second phase will peak,

etc. Three-phase motors provide a smooth and continuous source of power once they are started and driving the load. **(See Figure 16-2)**

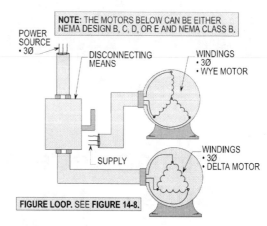

THREE-PHASE AC SQUIRREL-CAGE MOTORS

Figure 16-2. The above is an example of a three-phase AC squirrel-cage motor that is listed in **Table 430.52(C)(1)** and **Table 430.250.**

WOUND-ROTOR MOTORS

Wound-rotor motors are classified as three-phase induction motors. They are similar in design to squirrel-cage induction motors. Wound-rotor motors are three-phase motors that have two sets of leads. One set is the main leads to the motor windings (field poles) and the other set is the secondary leads to the rotor. The secondary leads are connected to the rotor through the slip rings, while the other ends of the leads are connected through a controller and a bank or resistors. The speed of the motor varies with the amount of resistance added in the motor circuit. The rotor will turn slower when the resistance is greater in the rotor, and vice versa. The resistance may be incorporated in the controller, or the resistor banks may be separate from the motor. **(See Figure 16-3)**

SYNCHRONOUS MOTORS

The following are two types of synchronous motors that are available:

(1) Nonexcited and

(2) Direct-current excited.

Synchronous motors are available in a wide range of sizes and types that are designed to run at designed speeds. A DC source is required to excite a DC-excited synchronous motor. The torque required to turn the rotor for a synchronous motor is produced when the DC current of the rotor field locks in with the magnetic field of the stator AC current. **(See Figure 16-4)**

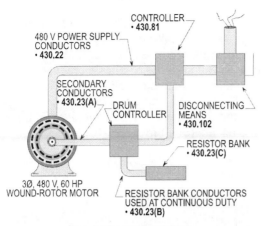

WOUND-ROTOR MOTORS

Figure 16-3. The above is an example of a three-phase wound-rotor motor that is listed in **Table 430.52(C)(1)** and **Table 430.250.**

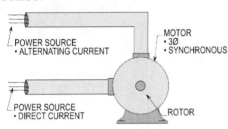

SYNCHRONOUS MOTORS

Figure 16-4. The above is an example of a three-phase synchronous motor that is listed in **Table 430.52(C)(1)** and **Table 430.250. (See Figure 15-33)**

DC MOTORS

Direct current only is used to operate DC related motors. A DC motor is designed with two main parts:

(1) The stator and

(2) The rotor.

The stationary frame of the motor is called the stator. The armature mounted on the drive shaft is known as the rotor. By applying direct current to the rotor, the speed may be adjusted for a DC motor that drives the driven load at a specific speed. **(See Figure 16-5)**

SERIES DC MOTORS

A very high starting torque of 300 to 375 percent of the full-load torque is provided when using series DC motors. Loads that are required to be driven with high torque and low speed regulate use of this type of motor. Depending on the load requirements, the speed varies. Series DC motors are used in installations such as traction work, where the speed varies depending on the load on the hoist. The armature and fields are connected in series. **(See Figure 16-6)**

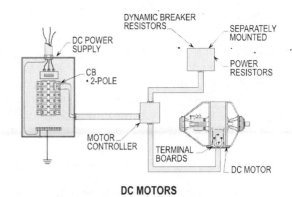

DC MOTORS

Figure 16-5. The above is an example of a DC motor that is listed in **Table 430.52(C)(1)** and **Table 430.247.**

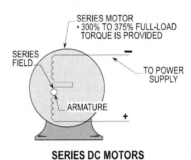

SERIES DC MOTORS

Figure 16-6. A series DC motor has a very high starting torque of 300 to 375 percent of the full-load torque.

SHUNT DC MOTORS

A high torque of 125 to 200 percent of the full-load torque is provided when using shunt DC motors. Loads that are required to be driven with constant or adjustable speeds and loads that do not require high starting torque use this type of motor. Loads such as woodworking machines, printing presses, and papermaking machines use shunt DC motors. **(See Figure 16-7)**

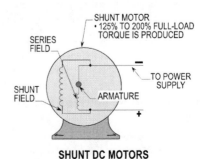

SHUNT DC MOTORS

Figure 16-7. A shunt DC motor provides a medium starting torque of 125 to 200 percent of the full-load torque.

COMPOUND DC MOTORS

A high torque of 180 to 260 percent of the full-load torque is provided when using compound DC motors. A fairly constant speed is obtained when using this type of motor. The compound DC motor is equipped with a series winding and shunt winding. A series winding is connected in series with the armature and the shunt winding is connected in parallel with the armature. This type of motor has the characteristics of both a series and shunt motor during operation. Loads such as crushers, reciprocating compressors, and punch presses use compound DC motors. **(See Figure 16-8)**

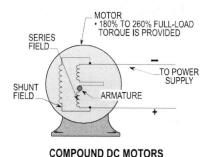

COMPOUND DC MOTORS

Figure 16-8. A compound DC motor provides a high torque of 180 to 260 percent of the full-load torque.

CALCULATING TORQUE

To accelerate and drive a piece of equipment, the motor must be capable of producing a torque. *Torque* is the turning or twisting force of the motor and is measured in foot-pounds or pound-feet.

FULL-LOAD TORQUE

The full-load torque of a motor is determined by dividing the horsepower times 5252, and dividing by the rpm of the motor.

> **Motor Tip:** The value of 5252 is found by dividing 33,000 foot-pounds per minute by 6.2831853 (33,000 ÷ 6.2831853 = 5252), which is found by multiplying π (3.14159265) by 2. **(See Figure 16-9)**

STARTING TORQUE

The starting torque of a motor varies with the classification of the motor. Motors are classified by NEMA as Design B, C, or D motors. These types of standardized motors are the most-used motors in the electrical industry. Other types of motors classified by NEMA are Design F or G motors.

A different rotor design is offered for each class of motor, which will create a different value of starting torque. A different value of torque, speed, current, and slip to start and drive the various types of loads is produced when using Design B, C, or D motors classified by NEMA. The design motor to be selected and used depends on the starting torque of the driven load and the running torque required to drive the load. **(See Figure 16-10)**

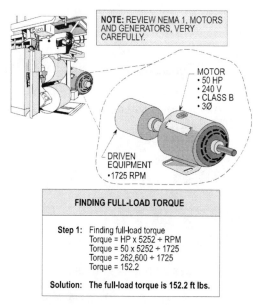

Figure 16-9. To find the full-load torque of a motor, multiply the horsepower rating times 5252 and divide by RPMs.

CLASS B MOTORS

The most-used motors in the electrical industry are Class B design motors.

For example, the starting torque of an induction motor will increase by 150 percent of the full-load torque when using Class B design motors. The starting torque of an induction motor is usually increased by less than 150 percent by most designers when using Class B motors to start and run loads. **(See Figure 16-10)**

CLASS C MOTORS

The starting torque of a squirrel-cage induction motor will increase about 225 percent of the full-load torque when using Class C design motors. However, to keep from overloading the starting torque of a motor, designers will often load a motor to a value less than 225 percent. **(See Figure 16-10)**

For example: What is the full-load torque and starting torque of a 40 HP, Class C design induction motor operating at 1725 RPM?

Step 1: Finding full-load torque
Torque = HP x 5252 ÷ RPM
Torque = 40 x 5252 ÷ 1725
Torque = 210,080 ÷ 1725
Torque = 121.8 ft lbs

Step 2: Finding starting torque
Full-load torque increased by 225%
Torque = 121.8 ft lbs x 225%
Torque = 274.05 ft lbs

Solution: The full-load torque is 122 ft lbs and the starting torque is 274 ft lbs.

For example: What is the full-load torque and starting torque of a 50 HP, Class D design induction motor operating at 1725 RPM?

Step 1: Finding full-load torque
Torque = HP x 5252 ÷ RPM
Torque = 50 x 5252 ÷ 1725
Torque = 262,600 ÷ 1725
Torque = 152.2 ft lbs

Step 2: Finding starting torque
Full-load current increased by 275%
Torque = 152.2 ft lbs x 275%
Torque = 418.6 ft lbs

Solution: The full-load torque is 152.2 ft lbs and the starting torque is 418.6 ft lbs.

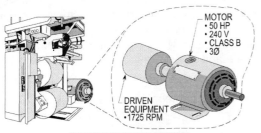

MOTOR	PERCENTAGE
B	150%
C	225%
D	275%

FINDING STARTING TORQUE

Step 1: Finding starting torque
Torque = HP x 5252 ÷ RPM
Torque = 50 x 5252 ÷ 1725
Torque = 262,600 ÷ 1725
Torque = 152.2

Step 2: Increasing torque by 150% for Class B
Torque = 152.2 x 150%
Torque = 228.3

Solution: The starting torque required is 228.3 ft lbs.

STARTING TORQUE

Figure 16-10. To find the starting torque of a motor (Class B, C, or D design), the full-load torque is multiplied by the percentages of the proper motor design letter.

CLASS D MOTORS

The starting torque of a squirrel-cage induction motor is increased about 275 percent of the full-load torque when using Class D design motors. However, to keep from overloading the starting torque of a motor, designers will often load a motor to a value less than 275 percent. **(See Figure 16-10)**

CLASS E AND NEMA B MOTORS

When designing and installing a high-efficiency motor, it is most important to know the starting and running torque of the load. The difference between the nominal and the minimum efficiency must also be determined. The motor must be sized to start and drive the load.

STARTING CURRENTS

Most high-efficiency motors do have higher starting currents and this presents a real problem where a standard motor is replaced with a high-efficiency motor. Nuisance tripping of the overcurrent protection device can occur during full-voltage start up. **[See Figures 14-7 and 18-12(c)]**

There are some high-efficiency motors that have starting currents as high as 1500 percent of the full-load current. If 1700 percent per **430.52(C)(3)(b)(2)b** does not permit the motor to start and run, reduced voltage starting or use of modern electronic types of motor start/run technologies must be utilized.

Note, starting currents of high-efficiency motors vary based on manufacturer and size. High-efficiency motors must be selected with enough starting torque and break-down torque to start and run the driven loads.

The nameplate on most motors will list the starting and running kVA of the motor. It is from these values and the manufacturer data that the overcurrent protection device and conductors shall be sized. The motor should be loaded based on the minimum efficiency and not the motor's nominal efficiency.

Note, a high-efficiency motor is equipped on its nameplate with a nominal and minimum efficiency full-load rating.

TWO-SPEED MOTORS

The full-load torque of a motor is determined by the RPM of the motor. A motor turning at 1800 RPM produces less torque than motor turning at 1200 RPM.

For example: What is the full-load torque for a two-speed motor, 30 HP motor operating at either 1200 RPM or 1800 RPM?

Step 1: Finding full-load torque (1200)
Torque = HP x 5252 ÷ RPM
Torque = 30 x 5252 ÷ 1200
Torque = 157,560 ÷ 1200
Torque = 131.3 ft lbs

Step 2: Finding full-load torque (1800)
Torque = HP x 5252 ÷ RPM
Torque = 30 x 5252 ÷ 1800
Torque = 157,560 ÷ 1800
Torque = 87.5 ft lbs

Solution: The full-load torque for 1200 RPM is 131.3 ft lbs and the full-load torque for 1800 RPM is 87.5 ft lbs

---

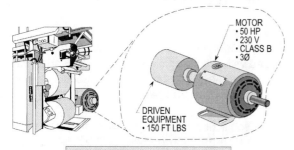

MOTOR
• 50 HP
• 230 V
• CLASS B
• 3Ø

DRIVEN EQUIPMENT
• 150 FT LBS

FINDING RESISTOR STARTING TORQUE

Step 1: Finding resistor starting torque
Torque = HP x 5252 ÷ RPM
Torque = 50 x 5252 ÷ 1725
Torque = 262,600 ÷ 1725
Torque = 152.2

Step 2: Increasing 150% for Class B
Torque = 152.2 x 150%
Torque = 228.3

Step 3: Reducing 42% for starting torque
Torque = 228.3 x 42%
Torque = 95.9

Solution: The reduced starting torque of 95.9 ft lbs for resistor starting will not start the driven load at 150 ft lbs.

RESISTOR- OR REACTOR-REDUCED STARTING

Figure 16-11. Resistor or reactor starting used to reduce the starting torque of a motor.

RESISTOR- OR REACTOR-REDUCED STARTING

To reduce the inrush starting current (LRC) of a motor, a resistor- or reactor-reduced starting method can be used. The starting current is reduced to 65 percent by using either method. The starting torque will be reduced to 42 percent (65% x 65% = 42%) if the starting current is reduced. When selecting a reduced starting method, care must be taken to ensure that enough foot-pounds are provided to accelerate the load. **(See Figure 16-11)**

CODE LETTERS
TABLES 430.7(B) AND 430.251

Code letters are installed on motors by manufacturers for calculating the locked-rotor current (LRC) in amps based upon the kVA per horsepower that is selected from the motor's code letter. Overcurrent protection devices shall be set above the locked-rotor current of the motor to prevent the overcurrent protection device from opening when the rotor of the motor is starting. The following two methods can be used to calculate and select the locked-rotor current of motors:

(1) Utilizing code letters to determine LRC and

(2) Utilizing horsepower to determine LRC.

UTILIZING CODE LETTERS TO FIND LRC 430.7(B) AND TABLE 430.7(B)

Code letters shall be marked on the nameplate, and such letters are used for designing locked-rotor current. Locked-rotor current for code letters is listed in **Table 430.7(B)** in kVA (kilovolt-amps) per horsepower, based on a particular code letter.

For example: What is the locked-rotor current rating for a three-phase, 208 volt, 20 horsepower motor with a code letter B marked on the nameplate of the motor?

Step 1: Finding LRC amps
Table 430.7(B)
A = (kVA per HP x 1000) ÷ (V x 1.732)
A = (3.54 x 20 x 1000) ÷ (208 V x 1.732)
A = 70,800 ÷ 360 V
A = 197

Solution: The locked-rotor current is 197 amps. Table 430.7(B) must be used to find LRCs of motors, based on their code letters per 1996 NEC and earlier editions.

LOCKED-ROTOR CURRENT UTILIZING HORSEPOWER TABLES 430.251(A) AND (B)

The locked-rotor current of a motor may be found in **Tables 430.251(A)** and **(B)**. The locked-rotor current for single-phase and three-phase motors is selected from one of these tables based upon the phases, voltage, and horsepower rating of the motor. For motors with code letters A through G, round the nameplate current in amps up to an even number (unit of ten) and multiply by 6 to obtain the LRC of the motor.

Note, code letters are not found in **Tables 430.251(A)** and **(B)**; they are listed on the motor's nameplate. Motors will be marked either as Design B, C, D, or E to indicate which locked-rotor currents are to be selected from **Tables 430.251(A)** and **(B)** based on horsepower, phases, and voltages. For motor code letters, see **Table 430.7(B)**.

For example: What is the locked-rotor current rating for a three-phase, 460 volt, 50 horsepower, Design B motor?

Table Method Using Design Letter

Step 1: Finding LRC amps
Table 430.251(B)
50 HP requires 363 A

Solution: The locked-rotor current is 363 amps.

For example: What is the locked-rotor current of a motor with a nameplate current of 63 amps, based upon code letters A through G?

Rule of Thumb Method Using Code Letter

Step 1: Finding even number (unit of 10)
Table 430.7(B)
Round up 63 A to 70 A

Step 2: Calculating LRC
Table 430.7(B)
70 A x 6 = 420 A

Solution: The locked-rotor current is 420 amps. This method can only be used for code letters A through G.

See Figures 16-12(a) and **(b)** for calculating and selecting the locked-rotor current of a motor.

Motor Tip: Engineers and electricians shall select the locked-rotor current rating from **Tables 430.251(A)** and **(B)** when using Design B, C, D, or E motors. The overcurrent protection device shall be set above the locked-rotor current of the motor so that the motor can start and run. See problem in **Figure 16-12(b)**.

When code letters are used, the locked-rotor current shall be calculated per **Table 430.7(B)** or the rule of thumb method applied, based on code letters A through G. See the problem and Quick Calc in **Figure 16-12(a)**.

See Figure 16-13 for a chart showing the different electrical characteristics for design type motors.

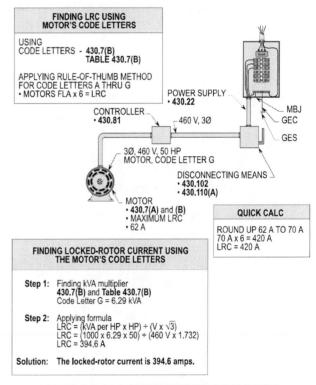

LOCKED-ROTOR CURRENT UTILIZING HORSEPOWER NEC TABLES 430.251(A) AND (B)

Figure 16-12(a). For motors having code letters instead of Design letters, the locked rotor current shall be calculated per **Table 430.7(B)** using the code letter of the motor.

Note, for calculating locked rotor current for DC motors, see **Figure 20-17**.

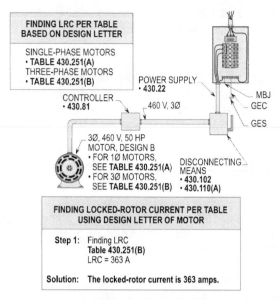

FINDING LRC PER TABLE
BASED ON DESIGN LETTER

SINGLE-PHASE MOTORS
• TABLE 430.251(A)
THREE-PHASE MOTORS
• TABLE 430.251(B)

FINDING LOCKED-ROTOR CURRENT PER TABLE
USING DESIGN LETTER OF MOTOR

Step 1:   Finding LRC
          Table 430.251(B)
          LRC = 363 A

Solution: The locked-rotor current is 363 amps.

**LOCKED-ROTOR CURRENT UTILIZING HORSEPOWER
NEC TABLES 430.251(A) AND (B)**

Figure 16-12(b). Tables 430.251(A) and **(B)** shall be used to determine the LRC in amps for motors with Design letters.

NEMA Design	Starting Torque	Starting Current	Breakdown Torque	Full-Load Slip
A	Normal	Normal	High	Low
B	Normal	Low	Medium	Low
C	High	Low	Normal	Low
D	Very high	Low	-	High

FOR MORE MOTOR FACTS, SEE **FIGURE 14-17.**

MOTOR DESIGN CHARACTERISTICS

Figure 16-13. The type of motor will determine the electrical characteristics of the design.

Note, NEMA has designated the above designs for polyphase motors. Design E motors are not listed.

For example: What size overcurrent protection device is required to permit the three-phase, 460 V, 50 HP motor in Figure 16-12(a) and (b) to start and run?

Step 1: Finding FLC of motor
Table 430.250
50 HP = 65 A

Step 2: Finding percentage to size OCPD (CB)
Table 430.52(C)(1)
Percentage = 250%

Step 3: Calculating amps
65A x 250% = 162.5 A

Step 4: Selecting OCPD (CB)
430.52(C)(1)(a) and **Table 240.6(A)**
162.5 A = 175 A CB

**Solution: A 175 amp circuit breaker will hold
about 525 A (175 A x 3 = 525 A)
for 4 to 9 seconds.**

Motor Tip: Inverse-time circuit breakers (600 V or less) will hold about three times their rating for different periods of time, based on their frame size.

Motor Tip: It does not matter if the code letter or Design letter is used to determine LRC (starting current). The size overcurrent protection device (circuit breaker), when used per **Table 430.52(C)(1)**, is large enought to hold such current and allow the motor to start and run.

Chapter 16: Design Letters and Code Letters

Section   Answer

1. The phase displacement for a single-phase AC squirrel-cage motor is about   _____   _____
   18 to _____ degrees in angular phase displacement.
   (a) 30   (b) 45
   (c) 60   (d) 90

2. A single-phase AC squirrel-cage motor operates on the running winding when   _____   _____
   the rotor starts turning and has established a running speed at about 75 to
   _____ percent of the motor's synchronous speed.
   (a) 78   (b) 80
   (c) 85   (d) 90

3. Three-phase AC squirrel-cage motors have three separate windings per pole   _____   _____
   on the stator that generate magnetic fields that are _____ degrees out-of-phase
   with each other.
   (a) 60   (b) 90
   (c) 110   (d) 120

4. A very high starting torque of 300 to _____ percent of the full-load torque is   _____   _____
   provided when using series DC motors.
   (a) 350   (b) 375
   (c) 400   (d) 450

5. A high torque of 125 to _____ percent of the full-load torque is provided when   _____   _____
   using shunt DC motors.
   (a) 150   (b) 175
   (c) 200   (d) 250

6. A high torque of 180 to _____ percent of the full-load torque is provided when   _____   _____
   using compound DC motors.
   (a) 200   (b) 220
   (c) 240   (d) 260

7. The full-load torque of a motor is determined by dividing the horsepower times   _____   _____
   _____, the RPM of the motor.
   (a) 2525   (b) 3636
   (c) 5252   (d) 6464

8. The most used motor in the electrical industry is Class _____ design motor.   _____   _____
   (a) B   (b) C
   (c) D   (d) E

9. The starting torque of an induction motor will increase by _____ percent of the   _____   _____
   full-load torque when using Class B design motors.
   (a) 125   (b) 150
   (c) 225   (d) 275

10. The starting torque of a squirrel-cage motor will increase about _____ percent   _____   _____
    of the full-load torque when using Class C motors.
    (a) 125   (b) 150
    (c) 225   (d) 275

_____ _____

11. The starting torque of a squirrel-cage induction motor is increased about _____ percent of the full-load torque when using Class D motors.
        (a) 125   (b) 150
        (c) 225   (d) 275

_____ _____

12. The starting current is reduced to _____ percent when using a reactor-reduced starting method.
        (a) 50   (b) 65
        (c) 75   (d) 80

_____ _____

13. Code letters are installed on motors by manufacturers for calculating the _____ based on the kVA per horsepower that is selected from the motor's code letter.
        (a) RPM   (b) amperage
        (c) locked-rotor current   (d) voltage

_____ _____

14. The full-load torque of a motor is determined by the _____ of the motor.
        (a) RPM   (b) amperage
        (c) locked-rotor current   (d) voltage

_____ _____

15. For motors with code letters A through G, round the nameplate current in amps up to an even number and multiply by _____ to obtain the locked-rotor current of the motor.
        (a) 3   (b) 6
        (c) 10   (d) 15

_____ _____

16. What is the full-load torque and starting torque of a 50 HP, Design C motor operating at 1725 RPM? (Round up the calculation.)

_____ _____

17. What is the full-load torque and starting torque of a 40 HP, Design D motor operating at 1725 RPM?

_____ _____

18. What is the full-load torque for a two-speed, 40 HP motor operating at either 1200 RPM or 1800 RPM? (Calculate each speed.)

_____ _____

19. What is the lowest (42 percent) reduced-resistor starting torque for a 240 volt, 40 HP, three-phase, Design B motor operating at 1725 RPM?

_____ _____

20. What is the locked-rotor current rating for a three-phase, 208 volt, 40 HP motor with a locked-rotor current code letter B marked on the nameplate of the motor?

_____ _____

21. What is the locked-rotor current rating for a three-phase, 460 volt, 40 HP, Design B motor using the locked-rotor current listed in **Table 430.251(B)**?

_____ _____

22. Consider a motor with a nameplate current of 58 amps and calculate the locked-rotor current of the motor based upon code letters A through G. (Use the rule-of-thumb method.)

_____ _____

23. What is the locked rotor amps for a 50 HP, 460 V, 3Ø Design B motor?

_____ _____

24. What is the LRA for a 40 HP, 208 V, 3Ø, Design B motor?

_____ _____

25. What is the LRA for a 7-1/2 HP, 230 V, 3Ø motor?

Starting Methods

The starting method of a motor must be considered when sizing the overcurrent protection device for the motor circuit. The starting method is determined and selected based on the amount of current required to be reduced. Overload protection for a circuit is used to allow a motor to start but will open if the motor develops overloads during operation. The starting methods are designed by using the external components in motor starters or the windings of the motor.

TYPES OF STARTING METHODS

The following seven starting methods, as oultined in NEMA 1, *Motors and Generators*, must be considered when sizing the overcurrent protection device:

- **(1)** Full-voltage starting,
- **(2)** Reactor starting,
- **(3)** Resistor starting,
- **(4)** Autotransformer starting,
- **(5)** Solid state starting,
- **(6)** Wye-delta starting, and
- **(7)** Part-winding starting.

Motor Starting Tip: The starting methods are no longer listed in **Table 430.52(C)(1)**. FYI - they can be found in Table 430-152 of the 1993 NEC.

FULL-VOLTAGE STARTING

Full-voltage starting applies 480 volts directly to the motor's windings when the supply voltage from the utility company is three-phase, 480 volts. A disconnecting switch or circuit breaker is used as a single main switch for connecting a motor across the line. The coil in a magnetic starter may be controlled by a start and stop pushbutton station or other control devices to bridge the line to the load terminals of the motor. **(See Figure 17-1)**

High torque is produced when using full-voltage starting. Full-voltage starting has a starting torque per ampere of line current that is the highest of all starting methods. Full-voltage starting for motors has an inrush starting current that varies from 3-1/2 to 10 times the normal full-load running amps. The power system for full-voltage starting must be capable of delivering its starting current without a voltage dip. Full-voltage starting for the driven equipment must be designed to withstand heavy currents. When selecting a starting method, full-voltage starting is usually selected because of its lower cost and maintenance. However, integral horsepower motors or high-voltage systems use full-voltage starting because the starting current of the motor is low due to the high voltage or lower horsepower.

> **For example:** What is the full-voltage starting current, in amps, applied across the line to the windings of a 240 volt, three-phase, Design B, 50 horsepower motor?
>
> **Step 1:**   Finding FLA
> **Table 430.251(B)**
> 50 HP = 725 A
>
> **Solution: The locked-rotor starting current is 725 amps.**

By using the design letter of the motor, the locked-rotor starting current of the motor is 725 amps per **Table 430.251(B)**. By using the code letter of the motor, if available, and calculating the locked-rotor current of the motor, the locked-rotor current may be less or greater per **Table 430.7(B)**.

The locked-rotor current of a motor, when calculated, is used to select the components that make up a motor circuit. A larger disconnect would be required for code letters selected above H due to the larger size fuses required to allow the motor to start and run.

REACTOR STARTING

Reduced-voltage starting is accomplished by placing a reactor in series with each phase of the motor. The insulation problems that are created – due to heat – when using resistor starting are not a problem when using reactor starting to reduce the voltage and current for starting a motor. Reactor starting is designed and installed mainly for motors with high-voltage systems. When using reactor starting, the torque efficiency is less than that of full-voltage starting. **(See Figure 17-2)**

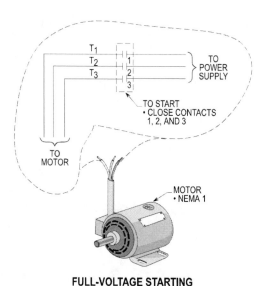

FULL-VOLTAGE STARTING

Figure 17-1. Supply voltage and starting current are applied to the motor windings when using full-voltage starting.

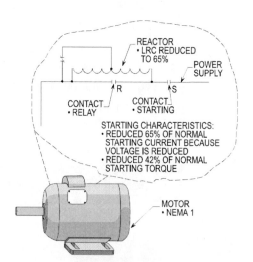

REACTOR STARTING

Figure 17-2. A percentage of reduced-voltage and starting current is applied to the motor when using reactor starting. Starting torque is also reduced.

The inrush starting current of a motor is reduced to about 65 percent when using reactor starting. The starting torque is reduced to about 42 percent of the normal starting torque. When applying either reactor or resistor starting, the starting current and starting torque of a motor will be reduced about the same. Reactor starting will affect the system's power factor.

Note, high-voltage systems over 1000 volts usually use reactor starting to start and run motor loads.

RESISTOR STARTING

Reduced voltage and current is accomplished by placing a resistor in series with each phase of a motor. When using resistor starting, the torque efficiency is less than that of full-voltage starting. **(See Figure 17-3)**

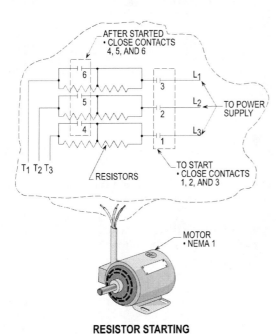

RESISTOR STARTING

Figure 17-3. A percentage of reduced-voltage and starting current is applied to the motor when using resistor starting.

Resistor starting is the least expensive reduced starting method. This type of starting method reduces the starting torque and provides smooth starting and acceleration up to the motor's running speed.

Resistor starting does not provide as high a starting torque and does not reduce the starting current to the same value as an autotransformer or a solid-state starter.

Motor Starting Tip: When using resistor starting, the starting current cannot be limited to the value of autotransformer starting.

The normal inrush starting current is reduced to about 65 percent of the locked-rotor current for resistor starting. The normal starting torque is reduced to about 42 percent of the starting torque. **(See Figure 17-4)**

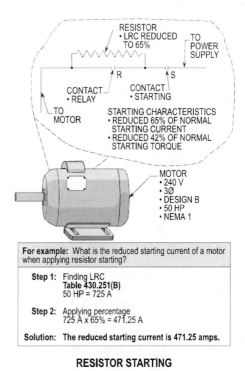

For example: What is the reduced starting current of a motor when applying resistor starting?

Step 1: Finding LRC
Table 430.251(B)
50 HP = 725 A

Step 2: Applying percentage
725 A x 65% = 471.25 A

Solution: The reduced starting current is 471.25 amps.

RESISTOR STARTING

Figure 17-4. By applying resistor starting, the inrush starting current is reduced to an acceptable level.

Care must be exercised to ensure that the amount of reduced torque will start the motor and driven load. When designing and selecting a reduced-voltage starting method, the amount of starting torque required to start the motor and driven load and then accelerate it to running speed must be considered.

Motors operating on low-voltage systems that are rated 600 volts or less are usually installed with resistor starting methods.

Note, the starting torque of a motor using resistor starting is reduced to about 42 percent of the full-load torque.

The reduced starting torque, using a one-step acceleration, may not be high enough to accelerate the motor up to its running speed. However, a resistor starting method with two steps of acceleration can be selected when this type of problem occurs. **(See Figure 17-5)**

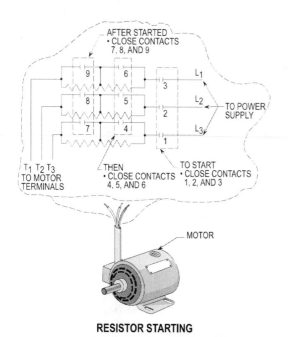

RESISTOR STARTING

Figure 17-5. Two steps of acceleration are selected to reduce starting voltage and current during acceleration.

AUTOTRANSFORMER STARTING

Autotransformer starting is designed and selected by providing taps to start the motor at 50, 65, or 80 percent of the applied line voltage. A tap of 50 percent can be provided to the line voltage to start a motor rated above 50 horsepower. When designing and installing autotransformer starting, an autotransformer with step-down taps and a switching device to start the motor are provided. Once started, the switching device switches the autotransformer out of the circuit and the motor is connected directly to the line. This type of reduced starting has the same effect as full-voltage starting because it provides good torque efficiency.

When determining the torque efficiency, the starting torque of the motor is divided by the locked-rotor current. The inrush starting current is reduced by switching the autotransformer into the motor circuit by contacts that connect to the desired tap. The autotransformer is switched or transferred out of the motor circuit when the motor accelerates up to its running speed. **(See Figure 17-6)**

Inrush starting current of a motor can be reduced by 50, 65, or 80 percent of the applied line voltage from the taps when using autotransformer starting. The percentages for autotransformer starting are based on voltage taps produced from 25 to 64 percent of the full-load starting torque.

> **For example,** 725 amps of locked-rotor starting current is listed for a 230 volt, three-phase, Design B, 50 horsepower motor, per **Table 430.251(B)**.

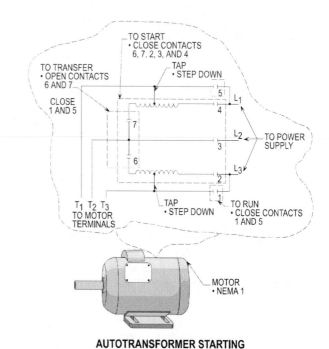

AUTOTRANSFORMER STARTING

Figure 17-6. The above illustrates the percentage applied for reducing voltage and starting current to a motor using autotransformer starting.

The percentage of the tap is squared to determine the starting torque (50% x 50% = 25%). When installing an autotransformer with a 50 percent tap, the starting torque will be reduced by 25 percent.

See Figure 17-7 for a detailed illustration about estimating the reduced starting torque and inrush current in a motor circuit, using an autotransformer reduced starting method.

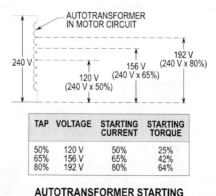

AUTOTRANSFORMER STARTING

TAP	VOLTAGE	STARTING CURRENT	STARTING TORQUE
50%	120 V	50%	25%
65%	156 V	65%	42%
80%	192 V	80%	64%

Figure 17-7. The reduced voltage for autotransformer starting is determined by using voltage taps.

When designing and installing an autotransformer starting method, care must be exercised when selecting the percentage of tap required to reduce the starting current. When selecting a tap, it must be sized large enough to provide starting torque for the driven load and to accelerate up to its running speed.

For example, 725 amps of locked-rotor starting current per **Table 430.251(B)** is needed for a 230 volt, three-phase, Design B, 50 horsepower motor.

The locked-rotor current (starting current) is altered per **Table 430.7(B)** when using the code letter on the nameplate of the motor. An autotransformer designed and installed with a 50 percent tap reduces the starting torque to 25 percent of the original value.

When applying a 50 percent voltage tap on an autotransformer with a (delta) motor starting current of 725 amps, the starting current is reduced to 210.25 amps for the transformation line-to-winding current (725 A x 50% x .58 = 210.25 A). Therefore, the current on the line conductors will be reduced to 210.25 amps. The current to the motor windings will be reduced to about 362.5 amps (725 A x 50% = 362.5 A). **(See Figure 17-8)**

Note, for the 58% rule, see **Figure 17-8** and **Figure 17-9**.

An autotransformer with a 65 percent tap is squared to determine the starting torque (65% x 65% = 42%). The starting current of a (delta) motor with 725 amps is reduced to 273.325 amps (725 A x 65% x 58% = 273.325 A). The locked-rotor current of 725 amps is multiplied by the 65 percent tap on the autotransformer to determine the winding current. Therefore, the motor's winding current is about 471.25 amps (725 A x 65% = 471.25 A).

An autotransformer with a 80 percent tap is squared to determine the starting torque of the motor (80% x 80% = 64%). The conductor's line current for the (delta) motor is found by multiplying 725 amps by 80 percent (725 A x 80% x 58% = 336.4 A). The locked-rotor current of 725 amps is multiplied by the 80 percent tap on the autotransformer to determine the motor's winding current. Therefore, the motor's winding current is about 580 amps (725 A x 80% = 580 A).

SOLID STATE STARTING

Solid state reduced starters use silicon controlled rectifiers (SCRs) to control voltage and current flow that is directed through the solid state reduced starters by a gate (terminal) to start and accelerate motors up to their running speeds. A low-voltage signal is applied to the gate, which switches the voltage and current ON and OFF through the solid state reduced starters.

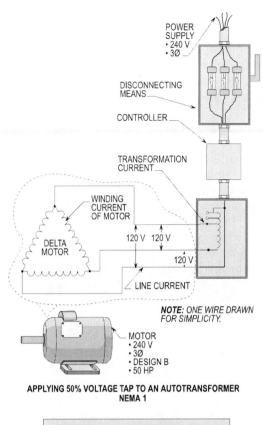

NOTE: *ONE WIRE DRAWN FOR SIMPLICITY.*

APPLYING 50% VOLTAGE TAP TO AN AUTOTRANSFORMER
NEMA 1

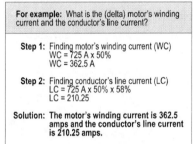

For example: What is the (delta) motor's winding current and the conductor's line current?

Step 1: Finding motor's winding current (WC)
WC = 725 A x 50%
WC = 362.5 A

Step 2: Finding conductor's line current (LC)
LC = 725 A x 50% x 58%
LC = 210.25

Solution: The motor's winding current is 362.5 amps and the conductor's line current is 210.25 amps.

AUTOTRANSFORMER STARTING

Figure 17-8. Autotransformer starting having a 50 percent voltage tap will have 50 percent winding and line current.

When applying AC power to the circuit, a signal is sent to the gate, allowing current to flow. This current flows in only one direction though the solid state reduced starter. The solid state reduced starters will turn OFF for each half cycle. The flow of current can be traced by using an AC waveform as the gate switches the flow of current through the solid state reduced starter. **(See Figure 17-9)**

B_1 sends a signal to the gate that turns the gate ON and causes current to flow. At C_2, the flow of current changes direction. E_4 sends a signal to the gate and causes current to flow for the last half of the cycle until F_5 turns the signal to the gate OFF.

When installing two solid state reduced starters, each solid state reduced starter is connected in parallel to the motor in opposite directions. The voltage supply to the motor is controlled by signals that are sent to the gate. The current flow through the windings is changed by solid state reduced starters each half cycle, and the circuit detects alternating current. By controlling the signals to the gate, the starting current and voltage can be adjusted to the desired level.

The circuit is energized to the motor windings when the power source is connected and the starting contacts close. By switching the signals to the gates and controlling the solid state reduced starters, acceleration of the motor is controlled. By turning ON the solid state reduced starters with gate signals, different voltage and current levels are obtained. The motor windings are connected directly to the supply line when the running contacts close, which brings the motor up to its running speed. The motor runs at full voltage when the solid state reduced starters are disconnected from the line by the opening of the starting contacts. **(See Figure 17-10)**

The starting current of a motor is approximately 100 to 400 percent of the motor's full-load current rating when using solid state starters. **(See Figure 17-11)**

Note, solid state reduced starters provide increments of starting torque that allow a motor to start and run its load in a very smooth operation.

For example: What is the reduced starting current for a solid state starter with a reduction of 300 percent of the full-load current rating for a 480 volt, three-phase, Design B, 400 horsepower motor? (See **Table 430.250** for FLC).

Step 1: Finding starting current
SC = FLC x %
SC = 477 A x 300%
SC = 1431 A

[Normal LRC = 2900 A per **Table 450.251(B)**]

**Solution: The starting current using a
solid state starter is 1431 amps.**

Motor Starting Tip: When using the rule-of-thumb method, the starting current for a motor without the use of a solid state starter is approximately 2862 amps (477 A x 6 = 2862 A).

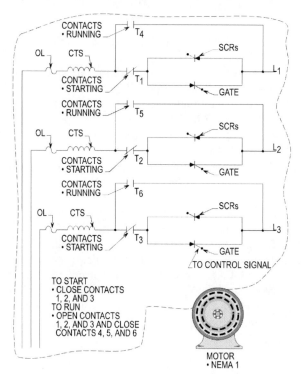

SOLID STATE STARTING

Figure 17-10. The motor is started by closing contacts 1, 2, and 3. When the motor reaches running speed, contacts 1, 2, and 3 open and contacts 4, 5, and 6 close to run the motor.

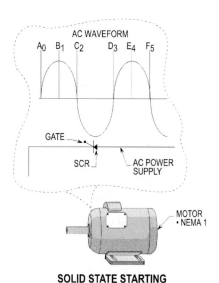

SOLID STATE STARTING

Figure 17-9. The above illustrates the use of an AC waveform. B_1 sends a signal to the gate and causes current to flow. At C_2, the flow of current changes direction. E_4 sends a signal to the gate and causes current to flow for the last half of the cycle.

Overloads can be set in a solid state starter to sense any amount of overload current that is higher than the running current of the motor. Therefore, all types of overload conditions are provided with closer protection for the windings. Overloads in a solid state starter can protect special motors by disconnecting the motor from the power supply where overloads exist. The power supply is connected again to the solid state starter and motor after the overload condition is corrected.

During the starting period, the starting torque will vary with the percentage of starting current. The motor's starting torque will be reduced to approximately 60 percent if the starting current is reduced to 400 percent, 40 percent if reduced to 300 percent, and 30 percent if reduced to 200 percent.

See Figure 17-12 for a detailed illustration of a solid state starter used to reduce the starting current and torque of a motor.

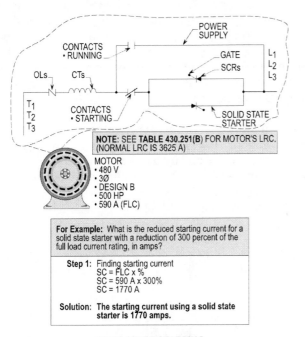

SOLID STATE STARTING

Figure 17-11. The above is an illustration using solid state starting to reduce starting current for a motor.

ADJUSTABLE FREQUENCY DRIVES

A basic adjustable frequency drive system consists of the following:

(1) AC squirrel-cage induction motor,

(2) Inverter, and

(3) Operator's control station.

Motor Starting Tip: A control station may be installed on an inverter cabinet, if necessary. (See Figure 17-13)

Adjustable frequency drives for AC squirrel-cage induction motors are used to control the speed by varying the frequency of the power supply to the motors.

A variety of sizes are available to give designers a broad selection of adjustable speed applications for an economical installation. Adjustable frequency drives have become a popular method by which designers and installers control the speed of a motor.

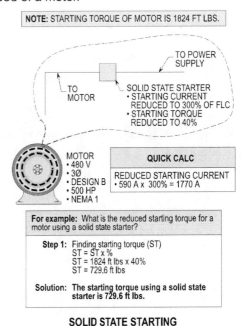

SOLID STATE STARTING

Figure 17-12. The above illustrates a solid state starter where the starting torque is reduced to 40 percent if the starting current is reduced to 300 percent.

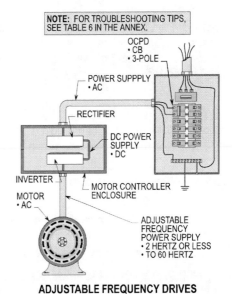

ADJUSTABLE FREQUENCY DRIVES

Figure 17-13. To start and run AC motors, adjustable frequency drives are installed to convert AC power to DC power. Rectifiers are used to convert AC to DC. The level of frequency is regulated by the use of an inverter to start and drive the AC squirrel-cage induction motor.

AC INDUCTION MOTOR

Class B, 460 volt, three-phase, AC squirrel-cage induction motors are usually used with adjustable frequency drives connected to a three-phase power supply.

Note, adjustable frequency drive systems can be fitted for any size AC squirrel-cage induction motor.

By reducing the applied frequency to a value of 2 hertz or less, an adjustable frequency drive system will start an AC squirrel-cage motor. The inrush current is reduced to approximately 150 percent of the rated current of the motor by using such a low frequency.

For example: What is the inrush current for a 460 volt, three-phase, Design B, 100 horsepower AC squirrel-cage induction motor?

Step 1: Finding A
Table 430.250 and **Table 430.251(B)**
100 HP = 124 A of FLC
100 HP = 725 A of LRC

Step 2: Calculating A
124 A x 150% = 186 A

Solution: The inrush current would be 186 amps using an adjustable frequency drive system.

Motor Starting Tip: By adjusting the frequency to 2 hertz or less, the AC squirrel-cage induction motor can be started at 186 amps and slowly brought up to the desired running speed.

See Figure 17-14 for a detailed illustration showing the varying percentages of torque and current due to the amount of frequency applied to the controller during starting.

INVERTERS

Inverters are solid state power conversion units that convert AC power to DC power or DC power to AC power. The following two stages of power conversion are used:

(1) Controlled or uncontrolled rectifier section (AC to DC) and

(2) Inverter (DC to AC).

A three-phase, 480 volt power supply at 60 hertz is used when inverters are installed. The AC squirrel-cage induction motor rotates at its maximum speed when the full 60 hertz is

applied to the inverter by the controller. The AC squirrel-cage induction motor rotates slower when the value of frequency applied is less than 60 hertz to the inverter by the controller. Torque would be less when applying more than 60 hertz from an inverter listed for the purpose, which would produce a higher output speed (RPMs) from the motor.

When designing and installing an inverter, care must be exercised in sizing and matching it to the AC squirrel-cage induction motor. Generally, an inverter and AC squirrel-cage induction motor can be used with the same horsepower rating. The motor rating in horsepower must equal the amount of current required to drive the load. This method is used when designing and selecting an AC squirrel-cage induction motor. The inverter is designed and selected based on this rating.

An inverter must be sized for the amount of current required for an AC squirrel-cage induction motor at the maximum operating torque when the motor is oversized to provide a wider range of speed control. The inverter output current rating must be equal to or greater than the current listed on the nameplate of the AC squirrel-cage induction motor if operating at full-load current.

A maximum ambient temperature of 40°C is used on most inverters. However, 50°C is used on some inverters. Inverters are oversized by one size for areas with a higher ambient temperature. Check with the manufacturer before designing and installing to verify this.

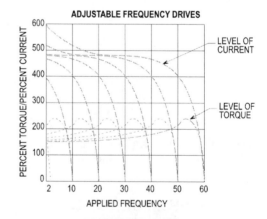

Figure 17-14. The percentage of torque and current vary with the amount of frequency applied by the controller.

CONTROL STATION

The operator's control station is equipped with start and stop pushbuttons that are normally open or normally closed contacts, which are designed and installed to start and stop the motor circuit. The rotating speed of an AC squirrel-cage induction motor is adjusted by using a speed-setting potentiometer. A potentiometer (rheostat or resistor) has three terminals, with one or more sliding contacts, that are adjustable and act as adjustable voltage dividers.

STARTING TORQUE

An AC squirrel-cage induction motor has an inrush current of approximately 600 percent of the motor's full-load current rating when started across the line at full voltage and full frequency. AC squirrel-cage induction motors marked with code letters A through H have 600 percent starting currents. Inrush current for AC squirrel-cage induction motors marked with code letters J through K shall be calculated based on individual code letters, per **Table 430.7(B)**.

> **For example:** What is the inrush current for a 460 volt, three-phase, 100 HP AC squirrel-cage induction motor with the code letter T?
>
> **Step 1:** Finding IC
> IC = (kVA x 1000 x HP) ÷ (V x 1.732)
> IC = (19.99 x 1000 x 100 HP) ÷ (460 x 1.732)
> IC = 2508 amps
>
> **Solution: The inrush current is 2508 amps.**

EDDY-CURRENT DRIVES

Eddy-current drives consist of soft iron bars (electromagnets) shaped like a U that are magnetized by applying DC voltage to the coil of insulated wire around the bases. An eddy-current clutch is developed by a solid ring or soft iron (drum assembly) that is added to encircle the poles of the electromagnets. **(See Figure 17-15)**

A wide range of stepless, adjustable speeds are obtained from eddy-current drives when used from AC power supply lines operating at standard frequencies. Eddy-current drives are designed and installed to consist of an AC squirrel-cage induction motor and a magnetic eddy-current clutch. Equipment requiring a variety of speed control or regulated torque is where eddy-current drives are used.

AC SQUIRREL-CAGE INDUCTION MOTORS

When designing and installing eddy-current drives, the AC supply power is converted to rotational power using AC squirrel-cage induction motors. AC squirrel-cage induction motors are designed and installed with basic output speeds

of 3600, 1800, and 1200 RPM. The full-load speeds of AC squirrel-cage induction motors are 2 to 5 percent less than synchronous speeds.

> **For example:** What is the actual speed if the synchronous speed is 1800 RPM and the motor is operating at 3 percent slip?
>
> **Step 1:**   Finding RPM
> RPM = 1800 RPM x 3% (.03)
> RPM = 54
> RPM = 1800 RPM - 54 RPM
> RPM = 1746
>
> **Solution: The actual speed of the motor is 1746 RPM.**

Note, by increasing DC voltage to the coil, the output shaft will speed up and slow down when the voltage is decreased. (See **page 17-11**)

The AC squirrel-cage induction motor has an eddy-current clutch added in which the motor drives to obtain variable output speeds.

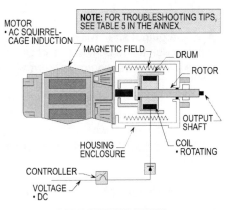

EDDY-CURRENT DRIVES

Figure 17-15. The above illustrates a basic eddy-current drive system, which consists of soft iron bars (electromagnets), a coil of insulating wire, and an iron ring (drum assembly).

PURPOSE OF CLUTCH

The following are the three main components of the eddy-current clutch:

(1) Drum,

(2) Rotor, and

(3) Rotating coil.

The drum (steel drum) of an eddy-current clutch is the input member that is driven by the AC squirrel-cage induction motor. The rotor of an eddy-current clutch is the output member and is free to rotate in the clutch drum. The rotating coil in an eddy-current clutch is wound around the rotor clutch and is supplied with DC voltage to produce a flux pattern through the drum and rotor.

Poles are cast in each section of the rotor, develops a north and south pole when the field coil is excited. The polarity is opposite that of the other section in each section of the rotor. Magnetic lines of force will flow through the north poles of the rotor into the drum and through the south poles of the rotor when the field coil is excited and then return to the field assembly.

The motion between the rotating drum and the rotor generates eddy currents in the drum. Circulating currents are induced in a conducting material when they cut the magnetic flux lines that are eddy currents. These small currents are produced by the voltage through the conducting material. Eddy currents also produce a second magnetic field. The rotor rotates in the same direction as the drum when the magnetic field, generated by the eddy currents, interacts with the magnetic field, generated by the field coil.

The rotor and drum will rotate freely, with no rotation of the output shaft, when no voltage is applied to the coil. The output shaft will pick up speed when voltage is applied and continue to increase its speed until it is rotating slightly less than the motor. The output shaft will not rotate at the same speed as the motor due to the percentage of slip generated by the difference in speed between the drum and rotor.

By adding or subtracting the amount of DC voltage applied to the coil, the output shaft speed can be varied. The speed of the output shaft will slow down when the voltage to the coil is decreased, and it will speed up when voltage to the coil is increased.

See Figure 17-15 for a detail illustration of a basic eddy-current drive.

CONTROLLER

The eddy-current controller changes the strength of the magnetic field on the rotating drum by the excitation voltage (which varies) to the clutch field coil. The output shaft of the clutch will speed up when the controller is set up to add more DC voltage to the coil. The output shaft of the clutch will slow down when the controller has less excitation voltage applied to the coil, which causes the magnetic field to be weaker on the drum.

The motor can be protected from overload by setting the controller being set at a moderate amount of current flow.

The motor can also be programmed to be shut off by the controller and reverse the motor's rotation, and then start again in the original rotation. This type of programming would be necessary where blockage could occur in the supply line.

Solid state transistorized boards are used with the controller, which helps facilitate troubleshooting procedures and replacement. These boards are easy to replace and can be repaired and used again. **(See Figure 17-16)**

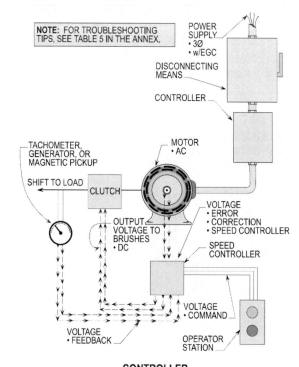

Figure 17-16. To increase or decrease the rotation speed of the eddy-current drive, the amount of excitation voltage is controlled by an operation station and controller.

TORQUE OUTPUT

The load will vary when the output speed of the clutch is increased or decreased by a fixed amount of excitation voltage applied to the coil.

By adjusting the level of excitation to the coil, the amount of torque transmitted from the AC squirrel-cage induction motor to the output shaft can be varied. The magnetic field will be greater on the drum and the faster the drum will rotate the output shaft as more excitation DC voltage is applied to the coil.

CONTROLLING SPEED OF THE MOTOR

A tachometer generator is designed to provide a signal that is proportional to the output speed of the shaft. The speed between the present speed of the controller and the actual speed of the load are realigned by this signal, which is designed to adjust the excitation to the coil. The tachometer generator is mounted integrally with the output shaft.

A drive regulator is installed for realigning the output speed to the present speed. **(See Figure 17-17)**

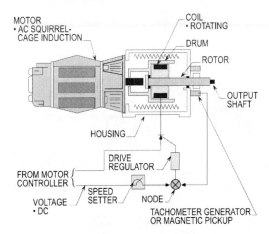

CONTROLLING SPEED OF THE MOTOR

Figure 17-17. Tachometer generators and drive regulators are designed to adjust and correct the realignment of speed between the actual output speed of the output shaft to the present speed where the load is varied.

WYE-DELTA STARTING MOTORS

A specially wound six-lead motor is required for a wye-delta starting method.

Note, the wye winding is used to start the motor, which then switches to the delta winding for the run operation of the motor. Lower current is produced in wye windings due to lower voltages.

The current in wye windings is equal to the line current and not 58 percent times the line current. Each wye winding has 139 volts (240 V x 58% = 139 V) impressed across it, instead of 240 volts as in delta windings. A three-phase, 240 volt supply is used to derive these values of voltages to the motor.

Wye-connected windings have different values of phase voltage and line current. The line voltage is equal to 1.732 times the voltage-to-ground.

> **For example,** the line voltage is 208 volts (120 V x 1.732 = 208 V) when the winding voltage is 120 volts. However, the line current and phase current have the same value for wye systems. The phase voltage in wye-connected windings can be found by multiplying the phase voltage (208 V x 58% = 120 V). **(See Figure 17-18)**

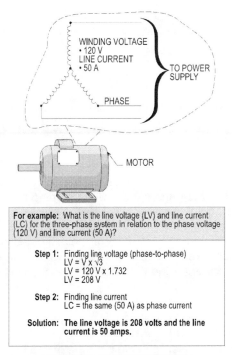

> **For example:** What is the line voltage (LV) and line current (LC) for the three-phase system in relation to the phase voltage (120 V) and line current (50 A)?
>
> **Step 1:** Finding line voltage (phase-to-phase)
> LV = V x √3
> LV = 120 V x 1.732
> LV = 208 V
>
> **Step 2:** Finding line current
> LC = the same (50 A) as phase current
>
> **Solution:** The line voltage is 208 volts and the line current is 50 amps.

WYE-DELTA STARTING MOTORS

Figure 17-18. Wye-connected windings produce the same values of phase current and line current.

Delta-connected windings produce the same value of phase voltage and line voltage. If the supplied phase voltage is 240 volts, the line voltage is 240 volts. If the line current is 50 amps, the phase current is multiplied by 58 percent (50 x 58% = 29 A). **(See Figure 17-19)**

> **Motor Starting Tip:** The reciprocal of the square root of 3 is found by dividing 1 by 1.732 to derive 58 percent (1 ÷ 1.732 = 58%).

The current flow into two phase windings connected to the line produces a different value between the phase current and line current. The phase current for delta-connected windings is found by multiplying the line current by 58 percent.

Note, the phase-to-phase voltage in a wye system is multiplied by 58% to derive the winding voltage, and in the delta system, the winding current is multiplied by the phase current to determine the winding current.

STARTING A MOTOR ON A WYE AND RUNNING ON A DELTA

Line currents and phase currents are the same currents in a wye-connected winding. However, the phase voltage is 58 percent of the line voltage. The voltage value does not change in a delta-connected winding, but the winding current value is 58 percent of the line current. The voltage and starting current are reduced when starting a motor on the wye winding. The circuit is automatically connected to the delta windings when the motor accelerates up to its running speed.

Motor Starting Tip: After a motor has been started by a wye and reaches its running speed, the wye windings are cut out and the motor then runs on a delta winding.

See Figure 17-20 for a detailed illustration pertaining to the values of voltage and current when starting a motor on a wye winding and running it on a delta winding.

The inrush starting current for a motor started on a wye connection is reduced to one-third the value of the locked-rotor line current. **(See Figure 17-21)**

For example: What is the inrush current for a 240 volt, three-phase, Design B, 50 HP motor with a wye-delta starting method?

Step 1: Finding amps
Table 430.251(B)
50 HP = 725 A

Step 2: Calculating amps
A = 725 A x .33
A = 239 A

Solution: The starting inrush current is 239 amps.

When designing and selecting the starting torque for a motor starting on a wye connection and running on a delta connection, the starting torque is reduced to one-third.

For example: What is the starting torque for a wye-delta connected motor with a torque of 216 foot-pounds?

Step 1: Finding ft lbs
216 ft lbs x .33 = 71 ft lbs

Solution: The starting torque is reduced to 71 ft lbs.

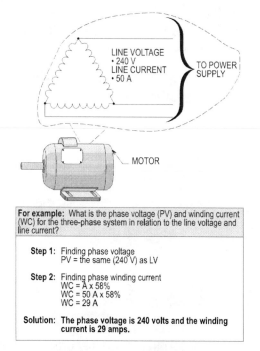

For example: What is the phase voltage (PV) and winding current (WC) for the three-phase system in relation to the line voltage and line current?

Step 1: Finding phase voltage
PV = the same (240 V) as LV

Step 2: Finding phase winding current
WC = A x 58%
WC = 50 A x 58%
WC = 29 A

Solution: The phase voltage is 240 volts and the winding current is 29 amps.

WYE-DELTA STARTING MOTORS

Figure 17-19. The phase voltage and line voltage have the same value, and the winding line current and phase current have different values for a delta-connected winding.

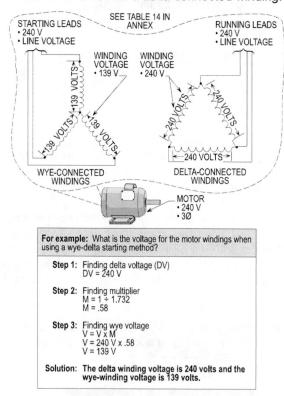

For example: What is the voltage for the motor windings when using a wye-delta starting method?

Step 1: Finding delta voltage (DV)
DV = 240 V

Step 2: Finding multiplier
M = 1 ÷ 1.732
M = .58

Step 3: Finding wye voltage
V = V x M
V = 240 V x .58
V = 139 V

Solution: The delta winding voltage is 240 volts and the wye-winding voltage is 139 volts.

STARTING A MOTOR ON A WYE AND RUNNING ON A DELTA

Figure 17-20. The above illustration shows the values of voltage and current when starting a motor on a wye winding and running it on a delta winding. The phase voltage in wye windings is 58 percent of the line voltage.

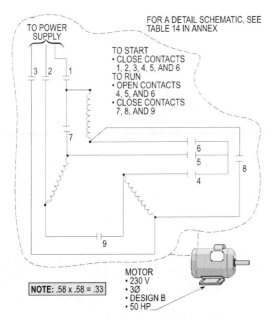

NOTE: .58 x .58 = .33

STARTING INRUSH CURRENT AND STARTING TORQUE

For example: What is the inrush current and starting torque for a wye-delta connected motor with a torque of 216 ft lbs?
Step 1: Finding A **Table 430.251(B)** 50 HP = 725 A
Step 2: Calculating A A = 725 A x .33 A = 239 A
Step 3: Finding ft lbs. 216 ft lbs. x .33 = 71 ft lbs
Solution: The starting inrush current is 239 amps and the starting torque is 71 ft lbs.

STARTING A MOTOR ON A WYE AND
RUNNING ON A DELTA

Figure 17-21. The inrush starting current and torque for a wye-delta connected motor is calculated at 33 percent of the normal current and torque.

PART-WINDING STARTING MOTORS

Part-winding starting is used mostly to reduce the voltage on weak power systems and prevent voltage disturbances. No voltage dip will occur when using a part-winding starting method during the starting and acceleration of the motor. Two separate parallel windings with two basic starting units are used for part-winding motors. Each individual starting unit is designed and selected for half the horsepower rating of the motor. When the motor is started, one winding of the motor is connected to the supply voltage. At the preset time, delay is used at a predetermined time to connect the second winding of the motor.

When using part-winding starting, only half of the motor's copper is utilized during the starting operation. The inrush starting current and starting torque are reduced by 65 percent when designing and installing part-winding starting methods. **(See Figure 17-22)**

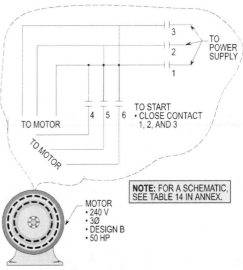

PART-WINDING STARTING MOTORS

Figure 17-22. The inrush starting current and starting torque is reduced by 65 percent when designing and installing part-winding starting methods.

OVERCURRENT PROTECTION
430.4

The requirements for sizing the overcurrent protection device for a part-winding motor are listed in **430.4**. When selecting the protective device per **430.52(C)(1)**, the percentages to be applied are found in **Table 430.52(C)(1)**. Since only half of the motor's horsepower is used for starting, only one half of the percentages listed in **Table 430.52(C)(1)** are used for selecting the overcurrent protection device. **(See Figure 17-23)**

Motor Starting Tip: The size overcurrent protection device can also be found by multiplying the FLC of the motor by the percentages in **Table 430.52(C)(1)** and dividing the size overcurrent protection device by 2.

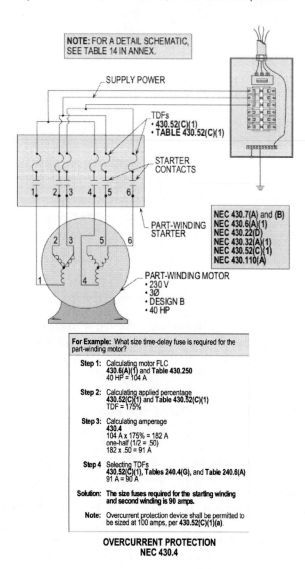

NOTE: FOR A DETAIL SCHEMATIC, SEE TABLE 14 IN ANNEX.

SUPPLY POWER

TDFs
• 430.52(C)(1)
• TABLE 430.52(C)(1)

STARTER CONTACTS

PART-WINDING STARTER

NEC 430.7(A) and (B)
NEC 430.6(A)(1)
NEC 430.22(D)
NEC 430.32(A)(1)
NEC 430.52(C)(1)
NEC 430.110(A)

PART-WINDING MOTOR
• 230 V
• 3Ø
• DESIGN B
• 40 HP

For Example: What size time-delay fuse is required for the part-winding motor?

Step 1: Calculating motor FLC
430.6(A)(1) and **Table 430.250**
40 HP = 104 A

Step 2: Calculating applied percentage
430.52(C)(1) and **Table 430.52(C)(1)**
TDF = 175%

Step 3: Calculating amperage
430.4
104 A x 175% = 182 A
one-half (1/2 = .50)
182 x .50 = 91 A

Step 4: Selecting TDFs
430.52(C)(1), **Tables 240.4(G)**, and **Table 240.6(A)**
91 A = 90 A

Solution: The size fuses required for the starting winding and second winding is 90 amps.

Note: Overcurrent protection device shall be permitted to be sized at 100 amps, per **430.52(C)(1)(a)**.

**OVERCURRENT PROTECTION
NEC 430.4**

Figure 17-23. Sizing time-delay fuses for a part-winding starting method to start and run a motor.

Chapter 17: Starting Methods

Section   Answer

1. Full-voltage starting for motors have an inrush starting current that varies from
   3-1/2 to _____ times the normal full-load running amps.
   (a) 5   (b) 10
   (c) 15   (d) 20

2. Reduced voltage starting is accomplished by placing a reactor in _____ with
   each phase of the motor.
   (a) series   (b) parallel
   (c) horizontal   (d) vertical

3. The inrush starting current of a motor is reduced to about _____ percent when
   using reactor starting.
   (a) 42   (b) 50
   (c) 65   (d) 75

4. The starting torque is reduced to about _____ percent of the normal starting
   torque when using reactor starting.
   (a) 42   (b) 50
   (c) 65   (d) 75

5. The normal inrush starting current is reduced to about _____ percent of the
   locked-rotor current for resistor starting.
   (a) 42   (b) 50
   (c) 65   (d) 75

6. A tap of _____ percent can be provided to the line voltage to start a motor
   rated above 50 HP when using autotransformer starting.
   (a) 42   (b) 50
   (c) 65   (d) 75

7. The percentages for autotransformer starting are based on voltage taps
   produced from 25 to _____ percent of the full-load starting torque.
   (a) 38   (b) 42
   (c) 57   (d) 64

8. Solid state reduced starters use silicon controlled _____to control voltage and
   current flow that is directed through the solid state reduced starters by a gate
   (terminal) to start and accelerate motors up to their running speeds.
   (a) rectifiers   (b) capacitors
   (c) reactors   (d) resistors

9. The starting current of a motor is approximately 100 to _____ percent of the
   motor's full-load current rating when using solid state starters.
   (a) 200   (b) 300
   (c) 400   (d) 600

10. Overloads can be set in a solid state starter to sense any amount of overload
    current higher than the _____ current of the motor.
    (a) winding   (b) coil
    (c) starting   (d) running

11. The motor's starting torque will be reduced to approximately _____ percent if the starting current is reduced to 400 percent when using solid state starting.
    (a) 50   (b) 60
    (c) 70   (d) 80

12. The motor's starting torque will be reduce to approximately _____ percent if the starting current is reduced to 200 percent when using solid state starting.
    (a) 10   (b) 20
    (c) 30   (d) 50

13. By reducing the applied frequency to a value of _____ hertz or less, an adjustable frequency drive system will start an AC squirrel-cage motor.
    (a) 2   (b) 24
    (c) 48   (d) 60

14. A three-phase, 480 volt power supply at _____ hertz is used when inverters are installed.
    (a) 2   (b) 24
    (c) 48   (d) 60

15. A maximum ambient temperature of _____ is used on most inverters.
    (a) 20ºC   (b) 40ºC
    (c) 75ºC   (d) 90ºC

16. An AC squirrel-cage induction motor has an inrush current of approximately _____ percent of the motors full-load current rating when started across the line at full voltage and full frequency.
    (a) 200   (b) 300
    (c) 400   (d) 600

17. An eddy-current clutch is developed by a solid ring or _____ iron (drum assembly) that is added to encircle the poles of the electromagnets.
    (a) soft   (b) hard
    (c) cast   (d) solid

18. When designing and installing eddy-current drives, the AC supply power is converted to _____ power using AC squirrel-cage induction motors.
    (a) DC   (b) directional
    (c) rotational   (d) varying

19. A special wound _____ lead motor is required for a wye-delta starting method.
    (a) 3   (b) 6
    (c) 9   (d) 12

20. The inrush starting current and starting torque is reduced by _____ percent when designing and installing part-winding starting methods.
    (a) 20   (b) 40
    (c) 50   (d) 65

21. Inverters can be used to _____ DC to AC or AC to DC power.
    (a) convert   (b) change
    (c) all of the above   (d) none of the above

22. What is the full-voltage starting current supplied to its windings for a 240 volt, three-phase, 40 HP, Design B motor?

23. What is the reduced starting current of a 240 volt, three-phase, 40 HP, Design B motor when applying resistor starting and using 65 percent resistance?

24. What is the winding current, line current, and transformation current for 208 volt, three-phase, 50 HP, Design B motor when applying autotransformer starting with a 50 percent tap?

25. What is the reduced starting current for a solid state starter with a reduction of 200 percent of the full-load current rating for a 480 volt, three-phase, 300 HP, Design B motor?

26. What is the inrush current for a 460 volt, three-phase, 125 HP, Design B, squirrel-cage induction motor? (Using an adjustable frequency drive system.)

27. What is the inrush current for a 460 volt, three-phase, 125 HP, Code Letter T, squirrel-cage induction motor? (Use code letter method.)

28. What is the actual speed if the synchronous speed for an induction motor is 1800 RPM and is operating at 5 percent slip where using eddy-current drive?

29. What is the inrush current for a 240 volt, three-phase, 40 HP, Design B motor with a wye-delta starting method?

30. What is the starting torque for wye-delta connected windings with a starting torque of 208 foot-pounds using wye-delta starting?

31. What size time-delay fuse is required for each winding of a 230 volt, three-phase, 50 HP, Design B, part-winding motor?

32. What is the starting current (LRC) of a 460 volt, three-phase, 50 HP Design B squirrel-cage induction motor?

33. The windings in a wye connected motor will pull _____% of the phase to phase current.

34. The windings of a delta connected motor will pull _____% of the phase to phase current.

35. If one phase is lost on the secondary side of a transformer, the motor will pull about _____ times the motor's running current.

36. The 58% in the delta connected motor is derived by dividing 1 by _____, which will produce the winding voltage.

37. An adjustable frequency drive can be used to start and run the _____ of a submersible pump.

38. Overloads can be installed in a solid state starter to protect the motor and circuit _____ from over-load conditions.

39. By controlling the _____ to the gate of a solid state controller, the starting current and voltage can be adjusted to the desired level for operation.

40. The voltage in the windings of a delta connected motor is _____% of the phase-to-phase voltage.

Overcurrent Protection for Individual Motors

The full-load current (FLC) from **Table 430.248** for single-phase and from **Table 430.250(C)(1)** for three-phase shall be used when designing and selecting the elements to make up circuits supplying power to motors. This current rating shall be used to size all the elements of the circuit except for the overload (OL) protection. **Table 430.7(B)** and **Tables 430.251(A)** or **(B)** are used to find the locked-rotor current (LRC). The overcurrent protection device shall be sized large enough to hold the LRC in amps and allow the motor to start and run.

SHORT CIRCUIT, GROUND FAULT, AND OVERLOAD PROTECTION
TABLE 430.52(C)(1), 430.52(C)(1), AND (C)(3)

The motor branch-circuit overcurrent protection device shall be capable of carrying the starting current of the motor. Short-circuit and ground-fault current is considered to be taken care of properly when the overcurrent protection device does not exceed the values in **Table 430.52(C)(1)**, as permitted by the provisions of **430.52(C)(1)** with **Exceptions**.

The overcurrent protection device shall be permitted to be sized greater than the full-load current of the motor or any other type of equipment that is outlined in **Table 240.4(G)**. References for sizing branch-circuit conductors are found in **Table 210.3** and **Table 220.3** in the NEC.

Different percentages are selected for particular overcurrent protection devices based on one of the four columns listed in **Table 430.52(C)(1)**. The percentages are used to size and select the proper size overcurrent protection device to allow a certain type of motor to start and run. The motor has a momentary starting current that is necessary for the motor to have power to start and drive the connected load at the driven equipment.

Note, the overcurrent protection device sized per **430.52(C)(1)** provides protection from short circuits and ground faults. Overload protection shall be provided for conductors and motor windings per **430.32(A)(1)** or **430.32(C). (See Figure 18-1)**

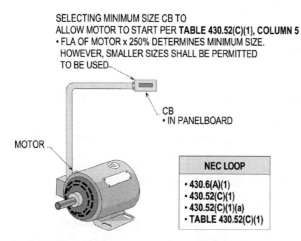

SELECTING MINIMUM SIZE CB TO
ALLOW MOTOR TO START PER **TABLE 430.52(C)(1), COLUMN 5**
• FLA OF MOTOR x 250% DETERMINES MINIMUM SIZE.
  HOWEVER, SMALLER SIZES SHALL BE PERMITTED
  TO BE USED

CB
• IN PANELBOARD

MOTOR

NEC LOOP
• 430.6(A)(1)
• 430.52(C)(1)
• 430.52(C)(1)(a)
• TABLE 430.52(C)(1)

**SHORT CIRCUIT, GROUND FAULT, AND OVERLOAD PROTECTION
NEC TABLE 430.52(C)(1), 430.52(C)(1), AND (C)(3)**

Figure 18-1. Selecting the percentages to determine the minimum size (rounding down), next size (rounding up), and maximum size circuit breaker to allow a motor to start and run.

> **Motor Tip:** In cases where the values for branch-circuit protective devices determined by **Table 430.52(C)(1)** do not correspond to the standard sizes or ratings of fuses, nonadjustable circuit breakers, or thermal devices, or possible settings of adjustable circuit breakers adequate to carry the starting currents of the motor, the next higher size rating or setting shall be permitted to be used.

APPLYING THE EXCEPTIONS 430.52(C)(1), a AND (b)

There are Exceptions that permit larger overcurrent protection devices to be used where the overcurrent protection device, as specified in **Table 430.52(C)(1),** will not permit the starting current of the motor to start and run. Where the motor fails to start and run because of excessive inrush starting currents, one of the following exceptions can be applied.

APPLYING (a)

If the values of the branch-circuit, short-circuit, and ground-fault protection devices determined from **Table 430.52(C)(1)** do not conform to standard sizes or ratings of fuses, nonadjustable circuit breakers, or possible settings on adjustable circuit breakers, it does not matter if they are capable or not capable of adequately carrying the load involved; the next higher setting or rating shall be permitted. In other words, you can round up or round down the size of the overcurrent protection device automatically by choice. **(See Figure 18-2)**

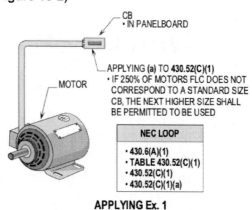

CB
• IN PANELBOARD

MOTOR

APPLYING (a) TO 430.52(C)(1)
• IF 250% OF MOTORS FLC DOES NOT
  CORRESPOND TO A STANDARD SIZE
  CB, THE NEXT HIGHER SIZE SHALL
  BE PERMITTED TO BE USED

NEC LOOP
• 430.6(A)(1)
• TABLE 430.52(C)(1)
• 430.52(C)(1)
• 430.52(C)(1)(a)

**APPLYING Ex. 1
NEC TABLE 430.52(C)(1) AND 430.52(C)(1)(a)**

Figure 18-2. Where the percentages of **Table 430.52(C)(1)** times the full-load current of motor does not correspond to a standard size overcurrent protection device, the next higher size rating above this percentage shall be permitted to be used.

APPLYING (b)

If the ratings listed in **Table 430.52(C)(1)** and **(a)** to **430.52(C)(1)** are not sufficient for the starting current of the motor, the overcurrent protection devices with percentages shown can be used to start and run motors that have high inrush starting currents. **(See Figure 18-3)**

When nontime-delay fuses are used and they do not exceed 600 amperes in rating, it shall be permitted to increase the fuse size up to 400 percent of the full-load current, but never over 400 percent.

Time-delay fuses (dual-element) shall not exceed 225 percent of the full-load current, but they may be increased up to this percentage.

Inverse time-element circuit breakers shall be permitted to be increased in rating. However:

- They shall not exceed 400 percent of the full-load current of the motor for 100 amperes or less or
- They may be increased to 300 percent where a full-load current is greater than 100 amperes.

See **Figure 18-4** for a detailed illustration on selecting percentages for sizing overcurrent protection devices.

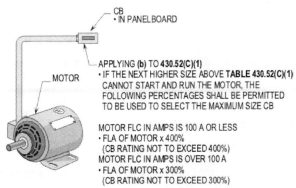

CB
• IN PANELBOARD

MOTOR

APPLYING (b) TO **430.52(C)(1)**
• IF THE NEXT HIGHER SIZE ABOVE **TABLE 430.52(C)(1)** CANNOT START AND RUN THE MOTOR, THE FOLLOWING PERCENTAGES SHALL BE PERMITTED TO BE USED TO SELECT THE MAXIMUM SIZE CB

MOTOR FLC IN AMPS IS 100 A OR LESS
• FLA OF MOTOR x 400%
  (CB RATING NOT TO EXCEED 400%)
MOTOR FLC IN AMPS IS OVER 100 A
• FLA OF MOTOR x 300%
  (CB RATING NOT TO EXCEED 300%)

APPLYING (b)
NEC TABLE 430.52 AND 430.52(C)(1)(b)

Figure 18-3. When the percentages of **Table 430.52(C)(1)** and **430.52(C)(1)(a)** will not allow the motor to start and run the driven load, the maximum size circuit breaker of **430.52(C)(1)(b)(3)** shall be permitted to be used.

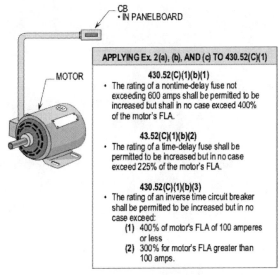

CB
• IN PANELBOARD

MOTOR

APPLYING Ex. 2(a), (b), AND (c) TO 430.52(C)(1)

430.52(C)(1)(b)(1)
• The rating of a nontime-delay fuse not exceeding 600 amps shall be permitted to be increased but shall in no case exceed 400% of the motor's FLA.

43.52(C)(1)(b)(2)
• The rating of a time-delay fuse shall be permitted to be increased but in no case exceed 225% of the motor's FLA.

430.52(C)(1)(b)(3)
• The rating of an inverse time circuit breaker shall be permitted to be increased but in no case exceed:
  (1) 400% of motor's FLA of 100 amperes or less
  (2) 300% for motor's FLA greater than 100 amps.

APPLYING (b)
NEC 430.52(C)(b)(1), (b)(2), and (b)(3)

Figure 18-4. When the percentages of **Table 430.52(C)(1)** and **430.52(C)(1)(a)** will not allow the motor to start and run, the maximum percentage of **430.52(C)(1).(b)(1), (b)(2)** and **(b)(3)** shall be permitted to be applied.

USING INSTANTANEOUS TRIP CIRCUIT BREAKERS
430.52(C)(3)(a)

An instantaneous trip circuit breaker shall be used only if it is adjustable, and is a part of a combination controller that has overcurrent protection in each conductor. Such combination, when used, has to be approved. An instantaneous trip circuit breaker is allowed to have a damping device, to limit the inrush current when the motor is started.

If the specified setting in **Table 430.52(C)(1)** is not sufficient for the starting current of the motor, the setting on an instantaneous trip circuit breaker shall be permitted to be increased, provided that in no instance it exceeds 1300 percent of the motor's full-load current ratings for motors marked Class B, C, or D.

> **Motor Tip:** For Design E and Design B NEMA high-efficiency motors, the setting on the instantaneous trip circuit breakers shall be permitted to be adjusted up to 1700 percent to allow the motor to start and run.

See **Figure 18-5** for adjusting the maximum trip settings on instantaneous trip circuit breakers to allow motors to start and accelerate their driven load.

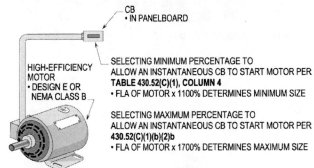

CB
• IN PANELBOARD

HIGH-EFFICIENCY MOTOR
• DESIGN E OR NEMA CLASS B

SELECTING MINIMUM PERCENTAGE TO ALLOW AN INSTANTANEOUS CB TO START MOTOR PER **TABLE 430.52(C)(1), COLUMN 4**
• FLA OF MOTOR x 1100% DETERMINES MINIMUM SIZE

SELECTING MAXIMUM PERCENTAGE TO ALLOW AN INSTANTANEOUS CB TO START MOTOR PER **430.52(C)(1)(b)(2)b**
• FLA OF MOTOR x 1700% DETERMINES MAXIMUM SIZE

USING INSTANTANEOUS TRIP CIRCUIT BREAKERS
NEC 430.52(C)(3)(b)(1)

Figure 18-5. Determining the minimum and maximum size setting on an instantaneous trip circuit breaker to allow the motor to start and run a driven load. **Note,** after the minimum setting of the overcurrent protection device has been determined, a smaller setting shall be permitted to be selected.

SIZING AND SELECTING OVERCURRENT PROTECTION DEVICES
TABLE 430.52(C)(1), COLUMNS 2, 3, 4, AND 5

The overcurrent protection device shall be sized for the starting current of the motor and selected to allow the motor to start and run. The overcurrent protection device per **Table 430.52(C)(1)** shall protect the branch-circuit conductors from short circuits and ground faults. The following four overcurrent protection devices selected from **Table 430.52(C)(1)** will start most motors under normal starting conditions:

(1) Nontime-delay fuses per Column 2

(2) Time-delay fuses per Column 3

(3) Instantaneous trip circuit breakers per Column 4

(4) Inverse-time circuit breakers per Column 5

NONTIME-DELAY FUSES
TABLE 430.52(C)(1), COLUMN 2

Nontime-delay fuses are installed with instantaneous trip features to detect short circuits and thermal characteristics to sense slow heat buildup in the circuit. A nontime-delay fuse will hold 5 times (500 percent) its rating for approximately 1/4 to 2 seconds based upon the type used.

For example: What is the holding time in amps for a nontime-delay fuse of 150 amps?

Step 1: Finding holding amps
A = fuse rating x 500%
A = 150 A x 500%
A = 750

Solution: The holding time in amps of a nontime-delay fuse is 750 amps.

Note, this fuse will blow in 1/4 to 2 seconds so the motor will have to start and accelerate the load quickly.

See Figure 18-6 for a detailed illustration of sizing nontime-delay fuses to allow motors to start and run.

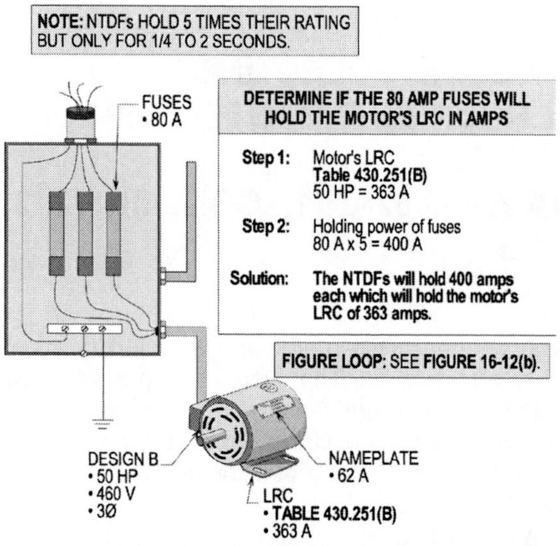

NOTE: NTDFs HOLD 5 TIMES THEIR RATING BUT ONLY FOR 1/4 TO 2 SECONDS.

FUSES
• 80 A

DETERMINE IF THE 80 AMP FUSES WILL HOLD THE MOTOR'S LRC IN AMPS

Step 1: Motor's LRC
Table 430.251(B)
50 HP = 363 A

Step 2: Holding power of fuses
80 A x 5 = 400 A

Solution: The NTDFs will hold 400 amps each which will hold the motor's LRC of 363 amps.

FIGURE LOOP: SEE FIGURE 16-12(b).

DESIGN B
• 50 HP
• 460 V
• 3Ø

NAMEPLATE
• 62 A

LRC
• TABLE 430.251(B)
• 363 A

NONTIME-DELAY FUSES
NEC TABLE 430.52(C)(1), COLUMN 2

Figure 18-6. Nontime-delay fuses will hold five times their rating, and when this rating is above the locked-rotor current it should allow the motor to start and run based on LRC.

TIME-DELAY FUSES
TABLE 430.52(C)(1), COLUMN 3

Time-delay fuses are also equipped with instantaneous trip features to detect short circuits and thermal characteristics to sense slow heat buildup in the circuit. Time-delay fuses are used because their time-delay action to allow a motor to start. Time-delay fuses will hold 5 times (500 percent) of their rating, which will permit most motors to start and accelerate the driven load.

Note, time-delay fuses that are sized at 125 percent or less of the motor's nameplate FLC rating can provide overload protection for the motor.

A time-delay fuse will hold 5 times its rating for 10 seconds, and this delayed action provides more acceleration time to allow the motor to start without tripping the overcurrent protection device.

For example: What is the holding power in amps for a time-delay fuse of 150 amps?

Step 1: Finding holding amps
A = fuse rating x 500%
A = 150 A x 500%
A = 750

Solution: The rating of the time-delay fuse is 750 amps.

Note, this fuse holds five times its rating for ten seconds without blowing and opening the circuit.

See Figure 18-7 for sizing time-delay fuses to hold the motor's locked-rotor current.

INSTANTANEOUS TRIP CIRCUIT BREAKERS
TABLE 430.52(C)(1), COLUMN 4

Instantaneous trip circuit breakers are installed with instantaneous values of current to respond from short circuits only. Thermal protection is not provided for instantaneous trip circuit breakers. Instantaneous trip circuit breakers will hold about three times their rating on the low setting and five times their next setting, seven times their next setting, and approximately ten times their rating on the high setting. Certain types allow such settings to be adjusted from 0 to 1700 percent. **(See Figure 18-8)**

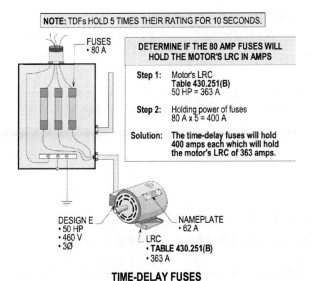

NOTE: TDFs HOLD 5 TIMES THEIR RATING FOR 10 SECONDS.

FUSES
• 80 A

DETERMINE IF THE 80 AMP FUSES WILL HOLD THE MOTOR'S LRC IN AMPS

Step 1:   Motor's LRC
           Table 430.251(B)
           50 HP = 363 A

Step 2:   Holding power of fuses
           80 A x 5 = 400 A

Solution: The time-delay fuses will hold
           400 amps each which will hold
           the motor's LRC of 363 amps.

DESIGN E
• 50 HP
• 460 V
• 3Ø

NAMEPLATE
• 62 A

LRC
• TABLE 430.251(B)
• 363 A

TIME-DELAY FUSES
NEC TABLE 430.52(C)(1), COLUMN 3

Figure 18-7. Time-delay fuses will hold five times their rating, and when this rating is above the locked-rotor current, it should allow the motor to start and run based on LRC.

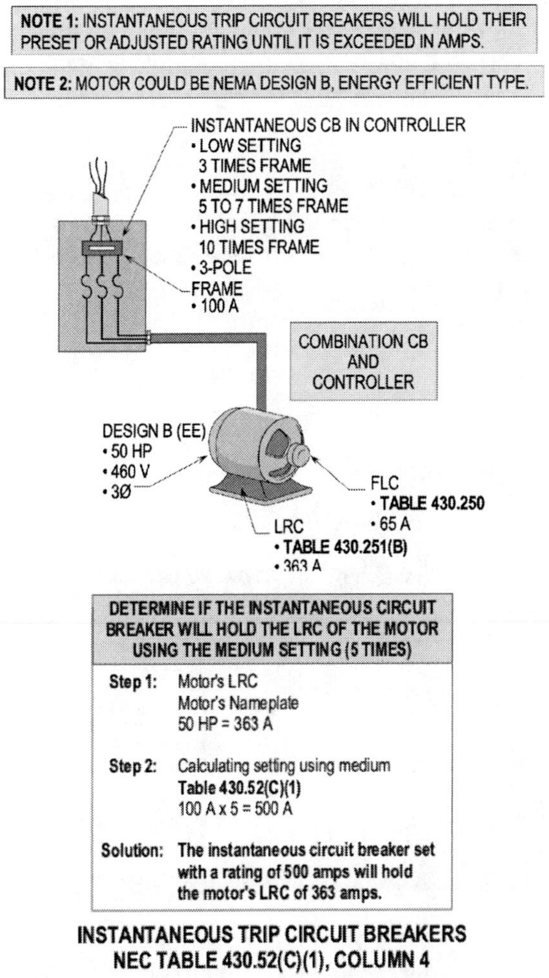

NOTE 1: INSTANTANEOUS TRIP CIRCUIT BREAKERS WILL HOLD THEIR PRESET OR ADJUSTED RATING UNTIL IT IS EXCEEDED IN AMPS.

NOTE 2: MOTOR COULD BE NEMA DESIGN B, ENERGY EFFICIENT TYPE.

INSTANTANEOUS CB IN CONTROLLER
• LOW SETTING
  3 TIMES FRAME
• MEDIUM SETTING
  5 TO 7 TIMES FRAME
• HIGH SETTING
  10 TIMES FRAME
• 3-POLE
FRAME
• 100 A

COMBINATION CB
AND
CONTROLLER

DESIGN B (EE)
• 50 HP
• 460 V
• 3Ø

FLC
• TABLE 430.250
• 65 A

LRC
• TABLE 430.251(B)
• 363 A

DETERMINE IF THE INSTANTANEOUS CIRCUIT BREAKER WILL HOLD THE LRC OF THE MOTOR USING THE MEDIUM SETTING (5 TIMES)

Step 1:   Motor's LRC
           Motor's Nameplate
           50 HP = 363 A

Step 2:   Calculating setting using medium
           Table 430.52(C)(1)
           100 A x 5 = 500 A

Solution: The instantaneous circuit breaker set
           with a rating of 500 amps will hold
           the motor's LRC of 363 amps.

INSTANTANEOUS TRIP CIRCUIT BREAKERS
NEC TABLE 430.52(C)(1), COLUMN 4

Figure 18-8. An instantaneous trip circuit breaker with its rating set above the locked-rotor current of a motor will allow the motor to start and run.

INVERSE-TIME CIRCUIT BREAKERS TABLE 430.52(C)(1), COLUMN 5

Inverse-time circuit breakers are designed with instantaneous trip features to detect short circuits and thermal characteristics to sense slow heat buildup in the circuit. If heat should occur in the windings of the motor, the instantaneous values of current will be detected by the thermal action of the circuit breaker and will trip open the circuit if it is sized properly. The magnetic action of the circuit breaker will clear the circuit if short circuits or ground faults should occur on the circuit elements or equipment served.

> **Motor Tip:** Inverse-time circuit breakers will hold about three times their rating for different periods of time based upon their frame size. A motor with a locked-rotor current of 585 amps can be started with a 200 amp circuit breaker.

This can be verified by multiplying the 200 amp circuit breaker by 3, which is equal to 600 amps; 585 amps divided by 3 is equal to 195 amps. By rounding up to the next size circuit breaker per **430.52(C)(1)(a)**, the size circuit breaker is 200 amps, per **240.6(A)**. This size circuit breaker allows the motor to start and run. **(See Figure 18-9)**

OBTAINING FLC RATINGS TABLES 430.247 THRU 430.250

The FLC ratings for single-phase and three-phase DC and AC motors are obtained from **Tables 430.247 through 430.250**. The starting currents (LRC) are obtained from **Tables 430.251(A)** and **(B)**.

FLC RATING FOR DC MOTORS TABLE 430.247

The FLC rating for DC motors is determined from the values listed in **Table 430.247** for motors running at base speed.

For example, the FLC rating for a 120 volt, 10 HP, DC motor is 76 amps.

FLC RATING FOR SINGLE-PHASE MOTORS TABLE 430.248

The FLC rating for a single-phase motor is determined from the values listed in **Table 430.248** for motors running at usual speeds and motors having normal torque characteristics.

For example, the FLC rating for a 208 volt, 5 HP, single-phase motor is 30.8 amps.

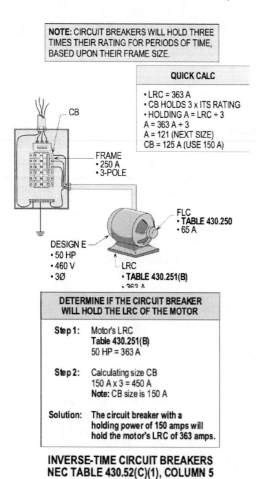

NOTE: CIRCUIT BREAKERS WILL HOLD THREE TIMES THEIR RATING FOR PERIODS OF TIME, BASED UPON THEIR FRAME SIZE.

QUICK CALC

- LRC = 363 A
- CB HOLDS 3 x ITS RATING
- HOLDING A = LRC ÷ 3
- A = 363 A ÷ 3
- A = 121 (NEXT SIZE)
- CB = 125 A (USE 150 A)

CB

FRAME
- 250 A
- 3-POLE

FLC
- **TABLE 430.250**
- 65 A

DESIGN E
- 50 HP
- 460 V
- 3Ø

LRC
- **TABLE 430.251(B)**
- 363 A

DETERMINE IF THE CIRCUIT BREAKER WILL HOLD THE LRC OF THE MOTOR

Step 1: Motor's LRC
Table 430.251(B)
50 HP = 363 A

Step 2: Calculating size CB
150 A x 3 = 450 A
Note: CB size is 150 A

Solution: **The circuit breaker with a holding power of 150 amps will hold the motor's LRC of 363 amps.**

INVERSE-TIME CIRCUIT BREAKERS NEC TABLE 430.52(C)(1), COLUMN 5

Figure 18-9. Circuit breakers sized at least three times their rating provide an amp rating above the locked-rotor current of the motor and will hold such LRC. [See **Figure 18-12(d)**]

FLC RATING FOR THREE-PHASE MOTORS TABLE 430.250

The FLC rating for a three-phase motor is determined from the values listed in **Table 430.250** for motors running at speeds used for belted motors and motors with normal torque characteristics.

For example, the FLC rating for 460 volt, 30 HP, three-phase motor is 40 amps.

STARTING CURRENTS FOR SINGLE-PHASE MOTORS TABLE 430.251(A)

The starting current (LRC) for a single-phase motor is determined from the values listed in **Table 430.251(A)**.

For example, the starting current (LRC) for a 230 volt, 7-1/2 HP, single-phase motor is 240 amps.

STARTING CURRENT FOR THREE-PHASE MOTORS TABLE 430.251(B)

The starting current (LRC) for a three-phase motor is determined from the values listed in **Table 430.251(B)**.

For example, the starting current (LRC) for a 208 volt, 50 HP, three-phase, Design B motor is 802 amps.

FLC FOR UNLISTED MOTORS TABLES 430.247 AND 430.250

The following methods can be used to determine the full-load current rating in amps for motors that are not listed in **Tables 430.247 through 430.250**.

(1) The horsepower rating of a listed motor shall be selected that is below the unlisted motor.

(2) The motor's full-load current rating shall be divided by its horsepower rating to obtain the multiplier.

(3) The multiplier times the horsepower of the unlisted motor derives FLC for the unlisted motor.

Motor Tip: The full-load current rating of the motor is determined by multiplying these values by the horsepower rating of the unlisted motor. **(See Figure 18-10)**

TO OCPD
- 430.52(C)(1)

SUPPLY CIRCUIT
- 430.22

MOTOR
- 45 HP
- 460 V
- 3Ø
- DESIGN B

SIZING MOTOR FLA RATING FOR A MOTOR NOT LISTED IN TABLE

Step 1: Finding FLA
Table 430.250
40 HP motor = 52 amps

Step 2: Finding multiplier
Multiplier = A ÷ HP
Multiplier = 52 A ÷ 40 HP
Multiplier = 1.3

Step 3: Applying multiplier
Multiplier x HP of unlisted motor
1.3 x 45 = 58.5 A

Solution: **The FLA rating of the unlisted motor is 58.5 amps.**

FLC FOR UNLISTED MOTORS NEC TABLES 430.247 THRU 430.250

Figure 18-10. The above illustrates the procedure for calculating the FLA of a motor not listed in **Tables 430.247 through 430.250**.

FLC RATINGS USING RULE-OF-THUMB METHOD

The full-load current of a motor may be found by applying the rule-of-thumb method to horsepower values in **Table 430.248** for single-phase and **Table 430.250** for three-phase. The table current will not always be exactly the same as the rule-of-thumb amps.

Overcurrent protection devices, conductors, and other elements can be sized with the full-load current ratings when using the rule-of-thumb method. The full-load current ratings are within a usable range when applying the rule-of-thumb method to determine the full-load current rating. These amperage ratings will provide values to calculate elements for a complete and safe electrical motor system. One of the following percentages (multipliers) can be applied when using a rule-of-thumb method to derive full-load amps for a particular size motor:

(1) When installing 550, 575, or 600 volt, three-phase motors, the horsepower rating of the motor shall be multiplied by 1.00 to obtain the full-load current in amps.

(2) When installing 440, 460, or 480 volt, three-phase motors, the horsepower rating of the motor shall be multiplied by 1.25 to obtain the full-load current in amps.

(3) When installing 220, 230, or 240 volt, three-phase motors, the horsepower rating of the motor shall be multiplied by 2.50 to obtain the full-load current in amps.

(4) When installing 220, 230, or 240 volt, single-phase motors, the horsepower rating of the motor shall be multiplied by 5.00 to obtain the full-load current in amps.

(5) When installing 110, 115, or 120 volt, single-phase motors, the horsepower rating of the motor shall be multiplied by 10.00 to obtain the full-load current in amps.

See Figure 18-11 for a detailed illustration of calculating full-load current for motors using the rule-of-thumb method.

SIZING MAXIMUM OVERCURRENT PROTECTION DEVICE 430.52(C)(1)(b)(1), (b)(2), AND (b)(3)

Where the rating specified in **Table 430.52(C)(1)** is not sufficient for the starting current of the motor, the following ratings (percentages) shall be applied:

(1) Nontime-delay fuses (400 percent)

(2) Time-delay fuses (225 percent)

(3) Inverse-time circuit breakers (400 and 300 percent)

(4) Instantaneous-trip circuit breakers (0-1700 percent based on Design letter or Code letter.)

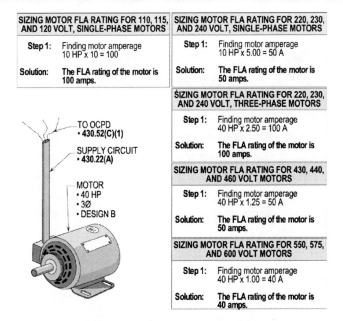

FLC RATINGS USING RULE-OF-THUMB METHOD

Figure 18-11. The above illustration is a method used by the electrical industry to determine the FLA of motors found in **Tables 430.247 through 430.250**.

SIZING OVERCURRENT PROTECTION DEVICES TO ALLOW MOTORS TO START AND RUN 430.52(C)(1) AND TABLE 430.52(C)(1)

The branch-circuit protection for a motor may be a fuse or circuit breaker located in the line at the point where the branch circuit originates. The fuse or circuit breaker is located either at a service cabinet or distribution panel or in the motor control center. When there is only one motor on a branch circuit, the fuse or circuit breaker is sized according to **Table 430.52(C)(1)** and **430.52(C)(1)**.

To use the table properly will require an explanation. There is the matter of "Design letters." A Design letter provides certain electrical characteristics of a particular motor that are needed to size the overcurrent protection device to permit the motor to start and accelerate its load. To apply **Table 430.52(C)(1)**, it is necessary to take the following steps:

(1) Select the phase of the motor
- Single-phase
- Three-phase (poly-phase)

(2) Select type of motor
- Squirrel-cage induction
- Wound-rotor
- DC
- Synchronous

Note, motors can be single-phase or three-phase types.

(3) Select the Design letter of the motor
- Design B
- Design C
- Design D
- Design E (from Europe, IEC)

(4) Select the type of overcurrent protection device
- Column 2 is for nontime-delay fuses
- Column 3 is for time-delay fuses
- Column 4 is for circuit breakers with instantaneous trip settings or adjustments
- Column 5 is for circuit breakers with both instantaneous trip settings and thermal trip characteristics

See Figures 18-12(a) through (d) for sizing and selecting the size overcurrent protection devices per **Table 430.52(C) (1)** to allow motors to start and run their driven load.

Note, the minimum (rounded down) and next size (rounded up) overcurrent protection device will be sized for a particular type and size motor.

NONTIME-DELAY FUSES USING THE MAXIMUM SIZE 430.52(C)(1)(b)(1)

If the minimum or next size overcurrent protection device does not allow the motor start and run, the maximum size rating of a nontime-delay fuse not exceeding 600 amps shall be permitted to be increased but shall in no case exceed 400 percent of the FLC of the motor. **(See Figure 18-13)**

TIME-DELAY FUSES USING MAXIMUM SIZE 430.52(C)(1)(b)(2)

To allow a motor to start and run, the rating of a time-delay fuse shall be permitted to be increased but shall in no case exceed 225 percent of the FLC of the motor. **(See Figure 18-14)**

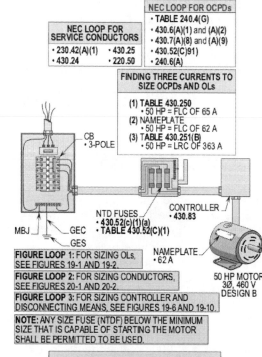

SIZING OVERCURRENT PROTECTION DEVICES TO ALLOW MOTORS TO START AND RUN

Figure 18-12(a). Determining the minimum and next size nontime-delay fuses per **Table 430.52(C)(1)** and **430.52(C) (1)** and **(a)** to start and run a motor. A smaller overcurrent protection device than the minimum size (rounded down) shall be permitted to be used, if it will start the motor.

INVERSE-TIME CIRCUIT BREAKERS 430.52(C)(1)(b)(3)

The rating for inverse-time circuit breakers shall be permitted to be increased but shall in no case exceed 400 percent for a full-load current of 100 amps or less. Full-load current greater than 100 amps shall be permitted to be increased up to 300 percent. **(See Figure 18-15)**

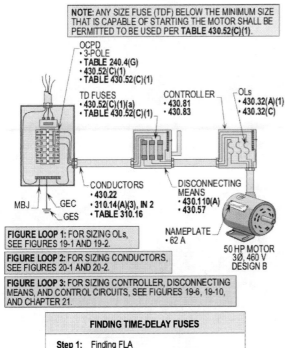

NOTE: ANY SIZE FUSE (TDF) BELOW THE MINIMUM SIZE THAT IS CAPABLE OF STARTING THE MOTOR SHALL BE PERMITTED TO BE USED PER **TABLE 430.52(C)(1)**.

OCPD
• 3-POLE
• **TABLE 240.4(G)**
• **430.52(C)(1)**
• **TABLE 430.52(C)(1)**

TD FUSES
• **430.52(C)(1)(a)**
• **TABLE 430.52(C)(1)**

CONTROLLER
• **430.81**
• **430.83**

OLs
• **430.32(A)(1)**
• **430.32(C)**

CONDUCTORS
• **430.22**
• **310.14(A)(3), IN 2**
• **TABLE 310.16**

DISCONNECTING MEANS
• **430.110(A)**
• **430.57**

NAMEPLATE
• 62 A

MBJ   GEC
      GES

50 HP MOTOR
3Ø, 460 V
DESIGN B

FIGURE LOOP 1: FOR SIZING OLs, SEE FIGURES 19-1 AND 19-2.

FIGURE LOOP 2: FOR SIZING CONDUCTORS, SEE FIGURES 20-1 AND 20-2.

FIGURE LOOP 3: FOR SIZING CONTROLLER, DISCONNECTING MEANS, AND CONTROL CIRCUITS, SEE FIGURES 19-6, 19-10, AND CHAPTER 21.

FINDING TIME-DELAY FUSES

Step 1: Finding FLA
430.6(A)(1) and **Table 430.250**
50 HP = 65 A

Step 2: Finding percentage
430.52(C)(1) and **Table 430.52(C)(1)**
Minimum size = 175%

Step 3: Calculating minimum size
430.52(C)(1)
Minimum size = 65 A x 175% = 113.75 A

Step 4: Calculating next-size
430.52(C)(1)(a)
113.75 permits 125 A

Step 5: Selecting TDFs
Table 240.6(A)
Minimum size = 110 A
Next size = 125 A

Solution : **The minimum size time-delay fuse is 110 amps and the next size is 125 amps.**

SIZING OVERCURRENT PROTECTION DEVICES TO ALLOW MOTORS TO START AND RUN

Figure 18-12(b). Determining the minimum and next size time-delay fuses per **Table 430.52(C)(1)** to start and run a motor. A smaller time-delay fuse than the minimum size (rounded down) shall be permitted to be used, if it will start the motor.

MOTORS CONNECTED TO INDIVIDUAL BRANCH CIRCUITS
430.53

Two or more motors, or one or more motors and other loads, shall be permitted to be connected to an individual branch circuit under the following conditions:

(1) motor not over 1 HP,

(2) smallest rated motor protected, and

(3) listed for other group installations.

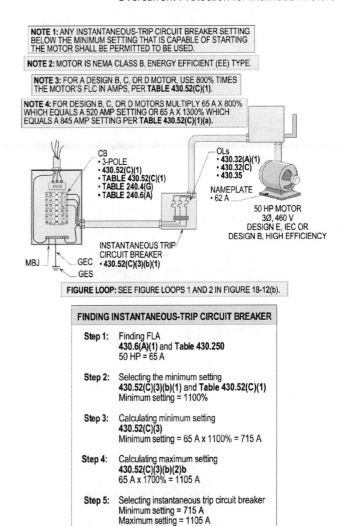

NOTE 1: ANY INSTANTANEOUS-TRIP CIRCUIT BREAKER SETTING BELOW THE MINIMUM SETTING THAT IS CAPABLE OF STARTING THE MOTOR SHALL BE PERMITTED TO BE USED.

NOTE 2: MOTOR IS NEMA CLASS B, ENERGY EFFICIENT (EE) TYPE.

NOTE 3: FOR A DESIGN B, C, OR D MOTOR, USE 800% TIMES THE MOTOR'S FLC IN AMPS, PER **TABLE 430.52(C)(1)**.

NOTE 4: FOR DESIGN B, C, OR D MOTORS MULTIPLY 65 A X 800% WHICH EQUALS A 520 AMP SETTING OR 65 A X 1300% WHICH EQUALS A 845 AMP SETTING PER **TABLE 430.52(C)(1)(a)**.

CB
• 3-POLE
• **430.52(C)(1)**
• **TABLE 430.52(C)(1)**
• **TABLE 240.4(G)**
• **TABLE 240.6(A)**

OLs
• **430.32(A)(1)**
• **430.32(C)**
• **430.35**

NAMEPLATE
• 62 A

50 HP MOTOR
3Ø, 460 V
DESIGN E, IEC OR
DESIGN B, HIGH EFFICIENCY

INSTANTANEOUS TRIP CIRCUIT BREAKER
• **430.52(C)(3)(b)(1)**

MBJ   GEC
      GES

FIGURE LOOP: SEE FIGURE LOOPS 1 AND 2 IN FIGURE 18-12(b).

FINDING INSTANTANEOUS-TRIP CIRCUIT BREAKER

Step 1: Finding FLA
430.6(A)(1) and **Table 430.250**
50 HP = 65 A

Step 2: Selecting the minimum setting
430.52(C)(3)(b)(1) and **Table 430.52(C)(1)**
Minimum setting = 1100%

Step 3: Calculating minimum setting
430.52(C)(3)
Minimum setting = 65 A x 1100% = 715 A

Step 4: Calculating maximum setting
430.52(C)(3)(b)(2)b
65 A x 1700% = 1105 A

Step 5: Selecting instantaneous trip circuit breaker
Minimum setting = 715 A
Maximum setting = 1105 A

Solution: **The minimum setting is 715 amps and the maximum setting is 1105 amps. However, a smaller setting shall be permitted to be used**

SIZING OVERCURRENT PROTECTION DEVICES TO ALLOW MOTORS TO START AND RUN
NEC 430.52(C)(1)(a)

Figure 18-12(c). Determining the minimum and maximum setting for an instantaneous trip circuit breaker to start and run a motor. A smaller minimum setting shall be permitted to be used, if it will start the motor.

MOTOR NOT OVER 1 HP
430.53(A)

Two or more motors may be installed without individual overcurrent protection devices if rated less than 1 HP each and if the full-load current rating of each motor does not exceed 6 amps. Motors not rated over 1 horsepower shall be within sight of the motor, manually started, and portable. Section **430.32** and **430.42** shall be applied for running overload protection for each motor if these conditions are not met.

The overcurrent protection device rated at 20 amps or less can protect a 120 volt or less branch circuit supplying these motors. Branch circuits of 600 volts or less can be protected by a 15 amp or less overcurrent protection device. **(See Figure 18-16)**

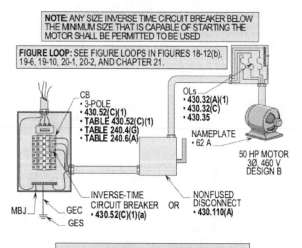

NOTE: ANY SIZE INVERSE TIME CIRCUIT BREAKER BELOW THE MINIMUM SIZE THAT IS CAPABLE OF STARTING THE MOTOR SHALL BE PERMITTED TO BE USED

FIGURE LOOP: SEE FIGURE LOOPS IN FIGURES 18-12(b), 19-6, 19-10, 20-1, 20-2, AND CHAPTER 21.

CB
• 3-POLE
• 430.52(C)(1)
• TABLE 430.52(C)(1)
• TABLE 240.4(G)
• TABLE 240.6(A)

OLs
• 430.32(A)(1)
• 430.32(C)
• 430.35

NAMEPLATE
• 62 A

50 HP MOTOR
3Ø, 460 V
DESIGN B

MBJ   GEC   GES

INVERSE-TIME
CIRCUIT BREAKER
• 430.52(C)(1)(a)

OR

NONFUSED
DISCONNECT
• 430.110(A)

FINDING INVERSE-TIME CIRCUIT BREAKER

Step 1:	Finding FLA 430.6(A)(1) and Table 430.250 50 HP = 65 A	
Step 2:	Finding percentage 430.52(C)(1) and Table 430.52(C)(1) Minimum size = 250%	
Step 3:	Calculating minimum size 430.52(C)(1) Minimum size = 65 A x 250% = 162.5 A	
Step 4:	Calculating next size 430.52(C)(1)(a) 162.5 A permits 175 A	
Step 5:	Selecting inverse-time circuit breaker Table 240.6(A) Minimum size = 150 A Next size = 175 A	
Solution:	The minimum size inverse-time circuit breaker is 150 amps and the next size is 175 amps.	

**SIZING OVERCURRENT PROTECTION DEVICES
TO ALLOW MOTORS TO START AND RUN
NEC 430.52(C)(1)(a)**

Figure 18-12(d). Determining the minimum and next size inverse-time circuit breaker to start and run a motor.

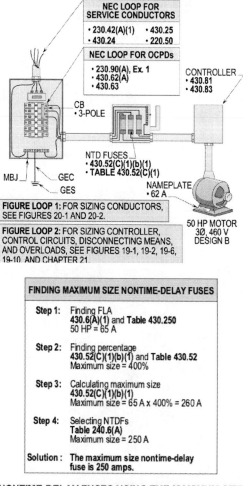

**NEC LOOP FOR
SERVICE CONDUCTORS**
• 230.42(A)(1)   • 430.25
• 430.24   • 220.50

NEC LOOP FOR OCPDs
• 230.90(A), Ex. 1
• 430.62(A)
• 430.63

CONTROLLER
• 430.81
• 430.83

CB
• 3-POLE

NTD FUSES
• 430.52(C)(1)(b)(1)
• TABLE 430.52(C)(1)

NAMEPLATE
• 62 A

MBJ   GEC   GES

50 HP MOTOR
3Ø, 460 V
DESIGN B

FIGURE LOOP 1: FOR SIZING CONDUCTORS, SEE FIGURES 20-1 AND 20-2.

FIGURE LOOP 2: FOR SIZING CONTROLLER, CONTROL CIRCUITS, DISCONNECTING MEANS, AND OVERLOADS, SEE FIGURES 19-1, 19-2, 19-6, 19-10, AND CHAPTER 21.

FINDING MAXIMUM SIZE NONTIME-DELAY FUSES

Step 1:	Finding FLA 430.6(A)(1) and Table 430.250 50 HP = 65 A	
Step 2:	Finding percentage 430.52(C)(1)(b)(1) and Table 430.52 Maximum size = 400%	
Step 3:	Calculating maximum size 430.52(C)(1)(b)(1) Maximum size = 65 A x 400% = 260 A	
Step 4:	Selecting NTDFs Table 240.6(A) Maximum size = 250 A	
Solution:	The maximum size nontime-delay fuse is 250 amps.	

**NONTIME-DELAY FUSES USING THE MAXIMUM SIZE
NEC 430.52(C)(1)(b)(1)**

Figure 18-13. Nontime-delay fuses shall be permitted to be increased to a maximum size of 400 percent of the motor's full-load current rating (smaller size permitted).

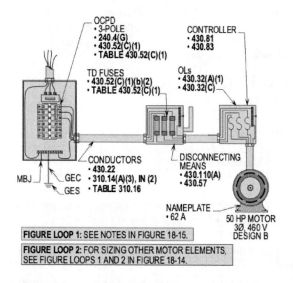

OCPD
• 3-POLE
• 240.4(G)
• 430.52(C)(1)
• TABLE 430.52(C)(1)

CONTROLLER
• 430.81
• 430.83

TD FUSES
• 430.52(C)(1)(b)(2)
• TABLE 430.52(C)(1)

OLs
• 430.32(A)(1)
• 430.32(C)

CONDUCTORS
• 430.22
• 310.14(A)(3), IN (2)
• TABLE 310.16

DISCONNECTING
MEANS
• 430.110(A)
• 430.57

MBJ   GEC   GES

NAMEPLATE
• 62 A

50 HP MOTOR
3Ø, 460 V
DESIGN B

FIGURE LOOP 1: SEE NOTES IN FIGURE 18-15.

FIGURE LOOP 2: FOR SIZING OTHER MOTOR ELEMENTS, SEE FIGURE LOOPS 1 AND 2 IN FIGURE 18-14.

FINDING MAXIMUM SIZE TIME-DELAY FUSES

Step 1:	Finding FLA 430.6(A)(1) and Table 430.250 50 HP = 65 A	
Step 2:	Finding percentage 430.52(C)(1)(b)(2) and Table 430.52(C)(1) Maximum size = 225%	
Step 3:	Calculating maximum size 430.52(C)(1)(b)(2) Maximum size = 65 A x 225% = 146 A	
Step 4:	Selecting TDFs Table 240.6(A) Maximum size = 125 A	
Solution:	The maximum size time-delay fuse is 125 amps.	

**TIME-DELAY FUSES USING MAXIMUM SIZE
NEC 430.52(C)(1)(b)(2)**

Figure 18-14. Determining the maximum size time-delay fuse to start and run a motor (smaller size permitted).

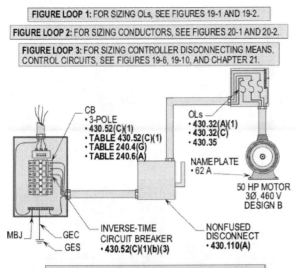

FIGURE LOOP 1: FOR SIZING OLs, SEE FIGURES 19-1 AND 19-2.

FIGURE LOOP 2: FOR SIZING CONDUCTORS, SEE FIGURES 20-1 AND 20-2.

FIGURE LOOP 3: FOR SIZING CONTROLLER DISCONNECTING MEANS, CONTROL CIRCUITS, SEE FIGURES 19-6, 19-10, AND CHAPTER 21.

FINDING MAXIMUM SIZE INVERSE-TIME CIRCUIT BREAKER

Step 1: Finding FLA
430.6(A)(1) and **Table 430.250**
50 HP = 65 A

Step 2: Finding percentage
430.52(C)(1)(b)(3) and **Table 430.52(C)(1)**
Maximum size = 400%

Step 3: Calculating maximum size
430.52(C)(1)(b)(3)
Maximum size = 65 A x 400% = 260 A

Step 5: Selecting inverse-time circuit breaker
Table 240.6(A)
Maximum size = 250 A

Solution: **The maximum size inverse-time circuit breaker is 250 amps.**

INVERSE-TIME CIRCUIT BREAKERS
NEC 430.52(C)(1)(b)(3)

Figure 18-15. An inverse-time circuit breaker shall be permitted to be increased to a maximum size of 400 percent of the motor's full-load current rating (smaller size permitted).

SMALLEST RATED MOTOR PROTECTED 430.53(B)

The branch-circuit overcurrent protection device shall be permitted to protect the smallest rated motor of the group for two or more motors of different ratings if the largest motor is permitted to start. The smallest rated motor of the group shall have its overcurrent protection device set at no higher value than permitted per **Table 430.52(C)(1)**. The smallest rated motor and other motors of the group shall be provided with overload protection if necessary per **430.32**. **(See Figure 18-17** and the **Ex's** to **430.87** and **430.112)**

OTHER GROUP INSTALLATIONS 430.53(C)

Two or more motors of any size shall be permitted to be installed and connected to an individual branch circuit. However, the largest motor of the group shall be protected

by the percentages listed in **Table 430.52** for sizing and selecting fuses or circuit breakers. Each motor controller and component installed in the group shall be approved for such use. The following are elements that shall be sized and selected properly:

(1) Overcurrent protection devices

(2) Controllers

(3) Running overload protection devices

The elements shall be permitted to be installed as a listed factory assembly or field installed as separate assemblies listed for such conditions of use.

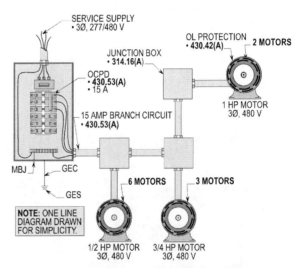

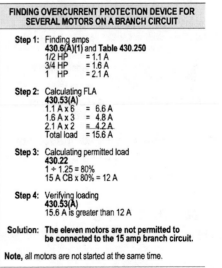

FINDING OVERCURRENT PROTECTION DEVICE FOR SEVERAL MOTORS ON A BRANCH CIRCUIT

Step 1: Finding amps
430.6(A)(1) and **Table 430.250**
1/2 HP   = 1.1 A
3/4 HP   = 1.6 A
1   HP   = 2.1 A

Step 2: Calculating FLA
430.53(A)
1.1 A x 6   = 6.6 A
1.6 A x 3   = 4.8 A
2.1 A x 2   = 4.2 A
Total load   = 15.6 A

Step 3: Calculating permitted load
430.22
1 ÷ 1.25 = 80%
15 A CB x 80% = 12 A

Step 4: Verifying loading
430.53(A)
15.6 A is greater than 12 A

Solution: **The eleven motors are not permitted to be connected to the 15 amp branch circuit.**

Note, all motors are not started at the same time.

MOTOR NOT OVER 1 HP
NEC 430.53(A)

Figure 18-16. Determining the number of motors permitted on a 15 amp branch circuit.

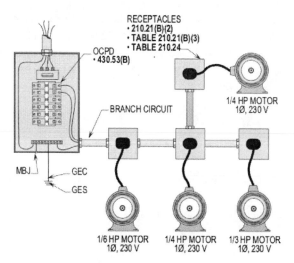

FINDING SEVERAL MOTORS ON A BRANCH CIRCUIT

Step 1: Finding amps
430.6(A)(1) and Table 430.248
1/6 HP = 2.2 A
1/4 HP = 2.9 A
1/4 HP = 2.9 A
1/3 HP = 3.6 A

Step 2: Calculating FLA
430.53(B)
2.2 A x 1   = 2.2 A
2.9 A x 1   = 2.9 A
2.9 A x 1   = 2.9 A
3.6 A x 1   = 3.6 A
Total load = 11.6 A

Step 3: Calculating permitted load
Table 210.21(B)(3)
1 ÷ 1.25 = 80%
15 A OCPD x 80% = 12 A

Step 4: Verifying loading
430.53(B) and Table 210.21(B)(3)
11.6 A is less than 12 A

Step 5: Protecting smaller motor
430.53(B) and Table 430.52
2.2 A x 250% = 5.5 A

Step 6: Selecting OCPD
430.53(B), 240.4(B), and Table 240.6(A)
5.5 A permits 15 A CB

Solution: Section 430.53(B) permits the next size circuit breaker which is 15 amps.

Note, most inspectors permit this concept since the next size circuit breaker is 15 amps.

SMALLEST RATED MOTOR PROTECTED
NEC 430.53(B)

Figure 18-17. Determining the number of motors permitted on a 15 amp branch circuit using a 15 amp circuit breaker per **240.6(B)** by permission of AHJ.

SINGLE MOTOR TAPS
430.53(D)

Any number of motor taps shall be permitted to be installed where a fuse or circuit breaker is installed at the point where each motor is tapped to the line. This type of installation made from a feeder per **430.28** and **430.53(D)** is often utilized. **(See Figure 18-18)**

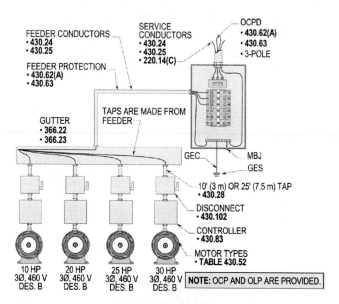

SINGLE MOTOR TAPS
NEC 430.53(D)

Figure 18-18. Taps can be made from a feeder with the proper conductor size and overcurrent protection device with each tap,

AUTOMATIC RESTARTING
430.43

A motor that can automatically restart after overloading (tripping) shall not be installed unless the motor is approved for such use. Automatic restarting of a motor after shutdown shall not be installed if the automatic restarting of the motor can cause injury to personnel. (Also, see **430.44.**)

SIZING AN OVERCURRENT PROTECTION DEVICE FOR TWO OR MORE MOTORS
430.62(A)

To determine the size overcurrent protection device to be installed for a feeder supplying two or motors, the following procedures shall be applied:

(1) Apply **Table 430.52(C)(1)** to select largest motor.

(2) Size largest overcurrent protection device for any one motor of the group.

(3) Add FLA of remaining motors.

(4) Do not exceed this value with overcurrent protection device rating.

See Figure 18-19 for a detailed procedure for sizing an overcurrent protection device for a feeder motor circuit.

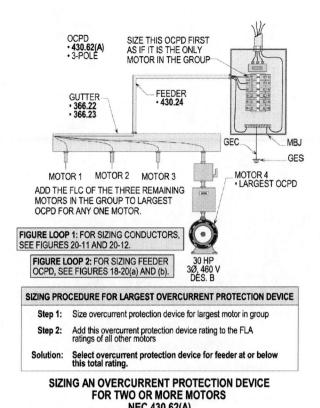

FIGURE LOOP 1: FOR SIZING CONDUCTORS, SEE FIGURES 20-11 AND 20-12.

FIGURE LOOP 2: FOR SIZING FEEDER OCPD, SEE FIGURES 18-20(a) AND (b).

SIZING PROCEDURE FOR LARGEST OVERCURRENT PROTECTION DEVICE

Step 1: Size overcurrent protection device for largest motor in group

Step 2: Add this overcurrent protection device rating to the FLA ratings of all other motors

Solution: Select overcurrent protection device for feeder at or below this total rating.

SIZING AN OVERCURRENT PROTECTION DEVICE FOR TWO OR MORE MOTORS
NEC 430.62(A)

Figure 18-19. Determining overcurrent protection device for a feeder with several motors being protected from short-circuit and ground-fault conditions.

OVERCURRENT PROTECTION DEVICE FOR MOTORS ON A FEEDER 430.62(A) AND (B)

The overcurrent protection device for a feeder with two or more motors shall be permitted to be sized by the following procedure:

(1) size overcurrent protection device based on motor's FLC,

(2) size overcurrent protection device based on conductor's ampacity, or

(3) conductors with ampacities greater than motor's FLC rating.

SIZING OVERCURRENT PROTECTION DEVICE BASED ON MOTOR'S FLC 430.62(A)

The overcurrent protection device for a feeder supplying two or more motors shall be based on the largest overcurrent protection device for any motor of the group plus the FLC of the remaining motors. This procedure requires a selection of overcurrent protection devices (rounding down) to find

the sum of the calculated value if it does not correspond to a standard device.

Note, the size overcurrent protection device for a feeder supplying two or more motors shall be determined by selecting the next lower rating if the calculation based on the percentages per **Table 430.52(C)(1)** times the FLA per **Table 430.250** does not correspond to a standard overcurrent protection device per **Table 240.6(A)**. **[See Figures 18-20(a) through (d)]**

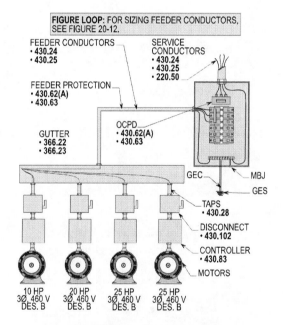

SIZING CIRCUIT BREAKER FOR A FEEDER

Step 1: Finding FLA of motors
430.6(A)(1) and Table 430.250
10 HP = 14 A
20 HP = 27 A
25 HP = 34 A
25 HP = 34 A

Note: CB for largest motor 34 A x 250% = 85 A (round up)

Step 2: Calculating feeder OCPD
430.52(C)(1), Table 430.52(C)(1), and 430.62(A)
34 A x 250% = 90 A + 34 A + 27 A + 14 A = 165 A

Step 3: Selecting OCPD
430.62(A), Table 240.4(G), and Table 240.6(A)
150 A is a standard OCPD

Solution: The size overcurrent protection device required for the feeder is 150 amps.

SIZING OVERCURRENT PROTECTION DEVICE BASED ON MOTOR'S FLC
NEC 430.62(A)

Figure 18-20(a). Sizing the circuit breaker for a feeder supplying two or more motors.

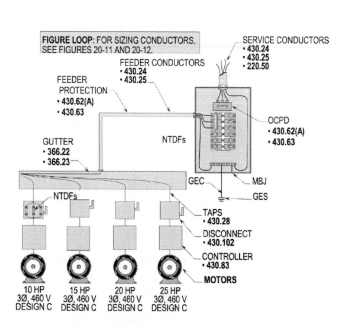

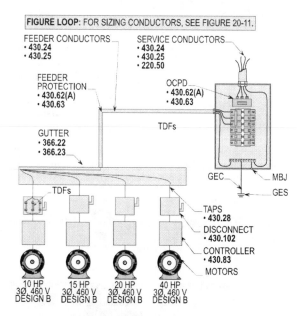

SIZING NONTIME-DELAY FUSES FOR A FEEDER

Step 1: Finding FLA of motors
430.6(A)(1) and **Table 430.250**
10 HP = 14 A
15 HP = 21 A
20 HP = 27 A
25 HP = 34 A

Step 2: Calculating largest OCPD
430.52(C)(1)(a), Table 430.52(C)(1), 430.62(A),
and **Table 240.6(A)**
34 A x 300% = 102 A requires 110 A NTDFs
27 A x 300% = 81 A requires 90 A NTDFs
21 A x 300% = 63 A requires 70 A NTDFs
14 A x 300% = 42 A requires 45 A NTDFs

Step 3: Calculating OCPD for feeder
430.62(A) and **430.52(C)(1)(a)**
Largest OCPD   = 110 A
Plus remaining motors = 27 A
                      = 21 A
                      = 14 A
Total amps   = 172 A

Step 4: Selecting OCPD for feeder
430.62(A), Table 240.4(G), and **Table 240.6(A)**
172 A requires 150 A NTDFs
(172 A is not a standard OCPD)

Solution: The size nontime-delay fuses for the feeder are 150 amps based on the motor's code letters.

Note, there is no **Ex.** in **430.62(A)** to permit the next higher size overcurrent protection device above 172 amps.

**SIZING OVERCURRENT PROTECTION DEVICE
BASED ON MOTOR'S FLC
NEC 430.62(A)**

Figure 18-20(b). Sizing nontime-delay fuses for a feeder supplying two or more motors.

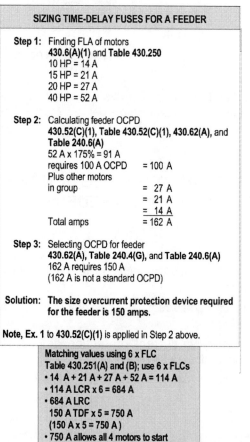

SIZING TIME-DELAY FUSES FOR A FEEDER

Step 1: Finding FLA of motors
430.6(A)(1) and **Table 430.250**
10 HP = 14 A
15 HP = 21 A
20 HP = 27 A
40 HP = 52 A

Step 2: Calculating feeder OCPD
430.52(C)(1), Table 430.52(C)(1), 430.62(A), and
Table 240.6(A)
52 A x 175% = 91 A
requires 100 A OCPD   = 100 A
Plus other motors
in group   = 27 A
                       = 21 A
                       = 14 A
Total amps   = 162 A

Step 3: Selecting OCPD for feeder
430.62(A), Table 240.4(G), and **Table 240.6(A)**
162 A requires 150 A
(162 A is not a standard OCPD)

Solution: The size overcurrent protection device required for the feeder is 150 amps.

Note, Ex. 1 to **430.52(C)(1)** is applied in Step 2 above.

Matching values using 6 x FLC
Table 430.251(A) and (B); use 6 x FLCs
• 14 A + 21 A + 27 A + 52 A = 114 A
• 114 A LCR x 6 = 684 A
• 684 A LRC
  150 A TDF x 5 = 750 A
  (150 A x 5 = 750 A)
• 750 A allows all 4 motors to start

**SIZING OVERCURRENT PROTECTION DEVICE
BASED ON MOTOR'S FLC
NEC 430.62(A)
BASED ON MOTOR'S FLC
NEC 430.62(A)**

Figure _____ feeder supplying two or more motors.

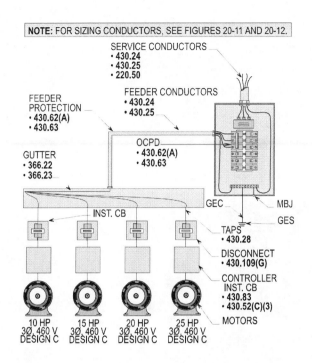

NOTE: FOR SIZING CONDUCTORS, SEE FIGURES 20-11 AND 20-12.

SERVICE CONDUCTORS
• 430.24
• 430.25
• 220.50

FEEDER CONDUCTORS
• 430.24
• 430.25

FEEDER PROTECTION
• 430.62(A)
• 430.63

OCPD
• 430.62(A)
• 430.63

GUTTER
• 366.22
• 366.23

INST. CB

GEC   MBJ
GES

TAPS
• 430.28

DISCONNECT
• 430.109(G)

CONTROLLER
INST. CB
• 430.83
• 430.52(C)(3)

MOTORS

10 HP / 15 HP / 20 HP / 25 HP
3Ø, 460 V DESIGN C

SIZING INSTANTANEOUS TRIP CIRCUIT BREAKER FOR FEEDER

Step 1: Finding FLA of motors
430.6(A)(1) and Table 430.250
10 HP = 14 A
15 HP = 21 A
20 HP = 27 A
25 HP = 34 A

Step 2: Calculating feeder OCPD
430.52(C)(3), Table 430.52(C)(1), 430.62(A), Ex. 1, and Table 240.6(A)
34 A x 800%   = 272 A
Plus other motors
in group   = 27 A
                      = 21 A
                      = 14 A
Total amps   = 334 A

Step 3: Selecting OCPD for feeder
430.62(A), Table 240.4(G), and Table 240.6(A)
334 A is the minimum setting

Solution: The minimum setting for the instantaneous circuit breaker for the feeder is 334 amps.

Matching values using 6 x FLC
Table 430.251(A) and (B); use 6 x FLCs
• 14 A + 21 A + 27 A + 34 A = 96 A
• 96 A LCR x 6 = 576 A
• 576 A LRC
  334 A setting = 334 A
• 334 A will not allow all 4 motors
  to start at the same time.

SIZING OVERCURRENT PROTECTION DEVICE BASED ON MOTOR'S FLC
NEC 430.62(A)

Figure 18-20(d). Sizing an instantaneous trip circuit breaker for a feeder supplying two or more motors.

SIZING OVERCURRENT PROTECTION DEVICE BASED ON CONDUCTOR'S AMPACITY
430.62(A)

The overcurrent protection device for a feeder supplying two or more motors shall be permitted to be selected based on the ampacity of the feeder conductors, if this procedure provides the greater size device. However, the overcurrent protection device sized per **Table 430.52(C)(1)** usually provides the largest device. **(See Figure 18-21)**

CONDUCTORS WITH AMPACITIES GREATER THAN MOTOR'S FLC
430.63

Feeders may be utilized in supplying one or more motors plus other loads. The size of the overcurrent protection device shall be calculated per **Articles 430** and **220**.

Note, if the ampacity of the conductors produces the largest overcurrent protection device, this size shall be used. **(See Figure 18-22)**

FUTURE ADDITIONS
430.62(B)

For large industrial plants or large capacity installations, feeders with greater capacity are usually installed to provide for a future addition of loads or changes that might be made. The ratings or settings of the feeder overcurrent protective devices shall be based on the rated ampacity of the feeder conductors.

Where a feeder carries a motor load in addition to lighting and/or the appliance loads, the capacity of the feeder shall be calculated per **Articles 210** and **220**. To this calculation is added the capacity of the motor or motors as in **430.62**. These totals are combined to find the ampacity of the feeder conductors and the overcurrent protection devices for such feeders.

Motor Tip: If two motors of the same HP are used, only one shall be considered as the larger. This motor is then used to calculate the overcurrent protection device rating and the sum is added to the other motors at 100 percent of their FLC rating.

Where two or more motors are started simultaneously, the feeder sizes and overcurrent protection devices shall be calculated accordingly and require higher ratings.

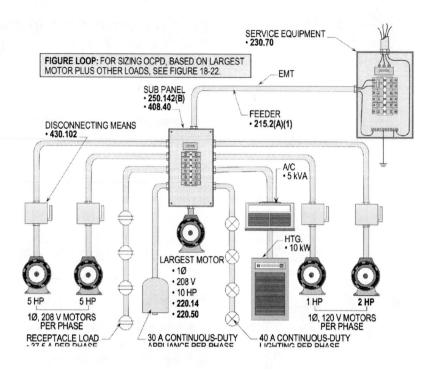

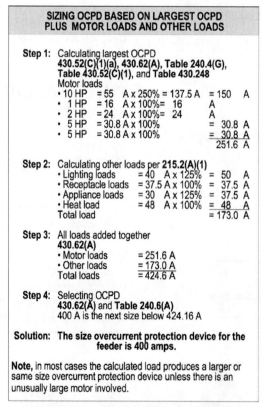

SIZING OCPD BASED ON LARGEST OCPD PLUS MOTOR LOADS AND OTHER LOADS

Step 1: Calculating largest OCPD
430.52(C)(1)(a), 430.62(A), Table 240.4(G), Table 430.52(C)(1), and Table 430.248
Motor loads
- 10 HP = 55 A x 250% = 137.5 A = 150 A
- 1 HP = 16 A x 100% = 16 A
- 2 HP = 24 A x 100% = 24 A
- 5 HP = 30.8 A x 100% = 30.8 A
- 5 HP = 30.8 A x 100% = 30.8 A
　　　　　　　　　　　　　　　　　251.6 A

Step 2: Calculating other loads per **215.2(A)(1)**
- Lighting loads = 40 A x 125% = 50 A
- Receptacle loads = 37.5 A x 100% = 37.5 A
- Appliance loads = 30 A x 125% = 37.5 A
- Heat load = 48 A x 100% = 48 A
Total load = 173.0 A

Step 3: All loads added together
430.62(A)
- Motor loads = 251.6 A
- Other loads = 173.0 A
Total loads = 424.6 A

Step 4: Selecting OCPD
430.62(A) and Table 240.6(A)
400 A is the next size below 424.16 A

Solution: **The size overcurrent protection device for the feeder is 400 amps.**

Note, in most cases the calculated load produces a larger or same size overcurrent protection device unless there is an unusually large motor involved.

SIZING OVERCURRENT PROTECTION DEVICE BASED ON CONDUCTOR'S AMPACITY NEC 430.62(A)

Figure 18-21. Sizing a circuit breaker for a feeder supplying two or more motors plus other loads. The motor's FLC shall be used to size the overcurrent protection device per **Table 430.52(C)(1)** and **430.62(A)**.

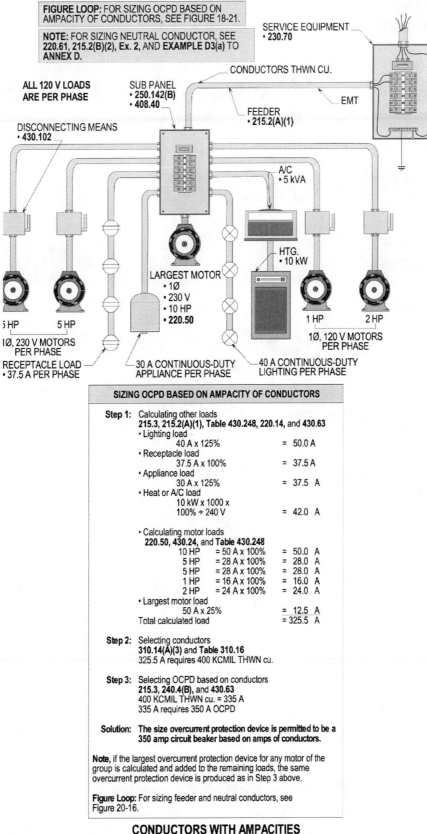

FIGURE LOOP: FOR SIZING OCPD BASED ON AMPACITY OF CONDUCTORS, SEE FIGURE 18-21.

NOTE: FOR SIZING NEUTRAL CONDUCTOR, SEE 220.61, 215.2(B)(2), Ex. 2, AND **EXAMPLE D3(a)** TO ANNEX D.

SERVICE EQUIPMENT
• 230.70

CONDUCTORS THWN CU.

ALL 120 V LOADS ARE PER PHASE

SUB PANEL
• 250.142(B)
• 408.40

FEEDER
• 215.2(A)(1)

EMT

DISCONNECTING MEANS
• 430.102

A/C
• 5 kVA

LARGEST MOTOR
• 1Ø
• 230 V
• 10 HP
• 220.50

HTG.
• 10 kW

5 HP   5 HP

1Ø, 230 V MOTORS
PER PHASE

1 HP   2 HP

1Ø, 120 V MOTORS
PER PHASE

RECEPTACLE LOAD
• 37.5 A PER PHASE

30 A CONTINUOUS-DUTY
APPLIANCE PER PHASE

40 A CONTINUOUS-DUTY
LIGHTING PER PHASE

SIZING OCPD BASED ON AMPACITY OF CONDUCTORS

Step 1: Calculating other loads
215.3, 215.2(A)(1), Table 430.248, 220.14, and 430.63

• Lighting load		
40 A x 125%	=	50.0 A
• Receptacle load		
37.5 A x 100%	=	37.5 A
• Appliance load		
30 A x 125%	=	37.5 A
• Heat or A/C load		
10 kW x 1000 x		
100% ÷ 240 V	=	42.0 A

• Calculating motor loads
220.50, 430.24, and Table 430.248

10 HP	= 50 A x 100%	=	50.0 A
5 HP	= 28 A x 100%	=	28.0 A
5 HP	= 28 A x 100%	=	28.0 A
1 HP	= 16 A x 100%	=	16.0 A
2 HP	= 24 A x 100%	=	24.0 A
• Largest motor load			
50 A x 25%		=	12.5 A
Total calculated load		=	325.5 A

Step 2: Selecting conductors
310.14(A)(3) and Table 310.16
325.5 A requires 400 KCMIL THWN cu.

Step 3: Selecting OCPD based on conductors
215.3, 240.4(B), and 430.63
400 KCMIL THWN cu. = 335 A
335 A requires 350 A OCPD

Solution: The size overcurrent protection device is permitted to be a 350 amp circuit beaker based on amps of conductors.

Note, if the largest overcurrent protection device for any motor of the group is calculated and added to the remaining loads, the same overcurrent protection device is produced as in Step 3 above.

Figure Loop: For sizing feeder and neutral conductors, see Figure 20-16.

**CONDUCTORS WITH AMPACITIES
GREATER THAN MOTOR'S FLC
NEC 430.63**

Figure 18-22. Sizing a circuit breaker for a feeder supplying two or more motors plus other loads with the overcurrent protection device sized on the conductor's ampacity.

OLP FOR MOTORS
(CUTLER HAMMER)

(A) For 50° C, 55° C, and 75° C rise motors and enclosed motors having a service factor of 1.0, selected one size smaller coil (OL).

(B) Ambient temperature of controller lower than motor by 47° F (26° C), use one size smaller coil (OL).

(C) Ambient temperature of controller higher than motor by 47° F (26° C) use one size larger coil (OL).

OLP FOR MOTORS
(ALLEN-BRADLEY)

(A) Same temperature at controller and motor
Selected based on motor's nameplate current

(B) Higher temperature at controller than motor
Selected higher size OL based on motor's (NPC) based on motor's NPC being less than Table current.

(C) Lower temperature at controller than motor
Selected lower size OL based on motor's NPC being less than Table current.

Note 1: (B) and (C) is based on the temperature differences not exceeding 18° F (10° C).

Note 2: For overload (OL) selection pertaining to size, see **Figures 19-1** and **19-2** in this book.

Chapter 18: Overcurrent Protection for Individual Motors

Section   Answer

1. The rating of a nontime-delay fuse not exceeding 600 amperes shall be
   permitted to be increased but shall in no case exceed _____ percent of the
   full-load current.
   (a) 225   (b) 250
   (c) 300   (d) 400

2. The rating of a time-delay (dual-element) fuse shall be permitted to be increased
   but shall in no case exceed _____ percent of the full-load current.
   (a) 225   (b) 250
   (c) 300   (d) 400

3. The rating of an inverse-time circuit breaker shall be permitted to be increased
   but shall in no case exceed _____ percent for full-load currents of 100 amperes
   or less.
   (a) 225   (b) 250
   (c) 300   (d) 400

4. The rating of an inverse-time circuit breaker shall be permitted to be increased
   but shall in no case exceed _____ percent for full-load currents greater than
   100 amperes.
   (a) 225   (b) 250
   (c) 300   (d) 400

5. For Design E and Design B NEMA motors, the setting on the instantaneous-
   trip circuit breaker shall be permitted to be adjusted up to _____ percent.
   (a) 1000   (b) 1100
   (c) 1500   (d) 1700

6. A nontime-delay fuse will hold _____ times its rating for approximately 1/4 to
   2 seconds based on the type used.
   (a) 2   (b) 3
   (c) 5   (d) 10

7. A time-delay fuse will hold 5 times its rating for _____ seconds.
   (a) 5   (b) 10
   (c) 15   (d) 20

8. Instantaneous-trip circuit breakers will hold about _____ times their rating on
   the low setting.
   (a) 3   (b) 5
   (c) 10   (d) 15

9. Inverse-time circuit breakers will hold about _____ times their rating for different
   periods of time based on their frame size.
   (a) 3   (b) 5
   (c) 10   (d) 15

10. When installing 575 volt, three-phase motors, the horsepower rating of the motor shall be multiplied by _____ to obtain the full-load current. (Rule-of-thumb method)
    (a) 1.00   (b) 1.25
    (c) 2.50   (d) 10.00

11. When installing 480 volt, three-phase motors, the horsepower rating of the motor shall be multiplied by _____ to obtain the full-load current. (Rule-of-thumb method)
    (a) 1.00   (b) 1.25
    (c) 5.00   (d) 10.00

12. When installing 220 volt, three-phase motors, the horsepower rating of the motor shall be multiplied by _____ to obtain the full-load current. (Rule-of-thumb method)
    (a) 1.25   (b) 2.50
    (c) 5.00   (d) 10.00

13. When installing 220 volt, single-phase motors, the horsepower rating of the motor shall be multiplied by _____ to obtain the full-load current. (Rule-of-thumb method)
    (a) 1.25   (b) 2.50
    (c) 5.00   (d) 10.00

14. When installing 120 volt, single-phase motors, the horsepower rating of the motor shall be multiplied by _____ to obtain the full-load current. (Rule-of-thumb method)
    (a) 1.25   (b) 2.50
    (c) 5.00   (d) 10.00

15. Two or more motors shall be permitted to be installed without individual overcurrent protection devices if rated less than 1 HP each and the full-load current rating of each does not exceed _____ amps.
    (a) 6   (b) 8
    (c) 10   (d) 20

16. Several motors, each not exceeding 1 HP in rating, shall be permitted on a nominal 120 volt branch circuit protected at not over _____ amps.
    (a) 20   (b) 25
    (c) 30   (d) 40

17. The overcurrent protection device for a feeder supplying two or more motors shall be based on the _____ overcurrent protection device for any motor of the group plus the FLC of the remaining motors.
    (a) smallest   (b) largest
    (c) next size   (d) none of the above

18. A motor overload device that can restart a motor automatically after overload tripping shall not be installed unless _____ for use with the motor it protects.
    (a) listed   (b) labeled
    (c) approved   (d) identified

19. The full-load current rating for a single-phase motor shall be determined from the values listed in _____ for motors running at usual speeds and motors having normal torque characteristics.

    (a) **Table 430.248**   (b) **Table 430.250**

    (c) **Table 430.251(A)**   (d) **Table 430.251(B)**

20. The locked-rotor current for a three-phase motor shall be determined from the values listed in _____.

    (a) **Table 430.248**   (b) **Table 430.250**

    (c) **Table 430.251(A)**   (d) **Table 430.251(B)**

21. What is the minimum (round down), per **430.52(C)(1)**, and the next size nontime-delay fuse, per **430.52(C)(1)(a)**, for allowing a 50 HP, 230 volt, three-phase, Design letter B motor to start and run?

22. What is the next, per **430.52(C)(1)**, maximum (round up) size time-delay fuse, per **430.52(C)(1)(b)(2)**, for a 50 HP, 230 volt, three-phase, Design B motor to start and run?

23. What is the minimum and maximum (setting) for an instantaneous-trip circuit breaker used for starting a 50 HP, 230 volt, three-phase, Design E motor?

24. What is the minimum (round down) and next size inverse-time circuit breaker used for starting a 50 HP, 230 volt, three-phase, Design B motor?

25. What is the maximum (round up) size nontime-delay fuse used for starting a 50 HP, 230 volt, three-phase, Design B motor?

26. What is the maximum (round up) size time-delay fuse used for starting a 50 HP, 230 volt, three-phase, Design B motor?

27. What is the maximum (round down) size inverse-time circuit breaker used for starting a 50 HP, 230 volt, three-phase, Design B motor?

28. What size overcurrent protection device (circuit breaker) is required to supply a feeder load having a group of 10 HP, 15 HP, 20 HP, and 25 HP, 460 volt, three-phase, Design B motors?

29. What size FLC rating is required for a 3 HP, 240 volt, single-phase, Design B motor, when applying the rule-of-thumb method?

30. What size FLC rating is required for a 30 HP, 220 volt, three-phase, Design B motor, when applying the rule-of-thumb method?

31. What size FLC rating is required for a 30 HP, 440 volt, three-phase, Design B motor, when applying the rule-of-thumb method?

32. What size FLC rating is required for a 30 HP, 575 volt, three-phase, Design B motor, when applying the rule-of-thumb method?

33. When derating for a feeder circuit, the largest of the derating factor in amps or the _____% rule is used.

34. When calculating the size time delay fuse for a feeder circuit, determine the _____ motor and add the remaining motors and select the size of the fuses.

———————— ———————— **35.** When sizing the conductors for a feeder circuit, take the largest motor at _____%.

———————— ———————— **36.** One disconnecting means and one controller can be used to connect and operate a _____ of motors.

———————— ———————— **37.** In a group rated installation of a number of motors, each motor shall be protected from _____ conditions

———————— ———————— **38.** The FLC of a 460 volt, three-phase, 50 HP motor is _____ amps when using the rule-of-thumb method.

———————— ———————— **39.** The maximum size time-delay fuse to start and run a motor is _____%.

———————— ———————— **40.** When a NEMA, Design B, energy efficient type motor is installed, an instantaneous circuit breaker can be adjusted to a maximum of _____%.

19

Overload Protection for Individual Motors

Devices such as thermal protectors, thermal relays, or fusetrons may be installed to provide running overload protection for motors rated more than 1 horsepower. The service factor or temperature rise of the motor shall be used when sizing and installing the running overload protection for motors. The running overload protection is set to open at 115 or 125 percent of the motor's full-load current. Under certain conditions of use, the running overload protection shall be set at 115 percent when the motor is not marked with a service factor or temperature rise. Time-delay fuses selected and sized at these percentages provide overload or backup overload protection.

MINIMUM SIZE OVERLOAD PROTECTION
430.32(A)(1)

The amperage for full-load current ratings listed in **Tables 430.247 through 430.250** shall not be used when sizing the running overload protection. The full-load current listed with the motor's nameplate shall be used to size the setting of the separate running overload protection.

Note, 430.32(C) will now permit an overload unit or fuse(s) to be used to protect motor winding(s) and conductors from harmful overload conditions.

The running overload protection shall be selected and rated no larger than the following minimum percentages based on the full-load current rating listed on the motor's nameplate:

(1) Motors with a marked service factor not less than 1.15, use 125 percent x FLA.

(2) Motors with a marked temperature rise not over 40°C, use 125 percent x FLA.

(3) All other motors, 115 percent x FLA.

See Figure 19-1 for a detailed illustration pertaining to determining the minimum size overloads based on service factors and temperature rise.

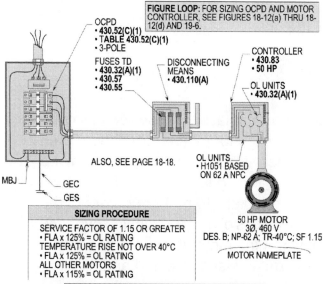

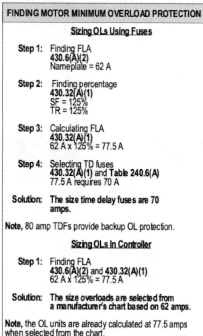

**MINIMUM SIZE OVERLOAD PROTECTION
NEC 430.32(A)(1)**

Figure 19-1. Determining the minimum size overloads based on service factor and temperature rise.

SERVICE FACTOR

For motors marked with a service factor of not less than 1.15 or a service factor less than 1.15, the following percentages of the motor's nameplate amps shall be used to ensure protection to the motor's insulation:

(1) Not less than 1.15, use 125 percent of the motor's nameplate rating.

(2) Less than 1.15, use 115 percent of the motor's nameplate rating.

TEMPERATURE RISE

The temperature rise in motor windings is affected by the altitude. Less heat is carried from the windings in higher altitudes because thinner air flows through the inlets and outlets of the motor. Elevations of 3300 ft or less allow thicker air to carry heat away effectively. Motors above elevations of 3300 ft must be derated. **For derating transformers, see pages 7-6 and 7-8** in this book.

Motors must be derated 1 percent for every 330 ft above 3300 ft.

For example, a 460 volt, 50 horsepower, three-phase motor pulling 62 amps and installed at an altitude of 3630 ft must be derated to a running current of 61.38 amps [(62 A x 1% = .62 A) (62 A - .62 = 61.38 A)].

Motors must be derated 10 percent for every 1000 ft above 3300 ft.

For example, a 460 volt, 50 horsepower, three-phase motor pulling 62 amps and installed at an altitude of 9300 ft (10% for every 1000 ft above 3300 ft = 60%) must be derated to a running current of 24.8 amps (62 A x 60% = 37.2 A (62 A - 37.2 = 24.8 A).

Note, 40 percent of 62 amps produces the same results.

For motors marked with a temperature rise of not over 40°C or a temperature rise over 40°C, the following percentages shall be used:

(1) Not over 40°C, use 125 percent of the motor's nameplate rating.

(2) Over 40°C, use 115 percent of the motor's nameplate rating.

(3) Motor not marked, use 115 percent of the motor's nameplate rating.

Due to the starting and running current period of the motor, the overload could trip open. A higher percentage shall be permitted to be applied per **430.32(C)** if the overloads should trip open. If the overloads should trip open after applying **430.32(C)(1)**, apply shunting rule per **430.35**.

OTHER CONDITIONS

For 50°C, 55°C, and 75°C rise motors, and enclosed motors having a service factor of 1.0, select one size smaller coil. When ambient temperature of the controller is lower than the motor by 26°C (47°F), use one size smaller coil.

When ambient temperature of the controller is higher than the motor by 26°C (47°F), use one size larger coil.

SIZING OVERLOADS FROM COVER

The motor's nameplate full-load running current is used when sizing the overloads from the cover of a magnetic starter or controller. The motor's full-load current rating is not increased by 125 percent when the overloads are selected using this procedure. **(See Figure 19-1)**

SIZING OVERLOADS FROM CHART

The motor's nameplate full-load current rating is used when sizing the overloads from the chart of a magnetic starter, a motor control center, or the manufacturer's catalog.

MAXIMUM SIZE OVERLOAD PROTECTION 430.32(C)

The selection of the running overload protection (overload relay) shall be permitted to be selected at higher percentages if the percentages of **430.32(A)(1)** are not sufficient. The running overload protection device or fuses shall be selected to trip or shall be rated no larger than the following percentages of the motor's (nameplate) full-load current rating:

(1) Motors with a marked service factor not less than 1.15, use 140 percent x FLA.

(2) Motors with a marked temperature rise not over 40°C, use 140 percent x FLA.

(3) All other motors, use 130 percent x FLA.

See Figure 19-2 for a detailed illustration pertaining to determining the maximum size overloads based on service factor and temperature rise.

SINGLE-PHASING

Overloads used in a magnetic starter shall be selected at 62 amps or less per **430.6(A)(2)** [using nameplate amps (62 A) of motor] to protect the motor windings from single-phasing or overheating due to the driven load. However, when the percentages per **430.32(A)(1)** are not exceeded, fuses or circuit breakers shall be permitted to be used.

For example, overload protection may be provided for a motor by a 70 amp fuse or circuit breaker if the motor will start and run using this size overcurrent protection device. A time delay fuse usually holds five times its rating for 10 seconds (70 A x 5 = 350 A).

Single-phasing occurs when one ungrounded (phase) conductor is lost in a three-wire system. Consider that if a motor is pulling 62 amps and Phase C is lost, the motor will be now be pulling 107.4 amps (62 A x 1.732 = 107.4 A).

For a detailed illustration, see **Figure 19-3.**

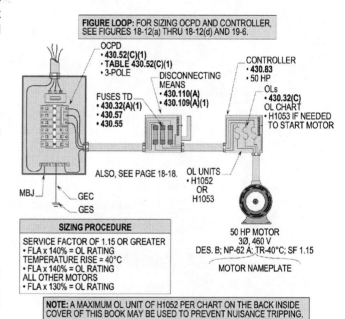

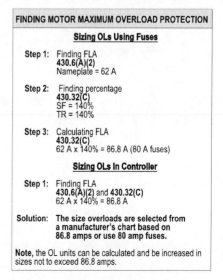

MAXIMUM SIZE OVERLOAD PROTECTION NEC 430.32(C)

Figure 19-2. Determining the maximum size overloads based on the service factor and temperature rise.

Based on the motor's nameplate rating, the 70 amp overcurrent protection device does not exceed 125 percent of the motor's nameplate FLC. The 70 amp overcurrent protection device trips open due to an overload of 107.4 amps on Phases A and B. **(See Figure 19-3)**

The percentage listed in **430.32(A)(1)** shall be permitted to be applied to the following types of devices:

(1) Circuit breakers

(2) Time-delay fuses

(3) Thermal cutouts

(4) Thermal relays

(5) Motor switches with thermal devices

(6) Thermal devices designed into motors

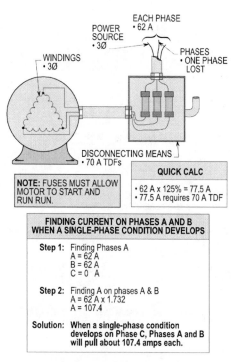

SINGLE-PHASING

Figure 19-3. Single-phasing occurs when one phase is lost in a three-wire system. The remaining phases will carry about 1.732 times the original running current of 62 amps.

SHUNTING OLs DURING STARTING PERIOD 430.35

The following two methods shall be used when shunting overloads during the motor's starting period:

(1) Nonautomatically started

(2) Automatically started

NONAUTOMATICALLY STARTED

The overload protection shall be permitted to be shunted for a nonautomatically started motor. However, it shall only be permitted to shunt or cut out the overload protection during start, provided the shunting device cannot be left in use after starting. Fuses or time-delay circuit breakers are installed and are rated or set so as not to exceed 400 percent of the full-load current rating of the motor.

AUTOMATICALLY STARTED

Automatically started motors shall not shunt or cut out overload protection. The following exceptions permit overload protection to be shunted or cut out when starting motors automatically:

(1) The starting period of the motor is greater than the time-delay of the available motor overload protective device.

(2) Where a listed means is provided that:

(a) Senses the motor rotation and will automatically prevent the shunting or cutout if the motor fails to start.

(b) The time of shunting is limited for the overload protection or cutout to a point that is less than the locked-rotor current rating of the motor that is being protected.

(c) Causes shutdown, if the running position has not been reached and the motor will have to be restarted manually.

SIZING CONTROLLERS 430.81 AND 430.83

The sizes and types of motor controllers shall be installed with a horsepower rating at least equal to the motor to be controlled. However, there is an exception to this rule for motors rated at and below a certain horsepower rating.

STATIONARY MOTORS OF 1/8 HORSEPOWER OR LESS 430.81(A)

The branch-circuit protection device shall be permitted to serve as the controller where the motor is rated 1/8 HP or less.

For example, motors less than 1/8 HP, where they are mounted stationary or permanent and the construction is such that one or more might fail during operation, the branch-circuit elements plus the motor won't be damaged. In other words, the components of the circuit won't be burned out, etc. **(See Figure 19-4)**

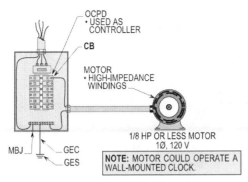

STATIONARY MOTORS OF 1/8 HORSEPOWER OR LESS
NEC 430.81(A)

Figure 19-4. The branch-circuit overcurrent protection device shall be permitted to serve as a controller for a 1/8 HP or less motor.

PORTABLE MOTOR OF 1/3 HORSEPOWER OR LESS 430.81(B)

The controller shall be permitted to be an attachment plug and receptacle or cord connector that is acceptable for use with portable motors rated 1/3 HP or less. **(See Figure 19-5)**

OTHER THAN HORSEPOWER RATED 430.83(A)

The following conditions, other than horsepower rated controllers, shall be permitted to be used for energizing and deenergizing circuits supplying motors:

(1) Inverse time circuit breakers

(2) Stationary motors rated 1/8 HP or less and portable motors rated 1/3 HP or less

(3) Stationary motors rated 2 HP or less (300 volts or less)

(4) Torque motors

HORSEPOWER RATINGS 430.83(A)(1) THRU (A)(3)

Controllers, other than inverse time circuit breakers and molded case switches, shall have horsepower ratings at the application voltage not lower than the horsepower rating of the motor. See the requirements below for circuit breakers and molded case switches.

A branch circuit inverse-time circuit breaker shall be permitted as a controller for all motors. Where this circuit breaker is also used for overload protection, it shall conform

to the appropriate provisions of this article governing overload protection.

A molded case switch shall be permitted as a controller for all motors. **(See Figures 19-7 and 19-11)**

Note, the controller shall be sized at least equal to the horsepower of the motor. Care must be exercised when replacing an existing motor with a high-efficiency motor and using the existing controller and electrical system.

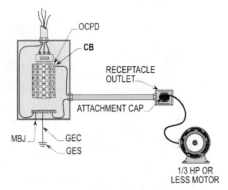

PORTABLE MOTOR OF 1/3 HORSEPOWER OR LESS
NEC 430.81(B)

Figure 19-5. The controller for a motor of 1/3 HP or less shall be permitted to be an attachment cap and receptacle or cord connector.

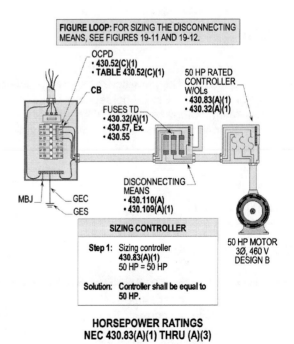

HORSEPOWER RATINGS
NEC 430.83(A)(1) THRU (A)(3)

Figure 19-6. Controllers shall have a horsepower rating at least equal to the horsepower of the motor.

INVERSE-TIME CIRCUIT BREAKERS
430.83(A)(2)

Inverse-time circuit breakers shall only be permitted to be installed as a controller where rated in amps. If such a circuit breaker is also used for motor overload protection, it shall be sized at 125 percent or less of the motor's nameplate current rating per **430.6(A)(2)** and **430.32(A)(1)**. **(See Figure 19-7)**

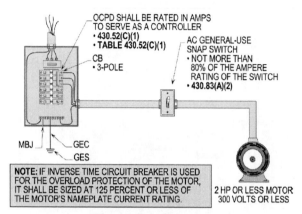

NOTE: IF INVERSE TIME CIRCUIT BREAKER IS USED FOR THE OVERLOAD PROTECTION OF THE MOTOR, IT SHALL BE SIZED AT 125 PERCENT OR LESS OF THE MOTOR'S NAMEPLATE CURRENT RATING.

INVERSE-TIME CIRCUIT BREAKERS
NEC 430.83(A)(2)

Figure 19-7. A circuit breaker rated at 125 percent of the motor's FLA shall be permitted to be used as a controller for the motor and also provide overload protection.

SMALL MOTORS
430.83(B)

Stationary motors rated 1/8 HP or less and portable motors rated 1/3 HP or less shall be permitted to serve as controllers and shall not be required to be horsepower rated. These horsepower-rated motors, because of their smaller locked-rotor currents, can be disconnected by cord-and-plug connections.

STATIONARY MOTORS OF 2 HORSEPOWER OR LESS
430.83(C)

For a stationary motor rated 2 HP or less, the controller shall be permitted to be a general-use switch rated for at least twice the motor's full-load current. An AC general-use snap switch shall be permitted to be installed as the controller where the full-load current rating of the switch does not exceed 80 percent (1 ÷ 1.25 = 80%) of the branch-circuit rating. **(See Figure 19-8)**

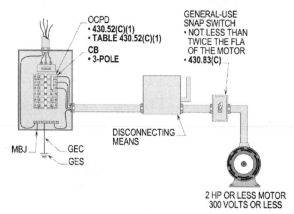

STATIONARY MOTORS OF 2 HORSEPOWER OR LESS
NEC 430.83(C)

Figure 19-8. For stationary motors rated 2 HP or less, a general-use snap switch shall be permitted to be used if sized not less than twice the motor's full-load current.

TORQUE MOTORS
430.83(D)

The motor controller for a torque motor shall have a continuous duty, full-load current rating not less than the nameplate current rating of the motor. **(See Figure 19-9)**

Motor Tip: If the motor controller is rated in horsepower and not marked or rated as above, to determine the amperage or horsepower rating, use **Table 430.247 through 430.250.**

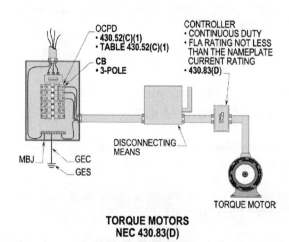

TORQUE MOTORS
NEC 430.83(D)

Figure 19-9. The controller for a torque motor shall be capable of holding the amps indefinitely.

VOLTAGE RATING
480.83(E)

A controller with a straight voltage rating of, for example, 240 volts or 480 volts, shall be permitted to be applied in a circuit in which the nominal voltage between any two conductors does not exceed the controller's voltage rating. A controller with a slash rating, for example, 120/240 volts or 480Y/277 volts, shall only be applied in a solidly grounded circuit in which the nominal voltage-to-ground from any conductor does not exceed the lower of the two values of the controller's voltage does not exceed the higher value of the controller's voltage rating. **(See Figure 19-10)**

SIZING THE DISCONNECTING MEANS TO DISCONNECT BOTH THE CONTROLLER AND MOTOR
430.109(A)(1) AND 430.110(A)

The disconnecting means for motor circuits shall have an amperage rating of at least 115 percent of the full-load current rating of the motor per **430.110(A)**. The disconnecting means shall be horsepower rated and capable of deenergizing locked-rotor currents per **Tables 430.251(A)** and **(B)**. For detailed rules, see **430.109(A)(1)**. **(See Figure 19-11)**

OTHER THAN HORSEPOWER RATED
430.109(B) THRU (G)

Sections **430.109(B) through (G)** permit other than a horsepower rated disconnecting means to be used to deenergize the power circuit to certain types of motors:

- Stationary motors rated 1/8 HP or less
- Stationary motors rated 2 HP or less (300 volts or less)
- Autotransformer-type controlled motors
- Torque motors

GENERAL REQUIREMENTS
430.109(A)

The disconnecting means shall be permitted to be one of the following, as specified in this section:

- A listed motor-circuit switch rated in horsepower,
- A listed molded case circuit breaker,
- A listed molded case switch,

- An instantaneous trip circuit breaker that is part of a listed combination motor controller, or
- A listed self-protected combination controller.

See Figure 19-12 and **19-13** for permitted disconnecting means to deenergize the power circuit.

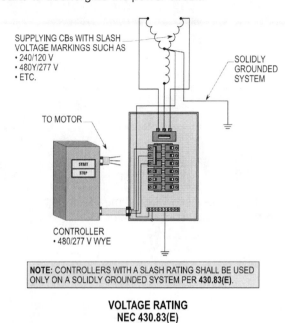

VOLTAGE RATING
NEC 430.83(E)

Figure 19-10. Controllers with a slash rating shall be used in a solidly grounded system only.

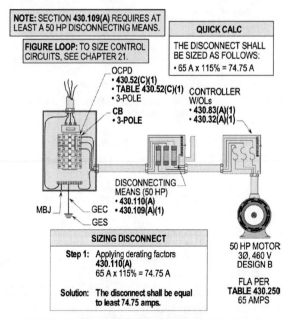

SIZING THE DISCONNECTING MEANS TO DISCONNECT BOTH THE CONTROLLER AND MOTOR
NEC 430.109(A)(1) AND 430.110(A)

Figure 19-11. The disconnecting means shall be sized by multiplying the motor's FLA by 115 percent.

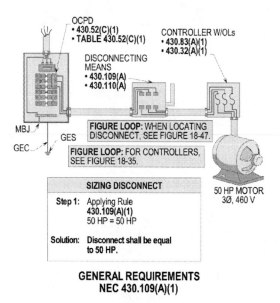

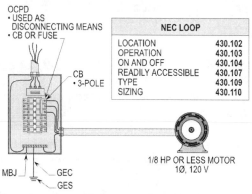

STATIONARY MOTORS OF 1/8 HORSEPOWER OR LESS
NEC 430.109(B)

Figure 19-12. The disconnecting means shall be at least equal to the horsepower of the motor.

Figure 19-14. Motors rated 1/8 horsepower or less shall be permitted to be disconnected by the overcurrent protection device located in the panelboard that is used to supply the circuit.

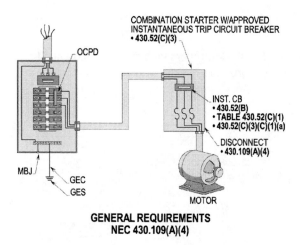

GENERAL REQUIREMENTS
NEC 430.109(A)(4)

Figure 19-13. The disconnecting means for a motor shall be permitted to be an approved instantaneous trip circuit breaker per **430.109(A)(4)**.

STATIONARY MOTORS OF 1/8 HORSEPOWER OR LESS 430.109(B)

For a stationary motor rated 1/8 HP or less, the branch-circuit overcurrent protection device shall be permitted to serve as the disconnecting means. This rule is permitted because the windings of such motors do not produce locked-rotor currents high enough to damage such motors, circuit conductors, or elements. **(See Figure 19-14)**

STATIONARY MOTORS OF 2 HORSEPOWER OR LESS 430.109(C)

For a stationary motor rated 2 HP or less, the controller shall be permitted to be a general-use switch rated for at least twice the motor's full-load current. An AC general-use snap switch shall be permitted to be installed as the controller, where the full-load current rating of the switch does not exceed 80 percent of the branch-circuit switch. **(See Figure 19-15)**

AUTOTRANSFORMER-TYPE CONTROLLED MOTORS 430.109(D)

Motors rated between 2 HP through 100 HP shall be permitted to be installed with a separate disconnecting means (general-use switch) if the motor is equipped with an autotransformer-type controller and complies with all the following conditions:

(1) The motor drives a generator that is provided with overload protection.

(2) The controller is capable of interrupting the locked-rotor current of the motor.

(3) The controller is provided with a no-voltage release.

(4) The controller is provided with running overload protection not exceeding 125 percent of the motor's full-load current rating.

(5) Separate fuses or an inverse-time circuit breaker is rated at 150 percent or more of the motor's full-load current rating. **(See Figure 19-16)**

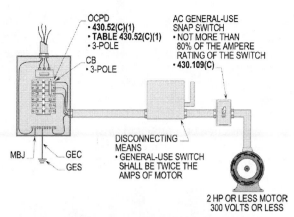

STATIONARY MOTORS OF 2 HORSEPOWER OR LESS
NEC 430.109(C)

Figure 19-15. This illustration lists the rules pertaining to the disconnecting means for motors rated 2 HP or less.

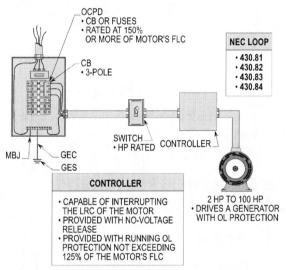

AUTOTRANSFORMER-TYPE CONTROLLED MOTORS
NEC 430.109(D)

Figure 19-16. This illustration lists the rules for a disconnecting means and controller used to disconnect and control motors rated between 2 HP to 100 HP.

ISOLATING SWITCHES
430.109(E)

The disconnecting means shall be permitted to be a general-use or isolating switch for DC stationary motors rated at 40 HP or greater and AC motors rated 100 HP or greater. However, such disconnects shall be plainly marked "Do not operate under load." **(See Figure 19-17)**

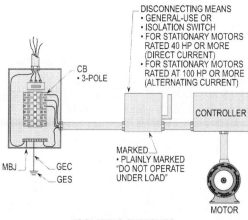

ISOLATING SWITCHES
NEC 430.109(E)

Figure 19-17. This illustration lists the rules for disconnecting means used to disconnect motors rated at 40 HP or more.

CORD-AND-PLUG CONNECTED MOTORS
430.109(F)

For a cord-and-plug-connected motor, a horsepower-rated attachment plug and receptacle, flanged surface inlet and cord connector having ratings no less than the motor ratings shall be permitted to serve as the disconnecting means. A horsepower-rated attachment plug and receptacle, flanged surface inlets, receptacles, or cord connectors shall not be required for a cord-and-plug-connected appliance in accordance with **422.33**, a room air conditioner in accordance with **440.63**, or a portable motor rated 1/3 HP or less. **(See Figure 19-18)**

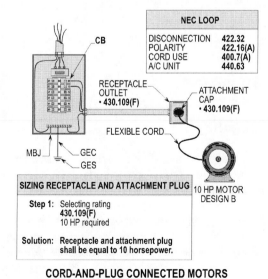

CORD-AND-PLUG CONNECTED MOTORS
NEC 430.109(F)

Figure 19-18. A receptacle and attachment cap used as a disconnecting means for motors shall be at least equal to motor's horsepower rating.

TORQUE MOTORS
430.109(G)

The disconnecting means for a torque motor shall be permitted to be installed as a general-use switch. Such switch shall be capable of handling the locked-rotor current of the motor indefinitely. **(See Figure 19-19)**

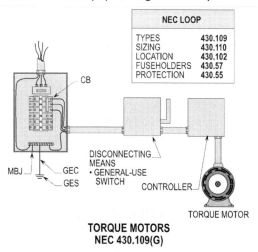

NEC LOOP	
TYPES	430.109
SIZING	430.110
LOCATION	430.102
FUSEHOLDERS	430.57
PROTECTION	430.55

TORQUE MOTORS
NEC 430.109(G)

Figure 19-19. The disconnecting means for a torque motor shall be permitted to be a general-use switch.

LOCATION OF THE DISCONNECTING MEANS FOR THE CONTROLLER AND MOTOR
430.102 AND 430.107

A motor and its driven machinery or load shall be installed within sight of the controller for the motor. This rule provides safety for electricians and maintenance personnel while servicing such machinery and circuit elements.

WITHIN SIGHT
ARTICLE 100, 430.102(A), AND
430.102(B)(2)

The disconnecting means shall be installed within sight of the motor controller. All of the ungrounded (phase) conductors shall be disconnected from both the motor and controller supplying the motor circuit. The disconnecting means shall be installed within sight of the motor and not more than 50 ft (15 m) from the motor. If such a disconnecting means is not installed within 50 ft (15 m) of the controller, motor, and driven equipment, other provisions for disconnecting the motor shall be made. The controller has a direct relationship to the disconnecting means and shall be installed within sight and within 50 ft (15 m) of the disconnecting means. The motor does not have a direct relationship with the controller. **(See Figure 19-20)**

Note, a disconnecting means shall always be required to be located in sight from the controller location. A single disconnecting means shall be permitted to be located adjacent to a group of coordinated controllers mounted adjacent one to another, such as on a multi-motor continuous process machine.

For further information pertaining to sizing, selecting, and locating such controllers and disconnecting means, review **430.83, 430.102, 430.103, 430.107, 430.109,** and **430.110** very carefully.

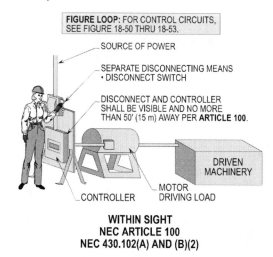

FIGURE LOOP: FOR CONTROL CIRCUITS, SEE FIGURE 18-50 THRU 18-53.

SOURCE OF POWER

SEPARATE DISCONNECTING MEANS
• DISCONNECT SWITCH

DISCONNECT AND CONTROLLER SHALL BE VISIBLE AND NO MORE THAN 50' (15 m) AWAY PER **ARTICLE 100**.

DRIVEN MACHINERY

CONTROLLER

MOTOR DRIVING LOAD

WITHIN SIGHT
NEC ARTICLE 100
NEC 430.102(A) AND (B)(2)

Figure 19-20. The disconnecting means shall be within sight and within 50 ft (15 m) of the controller, motor, and driven machinery.

LOCKED IN THE OPEN POSITION
430.102(A) AND (B)

Section **430.102(A)** and **(B)** permits the disconnect on the line side of the controller, if within sight and within 50 ft (15 m), and capable of being individually locked open, to serve as the disconnecting means for both the controller and motor. In this case, note that the motor shall be installed within sight and within 50 ft (15 m) of the disconnecting means of the controller. **[See Figures 19-21(a)** and **(b)]**

CANNOT BE LOCKED
IN THE OPEN POSITION
430.102(A) AND 430.102(B)

For motors rated 600 volts or less, an additional disconnecting means shall be mounted by the motor and within sight where the disconnecting means installed by the controller cannot be locked in the open position. The controller disconnecting means for a motor branch circuit over 1000 volts shall be permitted to be located out of sight of the motor branch-circuit controller and motor. However, the controller shall have a warning label that marks and lists the location and identification of the disconnecting means. To completely satisfy this rule, such disconnecting means shall be capable of being locked in the open position. **[See Figure 19-22(a)]**

APPLYING EXCEPTION 430.102(B)

Ex. (1) and **(2)** to **430.102(B)** do not require an additional disconnect to be installed within sight of the motor where the disconnecting means would be impractical or increase hazards. An additional disconnecting means is not required where it is located in an industrial installation that has written safety procedures and only qualified employees are permitted to work on the equipment involved. **[See Figure 19-22(b)]**

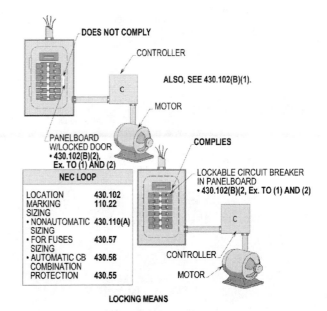

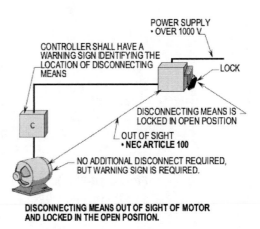

Figure 19-21(b). The locked door of a panelboard shall not be permitted to serve as the required disconnecting means for a motor. However, an individual locked circuit breaker shall be permitted to serve as the disconnecting means.

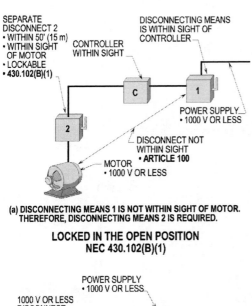

(a) DISCONNECTING MEANS 1 IS NOT WITHIN SIGHT OF MOTOR. THEREFORE, DISCONNECTING MEANS 2 IS REQUIRED.

LOCKED IN THE OPEN POSITION
NEC 430.102(B)(1)

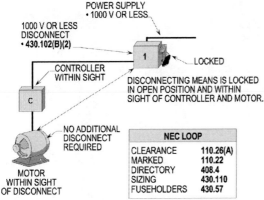

(b) DISCONNECTING MEANS 1 IS WITHIN SIGHT OF MOTOR AND CAN BE LOCKED IN THE OPEN POSITION.

LOCKED IN THE OPEN POSITION
430.102(B)(2), Ex. TO (1) AND (2)

DISCONNECTING MEANS OUT OF SIGHT OF MOTOR AND LOCKED IN THE OPEN POSITION.

DISCONNECT LOCKED IN THE OPEN POSITION
NEC 430.102(A), Ex. 1

Figure 19-22(a). If the disconnecting means is within sight and 50 ft (15 m) of controller and can be locked in the open position, an additional disconnecting means shall not be required to be installed by the motor.

Figure 19-21(a). Locating the disconnecting means to disconnect power conductors to motors rated 1000 volts or less.

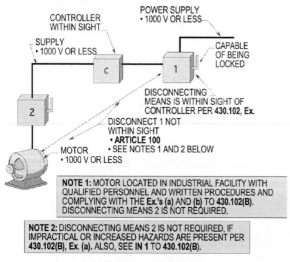

NOTE 1: MOTOR LOCATED IN INDUSTRIAL FACILITY WITH QUALIFIED PERSONNEL AND WRITTEN PROCEDURES AND COMPLYING WITH THE **Ex.'s (a)** AND **(b)** TO **430.102(B)**. DISCONNECTING MEANS 2 IS NOT REQUIRED.

NOTE 2: DISCONNECTING MEANS 2 IS NOT REQUIRED, IF IMPRACTICAL OR INCREASED HAZARDS ARE PRESENT PER **430.102(B), Ex. (a)**. ALSO, SEE **IN 1** TO **430.102(B)**.

APPLYING EXCEPTIONS
NEC 430.102(B)(2), EX. TO (1) AND (2)

Figure 19-22(b). Under certain conditions of use, an additional disconnecting means is not required to be installed within sight of the motor. When disconnecting valve actuator motors (vams) are involved, see **430.102(A), Ex. 3**. [See Figure **19-22(c)**]

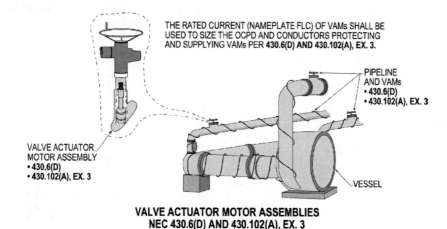

VALVE ACTUATOR MOTOR ASSEMBLIES
NEC 430.6(D) AND 430.102(A), EX. 3

Figure 19-22(c). No disconnecting means required per **Ex. 3** to **430.102(A)** for vams.

Chapter 19: Overload Protection for Individual Motors

Section   Answer

1. Motors with a temperature rise not over 40°C shall have their (minimum) running   _____ _____
   overload protection [per **430.32(A)(1)**] sized at _____ percent.
   (a) 100   (b) 115
   (c) 125   (d) 140

2. Motors above elevations of _____ ft shall be derated for temperature rise.   _____ _____
   (a) 1000   (b) 1800
   (c) 2600   (d) 3300

3. Motors shall be derated _____ percent for every 330 ft above 3300 ft for   _____ _____
   temperature rise.
   (a) 1   (b) 3
   (c) 5   (d) 10

4. Motors shall be derated _____ percent for every 1000 ft above 3300 ft for   _____ _____
   temperature rise.
   (a) 1   (b) 3
   (c) 5   (d) 10

5. Motors with a service factor not less than 1.15 shall have their (maximum)   _____ _____
   running overload protection [per **430.32(C)**] sized at _____ percent.
   (a) 100   (b) 115
   (c) 125   (d) 140

6. The branch-circuit protection device shall be permitted to serve as the controller   _____ _____
   where the motor is rated _____ horsepower or less.
   (a) 1/16   (b) 1/8
   (c) 1/3   (d) 1/2

7. The controller shall be permitted to be an attachment plug and receptacle, that   _____ _____
   is acceptable for use with portable motors rated _____ HP or less.
   (a) 1/16   (b) 1/8
   (c) 1/3   (d) 1/2

8. If an inverse-time circuit breaker is used for motor overload protection, it shall   _____ _____
   be sized at _____ percent or less of the motor's nameplate current rating.
   (a) 100   (b) 115
   (c) 125   (d) 150

9. Stationary motors rated _____ HP or less shall be permitted to serve as   _____ _____
   controllers and shall not be required to be horsepower rated.
   (a) 1/16   (b) 1/8
   (c) 1/3   (d) 1/2

10. For a stationary motor rated _____ HP or less, the controller shall be permitted   _____ _____
    to be a general-use switch rated for at least twice the motor's full-load current.
    (a) 2   (b) 5
    (c) 7-1/2   (d) 10

11. An AC general-use snap switch shall be permitted to be installed as the controller where the full-load current rating of the switch does not exceed _____ percent of the branch-circuit rating.
    (a) 50   (b) 80
    (c) 100   (d) 115

12. The disconnecting means for motor circuits shall have an ampere rating of at least _____ percent of the full-load current rating of the motor.
    (a) 50   (b) 80
    (c) 100   (d) 115

13. For a stationary motor rated _____ HP or less, the branch-circuit overcurrent protection device shall be permitted to serve as the disconnecting means.
    (a) 1/16   (b) 1/8
    (c) 1/3   (d) 1/2

14. Motors rated over 2 HP to _____ HP shall be permitted to be installed with a separate disconnecting means (general-use switch), if the motor is equipped with an autotransformer-type controller.
    (a) 40   (b) 50
    (c) 100   (d) 150

15. The disconnecting means shall be permitted to be a general-use or isolating switch for DC stationary motors rated at _____ HP or greater.
    (a) 40   (b) 50
    (c) 100   (d) 150

16. The disconnecting means shall be permitted to be a general-use or isolating switch for AC stationary motors rated at _____ HP or greater.
    (a) 40   (b) 50
    (c) 100   (d) 150

17. The disconnecting means shall be installed within sight of the motor and not more than _____ ft from the motor.
    (a) 25   (b) 50
    (c) 60   (d) 80

18. A horsepower-rated attachment plug and receptacle shall not be required for a portable motor rated _____ HP or less.
    (a) 1/16   (b) 1/8
    (c) 1/3   (d) 1/2

19. The disconnecting means for a torque motor shall be permitted to be installed as a(n) _____ switch.
    (a) horsepower   (b) AC
    (c) DC   (d) general-use

20. An additional disconnecting means is not required where it is located in a(n) _____ installation that has written safety procedures and only qualified employees are permitted to work on the equipment involved.
    (a) residential   (b) commercial
    (c) industrial   (d) agricultural

21. What size overload protection (minimum) is required for 20 HP, 460 volt, three-phase, Design B motor with a nameplate rating of 48 amps, temperature rise of 40°C, and a service factor of 1.15?

22. What size overload protection (maximum) is required for 20 HP, 460 volt, three-phase, Design B motor with a nameplate rating of 48 amps, temperature rise of 40°C, and a service factor of 1.15?

————————   ————————

23. What is the horsepower rating of the disconnecting means (motor rated switch) for a 50 HP, 460 volt, three-phase, Design B motor?

————————   ————————

24. What is the horsepower rating of the controller for a 25 HP, 460 volt, three-phase, Design B motor?

————————   ————————

25. What size horsepower rated receptacle and attachment plug is required for a 20 HP, Design B motor? **Note,** the installation is not designed to unplug under load.

————————   ————————

Motor Feeder and Branch-Circuit Conductors

Branch-circuit conductors shall be sized by the percentages based on the use of loads that they supply. These loads are rated as either continuous or noncontinuous. When sizing branch-circuit conductors, the continuous loads shall be calculated at 125 percent and the noncontinuous loads at 100 percent. The duty cycle operation of the driven load shall also be permitted to be used to size conductors.

Capacitors are installed when the power factor is low and the currents are high, thus correcting the power factor and reducing the currents.

To determine which section of the *National Electrical Code (NEC)* to use when sizing conductors to supply motors and other types of equipment loads, see **Table 210.3** and **Table 220.3**

SIZING CONDUCTORS FOR SINGLE MOTORS
430.6(A)(1) AND 430.22

Branch-circuit conductors supplying a single motor shall have an ampacity not less than 125 percent of the motor's full-load current rating as outlined in **Tables 430.247, 430.248, 430.249,** and **430.250,** respectively.

> **For example,** a 20 HP, 208 volt, three-phase motor per **Table 430.250** has a full-load current of 59.4 amps. The full-load amps (FLA) for sizing the conductors is determined by multiplying 59.4 amps x 125 percent which equals 74.25 amps.

A motor will normally have a starting current of 4 to 6 times the full-load current of the motor's FLA for motors marked with code letters A through G, and 8-1/2 to 15 times for NEMA B, high-efficiency motors. Design B, C, and D motors have a starting current of about 4 to 6 times the full-load amps when starting and driving a motor load.

There are heating effects on the conductors that develop when motors are starting and accelerating the driven load. To eliminate such effects, the conductor's current-carrying capacity is increased by taking 125 percent of the motor's full-load current rating.

For example, a motor with a FLC rating of 42 amps shall have conductors with a current-carrying capacity of at least 52.5 amps (42 A x 125% = 52.5 A) to safely carry the load and protect the insulation due to overload conditions.

SIZING CONDUCTORS FOR SINGLE-PHASE MOTORS
430.22

Section **430.6(A)(1)** requires the full-load current for single-phase motors to be obtained from **Table 430.248**. This FLC rating is then multiplied by 125 percent per **Table 210.3, Table 220.3**, and **430.22** to derive the total amps to select the conductors from **Table 310.16** to supply power to the motor windings. **(See Figure 20-1)**

SIZING CONDUCTORS FOR THREE-PHASE MOTORS
430.22

Section **430.6(A)(1)** requires the full-load current for three-phase motors to be obtained from **Table 430.250**. This FLC rating is multiplied by 125 percent per **Table 210.3, Table 220.3** and **430.22** to derive the total amps to select the conductors for the motor windings. **(See Figure 20-2)**

DIRECT-CURRENT MOTOR-RECTIFIER SUPPLIED
430.22(A)

The conductor ampacity on the inut of the rectifier shall not be less than 125 percent of the rated input current to the rectifier for DC motors operating from a rectified power supply. Where DC motors operate from a rectified single-phase power supply, the conductors between the field wiring output terminals of the rectifier and the motor shall have an ampacity of not less than the following percentages of the motor full load current rating:

- 190 percent, where a rectifier bridge of the single-phase, half-wave type is used.

- 150 percent, where a rectifier bridge of the single-phase, full-wave type is used.

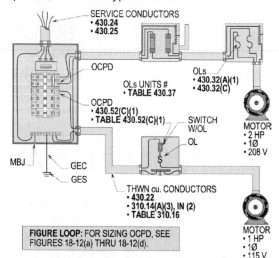

FINDING THWN COPPER CONDUCTORS

Single-phase motors (208 V)

Step 1: Finding FLA
430.6(A)(1) and Table 430.248
2 HP = 13.2 A

Step 2: Calculating load
430.22, Table 210.3, and Table 220.3
13.2 A x 125% = 16.5 A

Step 3: Selecting conductors
310.14(A)(3), IN (2) and Table 310.16
16.5 A requires 14 AWG cu.

Solution: The size THWN copper conductors are 14 AWG.

Single-phase motors (115 V)

Step 1: Finding FLA
430.6(A)(1) and Table 430.248
1 HP = 16 A

Step 2: Calculating load
430.22, Table 210.3, and Table 220.3
16 A x 125% = 20 A

Step 3: Selecting conductors
310.14(A)(3), IN (2) and Table 310.16
20 A requires 14 AWG cu.

Solution: The size THWN copper conductors are 14 AWG.

Note: See Asterisk to Table 310.16 and Table 240.4(G).

SIZING CONDUCTORS FOR SINGLE-PHASE MOTORS
NEC 430.22

Figure 20-1. Determining the size branch-circuit conductors to supply single-phase motors.

SIZING CONDUCTORS FOR MULTISPEED MOTORS
430.22(B)

The circuit conductors for multispeed motors shall be sized large enough, to the controller, to supply the highest nameplate full-load current rating of the multispeed motor winding involved. A single overcurrent protection device shall be permitted to serve each speed of a multispeed motor per **430.22(B)**. The speed with greater amps shall be used to size the overcurrent protection device and conductors.

Overload protection shall be provided for each speed to protect each winding from excessive current during an overload condition. **(See Figure 20-3)**

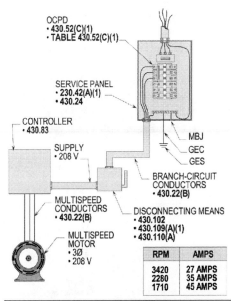

RPM	AMPS
3420	27 AMPS
2280	35 AMPS
1710	45 AMPS

FINDING THWN COPPER CONDUCTORS

Sizing branch-circuit conductors

Step 1: Finding FLA
430.22(B)
45 A largest amperage

Step 2: Calculating load
430.22(B)
45 A x 125% = 56.25

Step 3: Selecting conductors
310.14(A)(3), IN (2) and **Table 310.16**
56.25 A requires 6 AWG cu.

Solution: The size THWN copper conductors are 6 AWG.

Sizing multispeed conductors

Step 1: Finding FLA
430.22(B)
3420 RPM = 27 A
2280 RPM = 35 A
1710 RPM = 45 A

Step 2: Calculating load
430.22(B)
27 A x 125% = 33.75 A
35 A x 125% = 43.75 A
45 A x 125% = 56.25 A

Step 3: Selecting conductors
310.14(A)(3), IN (2) and **Table 310.16)**
33.75 A requires 10 AWG cu.
43.75 A requires 8 AWG cu.
56.25 A requires 6 AWG cu.

Solution: The size THWN copper conductors are 10 AWG cu., 8 AWG cu., and 6 AWG cu. for each speed.

**SIZING CONDUCTORS FOR MULTISPEED MOTORS
NEC 430.22(B)**

Figure 20-3. Determining the size branch-circuit conductors to supply multispeed motors.

SIZING CONDUCTORS FOR WYE-START AND DELTA-RUN MOTORS 430.22(C)

The branch-circuit conductors for wye-start and delta-run connected motors shall be selected based on the full-load current on the line side of the controller shall not be less than

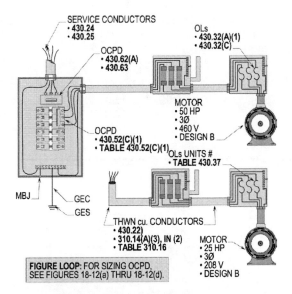

FINDING THWN COPPER CONDUCTORS

Three-phase motors (460 V)

Step 1: Finding FLA
430.6(A)(1) and **Table 430.250**
50 HP = 65 A

Step 2: Calculating load
430.22, Table 210.3, and **Table 220.3**
65 A x 125% = 81.25 A

Step 3: Selecting conductors
310.14(A)(3), IN 2 and **Table 310.16**
81.25 A requires 4 AWG cu.

Solution: The size THWN copper conductors are 4 AWG.

Three-phase motors (208 V)

Step 1: Finding FLA
430.6(A)(1) and **Table 430.250**
25 HP = 74.8 A

Step 2: Calculating load
430.22, Table 210.3, and **Table 220.3**
74.8 A x 125% = 93.5 A

Step 3: Selecting conductors
310.14(A)(3), IN (2) and **Table 310.16**
93.5 A requires 3 AWG cu.

Solution: The size THWN copper conductors are 3 AWG.

**SIZING CONDUCTORS FOR THREE-PHASE MOTORS
NEC 430.22**

Figure 20-2. Determining the size branch-circuit conductors to supply three-phase motors.

125 percent of the motor full-load current. The capacity of the conductors between the controller and the motor shall not be less than 72 percent of the motor full-load current rating.

Note, the selection of conductors between the controller and the motor shall be based on 58 percent (1 ÷ 1.732 = .58) of the motor's full-load current times 125 percent for continuous use. **(See Figure 20-4)**

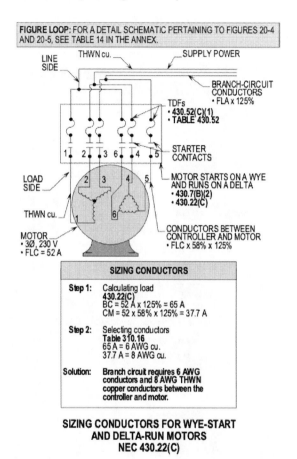

Figure 20-4. Determining the size conductors to supply motors starting on a wye and running on a delta.

SIZING CONDUCTORS FOR PART-WINDING MOTORS 430.22(D)

Induction or synchronous motors that have a part-winding start are designed so that when starting they energize the primary armature winding first. After starting, the remainder of the winding is energized in one or more steps. The purpose of this arrangement is to reduce the initial inrush current until the motor accelerates its running speed.

The inrush current at start is the locked-rotor current and at times can be quite high. A standard part-winding-start induction motor is designed so that only half of its winding is energized at the start; then, as it comes up to speed, the

other half is energized, so both halves are energized and carry equal current to drive the load.

Separate overload devices shall be used on a standard part-winding-start induction motor to protect the windings from excessive, damaging currents. This means that each half of the motor winding has to be individually provided with overload protection. These requirements are covered in **430.32** and **430.37**. Each half of each winding has a trip current value that is one half of the specified running current. As required by **430.52(C)(1)**, each of the two motor windings shall have branch-circuit, short-circuit, and ground-fault protection that is to be selected at not more than one half the percentages listed in **430.52(C)(1)** and **Table 430.52(C)(1)**. **(See Figure 20-5)**

> **Motor Tip:** Section **430.4, Ex.** permits a single device with this one half rating, for both windings, provided that it will permit the motor to start and run. If a time-delay (dual element) fuse is used as a single device for both windings, its rating shall be permitted if it does not exceed 150 percent of the motor's full-load current.

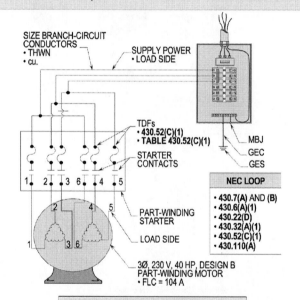

SIZING CONDUCTORS FOR PART-WINDING MOTORS NEC 430.22(D)

Figure 20-5. Determining the size branch-circuit conductors to supply part-winding motors.

SIZING CONDUCTORS FOR DUTY CYCLE MOTORS
430.22(E)

Conductors for a motor used for short-time, intermittent, periodic, or varying duty do not require conductors to be sized with a current-carrying capacity of 125 percent of the motor's full-load current. **Table 430.22(E)** permits the conductors to be sized with a percentage times the nameplate current rating based on the duty cycle classification of the motor.

When sizing conductors to supply individual motors that are used for short-time, intermittent, periodic, or varying duty, the requirements of **Table 430.22(E)** shall apply. Varying heat loads are produced on the conductors by the starting and stopping duration of operation cycles, which permits conductor sizing changes. In other words, such conductors are never subjected to continuous operation due to ON and OFF periods, and therefore conductors are never fully loaded for long intervals of time. For this reason, conductors can be downsized. **(See Figure 20-6)**

SIZING CONDUCTORS FOR ADJUSTABLE SPEED DRIVE SYSTEMS
430.122(A) AND ARTICLE 100

Power conversion equipment, when supplied from a branch circuit, includes all elements of the adjustable speed drive system. The rating in amps is used to size the conductors, which are based upon the power required by the conversion equipment. When the power conversion equipment provides overcurrent protection for the motor, no additional overload protection is required.

The disconnecting means can be installed in the line supplying the conversion equipment, and the rating of the disconnect shall not be less than 115 percent of the input current rating of the conversion unit.

Power conversion equipment requires the conductors to be sized at 125 percent of the rated input of such equipment.

Motor Tip: Power conversion equipment contains solid state units that change the cycles or chop part of the waveforms to vary the speed of squirrel cage motors as needed for the application. **(See Figure 20-7** and **Page 17-7)**

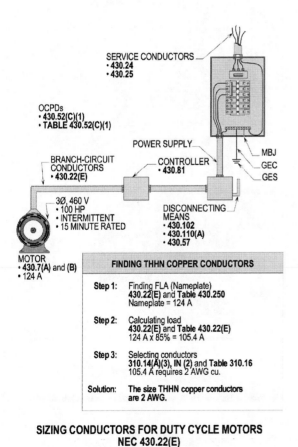

SIZING CONDUCTORS FOR DUTY CYCLE MOTORS
NEC 430.22(E)

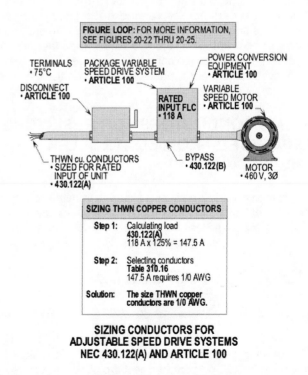

SIZING CONDUCTORS FOR ADJUSTABLE SPEED DRIVE SYSTEMS
NEC 430.122(A) AND ARTICLE 100

Figure 20-6. Determining the size conductors to supply duty cycle related motors.

Figure 20-7. Determining the size conductors to supply power conversion equipment.

WOUND-ROTOR SECONDARY
430.23

Wound-rotor motors are three-phase motors that are installed with two sets of leads. The main leads to the motor windings (field poles) are one set, and the secondary leads to the rotor are the other set. The secondary leads on one end connect to the rotor through slip rings, and the other of the leads connects through a controller and a bank of resistors. The speed of the motor varies when the amount of resistance in the motor circuit is varied. The rotor will turn slower when the resistance is greater in the rotor, and faster when such resistance is lowered.

SIZING CONDUCTORS FOR CONTINUOUS DUTY
430.23(A)

The conductors shall have an ampacity not less than 125 percent of the full-load secondary current of the motor where secondary leads are installed between the controller and the motor. The secondary full-load current rating is obtained from the manufacturer or found on the nameplate of the motor.

SIZING CONDUCTORS FOR OTHER THAN CONTINUOUS DUTY
430.23(B)

When installing a motor to be used for a short-time, intermittent, periodic, or varying duty, the secondary conductors shall be sized not less than 125 percent of the secondary current per **Table 430.22(E)**. The classification of service determines the correct percentages to select and apply, when sizing the conductors, based on the cycles of the motor.

SIZING CONDUCTORS FOR RESISTORS, SEPARATED FROM CONTROLLER
430.23(C)

Where the secondary resistor is separate from the controller, the ampacity of the conductors between the controller and resistor shall not be less than the resistor duty classification percentages listed in **Table 430.23(C)**. **(See Figure 20-8)**

SIZING CONDUCTORS FOR SEVERAL MOTORS
430.24

The full-load current rating of the largest motor shall be multiplied by 125 percent to select the size conductors for a feeder supplying a group of two or more motors. The remaining motors of the group shall have their full-load current ratings added to this value, and this total amperage is

then used to size the conductors. Noncontinuous nonmotor loads shall be sized at 100 percent. Continuous nonmotor loads shall be sized at 125 percent. **(See Figure 20-9)**

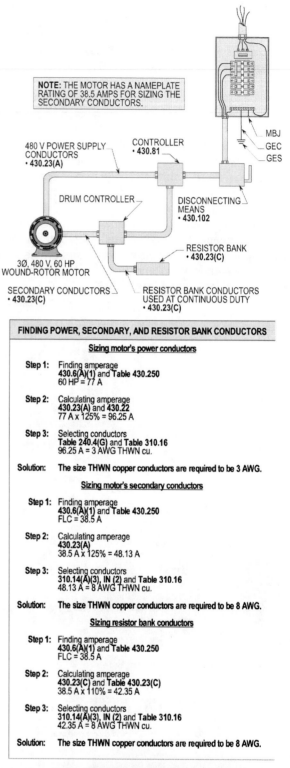

SIZING CONDUCTORS FOR RESISTORS,
SEPARATED FROM CONTROLLER
NEC 430.23(A) THRU (C)

Figure 20-8. Determining the size conductors to supply wound-rotor motors.

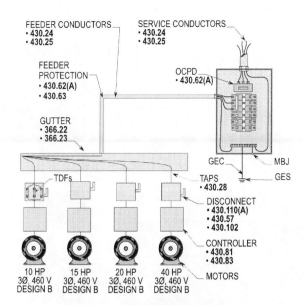

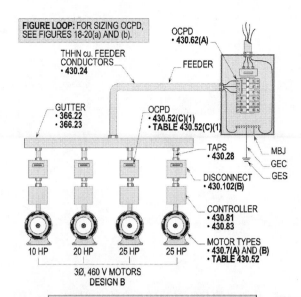

SIZING TIME-DELAY FUSES FOR FEEDER

Step 1: Finding FLA of motors
430.6(A)(1) and **Table 430.250**
10 HP = 14 A
15 HP = 21 A
20 HP = 27 A
40 HP = 52 A

Step 2: Calculating feeder OCPD
430.24, Table 210.3, and **Table 220.3**
52 A x 125%   = 65 A
Plus other motors
in group   = 27 A
                           = 21 A
                           = 14 A
Total amps   = 127 A

Step 3: Selecting conductors
310.14(A)(3), IN (2), 430.24, and
Table 310.16
127 A requires 1 AWG cu.

Solution: The size THWN copper conductors
are 1 AWG.

SIZING CONDUCTORS FOR SEVERAL MOTORS
NEC 430.24

Figure 20-9. Determining the size conductors for a feeder to supply several motors.

FINDING FEEDER THHN COPPER CONDUCTORS

Step 1: Finding FLA
430.6(A)(1) and **Table 430.250**
10 HP = 14 A
20 HP = 27 A
25 HP = 34 A
25 HP = 34 A

Step 2: Calculating load
430.24, Table 210.3, and **Table 220.3**
34 A x 125%   = 42.5 A
                   = 34 A
                   = 27 A
                   = 14 A
Total load   = 117.5 A

Step 3: Selecting conductors
310.14(A)(3), IN (2) and **Table 310.16**
117.5 A requires 1 AWG cu.

Solution: The size THHN copper conductors are 1 AWG.

SEVERAL MOTORS ON A FEEDER
NEC 430.24

Figure 20-10. Sizing the feeder conductors to supply power to a group of motors.

DETERMINING LARGEST MOTOR BASED ON THE DUTY CYCLE
430.24, Ex. 1

Feeder conductors supplying power to two or more motors utilized to serve duty-cycle loads per **430.22(E)** shall have the largest motor selected based on their conditions of use. **(See Figure 20-11)**

SEVERAL MOTORS ON A FEEDER
430.24

Feeder conductors supplying several motors shall be sized to carry 125 percent of the FLC rating of the highest rated current motor plus the sum of the FLC ratings of all remaining motors on the circuit. **(See Figure 20-10)**

MOTOR IN A HEATING UNIT
430.24, Ex. 2

Section **424.3(B)** shall be used to calculate the size conductors to supply power to fixed electric space heating units that are equipped with motor operated equipment. **(See Figure 20-12)**

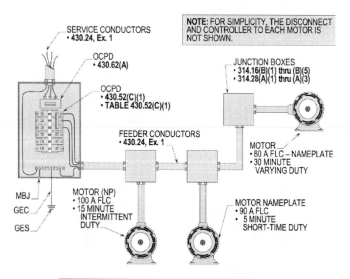

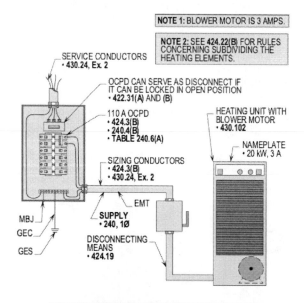

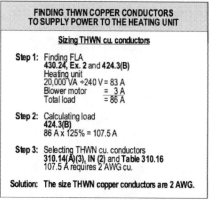

FINDING LARGEST LOAD AND THWN COPPER CONDUCTORS

Finding largest motor load

Step 1: Applying demand factors
430.24, Ex. 1, 430.22(E), and **Table 430.22(E)**
100 A x 85% = 85 A
90 A x 110 % = 99 A
80 A x 150% = 120 A

Solution: The largest motor load is 120 amps.

Sizing THWN cu. conductors

Step 1: Calculating load
430.24, Ex. 1
Largest motor load = 120 A
Plus others = 99 A
= 85 A
Total load = 304 A

Step 2: Selecting conductors
310.14(A)(3), IN (2) and **Table 310.16**
304 A requires 350 KCMIL cu.

Solution: The size THWN copper conductors are 350 KCMIL.

**DETERMINING LARGEST MOTOR
BASED ON THE DUTY CYCLE
NEC 430.24, Ex. 1**

Figure 20-11. Sizing feeder conductors for the largest motor load based on the duty cycle per **430.22(E)**.

MOTORS WITH INTERLOCKS
430.24, Ex. 3

Motors that operate with other loads and are interlocked so as not to operate at the same time shall be permitted to have the feeder conductors based on the interlocked group producing the greater FLA rating. **(See Figure 20-13)**

SIZING CONDUCTORS FOR MOTORS AND OTHER LOADS
430.25

The motor load shall be calculated per **430.22** or **430.24** when designing combination loads that consist of one or more motor loads on the same circuit with lights, receptacles, appliances, or any combination of such loads.

FINDING THWN COPPER CONDUCTORS
TO SUPPLY POWER TO THE HEATING UNIT

Sizing THWN cu. conductors

Step 1: Finding FLA
430.24, Ex. 2 and **424.3(B)**
Heating unit
20,000 VA ÷ 240 V = 83 A
Blower motor = 3 A
Total load = 86 A

Step 2: Calculating load
424.3(B)
86 A x 125% = 107.5 A

Step 3: Selecting THWN cu. conductors
310.14(A)(3), IN (2) and **Table 310.16**
107.5 A requires 2 AWG cu.

Solution: The size THWN copper conductors are 2 AWG.

**MOTOR IN A HEATING UNIT
NEC 430.24, Ex. 2**

Figure 20-12. Sizing conductors to supply heating unit.

For other than motor loads, **Article 220** and other applicable articles shall be used to calculate such loads. The ampacity required for the feeder conductors shall be equal to the total loads involved. The overcurrent protection devices used to protect conductors and elements from short circuits and ground faults shall be sized per **430.7(D)**, **430.7(D)(2)**, **430.24**, **430.62(A)** and **430.63**. **(See Figure 20-14)**

FEEDER DEMAND FACTORS
430.26

There are specific installations where there may be a number of motors connected to a feeder, and because of their operations, certain motors do not operate together. Therefore, the feeder conductors shall be sized according to the group that has the greater current rating per **430.24**. **(See Figure 20-15)**

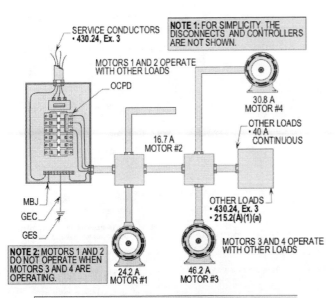

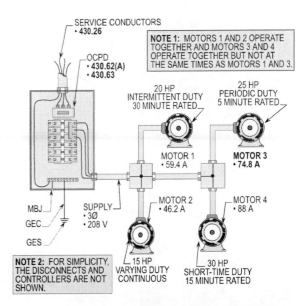

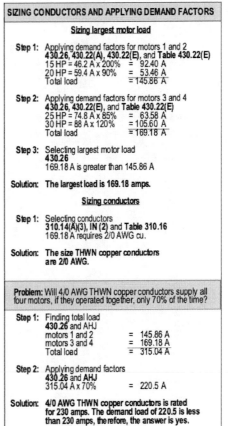

SIZING CONDUCTORS FOR THE MOTORS AND OTHER LOADS

Finding largest load

Step 1: Finding load for motors 1 and 2
430.24, Ex. 3 and 215.2(A)(1)
Motor 1   = 24.2 A x 125% = 30.25 A
Motor 2   = 16.7 A x 100% = 16.7 A
Other loads = 40   A x 125% = 50   A
Total load   = 96.95 A

Step 2: Finding load for motors 3 and 4
430.24, Ex. 3 and 215.2(A)(1)
Motor 3   = 46.2 A x 125% = 57.75 A
Motor 4   = 30.8 A x 100% = 30.8 A
Other loads = 40   A x 125% = 50   A
Total load   = 138.55 A

Step 3: Selecting largest load
430.24, Ex. 3
138.55 A is greater than 96.95 A

Solution: The greater interlocked load is **138.55 amps.**

Sizing conductors

Step 1: Selecting conductors
310.14(A)(3), IN (2) and **Table 310.16**, and Step 2 above
138.55 A requires 1/0 AWG cu.

Solution: The size THWN copper conductors are **1/0 AWG.**

MOTORS WITH INTERLOCKS
NEC 430.24, Ex. 3

Figure 20-13. Sizing conductors to supply power to the motors and other loads where they do not operate together.

DC MOTORS
430.29

Conductors connecting a motor controller to power accelerating and dynamic braking resistors in the armature circuit of DC motors shall be sized by the percentages listed in **Table 430.29. (See Figure 20-16)**

The conductors supplying power to a DC motor shall be sized at 125 percent of the FLC of the motor. Overcurrent protection devices shall be sized to carry the starting current of the motor. **(See Figure 20-17)**

SIZING CONDUCTORS AND APPLYING DEMAND FACTORS

Sizing largest motor load

Step 1: Applying demand factors for motors 1 and 2
430.26, 430.22(A), 430.22(E), and **Table 430.22(E)**
15 HP = 46.2 A x 200% = 92.40 A
20 HP = 59.4 A x 90%   = 53.46 A
Total load   = 145.86 A

Step 2: Applying demand factors for motors 3 and 4
430.26, 430.22(E), and **Table 430.22(E)**
25 HP = 74.8 A x 85%   = 63.58 A
30 HP = 88 A x 120%   = 105.60 A
Total load   = 169.18 A

Step 3: Selecting largest motor load
430.26
169.18 A is greater than 145.86 A

Solution: The largest load is 169.18 amps.

Sizing conductors

Step 1: Selecting conductors
310.14(A)(3), IN (2) and **Table 310.16**
169.18 A requires 2/0 AWG cu.

Solution: The size THWN copper conductors are 2/0 AWG.

Problem: Will 4/0 AWG THWN copper conductors supply all four motors, if they operated together, only 70% of the time?

Step 1: Finding total load
430.26 and AHJ
motors 1 and 2 = 145.86 A
motors 3 and 4 = 169.18 A
Total load   = 315.04 A

Step 2: Applying demand factors
430.26 and AHJ
315.04 A x 70% = 220.5 A

Solution: 4/0 AWG THWN copper conductors is rated for 230 amps. The demand load of 220.5 is less than 230 amps, therefore, the answer is yes.

FEEDER DEMAND FACTORS
NEC 430.26

Figure 20-15. Sizing feeder conductors when applying demand factors.

Note, DC circuitry is identified or color coding is used when required per **210.5(C)(1)** and **(C)(2).**

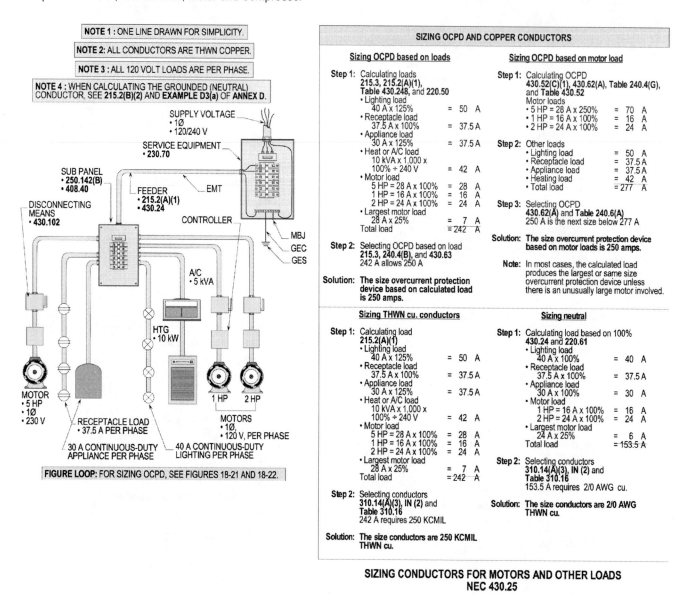

Figure 20-14. Calculating the size conductors for motors and other loads supplied by a feeder.

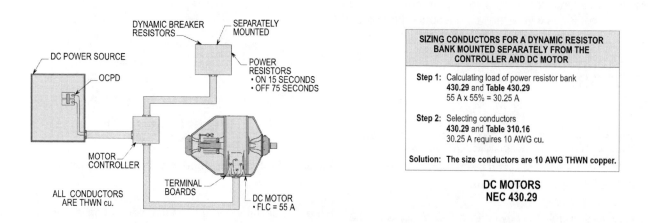

Figure 20-16. Sizing conductors for a dynamic resistor bank mounted separately from the controller and DC motor.

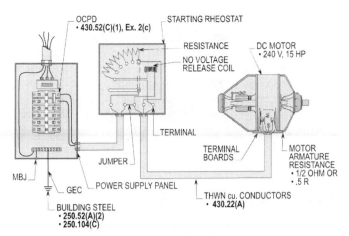

SIZING OCPD AND CONDUCTORS FOR DC MOTORS

Step 1: Calculating amps to size OCPD
430.52(C)(1)
LCR based on arm. (resistance)
= 240 V ÷ .5 (1/2 ohm)
LCR based on arm. = 480 A

Step 2: Calculating OCPD
Table 430.247, 430.52(C)(1), and **Table 430.5(C)(1)**
55 A x 150% = 82.5 A

Step 3: Selecting OCPD
240.4(G), Table 240.6(A), and **430.52(C)(1)(a)**
82.5 A requires 90 A

Step 4: Verifying starting of motor
• CB must hold 480 A starting current of motor
÷ 3 (CB holds about 3 times its rating) = 160 A
• 160 A requires 175 A CB
• 175 A CB holds 525 A (175 A x 3 = 525 A)
• 525 A will hold 480 A of LRC

Step 5: Applying maximum OCPD
430.52(C)(1)(b)(3)
Max. = 55 A x 400% = 220 A

Solution: **A 200 amp OCPD may be used. However, normally a 175 amp OCPD will allow the motor to start and run.**

Sizing conductors

Step 1: Finding FLA
430.6(A)(1) and **Table 430.247**
15 HP = 55 A

Step 2: Calculating load
430.22(A)
55 A x 125% = 68.75 A

Step 3: Selecting conductors
310.15 and **Table 310.16**
68.75 A requires 4 AWG cu.

Solution: **The size THWN copper conductors are 4 AWG.**

DC MOTORS
NEC 430.29

Figure 20-17. Sizing overcurrent protection device and conductors for a DC motor. [See **Figure 16-12(a)** and **128(b)**]

SIZING CONDUCTORS FOR CAPACITORS
460.8(A)

The ampacity of capacitor circuit conductors shall not be less than 135 percent of the rated current of the capacitor. The leads for a capacitor that supplies a motor shall not be less than one-third the ampacity of the motor circuit conductors. The larger of the two calculations shall be used for the capacitor supply conductors. **(See Figure 20-18)**

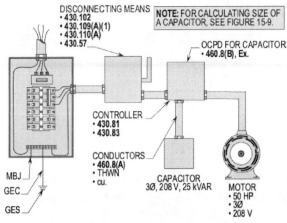

SIZING THWN CONDUCTORS TO CAPACITOR

Sizing conductors based on 1/3

Step 1: Finding FLA of motor
Table 430.250
50 HP = 143 A

Step 2: Calculating amps for conductors
430.22
143 A x 125% = 178.8 A

Step 3: Selecting conductors
310.14(A)(3), IN (2) and **Table 310.16**
178.8 A requires 3/0 AWG THWN cu.

Step 4: Calculating conductors at 1/3 of 3/0 AWG cu.
460.8(A) and **Table 310.16**
3/0 THWN cu. = 200 A
1/3 of 200 A = 66.7 A

Step 5: Selecting conductors
Table 310.16
66.7 A requires 4 AWG cu.

Solution: **The size THWN copper conductors based on 1/3 of branch circuit are 4 AWG cu.**

Sizing conductors based on 135%

Step 1: Calculating FLA of capacitor
460.8(A)
FLA = (kVAR x 1000) ÷ (V x √3)
FLA = (25 x 1000) ÷ (208 V x 1.732)
FLA = 69.4 A

Step 2: Calculating conductors
460.8(A)
69.4 A x 135% = 93.7 A

Step 3: Selecting conductors
310.14(A)(3), IN (2) and **Table 310.16**
93.7 A requires 3 AWG cu.

Solution: **The size THWN copper conductors based on 135 percent of FLA of capacitor are 3 AWG cu.**

Note: Section 460.8(A) requires the largest conductors calculated that are 3 AWG THWN copper.

SIZING CONDUCTORS FOR CAPACITORS
NEC 460.8(A)

Figure 20-18. There are two calculations to be performed, and one of them shall be selected to size the capacitor circuit conductors. **Note,** the greater of the 1/3 calculation or 135 percent calculation shall be used. **(See Figure 15-9)**

FINDING MICROFARADS

The microfarads for a capacitor may be found by applying the following equation:

$$C = \frac{159,300 \times A}{Hz \times V \times 1.732}$$

$$C = \frac{159,300 \times 143\,A}{60 \times 208\,V \times 1.732}$$

$$C = \frac{22,779,900}{21,615.36}$$

$$C = 1,053.9\ mF$$

The above microfarads (mF) were calculated based on the FLC of 143 amps from the 50 horsepower, three-phase, 208 volt motor in **Figures 20-18** and **15-9**.

Note, the number 159,300 is a constant that is always used when applying the above equation.

MOTOR CONTROL CENTERS
PART VIII OF ARTICLE 430

Motor control centers are used wherever centralized control of a number of motors is feasible and desired. They provide a control location where incoming and outgoing lines to branch circuits can be consolidated.

In addition to the obvious advantages of reduced installation cost, centralized control eliminates the need for time-consuming trips to remote areas in a plant to shut down equipment or restart a motor that has tripped out its circuit due to overload. In the event of a power failure, motor control centers provide a rapid, safe means of restoring power. Orderly and sequential start-up of process motors, fans, pumps, and blowers is critical. In some industrial operations, automatic restart is dangerous after a power interruption.

OVERCURRENT PROTECTION
430.94

Overcurrent protection shall be provided for these units based on the current rating of the power bus and the requirements of **Article 240**. This protection shall be provided either by an overcurrent device located ahead of the motor control center or by a main overcurrent protection device that is within sight of the center.

Motor Control Center Tip: The overcurrent protection cannot exceed the rating of the common power bus of a motor control center. It shall be permitted to use an overcurrent protective device with a rating less than the common power bus, provided it is of sufficient size to carry the load determined in accordance with **Part II** of **Article 430**.

SERVICE EQUIPMENT
430.95

When motor control centers are used as service equipment, they shall have a main disconnect that disconnects all ungrounded (phase) conductors. If necessary, a second service disconnect shall be permitted to be used to feed additional equipment. If a grounded (neutral) conductor is used, a main bonding jumper shall be installed.

See Figure 20-19(a), (b), and **(c)** to determine the size conductors and setting of an instantaneous trip circuit breaker to supply a 50 HP, three-phase, 460 volt motor from a motor control center (MCC).

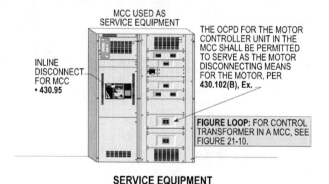

MCC USED AS
SERVICE EQUIPMENT

INLINE
DISCONNECT
FOR MCC
• 430.95

THE OCPD FOR THE MOTOR CONTROLLER UNIT IN THE MCC SHALL BE PERMITTED TO SERVE AS THE MOTOR DISCONNECTING MEANS FOR THE MOTOR, PER 430.102(B), Ex.

FIGURE LOOP: FOR CONTROL TRANSFORMER IN A MCC, SEE FIGURE 21-10.

SERVICE EQUIPMENT
NEC 430.95

Figure 20-19(a). Motor control center used as service equipment shall have a main disconnect to disconnect ungrounded (phase) conductors.

GROUNDING
430.96

All sections of motor control centers shall be connected together with an equipment grounding conductor or bus sized per **250.122**. All equipment grounding conductors shall be connected to this conductor or bus. (A bus is almost always used.) (See **Table 250.122** in the NEC)

SIZING CONDUCTORS FOR THREE-PHASE MOTORS

FINDING THWN COPPER CONDUCTORS FROM MCC TO MOTOR

Three-phase motors

Step 1: Finding FLA
430.6(A)(1) and Table 430.250
50 HP = 65 A

Step 2: Calculating load
430.22, Table 210.3, and Table 220.3
65 A x 125% = 81.25 A

Step 3: Selecting conductors
310.14(A)(3), IN (2) and Table 310.16
81.25 A requires 4 AWG cu.

Solution: The size THWN copper conductors are 4 AWG.

SERVICE EQUIPMENT
NEC 430.95

Figure 20-19(b). Sizing the conductor for a three-phase, 460 volt, 50 HP, Design B motor supplied from a motor control center. **(See Figure 21-10** for control transformer.)

SIZING OVERCURRENT PROTECTION DEVICES TO ALLOW MOTORS TO START AND RUN

SETTING AN INSTANTANEOUS TRIP CIRCUIT BREAKER IN CONTROL UNIT IN MCC

Step 1: Finding FLA
430.6(A)(1) and Table 430.250
50 HP = 65 A

Step 2: Selecting the minimum setting
430.52(C)(3) and Table 430.52(C)(1)
Minimum size = 800%

Step 3: Calculating minimum setting
430.52(C)(3)(b)(1) and Table 240.4(G)
Minimum size = 65 A x 800% = 520 A

Step 4: Calculating maximum setting
430.52(C)(3)(b)(2)a
65 A x 1300% = 845 A

Step 5: Selecting instantaneous trip circuit breaker
Minimum setting = 520 A
Maximum setting = 845 A

Solution: The minimum setting is 520 amps and the maximum setting is 845 amps. However, a smaller setting shall be permitted to be used.

SERVICE EQUIPMENT
NEC 430.95

Figure 20-19(c). Setting an instantaneous trip circuit breaker to start and run a 460 volt, 3Ø, 50 HP, Design B motor supplied from a motor control center.

BUSBARS AND CONDUCTORS
430.97

The following shall be considered for busbars and conductors:

- Support and arrangement
- Phase arrangement
- Minimum wire-bending space
- Spacing
- Barriers

SUPPORT AND ARRANGEMENT
430.97(A)

Busbars shall be protected and held rigidly in place. Conductors shouldn't be installed in vertical sections of the motor control center unless necessary or unless protected from the busbars by a barrier.

PHASE ARRANGEMENT
430.97(B)

The phase arrangement for three-phase systems shall be A, B, and C from front to back, top to bottom, or left to right. An exception is made for back-to-back units with vertical buswork. **(See Figure 20-20)**

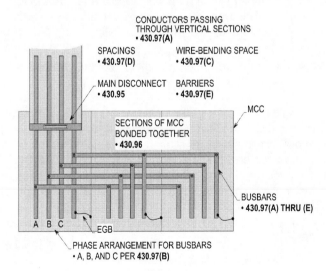

PHASE ARRANGEMENT
NEC 430.97(B)

Figure 20-20. Busbars and conductors shall be arranged and grounded per **430.97(A) through (E)**.

MINIMUM WIRE-BENDING SPACE
430.97(C)

The minimum wire-bending space at the motor control center terminals and minimum gutter space shall be as required in **Article 312**. [Also, see **Table 312.6(A)** and **(B)**]

SPACINGS
430.97(D)

Spacings between motor control center bus terminals and other bare metal parts shall not be less than specified in **Table 430.97(D)**.

BARRIERS
430.97(E)

Barriers shall be placed in all service-entrance motor control centers to isolate service busbars and terminals from the remainder of the motor control center.

MARKING OF MOTOR CONTROL CENTERS
430.98(A)

Motor control centers shall be marked according to **110.21**, and such marking shall be plainly visible after installation. Marking shall also include common power bus current rating and motor control center short-circuit rating.

Note, motor control units in a motor control center shall comply with **430.8**.

> **Motor Control Center Tip: Part VIII** to **Article 430** and **430.1** refers to installation requirements for motor control centers contained in **110.26(E)** and **408.18(B)**. The requirements of **110.26(E)** specify dedicated space for a motor control center and physical protection from mechanical systems that might leak or otherwise adversely impact a motor control center. **(See Figure 20-21)**

ADJUSTABLE-SPEED DRIVE SYSTEMS
PART X TO ARTICLE 430

When designing and installing electrical systems for adjustable-speed drives, the installation provisions of **Part I through Part IX** are applicable unless modified or supplemented by **Part X**.

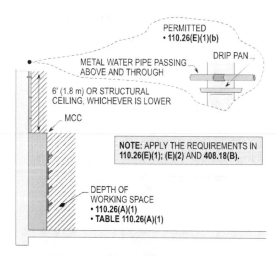

MARKING OF MOTOR CONTROL CENTERS
NEC 430.98(A)

Figure 20-21. The dedicated space above a motor control center shall be provided per **110.26(E)**.

BRANCH/FEEDER-CIRCUIT CONDUCTORS
430.122(A)

Circuit conductors supplying power conversion equipment included as part of an adjustable-speed drive system shall have an ampacity not less than 125 percent of the rated input to the power conversion equipment. **(See Figure 20-22)**

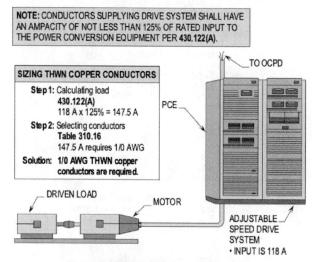

BRANCH/FEEDER-CIRCUIT CONDUCTORS
NEC 430.122(A)

Figure 20-22. The above illustrates the procedure for calculating the load in amps to size the conductors supplying the power conversion equipment.

Note, electrical resonance can result from the interaction of the nonsinusoidal currents from this type of load with power factor correction capacitors.

BYPASS DEVICE
430.122(B)

For an adjustable speed drive system that utilizes a bypass device, the conductor ampacity shall not be less than required by **430.6**. The ampacity of circuit conductors supplying power conversion equipment, included as part of an adjustable speed drive system that utilizes a bypass device shall be the larger of either of the following:

(1) 125 percent of the rated input to the power conversion equipment or

(2) 125 percent of the motor full-load current rating as determined by **430.6(A)(1)**.

For an illustrated description, see **Figure 20-23**.

OVERLOAD PROTECTION
430.124

Overload protection of the motor shall be provided.

INCLUDED IN POWER CONVERSION EQUIPMENT
430.124(A)

Where the power conversion equipment is marked to indicate that motor overload protection is included, additional overload protection shall not be required.

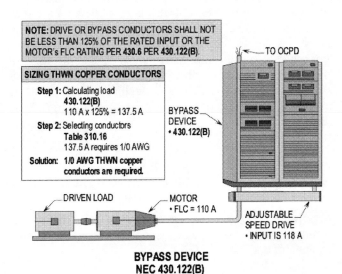

BYPASS DEVICE
NEC 430.122(B)

Figure 20-23. The above illustrates the procedures for calculating the load in amps to size the conductors for a bypass drive system.

BYPASS CIRCUITS
430.124(B)

For adjustable speed drive systems that utilize a bypass device to allow motor operation at rated full load speed, motor overload protection as described in **Article 430, Part III**, shall be provided in the bypass circuit.

MULTIPLE MOTOR APPLICATIONS
430.124(C)

For multiple motor application, individual motor overload protection shall be provided in accordance with **Article 430, Part III. (See Figure 20-24)**

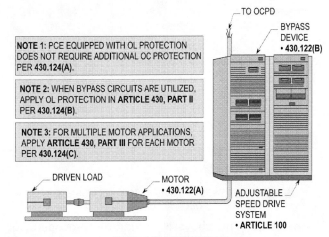

OVERLOAD PROTECTION
NEC 430.124(A) THRU (C)

Figure 20-24. The above illustrates the procedure for protecting the motor from overload when using a bypass device.

MOTOR OVERTEMPERATURE PROTECTION – GENERAL
430.126(A)

Adjustable speed drive systems shall protect against motor overtemperature conditions where the motor is not rated to operate at the nameplate rated current over the speed range required by the application. This protection shall be provided in addition to the conductor protection required in **430.32**. Protection shall be provided by one of the following means:

(1) Motor thermal protector in accordance with **430.32**

(2) Adjustable speed drive system with load- and speed-sensitive overload protection and thermal memory retention upon shutdown or power loss

Thermal memory retention upon shutdown or power loss is not required for continuous duty loads per **430.126(A)(2), Ex.**

(3) Overtemperature protection relay utilizing thermal sensors embedded in the motor and meeting the requirements of **430.32(A)(2)** or **(B)(2)**

(4) Thermal sensor embedded in the motor whose communications are received and acted upon by an adjustable speed drive system

For a detailed description of these requirements, see **Figure 20-25** and **IN** to **430.126(A)**.

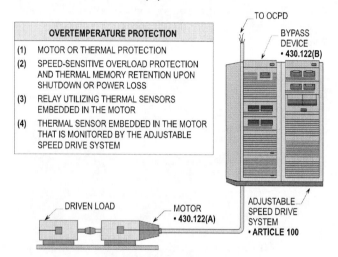

MOTOR OVERTEMPERATURE PROTECTION – GENERAL
NEC 430.126(A)

Figure 20-25. The above illustrates the procedure for determining protection for motor overtemperature problems.

MULTIPLE MOTOR APPLICATIONS
430.126(B)

For multiple motor application, individual motor overtemperature protection shall be provided per **430.126(A)**.

Note, the relationship between motor current and motor temperature changes when the motor is operated by an adjustable speed drive. When operated at reduced speed, overheating of motors may occur at current levels less than or equal to a motor's rated full load current. This is the result of reduced motor cooling when its shaft-mounted fan is operating at less than rated nameplate RPM.

AUTOMATIC RESTARTING AND ORDERLY SHUTDOWN
430.126(C)

The provisions of **430.43** and **430.44** shall apply to the motor overtemperature protection means.

DISCONNECTING MEANS
430.128

The disconnecting means shall be permitted to be in the incoming line to the conversion equipment and shall have a rating not less than 115 percent of the rated input current of the conversion unit.

PHASE CONVERTERS
455.6(A) AND 455.7(A)

Phase converters are used to convert single-phase power to three-phase power. The disconnecting means shall be located within 50 ft (15 m) and within sight per **455.8(A)**. Where the voltage is not the same, the output-to-input ratio shall be applied per **455.6(A)**.

Branch-circuit conductors shall be sized at 125 percent times the phase converter's nameplate single-phase input full-load current rating, in amps. The overcurrent protection device shall be sized at 125 percent times the phase converter's nameplate single-phase input full-load amps. The overcurrent protection device shall not exceed 125 percent but shall be equal to or lower than 125 percent. **(See Figure 20-26)**

Branch-circuit elements such as overcurrent protection devices and conductors supplying specific loads shall be calculated at 250 percent of the equipment's full-load amp rating. **(See Figure 20-27)**

Feeder conductors that convert single-phase power to three-phase power to supply power to two or more phase converters shall be sized at 250 percent times the three-phase amperage of all motors and other loads served. The overcurrent protection device shall be sized at 250 percent times the full-load three-phase amps of all motors and other loads. If the percentage does not correspond to a standard size, the next size overcurrent protection device above this percentage shall be permitted to be selected per **455.7**. **(See Figure 20-28)**

FIRE PUMPS
ARTICLE 695

Article 695 covers the installation of electric power sources, interconnecting circuits, and switching and control equipment dedicated to fire pumps.

Note, for more information on fire pump installations, see **NFPA 20, NFPA 37,** and for maintenance checks, **NFPA 110**.

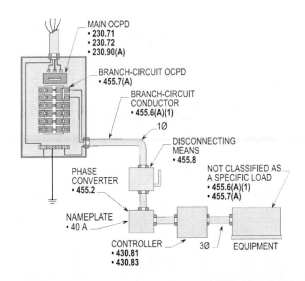

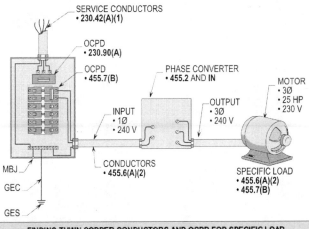

FINDING THWN CONDUCTORS AND OCPD FOR PHASE CONVERTER

Sizing conductors	Sizing OCPD
Step 1: Finding amperage 455.4 Nameplate = 40 A	**Step 1:** Finding amperage 455.4 Nameplate = 40 A
Step 2: Calculating amperage 240.4(G) and 455.6(A)(1) 40 A x 125% = 50 A	**Step 2:** Calculating amperage 455.7(A) 40 A x 125% = 50 A
Step 3: Selecting conductors Table 310.16 50 A = 8 AWG THWN cu.	**Step 3:** Selecting OCPD 455.7(A) and Table 240.6(A) 50 A = 50 A OCPD
Solution: The size THWN copper conductors are required to be 8 AWG.	**Solution:** A 50 amp overcurrent protection device is required.

PHASE CONVERTERS
NEC 455.6(A) AND 455.7(A)

Figure 20-26. Branch-circuit conductors shall be sized at 125 percent times the phase converter's nameplate single-phase input full-load amperage. The overcurrent protection device shall be sized at 125 percent times the phase converter's nameplate single-phase input full-load current, in amps.

POWER SOURCES
695.3(A)

Section **695.3(A)** covers power sources that are permitted to supply power to fire pump installations.

Power sources such as a reliable service, an on-site generator, a separately derived system, or a tap ahead of the service disconnecting means shall be considered dependable power supply systems when serving fire pumps and other related equipment. **(See Figure 20-29)**

FINDING THWN COPPER CONDUCTORS AND OCPD FOR SPECIFIC LOAD

Sizing conductors for input side	Sizing OCPD for input side
Step 1: Finding FLA of motor 430.6(A)(1) and Table 430.250 25 HP = 68 A	**Step 1:** Calculating OCPD 455.7(B): Step 1 above 68 A x 250% = 170 A
Step 2: Calculating conductors 455.6(A)(2) 68 A x 250% = 170 A	**Step 2:** Selecting OCPD 455.7(B), 240.4(G), and 240.6(A) 170 A requires 175 A
Step 3: Selecting conductors 310.14(A)(3), IN (2) and Table 310.16 170 A requires 2/0 AWG	**Solution:** The size overcurrent protection device is 175 amps.
Solution: The size THWN copper conductors are 2/0 AWG.	**Note:** See Table 240.4(G) and Table 240.6(A).

PHASE CONVERTERS
NEC 455.6(A)(2) AND 455.7(B)

Figure 20-27. Branch-circuit elements such as overcurrent protection devices and conductors supplying specific loads shall be calculated at 250 percent of the equipment's full-load current rating, in amps.

SIZING CONDUCTORS
695.6(C)(1) AND 430.22

Conductors shall be sized with enough capacity so that they are protected against short-circuit currents. By sizing the conductors to the fire pump motors at 125 percent of the motor's FLA, this should be accomplished. For sizing the conductors to one motor, see **430.22** and for more than one motor, plus other loads, see **430.24**. **(See Figure 20-30)**

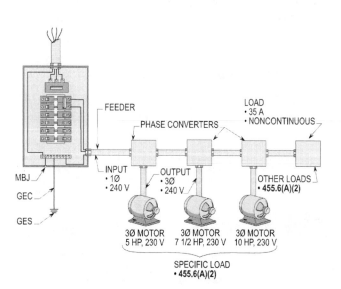

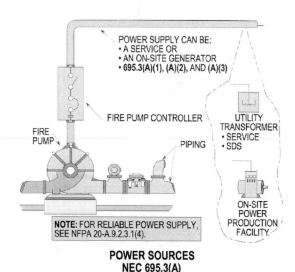

POWER SOURCES
NEC 695.3(A)

Figure 20-29. The above shows power sources that are permitted to supply fire pump installations.

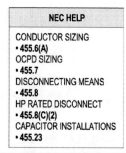

NEC HELP
CONDUCTOR SIZING
• 455.6(A)
OCPD SIZING
• 455.7
DISCONNECTING MEANS
• 455.8
HP RATED DISCONNECT
• 455.8(C)(2)
CAPACITOR INSTALLATIONS
• 455.23

FINDING OCPD AND THHN COPPER CONDUCTORS FOR FEEDER

Sizing conductors for input side

Step 1: Finding FLA for input side
430.6(A)(1) and **Table 430.250**
5 HP = 15.2 A
7 1/2 HP = 22.0 A
10 HP = 28.0 A

Step 2: Finding other loads
215.2(A)(1)
35 A x 100% = 35 A

Step 3: Calculating conductors
455.6(A)(2)
15.2 A + 22 A + 28 A + 35 A = 100.2 A
100.2 A x 250% = 250.5 A

Step 4: Selecting conductors
310.14(A)(3), IN (2) and
Table 310.16
250.5 A requires 250 KCMIL cu.

Solution: The size THWN copper conductors are 250 KCMIL copper.

Sizing OCPD for input side

Step 1: Calculating OCPD
455.7(B) and Step 3 above
100.2 A x 250% = 250.5 A

Step 2: Selecting OCPD
455.7(B) and **Table 240.6(A)**
250.5 A permits 250 A

Solution: The size overcurrent protection device is 250 amps.

PHASE CONVERTERS
NEC 455.6(A)(2), 455.7, AND 455.7(B)

Figure 20-28. Feeder conductors that convert single-phase power to three-phase power for supplying power to two or more phase converters shall be sized at 250 percent times the three-phase amperage of all motors and other loads served. The overcurrent protection device shall be sized at 250 times the full-load three-phase amps of all motors and other loads.

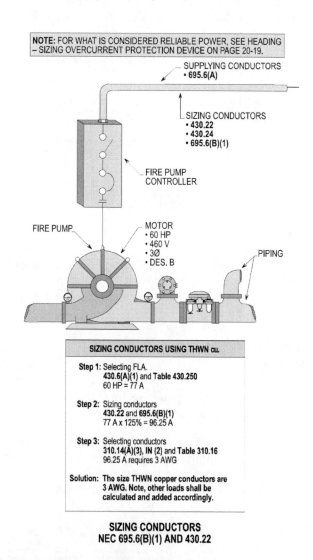

NOTE: FOR WHAT IS CONSIDERED RELIABLE POWER, SEE HEADING – SIZING OVERCURRENT PROTECTION DEVICE ON PAGE 20-19.

SIZING CONDUCTORS USING THWN cu.
Step 1: Selecting FLA.
430.6(A)(1) and **Table 430.250**
60 HP = 77 A
Step 2: Sizing conductors
430.22 and 695.6(B)(1)
77 A x 125% = 96.25 A
Step 3: Selecting conductors
310.14(A)(3), IN (2) and **Table 310.16**
96.25 A requires 3 AWG
Solution: The size THWN copper conductors are 3 AWG. Note, other loads shall be calculated and added accordingly.

SIZING CONDUCTORS
NEC 695.6(B)(1) AND 430.22

Figure 20-30. The above shows the procedure for sizing the conductors to supply a fire pump.

SIZING OVERCURRENT PROTECTION DEVICE
695.5(B), (C)(2), AND 230.90(A), Ex. 4

The overcurrent protection device shall protect the conductors and fire pump motor and accessories from short circuits. **(See Figure 20-31)**

Note, reliable power supply is a supply that won't shut down or fail more than four hours in a year as outlined in NFPA 20-A.9.2.3.1(4).

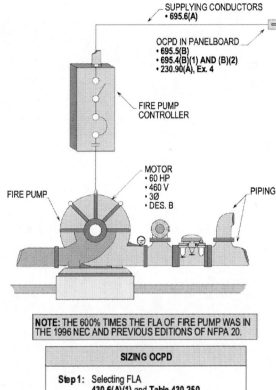

SUPPLYING CONDUCTORS
• 695.6(A)

OCPD IN PANELBOARD
• 695.5(B)
• 695.4(B)(1) AND (B)(2)
• 230.90(A), Ex. 4

FIRE PUMP CONTROLLER

FIRE PUMP

MOTOR
• 60 HP
• 460 V
• 3Ø
• DES. B

PIPING

NOTE: THE 600% TIMES THE FLA OF FIRE PUMP WAS IN THE 1996 NEC AND PREVIOUS EDITIONS OF NFPA 20.

SIZING OCPD

Step 1: Selecting FLA
430.6(A)(1) and **Table 430.250**
60 HP = 77 A

Step 2: Sizing OCPD
695.5(B), 695.5(C)(2), 695.4(B)(2)(a) and **230.90(A), Ex. 4**
77 A x 600% = 462

Step 3: Selecting OCPD
Table 240.6(A)
462 A permits 450 A OCPD

Solution: The overcurrent protection device is selected at 450 amps.

Note, other equipment and accessories loads shall be calculated and added accordingly.

SIZING OVERCURRENT PROTECTION DEVICE
NEC 695.5(B), 695.5(C)(2), AND 230.90(A), Ex. 4

Figure 20-31. The above shows the procedure for sizing the overcurrent protection device to allow a fire pump to operate until failure.

SIZING TRANSFORMER USED AS A SEPARATELY DERIVED SYSTEM
695.5(A) AND 695.6(B)(1)

Section **695.5(A)** permits a transformer dedicated to supplying a fire pump to be rated at a minimum of 125 percent of the sum of the rated full load of the fire pump motor(s), the rated full loads of pressure maintenance pump motor(s), and the full-load amps of any associated fire pump accessory equipment connected to the transformer.

Secondary overcurrent protection for the transformer shall not be permitted, and the primary overcurrent protection device shall not be set above 600 percent of the transformer's full-load current rating.

SIZING TRANSFORMER ELEMENTS

Section **695.5(A)** covers the requirements for sizing a separately derived system, **695.5(B)** deals with sizing the overcurrent protection device, and **695.5(B)(2)** outlines the rules that require the overcurrent protection device to carry the locked-rotor current of the transformer indefinitely.

SIZING OVERCURRENT PROTECTION DEVICE FOR A SEPARATELY DERIVED SYSTEM
695.5(B)

Section **696.5(B)** requires the overcurrent protection device on the primary side of a separately derived system, supplying power to a fire pump installation, to carry the secondary circuit indefinitely.

Note, such secondary currents include both normal full-load operating currents, as well as the locked-rotor current of the motor. **(See Figure 20-32)**

When separately derived systems are used to supply power to fire pumps and accessories, they are usually installed in the fire pump room with the fire pump controller.

Note, the transformer shall supply power until pump motor failure. This requirement allows the motor to pump water to fight the fire for as long as possible.

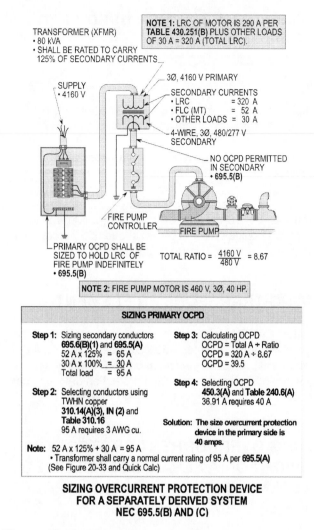

NOTE 1: LRC OF MOTOR IS 290 A PER TABLE 430.251(B) PLUS OTHER LOADS OF 30 A = 320 A (TOTAL LRC).

TRANSFORMER (XFMR)
• 80 kVA
• SHALL BE RATED TO CARRY 125% OF SECONDARY CURRENTS

SUPPLY
• 4160 V

3Ø, 4160 V PRIMARY

SECONDARY CURRENTS
• LRC   = 320 A
• FLC (MT)   = 52 A
• OTHER LOADS = 30 A

4-WIRE, 3Ø, 480/277 V SECONDARY

NO OCPD PERMITTED IN SECONDARY
• 695.5(B)

FIRE PUMP CONTROLLER

FIRE PUMP

PRIMARY OCPD SHALL BE SIZED TO HOLD LRC OF FIRE PUMP INDEFINITELY
• 695.5(B)

$$\text{TOTAL RATIO} = \frac{4160 \text{ V}}{480 \text{ V}} = 8.67$$

NOTE 2: FIRE PUMP MOTOR IS 460 V, 3Ø, 40 HP.

SIZING PRIMARY OCPD

Step 1: Sizing secondary conductors
695.6(B)(1) and **695.5(A)**
52 A x 125% = 65 A
30 A x 100% = 30 A
Total load   = 95 A

Step 2: Selecting conductors using TWHN copper
310.14(A)(3), IN (2) and **Table 310.16**
95 A requires 3 AWG cu.

Note: 52 A x 125% + 30 A = 95 A
• Transformer shall carry a normal current rating of 95 A per **695.5(A)**
(See Figure 20-33 and Quick Calc)

Step 3: Calculating OCPD
OCPD = Total A ÷ Ratio
OCPD = 320 A ÷ 8.67
OCPD = 39.5

Step 4: Selecting OCPD
450.3(A) and **Table 240.6(A)**
36.91 A requires 40 A

Solution: The size overcurrent protection device in the primary side is 40 amps.

**SIZING OVERCURRENT PROTECTION DEVICE
FOR A SEPARATELY DERIVED SYSTEM
NEC 695.5(B) AND (C)**

Figure 20-32. The above shows the procedure for sizing the transformer and primary overcurrent protection device for a fire pump installation.

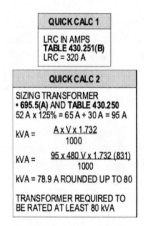

QUICK CALC 1

LRC IN AMPS
TABLE 430.251(B)
LRC = 320 A

QUICK CALC 2

SIZING TRANSFORMER
• **695.5(A)** AND **TABLE 430.250**
52 A x 125% = 65 A + 30 A = 95 A

$$kVA = \frac{A \times V \times 1.732}{1000}$$

$$kVA = \frac{95 \times 480 \text{ V} \times 1.732 \, (831)}{1000}$$

kVA = 78.9 A ROUNDED UP TO 80

TRANSFORMER REQUIRED TO BE RATED AT LEAST 80 kVA

Figure 20-33. Sizing the transformer to use as a separately derived system to supply a fire pump.

Chapter 20: Motor Feeder and Branch-Circuit Conductors

Section   Answer

1. Branch-circuit conductors supplying a single motor shall have an ampacity not   _____   _____
   less than _____ percent of the motor's full-load current rating.
   - (a) 100   (b) 115
   - (c) 125   (d) 135

2. When sizing conductors for wye start and delta run motor at continuous use,   _____   _____
   the selection of conductors between the controller and the motor shall be based
   on _____ percent of the motor's full-load current times 125 percent.
   - (a) 25   (b) 33
   - (c) 42   (d) 58

3. Conductors used for periodic duty with a continuous rated motor shall have a   _____   _____
   current-carrying capacity of _____ percent of the motor's full-load current.
   - (a) 125   (b) 140
   - (c) 150   (d) 175

4. The disconnecting means shall be permitted to be installed in the line supplying   _____   _____
   the conversion equipment and the rating of the disconnecting means shall
   not be less than _____ percent of the input current rating of the conversion
   equipment.
   - (a) 115   (b) 125
   - (c) 135   (d) 150

5. Power conversion equipment requires the conductors to be sized at _____   _____   _____
   percent of the rated input of such equipment or by the nameplate information.
   - (a) 115   (b) 125
   - (c) 135   (d) 150

6. The conductors supplying power to a DC motor (rated continuous) shall be   _____   _____
   sized at _____ percent of the full-load current of the motor.
   - (a) 100   (b) 115
   - (c) 125   (d) 135

7. Feeder conductors supplying several motors shall be sized to carry _____   _____   _____
   percent of the full-load current rating of the highest rated current motor plus
   the sum of the full-load current ratings of all remaining motors on the circuit.
   - (a) 85   (b) 100
   - (c) 115   (d) 125

8. The ampacity of capacitor circuit conductors shall not be less than _____   _____   _____
   percent of the rated current of the capacitor.
   - (a) 100   (b) 125
   - (c) 135   (d) 150

9. The phase arrangement (motor control centers) for three-phase systems shall   _____   _____
   be _____.
   - (a) front to back   (b) top to bottom
   - (c) left to right   (d) all of the above

10. When sizing conductors for continuous duty motors, the conductors shall have an ampacity of not less than _____ percent of the full-load secondary current of the motor.
    (a) 100   (b) 125
    (c) 150   (d) 200

11. What size THWN (branch-circuit) copper conductors are required for a 3 HP, 208 volt, single-phase, Design B motor?

12. What size THWN (branch-circuit) copper conductors are required for a 20 HP, 230 volt, three-phase, Design B motor?

13. What size THWN (branch-circuit) copper conductors are required for a 75 HP, 460 volt, three-phase, 15 minute rated intermittent duty cycle motor?

14. What size THWN (branch-circuit) copper conductors are required to supply power conversion equipment with a rated input of 112 amps?

15. What size THWN (branch-circuit) copper conductors (line side) are required to supply a 50 HP, 208 volt, three-phase, Design B part-winding motor?

16. What size THWN (feeder) copper conductors are required to supply 30 HP, 40 HP, and 50 HP, 460 volt, three-phase, Design B motors?

17. What size THWN (feeder) copper conductors are required to supply a 10 HP, 208 volt, three-phase, 5 minute rated intermittent duty cycle; 15 HP, 208 volt, three-phase, 15 minute rated intermittent duty cycle motor; and 20 HP, 208 volt, three-phase motor?

18. What size THWN (branch-circuit) copper conductors are required to supply a 20 kVAR, 208 volt, three-phase capacitor connected to a 40 HP, 208 volt, three-phase, Design B motor?

19. An overcurrent protection device for a fire pump can be sized at _____% under certain conditions of use.
    (a) 175   (b) 250
    (c) 300   (d) 600

20. A single-phase service can be used to supply a _____ -phase _____.
    (a) three   (b) converter
    (c) all of the above   (d) none of the above

21

Control Circuit Conductors and Components

Control circuit conductors are designed and installed so that they may be tapped from the motor power supply circuit or supplied from the service equipment. Overcurrent protection for control circuits that are tapped on the load side of controllers are designed and installed per **430.72**. Overcurrent protection for control circuits supplied from a source of power other than the motor circuit's source of power is designed and installed per **724.43** and **724.45**. Lower voltage may be provided by control transformers that are installed for controlling motor circuits and related systems.

TYPES OF CONTROL CIRCUITS
430.72 AND 724.43

A motor-control circuit tapped on the load side of fuses and circuit breakers utilized for motor branch circuits shall protect such conductors, or supplementary protection devices shall be provided.

The size of the control circuit conductors and the rating of the motor branch-circuit device will be determined by this method of protection. Motor-control circuits are classified as remote-control circuits where such circuits derive their power from other than the motor branch-circuit conductors. Various situations permit fuses or circuit breakers to be utilized to protect remote motor control circuits. For further information, see **724.43** and **724.4**

Note, also, see **725.60** and **Table 11(A)** or **(BB** to Chapter 9 in the NEC.

> **Motor Control Tip:** Remote-control circuits shall have their disconnecting means located immediately adjacent to the disconnecting means used to disconnect the branch-circuit conductors supplying the controller and motor. Sometimes an interlock in the disconnect for the motor controller is used for this purpose that allows the controller, motor-, and remote-control circuit to be disconnected simultaneously.

CONDUCTOR PROTECTION
430.72(B)

Conductors larger than 14 AWG are selected from **Tables 310.16 thru 310.19** for motor-control circuit conductors that are tapped from a motor power circuit. Overcurrent protection for conductors smaller than 14 AWG shall not exceed the values listed in **Table 430.72(B), Column A**. Conductors 18 AWG and 16 AWG shall be protected at the following amperage ratings:

(1) 18 AWG shall be protected at 7 amps when used for remote-control circuits.

(2) 16 AWG shall be protected at 10 amps when used for remote-control circuits.

Fuses selected at either 1 amp, 3 amp, 6 amp, or 10 amp are normally used to protect these conductors from short circuits, ground faults, and overloads. See **240.6(A)** and **Table 240.6(A)** for selection of such fuse sizes.

ONLY SHORT CIRCUIT PROTECTION
430.72(B), Ex. 1

Control-circuit conductors shall have short-circuit and ground-fault protection and shall be protected by the motor branch-circuit, short-circuit, and ground fault protection device, where a hazard is created by the opening of the control circuit.

CONDUCTORS FROM SECONDARY OF CONTROL TRANSFORMERS
430.72(B), Ex. 2

The secondary conductors of the control transformer circuit shall be permitted to be protected by the primary side of the transformer. The transformer shall be protected per **450.3(B)** and **Table 450.3(B)**. A two-wire secondary for a transformer installed outside or within the control starter enclosure shall be permitted to be protected per **240.4(F)** and **240.21(C)(1)**.

The secondary conductor ampacity shall be multiplied by the secondary-to-primary voltage ratio to provide protection in accordance with **450.3(B)** and **Table 450.3(B)**. Where the rated primary current is 9 amps or greater and 125 percent of this current does not correspond to a standard rating of a fuse or circuit breaker, the next higher standard size shall be permitted to be selected. Where the rated primary current is less than 9 amps, but is 2 amps or greater, an overcurrent protection device rated or set at not more than 167 percent of the primary current shall be permitted to be used. Where the rated primary current is less than 2 amps, an overcurrent protection device rated or set not greater than 300 to 500 percent shall be permitted to be used. **(See Figure 21-1)**

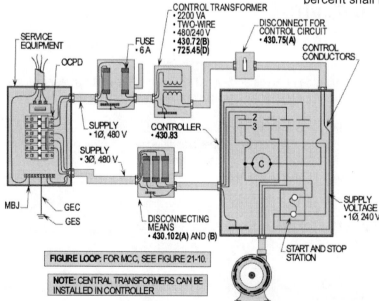

CONDUCTORS FROM SECONDARY OF CONTROL TRANSFORMERS
NEC 430.72(B), Ex. 2

Figure 21-1. Control-circuit conductors are supplied by a control transformer and protected by fuses on primary side.

For **example,** if the primary full-load current of a motor control transformer is less than 2 amps, the overcurrent protection device shall be permitted to be calculated and sized at 500 percent times such full-load current in amps per **430.72(C)(4)**.

CONDUCTORS IN ENCLOSURES
430.72(B)(2)

Motor-control circuit conductors that do not extend beyond the control equipment enclosure shall be permitted to be protected by the motor branch-circuit fuses or circuit breakers. **Table 430.72(B), Column B** permits this type of installation where the devices do not exceed 400 percent of the ampacity rating of sizes 14 AWG and larger conductors. Overcurrent protection for conductors smaller than 14 AWG shall not exceed the values listed in **Table 430.72(B), Column B**. Conductors rated 18 AWG through 10 AWG shall be permitted to be protected with the following sized overcurrent protection devices.

(1) 18 AWG = 25 amps
(7 A x 400% = 28 A and requires 25 A OCPD)

(2) 16 AWG = 40 amps
(10 A x 400% = 40 A and requires 40 A OCPD)

(3) 14 AWG = 100 amps
(25 A x 400% = 100 A and requires 100 A OCPD)

(4) 12 AWG = 120 amps
(30 A x 400% = 120 A and requires 110 A OCPD)

(5) 10 AWG = 160 amps
(40 A x 400% = 160 A and requires 150 A OCPD)

(6) 8 AWG and larger = 400 percent

> **Motor Control Tip:** The free air ampacities of **Table 310.17** for 60°C wire are used to determine the ampacity ratings for the control circuit conductors. This type of installation has more free space to dissipate the heat where control conductors are installed in the open air space of enclosures instead of enclosed raceways.

See Figure 21-2 for selecting such conductors based on the overcurrent protection device rating.

CONDUCTORS RUN REMOTE
430.72(B)(2)

Motor-control circuit conductors that extend beyond the control equipment enclosure shall be permitted to be protected by the motor's branch-circuit fuse or circuit breaker. **Table 430.72(B), Column C** permits this type of installation where the devices do not exceed 300 percent of

the ampacity rating of sizes 14 AWG and larger conductors. Overcurrent protection for conductors smaller than 14 AWG shall not exceed the values listed in **Table 430.72(B), Column C**.

Conductors rated 18 AWG through 10 AWG shall be permitted to be protected with the following sized overcurrent protection devices:

(1) 18 AWG = 7 amps
(requires 7 A OCPD)

(2) 16 AWG = 10 amps
(requires 10 A OCPD)

(3) 14 AWG = 45 amps
(15 A x 300% = 45 A and requires 45 A OCPD)

(4) 12 AWG = 60 amps
(20 A x 300% = 60 A and requires 60 A OCPD)

(5) 10 AWG = 90 amps
(30 A x 300% = 90 A and requires 90 A OCPD)

(6) Conductor 8 AWG and larger = 300 percent

Note, the above protection shall be required anytime the control circuit is used for remote control of a coil in a motor controller enclosure.

See Figure 21-3 for selecting such conductors based on the overcurrent protection device rating.

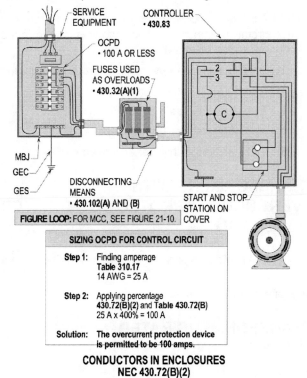

SIZING OCPD FOR CONTROL CIRCUIT

Step 1: Finding amperage
Table 310.17
14 AWG = 25 A

Step 2: Applying percentage
430.72(B)(2) and **Table 430.72(B)**
25 A x 400% = 100 A

Solution: The overcurrent protection device is permitted to be 100 amps.

CONDUCTORS IN ENCLOSURES
NEC 430.72(B)(2)

Figure 21-2. Control circuit conductors located in controller and protected by the branch-circuit overcurrent protection device.

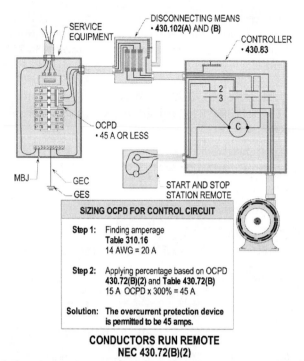

SIZING OCPD FOR CONTROL CIRCUIT

Step 1: Finding amperage
Table 310.16
14 AWG = 20 A

Step 2: Applying percentage based on OCPD
430.72(B)(2) and Table 430.72(B)
15 A OCPD x 300% = 45 A

Solution: The overcurrent protection device
is permitted to be 45 amps.

CONDUCTORS RUN REMOTE
NEC 430.72(B)(2)

Figure 21-3. Control circuit conductors are run remote and protected by the branch-circuit overcurrent protection device in the panelboard.

CONTROL CIRCUIT TRANSFORMERS 430.72(C)(1) THRU (C)(5)

Article 450 is used for designing the protection of control circuit transformers. The following control circuit transformers shall be sized accordingly:

(1) Transformers with overcurrent protection omitted.

(2) Transformers rated Class 1, 2, and 3,

(3) Transformers less than 50 VA,

(4) Transformers less than 2 amps, and

(5) Transformers with other approved means.

TRANSFORMERS WITH OVERCURRENT PROTECTION OMITTED 430.72(C), Ex.

Overcurrent protection shall be omitted where the opening of the control circuit would create a hazard, such as in the case of a control circuit for a fire pump motor.

TRANSFORMERS RATED CLASS 1, 2, AND 3 430.72(C)(1)

The FLC for a control circuit transformer that is rated 1000 volt-amps or less and 30 volts or less shall be increased 167 percent per **724.30 thru 724.52**, as well as **Part II** to **Article 725**.

Control circuit transformers with limited power sources are required per **724.40** and **725.60** to be designed and protected per **450.3(B)**. Section **430.72(C)(1)** refers to **724/30 thru 724.52** and **725.60,**, which requires overcurrent protection devices to be designed and placed in the secondary of Class 1 control circuit transformers per **450.3(B), Ex.**

TRANSFORMERS LESS THAN 50 VA 430.72(C)(3)

Protection shall not be needed for control transformers rated less than 50 VA that are located in the controller enclosure and an integral part of the controller. The motor circuit overcurrent protection device protects the transformer for this type of installation.

TRANSFORMERS LESS THAN 2 AMPS 430.72(C)(4)

Where the rated primary current is less than 2 amps, an overcurrent protection device rated or set not greater than 300 to 500 percent shall be permitted to be used.

For example, if the primary full-load current of a motor control transformer is less than 2 amps, the overcurrent protection device shall be permitted to be calculated and sized at 500 percent times such full-load current.

TRANSFORMERS WITH OTHER APPROVED MEANS 430.72(C)(5)

Control circuit transformers shall be permitted to be protected where provided with other approved means.

PROTECTION OF CONDUCTOR FROM PHYSICAL DAMAGE 430.73

Remote motor-control circuit conductors that are outside the control device shall be installed in a raceway or be suitably protected from physical damage if damage to the motor control circuit could create a hazard.

ELECTRICAL ARRANGEMENT OF CONTROL CIRCUITS 430.74

Motor-control circuits that are grounded on one side shall be arranged in such a manner that an accidental ground in control circuits remote from the motor controller will comply with the following:

(1) The motor will not start and

(2) The motor will not bypass manually operated shutdown devices or automatic safety shutdown devices.

DISCONNECTION OF CONTROL CIRCUIT CONDUCTORS AND POWER
430.75(A)

Motor control circuits shall be disconnected from all sources of supply when the disconnecting means is in the open position. The disconnecting means for the starter may be installed to serve as the disconnecting means for the motor circuit conductors if the control circuit conductors are tapped from the line terminal of the magnetic starter. An auxiliary contact shall be installed in the disconnecting means of the controller, or an additional disconnecting means shall be mounted adjacent to the controller, to disconnect the motor control circuit conductors if they are fed from another source and are not tapped from the starter conductors. **(See Figure 21-4)**

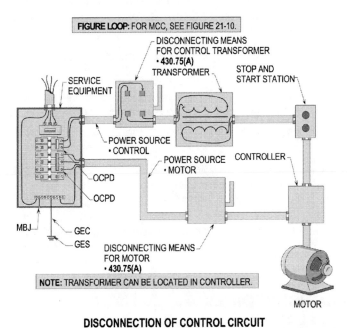

DISCONNECTION OF CONTROL CIRCUIT CONDUCTORS AND POWER NEC 430.75(A)

Figure 21-4. One disconnecting means or a number of disconnects may be required to disconnect a control circuit and power supply to a motor.

MORE THAN 12 CONDUCTORS
430.75(A), Ex. 1

A disconnecting means shall not be required to disconnect 12 or more control circuit conductors that are permitted to be located other than adjacent to each other when the following conditions are complied with:

(1) Access to energized parts is limited to qualified persons only.

(2) Access to live parts in motor control circuits is permitted by a warning sign that is permanently located on the outside of each equipment enclosure door or cover. The sign warns that the disconnecting means for the motor-control circuit is located remotely. Such sign shall also list the location and identify each disconnect and its use.

CLASS 1 CIRCUITS
724.40

Class 1 circuits are divided into two types: power-limited and remote-control and signaling circuits. Power-limited Class 1 circuits are limited to 30 volts and 1000 volt-amperes. Class 1 remote-control and signaling circuits are limited to 600 volts, but there are not any limitations on the power output of the source.

Note, the rules pertaining to Class 1 circuits for motor control are reviewed in this section.

POWER-LIMITED CIRCUITS
724.40

Class 1 power-limited circuits are supplied from a power source that has a rated output of not more than 30 volts and a power limitation of 1000 volt-amps. Class 1 power-limited circuits have a current limiter on the power source that supplies them. This limiter is an overcurrent protection device that restricts the amount of supply current to the circuit in the event of an overload, short circuit, or ground fault. These Class 1 circuits shall be permitted to be supplied from a transformer or other type of power supply such as generators or batteries.

REMOTE CONTROL OR SIGNALING CIRCUITS
CHAPTERS 1 THRU 4

Class 1 remote control and signaling circuits shall be permitted to operate at up to 600 volts and have no limitation on the power rating of the source. Class 1 systems generally shall meet most wiring requirements for power and light circuits. Class 1 remote control circuits are commonly used in motor controllers that operate mechanical processes, elevators, conveyors, and equipment that is controlled from one or more remote locations. Class 1 signaling circuits are used in nurses' call systems in hospitals, electric clocks, bank alarm systems, and factory call systems. **(See Figure 21-5)**

CLASS 2 AND 3 CIRCUITS
725.60(A) THRU (C)

Class 2 and Class 3 circuits are defined by two tables, one for AC current and one for DC current. In general, a Class 2 circuit operating at 24 volts with a power supply durably marked "Class 2" and not exceeding 100 volt-amperes is the type most commonly used.

A Class 2 circuit is defined as that portion of the wiring system between the load side of a Class 2 power source and the connected equipment. Because of its power limitations, a Class 2 circuit is considered safe from a fire initiation standpoint and provides acceptable protection from electric shock.

A Class 3 circuit is defined as that portion of the wiring system between the load side of a Class 3 power source and the connected equipment. Due to its power limitations, a Class 3 circuit is not considered safe from a fire-initiation standpoint. Since higher levels of voltage and current are permitted for Class 3 than for Class 2 circuits, additional safeguards are specified to provide protection from an electric shock hazard that might be encountered.

Power for Class 2 and Class 3 circuits is limited either inherently (in which no overcurrent protection is required) or by a combination of a power source and overcurrent protection scheme.

The maximum circuit voltage is 150 volts AC or DC for a Class 2 inherently limited power source, and 100 volts AC or DC for a Class 3 inherently limited power source. The maximum circuit voltage is 30 volts AC and 60 volts DC for a Class 2 power source limited by overcurrent protection, and 150 volts AC or DC for a Class 3 power source limited by overcurrent protection. **(See Figure 21-6)**

> **For example,** heating system thermostats are commonly Class 2 systems, and the majority of small bells, buzzers, and annunciator systems are Class 2 circuits. Class 2 also includes small intercommunicating telephone systems in which the voice circuit is supplied by a battery and the ringing circuit is supplied by a transformer.

Class 2 and 3 systems do not require the same wiring methods as power, light, and Class 1 systems. There are cases that require a 2 in. (50 mm) separation between these systems. (See **Tables 11(A) or (B)** to **Ch. 9 in the NEC.**)

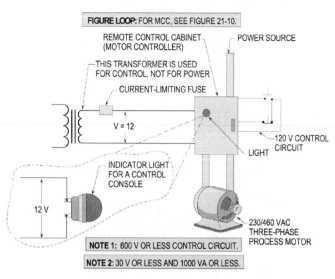

**REMOTE CONTROL OR SIGNALING CIRCUITS
CHAPTERS 1 THRU 4**

Figure 21-5. Class 1 remote control and signaling circuits shall be permitted to operate up to 600 volts with or without power limitations.

CONTROL CIRCUITS IN RACEWAYS, CABLES, AND ENCLOSURES
724.48

Class 1 control circuits shall be permitted to be installed in raceways, cables, and enclosures using the following installation procedures:

(1) Two or more Class 1 circuits and

(2) Class 1 circuits with power conductors.

TWO OR MORE CLASS 1 CIRCUITS
724.48(A)

Class 1 circuits shall be permitted to occupy the same cable, enclosure, or raceway without regard to whether the individual circuits are AC or DC current, provided all conductors are insulated for the maximum voltage of any conductor in the cable, enclosure, or raceway. **(See Figure 21-7)**

CLASS 1 CIRCUITS WITH POWER CONDUCTORS
724.48(B)(1)

Class 1 circuits and power supply circuits shall be permitted to occupy the same cable, enclosure, or raceway only in situations where the equipment power system is functionally associated. **(See Figure 21-7)**

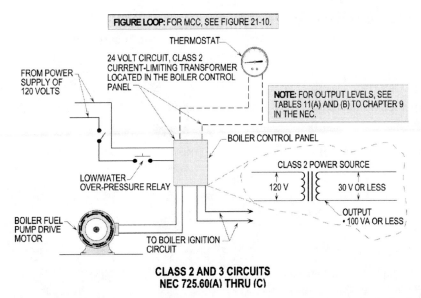

CLASS 2 AND 3 CIRCUITS
NEC 725.60(A) THRU (C)

Figure 21-6. The maximum voltage is usually 100 volts AC or DC for a Class 2 inherently limited power source, and 150 volts AC or DC for a Class 3 inherently limited power source.

NOTE 1: ALL CONDUCTORS ARE FUNCTIONALLY ASSOCIATED.

NOTE 2: OCPDs IN PANEL ARE 2- AND 3-POLE CIRCUIT BREAKERS.

LOW-VOLTAGE CONTROL TRANSFORMER INSTALLED HERE OR IN CONTROLLER

FIGURE LOOP: FOR MCC, SEE FIGURE 20-19(a) THRU (c) AND 21-10.

CONDUCTORS IN EMT
• 3 POWER
• 2 CONTROL

CONTROL WIRES IN RACEWAY WITH POWER WIRES
• 724.48(B)(1)
  CONTROL VOLTAGE
  • 30 V OR LESS

CONTROL WIRES IN ENCLOSURE WITH POWER WIRES
• 724.48(A) AND (B)

CLASS 1 CIRCUITS WITH POWER CONDUCTORS
NEC 724.48(A) AND (B)(1)

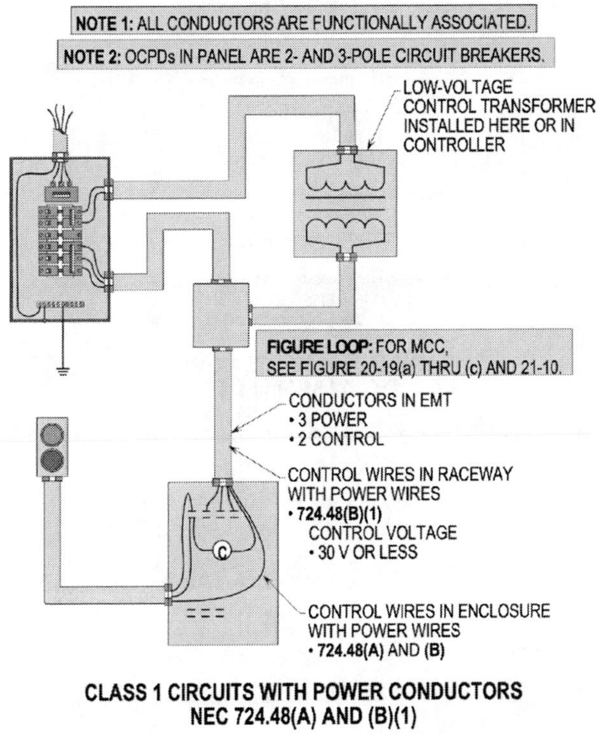

Figure 21-7. Class 1 circuits shall be permitted to occupy the same cable, enclosure, or raceway without regard to whether the individual circuits are AC or DC current, provided all conductors are insulated for the maximum voltage of any conductor in the cable, enclosure, or raceway.

Section **724.48(B)(2)** clarifies they shall be permitted to be mixed where installed in factory- or field-assembled control centers.

Section **724.48(B)(3)** permits mixing for underground conductors in a manhole if all of the following conditions are met:

(1) The power supply or Class 1 circuit conductors are in a metal-enclosed cable or Type UF cable.

(2) The conductors are permanently separated from the power supply conductors by a continuous, firmly fixed nonconductor, such as flexible tubing, in addition to the insulation on the wire.

(3) The conductors are permanently and effectively separated from the power supply conductors and securely fastened to racks, insulators, or other approved supporting means. **(See Figure 21-8)**

WHEN TO DERATE THE AMPACITY 724.51(A) AND (B)

Where only Class 1 circuit conductors are in a raceway, the number of conductors shall be permitted to be determined by the provisions of **300.17**. The ampacity adjustment factors given in **Table 310.15(C)(1)** apply only if such conductors carry continuous loads in excess of 10 percent of the ampacity of each control conductor routed through the raceway system.

The number of power supply conductors and Class 1 circuit conductors pulled through a raceway based on the rules of **724.48** shall be determined per **300.17**. The ampacity adjustment factors, given in **Article 310, Table 310.15(C)(1)** to Ampacity Tables of 0 to 2000 volts apply to the following conditions:

(1) All conductors where the Class 1 circuit conductors carry continuous loads in excess of 10 percent of the ampacity of each conductor and where the total number of conductors is four or more.

(2) The power supply conductors only, where the Class 1 circuit conductors do not carry continuous loads in excess of 10 percent of the ampacity of each conductor and where the number of power supply conductors is four or more. **(See Figure 21-9)**

> **Motor Control Tip:** Class 1 circuit conductors installed in cable tray systems shall comply with the rules and regulations of **392.22** and **392.80** as well as **Article 392.**

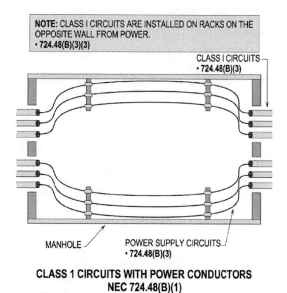

NOTE: CLASS I CIRCUITS ARE INSTALLED ON RACKS ON THE OPPOSITE WALL FROM POWER.
• 724.48(B)(3)(3)

CLASS I CIRCUITS
• 724.48(B)(3)

MANHOLE

POWER SUPPLY CIRCUITS
• 724.48(B)(3)

CLASS 1 CIRCUITS WITH POWER CONDUCTORS
NEC 724.48(B)(1)

Figure 21-8. Class I circuits, when properly installed, shall be permitted to be installed in manholes with power supply circuits.

MOTOR CONTROL CENTER TRANSFORMER
430.72(C)(4)

A primary and secondary control transformer installed in a motor control center can be used for controlling a coil in a magnetic starter in a controller unit. **(See Figure 21-10)**

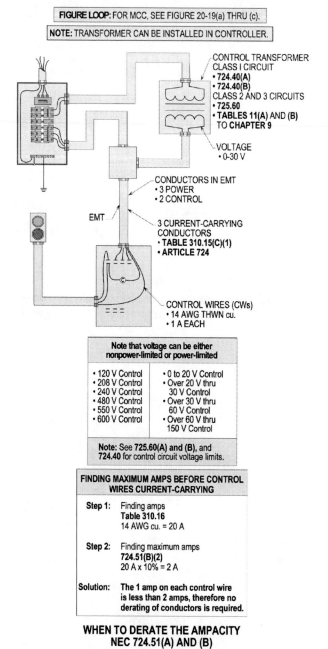

FIGURE LOOP: FOR MCC, SEE FIGURE 20-19(a) THRU (c).

NOTE: TRANSFORMER CAN BE INSTALLED IN CONTROLLER.

CONTROL TRANSFORMER
CLASS I CIRCUIT
• 724.40(A)
• 724.40(B)
CLASS 2 AND 3 CIRCUITS
• 725.60
• **TABLES 11(A) AND (B)**
TO **CHAPTER 9**

VOLTAGE
• 0-30 V

CONDUCTORS IN EMT
• 3 POWER
• 2 CONTROL

EMT

3 CURRENT-CARRYING CONDUCTORS
• **TABLE 310.15(C)(1)**
• **ARTICLE 724**

CONTROL WIRES (CWs)
• 14 AWG THWN cu.
• 1 A EACH

Note that voltage can be either nonpower-limited or power-limited	
• 120 V Control	• 0 to 20 V Control
• 208 V Control	• Over 20 V thru 30 V Control
• 240 V Control	
• 480 V Control	• Over 30 V thru 60 V Control
• 550 V Control	
• 600 V Control	• Over 60 V thru 150 V Control

Note: See 725.60(A) and (B), and 724.40 for control circuit voltage limits.

FINDING MAXIMUM AMPS BEFORE CONTROL WIRES CURRENT-CARRYING	
Step 1:	Finding amps Table 310.16 14 AWG cu. = 20 A
Step 2:	Finding maximum amps 724.51(B)(2) 20 A x 10% = 2 A
Solution:	The 1 amp on each control wire is less than 2 amps, therefore no derating of conductors is required.

WHEN TO DERATE THE AMPACITY
NEC 724.51(A) AND (B)

Figure 21-9. The derating factors given in **Table 310.15(C)(1)** apply only if such control conductors carry continuous loads in excess of 10 percent of the ampacity of each conductor routed through the raceway system.

Note, for determining if the grounded (neutral conductor is current-carrying, see **310.15(E)(3)** in the NEC.

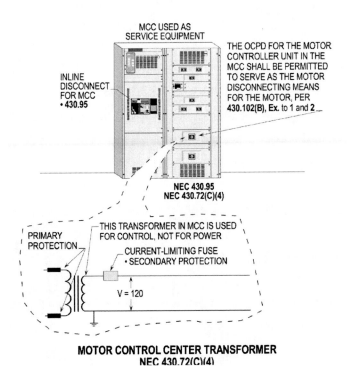

MCC USED AS
SERVICE EQUIPMENT

THE OCPD FOR THE MOTOR
CONTROLLER UNIT IN THE
MCC SHALL BE PERMITTED
TO SERVE AS THE MOTOR
DISCONNECTING MEANS
FOR THE MOTOR, PER
430.102(B), Ex. to 1 and 2

INLINE
DISCONNECT
FOR MCC
• 430.95

NEC 430.95
NEC 430.72(C)(4)

PRIMARY
PROTECTION

THIS TRANSFORMER IN MCC IS USED
FOR CONTROL, NOT FOR POWER

CURRENT-LIMITING FUSE
• SECONDARY PROTECTION

V = 120

MOTOR CONTROL CENTER TRANSFORMER
NEC 430.72(C)(4)

Figure 21-10. A primary and secondary protected control transformer installed in a motor control center for coil control of a magnetic starter used in a controller unit.

Note, for determining if the neutral or control circuits are current-carrying, see **724.51(B)(1); (2)** and **310.15(E)(3)** in the NEC.

Chapter 21. Control Circuit Conductors and Components

Section   Answer

1. Conductors _____ AWG shall be protected at 7 amps when used for remote   _____   _____
   control circuit conductors that extend beyond enclosure.
       (a) 18   (b) 16
       (c) 14   (d) 12

2. Conductors _____ AWG shall be protected at 10 amps when used for remote   _____   _____
   control circuit conductors that have separate protection provided.
       (a) 18   (b) 16
       (c) 14   (d) 12

3. Power sources other than transformers shall be permitted to be increased up   _____   _____
   to _____ percent per **724.40(B)**.
       (a) 110   (b) 115
       (c) 125   (d) 167

4. Protection is not needed or control transformers rated less than _____ volt-   _____   _____
   amps and are located in the controller enclosure and an integral part of the
   controller.
       (a) 15   (b) 20
       (c) 50   (d) 75

5. A disconnecting means shall not be required to disconnect _____ or more   _____   _____
   control circuit conductors that are permitted to be located other than adjacent
   to each other when access to energized parts is limited to qualified persons
   only and access to live parts in motor control circuits is permitted by a warning
   sign.
       (a) 6   (b) 12
       (c) 15   (d) 18

6. Class 1 power-limited circuits are supplied from a power source that has a   _____   _____
   rated output of not more than _____ volts and a power limitation of 1000 volt-
   amps or less.
       (a) 30   (b) 40
       (c) 50   (d) 75

7. The maximum circuit voltage is _____ volts AC or DC for a Class 2 inherently   _____   _____
   limited power source.
       (a) 100   (b) 120
       (c) 150   (d) 175

8. The maximum circuit voltage is _____ volts AC or DC for a Class 3 inherently   _____   _____
   limited power source.
       (a) 100   (b) 120
       (c) 150   (d) 175

9. Class 2 and Class 3 systems, installed in hoist ways, do not require the same   _____   _____
   wiring methods as power, light, and Class 1 systems. However, a _____ in.
   separation shall be required between these systems.
       (a) 1   (b) 2
       (c) 6   (d) 12

10. Where only Class 1 circuit conductors are in a raceway, the derating factors given in **Table 310.15(C)(1)** apply only if such conductors carry continuous loads in excess of _____ percent of the ampacity of each control conductor routed through the raceway system.
    (a) 2   (b) 5
    (c) 6   (d) 10

11. Control-circuits are considered current-carrying if the current in amps is greater than _____% of the conductor's amapcity.
    (a) 5   (b) 10
    (c) 15   (d) 20

12. The neutral is current-carrying if more than _____% of the neutral current is harmonic related.
    (a) 5   (b) 10
    (c) 25   (d) 50

13. A control transformer can be installed in a motor _____ center
    (a) control   (b) combination
    (c) all of the above   (d) none of the above

14. Under certain installation rules, a Class _____ can be run with the power conductors in a motor circuit.
    (a) 2   (b) 3
    (c) 1   (d) none of the above

15. A 120 volt control circuit is considered _____ limited.
    (a) power   (b) nonpower
    (c) all of the above   (d) none of the above

16. A Class 2 or 3 circuit shall be _____ and marked as such.
    (a) listed   (b) approved
    (c) identified   (d) none of the above

17. Two or more Class 2 circuits can be routed through the same _____.
    (a) cable   (b) raceway
    (c) enclosure   (d) all of the above

18. What size overcurrent protection device is permitted for motor-control circuit conductors that are located in the enclosure and supplied by 12 AWG copper conductors?

19. What size overcurrent protection device is permitted for motor-control circuit conductors that are run remote and supplied by 12 AWG copper conductors?

20. What size overcurrent protection device is required for motor-control circuit conductors that are supplied by a 2400 VA, 480 volt, two-wire control transformer?

22

Connecting Controls
for Operation

A means for starting and stopping shall be provided for all electric motors and their driven load. Either manual magnetic starters or motor control centers are used as a controlling means for commercial and industrial motors.

The power supply is connected to the manual starter in series through the contacts to the motor leads. Magnetic starters are controlled by pressure, temperature, light, start-and-stop buttons, etc., which provide automatic starting and stopping of motors.

Note, review Chapter 23 and Tables 1 through 14 of Annex A for troubleshooting techniques on control circuits and components.

MAGNETIC STARTERS

Magnetic starters are the most common type of controllers in the electrical industry. They are equipped with normally open (NO) power contacts that can be closed by applying voltage to their closing coils. Coil voltages may range in values from 24 to 480 volts. Control voltage is used to close the contacts and provide power to the motor. The device used to control the voltage to the coil may be manually or automatically controlled. Different wiring procedures are required for each method. The motor windings are protected from overload conditions by an overload relay unit that is provided in the magnetic starter circuitry. **(See Figure 22-1)**

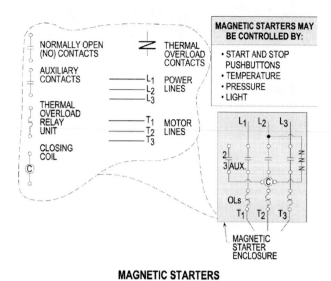

MAGNETIC STARTERS

Figure 22-1. This illustration shows a magnetic starter that is designed to be controlled automatically or nonautomatically.

COMPONENTS

The terminals L_1, L_2, and L_3 are the terminals used to connect the branch-circuit conductors from the power line to the magnetic starter. The branch-circuit conductors for the magnetic starter shall be sized and selected per **430.22** and **Table 310.16**.

The terminals T_1, T_2, and T_3 are used to connect the magnetic starter to the motor leads. The minimum wire bending space at the terminals within the enclosure housing for the magnetic starter shall comply with **Table 430.10(B)**. Where terminal housings are provided on motors, the minimum space required shall comply with **430.12**.

The branch-circuit conductors are connected from the power supply to the motor leads by stationary contacts. Contacts will eventually become tarnished from the making and breaking when starting and stopping motors with their driven loads. The contacts are energized and deenergized by the closing coil. The control circuit operating this coil shall be designed and selected per **430.72** and **724.43**. The connection of the power circuit conductors to the motor leads are bridged from auxiliary contact points 2 and 3. The temperature rise in the motor windings is sensed by the thermal overload relay unit. If the setting of the overload relay is exceeded by the temperature rise in the motor windings, the coil circuit is opened by the overload contacts, dropping out the power circuit conductors to the motor. Overload contacts are designed to be connected in series from L_2 to the coil and from that point to the controlling devices supplied by L_1. The coil control circuit is opened by the overload contacts due to the heat of an overload condition.

For example: What is the minimum wire bending space required for 1 - 2 AWG conductor per terminal within the enclosure housing for a magnetic starter?

Step 1: Finding space
Table 430.10(B)
2 AWG conductor = 2-1/2"

Solution: **The minimum wire bending space required is 2-1/2 in.**

TWO-WIRE CONTROL SYSTEMS

Two-wire control circuits are designed and installed to eliminate a voltage release during a power failure. This type of installation (no voltage release) means that the coil circuit is maintained through the contacts of the pilot device until it is disconnected. The contacts to the pilot device controlling the circuit to the coil usually remains closed and connects power immediately to the coil when the power to the circuit is restored. Two-wire devices are designed and installed to be used for two-wire control circuits. These types of devices include single-pole switches, pressure switches, float switches, thermostats, limit switches, etc. **(See Figure 22-2)**

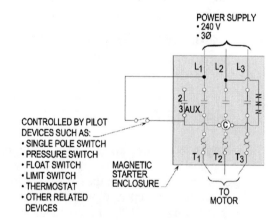

TWO-WIRE CONTROL SYSTEMS

Figure 22-2. This illustration shows a magnetic starter that is controlled by a two-wire control circuit.

THREE-WIRE CONTROL SYSTEMS

Three-wire control circuits are designed and installed to provide a voltage release during a power failure. Power is energized to the coil by pushing the starting button, which is normally open (NO), causing the contacts to close and energize power to the motor.

A three-wire control circuit consists of a start button with normally open (NO) contacts and a stop button with normally closed (NC) contacts. The auxiliary contacts are connected in parallel for the start button and in series for the stop button. No voltage protection means that the coil circuit is maintained through the normally closed contacts of the stop button. The control circuit is completed with an extra set of contacts (auxiliary contacts 2 and 3) through the stop button, and it holds power to the circuit until the stop button is pressed, which deenergizes the circuit to the coil and drops out the control circuit. The extra set of contacts (auxiliaries 2 and 3) will not close again until the coil has been energized by the start button. **(See Figure 22-3)**

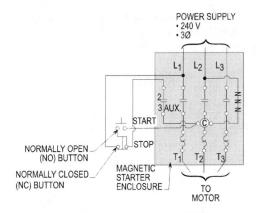

THREE-WIRE CONTROL SYSTEMS

Figure 22-3. A three-wire circuit installed to control voltage to the coil of a magnetic starter.

By pressing the normally open start button in a three-wire control circuit, power energizes the coil and closes the motor starter contacts. By pressing the normally closed stop button in a three-wire control circuit, power is deenergized to the holding circuit to the coil, opening the motor starter contacts and disconnecting voltage to the motor. **(See Figure 22-4)**

CONTROL DEVICES

Motor control circuits may be equipped with control devices to perform a variety of operations. The following types of control devices may be added to the control circuit to regulate the starting and stopping of the motor:

(1) Start buttons,

(2) Stop buttons,

(3) Jog buttons,

(4) Auxiliary contacts,

(5) Emergency or extra motor stop buttons,

(6) Hand-off automatic switches,

(7) Forward-reverse stop stations,

(8) Float switches, and

(9) Pressure switches, etc.

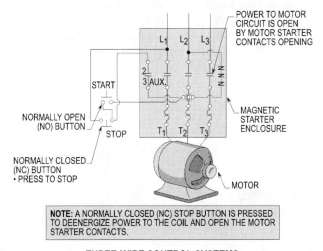

NOTE: A NORMALLY OPEN (NO) START BUTTON IS PRESSED TO ENERGIZE POWER TO THE COIL AND CLOSE THE MOTOR STARTER CONTACTS.

THREE-WIRE CONTROL SYSTEMS

NOTE: A NORMALLY CLOSED (NC) STOP BUTTON IS PRESSED TO DEENERGIZE POWER TO THE COIL AND OPEN THE MOTOR STARTER CONTACTS.

THREE-WIRE CONTROL SYSTEMS

Figure 22-4. The normally open start button connects power to the coil and the normally closed stop button disconnects power to the holding circuit to the coil in a three-wire control circuit.

START STATIONS

Extra start buttons may be added as needed for control purposes, but they must be connected in parallel with the start button to energize the control circuit to the coil. These contacts close and start the motor. **(See Figure 22-5)**

STOP STATIONS

Extra stop buttons can be added as needed for control purposes, but they must be connected in series to deenergize power to the coil of the magnetic starter. These extra stop buttons may be located at various locations to stop the motor. **(See Figure 22-6)**

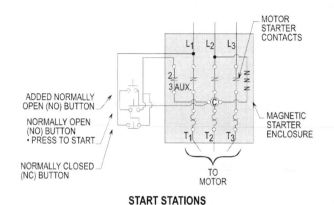

START STATIONS

Figure 22-5. Extra start buttons may be added for the control of motor control circuits and power circuits.

Control Tip: A motor may be stopped by any type of switch that is connected in series with the holding circuit (auxiliary contacts 2 and 3) to the coil. **Note,** contacts connected in series interrupt the power source and disconnect the circuit.

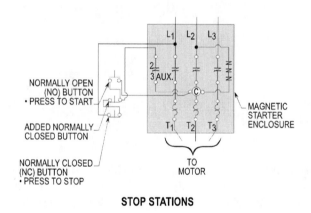

STOP STATIONS

Figure 22-6. Extra stop buttons may be added for the motor control and power circuits.

JOG STATIONS

Jog buttons are installed for jogging, and they let the motor run as long as the jog button is depresssed. When jogging the motor, the magnetic starter must be wired with a jog relay in the control circuit so that there is no chance of locking in. The jog button has normally open contacts that are connected in parallel with the start button and two normally closed contacts (CR&M) that are connected in series with the stop button and auxiliary terminal No. 3. The jog button is held down to connect the power to the main coil and jog the motor. The jog button's normally open contacts will prevent the holding coil from locking in and running the motor. **(See Figure 22-7)**

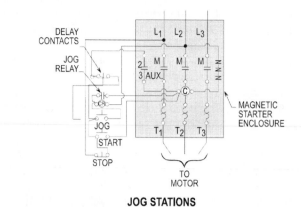

JOG STATIONS

Figure 22.7. When jogging the motor, the magnetic starter must be wired with a jog relay in the control circuit so that there is no chance of locking in the circuit.

AUXILIARY CONTACTS

An extra auxiliary contact may be added to one side of a magnetic starter to control a circuit to another coil or device. The extra auxiliary contact may be installed either normally open or normally closed. If the auxiliary contact is normally open, its function is to close the control circuit. Auxiliary contacts are installed with one side being connected to L_1 and the other side being routed and connected to the coil to be controlled. **(See Figure 22-8)**

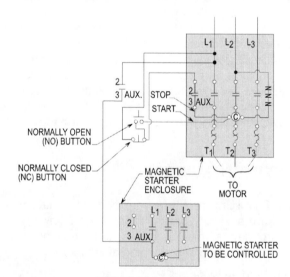

AUXILLARY CONTACTS

Figure 22-8. An extra auxiliary contact may be added to one side of a magnetic starter to control a circuit to another coil or device.

MOTOR STOP STATIONS

A master stop button may be installed for safety when it is connected in series with the wire from L_1 to the first stop button in the control circuit. The contacts remain in the open position when the master stop button is turned off manually. The coil of the magnetic starter cannot be energized since the contacts of the stop button are in the open position, which disconnects the power of L_1 from the components of the control circuit. **(See Figure 22-9)**

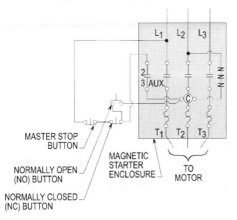

MOTOR STOP STATIONS

Figure 22-9. A master stop button may be installed for safety when it is connected in series with the wire from L_1 to the first stop button in the control circuit.

HAND-OFF AUTOMATIC SWITCHES

A motor may be started manually or automatically by installing a hand-off automatic switch. When starting the motor automatically, a remote control device may be installed. The coil may be energized to start the motor by installing pilot devices such as float switches, limit switches, and pressure switches, etc. **(See Figure 22-10)**

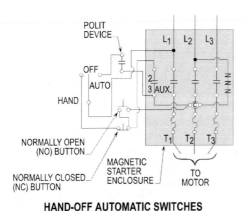

HAND-OFF AUTOMATIC SWITCHES

Figure 22-10. Installing a hand-off automatic switch in the control circuit to start a motor.

FORWARD-REVERSE STOP STATIONS

The motor may be wired to rotate in the forward or reverse direction by installing a forward-reverse stop pushbutton station. The rotation of the motor is stopped by pressing the stop button. By pressing the forward button, terminal 3 and terminals 3 through 6 are connected to one side of the forward control coil. The power circuit conductors are connected to the motor by the contacts of the forward magnetic starter being closed and energizing the coil. The reverse button for reverse rotation must not be pressed until the stop button is pressed and the motor has stopped. By pressing the reverse button, terminals 5 through 7 are energized to one side of the reverse control coil. The power circuit conductors are connected to the motor by the contacts of the reverse magnetic starter being closed and energizing the coil. **(See Figure 22-11)**

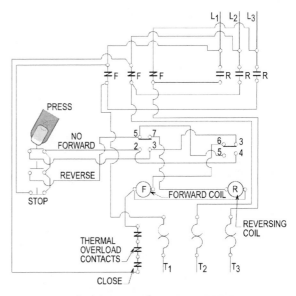

FORWARD-REVERSE STOP BUTTONS

Figure 22-11. The coil is energized by pressing the forward button for forward rotation and pressing the reverse button for reverse rotation.

FLOAT SWITCHES

Float switches (liquid level switches) may be installed and controlled by hardware that floats on a liquid.

For example, a sump pump in a basement is controlled by the use of a float switch. The float permits the switch to turn the pump motor on when the water reaches a level in the sump. The float of the switch will turn the pump motor off when the water reaches a lower level.

PRESSURE SWITCHES

Pressure switches (pressure operated) are vacuum switches that are defined as the absence of pressure. Pressure switches are designed and installed in applications where fluids (gases or liquids) are placed under pressure and turn equipment ON or OFF at some preset operating pressure, or at a pressure level beyond which it would be unsafe to operate.

> **For example,** pressure switches are installed in steam generators and electrically operated air compressors to maintain the correct operating pressures and to detect the pressure level beyond which it would be unsafe to operate.

Chapter 22. Connecting Controls for Operation

Section   Answer

1. The terminals _____ are used to connect the branch-circuit conductors from the power line to the magnetic starter.
   - (a) L_1, L_2, and L_3
   - (b) M_1, M_2, and M_3
   - (c) S_1, S_2, and S_3
   - (d) T_1, T_2, and T_3

2. The terminals _____ are used to connect the magnetic starter to the motor leads.
   - (a) L_1, L_2, and L_3
   - (b) M_1, M_2, and M_3
   - (c) S_1, S_2, and S_3
   - (d) T_1, T_2, and T_3

3. _____ control circuits are designed and installed to eliminate a voltage release during a power failure.
   - (a) Two-wire
   - (b) Three-wire
   - (c) both (a) and (b)
   - (d) neither (a) nor (b)

4. Which of the following types of control device may added to the control circuit to regulate the starting and stopping of the motor?
   - (a) start buttons
   - (b) auxiliary contacts
   - (c) float switches
   - (d) all of the above

5. Extra start buttons may be added as needed for control purposes but they must be connected in _____ with the start button to energize the control circuit to the coil.
   - (a) series
   - (b) parallel
   - (c) rotationally
   - (d) directionally

6. Extra stop buttons may be added as needed for control purposes but they must be connected in _____ to deenergize power to the coil of the magnetic starter.
   - (a) series
   - (b) parallel
   - (c) rotationally
   - (d) directionally

7. When using a jog button to jog the motor, the magnetic starter must be wired with a jog _____ in the control circuit so that there is no chance of locking in.
   - (a) contact
   - (b) switch
   - (c) relay
   - (d) coil

8. Auxiliary contacts are installed with one side being connected to _____ and the other side being routed and connected to the coil to be controlled.
   - (a) L_1
   - (b) M_1
   - (c) S_1
   - (d) T_1

9. A master stop button may be installed for safety when it is connected in series with the wire from _____ to the first stop button in the control circuit.
   - (a) L_1
   - (b) L_2
   - (c) T_1
   - (d) T_2

10. A motor may be started _____ by installing a hand-off automatic switch.
    - (a) manually
    - (b) automatically
    - (c) both (a) and (b)
    - (d) neither (a) nor (b)

_____ _____   **11.** What are the components marked A through I?

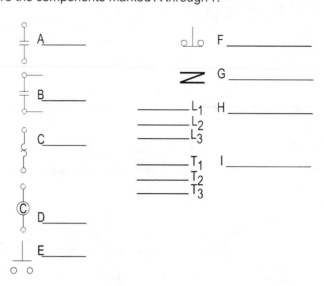

A_____   F_____

B_____   G_____

C_____   H_____

D_____   I_____

E_____

_____ _____   **12.** Connect the magnetic starter for two-wire operation.

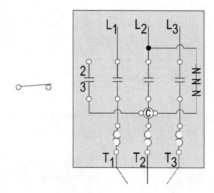

_____ _____   **13.** Connect the three-wire circuit to control a magnetic starter.

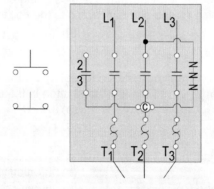

14. Connect the additional stop button for the magnetic starter.   _____ _____

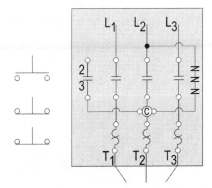

15. Connect the additional start button for the magnetic starter.   _____ _____

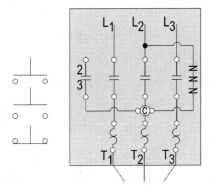

16. Connect the jog button to the magnetic starter for the jogging of the motor.   _____ _____

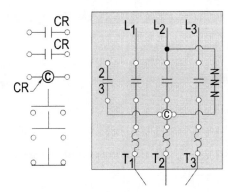

_____ _____ **17.** Connect the additional auxiliary contact to the magnetic starter to control a circuit to another coil or device.

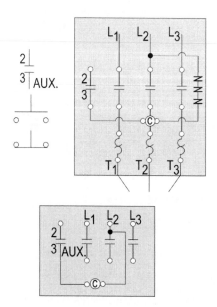

_____ _____ **18.** Connect the master stop button for disconnecting the control circuit.

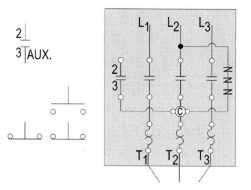

_____ _____ **19.** Connect the hand-off automatic switch in the control circuit to start a motor.

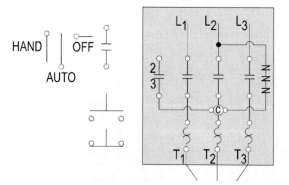

_____ _____ **20.** Two or three-wire _____ circuits can be wired to start and stop one or more motors.

    (a) control   (b) feeder
    (c) both (a) and (b)   (d) neither (a) nor (b)

23

Troubleshooting Motor Windings and Components

Most commercial and industrial motor applications require the controller to be capable of being operated from remote locations. This scheme of automatic operation occurs in response to signals from such pilot devices as thermostats, float switch pressure, limit switches, etc. These devices allow the magnetic starter to be controlled as necessary from any location. However, manual control can also be used with the starter, mounted so that the operator has easy access to the controls.

A motor that fails to run must be checked to determine the problem. These problems can be defective windings in the motor or a defective electrical apparatus associated with the operation of the motor.

This chapter covers the techniques necessary to troubleshoot electrical motors and components pertaining to their operation and control.

Note, review Chapter 22 for control connections. For troubleshooting tips, see Tables 1 through 14 of Annex A in the back of this book.

TROUBLESHOOTING SPLIT-PHASE MOTORS

When troubleshooting single-phase, split-phase motors, there are various components with different electrical characteristics that have to be considered before attempting to test for and determine operating problems.

CONNECTING LEADS AND WINDINGS

There are basically two procedures for connecting the leads of motors to the power supply line. The first step is to identify the motor winding conductors. The NEMA tagging method for new motors identify the running winding leads as T_1 and T_2. The starting winding leads are tagged T_3 and T_4. For older motors, the identification method of tagging winding leads is M_1 and M_2 for the running windings and S_1 and S_2 for the starting windings. However, some leads in older motors are tagged as follows:

(1) S_1 and S_2 for starting

(2) R_3 and R_4 for running

For some motors, the leads may be color-coded as follows:

(1) Red is T_1,

(2) Blue is T_2,

(3) Yellow is T_3, and

(4) Black is T_4.

The above color coding is typical. However, color coding can vary greatly from manufacturer to manufacturer.

See Figure 23-1 for a detailed illustration of connecting the leads of a motor based on its tagging method.

SINGLE-PHASE, SQUIRREL-CAGE INDUCTION MOTORS

Single-phase, split-phase induction motors consist of a housing and a laminated iron core stator with embedded windings located inside the motor housing. A rotor made of copper bars is set in slots in an iron core and connected by copper rings around both ends of the core with plates that are bolted to the housing. The motor enclosure also supports the bearings, the rotor shaft, and centrifugal switch. The centrifugal switch opens the circuit to the starting winding when the motor reaches its running speed.

> **Motor Tip:** The type of rotor mentioned above is often called a squirrel-cage rotor since the configuration of the copper bars resembles a cage.

TESTING WINDINGS

To detect defects in a single-phase, split-phase induction motor, both the running and starting windings must be tested for:

(1) grounds,

(2) open circuits, and

(3) short circuits.

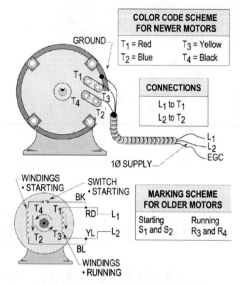

CONNECTING LEADS AND WINDINGS

Figure 23-1. The above illustration shows the windings of a single-phase motor being connected by markings and color coding of leads.

TESTING FOR GROUNDS

A winding is grounded if it makes electrical contact with the metal of the motor housing, etc. To determine whether the winding is grounded, a continuity tester may be used. One test lead of the tester must be connected to the winding and the other lead to the motor frame. If a reading is taken, the winding is grounded to the motor's enclosure in some way. In like manner, one lead of the ohmmeter is connected to the winding and the other to the motor's frame and if a reading can be made, the winding is grounded.

TESTING FOR OPEN CIRCUITS

The cause of an open circuit in a split-phase motor can be a loose or dirty connection or broken conductor, which may be in either the running or the starting winding, or the centrifugal switch.

To determine whether the running winding is open or not, the leads of the tester or ohmmeter are connected to the ends of the winding. If the tester or the ohmmeter has a reading, the circuit is complete. If there is no continuity on the tester or no reading on the ohmmeter, there is an open circuit. **(See Figure 23-2)**

TESTING FOR SHORT CIRCUITS

Two or more turns of wire that make contact with each other electrically are the cause of short circuits. There are other cases where excessive heat develops from overloads and makes the insulation defective and causes shorts to occur. A short circuit is easy to spot because smoke comes from the winding while the motor is running or drawing excessive current at no load conditions. Any one of the following can be utilized to find a short circuit:

(1) Run the motor and locate the hot winding. This winding is normally the one that is short circuited when tested.

(2) Place a growler on the core of the stator and move it from slot to slot until a rapid vibration occurs. This coil is short circuited.

(3) Connect the winding to a low DC voltage and take a voltage measurement. The winding with the least voltage drop is the one that is short circuited.

See Figure 23-3 for a detailed illustration of how to locate short circuits using the growler method.

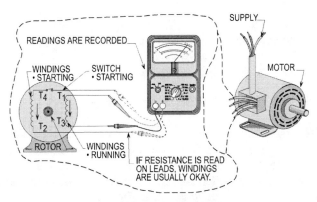

TESTING FOR OPEN CIRCUITS

Figure 23-2. If the windings to the run and start show continuity using a ohmmeter, the windings are usually okay.

TESTING CAPACITORS

The reasons for a capacitor to suddenly become defective can be caused by either of the following:

(1) Overheating or

(2) Excessive voltage.

Note, a defective capacitor must be replaced with one that has about the same value of capacitance. If one with a different capacitance value is used, the motor may not have the necessary starting torque to start and run.

When checking capacitors, they must be removed from the circuit and have their capacitance measured. Such measurement will detect either open or shorted capacitors. For best results, measure the resistance of a capacitor with an ohmmeter; if the capacitor is shorted, the meter will read less than 10 ohms. However, if the capacitor is good, the resistance reading will be about 50 ohms or greater.

An open circuit on a capacitor can be checked by using a neon voltage tester. If the neon tester does not glow during the test, the capacitor can be considered defective.

Note, this tester is not to be used on mica grid capacitors.

Capacitors can be checked by placing the leads of an ohmmeter to the capacitor bridge. If the needle pegs and then falls to zero, the capacitor is good. An in-line fuse can be connected to one side of the capacitor's terminal. If the fuse does not blow, the capacitor is good.

See Figure 23-4 for a detailed illustration of how to test capacitors for an open or short circuit.

Motor Testing Tip: Check the type of capacitor used before selecting the testing method to test it.

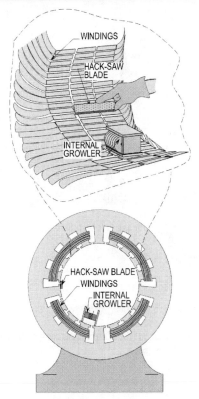

TESTING FOR SHORT CIRCUITS

Figure 23-3. The above illustration shows a growler and hacksaw blade being utilized to test for short circuits.

TESTING CENTRIFUGAL SWITCHES

A centrifugal switch that is defective causes considerable trouble that is difficult to find unless the troubleshooter is familiar with the operating characteristics of such switches. If the switch fails to close when the rotor stops, the motor will not start again when supplied with line power. The switch's failure to close normally is caused by dirt, grit, or some other foreign material getting into the contacts of the switch.

If the centrifugal switch and the starting windings are to be tested for an open circuit, connect the test leads to the starting winding circuit. If there is no reading, the contacts of the centrifugal switch may not be closed.

To verify this condition, the rotor can be pushed lengthwise toward the front end. If this causes the contacts to close, the tester will show a reading. Such trouble can be corrected by adding several insulating washers to the pulley end of the motor shaft to push the rotor forward. If a reading of the tester cannot be taken, the trouble is in the centrifugal switch (starting switch). **See Figure 23-5** for the testing procedure to verify if a centrifugal switch is good or bad.

Motor Testing Tip: If the fiber insulating washers do not correct the problem, the switch must be changed.

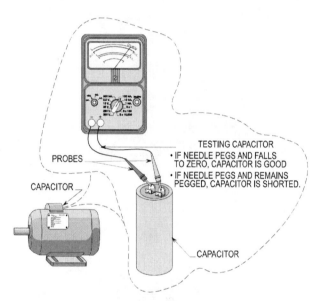

TESTING CAPACITORS

Figure 23-4. The above illustration shows a capacitor being tested with an ohmmeter.

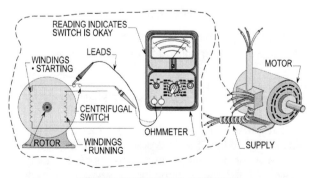

TESTING CENTRIFUGAL SWITCHES

Figure 23-5. The above illustration shows the testing of a centrifugal switch using an ohmmeter.

SINGLE-PHASE, SHADED-POLE MOTORS

Shaded-pole motors are single-phase induction motors equipped with a short circuited auxiliary winding that is displaced in a magnetic position from the main winding. The auxiliary winding is called the shading coil and surrounds a portion of the pole. The main winding surrounds the entire pole and may consist of one or more coils per pole to provide the proper running power.

TESTING WINDINGS

The windings can be tested by using an ohmmeter. If the windings are not defective, the ohmmeter will have a reading that proves that the windings have continuity. A battery test light or lamp also can be used to make such test.

For example, the test light will glow if the windings have continuity and will not glow if the windings are broken. **(See Figure 23-6)**

TESTING REVERSE SWITCHES

Reverse switches can be tested by placing one of the tester leads to the line side of the switch and the other lead to the load side. If a reading is taken, the switch contacts are good. A multiposition switch with two or more speeds is checked using the same procedure. **(See Figure 23-7)**

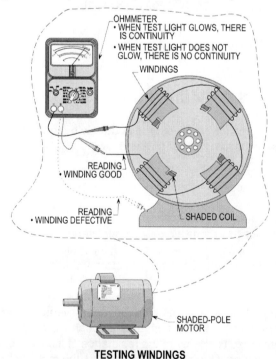

TESTING WINDINGS

Figure 23-6. The above illustration shows the windings of a shaded-pole motor being tested for continuity.

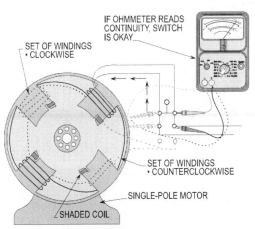

TESTING REVERSE SWITCHES

Figure 23-7. The above illustrates the procedure for testing the reversing switch to a shaded-pole motor.

UNIVERSAL MOTORS

Universal motors are an adaptation of series-connected DC motors and they are named "universal" because they can be connected on either AC or DC and they operate in the same manner.

Basically, the universal motor contains field windings on the stator within the frame and armature with the ends of its windings brought out to a commutator at one end. Carbon brushes are held in place by the motor's end plate, which allows them to have contact with the commutator.

When an AC or DC current is applied to a universal motor, such current flows through the field coils and the armature windings, which are in series. The magnetic field set up by the field coils in the stator reacts with the current-carrying wires on the armature and produces the desired rotation of the motor and the equipment served.

TESTING WINDINGS

To ensure winding continuity, the field windings of a universal motor must be measured using an ohmmeter or light tester. If a reading cannot be measured, an open circuit is present and the following test must be performed:

(1) Test motor leads for an open circuit.

(2) Check brushes for the right setting.

(3) Check the cleanness of the commutator.

(4) Check the spring tension of the brushes riding on the commutator.

(5) Test the windings for grounds.

See Figure 23-8 for a detailed illustration of troubleshooting a universal motor.

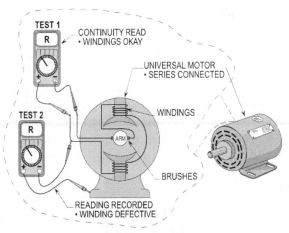

TESTING WINDINGS

Figure 23-8. The above illustration shows the procedure for testing the windings of a universal motor.

TESTING BRUSHES

The continuity of the brushes through the armature winding can be tested by placing one lead of the ohmmeter to one side of the brushes and other lead to the other side of the brushes. If a measurement can be read, the brushes are setting properly on the commutator. Therefore, good continuity should be made. If a reading is not obtained, the setting of the brushes must be checked as follows:

(1) Check for the wrong brush position.

(2) Check for brushes off-neutral plane.

(3) Check the setting of brushes riding on the commutator.

See Figure 23-9 for a detailed illustration on how to check the continuity of brushes.

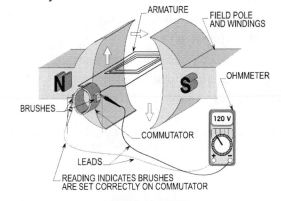

TESTING BRUSHES

Figure 23-9. The above illustration shows one of the methods used to test brushes on a universal motor.

SINGLE-PHASE REPULSION MOTORS

Single-phase repulsion motors are divided into the following types:

(1) repulsion,

(2) repulsion induction-run,

(3) repulsion induction start, and

(4) induction run.

Even though there are several motor types, there are specific construction characteristics that are definitely common to each type. Such characteristics are as follows:

(1) Each has a stator with a running winding similar to that of a split-phase motor.

(2) The rotor has a slotted core with embedded windings.

(3) Bearings are mounted in the end plates to support the rotor shaft.

(4) Carbon brushes are fitted in holders and ride on the commutator.

(5) Either the front end plate or the rotor shaft supports the brush holders.

Troubleshooting techniques are based on the type of repulsion motor under test.

TESTING WINDINGS

The windings of repulsion motors can be tested phase-to-ground by the use of an ohmmeter. If there is a reading from one lead of the motor windings to the frame of the motor, there is a short circuit of some kind.

If the motor fails to start and run when the switch is energized, the trouble may be any one of the following:

(1) Burned out fuse or tripped circuit breaker.

(2) Worn bearings.

(3) Brushes stuck in the holder.

(4) Worn brushes.

(5) Open circuit in the stator or armature.

(6) Wrong brush-holder position.

(7) Shorted armature.

See Figure 23-10 for a detailed illustration of how to test the windings of repulsion motors for continuity.

TESTING BRUSHES

Brushes can be tested by placing one lead of the ohmmeter to one side of the brushes and the other lead to the other side of the brushes. If a reading is measured, the continuity of the brushes to the commutator and armature windings is usually good. **(See Figure 23-11)**

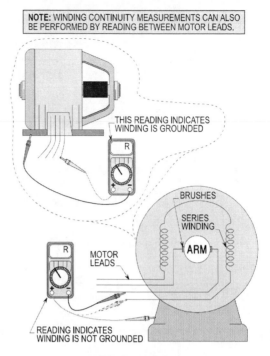

TESTING WINDINGS

Figure 23-10. The above illustration shows the procedure for testing the windings of a repulsion motor.

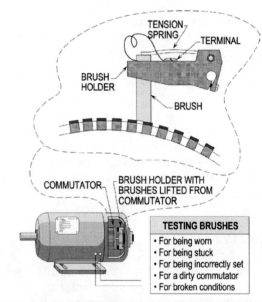

TESTING BRUSHES
- For being worn
- For being stuck
- For being incorrectly set
- For a dirty commutator
- For broken conditions

See Figure 23-11. This figure illustrates the procedures to use when testing the conductivity of the brushes and their relationship to the commutator and armature windings.

TROUBLESHOOTING THREE-PHASE INDUCTION MOTORS

A typical three-phase induction motor has three main parts, which are as follows:

(1) Stator,

(2) Rotor, and

(3) End plates.

The stator consists of a steel frame and a laminated iron core and winding formed of individual coils placed in slots. The rotor may be constructed of a squirrel-cage or wound rotor type.

Three-phase induction motors have relatively constant speed characteristics and are available in designs that provide a variety of torque values. Some are designed to have a high starting torque and others have a low starting torque. Some draw a normal starting current while others are designed with a high starting current.

The end plates or brackets are bolted to each side of the stator enclosure and contain the bearings in which the shaft rotates freely.

CONNECTING LEADS AND WINDINGS

There are two methods by which to connect the stator windings of a three-phase induction motor to a three-phase power supply:

(1) Wye or star (⋏)

(2) Delta or triangle (Δ)

When using either method, the windings are so connected that only three leads come from the windings in the stator, which make the line connections a very simple task.

See Figures 23-12 (a) and **(b)** for a detailed illustration of how to connect the leads from the windings of three-phase motors to the power supply leads.

TESTING AND FINDING THE LEADS OF WYE MOTORS

Wye-connected motors have four individual circuits to find and mark :

(1) Three circuits with two leads each and

(2) One circuit with three leads.

TAKING MEASUREMENTS

The leads and internal connections can easily be identified by drawing the windings to resemble a wye and then in a right handed motion spirally decrease and number each winding end as shown in **Figure 23-13**.

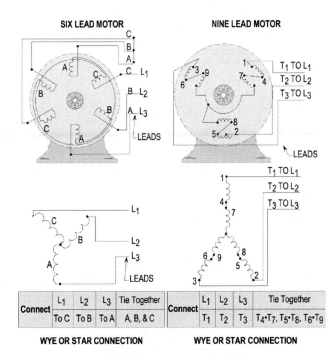

Figure 23-12(a). The above illustration shows the procedure for connecting six- and nine-lead motors in a wye configuration.

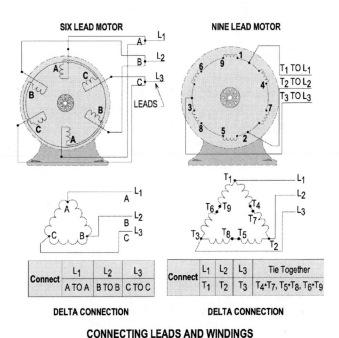

Figure 23-12(b). The above illustration shows the procedure for connecting six- and nine-lead motors in a delta configuration.

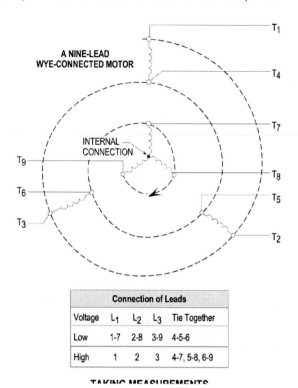

A NINE-LEAD
WYE-CONNECTED MOTOR

INTERNAL
CONNECTION

Connection of Leads				
Voltage	L₁	L₂	L₃	Tie Together
Low	1-7	2-8	3-9	4-5-6
High	1	2	3	4-7, 5-8, 6-9

TAKING MEASUREMENTS

Figure 23-13. The above illustrates the procedure for marking the leads of a wye motor by drawing and following a decreasing spiral (circle) and numbering each lead as shown.

Each circuit winding can be determined by using an ohmmeter or continuity tester as follows:

(1) Connect one lead of the tester to any selected lead of the circuit and read for continuity between each of the other eight leads.

(2) When a continuity measurement between two other leads is found, the three-wire circuits have been found that make up the internal winding of the wye.

(3) Readings must be continually made until all four circuits have been found.

(4) After finding and isolating the leads, mark the three-wire leads T_7, T_8, and T_9.

(5) Temporarily mark the other leads as follows:
  (a) T_1 and T_4 for one-circuit winding.
  (b) T_2 and T_5 for the second-circuit winding.
  (c) T_3 and T_6 for the third-circuit winding.

> **Testing Tip:** The circuit windings are now marked and ready for voltage testing.

See Figure 23-14(a) for a detailed illustration of applying this procedure.

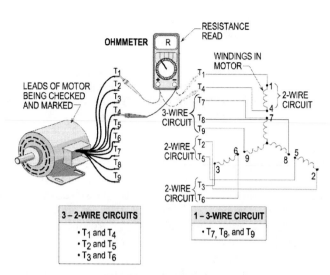

3 – 2-WIRE CIRCUITS
• T_1 and T_4
• T_2 and T_5
• T_3 and T_6

1 – 3-WIRE CIRCUIT
• T_7, T_8, and T_9

TAKING MEASUREMENTS

Figure 23-14(a). The above illustration shows the procedure for determining the number of circuits in a wye motor and temporarily marking them for testing procedures.

VOLTAGE TESTING WINDING CIRCUITS

The windings of wye-connected motors can be tested for correct markings by applying 240 volts to leads T_7, T_8, and T_9 respectively. Windings T_1 and T_4, T_2 and T_5, and T_3 and T_6 will act like the secondary of a transformer, with T_7, T_8, and T_9 serving as the primary. In other words, a voltage is set up in the secondary by the applied voltage in the primary. There is a transformer relationship taking place in the windings of the motor. After starting the motor, once it is running, take readings on the induced windings (T_1 and T_4, T_2 and T_5, and T_3 and T_6) by using a voltmeter as follows:

(1) Read each circuit,

(2) Voltage reading should be about 125 to 130 volts,

(3) Voltage readings could be less than 125 to 130 volts, and

(4) Readings may be 75 to 85 volts, which is okay as long as they are about equal.

See Figure 23-14(b) for a detailed illustration of applying this procedure.

TESTING OTHER LEADS

With the motor running, the other lead that is temporarily identified as T_4 must be connected to T_7 and tested as follows:

(1) Read the voltage between T_1 and T_8 and

(2) Read the voltage between T_1 and T_9.

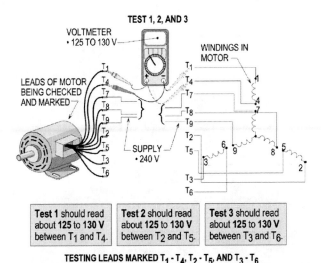

Test 1 should read about **125 to 130 V** between T₁ and T₄.

Test 2 should read about **125 to 130 V** between T₂ and T₅.

Test 3 should read about **125 to 130 V** between T₃ and T₆.

TESTING LEADS MARKED T₁ - T₄, T₂ - T₅, AND T₃ - T₆

VOLTAGE TESTING WINDING CIRCUITS

Figure 23-14(b). The above illustration shows leads T_7, T_8, and T_9 being supplied by 240 volts and leads T_1 and T_4, T_2 and T_5, and T_3 and T_6 being read to check if such circuits measure about 125 to 130 volts each. Motor is ready to test other leads.

If both readings are measured with values of about 330 to 340 volts, leads T_1 and T_4 can be permanently marked T_1 and T_4. However, if such readings are about 125 to 130 volts, reverse T_1 to T_4 and test the remaining leads as follows:

(1) If readings between T_1 and T_8, and T_1 and T_9 are not equal,

    a. Disconnect T_4 from T_7 and connect T_4 to T_8 and the supply line.

    b. Read the voltage between T_1 and T_7 and T_1 and T_9.

(2) If voltage readings are equal and about 330 to 340 volts.

    a. Mark T_1 as T_2 permanently.

    b. Mark T_4 as T_5 permanently.

However, if readings are about equal between 125 to 130 volts, mark the leads as follows:

(1) Disconnect leads T_1 and T_4.

(2) Interchange and mark T_2 and T_5.

(3) Change T_1 to T_5.

(4) Change T_4 to T_2.

If the voltage readings are different, disconnect and reconnect as follows:

(1) Disconnect T_4 from T_8.

(2) Read between T_1 and T_7 and T_1 and T_8.

(3) If readings are about 330 to 340 volts are measured, permanently identify T_3 and T_6.

See Figures 23-14(c) and **(d)** for a detailed illustration of applying the above procedures.

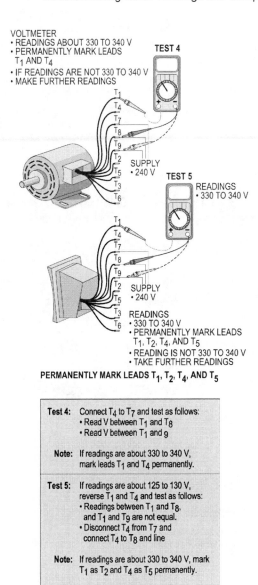

Test 4:	Connect T₄ to T₇ and test as follows: • Read V between T₁ and T₈ • Read V between T₁ and 9
Note:	If readings are about 330 to 340 V, mark leads T₁ and T₄ permanently.
Test 5:	If readings are about 125 to 130 V, reverse T₁ and T₄ and test as follows: • Readings between T₁ and T₈, and T₁ and T₉ are not equal. • Disconnect T₄ from T₇ and connect T₄ to T₈ and line
Note:	If readings are about 330 to 340 V, mark T₁ as T₂ and T₄ as T₅ permanently.

TESTING OTHER LEADS

Figure 23-14(c). The above illustrates the procedure for identifying the leads of a wye motor.

Note, the same method of identification is used for the other two circuits that are temporarily marked T_2 and T_5 and T_3 and T_6. A position must be determined where both circuits have readings that are about equal and measure 330 to 340 volts. **[See Figure 23-14(e)]**

After all the leads of the circuits have been marked, leads T_4, T_5, and T_6 must be connected together and voltage readings must be taken between T_1, T_2, and T_3. Such readings should have voltages measuring about 230 volts.

With the motor power off, disconnect leads T_7, T_8, and T_9, and then connect leads T_1, T_2, and T_3 to the power supply line. T_1 must be connected to the line to which T_7 was previously connected and T_2 to the same line as T_8 was connected. T_3 has to be connected to the same line as T_9 and T_4; T_5 and T_6 are still connected together to make up the wye connection.

Start the motor unloaded, and if all lead markings are right, the motor rotation in relationship with T_1, T_2, and T_3 should be connected in the same manner as when T_7, T_8, and T_9 were connected.

> **Motor Testing Tip:** The above voltage readings are based on a three-phase, 230/460 volt, induction motor. Voltage readings will vary for a motor that has a different voltage.

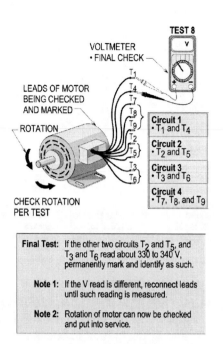

Final Test: If the other two circuits T_2 and T_5, and T_3 and T_6 read about 330 to 340 V, permanently mark and identify as such.

Note 1: If the V read is different, reconnect leads until such reading is measured.

Note 2: Rotation of motor can now be checked and put into service.

TESTING OTHER LEADS

Figure 23-14(e). The above is the final procedure for testing, checking, and marking leads of a wye-connected motor.

TESTING AND FINDING THE LEADS OF DELTA MOTORS

Delta-connected motors with nine leads have only three circuits with three leads to find and mark on each.

TAKING MEASUREMENTS

The leads can be easily found by drawing the windings to resemble a delta triangle, and then in a right hand motion spirally decrease and number each coil end as shown in **Figure 23-15.**

Each circuit winding can be determined by using a ohmmeter or continuity tester as follows:

(1) Read the resistance between one lead and the others until two match up to one winding of leads.

(2) The first lead is used to find the other two common windings.

(3) The common lead is marked T_1 and the other leads temporarily marked T_4 and T_9.

(4) The common lead of the next group is determined and marked T_2 with the other leads temporarily being marked T_5 and T_7.

(5) The common lead of the final group is found and marked T_3 with the other leads being temporarily marked T_6 and T_8.

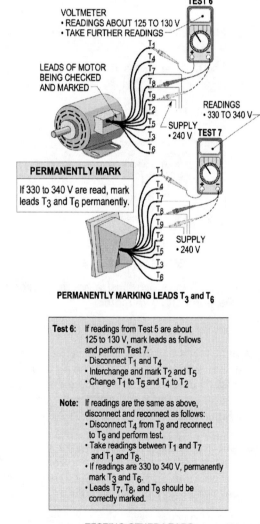

PERMANENTLY MARKING LEADS T_3 and T_6

Test 6: If readings from Test 5 are about 125 to 130 V, mark leads as follows and perform Test 7.
- Disconnect T_1 and T_4
- Interchange and mark T_2 and T_5
- Change T_1 to T_5 and T_4 to T_2

Note: If readings are the same as above, disconnect and reconnect as follows:
- Disconnect T_4 from T_8 and reconnect to T_9 and perform test.
- Take readings between T_1 and T_7 and T_1 and T_8.
- If readings are 330 to 340 V, permanently mark T_3 and T_6.
- Leads T_7, T_8, and T_9 should be correctly marked.

TESTING OTHER LEADS

Figure 23-14(d). The above illustrates the procedure for identifying the leads of a wye motor.

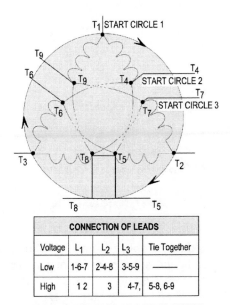

CONNECTION OF LEADS				
Voltage	L_1	L_2	L_3	Tie Together
Low	1-6-7	2-4-8	3-5-9	—
High	1 2	3	4-7,	5-8, 6-9

MARKING THE LEADS OF A DELTA MOTOR

TAKING MEASUREMENTS

Figure 23-15. The above illustrates the procedure for marking the leads of a delta motor by drawing a decreasing spiral (circle) and numbering each lead as shown.

After properly marking the leads, T_1, T_4, and T_9 are connected to a 240 volt power supply. With the motor subjected to no load conditions, lead T_7 is then connected to the power supply line. **[See Figure 23-16(a)]**

Voltage readings are taken as follows, to find and mark the leads of the motor:

(1) Read the voltage between T_1 and T_2.

(2) If the voltage reads about 460 volts, the markings are right and can be permanently identified.

(3) If readings are of 400 volts or less, interchange T_5 and T_7 or T_4 and T_9.

(4) Read the voltage again; if readings of about 230 volts are measured, then read 5.

(5) Interchange leads T_5 with T_7 and T_4 with T_9.

(6) The readings should now measure about 460 volts between T_1 and T_2.

(7) The leads connected together as T_4 and T_7 can be permanently identified.

(8) The remaining leads in each group can be marked as T_9 and T_5.

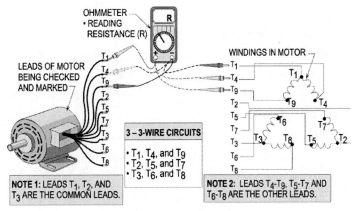

FINDING NUMBER OF CIRCUITS

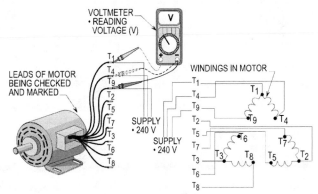

CONNECTING 240 V TO MOTOR LEADS

TAKING MEASUREMENTS

Figure 23-16(a). The above illustration shows the procedure for determining the number of circuits in a delta motor and temporarily marking them for testing purposes.

FINAL READINGS

Connect one of the leads to the last winding of the group and measure T_9; identify as follows:

(1) If about 460 volts is read between T_1 and T_3, the lead can be permanently marked as T_6.

(2) If a reading of 400 volts or less is measured, interchange T_6 and T_8.

(3) If 460 volts is read between T_1 and T_3, T_6 is changed to T_8 and permanently identified. **Note,** T_8 is changed to T_6.

(4) If about 460 volts can be read between leads T_1, T_2, and T_3, the leads are considered correctly marked.

See Figures 23-16(b) through (g) for testing procedures pertaining to Test 1 through Test 6.

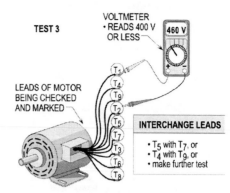

READING VOLTAGE AND MARKING LEADS

FINAL READINGS

Figure 23-16(d). The above illustration shows a voltage reading on leads and either permanently marking them or making further tests to determine the permanent markings.

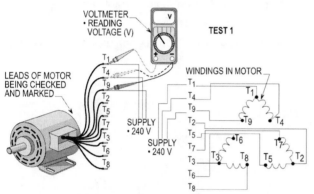

CONNECTING 240 V TO MOTOR LEADS

FINAL READINGS

Figure 23-16(b). The above illustration shows 240 volt supply being connected to leads T_1, T_4, and T_9 so that the windings can be tested and permanently marked.

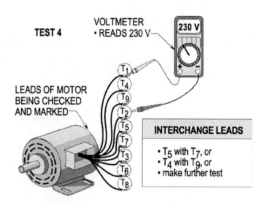

READING VOLTAGE AND MARKING LEADS

Figure 23-16(e). The above illustration shows a voltage reading on leads and either permanently marking them, or making further test.

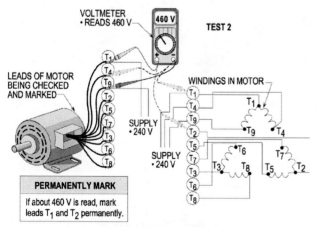

READING LEADS AND MARKING THEM

FINAL READINGS

Figure 23-16(c). The above illustration shows the procedure for reading voltage on leads and marking them based on voltage measurements.

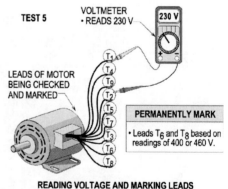

READING VOLTAGE AND MARKING LEADS

FINAL READINGS

Figure 23-16(f). The above illustrations shows a voltage reading on leads; either they are permanently marked, or further testing is done.

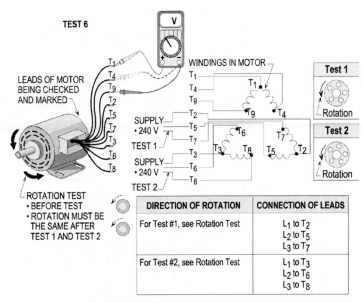

FINAL READINGS

Figure 23-16(g). Two tests are performed to identify all leads of a delta-connected motor. If the previous connections of T_1, T_4, and T_9 do not produce proper voltage measurements, connect leads T_5 with T_7 or T_4 with T_9 and then apply test 2 and the rotor of the motor should rotate in the same direction as in test 1. (See rotation test above.)

DOUBLE CHECK MARKINGS

With the motor supply off, reconnect T_2, T_5, and T_7 to the supply line. Lead T_2 is connected to the line as T_1. Lead T_5 is connected to the location that T_4 was previously connected. In like manner, line T_7 is connected where T_9 was connected. The motor should rotate in the same direction as it did before.

After stopping the motor and disconnecting the power source, connect leads T_3, T_6, and T_8 to the power supply line where T_2, T_5, and T_7 were previously connected. The motor should rotate in the same direction as it did before. **[See Figure 23-16(g)]**

> **Motor Testing Tip:** The above voltage readings are based on a three-phase, 230/460 volt, induction motor. Voltage readings will vary for motors that have a different voltage.

TROUBLESHOOTING WOUND-ROTOR MOTORS

Wound-rotor motors are induction motors that are equipped with stator windings, called primary windings, that are connected in a three-phase wye or delta configuration.

The rotors of such motors are wound with insulated windings that are connected with slip rings mounted on the rotors. Rotor windings are called secondary windings and they have the same number of poles as the stator windings.

Rotor windings are connected to external resistors by brushes and slip rings. The resistors can be used to reduce the starting current of the motor and also to regulate the speed of the motor. Reduce the resistance in the rotor and the motor will speed up. Increase the resistance in the rotor and the motor will slow down.

TESTING SLIP RINGS

The continuity between the slip rings and brushes to the rotor can be interrupted by any of the following conditions:

  (1) Slip rings are dirty.

  (2) Slip rings are not set against the rotor.

  (3) Slip rings are broken.

Any condition above can be corrected by cleaning slip rings or refitting brushes to make good electrical contact. If slip rings are broken, they must be replaced. **(See Figure 23-17)**

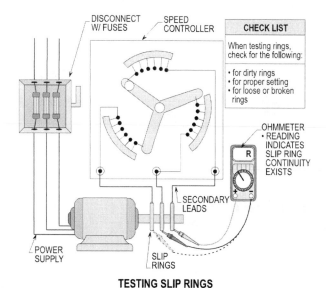

TESTING SLIP RINGS

Figure 23-17. The above illustration shows the main items to check when slip rings are considered the source of trouble.

TESTING BRUSHES

The continuity of the brushes to the rotor can be interrupted by any one of the following conditions:

(1) Brushes are chipped or broken.

(2) Brushes are not making proper contact.

(3) Variac setting is not correct.

Any condition above can be corrected by replacing brushes or readjusting spring tension or completely replacing. Reset variac as necessary to make proper continuity. **(See Figure 23-18)**

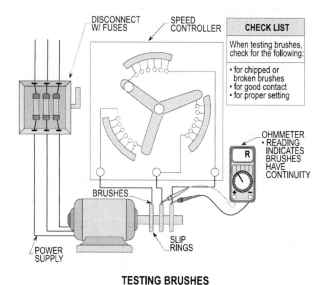

TESTING BRUSHES

Figure 23-18. The above illustration shows the procedure for checking the continuity of the brushes to the commutator.

TESTING CONTROLLER AND RESISTORS

The circuitry from the resistor bank or drum controller may be open. Such a condition will not allow the resistance to be increased or decreased to the rotor for starting or speed control. Any one of the following conditions can cause this problem:

(1) Fuse may be blown.

(2) Circuit breaker may be open.

(3) Windings of rheostat may be open.

To solve such a problem, check fuses and replace any that is blown, or verify if a circuit breaker is tripped open. Replace rheostat if it is defective, or bridge across the resistor windings to complete the circuit. **(See Figure 23-19)**

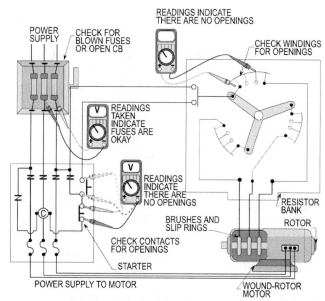

TESTING CONTROLLER AND RESISTORS

Figure 23-19. When checking the starting and running problems of wound-rotor motors, test for open contacts of start and stop buttons and resistor (rheostat) windings. Also test for blown fuses and circuit breakers in primary windings that may be tripped open.

TESTING WINDINGS

To test windings, connect one lead of the ohmmeter to the frame of the motor and the other lead to one of the motor leads. If a reading is measured, then the winding is grounded. To ensure the test is adequately performed, move the test lead to each lead of the motor. However, if a measurement is not read to the frame of the motor, check the leads to the windings and a reading should be obtained. **(See Figure 23-20)**

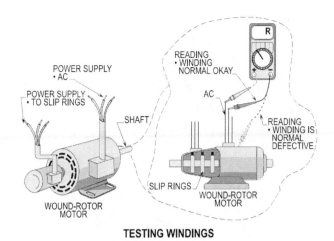

TESTING WINDINGS

Figure 23-20. The above illustration shows the procedure for checking the continuity of windings between phases and the ground. **Note,** the metal frame of the motor is grounded to the metal conduit or equipment grounding conductor in the circuit.

TROUBLESHOOTING SYNCHRONOUS MOTORS

Synchronous motors have stators that are constructed in the same manner as regular squirrel-cage induction motors. In addition, the rotors of synchronous motors have coils (damper windings) wound on laminated poles and connected to slip rings on shafts. A squirrel-cage winding is usually embedded in the pole faces to start the motor. For control, a small DC generator called an exciter is used to energize the rotor coils.

Note, synchronous motors operate at synchronous speed. They can be controlled to produce leading current and thus improve on power factor.

TESTING EXCITER

Another motor or damper windings on a rotor can be used to start a synchronous motor. At some point, slightly below the motor's synchronous speed, a DC source of power is fed into the rotor through slip rings and the motor will run at its synchronous speed. The following test can be made to determine if the exciter is delivering DC current to the rotor:

(1) Test for a defective exciter,

(2) Test for DC power (voltage),

(3) Test for an open exciter circuit, and

(4) Test for a low exciter output.

If any of the above problems exist, they can be corrected by applying one of the following troubleshooting techniques:

(1) Turn the rotor by hand and check the exciter output.

(2) Check for a DC open circuit.

(3) Check for a blown fuse.

(4) Check for an open circuit breaker.

(5) Check the variac windings for an open circuit.

(6) Check the exciter variac for proper setting.

(7) Check the exciter variac for a short.

If any of these defects are found, fix or replace as necessary. **(See Figure 23-21)**

TESTING SLIP RINGS

DC voltage is applied through brushes to slip rings and then to the rotor. If the slip rings fail to conduct this voltage to the rotor, the motor will not function properly. Any one of the following problems can cause the slip rings to interrupt the DC supply to the rotor:

(1) Dirt on slip rings.

(2) Slip rings are broken.

(3) Slip rings are open.

(4) Open circuit from the DC source.

Anyone of the conditions above can be corrected by cleaning or resetting the slip rings and by checking the circuitry to see if an open circuit exists. A blown fuse must be replaced and a tripped circuit breaker must be reset to restore the DC power voltage to the rotor windings.

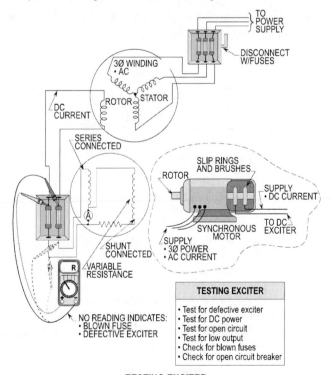

TESTING EXCITER

Figure 23-21. The above illustration shows the testing procedure for determining the output of the exciter power for a synchronous motor.

TROUBLESHOOTING DC MOTORS

The major parts of DC motors are the armature, field poles, frames, end brackets, and brush riggings. Armatures are the rotating parts of such motors, and they consist of laminated iron cores with slots. Coils of wire are placed in these slots. Each core is pressed on a steel shaft that holds the commutator of a DC motor, and current is conducted from the brushes to the coils in the slots.

TESTING THE OUTPUT

To check the output for an open circuit, there are three complete circuits to be tested. **[See Figures 23-22(a) and (b)]**

The testing can be performed as follows:

(1) Test for an opening in the armature circuit.

(2) Test for a problem in the brushes.

(3) Test for connection to the brushes.

(4) Test for openings in the series or shunt field.

(5) Test for a circuit reading from one winding to another.

Any one of the above problems can be corrected by replacing or resetting the brushes as needed. If there is an opening in the series or shunt field, correct it by fixing the loose connection on the open winding.

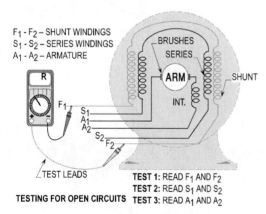

TESTING FOR OPEN CIRCUITS

TEST 1: READ F_1 AND F_2
TEST 2: READ S_1 AND S_2
TEST 3: READ A_1 AND A_2

TESTING PROCEDURE
• For opening of shunt windings, test between F_1 and F_2.
• For opening of series windings, test between S_1 and S_2.
• For opening of armature winding, test between A_1 and A_2.
Note, three tests must be performed.

TESTING THE OUTPUT

Figure 23-22(a). The above illustrates the procedure for testing the armature, shunt windings, and series windings for open circuits.

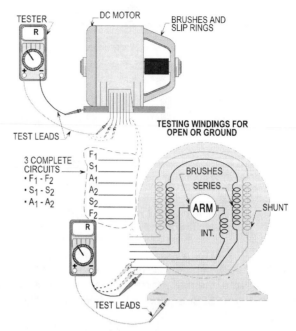

TESTING THE OUTPUT

Figure 23-22(b). The above illustration shows the procedure for testing the windings of a DC motor.

TESTING WINDINGS

The leads to DC motors can be identified by using an ohmmeter or continuity tester as follows:

(1) The first step is to find the three circuits of the armature, the series field, and the shunt field.

(2) By performing the test above, three pairs of leads are obtained.

(3) The ohmmeter will read a higher resistance for one pair of leads (shunt winding).

(4) The ohmmeter will read a lower resistance for the remaining two sets of leads.

MARKING LEADS

By removing the brushes, readings can be taken and the ohmmeter should not record a measurement. These leads are to be connected to the armature and must be marked A_1 and A_2.

The remaining pair should be connected to the series field leads. Such leads should be marked as follows:

(1) The shunt field leads must be marked F_1 and F_2.

(2) The series field leads must be marked S_1 and S_2.

After final checks, the motor is ready to be connected to the power supply and put into service. **[See Figures 23-22(a) and (b)]**

TROUBLESHOOTING CONTROL CIRCUITS

Before attempting to troubleshoot a control circuit, it is necessary to understand the basic operation and construction of magnetic starters.

A typical magnetic starter consists of a magnet assembly, a coil, an armature, and contacts. The armature is controlled by current through such coil. The contacts are mechanically connected to the armature so that when the armature is in the closed position, the contacts are closed. This action of the starter connects power to the motor. When the coil is energized and the armature and contacts are in the closed position, the starter is in the picked-up position and the armature is in the sealed-in position.

Note, the coil has a fair amount of inrush current when energized by the control device. Such inrush current can be as high as 5 to 10 times the sealed-in current.

DETERMINING INRUSH CURRENT

Information on magnetic coils are normally listed in units of volt-amperes (VA) per manufacturer's specifications.

For example, for a magnetic starter rated 500 VA inrush and 50 VA sealed-in, the inrush current of a 120 volt coil is 500/120 volt, or 4.2 amps. A starter with a 480 volt coil pulls only 500/480 volt, or 1.04 amps inrush, and 50/480 volt, or .104 amps sealed-in current. (50 VA x 10 = 500 VA)

See Figure 23-23 for a detailed illustration of how to calculate such inrush current.

TESTING FUSES

When testing fuses, first test the incoming power supply line to verify if there is a voltage. If a reading between the ungrounded (phase) conductors cannot be measured, check for the following:

(1) Blown fuse,

(2) Open circuit breaker,

(3) Poor connections, and

(4) Broken switch blades.

A voltage tester rated for the correct voltage can be used as follows:

(1) Test for voltage between L_1 and L_2.

(2) Test for voltage between L_1 and L_3.

(3) Test for voltage between L_2 and L_3.

If voltage readings are measured and they are the same as the supply voltage to the starter, there is not a problem with the circuit supplying the voltage to the line side of the magnetic starter. **(See Figure 23-24)**

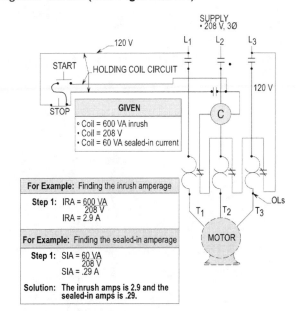

DETERMINING INRUSH CURRENT

Figure 23-23. The above illustrates the procedure for calculating the inrush and seal-in amps for a coil in a magnetic starter.

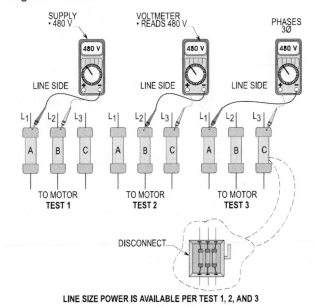

LINE SIZE POWER IS AVAILABLE PER TEST 1, 2, AND 3

TESTING FUSES

Figure 23-24. The above illustrates the procedure for testing fuses. Tests 1, 2, and 3 show fuses are good because they have readings of 480 volts.

Motor Testing Tip: The above test must never be taken for L_1, L_2, or L_3 to ground because a back-feed through the motor windings can be read with one blown fuse, and the other two fuses can still be energized.

The fuses in the disconnect switch should be tested for defects where the three-phase supply circuit is rated at 480 volts. A measurement of 480 volts to the load side of fuses L_1 and L_2 indicates L_1 and L_2 are not defective.

As shown in **Figure 23-25,** measurements between L_1 and L_2, L_1 and L_3, and L_2 and L_3 indicates that fuse B is defective.

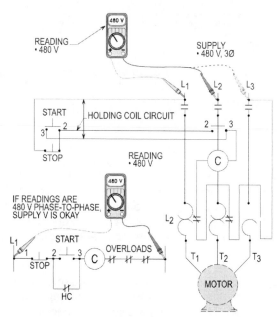

TESTING FOR POWER TO MAGNETIC STARTERS

Figure 23-26. The above illustrates the procedure for testing the voltage to the line side of the magnetic starter.

(1) Check overloads for open contacts.

(2) Reset overloads for continuity.

(3) Check for loose wires.

(4) Check for burned or discolored elements.

If the above trouble points are checked and measurements are read and they turn out to be correct, the overloads can be eliminated as a source of trouble. However, if readings are not recorded, the overloads could be the source of trouble. The procedure for Test 2 is to read the voltage from L_1 to the control side of the coil.

> **Motor Testing Tip:** Do not read from the overload side of the coil to obtain measurement.

If a reading is measured here, the coil is usually good. However, if a reading is not obtained, the coil is normally defective and has an open path. For such a problem, check for the following:

(1) Loose wire,

(2) Broken wire, or

(3) Defective coil.

To correct the above problem, fix the loose or broken wire or replace the coil if necessary. To continue the procedure for Test 2, read the voltage between L_1 and the load side terminal of the same overloads. **(See Figure 23-28)**

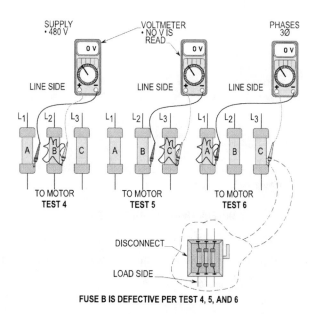

TESTING FUSES

Figure 23-25. The above illustrates the procedures for testing fuses. Tests 4, 5, and 6 show fuses B, C, and A are defective because they do not have readings of 480 volts.

TESTING FOR POWER TO MAGNETIC STARTERS

At the line side of the magnetic starter, measure the voltage between L_1, L_2, and L_3. Readings of 480 volts between all three phases indicate that supply voltage is available at these terminals. **(See Figure 23-26)**

TESTING OVERLOADS

The procedure for testing the overloads (Test 1) is to read the voltage from L_1 to the line side of L_2, the overload terminals. **(See Figure 23-27)**

If a reading is not measured, there is a broken or loose wire from L_1 to the line side terminal of the overloads previously checked. If a reading is recorded between L_1 and the load side terminal of the overloads, this indicates an open wire or overload contact is present. The following trouble points should be checked for a problem:

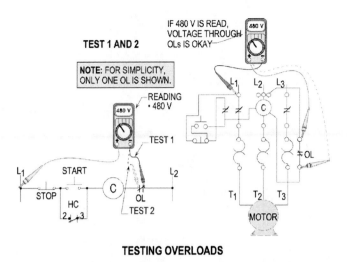

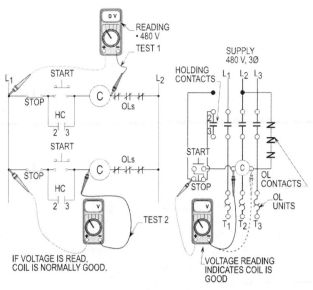

Figure 23-27. This illustration shows the procedure for testing the voltage through the overloads and to the coil.

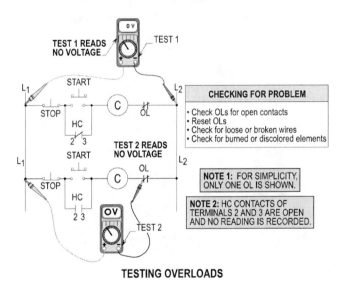

Figure 23-28. The above illustrates common problems that could cause interruption of the voltage through the overloads to the coil terminals.

Figure 23-29. The above illustration shows the procedure for testing the voltage to a coil to determine if it is defective.

TESTING CONTROL DEVICES

There are many types of control devices that are used to energize and deenergize the power to the coil that causes the contacts in the magnetic starter to close. The closing of these contacts provides line voltage to the windings of the motor. The following are procedures used to troubleshoot two-wire or three-wire control devices.

TESTING COIL

To perform Test 1 above, read between L₁ and the side of the coil that is connected to the overloads. If a reading can be measured, the wire between the coil and overload is not defective. However, no recorded measurement indicates a loose connection, broken wire, or defective coil.

Test 2 is accomplished by reading between L₁ and the control device side of the coil. If a measurement is recorded, the coil should be good. No reading between these points indicates that there is an open path. This open path can be caused by a defective coil, loose connection, or defective overload. **(See Figure 23-29)**

TESTING TWO-WIRE DEVICES

First perform a reading between L₁ and the side of the two-wire device connected to the coil. If a reading is measured here, the two-wire switch to the coil is not defective. The two-wire switch can be checked by reading each side of the switch. If a reading between the terminals of the switch can be read, the switch is not defective. If no measurement is recorded, it is an indication that the switch is open or defective and must be replaced. However, loose or bad connections between conductors and switch terminals are often the source of trouble. Therefore, always check for these problems by visually looking for arcing, burning, or discolored wire and terminals. **(See Figure 23-30)**

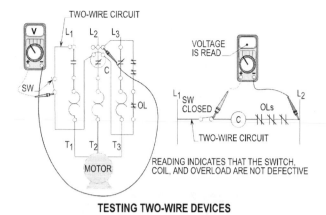

TESTING TWO-WIRE DEVICES

Figure 23-30. The above illustration shows the procedure for testing the voltage of a two-wire control circuit. If the switch or overload contacts are good, voltage should be read at the coil.

TESTING THREE-WIRE DEVICES

The general procedure for troubleshooting a problem in a three-wire control circuit such as a start-and-stop push button station can be performed as follows:

(1) Check the circuit overcurrent protection device for:

(a) Power circuit voltage.

(b) Control circuit voltage.

(2) Open contacts of the stop button.

(3) Closed contacts of the start button.

(4) Open overload contacts.

(5) Defective coil.

(6) Holding contacts of the magnetic starter.

TESTING THE CIRCUIT

Test for voltage between L_1 and L_2, including L_3 if necessary. If there is no voltage measured, one or more fuses are blown or a circuit breaker has opened. Don't overlook broken or loose wires, for often they can be the cause of lost power. However, if voltage readings are present, eliminate problem number 1 as a source of trouble and move on to problem number 2. **(See Figure 23-31)**

TESTING FOR OPEN CONTACTS ON THE STOP BUTTON (NO POWER)

To perform an ohmmeter test, read between L_1 and the side of the stop button that is connected to the start button and terminal 2 of the holding contacts. If a reading is measured, problem number 2 of open contacts in the stop button can be eliminated and problem number 3 is now considered. **(See Figure 23-32)**

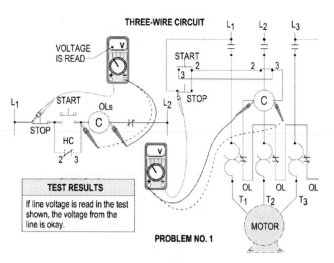

TESTING THE CIRCUIT

Figure 23-31. The above illustration shows the procedure for testing the line voltage from the line to the contacts of the stop and start button and coil.

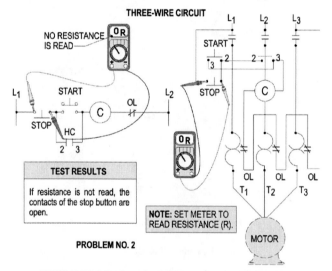

TESTING FOR OPEN CONTACTS ON THE STOP BUTTON
(NO POWER)

Figure 23-32. The above illustration shows the procedure for testing the contacts of a stop button in a three-wire control circuit, using a resistance testing procedure.

TESTING FOR CLOSED CONTACTS ON THE START BUTTON (NO POWER)

To perform this test, read from the side of the stop button connected to L_1 and to the side of the start button terminated to the holding coil. If no resistance can be read, the contacts of the start button are open.

Note, a recorded measurement indicates that a jammed contact or loose wire is the source of trouble. By eliminating problem number 3 as the trouble, move on to problem number 4 and test for voltage through the overloads. **(See Figure 23-33)**

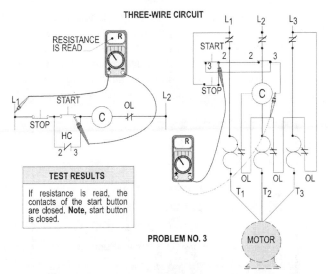

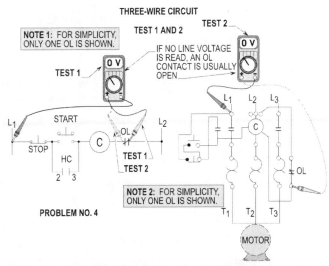

TESTING FOR CLOSED CONTACTS ON THE START BUTTON (NO POWER)

Figure 23-33. The above illustration shows the procedure for testing the contacts of a start button in a three-wire control circuit.

TESTING FOR OPEN OVERLOAD CONTACTS

Figure 23-34. The above illustration shows the procedure for testing the contacts of the overloads in a three-wire control circuit.

TESTING FOR OPEN OVERLOAD CONTACTS

Using the leads of the tester, read for voltage between L_1 and the side of the overloads connected to L_2. If no voltage measurement can be read in Test 1, there is a loose or broken wire from L_2 through the overloads. If the reading in Test 2 is okay, eliminate problem number 4 and move on to problem number 5. **(See Figure 23-34)**

TESTING FOR DEFECTIVE COILS

To perform this test, read from L_1 to the side of the coil connected to the start button contacts and the holding coil contacts. If a voltage reading is recorded by the voltmeter, the coil is assumed to be okay. To be certain, read the coil for continuity using an ohmmeter, after removing the coil from the circuit. **(See Figure 23-35)**

TESTING HOLDING CONTACTS

This test is made by testing from L_1 to terminal L_2 of the holding coil with the start button energized. A voltage reading should be measured, indicating that the contacts are closing when the coil circuit is made. If no voltage reading is recorded, the voltage to the coil is restricted by open contacts in the start button. As always, consider the possibility of loose or broken wires at the contacts of the stop or start buttons, etc. **(See Figure 23-36)**

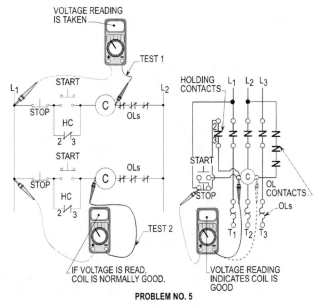

TESTING FOR DEFECTIVE COILS

Figure 23-35. The above illustration shows the procedure for testing a coil in a three-wire circuit to determine if it is defective.

TROUBLESHOOTING VARIABLE FREQUENCY DRIVES (VFD)

First of all, the drive should be installed away from any high heat-producing apparatus. The airflow around the drive unit must be maintained at all times, with no other equipment or materials restricting air flow. Air conditioning should be provided to help cool the drive unit and its components.

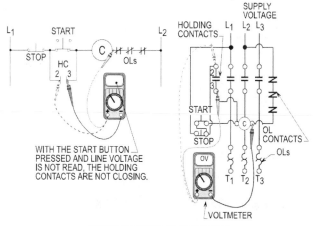

TESTING HOLDING CONTACTS

Figure 23-36. The above illustrates the procedure for testing the contacts of the holding circuits in a three-wire control circuit.

Most troubleshooting procedures may be performed with the following tools: voltmeter, oscilloscope, digital voltmeter, AC ammeter, clamp-on ammeter, and standard hand tools.

Today's VFD systems have self-diagnostic readouts. It is imperative to have the manufacturer's manual for a particular unit and to follow the manufacturer's instructions on the use of the diagnostic system.

For basic troubleshooting:

(1) Check incoming AC power supply;

(2) Check all overcurrent protection devices;

(3) Check output to motor;

(4) Check tach feedback to controller if used;

(5) If need be, consult manufacturer's manual for correct troubleshooting procedure.

Figure 23-37 illustrates the troubleshooting procedures using a readout board to determine the cause of trouble.

Note, within the adjustable speed drive system, there are low and high voltages of both AC and DC present.

For safety, ALWAYS:

(1) check all AC power sources.

(2) check the DC bus for voltage.
   a. allow sufficient time to discharge any power supply capacitors.

Note, the equipment ground and DC bus ground may not be the same potential. Most DC bus grounds float. Do not let the oscilloscope cabinet touch the chassis of the adjustable speed controller. Remember that incorrectly connecting the leads to the silicon-controlled rectifiers (SCRs) will damage them.

Shorted diodes or silicone-controlled rectifiers easily can be determined by checking across their terminals with a volt-ohmmeter. Good rectifier cells have infinite resistance with reverse polarity and read approximately mid-scale with forward polarity. Silicone controlled rectifiers have resistance readings ranging from 12,000 to infinity. **(See Figure 23-38)**

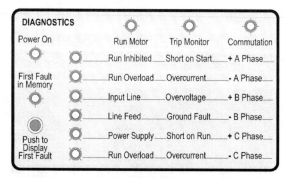

TROUBLESHOOTING VARIABLE FREQUENCY DRIVES (VFD)

Figure 23-37. The above illustration shows a readout board being used to troubleshoot a problem with the operation of an adjustment speed drive unit. **Note,** this is just one of the readout solutions that can be performed when troubleshooting a drive unit. For troubleshooting tips, see **Table 6** of the **Annex.**

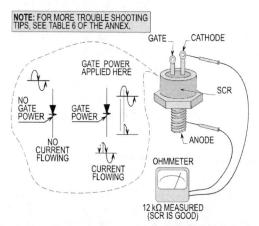

TROUBLESHOOTING VARIABLE FREQUENCY DRIVES (VFD)

Figure 23-38. Silicone-controlled rectifiers can be tested by using an ohmmeter. The ohmmeter will either measure 12,000 ohms, or the needle will peg if the silicone-controlled rectifier is good.

TROUBLESHOOTING EDDY-CURRENT DRIVES

Eddy-current drive controllers usually consist of a voltage reference circuit, anti-hertz circuit, DC amplifier circuit, feedback circuit, and various potentiometers for controlling output speed of the magnetic drive system.

If a higher drive speed is designed, the speed potentiometer can be turned to a higher setting, which results in the following:

(1) The DC output voltage of the potentiometer is increased. (Command Voltage)

(2) When the command voltage is increased, an error voltage is produced between the command voltage and the feedback voltage coming from the tachometer generator (or magnetic pickup frequency to voltage converter). The error causes an increased voltage to be applied to the magnetic drive coupling field through a silicon-controlled rectifier. This increased field excitation causes the magnetic drive coupling to accelerate until the feedback voltage signal again aligns to the command voltage signal.

Note, the difference between the command voltage and the feedback voltage is the error voltage. When the drive is operating at a steady speed, the error voltage is practically zero. For more detailed information on troubleshooting eddy-current drives, see **Table 5** of the **Annex**.

TESTING CERTAIN COMPONENTS

Testing a diode can be done by using an ohmmeter. If a diode (forward biased) measures a low resistance with the ohmmeter connected across it and a high resistance with the diode reversed (reversed biased), the diode is in all probability okay. However, if the diode shows either high or low resistance in both directions, it is usually open or shorted and needs replacing. **(See Figure 23-39)**

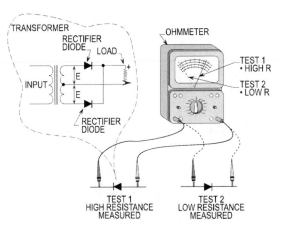

TESTING CERTAIN COMPONENTS

Figure 23-39. If a diode has a high resistance measurement in one direction and a low resistance reading in the reverse direction, the diode is normally good.

It is much more difficult to test diodes for triacs and diacs. When using an ohmmeter, both devices should normally show an open circuit in both directions. If they do not, they are almost always defective. **[See Figures 23-40(a) and (b)]**

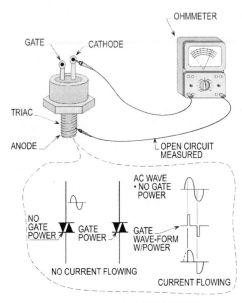

TESTING CERTAIN COMPONENTS

Figure 23-40(a). When testing a triac with an ohmmeter, the triac is usually not defective if the measurement reads an open circuit.

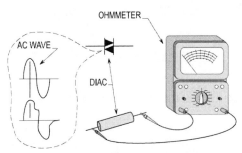

TESTING CERTAIN COMPONENTS

Figure 23-40(b). When testing a diac with an ohmmeter, the diac is normally not defective if the measurement reads an open circuit.

TROUBLESHOOTING THE WINDINGS OF A WYE MOTOR FOR GROUNDS

To test for grounds in a wye-connected motor, connect one test lead to the frame of the motor and one test lead to one of the leads of the motor. If a resistance reading is measured, a winding is grounded. To ensure a more accurate test, move the test lead to each lead of the motor and take resistance measurements.

For checking each winding individually in a star-connected motor, disconnect the windings at the star point and test each winding for a ground. **(See A in Figure 23-41)**

Part B in **Figure 23-41** shows the procedure for checking all the windings for a ground to the frame of the motor.

TROUBLESHOOTING THE WINDINGS OF A DELTA MOTOR FOR GROUNDS

To test for grounds in a delta-connected motor, connect one test lead to the frame of the motor and one test lead to one of the leads of the motor. If a resistance reading is measured, a winding is grounded. To ensure a more accurate test, move the test lead to each lead of the motor and take resistance measurements.

For checking each winding individually in a delta-connected motor, disconnect the windings at the delta point and test each winding for a ground. **(Part A in Figure 23-42)**

Part B in **Figure 23-42** shows the procedure for testing all the windings for a ground to the frame of the motor.

Note, for more troubleshooting tips, see **Tables 1 through 11** of **Annex A** in the back of this book.

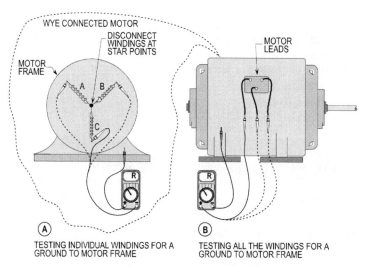

Figure 23-41. If a resistance is read on any winding or all the windings, a ground to the frame of the motor is usually present.

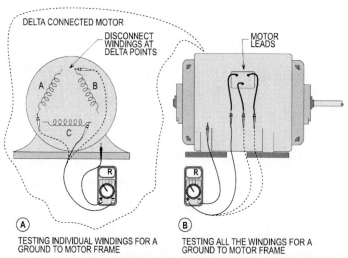

Figure 23-42. If a resistance is read on any winding or all the windings, a ground to the frame of the motor is usually present.

TROUBLESHOOTING SOLID STATE CIRCUIT BOARDS

Assuming that a motor in a process machine will not start and run, the procedure for troubleshooting the circuitry to and from the solid state board(s) can be performed as shown in **Figure 23-43**.

Note, the problem can be the circuitry leading into or out of the solid state board. However, if the circuitry or the solid state board is not the cause of trouble, then it would be logical to conclude that there are mechanical problems or there is a defective motor.

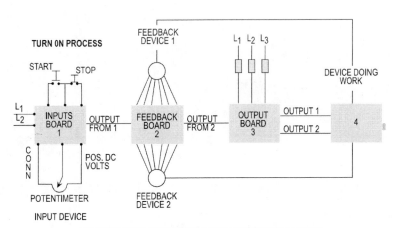

TROUBLESHOOTING SOLID STATE CIRCUIT BOARDS

Figure 23-43. The above diagram shows the components that are checked to determine why the motor will not start and run. (See the Troubleshooting Procedures)

Note: For troubleshooting tips, see Table 15 in Annex A of this book.

Chapter 23: Troubleshooting Motor Windings and Components

	Section	Answer

1. The NEMA tagging method for new motors identifies the running windings leads as _____.   _____ _____
   (a) L_1 and L_2 (b) M_1 and M_2
   (c) S_1 and S_2 (d) T_1 and T_2

2. The NEMA tagging method for new motors identifies the starting winding leads as _____.   _____ _____
   (a) L_3 and L_4 (b) M_3 and M_4
   (c) S_3 and S_4 (d) T_3 and T_4

3. For older motors, the identification method for tagging winding leads is _____   _____ _____
   for the running windings.
   (a) L_1 and L_2 (b) M_1 and M_2
   (c) S_1 and S_2 (d) T_1 and T_2

4. For older motors, the identification method for tagging running windings is   _____ _____
   _____ for the starting windings.
   (a) L_1 and L_2 (b) M_1 and M_2
   (c) S_1 and S_2 (d) T_1 and T_2

5. To detect defects in a single-phase, split-phase induction motor, both the   _____ _____
   running and starting windings must be tested for:
   (a) grounds   (b) open circuits
   (c) short circuits   (d) all of the above

6. The cause of an open circuit in a split-phase, squirrel-cage induction motor   _____ _____
   can be a loose or dirty connection or broken conductor, which may be in the

   _____.
   (a) running winding   b) starting winding
   (c) centrifugal switch   (d) all of the above

7. The windings for a single-phase, shaded-pole motor can be tested by using   _____ _____
   a(n) _____.
   (a) ohmmeter   (b) voltmeter
   (c) ampmeter   (d) none of the above

8. To ensure winding continuity, the _____ windings of a universal motor must   _____ _____
   be measured using an ohmmeter or light tester.
   (a) running   (b) starting
   (c) field   (d) rotational

9. The continuity of the brushes through the _____ winding can be tested by   _____ _____
   placing one lead of the ohmmeter to one side of the brushes and the other
   lead to the other side of the brushes for an universal motor.
   (a) stator   (b) armature
   (c) field   (d) coil

_____ _____

10. If a single-phase repulsion motor fails to start and run when the switch is energized, the trouble may be:

(a) worn bearings   (b) brushes stuck in the holder

(c) shorted armature   (d) all of the above

_____ _____

11. The windings of wye-connected motors can be tested for correct markings by applying 240 volts to leads _____.

(a) T_1, T_2, and T_3 (b) T_4, T_5, and T_6

(c) T_7, T_8, and T_9 (d) T_1, T_3, and T_5

_____ _____

12. Windings _____ of a wye-connected motor will act like the secondary of a transformer.

(a) T_1 and T_2, T_3 and T_4, and T_5 and T_6

(b) T_1 and T_3, T_2 and T_6, and T_4 and T_5

(c) T_1 and T_4, T_2 and T_5, and T_3 and T_6

(d) T_1 and T_5, T_2 and T_6, and T_3 and T_4

_____ _____

13. If the slip rings for a synchronous motor fail to conduct voltage to the _____, the motor will not function properly.

(a) rotor   (b) stator

(c) armature   (d) coil.

_____ _____

14. By removing the _____ of a DC motor, a reading can be taken and the ohmmeter should not record a measurement.

(a) centrifugal switch   (b) brushes

(c) stator   (d) armature

_____ _____

15. Information on magnetic coils is normally listed in units of _____ per manufacturers specifications for determining inrush current.

(a) amps   (b) voltage

(c) resistance   (d) volt-amps

_____ _____

16. A voltage tester rated for the correct voltage can be used for testing the voltage for fuses between _____.

(a) L_1 and L_2 (b) L_1 and L_3

(c) L_2 and L_3 (d) all of the above

_____ _____

17. The procedure for testing the overloads (Test 1) is to read the voltage from L_1 to the line side of _____.

(a) L_2 (b) L_3

(c) L_5 (d) L_6

_____ _____

18. To perform an ohmmeter test for open contacts on the stop button, read between L_1 and the side of the stop button that is connected to the start button and terminal _____ of the holding contacts.

(a) 1   (b) 2

(c) 3   (d) 6

_____ _____

19. To perform testing for closed contacts on the start button, read from the side of the stop button connected to L_1 and to the side of the start button terminated to the holding _____.

(a) winding   (b) stator

(c) coil   (d) armature

20. To test for grounds in a wye-connected motor, connect one test lead to the _____ of the motor and one test lead to one of the lead of the motor.
    (a) coil   (b) frame
    (c) stator   (d) rotor

21. Connect the leads for a wye configuration six-lead motor.

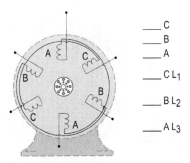

SIX-LEAD WYE MOTOR

22. Connect the leads for a delta configuration six-lead motor.

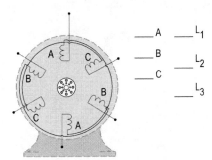

SIX-LEAD DELTA MOTOR

23. Number the leads for each winding in a delta configuration nine-lead motor.

A_____

B_____

C_____

D_____

E_____

F_____

G_____

H_____

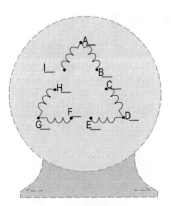

NINE-LEAD DELTA MOTOR

I_____

_____ A_____ **24.** Number the leads for each winding in a wye configuration nine-lead motor.

B_____

C_____

D_____

E_____

F_____

G_____

H_____

I_____

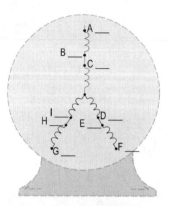

NINE-LEAD WYE CONNECTOR

_____ _____ **25.** Mark where the testing leads are to be placed when testing the voltage to the line side of the magnetic starter. (For simplicity, test each overload.)

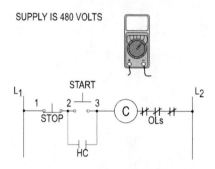

SUPPLY IS 480 VOLTS

_____ _____ **26.** Mark where the testing leads are to be placed when testing the voltage through the overloads and to the coil.

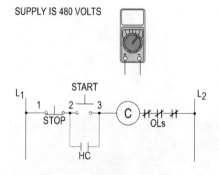

SUPPLY IS 480 VOLTS

27. Mark where the testing leads are to be placed in two different tests to determine the common problems that could cause the interruption of voltage through the overloads to the coil terminals.

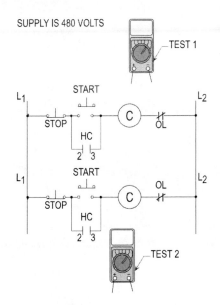

28. Mark where the testing leads are to be placed from two different tests to determine the voltage to a coil if it is defective. (Voltage is measured at Test 1 and Test 2.)

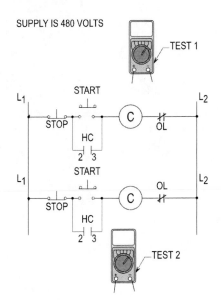

_____ _____ **29.** Mark where the testing leads are to be placed when testing the line voltage to the contacts (HC) of the stop and start buttons.

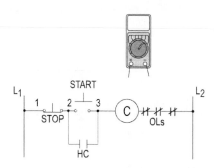

_____ _____ **30.** Mark where the testing leads are to be placed when testing the contacts of a stop button in a three-wire control circuit using resistance.

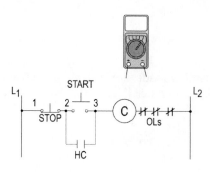

_____ _____ **31.** Mark where the testing leads are to be placed when testing the contacts of a start button in a three-wire control circuit.

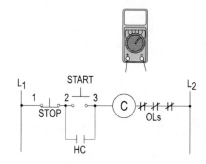

32. Mark where the testing leads are to be placed in two different tests for testing the contacts of the overloads in a three-wire control circuit.

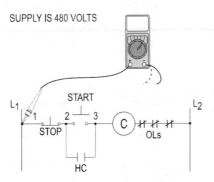

SUPPLY IS 480 VOLTS

33. Mark where the testing leads are to be placed in two different tests for testing a coil in a three-wire circuit to determine if it's defective. (No voltage is measured at Test 1.)

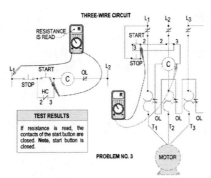

34. Mark where the testing leads are to be placed when testing the contacts of the holding circuit in a three-wire control circuit with the start button held closed.

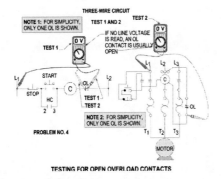

_____ _____ **35.** Referring to problems 25 through 34, one basic troubleshooting method is to check the _____ power supply.
    (a) outgoing   (b) incoming
    (c) all of the above   (d) none of the above

_____ _____ **36.** The _____ contacts keep the contactor energized and powers the motor.
    (a) holding   (b) release
    (c) all of the above   (d) none of the above

_____ _____ **37.** Silicon-controlled rectifiers can be tested by using an _____.
    (a) ohmmeter   (b) voltmaster
    (c) ampmeter   (d) all of the above

_____ _____ **38.** When testing the contacts of a stop button and resistance is not read, the stop button is _____.
    (a) closed   (b) open
    (c) all of the above   (d) none of the above

_____ _____ **39.** The contacts for the _____ button are usually marked 2 and 3.
    (a) stop   (b) jog
    (c) start   (d) all of the above

_____ _____ **40.** Overloads are installed on the side of the coil and supplied from _____ and contact 3.
    (a) L_1 (b) L_2
    (c) L_4 (d) L_5

24

Compressor Motors

Article 440 deals with individual or group installations having hermetically sealed motor compressors. The techniques for designing the proper size conductors, disconnecting means, and controllers are discussed.

The conductors supplying power to heating, air-conditioning, and refrigeration (HACR) equipment are sized from the full-load amp (FLA) ratings of the compressor and condenser motor. These FLA ratings are increased by 125 percent per **440.32** to compensate for the starting periods and overload conditions.

The overcurrent protection devices protecting the branch circuits from short-circuit and ground-fault currents are sized from the provisions listed in **440.22(A) or Ex. 1 and Ex. 2**, which requires the FLA ratings to be increased from 175 percent up to 225 percent to allow the HACR equipment to start and run without tripping the overcurrent protection device ahead of the circuit.

Note, the elements used to supply the branch circuits to HACR equipment may be required to be selected by the branch-circuit selection currents listed on the nameplate of the equipment per **440.4(C)** and **110.3(B)**.

Note, also the exceptions that have been added to **440.22(A)** to recognize the round-up or round-down of the overcurrent protection device.

SCOPE
440.1

The overcurrent protection devices, running overload protection devices, conductors, disconnecting means, and controllers shall be sized and selected by the information provided on the nameplate listing for air-conditioning and refrigeration equipment. The information on the nameplate is very important to installers and service personnel; therefore, the nameplate shall never be removed from the air-conditioner or refrigeration equipment.

MARKINGS ON HERMETIC REFRIGERANT MOTOR-COMPRESSORS AND EQUIPMENT
440.4(A) AND (B)

Hermetic refrigerant motor-compressors shall be provided with a marking on the nameplate giving the manufacturer's name, trademark, or symbol and designating the identification, number of phases, voltage, and frequency. The information provided on the nameplate of the hermetic refrigerant motor-compressor is used to determine the ratings of branch-circuit conductors, ground fault protection, short circuits, disconnecting means, controllers, and other components of the electrical system.

MARKINGS ON CONTROLLERS
440.5

Controllers shall be marked with information that lists the manufacturer's name, trademark, or symbol, identifying voltage, phases, full-load current, locked-rotor current rating, or horsepower.

AMPACITY AND RATING
440.6

The full-load current rating listed on the nameplate of the motor-compressor shall be used to determine the branch-circuit conductor rating, short-circuit protection rating, motor overload protection rating, controller rating, or disconnecting means rating. The branch-circuit selection current (if greater) shall be applied if shown instead of the full-load current rating. The full-load current rating shall be used to determine the motor's overload protection rating. The full-load current rating listed on the compressor nameplate shall be used when the nameplate for the equipment does not list a full-load current rating based on the branch-circuit selection current. (See Figure 24-1)

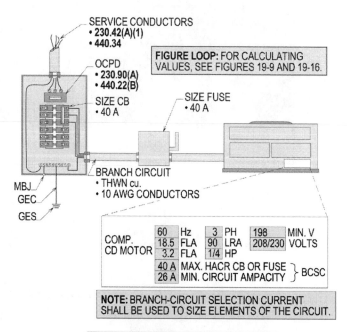

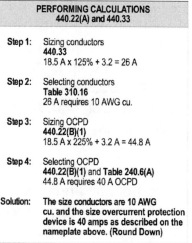

Figure 24-1. If the branch-circuit selection current (BCSC) on the nameplate calls for a certain circuit size and overcurrent protection device size, this rating shall be used instead of actually calculating such values and sizes per **440.22(A)** and **440.32**. (OCPD round down size)

HIGHEST RATED (LARGEST) MOTOR
440.7

When sizing the conductors for a feeder supplying air-conditioning units and motors per **430.24**, the full-load current of the largest motor is multiplied by 125 percent. The full-load current ratings of the remaining motors are added to this total to derive the total FLA.

See Figures 20-11 and **20-12** for illustrations pertaining to this rule.

When sizing the overcurrent protection device for two or more motors per **430.62(A)**, the full-load current of the largest motor is multiplied by the percentages listed in **Table 430.52(C)(1)**. The full-load current ratings of the remaining motors are added to this total to derive the FLA.

The full-load current ratings listed on the nameplate of the motor-compressor shall be used to determine the size conductors and overcurrent protection device using the same procedure. The larger of the two shall be used.

See Figure 24-2 for a feeder supplying motors and air-conditioning units.

Note, the air-conditioning unit is the largest motor and not one of the motors in the group.

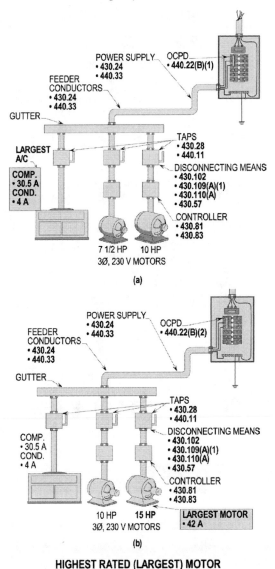

HIGHEST RATED (LARGEST) MOTOR
NEC 440.7

Figure 24-2. The above shows the calculation procedure for sizing conductors and overcurrent protection devices where the air-conditioning unit or motor is the largest in the group of air-conditioning units and motors.

SINGLE MACHINE
440.8

Each motor controller shall be provided with an disconnecting means. Air-conditioning and refrigeration systems are considered to be a single machine even though they consist of any number of motors. The number of disconnecting means to be provided are determined by applying **430.87, Ex.** and **430.112, Ex. (See Ex. to 440.8.)**

DISCONNECTING MEANS
440.11

The full-load current rating of the nameplate or the nameplate branch-circuit selection current of the compressor, whichever is greater, shall be used to size the branch-circuit conductors and the disconnecting means to disconnect air-conditioning and refrigeration equipment. **(See Tool or Locking Rule.)**

RATING AND INTERRUPTING CAPACITY
440.12

The full-load current rating of the nameplate or the nameplate branch-circuit selection current of the compressor, whichever is greater, shall be sized at 115 percent to size the disconnecting means. A horsepower rated switch, circuit breaker, or other switches shall be permitted to be used as the disconnecting means per **430.109(A)(1)** and **430.110(A)**. **(See Figure 24-3)**

> **Design Tip:** A minimum load is derived when applying 115 percent for sizing the disconnecting means. Therefore, on larger units the 115 percent may not be of sufficient ampacity for opening the circuit under load.

The horsepower amperage rating may be selected from **Tables 430.247 through 430.250** when corresponding to the nameplate current rating or branch-circuit selection current of the motor-compressor or equipment when listed in amperage and not horsepower. The horsepower amperage rating for locked-rotor current shall be selected from **Tables 430.251(A)** and **(B)** when the nameplate fails to list the locked-rotor current.

Note, the disconnecting means shall be sized with enough capacity in horsepower to be capable of disconnecting the total locked-rotor current. **(See Figure 24-4)**

The full-load current rating of the nameplate shall be permitted to be used to size a circuit breaker at 115 percent or more to disconnect a hermetically sealed motor from the power circuit. **(See Figure 24-5)**

Design Tip: The circuit breaker shall be sized at 115 percent or more of the branch-circuit selection current if it is greater in rating, so as to be capable of disconnecting the circuit safely.

Two or more hermetic motors or combination loads such as hermetic motor loads, standard motor loads, and other loads shall have their separate values totaled to determine the rating of a single disconnecting means. This total rating shall be sized at 115 percent to determine the size disconnecting means required to disconnect the circuits and components in a safe and reliable manner. **(See Figure 24-6)**

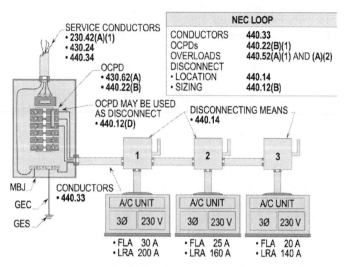

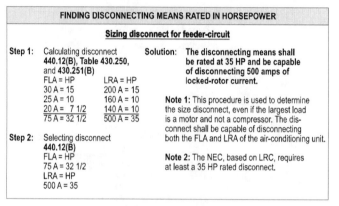

RATING AND INTERRUPTING CAPACITY
NEC 440.12(B)

Figure 24-4. Sizing horsepower rating to select disconnecting means based on the locked-rotor current.

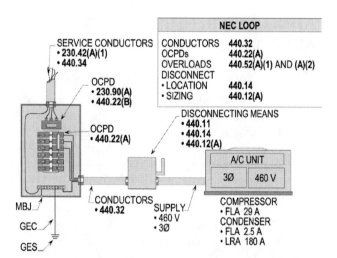

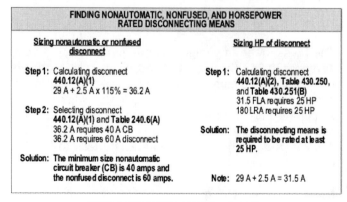

RATING AND INTERRUPTING CAPACITY
NEC 440.12(A)

Figure 24-3. The full-load current rating of the nameplate or the nameplate branch-circuit selection current of the compressor, whichever is greater, shall be sized at 115 percent to size the disconnecting means.

CORD-CONNECTED EQUIPMENT 440.13

For cord-and-plug connected equipment such as room air-conditioners, home refrigerators and freezers, drinking water coolers, and beverage dispensers, a separable connector or attachment plug and receptacle shall be permitted to be used to serve as a disconnecting means. **(See Figure 24-7)**

Design Tip: In some cases, room air-conditioners shall not be permitted to have a cord-and-plug connection to serve as their disconnecting means, as when unit switches for manual control are installed in air-conditioners mounted over 6 ft (1.8 m) above finished grade.

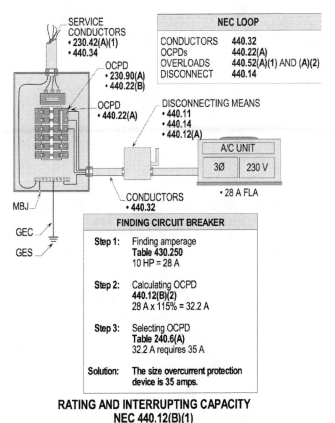

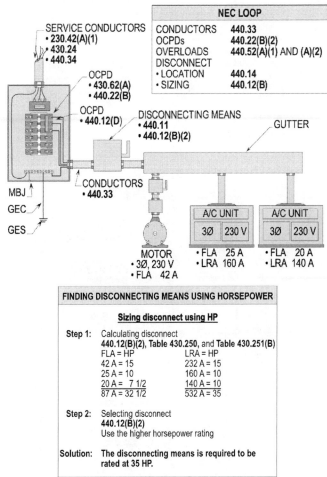

**RATING AND INTERRUPTING CAPACITY
NEC 440.12(B)(1)
NEC TABLE 430.250**

Figure 24-5. The full-load current rating of the nameplate shall be permitted to be used to size a circuit breaker at 115 percent or more to disconnect a hermetically sealed compressor motor from the power circuit.

**RATING AND INTERRUPTING CAPACITY
NEC 440.12(B)(2)**

Figure 24-6. Two or more hermetic motors or combination loads, such as hermetic motor loads, standard motor loads, and other loads, shall have their separate values totaled to determine the rating of a single disconnecting means.

LOCATION
440.14

The disconnecting means for air-conditioning or refrigeration equipment shall be located within sight and within 50 ft (15 m) and shall be readily accessible to the user. An additional circuit breaker or disconnecting switch shall be provided at the equipment if the air-conditioning or refrigeration equipment is not within sight or within 50 ft (15 m). The disconnecting means shall be permitted to be installed within or on the air-conditioning or refrigeration equipment. For the use of unit switches located in air-conditioning units, review **422.34** per AHJ. **(See Figure 24-8)**

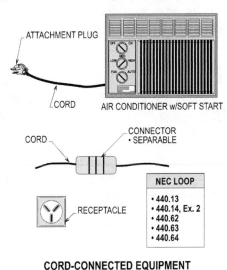

**CORD-CONNECTED EQUIPMENT
NEC 440.13**

Figure 24-7. Cord-and-plug connected equipment such as room air-conditioners, home refrigerators and freezers, drinking water coolers, and beverage dispensers shall be permitted to be disconnected by a cord and receptacle. A separable connector or an attachment plug and receptacle shall be permitted to be used to serve as such disconnecting means.

Safety Tip: If the disconnectng means is readily accessible to unqualified persons, any enclosure door or hinged cover of the disconnecting means enclosure exposes energized parts when open shall require a tool to open or be capable of being locked per **440.11.**

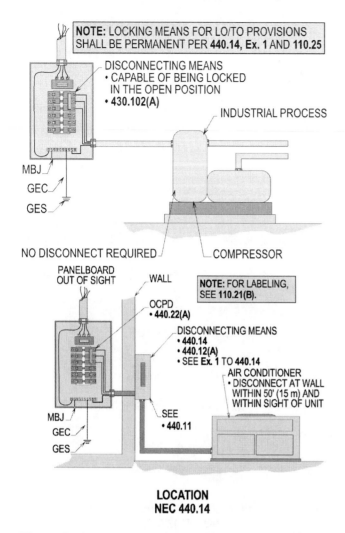

NOTE: LOCKING MEANS FOR LO/TO PROVISIONS SHALL BE PERMANENT PER **440.14, Ex. 1** AND **110.25**

DISCONNECTING MEANS
• CAPABLE OF BEING LOCKED IN THE OPEN POSITION
• **430.102(A)**

INDUSTRIAL PROCESS

MBJ
GEC
GES

NO DISCONNECT REQUIRED

COMPRESSOR

PANELBOARD OUT OF SIGHT

WALL

NOTE: FOR LABELING, SEE **110.21(B)**.

OCPD
• **440.22(A)**

DISCONNECTING MEANS
• **440.14**
• **440.12(A)**
• SEE **Ex. 1** TO **440.14**

AIR CONDITIONER
• DISCONNECT AT WALL WITHIN 50' (15 m) AND WITHIN SIGHT OF UNIT

MBJ
GEC
GES

SEE
• **440.11**

LOCATION
NEC 440.14

Figure 24-8. The disconnecting means for air-conditioning or refrigeration equipment shall be located within sight and within 50 ft (15 m) and be readily accessible to the user. An additional circuit breaker or disconnecting switch shall be provided at the equipment if the air-conditioning or refrigeration equipment is not within sight or within 50 ft (15 m).

APPLICATION AND SELECTION
440.22

The branch-circuit fuse or circuit breaker ratings for hermetically sealed motors shall be sized with enough capacity to allow the motor to start and develop speed without tripping open the overcurrent protection device due to the momentary inrush current of the compressor and other elements. Maximum protection is always provided by the ratings and settings of the overcurrent protection device being sized with values as low as possible. Hermetic refrigerant motor-compressors shall be protected by properly sizing and selecting the ratings and settings of the overcurrent protection devices to protect the branch-circuit conductors and other elements in the circuit from short-circuit and ground-fault conditions.

RATING AND SETTING FOR INDIVIDUAL MOTOR-COMPRESSORS
440.22(A) OR Ex. 1 OR 2

The overcurrent protection device for hermetically sealed compressors shall be selected at 175 percent (for minimum) or 225 percent (for maximum) of the compressor FLA rating or the branch-circuit selection circuit current, whichever is greater. **(See Figure 24-9)**

Overcurrent protection devices for hermetically sealed compressors shall be permitted to be selected up to 225 percent to permit the motor to start if the compressor will not start and develop speed when the rating is 175 percent or less. **Note,** OCPD can be rounded up or down.

> **Design Tip:** A normal circuit breaker shall not be installed when the equipment is marked for a particular fuse size or HACR circuit breaker rating. The branch-circuit conductors shall be protected only by that specified fuse size or HACR circuit breaker rating.

RATING OR SETTING FOR EQUIPMENT
440.22(B)

When sizing the overcurrent protection device, the rating or setting shall be selected to comply with the number of hermetic motors, or combination of hermetic motors, and standard motors installed on a circuit.

SIZING OVERCURRENT PROTECTION DEVICES FOR TWO OR MORE HERMETIC MOTORS
440.22(B)(1)

The overcurrent protection device for a feeder supplying two or more air-conditioning or refrigerating units shall be sized to allow the largest unit to start and allow the other units to start at different intervals of time. The full-load current rating of the nameplate or the branch-circuit selection current rating of the largest motor, whichever is greater, shall be sized at 175 percent if there are two or more hermetically sealed motors installed on the same feeder. **(See Figure 24-10)**

Overcurrent protection devices for hermetically sealed motors shall be permitted to be selected up to 225 percent to allow the motor to start if the motor will not start and develop speed when the rating is selected at 175 percent or less. **(See Figure 24-11)**

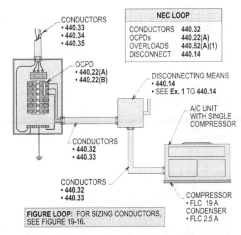

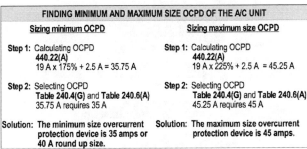

FINDING MINIMUM AND MAXIMUM SIZE OCPD OF THE A/C UNIT	
Sizing minimum OCPD	**Sizing maximum size OCPD**
Step 1: Calculating OCPD **440.22(A)** 19 A x 175% + 2.5 A = 35.75 A	**Step 1:** Calculating OCPD **440.22(A)** 19 A x 225% + 2.5 A = 45.25 A
Step 2: Selecting OCPD **Table 240.4(G)** and **Table 240.6(A)** 35.75 A requires 35 A	**Step 2:** Selecting OCPD **Table 240.4(G)** and **Table 240.6(A)** 45.25 A requires 45 A
Solution: The minimum size overcurrent protection device is 35 amps or 40 A round up size.	**Solution:** The maximum size overcurrent protection device is 45 amps.

**RATING AND SETTING FOR INDIVIDUAL MOTOR-COMPRESSORS
NEC 440.22(A)**

Figure 24-9. The overcurrent protection device for hermetically sealed compressors shall be selected at 175 percent (for minimum) or 225 percent (for maximum) of the compressor's FLA rating or the branch-circuit selection circuit current, whichever is greater. **Note,** a smaller size overcurrent protection device shall be permitted to be used then selected per solution, if air-conditioning unit will start and run. Review **Ex. 1** and **Ex. 2** for round up or round down size.

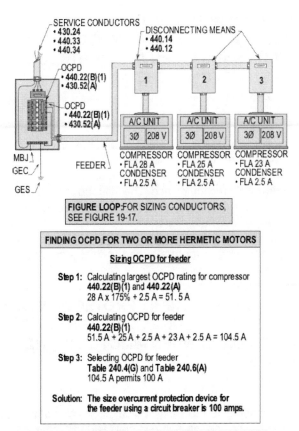

FINDING OCPD FOR TWO OR MORE HERMETIC MOTORS
Sizing OCPD for feeder
Step 1: Calculating largest OCPD rating for compressor **440.22(B)(1)** and **440.22(A)** 28 A x 175% + 2.5 A = 51.5 A
Step 2: Calculating OCPD for feeder **440.22(B)(1)** 51.5 + 25 A + 2.5 A + 23 A + 2.5 A = 104.5 A
Step 3: Selecting OCPD for feeder **Table 240.4(G)** and **Table 240.6(A)** 104.5 A permits 100 A
Solution: The size overcurrent protection device for the feeder using a circuit breaker is 100 amps.

**SIZING OVERCURRENT PROTECTION DEVICE FOR
TWO OR MORE HERMETIC MOTORS**

Figure 24-10. The full-load current rating of the nameplate or the branch-circuit selection current rating of the largest motor, whichever is greater, shall be sized at 175 percent if there are two or more hermetically sealed motors installed on the same feeder.

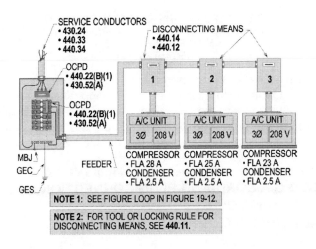

FINDING OCPD FOR TWO OR MORE HERMETIC MOTORS
Sizing OCPD for feeder
Step 1: Calculating largest OCPD rating for compressor **440.22(B)(1)** and **440.22(A)** 28 A x 225% + 2.5 A = 65.5 A
Step 2: Calculating OCPD for feeder **440.22(B)(1)** 65.5 A + 25 A + 2.5 A + 23 A + 2.5 A = 118.5 A
Step 3: Selecting OCPD for feeder **Table 240.4(G)** and **Table 240.6(A)** 118.5 A allows 110 A
Solution: The size overcurrent protection device for the feeder using a circuit breaker is 110 amps.

**SIZING OVERCURRENT PROTECTION DEVICE FOR
TWO OR MORE HERMETIC MOTORS
NEC 440.22(B)(1)**

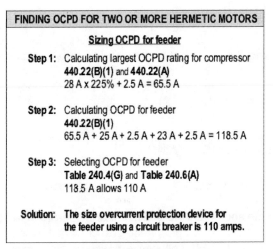

Figure 24-11. Overcurrent protection devices for hermetically sealed motors shall be permitted to be selected up to 225 percent to allow the motor to start if the motor will not start and develop speed.

SIZING OVERCURRENT PROTECTION DEVICES FOR HERMETIC MOTORS AND OTHER LOADS WHEN A HERMETICALLY SEALED MOTOR IS THE LARGEST
440.22(B)(1)

When installing hermetically sealed motors and other loads such as motors on the same circuit, and the largest motor of the group is hermetic, the same procedure used for two or more hermetic motors on a feeder shall be used to size the overcurrent protection device. The full-load current rating of the nameplate or the branch-circuit selection current rating of the largest hermetic motor, whichever is greater, shall be sized at 175 percent, and the sum of the full-load current ratings of the other motors added to this largest hermetic motor load.

SIZING OVERCURRENT PROTECTION DEVICES FOR HERMETIC MOTORS AND OTHER LOADS WHEN A MOTOR IS THE LARGEST
440.22(B)(2)

When installing hermetically sealed motors and other loads such as motors on the same circuit, and the largest in the group is a motor, the overcurrent protection device shall be sized and selected based on the percentages from **Table 430.52(C)(1)**. The maximum branch-circuit overcurrent protection device shall be used when the standard motor is the largest of the group, and the sum of the full-load current ratings of the remaining hermetically sealed motor and other motors of the group added to the largest motor. The next lower standard size overcurrent protection device below this total sum shall be installed per **240.6(A)**. **(See Figure 24-12)**

> **Design Tip:** The next larger standard size overcurrent protection device is not permitted to be installed, for there is not an exception to permit the next higher size per **440.22(B)(2)** or **430.62(A)**.

USING A 15 OR 20 AMP OVERCURRENT PROTECTION DEVICE
440.22(B)(2), Ex. 1

When the equipment will start, run, and operate on a 15 or 20 amp, 120 volt, single-phase branch circuit, or on a 15 amp, 208 volt or 240 volt, single-phase branch circuit, with a 15 or 20 amp overcurrent protection device, such device shall be permitted to be used to protect the branch circuit. However, the values of the overcurrent protection device in the branch circuit shall not exceed the values marked on the

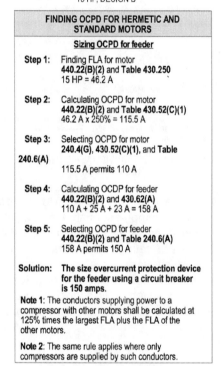

FINDING OCPD FOR HERMETIC AND STANDARD MOTORS

Sizing OCPD for feeder

Step 1:	Finding FLA for motor **440.22(B)(2)** and **Table 430.250** 15 HP = 46.2 A
Step 2:	Calculating OCPD for motor **440.22(B)(2)** and **Table 430.52(C)(1)** 46.2 A x 250% = 115.5 A
Step 3: **240.6(A)**	Selecting OCPD for motor **240.4(G)**, **430.52(C)(1)**, and **Table** 115.5 A permits 110 A
Step 4:	Calculating OCDP for feeder **440.22(B)(2)** and **430.62(A)** 110 A + 25 A + 23 A = 158 A
Step 5:	Selecting OCPD for feeder **440.22(B)(2)** and **Table 240.6(A)** 158 A permits 150 A
Solution:	**The size overcurrent protection device for the feeder using a circuit breaker is 150 amps.**

Note 1: The conductors supplying power to a compressor with other motors shall be calculated at 125% times the largest FLA plus the FLA of the other motors.

Note 2: The same rule applies where only compressors are supplied by such conductors.

SIZING OVERCURRENT PROTECTION DEVICE FOR HERMETIC MOTORS AND OTHER LOADS WHEN A MOTOR IS THE LARGEST NEC 440.22(B)(2)

Figure 24-12. When hermetically sealed motors and other loads, such as motors, are being installed on the same circuit, and the largest in the group is a motor, the overcurrent protection device shall be sized and selected based on the percentages from **Table 430.52(C)(1)**.

nameplate of the equipment. **(See Figure 24-13)**

USING A CORD-AND-PLUG CONNECTION NOT OVER 250 VOLTS
440.22(B)(2), Ex. 2

The rating of the overcurrent protection device shall be determined by using the rating on the nameplate of the cord-and-plug connected equipment serving single-phase, 250 volt or less, hermetically sealed motor. **(See Figure 24-14)**

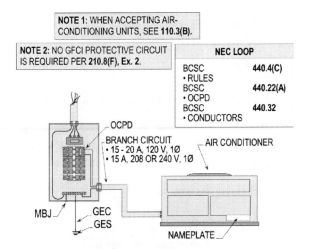

NEC LOOP	
BCSC • RULES	440.4(C)
BCSC • OCPD	440.22(A)
BCSC • CONDUCTORS	440.32

USING A 15 OR 20 AMP OVERCURRENT PROTECTION DEVICE NEC 440.22(B)(2), Ex. 1

Figure 24-13. Where the equipment will start, run, and operate on a 15 or 20 amp, 120 volt, single-phase branch circuit, or on a 15 amp, 208 volt or 240 volt, single-phase branch circuit, a 15 or 20 amp overcurrent protection device shall be permitted to be used to protect the branch circuit.
• No GFCI protective circuit is required per **210.8(F), Ex. 2.**

PROTECTIVE DEVICE RATING NOT TO EXCEED THE MANUFACTURER'S VALUES
440.22(C)

The manufacturer's values marked on the equipment shall not be exceeded by the overcurrent protection device rating, where the maximum overcurrent protection device ratings on the manufacturer's heater table for use with a motor controller are less than the rating or setting per **440.22(A)** and **(B)**. **(See Figure 24-15)**

BRANCH-CIRCUIT CONDUCTORS
440.31

In general, to prevent conductors and motor elements of the branch circuit from overheating, the conductors shall be sized with enough capacity to allow a hermetic motor to start and run. To ensure adequate sizing, a derating factor of 80 percent shall be applied to the branch-circuit conductors or such conductors shall be sized at 125 percent of the load.

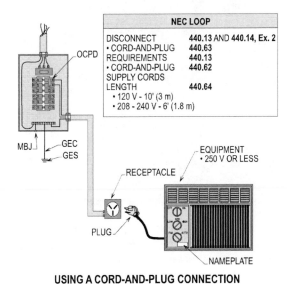

NEC LOOP	
DISCONNECT	440.13 AND 440.14, Ex. 2
• CORD-AND-PLUG REQUIREMENTS	440.63 440.13
• CORD-AND-PLUG SUPPLY CORDS	440.62
LENGTH • 120 V - 10' (3 m) • 208 - 240 V - 6' (1.8 m)	440.64

USING A CORD-AND-PLUG CONNECTION NOT OVER 250 VOLTS NEC 440.22(B)(2), Ex. 2

Figure 24-14. The rating of the overcurrent protection device shall be determined by using the rating of the nameplate of the cord-and-plug connected equipment having a single-phase, 250 volt or less, hermetically sealed motor.

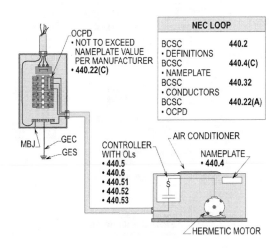

NEC LOOP	
BCSC • DEFINITIONS	440.2
BCSC • NAMEPLATE	440.4(C)
BCSC • CONDUCTORS	440.32
BCSC • OCPD	440.22(A)

PROTECTIVE DEVICE RATING NOT TO EXCEED THE MANUFACTURER'S VALUES NEC 440.22(C)

Figure 24-15. The manufacturer's values marked on the equipment shall not be exceeded by the overcurrent protection device rating where the maximum overcurrent protective device ratings on the manufacturer's heater table for use with a motor controller are less than the rating or setting per **440.22(A)** and **(B)**.

SINGLE MOTOR-COMPRESSORS
440.32

The conductors supplying power to an air-conditioning or refrigerating unit shall be sized to carry the load of the unit plus an overload for a period of time that will not damage the elements. The full-load current rating of the nameplate or branch-circuit selection current, whichever is greater, shall be sized at 125 percent to size and select the conductors supplying hermetically sealed motors. **(See Figure 24-16)**

TWO OR MORE MOTOR COMPRESSORS
440.33

Two or more compressors plus other motor loads can be connected to a feeder. The largest compressor shall be calculated at 125 percent of its FLA, and the remaining compressor loads are added to this total at 100 percent of their FLA ratings. For units with a branch-circuit selection current, the circuit conductors are selected and based on the nameplate values. **(See Figure 24-17)**

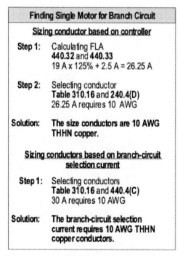

SINGLE MOTOR-COMPRESSORS
NEC 440.32

Figure 24-16. The full-load current rating of the nameplate or branch-circuit selection current, whichever is greater, shall be sized at 125 percent to size and select the conductors supplying hermetically sealed motors.

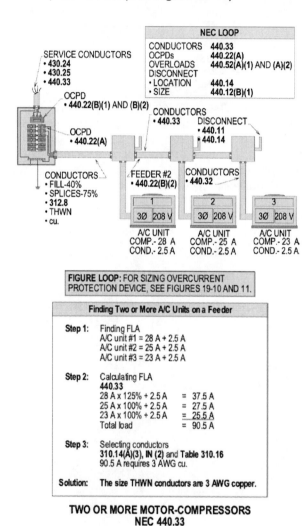

TWO OR MORE MOTOR-COMPRESSORS
NEC 440.33

Figure 24-17. Two or more compressors plus the other motor loads can be connected to a feeder. The largest compressor shall be calculated at 125 percent of its FLA and the remaining compressor loads are added to this total at 100 percent of their FLA ratings.

COMBINATION LOADS
440.34

Two or more motor-compressors with motor loads plus other loads may be connected to a feeder or service conductors. The largest compressor or motor load shall be calculated at 125 percent plus 100 percent of the remaining compressors and motors. The other loads shall be calculated at 125 percent for continuous and 100 percent for noncontinuous operation per **215.2(A)(1)**, and these total values used to select conductors. **(See Figure 24-18)**

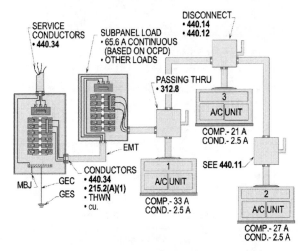

COMBINATION LOAD
NEC 440.34

Figure 24-18. Two or more motor-compressors with motor loads plus other loads may be connected to a feeder or service conductors. The largest compressor or motor load shall be calculated at 125 percent, plus 100 percent of the remaining compressors and motors, plus the other loads.

MULTIMOTOR AND COMBINATION LOAD EQUIPMENT
440.35

The marking on the nameplate shall be used when sizing the branch-circuit conductors for multimotor and combination load equipment. The conductors shall be installed to have a rating equal to the nameplate rating. Each individual motor or load contained in the unit shall not be required to be calculated individually to size and select the conductors.

CONTROLLERS FOR MOTOR-COMPRESSORS
440.41

When installing the wiring for a motor-controller, the circuit supply conductors are run from a motor controller and connected to the terminals of the compressor. The full-load current rating and the locked-rotor current rating of the compressor motor shall be sized at continuous operation.

MOTOR-COMPRESSOR CONTROLLER RATING
440.41(A)

The full-load current rating on the nameplate or the branch-circuit selection current ratings, whichever is greater, shall be used to size and select the motor controller. If necessary, the locked-rotor current rating of the motor shall be permitted to be used to size and select the motor controller. **(See Figure 24-19)**

> **Design Tip:** The motor controller shall be sized and selected using the same procedure as used for the sizing of the disconnecting means.

MOTOR-COMPRESSOR AND BRANCH-CIRCUIT OVERLOAD PROTECTION
440.51

The overload (OL) protection for compressors may be accomplished by using overcurrent protection devices in separate enclosures, separate overload relays, or thermal protectors that are an integral part of the compressor.

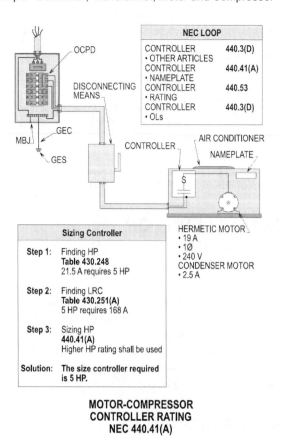

**MOTOR-COMPRESSOR
CONTROLLER RATING
NEC 440.41(A)**

Figure 24-19. The full-load current rating of the nameplate or the branch-circuit selection current ratings, whichever is greater, shall be used to size and select the motor controller.

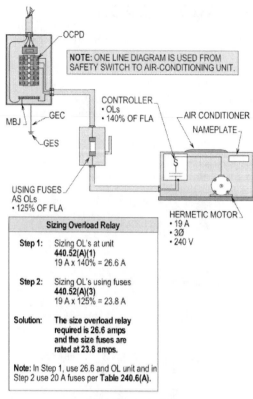

**APPLICATION AND SELECTION
NEC 440.52(A)(1)
NEC 440.52(A)(3)**

Figure 24-20. The overload relay for the motor-compressor shall trip at not more than 140 percent of the full-load current rating. If a fuse or circuit breaker is used for the protection of the motor-compressor, it shall trip at not more than 125 percent of the full-load current rating.

APPLICATION AND SELECTION 440.52

The overload relay for a motor-compressor shall trip at not more than 140 percent of the full-load current rating. If a fuse or circuit breaker is used for the protection of the motor-compressor, it shall trip at not more than 125 percent of the full-load current rating. **(See Figure 24-20)**

OVERLOAD RELAYS 440.53

Short-circuit and ground-fault protection is not provided by overload relays and thermal protectors. Overload relays and thermal protectors respond to any type of heat buildup and open with a delay action that will not operate instantly, even on short circuits or ground faults. The branch-circuit overcurrent protection device for the circuit shall operate and clear the circuit under short-circuit and ground-fault conditions.

MOTOR-COMPRESSORS AND EQUIPMENT ON A 15 OR 20 AMP BRANCH CIRCUIT NOT CORD-AND-PLUG CONNECTED 440.54

Overload protection shall be provided for direct- or fixed-wired motor-compressors and equipment that is connected to 15 or 20 amp, 120 volt, single-phase branch circuits.

Note, a 15 amp overcurrent protection device is required for 240 volt, single-phase branch circuits.

The full-load current rating of the hermetically sealed motor shall be selected at 140 percent when sizing separate overload relays. Hermetic motors shall be provided with fuses or circuit breakers that provide sufficient time delay to allow the motor to come up to running speed without tripping open the circuit due to the high inrush current. **(See Figure 24-21)**

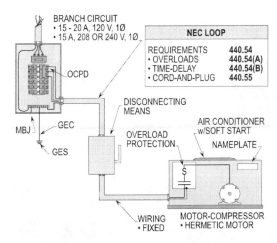

MOTOR-COMPRESSORS AND EQUIPMENT
ON A 15 OR 20 AMP BRANCH CIRCUIT NOT
CORD-AND-PLUG CONNECTED
NEC 440.54

Figure 24-21. Overload protection shall be provided for direct- or fixed-wired motor compressors and equipment that is connected to 15 or 20 amp, 120 volt, single-phase branch circuits.

CORD-AND-ATTACHMENT PLUG CONNECTED MOTOR-COMPRESSORS AND EQUIPMENT ON 15 OR 20 AMP BRANCH CIRCUITS 440.55

When attachment plugs and receptacles or cord connectors are used for circuit connection they shall be rated no higher than 15 or 20 amps for 120 volt, single-phase circuits, or 15 amps, for 208 or 240 volt, single-phase branch circuits. **(See Figure 24-22)**

ROOM AIR-CONDITIONERS 440.60

Room air-conditioners are usually cord-and-plug connected when installed on 120/240 volt, single-phase systems. However, they may be hard-wired. Air-conditioners are always hard-wired when installed on three-phase systems or on electrical supply systems over 250 volts.

GROUNDING 440.61

The following wiring methods, when utilized to wire in room air-conditioners, shall be connected to an equipment grounding conductor:

(1) Cord-and-plug connected

(2) Hard-wired (if within reach of the ground or grounded object)

(3) In contact with metal

(4) Operating over 150 volts-to-ground

(5) Wired with metal-clad wiring

(6) Located in a hazardous location

(7) Installed in damp location (within reach of the user)

See Figure 24-23 for the wiring methods that shall be permitted to be used to ground room air-conditioners.

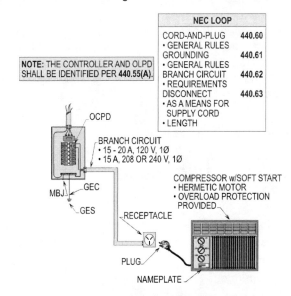

CORD-AND-ATTACHMENT PLUG CONNECTED
MOTOR-COMPRESSORS AND EQUIPMENT ON
15 OR 20 AMP BRANCH CIRCUITS
NEC 440.55

Figure 24-22. When attachment plugs and receptacles or cord connectors are used for circuit connection, they shall be rated no higher than 15 or 20 amps, for 120 volt, single-phase circuits, or 15 amps, for 208 or 240 volt, single-phase branch circuits.

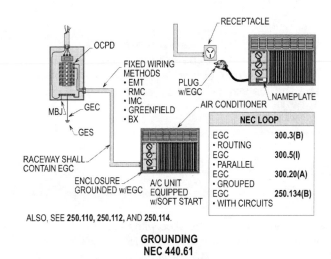

GROUNDING
NEC 440.61

Figure 24-23. The above shows wiring methods that shall be permitted to be used to ground room air-conditioners.

BRANCH CIRCUIT REQUIREMENTS
440.62

The full-load current rating of a room air-conditioner shall be marked on the nameplate and shall not operate at more than 40 amps on 250 volts. The branch-circuit overcurrent protection device shall be installed with a rating no greater than the circuit conductor's ampacity or the rating of the receptacle serving the unit, whichever is less. The ampacity of a cord-and-plug connected air-conditioning window unit shall not exceed 80 percent of the branch circuit where no other loads are served. If other loads are served by the branch circuit, the cord-and-plug connected air-conditioner unit shall not exceed 50 percent of the branch circuit. **[See Figures 24-24(a) and (b)]**

DISCONNECTING MEANS
440.63

A cord-and-plug shall be permitted to serve as the disconnecting means for the room air-conditioner if all the following conditions are met:

(1) Operates at 250 volts or less

(2) Controls are manually operated

(3) Controls are within 6 ft (1.8 m) of the floor

(4) Controls are readily accessible to the user

A room air-conditioner shall be permitted to be hard-wired and located within sight of the service equipment, or it may be wired so that it is readily accessible to a disconnecting switch for the user. However, such switch shall be located within sight and/or within the unit. **[See Figures 24-25(a) and (b)]**

> **Design Tip:** The rules for three-phase room air-conditioners shall not be used for these type of units. Three-phase room air-conditioners shall be hard-wired and shall be installed with a disconnecting means that is readily accessible to the user.

SUPPLY CORDS
440.64

Room air-conditioners installed with flexible cords shall be a length that is limited to 10 ft (3 m) for 120 volt circuits and 6 ft (1.8 m) for 208 or 240 volt circuits. Long cords shall not be used because they are dangerous. Long cords can also be a shock or fire hazard. **(See Figure 24-26)**

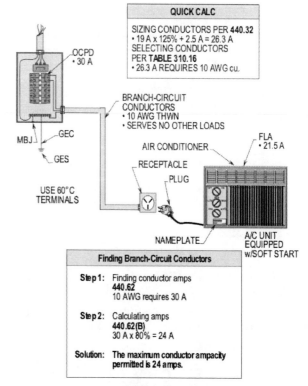

QUICK CALC

SIZING CONDUCTORS PER **440.32**
• 19 A x 125% + 2.5 A = 26.3 A
SELECTING CONDUCTORS
PER **TABLE 310.16**
• 26.3 A REQUIRES 10 AWG cu.

Finding Branch-Circuit Conductors

Step 1: Finding conductor amps
440.62
10 AWG requires 30 A

Step 2: Calculating amps
440.62(B)
30 A x 80% = 24 A

Solution: The maximum conductor ampacity permitted is 24 amps.

BRANCH-CIRCUIT REQUIREMENTS
NEC 440.62(B)

Figure 24-24(a). The ampacity of a cord-and-plug connected air-conditioning window unit shall not exceed 80 percent of the branch circuit where no other loads are served.

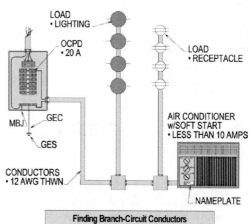

Finding Branch-Circuit Conductors

Step 1: Finding A
440.62 and **Table 210.24(1)**
12 AWG requires 20 A

Step 2: Calculating A
440.62(C) and **210.23(A)**
20 A x 50% = 10 A

Solution: The maximum conductor ampacity permitted is 10 amps.

BRANCH-CIRCUIT REQUIREMENTS
NEC 440.62(C)

Figure 24-24(b). If other loads are served by the branch circuit, the cord-and-plug connected air-conditioner unit shall not exceed 50 percent of the branch circuit.

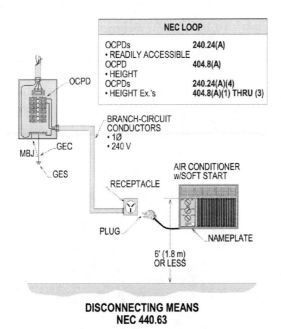

NEC LOOP	
OCPDs	240.24(A)
• READILY ACCESSIBLE	
OCPD	404.8(A)
• HEIGHT	
OCPDs	240.24(A)(4)
• HEIGHT Ex.'s	404.8(A)(1) THRU (3)

**DISCONNECTING MEANS
NEC 440.63**

Figure 24-25(a). A cord-and-plug shall be permitted to serve as the disconnecting means for a room air-conditioner if it operates at 250 volts or less and its controls are manually operated, within 6 ft (1.8 m) of the floor, and readily accessible to the user.

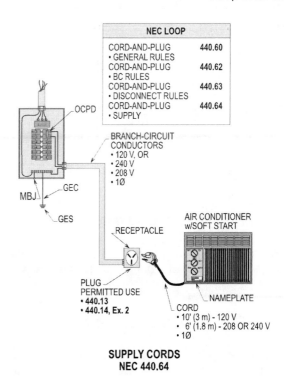

NEC LOOP	
CORD-AND-PLUG	440.60
• GENERAL RULES	
CORD-AND-PLUG	440.62
• BC RULES	
CORD-AND-PLUG	440.63
• DISCONNECT RULES	
CORD-AND-PLUG	440.64
• SUPPLY	

**SUPPLY CORDS
NEC 440.64**

Figure 24-26. Room air-conditioners installed with flexible cords shall have a length that is limited to 10 ft (3 m) for 120 volt circuits and 6 ft (1.8 m) for 208 or 240 volt circuits.

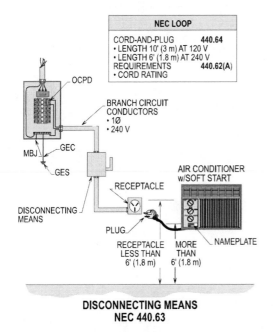

NEC LOOP	
CORD-AND-PLUG	440.64
• LENGTH 10' (3 m) AT 120 V	
• LENGTH 6' (1.8 m) AT 240 V	
REQUIREMENTS	440.62(A)
• CORD RATING	

**DISCONNECTING MEANS
NEC 440.63**

Figure 24-25(b). A cord-and-plug shall be permitted to serve as the disconnecting means even if the room air conditioner's manual controls are located above 6 ft (1.8 m) from finished grade.

TROUBLESHOOTING A COMPRESSOR MOTOR

To check the motor-compressor safely, turn off the disconnect switch and disconnect all wiring from the motor terminals in the terminal box. The terminal at the right when facing the compressor motor, will be the starting terminal.

Note, the center terminal is the common and the left terminal is the running winding terminal.

Using an ohmmeter, troubleshoot the windings for grounds as follows.

TESTING RUNNING WINDINGS

The first step in testing running windings is to disconnect all wires from the motor terminals. To check for resistance in the running winding, touch the ohmmeter leads to the "common" and "running" terminals and take a measurement. **(See Figure 24-27)**

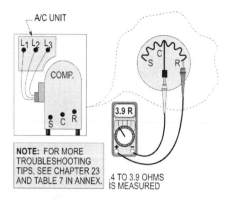

TESTING RUNNING WINDINGS

Figure 24-27. The running winding is usually not defective if a resistance reading of a 0.4 to 3.9 ohms is measured.

TESTING STARTING WINDINGS

The second step is to test the resistance in the starting winding; this test can be performed by touching the ohmmeter leads to the "common" and "starting" terminals. The resistance reading in the running winding from R to C will measure the lowest, and the starting winding from S to C will be higher. Between R and S, the reading is the total of the two, from 2.4 to 22.9 ohms. (0.4 R + 2 R = 2.4 R - 3.9 R + 19 = 22.9 R) **(See Figure 24-28)**

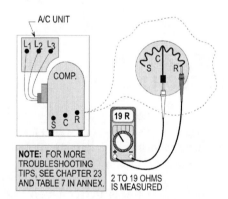

TESTING STARTING WINDINGS

Figure 24-28. The starting winding is usually not defective if a resistance reading of 2 to 19 ohms is measured.

TESTING FOR GROUNDS

The ohmmeter method can be used for testing grounds. One test lead is touched to the motor frame and the other is touched to each motor terminal. If the resistance measured is below one million ohms, a ground from a winding is assumed. **(See Figure 24-29)**

Note, for more troubleshooting tips, see the illustrations in Chapter 23 and **Table 7** of **Annex A**.

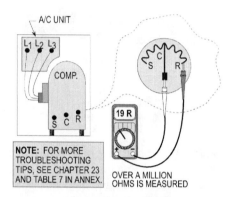

TESTING FOR GROUNDS

Figure 24-29. If a reading of over one million ohms-to-ground is measured, there is usually no ground present.

Note, in accordance with **210.8(B), Ex. 2** no GFCI for AC/ units is required.

Chapter 24. Compressor Motors

Section   Answer

1. The full-load current rating of the nameplate or the nameplate branch-circuit selection current of the compressor, whichever is greater, shall be sized at _____ percent to size the disconnecting means.
   (a) 100   (b) 115
   (c) 125   (d) 135

2. The disconnecting means for air-conditioning or refrigeration equipment shall be located within sight and within _____ ft, and shall be readily accessible to the user.
   (a) 10   (b) 20
   (c) 25   (d) 50

3. The overcurrent protection device for hermetically sealed compressors shall be selected at _____ percent (minimum) of the compressor's FLA rating.
   (a) 175 [See **Ex. 1** to **440.22(A)**]   (b) 200
   (c) 225   (d) 250

4. The overcurrent protection device for hermetically sealed compressors shall be selected at _____ percent (maximum) of the compressor's FLA rating.
   (a) 175   (b) 200
   (c) 225   (d) 250

5. The rating of the overcurrent protection device shall be determined by using the rating on the nameplate of the cord-and-plug connected equipment serving a single-phase, _____ volt or less hermetically sealed motor.
   (a) 120   (b) 250
   (c) 277   (d) 480

6. Two or more compressors plus the other motor loads can be connected to a feeder. The largest compressor is calculated at 125 percent of its FLC, and the remaining compressor loads are added to this total at _____ percent of their FLA ratings.
   (a) 100   (b) 125
   (c) 150   (d) 175

7. The overload relay for a motor-compressor shall trip at not more than _____ percent of the full-load current rating.
   (a) 110   (b) 115
   (c) 125   (d) 140

8. Overload protection shall be provided for direct- or fixed-wired motor-compressors and equipment that is connected to _____, 120 volt, single-phase branch-circuits.
   (a) 15 or 20   (b) 20 or 30
   (c) 30 or 40   (d) 40 or 50

9. Room air conditioners shall be grounded to an equipment grounding conductor when operating over _____ volts-to-ground.
   (a) 100   (b) 120
   (c) 150   (d) none of the above

10. The full-load current rating of a room air conditioner shall be marked on the nameplate and shall not operate at more than _____ amps on 250 volts.
    (a) 30   (b) 40
    (c) 50   (d) 100

11. A cord-and-plug shall be permitted to serve as the disconnecting means for the room air conditioner if it operates at _____ volts or less.
    (a) 50   (b) 120
    (c) 150   (d) 250

12. A cord-and-plug shall be permitted to serve as the disconnecting means for the room air conditioner if the controls are within _____ ft of the floor.
    (a) 6   (b) 8
    (c) 10   (d) 12

13. Room air conditioners installed with flexible cords shall be a length that is limited to _____ ft for 120 volt circuits.
    (a) 6   (b) 10
    (c) 12   (d) 15

14. Room air conditioners installed with flexible cords shall be a length that is limited to _____ ft for 208 or 240 volt circuits.
    (a) 6   (b) 10
    (c) 12   (d) 15

15. The ampacity of a cord-and-plug connected air-conditioning window unit shall not exceed _____ percent of the branch circuit where no other loads are served.
    (a) 25   (b) 50
    (c) 80   (d) 100

16. A disconnect means shall be placed within _____ ft. of the A/C unit.
    (a) 50   (b) 75
    (c) 100   (d) none of the above

17. The starting winding of a compressor is usually not defective if a resistance of _____ to _____ ohms is measured.
    (a) 2 to 19   (b) 3 to 25
    (c) 4 to 21   (d) none of the above

18. Cord and plug connected A/C units (window type) shall not be supplied with _____-phase circuits.
    (a) single   (b) two
    (c) three   (d) none of the above

19. When time-delay fuses are used to provide overload protection, they shall exceed _____% of the motor compressor.
    (a) 125   (b) 150
    (c) all of the above   (d) none of the above

20. When testing a motor compressor for a ground, if over _____ ohms is read, there is usually no grounded condition.
    (a) 25,000   (b) 50,000
    (c) 75,000   (d) 1,000,000

21. The running winding of a motor compressor is usually not defective if a   _____   _____
     resistance reading of _____ to _____ ohms is measured.
       (a) 0.4 to 3.0   (b) 0.5 to 2.1
       (c) all of the above   (d) none of the above

22. What size nonautomatic circuit breaker is required for an air-conditioning unit   _____   _____
     with a compressor rated at 29 amps and the condenser fan rated at 2.5 amps?

23. What size nonfused disconnect is required for an air-conditioning unit with a   _____   _____
     compressor rated at 29 amps and the condenser fan rated at 2.5 amps?

24. What size horsepower rated disconnect is required for an air-conditioning with   _____   _____
     a compressor rated at 29 amps and the condenser fan rated at 2.5 amps with
     a 200 amp locked-rotor current rating? **Note,** the supply voltage is 480 volt,
     three-phase.

25. What size horsepower rated disconnect is required for the following loads on   _____   _____
     a three-phase, 230 volt system:
      • Air-conditioning unit with a compressor rated at 29 amps with a 200
        amp locked-rotor current rating
      • Air-conditioning unit with a compressor rated at 24 amps with a 150
        amp locked-rotor current rating
      • Air-conditioning unit with a compressor rated at 20 amps with a 140
        amp locked-rotor current rating

26. What size circuit breaker (nonautomatic) is required to disconnect a hermetic   _____   _____
     sealed motor for an air-conditioning unit rated at 29 amps? (Supply voltage is
     208 volt, three-phase.)

27. What size horsepower rated disconnecting means is required to disconnect   _____   _____
     the following motor loads on a three-phase, 230 volt system:
      • Motor rated at 38 amps with a 212 amp locked-rotor current rating
      • Air-conditioning unit with a compressor rated at 28 amps with a 160
        amp locked-rotor current rating
      • Air-conditioning unit with a compressor rated at 24 amps with a 160
        amp locked-rotor current rating

28. What is the minimum size overcurrent protection device, per **440.22(A)**,   _____   _____
     required for an individual air-conditioning unit with a compressor rated at 20
     amps and the condenser rated at 2.5 amps? [**See Ex. 1 to 440.22(A)**]

29. What is the maximum size overcurrent protection device, per **440.22(A)**,   _____   _____
     required for an individual air-conditioning unit with a compressor rated at 20
     amps and the condenser rated at 2.5 amps. [**See Ex. 2 to 440.22(A)**]

30. What is the minimum size overcurrent protection device, per **440.22(B)(1)**,   _____   _____
     required for a feeder with the following loads on a 230 volt, three-phase system:
      • Air-conditioning unit with a compressor rated at 29 amps and the con-
        denser fan rated at 2.5 amps
      • Air-conditioning unit with a compressor rated at 26 amps and the con-
        denser fan rated at 2.5 amps
      • Air-conditioning unit with a compressor rated at 22 amps and the con-
        denser fan rated at 2.5 amps

31. What is the maximum size overcurrent protection device, per **440.22(B)(1)**, required for a feeder with the following loads on a 230 volt, three-phase system:
   - Air-conditioning unit with a compressor rated at 29 amps and the condenser rated at 2.5 amps
   - Air-conditioning unit with a compressor rated at 26 amps and the condenser rated at 2.5 amps
   - Air-conditioning unit with a compressor rated at 22 amps and the condenser rated at 2.5 amps

32. What size overcurrent protection device is required for a feeder with the following loads on a 230 volt, three-phase system:
   - Air-conditioning unit with a compressor rated at 26 amps and the condenser fan rated at 2.5 amps
   - Air-conditioning unit with a compressor rated at 24 amps and the condenser fan rated at 2.5 amps
   - 10 HP, 230 volt, three-phase, Design Letter B motor

33. What size THHN copper conductors are required to supply an air-conditioning unit with a compressor rated at 20 amps and the condenser fan rated at 2.5 amps?

34. What size THHN copper conductors are required to supply an individual air-conditioning unit with a branch-circuit selection current of 30 amps?

35. What size THWN copper conductors are required for a feeder with the following loads on a 208 volt, three-phase system:
   - Air-conditioning unit with a compressor rated at 30 amps and the condenser fan rated at 3 amps
   - Air-conditioning unit with a compressor rated at 28 amps and the condenser fan rated at 2.5 amps
   - Air-conditioning unit with a compressor rated at 24 amps and the condenser fan rated at 2.5 amps

36. What size THWN copper conductors are required for a feeder with the following loads on a 208 volt, three-phase system:
   - Air-conditioning unit with a compressor rated at 30 amps and the condenser fan rated at 3 amps
   - Air-conditioning unit with a compressor rated at 28 amps and the condenser fan rated at 2.5 amps
   - Other loads of 80 amps (continuous)

37. What size controller is required for an individual air-conditioning unit with a compressor rated at 20 amps (BSCS) and the condenser fan rated at 2.5 amps on a 230 volt, single-phase system?

38. What size overload relay and fuses are required for an air-conditioning unit with a compressor rated at 20 amps on a 240 volt, three-phase system?

39. What is the maximum value for a THWN copper conductor ampacity for a 10 AWG branch-circuit conductor supplying an air-conditioning window unit?

40. What is the maximum value for a THWN copper conductor ampacity for a 10 AWG branch-circuit conductor supplying an air-conditioning window unit with other loads such as lighting and receptacle loads?

Annex

Troubleshooting Tables

Qualified personnel with proper testing equipment and tools may use the tables in this annex for troubleshooting problems related to motors, controls, adjustable speed drives, and eddy-current drives. However, these instructions do not cover all details or variations in equipment, nor do they provide for every possible condition to be met in actual practice.

The following tables in this annex can be used for troubleshooting tips:

TROUBLESHOOTING INDUCTION MOTORS

What To Do

Symptoms	AC Single-Phase Motors			Shaded Poles	AC Three Phase Motors	Motors With Brushes
	Split Phase	Capacitor Start	Capacitor Start & Run			
Fails to start and run	A, B, F, C	A, B, F, H, C	A, B, H, I, Q	A, B, I, P, Q	A, B, E	A, B, L, M
Motor does not always start, even without a load. Runs forward or in reverse when started by manual means	F, C	F, H, C	H, E		E	
Starts and runs but heats very rapidly	G, D	G, D	H, D	D	D	D
Starts and runs but overheats	D	D	H, D	D	D	D
Sparking and arcing at brushes						J, K, L, M, N
Severely high speed with sparking at the brushes						O
Increase in amps and motor overheats	D, P, Q	D, P, Q	D, P, Q	D, P, Q	D, P, Q	L, P, Q
Motor blows OCPD and continues to operate when switch is off	D, R	D, R	D, R	D, R	D, R	D, R
Problems with vibration						J, K, L, M, N, S

Possible Causes

A — Open circuit
B — Circuit open in motor winding (See **Figure 15-4** in Chapter 15)
C — Circuit open in starting winding
D — Winding is short-circuited or grounded
E — More than one winding is open
F — Open contacts in centrifugal switch
G — Centrifugal starting switch is not operating properly
H — Capacitor is defective
I — Motor is overloaded
J — Problems between mica and commutator

K — Commutator is dirty
L — Brushes are worn
M — Armature winding is shorted or open
N — Brushes not aligned and set
O — Shunt winding is open
P — Problems with bearings
Q — Rotor problems
R — Winding is grounded
S — Armature winding is shorted

TABLE 1

TROUBLESHOOTING REPULSION AND UNIVERSAL MOTORS

Symptoms	What To Do
• Failure to start	A, B, C, D, E, F, G, H, I J, K, L
• Excessive noise	M, N, O, P, Q
• Bearings overheating	P, Q, R, S, T, U, V, X, Y, Z, AA, BB
• Excessive brush wear	CC, DD, EE, FF, GG, HH
• Overheating of motor	II, JJ
• Commutator burned out	KK, LL, MM, NN, OO
• Governor problems	PP, QQ, RR, SS, TT, UU, VV, XX

Possible Causes

A	Blown fuse	AA	Excessive end thrust
B	Circuit breaker open	BB	Excessive side pull
C	Low voltage	CC	Dirty commutator
D	No voltage	DD	Improper contact with commutator
E	Open circuit	EE	Excessive load
F	Improper line connections	FF	Governor not acting promptly
G	Excessive load	GG	High mica
H	Brushes are worn or sticking	HH	Rough commutator
I	Brushes are incorrectly set	II	Obstruction of ventilation system
K	Excessive end play	JJ	Overloading
L	Bearings are frozen	KK	Worn bearings
M	Unbalance conditions	LL	Moisture
N	Bent shaft or loose parts	MM	Acids or alkalies
O	Faulty alignment or worn bearings	NN	Harmful dust accumulation
P	Dirt in air gap	OO	Overloading
Q	Uneven air gap	PP	Governor mechanism sticking
R	Motor needs oil	QQ	Worn or sticking brushes
S	Dirty oil	RR	Low frequency in supply circuit
T	Oil not reaching shaft	SS	Low voltage
U	Excessive grease	TT	Incorrect connections or incorrect brush settings
V	Excessive belt tension		
X	Rough bearing surface	UU	Excessive load
Y	Bent shaft	VV	Incorrect spring tension
Z	Misalignment of shaft and bearing		

TABLE 2

TROUBLESHOOTING WOUND-ROTOR MOTORS

Symptoms	What To Do
• Failure to start	A, B, C, D, E,
• Motor will not come up to speed	F, G, H, I, J, K, L, M, BB, CC
• Excessive noise	N, O, P, Q, R, S, T,
• Overheating of bearings	U, V, W, X, Y, Z, AA
• Overheating of motor	DD, EE
• Rotor or stator burned out	FF, GG, HH, II

Possible Causes

A — Blown OCPD
B — Low or no AC field supply
C — Bearings stuck or binding load
D — Open or shorted field
E — Open or shorted rotor
F — Broken slip rings
G — Open control device
H — Low AC supply voltage
I — Binding load
K — Insufficient oil or grease
L — Low frequency in supply circuit
M — Dirt on slip rings
N — Vibration
O — Bent shaft
P — Loose parts
Q — Faulty alignment
R — Worn bearings

S — Dirt in air gap
T — Uneven air gap
U — Motor needs oil
V — Dirty oil
W — Oil not reaching shaft
X — Excessive grease
Y — Rough bearing surface
Z — Bent shaft
AA — Misalignment of shaft and bearing
BB — Broken or chipped brushes
CC — Improper brush contact
DD — Obstruction of ventilating system
EE — Overloading
FF — Worn bearings
GG — Moisture
HH — Dust accumulation

TABLE 3

| TROUBLESHOOTING SYNCHRONOUS MOTORS ||
Symptoms	What To Do
• Motor will not start and run	A, B, C, D, E, F, G, H, I, J, K, L,
• Motor will not accelerate to speed	J, K, L, N
• Motor fails to pull into step	M, L, N
• Motor pulls out of step or trips OCPD	O, P, Q, R, S, T, U, V
• Overheating	W, X, Y

Possible Causes

A — Faulty connections
B — Open circuit on one circuit
C — Short circuit on one phase
D — Voltage falls too low
E — Friction too high
F — Field excited
G — Too great of load
H — Automatic field relay not working
I — Wrong direction of rotation
K — Low voltage
L — Field excited
M — No field excitation
N — Inertia of load excessive

O — Exciter voltage low
P — Open circuit in field and exciter circuit
Q — Short-circuit in field
R — Reversed field
S — Load fluctuates widely
T — Excessive torque peak
U — Power fails
V — Line voltage too low
W — Overload condition
X — Over or under excitation
Y — No field excitation

TABLE 4

TROUBLESHOOTING EDDY-CURRENT DRIVES

Symptoms	What To Do
• Motor does not start	A, B, C, D, E, F
• Motor runs but has no output	S, T, U, V, W, X
• Drive stops during operation	G, H, I, J ,K, L
• Unit overheats	Y, Z, AA, BB, CC
• Erratic operation	M, N, O, P, Q, R
• Runs at full speed only	DD, EE, FF
• Magnetic drive at stand-still or lower speed than expected with the speed potentiometer set at a higher speed	GG, HH, II
• Magnetic drive set at 100% speed with no control	JJ, KK
• Magnetic drive has intermitten speed up or slow down	LL, MM, NN

Possible Causes

A — Loss of AC power
B — Defective switch or breaker
C — Blown fuse
D — Motor starter not closing
E — Overload or safety interlock open
F — Loose or incorrect wiring or defective motor
G — Controller malfunction, check controller
H — Drive is overloaded
I — Safety interlock
K — Loose connection
L — Open or defective clutch coil, check brushes first
M — Controller malfunction
N — Velocity feedback malfunction (Tach. Gen. or Mag. Pickup malfunction)
O — Electric noise or radio frequency interference
P — Loose wiring connection
Q — Contaminated slip rings
R — Sticking or worn out brushes
S — Check controller for input voltage
T — Loose or incorrect wiring
U — Open safety interlock
V — Brushes not making contact
W — Brake not releasing
X — Open or defective clutch coil
Y — Overload, check motor current
Z — Operating below minimum speed
AA — Air passages blocked on magnetic drive unit
BB — Recirculating cooling air or ambient temperature too high

CC — Brake not releasing or machine binding
DD — Controller malfunction, check controller
EE — Loss of velocity feedback signal (Tach. Gen. or Mag. Pickup)
FF — Mechanical lock up of clutch drum and rotor
GG — Possible stall conditions or overload on the drive unit. Turn off control. Check driven load for restriction or fault condition.
HH — Possible open circuit in the drive unit field circuit. Check brushes and slip rings for continuity.
II — Check output voltage to the drive unit. If no or incorrect voltage check the silicon controller rectifiers (SCRs), if the gate pulse board is not sending pulse to the SCRs, replace SCRs and pulse board as needed.
JJ — If voltage to drive unit is correct, then check "Feedback" voltage from the tachometer generator (magnetic pickup).
KK — Check pulse board and SCRs.
LL — Check brushes and collector rings on drive unit
MM — Check for loose or broken wires on the tachometer generator (or magnetic pickup).
NN — Check for proper adjustment of the tach generator or magnetic pickup.

TABLE 5

TROUBLESHOOTING ADJUSTABLE SPEED DRIVES

Symptoms	What To Do
• Overcurrent	A, B, C, D
• Tachometer loss	E, F, G, H, I, J, K, L, M, N
• Overspeed	O, P, Q, R, S
• Field current loss	T, U, V, W, X
• Sustained overload	Y, Z, AA
• Blower motor starter open	BB, CC, DD
• Open armature	EE, FF, GG
• Motor thermostat trip	HH, II, JJ, KK, LL, MM, NN, OO
• Controller thermostat trip	PP, QQ, RR, SS
• AC line synchronization fault	TT, UU, VV, WW, XX

Possible Causes

A — Incorrect armature current feedback scaling

B — One or more thyristors not operating

C — Improper current minor loop tuning

D — Motor armature winding damaged

E — Tach coupling failure

F — Disconnected, loosely connected, or damaged tach wires

G — Pulse tach supply voltage low

H — Incorrect tach polarity

I — Incorrect analog tach scaling

K — Motor armature winding not connected or open circuit

L — Blown inverting fault

M — Inverting fault breaker tripped

N — Tachometer failure

O — Incorrect tach scaling

P — Blown field supply

Q — Improper speed loop tuning

R — Pulse tach quadrature set to ON for a non-regenerative drive

S — Incorrect pulse tach wiring

T — Motor field wiring

U — Blown field supply fuse(s)

V — Blown AC line fuse(s)

W — Field supply failure

X — Disconnected, loosely connected, or damaged wiring harness

Y — Incorrect armature current feedback scaling

Z — Blown field supply fuse(s)

AA — Mechanical binding preventing the motor shaft from rotating freely

BB — Blown blower motor starter fuse(s)

CC — Disconnected, loosely connected, or damaged blower motor starter wiring

DD — Blower motor overload

EE — Motor armature winding not connected or open circuit

FF — Blown inverting fault (DC) fuse

GG — Inverting fault breaker tripped

HH — Damaged or disconnected motor thermostat wiring

II — Inadequate ventilation

JJ — Blower motor failure

KK — Incorrect blower rotation

LL — Blocked ventilation slots

MM — Clogged filters

NN — Excessive armature

OO — One or more thyristors not operating

PP — Inadequate heat sink ventilation

QQ — Inadequate cabinet ventilation

RR — Heat sink fan failure

SS — Damaged or disconnected controller thermostat wiring

TT — Blown AC line fuse(s)

UU — AC line frequency not within required range of 48 - 62 Hz

VV — Excessive AC line noise or distortion

WW — Unstable AC frequency

XX — Disconnected, loosely connected, or damaged J6 ribbon cable

TABLE 6

TROUBLESHOOTING COMPRESSOR MOTORS	
Symptoms	**What To Do**
• Compressor hums and fails to start	A, B, C, D, E, F
• Compressor hums and cycles on overload protector, but fails to start	G, H, I, J
• Starting winding remains in circuit after the compressor starts	G, K, L, M, N
• Compressor starts but cycles on overload	F, G, M, O, P
Possible Causes	

A — Disconnect switch is open	J — Compressor motor is defective
B — Blown fuse or CB is open	K — Starting relay is defective
C — Defective wiring	L — Starting capacitor is weak
D — Overload protector is tripped	M — Running capacitor is defective
E — Control contacts are open	N — Compressor motor is defective
F — Overload protector is defective	O — Compressor motor partially grounded
G — Low voltage	P — Unbalanced line voltage (3Ø supply)
H — Starting capacitor is defective	
I — Starting relay contacts are not closing	

TABLE 7

TROUBLESHOOTING GENERATORS	
Symptoms	**What To Do**
• Commutator	A
• Armature	B, C, G
• Brushes	D, E, F
• Overloaded	R
• Short circuit	S
• Broken circuit	T
• Open circuit	G, H, I, J, K, L
• Excessive current — in shunt winding — in series winding	 U, V
Possible Causes	

A — Check for worn-in grooves or ridges out of round
B — Check for short-circuit coils
C — Check for broken coils
D — Check setting at neutral points
E — Check and verify if they are in line
F — Check and verify if they are making good contact
G — Check for broken wires
H — Check for open switch
I — Check for safety fuses melted or broken
J — Check for faulty connections
K — Check for external circuit opening
L — Check for brushes not in contact
M — Check for excessive loading

N — Check for a ground and leak from short-circuit on line
O — Check for a dead short circuit on line
P — Check for excessive current
Q — Check for eddy currents
R — Too many amps taken from machine
S — Usually caused by dirt and such at commutator bars
T — Usually caused by a loose or broken band or wire, and such
U — Reduce speed and decrease voltage at terminals
V — By shunting, decrease current through field (remove some of field winding)

TABLE 8

TROUBLESHOOTING CONTACTORS AND RELAYS

Symptoms	What To Do
• Failure to energize	A, B, C, D, E, F, G, H, I, J,
• Failure to deenergize	K, O, P, Q
• Equipment fails to operate with contactor closed	L, M, N
• Pitted or discolored contacts	R, S, T
• Chatter or humming contactor	U, Z
• Coil has excessive temperature	V, W, X, Y

Possible Causes

A — Blown fuse, open line switch, or break in wiring

B — Line voltage is below normal

C — Overload relay is open or set too low

D — Control lever or start button is in OFF position

E — Pull-in circuit open, shorted, or grounded

F — Contacts in protective or controlling circuit open or a pigtail connection is broken

G — Operating coil open or grounded circuit

H — Loose or disconnected coil wire

I — Test coil and replace if necessary

J — Normally closed contacts are welded together

K — Normally opened contacts are welded together

L — One contact is not closing

M — Contacts are burned

N — Contact pigtail connection is broken

O — Contacts in controlling or protective tripping circuits are closed, shorted, or shunted

P — Tripping devices are defective, such as undervoltage relay plunger stuck or out of adjustment, defective stop button, or defective time-relay

Q — Contact pressure spring or armature spring is too weak or improperly adjusted

R — Contacts are overheated from overload

S — Contacts are not fitted properly

T — Wiping action of contacts on closing is insufficient

U — Free movement of armature is hindered due to deformed parts, dirt, or lint

V — Excessive current or voltage is measured

W — Short circuit is found in coil

X — Excessive eddy current and hysteresis is measured

Y — High room temperature is detected

Z — Voltage drop is measured at coil when closing

TABLE 9

TROUBLESHOOTING DRY TYPE TRANSFORMERS

Symptoms	What To Do
• Overheating	A, B, C, D, E
• Cable overheating	P
• Insulation is burned	R, S, T
• Failure of insulation	J, K, L, M, N
• Secondary voltage is too high	G
• CB is open or fuse is blown	O
• Excessive vibration and noise	Q

Possible Causes

A — Continuous overload problems

B — Wrong external connections are found

C — Poor ventilation is detected

D — High surrounding air temperatures are present

E — Clogged air ducts or inadequate ventilation problems

F — Loose connections to transformer terminal are found

G — Input voltage high or dirt accumulations on primary terminal leads are found

H — Terminal boards are not on correct tap position

I — Coils are short-circuited

J — Continuous overloads are measured

K — Dirt accumulations are found on coils

L — Mechanical damage is found

M — Lightning surges are detected

N — High core temperature due to high input voltage or low frequency is measured

O — Short circuits, ground-faults, or overloads are detected

P — Improperly bolted connections are found

Q — Core clamps are loose or other loose hardware is found on enclosure

R — Lightning surge is found

S — Switching or line disturbance is detected

T — Broken bushings are found

TABLE 10

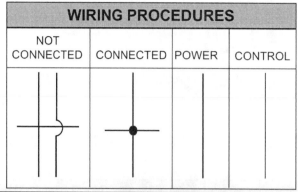

WIRING PROCEDURES			
NOT CONNECTED	CONNECTED	POWER	CONTROL

CONTACT IDENTIFICATION

SPST – Single Pole Single Throw		SPST – Single Pole Single Throw		SPST – Single Pole Double Throw	
Single Break	Double Break	Single Break	Double Break	Single Break	Double Break
NO	NO	NC	NC	NC	NC

DPST – Double Pole Single Throw				DPDT – Double Pole Double Throw	
Single Break	Double Break	Single Break	Double Break	Single Break	Double Break
NO	NO	NC	NC	NC	NC

IDENTIFICATION OF POWER CONDUCTORS & TERMINALS

Phases	Single-phase	Single-phase	Three-Phase
Line Markings	L_1	L_1, L_2	L_1, L_2, L_3
Terminal Markings	T_1	T_1, T_2	T_1, T_2, T_3

WIRING METHODS

AC	Armored Cable	NMC	Nonmetallic-Sheathed Cable
BX	Trade Name for AC	NPLFA	Nonpower-Limited Fire Alarm Circuit
EMT	Electrical Metallic Tubing	OFNP	Nonconductive Optical Fiber Plenum Cable
ENT	Electrical Nonmetallic Tubing		
FMC	Flexible Metal Conduit	PLFA	Power-Limited Fire Alarm Circuit
ITC	Instrument Tray Cable	PLTC	Power-Limited Tray Cable
IMC	Intermediate Metal Conduit	PVC	Plastic Conduit
LTFMC	Liquidtight Flexible Metal Conduit	RMC	Rigid Metallic Conduit
LTFNC	Liquidtight Flexible Non-Metallic Conduit	RNMC	Rigid Nonmetallic Conduit
		SE	Service-Entrance Cable
MC	Metal-Clad Cable	SNM	Shielded Nonmetallic Sheathed Cable
MI	Mineral Insulated Metal-Sheathed Cable	TC	Tray Cable
		USE	Underground Service-Entrance Cable
NM	Nonmetallic-Sheathed Cable		

TABLE 11

DETERMINING FLC (in amps) OF TRANSFORMERS AND MOTORS

AC MOTORS			
SINGLE-PHASE			
FULL LOAD AMPERES			
HP	115 V	208 V	230 V	MIN. TRANSFORMER kVA
1/6	4.4	2.4	2.2	.53
1/4	5.8	3.2	2.9	.70
1/3	7.2	4.0	3.6	.87
1/2	9.8	5.4	4.9	1.18
3/4	13.8	7.6	6.9	1.66
1	16	8.8	8	1.92
1 1/2	20	11	10	2.4
2	24	13.2	12	2.88
3	34	18.7	17	4.1
5	56	30.8	28	6.72
7 1/2	80	44	40	9.6
10	100	55	50	12

THREE-PHASE				
FULL LOAD AMPERES				
HP	208 V	230 V	460 V	575 V	MIN. TRANSFORMER kVA
1/2	2.4	2.2	1.1	0.9	0.9
3/4	3.5	3.2	1.6	1.3	1.2
1	4.6	4.2	2.1	1.7	1.5
1 1/2	6.6	6	3	2.4	2.1
2	7.5	6.8	3.4	2.7	2.7
3	10.6	9.6	4.8	3.9	3.8
5	16.7	15.2	7.6	6.1	6.3
7 1/2	24.2	22	11	9	9.2
10	30.8	28	14	11	11.2
15	46.2	42	21	17	16.6
20	59.4	54	27	22	21.6
25	74.8	68	34	27	26.6
30	88	80	40	32	32.4
40	114	104	52	41	43.2
50	143	130	65	52	52
60	169	154	77	62	64
75	211	192	96	77	80
100	273	248	124	99	103
125	343	312	156	125	130
150	396	360	180	144	150
200	528	480	240	192	200
250	—	—	302	242	
300	—	—	361	289	
350	—	—	414	336	
400	—	—	477	382	
450	—	—	515	412	
500	—	—	590	472	

TRANSFORMERS				
SINGLE-PHASE				
	AMPERES			
kVA RATING	120 V	240 V	480 V	600 V
1	8.33	4.17	2.08	1.67
1 1/2	12..5	6.25	3.13	2.50
2	16.7	8.33	4.17	3.33
3	25.0	12.5	6.25	5.00
5	41.7	20.8	10.4	8.33
7 1/2	62.5	31.3	15.6	12.5
10	83.3	41.7	20.8	16.7
15	125	62.5	31.3	25.0
20	167	83.3	41.7	33.3
25	208	104	52.1	41.7
30	250	125	62.5	50
37 1/2	313	156	78.0	62.5
50	417	208	104	83.3
75	625	313	156	125
100	833	417	208	167
150	1,250	625	313	250
167	1,392	696	348	278
200	1,667	833	417	333
250	2,083	1,042	521	417
333	2,775	1,388	694	555
500	4,167	2,083	1,042	833

THREE-PHASE				
	AMPERES			
kVA RATING	120 V	240 V	480 V	600 V
3	8.3	7.2	3.6	2.9
6	16.6	14.4	7.2	5.8
9	25.0	21.6	10.8	8.7
15	41.6	36	18	14.4
20	55.6	48.2	24.1	19.3
25	69.5	60.2	30.1	24.1
30	83.0	72	36	28.8
37 1/2	104	90.3	45.2	36.1
45	125	108	54	43
50	139	120	60.2	48.2
60	167	145	72.3	57.8
75	208	180	90	72
100	278	241	120	96.3
112.5	312	270	135	108
150	415	360	180	144
200	554	480	240	192
225	625	540	270	216
300	830	720	360	288
400	1,110	960	480	384
500	1,380	1,200	600	480
750	2,080	1,800	900	720
1,000	2,780	2,400	1,200	960
1,500	4,150	3,600	1,800	1,440
2,000	5,540	4,800	2,400	1,920

TABLE 12 A

Rated Horsepower	Maximum Locked-Rotor Current in Amperes, Single Phase		
	115 Volts	208 Volts	230 Volts
1/2	58.8	32.5	29.4
3/4	82.8	45.8	41.4
1	96	53	48
1-1/2	120	66	60
2	144	80	72
3	204	113	102
5	336	186	168
7-1/2	480	265	240
10	1000	332	300

Rated Horsepower	Maximum Motor Locked-Rotor Current in Amperes, Two- and Three-Phase, Design B, C, and D*					
	115 Volts	200 Volts	208 Volts	230 Volts	460 Volts	575 Volts
	B, C, D	B, C, D	B, C, D	B, C, D	B, C, D	B, C, D
1/2	40	23	22.1	20	10	8
3/4	50	28.8	27.6	25	12.5	10
1	60	34.5	33	30	15	12
1-1/2	80	46	44	40	20	16
2	100	57.5	55	50	25	20
3	-----	73.6	71	64	32	25.6
5	-----	105.8	102	92	46	36.8
7-1/2	-----	146	140	127	63.5	50.8
10	-----	186.3	179	162	81	64.8
15	-----	267	257	232	116	93
20	-----	334	321	290	145	116
25	-----	420	404	365	183	146
30	-----	500	481	435	218	174
40	-----	667	641	580	290	232
50	-----	834	802	725	363	290
60	-----	1001	962	870	435	348
75	-----	1248	1200	1085	543	434
100	-----	1668	1603	1450	725	580
125	-----	2087	2007	1815	908	726
150	-----	2496	2400	2170	1085	868
200	-----	3335	3207	2900	1450	1160
250	-----	-----	-----	-----	1825	1460
300	-----	-----	-----	-----	2200	1760
350	-----	-----	-----	-----	2550	2040
400	-----	-----	-----	-----	2900	2320
450	-----	-----	-----	-----	3250	2600
500	-----	-----	-----	-----	3625	2900

TABLE 12 B

The following table represents heater selection tables applicable to the overload relays used in Westinghouse Control Centers.

DETERMINING THE SIZE OVERLOADS		
Compensated Ambient (Black reset rod)	Compensated Ambient (Black reset rod)	Heater Code Marking
.51 – .55	.48 – .51	FH10
.56 – .62	.52 – .57	FH11
.63 – .68	.58 – .63	FH12
.69 – .75	.64 – .70	FH13
.76 – .83	.71 – .77	FH14
.84 – .91	.78 – .85	FH15
.92 – 1.00	.86 – .93	FH16
1.01 – 1.11	.94 – 1.03	FH17
1.12 – 1.22	1.04 – 1.13	FH18
1.23 – 1.34	1.14 – 1.25	FH19
1.35 – 1.47	1.26 – 1.37	FH20
1.48 – 1.62	1.38 – 1.51	FH21
1.63 – 1.78	1.52 – 1.65	FH22
1.79 – 1.95	1.66 – 1.81	FH23
1.96 – 2.15	1.82 – 1.99	FH24
2.16 – 2.35	2.00 – 2.19	FH25
2.36 – 2.58	2.20 – 2.39	FH26
2.59 – 2.83	2.40 – 2.63	FH27
2.84 – 3.11	2.64 – 2.89	FH28
3.12 – 3.42	2.90 – 3.17	FH29
3.43 – 3.73	3.18 – 3.47	FH30
3.74 – 4.07	3.48 – 3.79	FH31
4.08 – 4.39	3.80 – 4.11	FH32
4.40 – 4.87	4.12 – 4.55	FH33
4.88 – 5.3	4.56 – 5.0	FH34
5.4 – 5.9	5.1 – 5.5	FH35
6.0 – 6.4	5.6 – 5.9	FH36
6.5 – 7.1	6.0 – 6.6	FH37
7.2 – 7.8	6.7 – 7.2	FH38
7.9 – 8.5	7.3 – 7.9	FH30
8.6 – 9.4	8.0 – 8.7	FH40
9.5 – 10.3	8.8 – 9.5	FH41
10.4 – 11.3	9.6 – 10.5	FH42
11.4 – 12.4	10.6 – 11.5	FH43
12.5 – 13.5	11.6 – 12.6	FH44
13.6 – 14.9	12.7 – 13.8	FH45
15.0 – 16.3	13.9 – 15.1	FH46
16.4 – 18.0	15.2 – 16.7	FH47
18.1 – 19.1	16.8 – 18.3	FH48
19.9 – 21.7	18.4 – 20.2	FH49
21.8 – 23.9	20.3 – 22.2	FH50
24.0 – 26.2	22.3 – 24.3	FH51
26.3 – 28.7	24.4 – 26.6	FH52

FOR STARTER SIZE 2

28.8 – 31.4	26.7 – 29.1	FH53
31.5 – 34.5	29.2 – 32.0	FH54
34.6 – 37.9	32.1 – 35.2	FH55
38.0 – 41.5	35.3 – 38.5	FH56
41.6 – 45.0	38.6 – 42.3	FH57

FOR STARTER SIZES 3 & 4

19.0 – 20.8	17.5 – 19.1	FH72
29.9 – 22.9	19.2 – 21.1	FH73
23.0 – 25.2	21.2 – 23.2	FH74
25.3 – 27.8	23.3 – 25.6	FH75
27.9 – 30.6	25.7 – 28.1	FH76
30.7 – 33.5	28.2 – 30.8	FH77
33.6 – 37.5	30.9 – 34.5	FH78
37.6 – 41.5	34.6 – 38.2	FH79
41.6 – 46.3	38.3 – 42.6	FH80
46.4 – 50.	42.7 – 46.	FH81
51. – 55.	47. – 51.	FH82
56. – 61.	52. – 56.	FH83
62. – 66.	57. – 61.	FH84
67. – 73.	62. – 67.	FH85
74. – 79.	78. – 73.	FH86
80. – 87.	74. – 80.	FH87
88. – 90.	81. – 87.	FH88

FOR STARTER SIZE 4

88. – 50.	88. – 95.	FH88
96. – 105.	96. – 105.	FH89
106. – 116.	106. – 116.	FH90
117. – 128.	117. – 128.	FH91

DETERMINING THE SIZE OVERLOADS		
Compensated Ambient (Black reset rod)	Compensated Ambient (Black reset rod)	Heater Code Marking

FOR STARTER SIZE GCA 5

118. – 129.	110. – 119.	FH24
130. – 141.	120. – 131.	FH25
142. – 155.	132. – 143.	FH26
156. – 170.	144. – 158.	FH27
171. – 187.	159. – 173.	FH28
188. – 205.	174. – 190.	FH29
206. – 224.	191. – 208.	FH30
225. – 244.	209. – 227.	FH31
245. – 263.	228. – 247.	FH32
264. – 270.	248. – 270.	FH33

FOR STARTER SIZE GCA 6

236. – 259.	219. – 239.	FH24
260. – 283.	240. – 263.	FH25
284. – 310.	264. – 287.	FH26
311. – 340.	288. – 316.	FH27
341. – 374.	317. – 347.	FH28
374. – 411.	348. – 381.	FH29
412. – 448.	381. – 417.	FH30
449. – 489.	418. – 455.	FH31
490. – 527.	456. – 494.	FH32
528. – 540.	495. – 540.	FH33

Note:

When selecting heating coils based on "other calculations," see **pages 19-1** and **19-2** in this book.

TABLE 13

CONNECTION OF STARTING ON A WYE AND RUNNING ON A DELTA

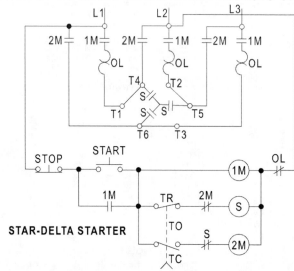

STAR-DELTA STARTER

CONNECTION OF PART-WINDING MOTORS

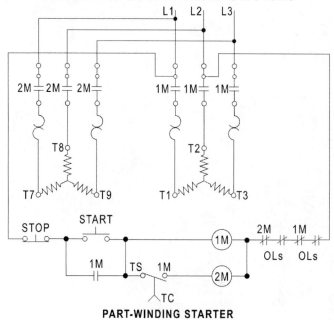

PART-WINDING STARTER

TABLE 14

TROUBLESHOOTING PROCEDURES FOR
DETERMINING WHY THE MOTOR WILL NOT START AND RUN

1. Check to see if there is proper voltage going to L_1 and L_2 on the input board.
2. Check to see if there is proper voltage going to L_1, L_2, and L_3 on the output board.
3. Check the output coming from the feedback board. If output is present, go to step 11.
4. Check the output coming from the input board. If output is present, go to step 8.
5. Check that the start/stop circuit works properly.
6. Check the input device for a proper signal going to input board.
7. Replace the input board. Problem should now be taken care of.
8. Check feedback device #1 for proper feedback.
9. Check feedback device #2 for proper feedback.
10. Replace the feedback board. Problem should now be take care of.
11. Check the output coming from the output board. if output is present, go to step 14.
12. Make sure there is power going to the output board.
13. Replace the output board.
14. Check if there is anything mechanically wrong with the system.
15. Replace the motor, if necessary.

TABLE 15

Abbreviations

A

A – amps
AC – alternating current
A/C – air conditioning
AEGCP – assured equipment grounding conductor program
AHJ – authority having jurisdiction
Alu. – aluminum
ASCC – available short–circuit current
AWG – American Wire Gauge
AXFMR – autotransformer

B

BC – branch circuit
BCSC – branch–circuit selection current
BJ – bonding jumper
BK – black
BL – blue
BR – brown

C

°C – Celsius
CB – circuit breaker
CEE – concrete–encased electrode
CL – code letter
CM – circular mills
CMP – Codemaking Panel
Comp. – compressor
Cond. – condenser
Cont. – continuous
cu. – copper
cu. in. – cubic inches

D

dia. – diameter
DC – direct–current
DPCB – double pole circuit breaker

E

EBJ – equipment bonding jumper
Eff. – efficiency
EGB – equipment grounding bar
EGC – equipment grounding conductor
EMT – electrical metallic tubing
ENT or ENMT – electrical nonmetallic tubing
Ex. – Exception
EExde – increase safety
Eexe – flameproof/increased safety components
Epf – explosionproof

F

°F – Fahrenheit
FLA – full–load amperage
FLC – full–load current
FMC – flexible metal conduit
FPN – fine print note
FREQ. – frequency
ft – foot

G

G – ground
GE – grounding electrode
GEC – grounding electrode conductor
GES – grounding electrode system
GFL – ground–fault limiter
GFCI – ground–fault circuit interrupter
GFPE – ground–fault protection of equipment
GR – green
GRY – gray
GSC – Grounded service conductor

H

H – hot conductor
HACR – heating, air conditioning, cooling, and refrigeration
HP – horsepower
Htg. – heating
Hz – hertz

I

I – amperage or current
IEC – International Electrotechnical Commission
IG – Isolated ground
in. – inches
INVT – inverse–time circuit breaker
INST. CB – instantaneous trip circuit breaker
INTP – interpole
IRA – inrush amps
ITSC – intrinsically safe circuits

K

kFT – 1000'
kV – kilovolts
kVA – kilovolt–amps
kvar – kilovar
kW – kilowatts
kWH – kilowatt–hour

L

L – length of conductor
Ld. – load
LPB – lighting panelboard
LRA – locked rotor amps
LRC – locked–rotor current
LTFMC – liquidtight flexible metal conduit
LTR – long time rated

M

MA – milli–amps
max. – maximum
MEL – maximum energy level
mf – microfarads
MGFA – maximum ground–fault available
min. – minimum
min. – minute
MR – momentary rated
Mt. – motor

N

N – neutral
NACB – nonautomatic circuit breaker
NB – neutral bar
NEC – National Electrical Code®
NEMA – National Electrical Manufacturers Association®
NFD – nonfused disconnect
NFPA – National Fire Protection Association®
NLTFMC – nonmetallic liquidtight flexible metal conduit
NTDF – nontime–delay fuse

O

OCP – overcurrent protection
OCPD – overcurrent protection device
OL – overload
OLP – overload protection
OLs – overloads
OR – orange
OSHA – Occupational Safety and Health Administration

P

PF – power factor
Ph. – phases (hots)
pri. – primary
PSA – power supply assembly
PU – purple

R

R – ohms or resistance
RD – red
REC. – receptacle
RMC – rigid metal conduit

S

SBS – structural building steel
SCC – short–circuit current
sec. – secondary
SDS – separately derived system
SF – service factor
SIA – seal–in amps
SP – single–pole
S/P – single–phase
SPCB – single–pole circuit breaker
sq. ft – square foot (feet)
sq. in. – square inches
SS – synchronous speed
STR – short–time rated
SWD – switched disconnect
SWG – switchgear

T

TDC – time–delay cycle
TDF – time–delay fuse
TDL – time–delay limiter
TP – thermal protector
TR – temperature rise
Tran. – transformer
TS – trip setting
TV – touch voltage

U

UF – underground feeder

V

V – volts
VA – volt–amps
VD – voltage drop

W

W – watts
WC – winding current
WT – white
WP – weatherproof
WV – winding voltage

X

XFMR – transformer

Y

YEL – yellow

Glossary of Terms

A

Across-the-line starter is a device consisting of contactor and overload relay that is used to start an electric motor by connecting it directly to the supply line.

Active power is the true electrical power or real power supplying the load.

Air gap is the air space between two electrically related parts such as the space between poles of a magnet or poles in an electric motor.

Alternating current (AC) is the current in an electrical circuit that alternates in flowing, first with a positive polarity and then with a negative polarity.

Alternator is a rotating machine whose output is AC.

Ambient conditions are the conditions of the atmosphere adjacent to electrical equipment.

Ambient temperature is the temperature of the surrounding atmosphere cooling medium, which comes into contact with the heated parts of equipment.

Ambient temperature compensated is a device, such as an overload relay, which is not affected by the temperature surrounding it.

Ampacity is the current, in amperes, that a conductor can carry continuously under the conditions of use without exceeding its temperature rating.

Ampere is a unit of intensity of electrical current produced in a conductor by an applied voltage.

Ampere is an unit of measure for current flow. Note that one ampere equals a flow of one coulomb of charge per second.

Apparatus is a set of control devices used to help perform the intended control functions, operating by its own means.

Apparent power is the sum of active power and reactive power. It is determined by multiplying voltage times current.

Arc-chute is a cover around contacts designed to protect surrounding parts from arcing effects.

Armature is a special designed rotor.

Armature reaction is the reaction of the magnetic field produced by the current on the magnetic lines of force which are produced by the field coil of an electric motor or generator.

Automatic is a means of self acting that operates by its own mechanism, such as a change in pressure or temperature.

Automatic controller is a motor or other control mechanism which uses automatic pilot devices as activating devices. These devices may be pressure switches, level switches, or thermostats.

Autotransformer starter is equipped with an autotransformer designed to reduce the voltage to the motor terminals and reduce the starting current. It will still start the motor.

Auxiliary contacts are contacts in addition to the main-circuit contacts and function with their movement.

Auxiliary device is any device other than motors and motor starters necessary to fully operate the machine or equipment.

Auxiliary interlock:

- Mechanical – A physical device or arm so arranged that it cannot close both starter circuits at the same time.

- Electrical – An additional contact mounted on the side of a magnetic starter.

B

Bearings are devices used to support the motor shaft; they allow it to rotate smoothly.

Bimetallic disc is a disc made up of two strips of dissimilar metals combined to form a single strip.

Branch circuit is that portion of a wiring system extending beyond the final overcurrent device protecting the circuit.

Breakdown torque is the maximum torque that a motor develops under increasing load conditions at rated voltage and frequency without an sudden drop in rotating speed.

Brushes are sliding contacts, usually made of carbon, which are located between a commutator and the outside circuit in a generator or motor.

C

Capacitance is the ability to store electricity in an electrostatic field.

Capacitor is a device that is designed to introduce capacitance into an electric circuit.

Capacitor-start motor is an AC split-phase induction motor that has a capacitor connected in series with an auxiliary winding which provides a way for it to start. This auxiliary circuit is designed to disconnect to the motor when it reaches its speed.

Circuit is an electrical network of conductors that provides one or more paths for current.

Circuit breaker is a device designed to open and close a circuit either by a nonautomatic means or by an automatic means due to a predetermined overload of current.

Combination starter is a magnetic starter having a manually operated disconnecting means built into the enclosure that houses the magnetic contactor or starter.

Commutator is a device which reverses the connections to the revolving loops on the armature.

Compensating windings are the windings embedded in the main pole pieces of a compound DC motor.

Component is the smallest element of a circuit.

Contacts are connecting parts which co-act with other parts to connect or disconnect a circuit.

Contactor is a electromechanical device for connecting and disconnecting an electric power circuit.

Control is a device or group of devices used in some predetermined manner to govern the electric power delivered to an apparatus.

Control circuit carries the signals directing the performance of the controller.

Control circuit transformer is a control circuit transformer utilized to supply a reduced voltage suitable for the operation of control devices.

Control circuit voltage is the control circuit voltage providing the operation to the coils of magnetic devices.

Control, three-wire is a control function which utilizes a momentary contact pilot device and a holding circuit contact to provide voltage to the coil of a controller. The holding circuit maintains the control circuit voltage.

Control, two-wire is a control function which utilizes a maintained contact type pilot device to provide undervoltage release.

Controller is a device, or group of devices, that is used in some predetermined manner to connect and disconnect the electric power delivered to the apparatus.

Copper loss is the electrical power lost through the resistance of the coils due to the current flowing through the wire of the coils.

Core is the magnetic path through the center of the coil or the transformer.

Core losses are the losses of power in the coil (core) due to eddy currents and hysteresis.

Core transformer is an electrical transformer with the core inside of the coils.

Counterelectromotive force is the voltage induced in the armature coil of an electric motor.

Counter torque is a repulsion force between two magnetic fields.

D

Delta-delta connected is a coil connection in which the primary and secondary coils are delta connected.

Delta-wye connected is a connection in which the primary are delta connected while the secondary windings are wye connected.

Diagram shows the electrical connection between the parts of the control, and external connections.

Direct-current (DC) is a current that always flows in only one direction.

Disconnect means is a motor circuit switch intended to connect and disconnect a circuit to a motor. It must be rated in horsepower and capable of interrupting the maximum current.

E

Eddy currents are the electrical currents circulating in the core of a transformer as the result of induction.

Efficiency is the ratio of output power (watts) to input power (watts).

Electric motor is a machine that converts electrical energy to mechanical energy.

Electricity is electrical charges in motion. Such movement is called current and is measured in amps.

Electrolytic capacitor is a capacitor that uses a liquid or past as one of its electrical storage plates.

Electromagnet is a magnet comprised of a coil of wire wound around a soft-iron core. When current is passed through the wire, a magnetic field is produced.

Electromagnet is a temporary magnet created by passing an electric current through a coil wound around a soft iron or other magnetic core.

Electromagnetism is a magnetic field that exists around a wire or other conductor if a current is passing through it.

Electromechanical is a device that uses electrical energy to create mechanical motion of force.

Electromotive force is a voltage or force that causes free electrons to move in a conductor.

Electron is a negative electric charge.

Electron flow is the flow of electrons from a negative point to a positive point in a conductor.

Electrostatic charge is the electrical charge stored by a capacitor.

Electrostatic field is the stored electrical charge on the surface of an insulator.

Excitation is creating a magnetic field to be used to create electromagnetics when an electric current is passed through a coil.

F

Feeder is the conductors between the service equipment and the branch-circuit overcurrent device.

Float switch is a switch operated by a float and is responsive for the level of liquid.

Foot switch is a switch suitable for operation by an operator's foot.

Frequency is the rate at which AC changes its direction of flow; it is normally expressed in terms of hertz (cycles) per second.

Fuse is an overcurrent protection device with a circuit opening fuseable member that opens when overheated by current passing through it.

G

Gate is one of the leads on a thyristor. This lead is the one that normally controls output when it is correctly biased.

Generator is a rotating machine that changes mechanical energy into DC.

Generator action induces voltage into a wire that cuts a magnetic field.

Ground is any point on a motor component at which the ohmic resistance between the component and the motor frame is one megaohm or less.

Guarded is covered, shielded, fenced, enclosed, or otherwise protected by means of suitable covers or casings, barriers, rails or screens, mats or platforms, removing the likelihood of dangerous contact or approach by persons or objects to a point of danger.

H

Hermetic refrigerant motor compressor is a combination consisting of a compressor and motor, both of which are enclosed in the same housing, with no external shaft or shaft seals, the motor operating in the refrigerant.

Hertz is a measurement of frequency and it actually means cycles per second of AC.

High side marking in a transformer indicates the high-voltage winding.

Horsepower is a unit of measure for power and it represents the force times distance times time. For example, one horsepower (HP) equals 746 watts, or 33,000 ft lb per minute, or 550 ft lb per second.

Hysteresis is the property of a magnetic substance that causes the magnetization to lag behind the magnetizing force.

I

Impedance is the total opposition to current flow in a circuit and is measured in ohms.

Induced current is the current that flows in a conductor because of a changing magnetic field.

Inductance is electromotive force that results from a change in magnetic flux surrounding a circuit or conductor.

Induction is the generation of electricity by magnetism.

Inductive reactance is the opposition in ohms to an AC as a result of induction. This is voltage resulting from cutting lines of magnetic force.

Interlock is an electrical or mechanical device actuated by the operation of a different device in which it is directly related.

Intermittent duty is a requirement or service that demands operations for alternate intervals of (1) load and no load; or (2) load and rest; or (3) load, no load, and rest; such alternate intervals being definitely specified.

Inverter is a circuit capable of receiving a positive signal and sends out a negative one or vice versa. It is a device that changes AC to DC or vice versa.

Isolating transformer is used to electrically isolate one circuit from another.

J

Jogging is the rapid and repeated opening and closing of the circuit to start a motor from rest for the purpose of creating small movements of the motor or driven load.

K

kVA is the term used to rate transformers.

kvar is the reactive power in a circuit.

kW is used to rate the load of certain types of equipment and such.

L

Lamination consist of sheet material sandwiched together to construct a stator or rotor of a rotating machine.

Limit switch is operated by a part or motion of a power-driven piece of equipment. Such operation alters the electric or electronic circuits related to the equipment.

Locked-rotor current of a motor is taken from the line when the motor starts or the rotor becomes locked in place.

Low side in a transformer, this marking indicates the low-voltage winding.

M

Magnetic drive (magnetic clutch) is an electromagnetic device that is connected between a three-phase motor and its load. Its main purpose is regulating the speed at load rotated speed.

Magnetic fields are the invisible lines of force found between the north and south poles of a magnet.

Magnetic lines of force in a magnetic field are imaginary lines that show the direction of the magnetic flux.

Magnetic starter is actuated by an electro-magnetic means.

Maintained contacts close the circuit when the push button is pressed and will open the circuit when the push button is pressed again.

Manual controller is a device that is manually closed or opened.

Manual reset is a device that requires manual action to re-engage the contacts after an overload.

Megaohm is one million ohms.

Motor action is the mechanical force that exist between magnets. Two magnets approaching each other will either pull toward or push away from the other. In other words, there is a pull and push action between the rotor and field poles of the motor.

Multi-speed motor is a motor capable of operating at two or more fixed speeds.

N

NEMA (National Electrical Manufacturers Association) is an organization that establishes certain voluntary standards relating to motors such as operating characteristics, terminology, basic dimensions, ratings, and testing.

No-load speed is the speed reached by the rotor or armature when it rotates.

Nonautomatic requires personal action and operation of devices for its control means.

Nonreversing is a control function that provides for operation in one direction only.

Normally open and normally closed is a term that when applied to a magnetically operated switching device, signifies the position that the contacts are in.

Normally closed contacts are motor control contacts (set) that are open when the push button is depressed.

Normally open contacts are contacts (set) that are closed when the push button is depressed.

O

Ohm is a unit of electrical resistance of a conductor.

Out-of-phase is a condition in which two or more phases of AC are changing direction at different intervals of time.

Overexcited is a condition in which a synchronous motor is equipped with a DC field that supplies more magnetization than is needed.

Overload protector is a device affected by an abnormal operating condition that causes the interruption of current flow to the device governed.

Overload relay is a device that provides overload protection for conductors and electrical equipment.

Overcurrent protective device (OCPD) is a device that operates on excessive current that causes the interruption of power to the circuit if necessary.

P

Parallel circuit is a circuit in which all positive terminals are connected at a common point and all negative terminals are connected to another point.

Periodic duty is a type of intermittent duty in which the load conditions are regularly recurrent.

Permanent-capacitor motor is a single-phase electric motor that uses a phase winding and capacitor in conjunction with the main winding. The phase winding is controlled by the capacitor, which remains in the circuit at all times.

Permanent magnetism is magnet that will keep its magnetic properties indefinitely.

Permeability is a condition in which domains in a magnetic core can be made to line up to create magnetism.

Phase is the relationship of two wave forms that have the same frequency.

Phase angle is the difference in angle between two sine wave vectors.

Phase shift is the creation of a lag or advance in voltage or current in relation to another voltage or current in the same electrical circuit.

Phase voltage is the voltage across a coil.

Polarity is a condition in which a magnet has north and south poles that are positive and negative charge.

Polyphase is more than one phase, usually three-phase, when related to generators, transformers, and motors.

Pounds force is an English unit of conventional measurement for force.

Power factor is the figure that indicates what portion of the current delivered to the motor is used to do work.

Primary coil is one of two coils in a transformer.

Prime mover is the primary power source that can be used to drive a generator.

Pull-in to torque is the maximum torque at which an induction motor will pull into step.

Pull-out torque is the maximum torque developed by a motor for one minute, before it pulls out of step due to an overload.

Pull-up torque is the minimum torque developed by an induction motor during the period of acceleration from rest to full speed.

Push button control is the control and operation of equipment through push buttons used to activate relays.

Push button switch is a switch utilizing a button for activating a coil and contact to open or close a circuit.

R

Rainproof is an enclosure constructed to prevent rain from interfering with operation of the apparatus.

Raintight is an enclosure constructed to exclude rain under specified test conditions.

Rated-load current is the load rated-load current for a hermetic refrigerant motor-compressor if the current resulting when the motor-compressor is operated at the rated load, rated voltage, and rated frequency of the equipment it serves.

Rating is a designated limit of operating characteristics based on conditions of use such as load, voltage, frequency, and so on.

Rating, continuous is the rating that defines the substantially constant load that can be carried for an indefinitely long time.

Reactive power is the reactive voltage times the current, or voltage times the reactive current, in an AC circuit.

Rectifier is an electrical device that converts AC to DC by allowing the current to move in only one direction.

Relay is a device that operates by a variation of a condition that affects the operation of other devices in an electric circuit.

Relay contacts are closed or opened by movement of a relay armature.

Reluctance is the ratio between the magnetomotive force and the resulting flux.

Reset is to restore a mechanism or device to a prescribed state.

Reset, automatic is a function that operates automatically to reestablish certain circuit conditions.

Reset, manual is a function that requires a manual operation to reestablish certain circuit conditions.

Residual magnetism is the magnetism remaining in the core of a coil or an electromagnet after the current flow has been removed.

Resistance is a property of conductors that makes them resist the movement of current flow.

Resistance starting is a reduced-voltage starting method employing resistances that are short-circuited in one or more steps to complete the starting cycle of a motor, and such.

Resistors are electrical-electronic devices which are attached to a circuit to produce resistance to current flow.

Rheostat is a variable resistor with a fixed terminal and a movable contact.

Rotor is the rotating section that rotates within the stator of a motor.

Rotor impedance is the phasor sum of resistance and inductive reactance.

RPM is the revolutions per minute.

Running torque is the torque or turning effort determined by the horsepower and speed of a motor at any given point of operation.

S

Saturated is when an electrical or magnetic component cannot receive any more electrical current or magnetism.

Saturation is a point at which a magnet will not receive any more flux density.

Sealing, voltage or current is the voltage or current required to seat the armature of a magnetic circuit closing device to the make position.

Secondary coil is the coil that is connected to the load in the electrical circuit.

Service factor is the number by which the horsepower rating is multiplied to determine the maximum safe load that a motor can carry continuously at its rated voltage and frequency.

Self excitation is a condition of supplying excitation voltages by a device on the generator rather than from an outside source.

Self induction is a counterelectromotive force produced in a conductor when the magnetic field produced by the conductor collapses or expands after a change in current flow.

Separate excitation is a condition of producing generator field current from an independent source.

Series circuit is a circuit in which all resistances and other components are connected so that the same current flows from point to point.

Series field is the total magnetic flux caused by the action of the series winding in a rotating piece of machine.

Series motor is a motor in which the field and armature circuits are connected in series.

Shaded-pole motor is a single-phase squirrel cage induction motor with stator poles slotted and used to create two sections in each pole.

Shading coil is a copper ring or coil that is set into a section of the pole piece and its function is to produce the lagging part of a rotating magnetic field for starting torque.

Short is any two points of a motor with zero, or extremely low, resistance between them or between two motor components.

Short-time rating is referring to the motor load that can be carried for a short and definitely specified time.

Shunt field is a type of field coil designed for a DC motor that is connected in parallel with the armature.

Silicon-controlled rectifier (SCR) is a semiconductor device that has the ability to block a voltage that is applied in either direction. On a signal applied to its gate, it is capable of conducting current even when the signal has been removed.

Single-phase is having only one AC or voltage in a circuit.

Slip is the difference between the synchronous speed of a motor and the speed at which it operates.

Slip-ring motor has a rotor with the same number of magnetic poles at the stator.

Slip rings are equipped with circular bands on a rotor which are used to transmit current from rotor coils to brushes.

Slip speed is the difference between the rotor speed and synchronous speed in an induction motor.

Soft neutral position is a condition in which the brushes of a repulsion electric motor are aligned with the stator field.

Solid state devices contain circuits and components using semiconductors.

Solid state controls are devices that control current to motors through semiconductors.

Solid state relay uses semiconductor devices.

Split-phase (resistance-start) motor is a single-phase induction motor equipped with an auxiliary winding connected in parallel with the main winding.

Squirrel-cage rotor is designed with a rotor made up of metal bars that are short-circuited at each end.

Starter is a controller for accelerating a motor from rest to its running speed.

Starter, automatic is a starter that automatically controls the starting of a motor.

Starter, autotransformer is a starter which is provided with an autotransformer that provides a reduced voltage for starting.

Stall torque of an energized motor produces when the rotor is not rotating.

Starter, part-winding applied voltage to partial sections of the primary winding of an AC motor.

Starter, reactor includes a resistor that is connected in series with the primary winding of an induction motor to provide reduced voltage for starting.

Starter, wye-delta connects the motor leads in a wye configuration for reduced voltage starting and reconnects the leads in a delta configuration for the run position.

Starting torque is the amount of torque produced by a motor as it breaks the motor shaft from standstill and accelerates to its running speed.

Static electricity is electricity at rest. It is also known in the industry as a static charge.

Stator is the portion that contains the stationary parts of the magnetic circuit with associated windings when installed in a motor.

Stator field contains a magnetic field set up in the electric motor when the motor is energized and electric current is flowing.

Stator poles are the shoes on an electric motor stator that hold the windings and the magnetic poles of the stator.

Switch is a device for making, breaking, or changing the connections in an electric circuit.

Switch, float is responsive to the level of a liquid.

Switch, foot is a switch that is operated by an operator's foot.

Switch, general-use is a general-use type non-horse rated switch capable of interrupting the rated current at the rated voltage.

Switch, limit is operated by some part or motion that alters the electrical circuit associated with the equipment.

Switch, master controls the operation of contactors, relays, or other similar operated devices.

Switch, motor circuit is rated in horsepower, and is capable of interrupting the maximum operating current of the motor.

Switch, pressure is operated by fluid pressure and such.

Switch, selector is a manually operated multiposition switch that is used for selecting an alternative control circuit.

Synchronous is a condition in which the currents and voltages are in-step or in-phase.

Synchronous motor is an induction motor that runs at synchronous speed.

Synchronous speed is the constant speed to which an AC motor adjusts itself, depending on the frequency of the power source and the number of poles in the motor.

T

Tachometer is a device that is capable of measuring rotational speed of rotating machines.

Tap changer is a mechanical device that has the ability to change the voltage output of a transformer.

Taps are fixed electrical connections located at specific positions on a transformers coil.

Temperature, ambient is the temperature of the medium such as air, oil, and such into which the heat of the equipment is dissipated.

Terminal is a point at which an electrical element may be connected to another electrical element.

Terminal board is an insulating base equipped with one or more terminal connectors used for making electrical connections.

Thermal, cutout is an overcurrent protective device having a heater element that affects a fusible member that opens, the circuit due to an overload.

Thermal protector is a protective device that is an integral part of the motor designed to protect the motor windings from dangerous overloads.

Thermocouple is a device that consists of two unlike metals joined together, and when heat is applied, a current will flow.

Thermostat is an instrument that responds to changes in temperature to effect control over an operating condition.

Three-phase alternator is a rotating machine that generates three separate phases of AC.

Three-phase electric motor is a motor that operates from a three-phase power supply.

Timer is a device designed to delay the closing or opening of a circuit for a specific period of time.

Torque is a force that produces a rotating or twisting action.

Torque, breakdown is the maximum torque that a motor develops with rated voltage when applied at rated frequency.

Torque, locked rotor is the minimum torque that a motor develops at standstill when rated voltage is applied at rated frequency.

Transformer is an device designed to change the voltage in an AC electrical circuit. Step-up transformers increase the voltage and lower the current. Step-down transformers decrease the voltage and raise the current.

Transformer efficiency is the ratio of input to output power.

Turns ratio is the ratio of the number of turns in the primary winding of a transformer to the number of turns in the secondary winding.

Two-capacitor motor is an induction motor that uses one capacitor for starting and one for running.

U

Under excited is a term used to describe the magnetizing power of synchronous motor.

Undervoltage protection is a device that operates on the reduction or failure of voltage and has the ability to maintain the interruption of power.

Undervoltage release is a device that operates on the reduction or failure of voltage and has the ability to interrupt the power but not to prevent the reestablishment of the circuit.

Unity power factor is a power factor of 1, and this is the best PF that can be obtained in an electrical system.

V

Vector is an in-phasor diagram having lines with a specific length and direction.

Voltage is a force that, when applied to a conductor, produces a current in the conductor.

W

Watt is a unit of electrical power and is the product of voltage and amperage.

Wattmeter is an instrument used for measuring electrical power.

Wye or star connection is an electrical connection in which all of the terminals are joined at the neutral junction. After it is connected it resembles a wye connection.

Wye-wye connection is the coil arrangement in which both the primary and the secondary coils are wye-connected.

Answer Key

Chapter 1
Magnetism and Electromagnetism

Answer	Section
1. (a)	Theory of magnets
2. (c)	Magnetic fields
3. (b)	Magnetic field
4. (c)	Electromagnetic induction
5. (a)	Electrmagnetic induction
6. (d)	**490.2**
7. (d)	Figure 1-10(b)
8. (d)	**250.26**
9. (c)	Figure 1-4
10. (c)	Figure 1-2

Chapter 2
Generator Principles

Answer	Section
1. (d)	Basic operation of generators
2. (b)	Commutator
3. (a)	Commutation
4. (d)	Armature reaction
5. (c)	Single-phase output
6. (a)	Single-phase output
7. (b)	Three-phase output
8. (d)	Typical synchronous generator
9. (c)	Generator exciters
10. (b)	DC exciters
11. (c)	Gasoline engines
12. (b)	Diesel engines
13. (a)	Single-phase generators
14. (d)	Three-phase generators
15. (c)	Frame
16. (b)	Core
17. (a)	Wye-connected systems
18. (c)	Salient pole rotors
19. (c)	Gas-to-water heat exchanger
20. (a)	Automatic synchronization of generators

Chapter 3
Generators and the *National Electrical Code*

Answer	Section
1. (d)	**445.11**
2. (a)	**445.12(B)**

3. (b)	445.12(C)
4. (c)	445.13
5. (b)	445.13, Ex.
6. (a)	445.14
7. (c)	445.15; 430.232, Ex.; 430.233
8. (d)	445.16
9. (b)	445.18; 110.25; 110.21
10. (d)	445.18(B); 445.18(C); 700.10(A)(1)

Chapter 4
Emergency System Generators

Answer	Section
1. (d)	**700.12(D)(1)**
2. (c)	**700.12(C)(1)**
3. (a)	**700.12(D)(3)**
4. (b)	**700.4(A) and (B)**
5. (b)	**700.10(D)(2)(2)**
6. (b)	**700.10(D)(2)(5)**
7. (b)	**700.10(D)(2)(4)**
8. (d)	**700.10(D)(3)**
9. (c)	**700.10(D)(4)**
10. (d)	**700.10(D)(1)**

Chapter 5
Legally Required and Optional Standby Systems

Answer	Section
1. (b)	**701.12(D)(1)**
2. (c)	**701.12(C)(1)**
3. (a)	**700.4(A)**
4. (b)	**701.5 and 702.5**
5. (a)	**702.11(B)**
6. (a)	**445.20(A), Ex.**
7. (b)	**701.7(B) and 702.7(B)**
8. (c)	**250.35, 701.12(D)(3)**
9. (d)	**701.4(B)**
10. (a)	**701.30**

Chapter 6
Generators Supplying Essential Loads for Hospitals

Answer	Section
1. (b)	**517.32(B) and 517.30(B)(3)(c)**
2. (a)	**517.3(B)**
3. (c)	**Figure 517.31(B)(1)**

4. (d)	**250.35(B)**
5. (a)	Low-resistance grounding **250.36**
6. (c)	High-resistance grounding **250.36**
7. (b)	**517.30(B)(2)** and **Article 100**
8. (d)	**517.31(C)(1)**
9. (b)	**517.31(C)(3)(2)**
10. (c)	**517.19(E)** and **250.4(A)(1)**

Chapter 7
Transformer Theory

Answer	Section
1. (a)	Single-phase output
2. (b)	Single-phase output
3. (c)	Balanced current flow
4. (a)	Wye-connected transformers
5. (d)	Balanced current flow and three/phase balancing
6. (b)	Open connected windings
7. (c)	Close connected wiindings
8. (a)	Balanced current flow
9. (b)	Single-phase load balancing
10. (c)	Wye-connected transformers

Chapter 8
Installing Transformers

Answer	Section
1. (d)	**450.11**
2. (b)	**450.8(C)** and **110.27(A)(4)**
3. (c)	**450.13**
4. (b)	**450.13(B)**
5. (c)	**450.21(A)**
6. (c)	**450.21(C)**
7. (a)	**450.23(A)(2)**
8. (d)	**450.25**
9. (b)	**450.26, Ex. 4**
10. (a)	**450.26, Ex. 2**

Chapter 9
Transformer Vaults

Answer	Section
1. (b)	**450.42**
2. (d)	**450.42, IN 2**
3. (c)	**450.42**
4. (c)	**450.43(B)**
5. (d)	**450.43(C)**
6. (b)	**450.45(C)**

7. (a)	**450.43(C)**
8. (d)	**450.47**
9. (a)	**450.45(E)**
10. (b)	**450.43(A)**

Chapter 10
Sizing Transformers and Connections

Answer	Section
1. (d)	Sizing closed delta-connected secondaries
2. (a)	Sizing closed delta-connected secondaries
3. (c)	Sizing open delta-connected secondaries
4. (b)	**240.21(B)(3)** and **240.21(C)(5)**
5. (d)	**240.92(C)(1)(1)**
6. (c)	**240.92(C)(2)**
7. (b)	**240.21(C)(2)(4)**
8. (a)	**240.92(C)(1), (1)**
9. (d)	**240.92(C)(1)(3)**
10. (a)	Sizing closed delta-connected secondaries
11. (d)	**240.21(C)(6)**

12. **Wye-connected secondaries**

Step 1: Finding kVA load for three transformers
GE manual
Single-phase (1/3):25 kVA x .33 = 8.25 kVA
Three-phase (1/3):40 kVA x .33 = 13.20 kVA
Total load = 21.45 kVA

Step 2: Sizing individual transformers
Three 25 kVA lighting and power transformers of the same size are to be installed

Step 3: Sizing kVA for one transformer
25 kVA + 40 kVA = 65 kVA

Solution: **Three transformers of 25 kVA each and one transformer of at least 65 kVA must be installed. Wye-connected secondaries.**

13. **Closed delta-connected secondaries**

Step 1: Finding kVA load for lighting transformers
Single-phase (2/3):25 kVA x .67 = 16.75 kVA
Three-phase (1/3):40 kVA x .33 = 13.20 kVA
Total load = 29.95 kVA

Solution: **Lighting transformers is 30 kVA.**
Step 1: Finding kVA load for power transformers
Single-phase (1/3):25 kVA x .33 = 8.25 kVA
Three-phase (1/3):40 kVA x .33 = 13.20 kVA
Total load = 21.45 kVA

Solution: **Two power transformers of 25 kVA each are required.**

Note: Lighting transformer is 30 kVA and the two power transformers are 25 kVA each.

14. Open delta-connected secondaries

Step 1: Finding kVA load for lighting and power transformer
Single-phase:25 kVA x 1.00   = 25   kVA
Three-phase (1 ÷ 1.732):40 kVA x .58   = 23.2 kVA
Total load   = 48.2 kVA

Solution: **One transformer of 50 kVA is required to be installed.**

Step 1: Finding kVA load for power transformers
Single-phase:40 kVA x .58   = 23.2 kVA

Solution: **One transformer of 25 kVA is required to be installed.**

15. Autotransformer secondary

Step 1: Finding secondary amps
Secondary A = kVA x 1000 ÷ secondary V
Secondary A = 2 kVA x 1000 ÷ 24 V
Secondary A = 83

Solution: **The secondary amperage is 83 amps.**

16. Sizing autotransformer

Step 1: Finding amps
A = load served ÷ supply V
A = 10,000 VA ÷ 230 V
A = 44
Step 2: Sizing autotransformer
AXFMR = A x secondary V
AXFMR = 44 A x 24 V
AXFMR = 1056 VA

Solution: **The size autotransformer to supply the load is 1.056 kVA.**
(1056 VA ÷ 1000 = 1.056 kVA)

17. 240.21(C)(2)(1)a, Table 310.16, and 240.4(B)

Step 1: Calculating minimum size tap
240.21(C)(2)(1)a
Calculated load is 168 A
Step 2: Sizing conductors
Table 310.16
2/0 AWG THWN cu. = 175 A
Step 3: Verifying size
240.21(C)(2)(1)a
175 A is greater than 168 A

Solution: **The THWN copper conductors are 2/0 AWG rated at 175 amps.**

Step 1: Calculating OCPD
240.4(E), 240.21(C)(2)(1)a, and 240.4(B)
2/0 AWG cu. = 175 A
OCPD rated at 175 A protects conductors from overload

Solution: **The overcurrent protecton device is permitted to be 175 amps.**

18. 240.21(B)(3)(1), Table 310.15(B)(16), 240.4(E), and 240.6(A)

Step 1: Calculating primary tap
240.21(B)(3)(1)
1/3 of 200 A = 67 A
Step 2: Selecting conductors
Table 310.16
67 A requires 4 AWG cu.

Solution: **The THWN copper conductors are 4 AWG.**

Step 1: Calculating secondary tap
240.21(B)(3)(2)
480 V ÷ 208 V x 1/3 x 200 A = 153.9 A
Step 2: Selecting conductors
Table 310.16
153.9 A requires 2/0 AWG cu.

Solution: **The THWN copper conductors are 2/0 AWG.**

Step 1: Selecting OCPD in secondary tap
240.4(E), 240.21(B)(3)(2), and Table 240.6(A)
175 A (2/0 AWG cu.) requires 175 A

Solution: **The overcurrent protection device is 175 amps.**

19. 240.21(C)(3)(1), Table 310.15(B)(16), 240.4(E), and 240.6(A)

Step 1: Calculating minimum size tap
240.21(C)(3)(1)
Calculated load is 312 A
Step 2: Sizing conductors
Table 310.16
400 KCMIL THWN cu. = 335 A
Step 3: Verifying size
240.21(C)(3)(1)
335 A is greater than 312 A

Solution: **The THWN copper conductors are 400 KCMIL rated at 335 amps.**

Step 1: Calculating OCPD
240.4(E), 240.21(C)(3)(1), and 240.4(B)
400 KCMIL cu. = 335 A
OCPD rated at 300 A protects conductors from overload

Solution: **The overcurrent protection device is permitted to be 300 amps.**

20. Outside taps

Step 1: Sizing conductors
Table 310.16
280 A requires 300 KCMIL cu.

Solution: **The THWN copper conductors are 300 KCMIL.**

Step 1: Sizing OCPD
240.4 and Table 240.6(A)
280 A output requires 250 A OCPD

Solution: **The overcurrent protection device is required to be 250 amps.**

Chapter 11
Protecting Transformers

Answer	Section
1. (b)	Table 450.3(A)
2. (a)	Table 450.3(A), Item 1
3. (c)	Table 450.3(A)
4. (b)	Table 450.3(A)
5. (b)	Table 450.3(B)
6. (c)	Table 450.3(B)
7. (d)	Table 450.3(B)
8. (c)	Table 450.3(B)
9. (a)	450.4(A)
10. (b)	450.4(A), Ex.

11. Finding amperage

Step 1: Finding primary amps
A = (kVA x 1000) ÷ V
A = (20 kVA x 1000) ÷ 480 V
A = 41.7 A

Step 2: Finding secondary amps
A = (kVA x 1000) ÷ V
A = (20 kVA x 1000) ÷ 240 V
A = 83.3 A

Solution: **The primary amperage is 41.7 amps and the secondary amperage is 83.3 amps.**

12. Finding amperage

Step 1: Finding primary amps
A = (kVA x 1000) ÷ (V x 1.732)
A = (20 kVA x 1000) ÷ (480 V x 1.732)
A = 24 A

Step 2: Finding secondary amps
A = (kVA x 1000) ÷ (V x 1.732)
A = (20 kVA x 1000) ÷ (240 V x 1.732)
A = 48 A

Solution: **The primary amperage is 24 amps and the secondary amperage is 48 amps.**

13. Finding interrupting capacity (IC)

Step 1: Finding FLC
FLC = (kVA x 1000) ÷ V
FLC = (20 kVA x 1000) ÷ 240 V
FLC = 83.3 A

Step 2: Finding IC
IC = FLC ÷ impedance
IC = 83.3 A ÷ .015
IC = 5553. 3 A

Solution: **The interrupting capacity is 5553.3 amps.**

14. 450.3(A), Table 450.3(A), and Table 240.6(A)

Step 1: Finding FLA of primary
450.3(A)
FLA = (kVA x 1000) ÷ (V x 1.732)
FLA = (1500 kVA x 1000) ÷ (12,470 x 1.732)
FLA = 69.45

Step 2: Calculating FLA for OCPD
450.3(A) and **Table 450.3(A)**
69.45 A x 300% = 208.4 A

Step 3: Selecting OCPD
Table 450.3(A), Ite, 1 and **Table 240.6(A)**
208.4 A requires 225 A

Solution: **The size circuit breaker is 225 amps.**

15. 450.3(A), Table 450.3(A), and Table 240.6(A)

Step 1: Finding FLA of transformer (primary)
FLA = (kVA x 1000) ÷ (V x 1.732)
FLA = (400 kVA x 1000) ÷ (4160 V x 1.732)
FLA = 55.5 A

Step 2: Calculating FLA for OCPD (primary)
450.3(A) and **Table 450.3(A)**
FLA = 55.5 A x 600%
FLA = 333 A

Step 3: Selecting OCPD (primary)
Table 450.3(A), Item 3 and **Table 240.6(A)**
333 A requires 350 A OCPD

Step 4: Finding FLA of transformer (secondary)
FLA = (kVA x 1000) ÷ (V x 1.7323)
FLA = (400 kVA x 1000) ÷ (480 V x 1.732)
FLA = 481.4 A

Step 5: Calculating FLA for OCPD (secondary)
450.3(A) and **Table 450.3(A)**
FLA = 481.4 A x 250%
FLA = 1203.5 A

Step 6: Selecting OCPD (secondary)
Table 450.3(A), Item 3 and **Table 240.6(A)**
1203.5 A permits 1200 A OCPD

Solution: **The size overcurrent protection device for the primary side is 350 amps and the size overcurrent protection device for the secondary side is 1200 amps.**

16. 450.3(A), Table 450.3(A), and Table 240.6(A)

Step 1: Finding FLA of transformer
FLA = (kVA x 1000) ÷ (V x 1.732)
FLA = (500 kVA x 1000) ÷ (13,800 V x 1.732)
FLA = 20.92 A

Step 2: Calculating FLA for OCPD
450.3(A) and **Table 450.3(A)**
FLA = 20.92 A x 600%
FLA = 125.5 A

Step 3: Selecting OCPD
Table 450.3(A), Item 3 and **Table 240.6(A)**
125.5 A permits 125 A

Solution: **The size overcurrent protection device for the primary side is a 125 amp circuit breaker.**

Step 1: Finding FLA of transformer
FLA = (kVA x 1000) ÷ (V x 1.732)
FLA = (500 kVA x 1000) ÷ (4160 V x 1.732)
FLA = 69.4 A

Step 2: Calculating FLA for OCPD
450.3(A) and **Table 450.3(A)**
FLA = 69.4 A x 250%
FLA = 173.5 A

Step 3: Selecting OCPD
Table 450.3(A), Item 3 and **Table 240.6(A)**
173.5 A permits 150 A

Solution: **The size overcurrent protection device for secondary side is 150 amp fuses.**

17. Finding amperage

Step 1: Finding ratio amps (3 AWG THWN cu. = 100 A)
(240 V ÷ 480 V) x 100 A = 50 A

Solution: **A 50 amp overcurrent protection device on the primary can protect the secondary.**

18. **Finding amperage (500 KCMIL cu. = 380 A)**

Step 1: Finding ratio amps
(240 V ÷ 480 V) x 380 A = 190 A

Solution: **A 175 amp overcurrent protection device on the primary can protect the secondary.**

19. **450.3(A), Table 450.3(A),** and **Table 240.6(A)**

Step 1: Finding FLA of transformer (primary)
FLA = (kVA x 1000) ÷ (V x 1.732)
FLA = (400 kVA x 1000) ÷ (4160 V x 1.732)
FLA = 55.5 A

Step 2: Calculating FLA for OCPD (primary)
450.3(A) and **Table 450.3(A)**
FLA = 55.5 A x 600% = 333 A

Step 3: Selecting OCPD (primary)
Table 450.3(A), Item 1 and **Table 240.6(A)**
333 A requires 350 A OCPD

Step 4: Finding FLA of transformer (secondary)
FLA = (kVA x 1000) ÷ (V x 1.732)
FLA = (400 kVA x 1000) ÷ (480 V x 1.732)
FLA = 481.4 A

Step 5: Calculating FLA for OCPD (secondary)
450.3(A) and **Table 450.3(A)**
FLA = 481.4 A x 125%
FLA = 601.8 A

Step 6: Selecting OCPD (secondary)
Table 450.3(A), Item 1 and **Table 240.6(A)**
601.8 A permits 700 A OCPD (or 600 A OCPD)

Solution: **The size overcurrent protection device for the primary side is 350 amps and the size overcurrent protection device for the secondary side is 700 amps.**

20. **450.3(B), Table 450.3(B),** and **240.6(A)**

Step 1: Finding FLA of primary
FLA = (kVA x 1000) ÷ V
FLA = (25 kVA x 1000) ÷ 240 V
FLA = 104.2 A

Step 2: Calculating OCPD
450.3(B) and **Table 450.3(B)**
104.2 A x 125% = 130.3 A

Solution: **The size overcurrent protection device in the primary side is 125 amps.**

21. **450.3(B), Table 450.3(B), Table 240.6(A),** and **430.72(C)(4)**

Step 1: Finding FLA of primary
FLA = (kVA x 1000) ÷ V
FLA = (.7 kVA x 1000) ÷ 480 V
FLA = 1.5 A

Step 2: Calculating OCPD
450.3(B) and **Table 450.3(B)**
1.5 A x 300% = 4.5 A

Step 3: Selecting OCPD
450.3(B) and **Table 240.6(A)**
4.5 A permits 3 A

Solution: **The minimum size overcurrent protection device in the primary side is 3 amps.**

Step 1: Calculating OCPD for control transformer
430.72(C)(4) and **Step 1**
1.5 A x 500% = 7.5 A

Step 2: Selecting OCPD
430.72(C)(4) and **Table 240.6(A)**
7.5 A permits 6 A

Solution: **The maximum size overcurrent protection device in the primary side is 6 amps.**

Note: The secondary side is a motor controller circuit.

22. **450.3(B), Table 450.3(B),** and **Table 240.6(A)**

Step 1: Finding FLA of primary
FLA = (kVA x 1000) ÷ (V x 1.732)
FLA = (40 kVA x 1000) ÷ (480 V x 1.732)
FLA = 48.2 A

Step 2: Calculating OCPD
450.3(B) and **Table 450.3(B)**
48.2 A x 250% = 120.5 A

Step 3: Selecting OCPD
450.3(B) and **Table 240.6(A)**
120.5 A permits 110 A

Solution: **The maximum size overcurrent protection device in the primary side is 110 amps.**

Note: The size of the overcurrent protection device in primary shall not exceed the 250% x FLA of primary.

Step 1: Finding FLA of secondary
FLA = (kVA x 1000) ÷ (V x 1.732)
FLA = (40 kVA x 1000) ÷ (208 V x 1.732)
FLA = 111.1 A

Step 2: Calculating OCPD
450.3(B) and Table 450.3(B), Item 1
111.1 A x 125% = 138.9 A

Step 3: Selecting OCPD
450.3(B) and Table 240.6(A)
138.9 A permits 150 A

Solution: **The maximum size overcurrent protection device in the secondary side is 150 amps.**

Note: **Table 450.3(B), Note 1** permits the next higher size overcurrent protection device to be used.

23. **450.5(A)(2)**

Step 1: Calculating current
450.5(A)(2)
150 A x 125% = 187.5 A

Solution: **A current of 187.5 amps or greater will cause the service overcurrent protection device to trip open.**

Answer	Section
24. (a)	**Table 450.3(B)**
25. (a)	**Table 450.3(B)**

Chapter 12
Secondary Ties

Answer	Section
1. (c)	**450.6(A)(1)**
2. (a)	**450.6(A)(2)**
3. (c)	**450.6(A)(5)**
4. (b)	**450.6(B)**
5. (d)	Bus-tie loops
6. (d)	**450.6(A)(2)**
7. (c)	**450.6(A)(1)**
8. (c)	**450.6(A)(5)**
9. (a)	**450.6(B)**
10. (a)	**Figure 12-5**

Chapter 13
Windings and Components

Answer	Section
1. (a)	Additive polarity
2. (b)	Subtractive polarity
3. (c)	Polarity connections and identifying terminals
4. (d)	Polarity connections and identifying terminals
5. (b)	120/204 volt, single-phase transformers
6. (d)	Three-phase, wye-connected system
7. (a)	**Table 250.102(C)(1), Note 1** and **250.30(A)(1)**
8. (c)	**250.30(A)(4), 250.52(A)(2), 250.68(C)(2)** and **Table 250.66**
9. (b)	**250.30(A)(4) Ex. 1** and **250.66(A)**
10. (d)	**250.30(A)(5)** and **Table 250.66**

11. (b)	**250.30(A)(1)**
12. (a)	**250.30(A)(1)**
13. (d)	**Text in workbook**
14. (c)	**450.11(B)**
15. (c)	**450.14**
16. (d)	**450.21(A)**
17. (d)	**450.21(C)**
18. (d)	**450.43(A)**
19. (d)	**450.43(B)**

20. **250.102(C)(1)** and **Table 250.102(C)(1)**

Step 1: Finding size supply-side bonding jumper
250.102(C)(a) and **Table 250.102(C)(1)**
2/0 AWG THWN requires a 4 AWG THWN cu.
2/0 AWG THWN requires a 2 AWG THWN alu.

Solution: **A 4 AWG THWN copper or a 2 AWG aluminum supply-side bonding jumper is required.**

21. **Table 250.66, Columns 3** or **4**

Step 1: Finding grounding electrode conductor
Table 250.66, Columns 3 or **4**
2/0 AWG THWN requires a 4 AWG THWN cu.
2/0 THWN requires a 2 AWG THWN alu.

Solution: **A 4 AWG THWN copper or a 2 AWG aluminum grounding electrode conductor is required.**

22. **Voltage for additive polarity**
- Primary   = 480 V
- Secondary   = 240 V
- Total   = 720 V

23. **Voltage for subtractive polarity**
- Primary   = 480 V
- Secondary   = 240 V
- Total   = 240 V

24. **Voltage for phase-to-phase**
- 240 V

25. **Voltage for phase-to-ground**
- 120 V

Chapter 14
Motor Theory

Answer	Section
1. (b)	Electromagnets
2. (c)	Poles
3. (a)	Basic induction motors
4. (d)	Basic induction motors
5. (c)	Basic induction motors
6. (b)	Rotor
7. (b)	Class B motors
8. (c)	Class B motors

9. (a)   Class C motors

10. (d)   Class D motors

11. (a)   I²R losses

12. (b)   Core losses

13. (d)   Operating torque and slip

14. (b)   Power Factor

15. (c)   Reactive Power

16. (a)   Apparent Power

17. (b)   Actual Power

18. (d)   Torque

19. (b)   Slip

20. (c)   Current

21. **Finding synchronous and actual speed**

   Step 1:   Finding synchronous speed
   Synchronous speed = (120 x Frequency) ÷ (# of poles)
   Synchronous speed = (120 x 60 cps) ÷ 4
   Synchronous speed = 1800 rpm

   Step 2:   Using alternate method
   Synchronous speed. = (cps x cps) ÷ (pair of poles)
   Synchronous speed = (60 cps x 60 cps) ÷ 2
   Synchronous speed = 1800 rpm

   Step 3:   Finding actual speed
   Actual speed = rpm x slip
   Actual speed = 1800 rpm x 5% slip
   Actual speed.= 90 rpm
   Actual speed = 1800 rpm - 90 rpm
   Actual speed = 1710 rpm

   Solution: **The synchronous speed is 1800 rpm and the actual speed is 1710 rpm.**

22. **Finding watts**

   Step 1:   Finding W
   W = V x A
   W = 240 V x 30 A
   W = 7200

   Solution: **The actual power for the water heater is 7200 watts.**

23. **Finding watts**

   Step 1:   Finding W
   W = V x A x PF
   W = 240 V x 30 A x 70%
   W = 5.040

   Solution: **The actual power for the water heater is 5,040 watts.**

24. **Finding watts**

   Step 1:   Finding W
   W = V x 1.732 x A x PF
   W = 480 V x 1.732 x 50 x 80%
   W = 33,240

   Solution: **The actual power for the motor is 33,240 watts**.

Answer	Section
25. (b)	**Table 430.7(B)**

Chapter 15
Types of Motors

Answer	Section
1. (c)	Split-phase motors
2. (d)	With capacitors
3. (a)	Identification of leads
4. (b)	Identification of leads
5. (c)	Identification of leads
6. (c)	Identification of leads
7. (a)	Identification of leads
8. (d)	Identification of leads
9. (b)	Identification of leads
10. (a)	Capacitor start motors
11. (d)	Capacitor start motors
12. (c)	Permanent split-capacitor motors
13. (b)	Shaded-pole motors
14. (a)	Regulating speeds
15. (b)	Universal motors
16. (d)	Universal motors
17. (c)	Reversing direction
18. (d)	Standard repulsion motors
19. (a)	Reversing direction
20. (b)	Connecting leads
21. (c)	Six-lead motors
22. (a)	Wound rotor motors
23. (a)	NEMA Type 1 enclosures
24. (b)	NEMA Type 3 enclosures
25. (d)	NEMA Type 5 enclosures

Chapter 16
Design Letters and Code Letters

1. (a)	Single-phase AC squirrel-cage motors
2. (b)	Single-phase AC squirrel-cage motors
3. (d)	Three-phase AC squirrel-cage motors
4. (b)	Series DC motors
5. (c)	Shunt DC motors
6. (d)	Compound DC motors
7. (c)	Full-load torque
8. (a)	Class B motors
9. (b)	Class B motors
10. (c)	Class C motors
11. (d)	Class D motors
12. (b)	Resistor- or reactor-reduced starting
13. (c)	Code letters

14. (a)   Two-speed motors

15. (b)   Locked-rotor current utilizing horsepower

16. **Finding full-load and starting torque**

Step 1: Finding full-load torque
Torque = (HP x 5252) ÷ rpm
Torque = (50 HP x 5252) ÷ 1725 rpm
Torque = 262,600 ÷ 1725
Torque = 152.23 ft lbs

Step 2: Finding starting torque
Full-load torque increased by 225%
Torque = 152.23 ft lbs x 225%
Torque = 342.5 ft lbs

Solution: **The full-load torque is 152.23 ft lbs and the starting torque is 342.5 ft lbs.**

17. **Finding full-load and starting torque**

Step 1: Finding full-load torque
Torque = (HP x 5252) ÷ rpm
Torque = (40 HP x 5252) ÷ 1725 rpm
Torque = 210,080 ÷ 1725
Torque = 121.8 ft lbs

Step 2: Finding starting torque
Full-load torque increased by 275%
Torque = 121.8 ft lbs x 275%
Torque = 335 ft lbs

Solution: **The full-load torque is 121.8 ft lbs and the starting torque is 335 ft lbs.**

18. **Finding full-load torque**

Step 1: Finding full-load torque (1200)
Torque = (HP x 5252) ÷ rpm
Torque = (40 HP x 5252) ÷ 1200 rpm
Torque = 210,080 ÷ 1200
Torque = 175.1 ft lbs

Step 2: Finding full-load torque (1800)
Torque = (HP x 5252) ÷ rpm
Torque = (40 HP x 5252) ÷ 1800 rpm
Torque = 210,080 ÷ 1800
Torque = 116.7 ft lbs

Solution: **The full-load torque for 1200 rpm is 175.1 ft lbs and the full-load torque for 1800 rpm is 116.7 ft lbs.**

19. **Finding resistor starting torque**

Step 1: Finding resistor starting torque
Torque = (HP x 5252) ÷ rpm
Torque = (40 HP x 5252) ÷ 1725
Torque = 210,080 ÷ 1725
Torque = 121.875 ft lbs

Step 2: Increasing 150% for Class B
Torque = 121.785 ft lbs x 150%
Torque = 182.678

Step 3: Reducing 42% for starting torque
Torque = 182.678 x 42%
Torque = 76.724

Solution: **The reduced starting torque is 76.724 ft lbs.**

20. **Table 430.7(B)**

Step 1: Finding LRC amps
Table 430.7(B)
A = (kVA per HP x 1000) ÷ (V x 1.732)
A = (3.54 x 40 x 1000) ÷ (208 V x 1.732)
A = 141,600 ÷ 360 V
A = 393.3

Solution: **The locked-rotor current is 393.3 amps. Note, Table 430.7(B) shall be used to find LRCs of motor based on their code letters per the 1996 NEC and earlier editions.**

21. **Table 430.251(B)**

Step 1: Finding LRC amps
Table 430.251(B)
40 HP requires 290 A

Solution: **The locked-rotor current is 290 amps.**

22. **Table 430.7(B)**

Step 1: Finding even number
Table 430.7(B)
Round up 58 amps A to 60 A

Step 2: Calculating LRC
Table 430.7(B)
60 A x 6 = 360 A

Solution: **The locked-rotor current is 360 amps.**

Note: This method should be used only for code letters A through G.

23. 363 A   **Table 430.251(B)**
24. 641 A   **Table 430.251(B)**
25. 127 A   **Table 430.251(B)**

Chapter 17
Starting Methods

Answer	Section
1. (b)	Full-voltage starting
2. (a)	Reactor starting
3. (c)	Reactor starting
4. (a)	Reactor starting
5. (c)	Resistor starting
6. (b)	Autotransformer starting
7. (d)	Autotransformer starting
8. (a)	Solid state starting
9. (c)	Solid state starting
10. (d)	Solid state starting

11. (b)   Solid state starting

12. (c)   Solid state starting

13. (a)   AC induction motor

14. (d)   Inverters

15. (b)   Inverters

16. (d)   Starting torque

17. (a)   Eddy-current drives

18. (c)   AC squirrel-cage induction motors

19. (b)   Wye-delta starting motors

20. (d)   Part-winding starting motors

21. (c)   Text in workbook

22. **Table 430.251(B)**

    Step 1: Finding FLA
             Table 430.251(B)
             40 HP = 580 A

    Solution: **The locked-rotor starting current is 580 amps.**

23. **Table 430.251(B)**

    Step 1: Finding LRC
             Table 430.251(B)
             40 HP = 580 A
    Step 2: Applying percentage
             580 A x 65% = 377 A

    Solution: **The reduced starting current is 377 amps.**

24. **Finding winding current, line current, and transformation current**

    Step 1: Finding winding current (WC)
             WC = 802 A x 50%
             WC = 401 A

    Step 2: Finding line current (LC)
             LC = 401 A x 50%
             LC = 200.5 A

    Step 3: Finding transformation current (TC)
             TC = 401 A - 200.5 A
             TC = 200.5 A

    Solution: **The winding current is 401 amps, line current is 200.5 amps, and the transformation current is 200.5 amps.**

25. **Finding reduced starting current for solid state starter**

    Step 1: Finding starting current
             SC = FLC x %
             SC = 361 A x 200%
             SC = 722 A

    Solution: **The starting current using a solid state is 722 amps.**

26. **Finding inrush current**

    Step 1: Finding amps
             Table 430.250
             125 HP = 156 A of LRC
             125 HP = 903 A of LRC

    Step 2: Calculating amps
             156 A x 150% = 234 A

    Solution: **The inrush current would be 234 amps using an adjustable frequency drive system.**

27. **Finding inrush current**

    Step 1: Finding IC
             IC = (kVA x HP) ÷ (V x 1.732)
             IC = (19.99 x 1000 x 125 HP) ÷ (460 V x 1.732)
             IC = 2498.8 ÷ 797 V
             IC = 3135

    Solution: **The inrush current is 3135 amps.**

28. **Finding actual speed**

    Step 1: Finding rpm
             rpm = 1800 rpm x .05
             rpm = 90
             rpm = 1800 rpm - 90
             rpm = 1710 or (1800 rpm x .95 = 1710 rpm)

    Solution: **The actual speed of the motor is 1710 rpm.**

29. **Table 430.251(B)**

    Step 1: Finding amps
             Table 430.251(B)
             40 HP = 580 A

    Step 2: Calculating amps
             A = 580 A x 33%
             A = 191.4

    Solution: **The starting inrush current is 191.4 amps.**

30. **Finding starting torque**

    Step 1: Finding ft lbs
             208 ft lbs x 33% = 68.6 ft lbs

    Solution: **The starting torque is reduced to 68.6 ft lbs.**

31. **430.6(A), Table 430.250, 430.52(C)(1),** and **Table 430.52**

    Step 1: Calculating motor FLC
        430.6(A)(1) and **Table 430.250**
        50 HP = 130 A

    Step 2: Calculating applied percentage
        430.52(C)(1) and **Table 430.52(C)(1)**
        TDF = 175%

    Step 3: Calculating amperage
        430.4
        130 A x 175% = 227.5 A
        One-half (1/2 = .50)
        227.5 x .50 = 113.75 A

    Step 4: Selecting time-delay fuses
        430.52(C)(1), 240.4(G), and **Table 240.6(A)**
        113.75 A requires 110 A

    Solution: **The size fuses required for the starting winding and second winding is 110 amps.**

       Note: Overcurrent protection device shall be permitted to be sized at 125 amps, per **430.52(C)(1)(a)**.

32. 363 A   **Table 430.251(B)**
33. 100%   Text in workbook
34. 58%   Text in workbook
35. 1.732   Text in workbook
36. 1.732   Text in workbook
37. motor   Text in workbook
38. conductors   Text in workbook
39. signals   Text in workbook
40. 100%   Text in workbook

Chapter 18
Overcurrent Protection for Individual Motors

Answer	Section
1. (d)	**430.52(C)(1)(b)(1)**
2. (a)	**430.52(C)(1)(b)(2)**
3. (d)	**430.52(C)(1)(b)(3)**
4. (c)	**430.52(C)(1)(b)(3)**
5. (d)	**430.52(C)(3)(b)(2)b**
6. (c)	Nontime-delay fuses, **Table 430.52, Column 2**
7. (b)	Time-delay fuses, **Table 430.52(C)(1), Column 3**
8. (a)	Instantaneous trip circuit breaker, **Table 430.52(C)(1), Column 4**
9. (a)	Inverse-time circuit breaker, **Table 430.52(C)(1), Colum 5**
10. (a)	FLC ratings using rule-of-thumb method
11. (b)	FLC ratings using rule-of-thumb method
12. (b)	FLC ratings using rule-of-thumb method
13. (c)	FLC ratings using rule-of-thumb method
14. (d)	FLC ratings using rule-of-thumb method
15. (a)	**430.53(A)**
16. (a)	**430.53(A)**
17. (b)	**430.62(A)**
18. (c)	**430.43**

19. (a)	**Table 430.248**
20. (d)	**Table 430.251(B)**

21. **430.52(C)(1)** and **(a), 430.6(A)(1), Table 430.250,** and **Table 430.52(C)(1)**

    Step 1: Finding FLA
        430.6(A)(1) and **Table 430.250**
        50 HP = 130 A

    Step 2: Finding percentage
        430.52(C)(1) and **Table 430.52(C)(1)**
        Minimum size = 300%

    Step 3: Calculating minimum size
        430.52(C)(1) and **Table 430.52(C)(1)**
        130 A x 300% = 390 A

    Step 4: Calculating next size
        430.52(C)(1)(a)
        390 A permits 400 A

    Step 5: Selecting nontime-delay fuses
        Minimum size = 350 A
        Next size = 400 A

    Solution: **The minimum size nontime-delay fuse is 350 amps and the next size is 400 amps.**

22. **430.52(C)(1)(a), (b)(1), 430.6(A)(1), Table 430.250,** and **Table 430.52(C)(1)**

    Step 1: Finding FLA
        430.6(A)(1) and **Table 430.250**
        50 HP = 130 A

    Step 2: Finding percentage
        430.52(C)(1) and **Table 430.52(C)(1)**
        Minimum size = 175%

    Step 3: Calculating next size
        430.52(C)(1) and **(a)**
        130 A x 175% = 227.5 A
        permits 250 A

    Step 4: Calculating maximum size
        430.52(C)(1)(b)(3)
        130 x 225% = 292.5 A
        permits 250 A

    Step 5: Selecting time-delay fuses
        Next size = 250 A
        Maximum size = 250 A

    Solution: **The minimum size time-delay fuse is 250 amps and the next size is 250 amps.**

23. **430.52(C)(3)** and **Ex. 1**, **430.6(A)(1)**, **Table 430.250**, and **Table 430.52**

   Step 1: Finding FLA
   430.6(A)(1) and **Table 430.250**
   50 HP = 130 A

   Step 2: Selecting the minimum size
   430.52(C)(3)(b)(1) and **Table 430.52(C)(1)**
   Minimum size = 1100%

   Step 3: Calculating minimum size
   430.52(C)(3)(a)
   130 A x 1100% = 1430 A

   Step 4: Calculating maximum size
   430.52(C)(3), Ex. 1
   130 A x 1700% = 2210 A

   Step 5: Selecting instantaneous-trip circuit breaker
   Minimum size = 1430 A
   Maximum size = 2210 A

   Solution: **The minimum setting is 1430 amps and the maximum setting is 2210 amps.**

24. **430.52(C)(1)**, **Ex. 1**, **430.6(A)(1)**, **Table 430.250**, and **Table 430.52(C)(1)**

   Step 1: Finding FLA
   430.6(A)(1) and **Table 430.250**
   50 HP = 130 A

   Step 2: Finding percentage
   430.52(C)(1), Ex. 1 and **Table 430.52(C)(1)**
   Minimum size = 250%
   Step 3: Calculating minimum size
   430.52(C)(a)
   130 A x 250% = 325 A

   Step 4: Calculating next size
   430.52(C)(1)(a)
   325 A permits 350 A

   Step 5: Selecting inverse-time circuit breaker
   Minimum size = 300 A
   Next size = 350 A

   Solution: **The minimum size inverse-time circuit breaker is 300 amps and the next size is 350 amps.**

25. **430.52(C)(1)(b)(1)**, **430.6(A)(1)**, **Table 430.250**, and **Table 430.52(C)(1)**

   Step 1: Finding FLA
   430.6(A)(1) and **Table 430.250**
   50 HP = 130 A

   Step 2: Finding percentage
   430.52(C)(1)(b)(1) and **Table 430.250**
   Maximum size = 400%

   Step 3: Calculating maximum size
   430.52(C)(1)(b)(1)
   130 A x 400% = 520 A

   Step 4: Selecting nontime-delay fuses
   Maximum size = 500 A

   Solution: **The maximum size nontime-delay fuse is 500 amps.**

26. **430.52(C)(1)**, **Ex. 2(b)**, **430.6(A)(1)**, **Table 430.250**, and **Table 430.52**

   Step 1: Finding FLA
   430.6(A)(1) and **Table 430.250**
   50 HP = 130 A

   Step 2: Finding percentage
   430.52(C)(1)(b)(2)
   Maximum size = 225%

   Step 3: Calculating maximum size
   430.52(C)(1)(b)(2)
   130 A x 225% = 292.5 A

   Step 4: Selecting time-delay fuses
   Maximum size = 250 A

   Solution: **The maximum size time-delay fuse is 250 amps.**

27. **430.52(C)(1)(b)(3)**, **430.6(A)(1)**, **Table 430.250**, and **Table 430.52(C)(1)**

   Step 1: Finding FLA
   430.6(A)(1) and **Table 430.250**
   50 HP = 130A

   Step 2: Finding percentage
   430.52(C)(1)(b)(3)
   Maximum size = 300%

   Step 3: Calculating maximum size
   430.52(C)(1)(b)(3)
   130 A x 300% = 390A

   Step 4: Selecting inverse-time circuit breaker
   Maximum size = 350A

   Solution: **The maximum size inverse-time circuit breaker is 500 amps.**

28. **430.62(A)**, **430.52(A)**, **430.6(A)(1)**, **Table 430.250**, and **Table 430.52(C)(1)**

   Step 1: Finding FLA of motors
   430.6(A)(1) and **Table 430.250**
   10 HP = 14 A
   15 HP = 21 A
   20 HP = 27 A
   25 HP = 34 A

   Step 2: Calculating feeder OCPD
   430.62(A), **Table 430.52(C)(1)**, and **430.62(A)**
   34 A x 250% = 85 A = 90 A
                       = 14 A
                       = 21 A
                       = 27 A
   Total   = 152 A

   Step 3: Selecting OCPD
   430.62(A), **240.4(G)**, and **Table 240.6(A)**
   152 A permits 150 A OCPD

   Solution: **The size overcurrent protection device required for the feeder is 150 amps.**

29. Rule-of-thumb method (Figure 18-11)

  Step 1: Finding motor amperage
  3 HP x 5 = 15 A

  Solution: The FLA rating of the motor is 15 amps.

30. Rule-of-thumb method (Figure 18-11)

  Step 1: Finding motor amperage
  30 HP x 2.50 = 75 A

  Solution: The FLA rating of the motor is 75 amps.

31. Rule-of-thumb method (Figure 18-11)

  Step 1: Finding motor amperage
  30 HP x 1.25 = 37.5 A

  Solution: The FLA rating of the motor is 37.5 amps.

32. Rule-of-thumb method (Figure 18-11)

  Step 1: Finding motor amperage
  30 HP x 1.00 = 30 A

  Solution: The FLA rating of the motor is 30 amps.

33.	125	**215.2(A)(1) or (A)(1), Ex. 1**
34.	largest	**430.62(A)**
35.	125	**430.24**
36.	number	**430.112, Ex. and 430.87, Ex.**
37.	overload	**430.53(B)**
38.	62.5	**4360.6(A)(2) and Text in workbook (62 A x 125%)**
39.	225	**430.52(C)(1)(b)(2)**
40.	1700	**430.52(C)(3)(b)(1)**

Chapter 19
Overload Protection for Individual Motors

Answer	Section
1. (c)	**430.32(A)(1)**
2. (d)	Temperature rise
3. (a)	Temperature rise
4. (d)	Temperature rise
5. (d)	**430.32(C)**
6. (b)	**430.81(A)**
7. (c)	**430.81(B)**
8. (c)	**430.83(A)(2)**
9. (b)	**430.83(B)**
10. (a)	**430.83(C)**
11. (b)	**430.83(C)**
12. (d)	**430.110(A)**
13. (b)	**430.109(B)**
14. (c)	**430.109(D)**
15. (a)	**430.109(E)**
16. (c)	**430.109(E)**

17. (b)	**Article 100** and **430.102**
18. (c)	**430.109(F)**
19. (d)	**430.109(G)**
20. (c)	**430.102(B)(2), Ex.** to **(1)** and **(2)**

21. 430.32(A)(1) and 430.6(A)(2)

  Step 1: Finding FLA
  430.6(A)(2)
  Nameplate = 48 A

  Step 2: Finding percentage
  430.32(A)(1)
  SF = 125%
  TR = 125%

  Step 3: Calculating FLA
  430.32(A)(1)
  48 A x 125% = 60 A

  Step 4: Selecting time-delay fuses
  430.32(A)(1) and **Table 240.6(A)**
  60 A requires 60 A

  Solution: The size time-delay fuses are 60 amps.

22. 430.33(C) and 430.6(A)(2)

  Step 1: Finding FLA
  430.6(A)(2)
  Nameplate = 48 A

  Step 2: Finding amperage
  430.32(C)
  SF = 140%
  TR = 140%

  Step 3: Calculating FLA
  430.32(C)
  48 A x 140% = 67.2 A

  Step 4: Selecting time-delay fuses
  430.32(C) and **Table 240.6(A)**
  67.2 A requires 60 A

  Solution: The size time-delay fuses are 60 amps.

23. 430.109(A)(1)

  Step 1: Applying HP
  430.109(A)(1)
  50 HP requires at least 50 HP

  Solution: Disconnect (motor rated switch) shall be equal to 50 HP.

24. 430.83(A)(1)

  Step 1: Applying HP
  430.83(A)(1)
  25 HP requires 25HP

  Solution: Controller shall be equal to 25 HP.

25. **430.109(F)**

    Step 1: Selective Elements
        430.109(F)
        20 HP requires 20 HP

    Solution: Receptacle and attachment plug shall be equal to 20 HP.

Chapter 20
Motor Feeder and Branch-Circuit Conductors

1. (c)   **430.22**
2. (d)   **430.22(C)** and **IN**
3. (b)   **430.22(E)** and **Table 430.22(E)**
4. (a)   **430.122(A)**
5. (b)   **430.122(A)**
6. (b)   **430.29**
7. (d)   **430.24**
8. (c)   **460.8(A)**
9. (d)   **430.97(B)**
10. (b)   **430.23(A)**

11. **430.6(A)(1), 430.22,** and **Table 430.248**

    Step 1: Finding FLA
        430.6(A)(1) and **Table 430.248**
        3 HP = 18.7 A

    Step 2: Calculating load
        430.22
        18.7 A x 125% = 23.4 A

    Step 3: Selecting conductors
        310.14(A)(3), IN (2), Table 310.16, Table 240.4(G), and **240.4(D)**
        23.4 A requires 12 AWG cu.

    Solution: The size THWN copper conductors is 12 AWG.

12. **430.6(A)(1), 430.22,** and **Table 430.250**

    Step 1: Finding FLA
        430.6(A)(1) and **Table 430.250**
        20 HP = 54 A

    Step 2: Calculating load
        430.22
        54 A x 125% = 67.5 A

    Step 3: Selecting conductors
        310.14(A)(3), IN (2) and **Table 310.16**
        67.5 A requires 4 AWG cu.

    Solution: The size THWN copper conductors is 4 AWG.

13. **430.22(E), Table 430.250,** and **Table 430.22(E)**

    Step 1: Finding FLA
        430.22(E) and **Table 430.250**
        75 HP = 96 A

    Step 2: Calculating load
        430.22(E) and **Table 430.22(E)**
        96 A x 85% = 81.6 A

    Step 3: Selecting conductors
        310.14(A)(3), IN (2) and **Table 310.16**
        81.6 A requires 4 AWG cu.

    Solution: The size THWN copper conductors are 4 AWG.

14. **430.122(A)** and **Table 310.16**

    Step 1: Calculating load
        430.122(A)
        112 A x 125% = 140 A

    Step 2: Selecting conductors
        Table 310.16
        140 A requires 1/0 AWG cu.

    Solution: 1/0 AWG THWN copper conductors are required.

15. **430.22(D), 430.6(A)(1), Table 430.250,** and **Table 310.16**

    Step 1: Finding FLA
        430.6(A)(1) and **Table 430.250**
        50 HP = 143 A

    Step 2: Sizing conductors
        430.22
        143 A x 125% = 178.75 A

    Step 3: Selecting conductors
        Table 310.16
        178.75 A requires 3/0 AWG cu.

    Solution: The size conductors are 3/0 AWG THWN copper.

16. **430.24, 430.6(A)(1), Table 430.250,** and **Table 310.16**

    Step 1: Finding amperage
        430.6(A)(1) and **Table 430.250**
        30 HP = 40 A
        40 HP = 52 A
        50 HP = 65 A

    Step 2: Calculating amperage
        430.24
        65 A x 125%   = 81.25 A
                     = 40 A
                     = 52 A
        Total   = 173.25 A

    Step 3: Selecting conductors
        310.14(A)(3), IN (2) and **Table 310.16**
        173.25 A requires 2/0 AWG cu.

    Solution: The size THWN copper conductors are 2/0 AWG.

17. **430.24, Table 430.22(E), 430.6(A)(1), Table 430.250,** and **Table 310.16**

    Step 1: Finding amperage
             430.6(A)(1) and **Table 430.250**
             10 HP = 30.8 A
             15 HP = 46.2 A
             20 HP = 59.4 A

    Step 2: Calculating percentage
             430.24 and **Table 430.22(E)**
             59.4 A x 125%   = 74.25 A
             30.8 A x 85%   = 26.18 A
             46.2 A x 85%   = 39.27 A
             Total   = 139.7 A

    Step 3: Selecting conductors
             Table 310.16
             139.7 A requires 1/0 AWG cu.

    Solution: **The size THWN copper conductors are 1/0 AWG.**

18. **460.8(A), 430.22,** and **Table 310.16**

        Sizing conductors based on 1/3

    Step 1: Finding FLA of motor
             40 HP = 114 A

    Step 2: Calculating conductors
             430.22
             114 A x 125% = 142.5 A

    Step 3: Selecting conductors
             310.14(A)(3), IN (2) and **Table 310.16**
             142.5 A requires 1/0 AWG cu.

    Step 4: Calculating conductors at 1/3 of 1/0 AWG cu.
             460.8(A) and **Table 310.16**
             1/0 AWG cu. = 150 A
             1/3 of 150 A = 50 A

    Step 5: Selecting conductors
             Table 310.16
             50 A requires 8 AWG cu.

    Solution: **The size THWN copper conductors based on 1/3 of branch circuit is 8 AWG.**

        Sizing conductors based on 135%

    Step 1: Calculating FLA of motor
             460.8(A)
             FLA = (kVA x 1000) ÷ (V x 1.732)
             FLA = (20 kVA x 1000) ÷ (208 x 1.732)
             FLA = 55.5 A

    Step 2: Calculating conductors
             460.8(A)
             55.6 A x 135% = 75 A

    Step 3: Selecting conductors
             310.14(A)(3), IN (2) and **Table 310.16**
             75 A requires 4 AWG cu.

    Solution: **The size THWN copper conductors based on 135 percent of FLA of capacitor are 4 AWG.**

19. (d)   **695.4(B)(2)(2)(a)**
20. (3)   **455.2**

Chapter 21
Control Circuit Conductors and Components

1. (a)   **Table 430.72(B)**
2. (b)   **Table 430.72(B)**
3. (d)   **724.40(B)**
4. (c)   **430.72(C)(3)**
5. (b)   **430.75(A), Ex. 1**
6. (a)   **724.40(A)**
7. (c)   **725.60(A), Ex. 2 and 3** and **Tables 11(A)** and **(B) to Ch. 9**
8. (a)   **725.60(A), Ex. 2 and 3** and **Tables 11(A)** and **(B) to Ch. 9**
9. (b)   **725.136(I)**
10. (d)   **724.51(B)(1)** and **(2)**
11. (b)   **724.51(B)(2)**
12. (d)   **310.15((E)(3)** and **400.5(A)**
13. (a)   Text in workbook
14. (c)   **430.72(A), 724.48(B)(1)**
15. (b)   **Chapters 1 thru 4**
16. (a)   **725.60(A)** and **(B)**
17. (d)   **725.139(A)**

18. **430.72(B)(2)** and **Table 310.16**

    Step 1: Finding amperage
             Table 310.16
             12 AWG cu. = 30 A

    Step 2: Applying percentage
             430.72(B)(2), Table 430.72(B), and **Table 240.6(A)**
             30 A x 400% = 120 A

    Solution: **The overcurrent protection device is 110 amps.**

19. **430.72(B)(2)** and **Table 310.16**

    Step 1: Finding amperage
             Table 310.16
             12 AWG = 25 A
             OCPD = 20 A

    Step 2: Applying percentage based on OCPD
             430.72(B)(2), Table 430.72(B), and **Table 240.6(A)**
             20 A OCPD x 300% = 60 A

    Solution: **The overcurrent protection device is 60 amps.**

20. **430.72(B), Ex. 2, 450.3(B), Table 450.3(B),** and **Table 240.6(A)**

Step 1: Finding amperage
430.72(B), Ex. 2
I = VA ÷ V
I = 2400 VA ÷ 480 V
I = 5 A

Step 2: Applying percentage
450.3(B and **Table 450.3(B)**
5 A x 167% = 8.35 A

Step 3: Selecting OCPD
Table 240.6(A)
8.35 A requires 6 A

Solution: **The overcurrent protection device is 6 amps.**

Note: The amps of the control transformer is 5 amps, so
Table 450.3(B) had to be used instead of **430.72(C)(4).**

Chapter 22
Connecting Controls for Operation

Answer	Section
1. (a)	Components
2. (d)	Components
3. (c)	Two-wire and three-wire control systems
4. (d)	Control devices
5. (b)	Start stations
6. (a)	Stop stations
7. (c)	Jog stations
8. (a)	Auxiliary contacts
9. (a)	Master stop stations
10. (c)	Hands-off automatic switches

11. Finding components

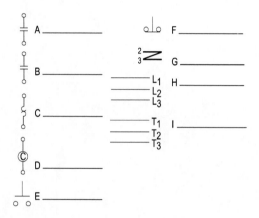

A: Normally open (NO) contacts
B: Auxiliary contacts
C: Thermal overload relay unit
D: Closing coil
E: Start button
F: Stop button
G: Thermal overload contact
H: Power lines
I: Motor leads

12. Connecting a magnetic starter for two-wire operation

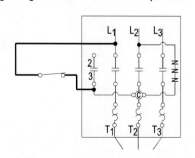

13. Connecting a magnetic starter for three-wire operation

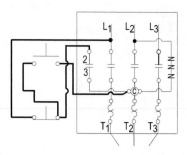

14. Connecting an additional stop button

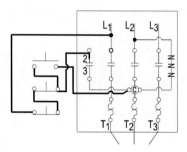

15. Connecting an additional start button

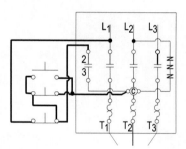

16. Connecting a jog button

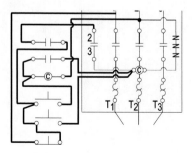

17. Connecting an additional auxiliary contact

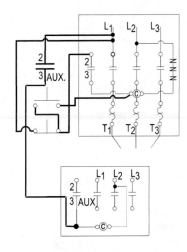

18. Connecting a master stop button

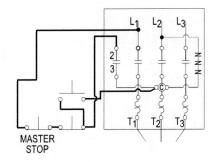

19. Connecting a hand-off automatic switch

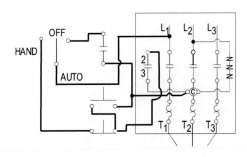

Answer	Section
20. (a)	Text in workbook

Chapter 23
Troubleshooting Motor Windings and Components

Answer	Section
1. (a)	Connecting leads and windings
2. (d)	Connecting leads and windings
3. (b)	Connecting leads and windings
4. (c)	Connecting leads and windings
5. (d)	Testing windings
6. (d)	Testing for open circuits
7. (a)	Single-phase, shaded-pole motors
8. (c)	Testing windings
9. (b)	Testing brushes
10. (d)	Testing windings
11. (c)	Voltage testing winding circuits
12. (c)	Voltage testing winding circuits
13. (a)	Testing slip rings
14. (b)	Marking leads
15. (d)	Determining inrush current
16. (d)	Testing fuses
17. (a)	Testing overloads
18. (b)	Testing for open contacts on the stop button
19. (c)	Testing for closed contacts on the stop button
20. (b)	Troubleshooting the windings of a wye motor for grounds

21. Connecting the leads for wye configuration six-lead motor

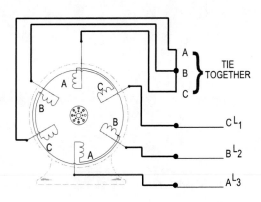

SIX-LEAD WYE MOTOR

22. Connecting the leads for delta configuration six-lead motor

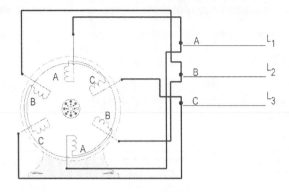

SIX-LEAD DELTA MOTOR

23. Nine-lead delta motor

A: T_1

B: T_4

C: T_7

D: T_2

E: T_5

F: T_8

G: T_3

H: T_6

I: T_9

24. Nine-lead wye motor

A: 1

B: 4

C: 7

D: 8

E: 5

F: 2

G: 3

H: 6

I: 9

25. Placement of test leads for measuring line side voltage.

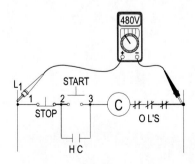

26. Placement of leads for testing voltage through the overloads and to the coil.

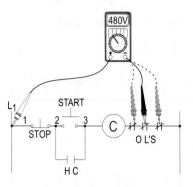

27. Placement of leads when testing interruption of voltage through the OLs to the coil terminals.

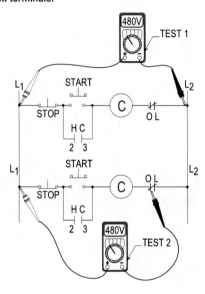

28. Placement of leads when testing the voltage to a coil to determine if it is defective.

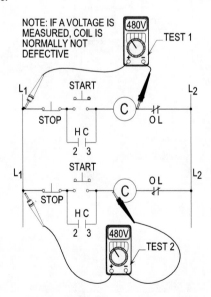

29. Placement of leads when testing the line voltage to the coil contacts of the stop and start buttons.

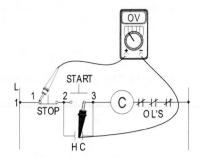

30. Placement of leads when testing the contacts of a stop button in a three-wire control circuit.

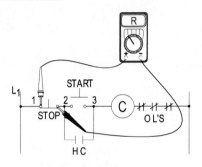

31. Placement of leads when testing the contacts of a start button in a three-wire control circuit.

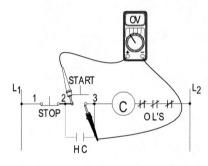

32. Placement of leads when testing the contacts of the overloads in a three-wire control circuit.

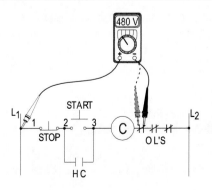

33. Placement of leads when testing the coil in a three-wire to determine if it is defective.

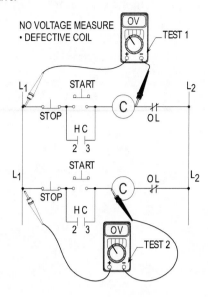

34. Placement of leads when testing the contacts of the holding circuit in a three-wire control circuit.

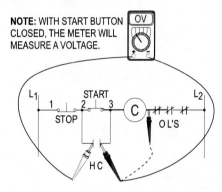

Answer	Section
35. (b)	Text in workbook
36. (a)	Text in workbook
37. (a)	Text in workbook
38. (b)	Text in workbook
39. (c)	Text in workbook
40. (b)	Text in workbook

Chapter 24
Compressor Motors

1. (c)		**440.4(C)**
2. (d)		**440.14, Article 100**
3. (a)		**440.22(A)**
4. (c)		**440.22(A)**
5. (b)		**440.22(B)(2), Ex. 2**
6. (a)		**440.33, 440.34**
7. (d)		**440.52(A)(1)**
8. (a)		**440.54**
9. (d)		**440.61**
10. (b)		**440.62(A)(2)**
11. (d)		**440.63**
12. (a)		**440.63**
13. (b)		**440.64**
14. (a)		**440.64**
15. (c)		**440.62**
16. (a)		**440.14, Article 100**
17. (a)		Text in workbook
18. (c)		**440.60**
19. (a)		**440.52(A)(1) and (A)(3)**
20. (d)		Text in workbook
21. (a)		Text in workbook

22. **440.12(A)(1)** and **Table 240.6(A)**

   Step 1: Calculating nonautomatic circuit breaker
   440.12(A)(1)
   29 A + 2.5 A x 115% = 36.23 A

   Step 2: Selecting disconnect
   440.12(A)(1) and **240.6(A)**
   36.23 A requires 40 A CB

   Solution: **The minimum size nonautomatic circuit breaker is 40 amps.**

23. **440.12(A)(1)** and **Table 240.6(A)**

   Step 1: Calculating nonfused disconnect
   440.12(A)(1)
   29 A + 2.5 A x 115% = 36.23 A

   Step 2: Selecting disconnect
   440.12(A)(1) and **Table 240.6(A)**
   36.23 A requires 60 A disconnect

   Solution: **The minimum size nonfused disconnect is 60 amps.**

24. **440.12(A)(2), Table 430.250,** and **Table 430.251(B)**

   Step 1: Calculating disconnect
   440.12(A)(2), Table 430.250, and **Table 430.251(B)**
   31.5 FLA requires 25 HP
   200 LRA requires 30 HP

   Solution: **The disconnecting means is required to be rated at least 30 HP.**

25. **440.12(B), Table 430.250,** and **Table 430.251(B)**

   Step 1: Calculating disconnect
   440.12(B), Table 430.250, and **Table 430.251(B)**

FLA = HP	LRA = HP
29 A = 15	200 A = 15
24 A = 10	150 A = 10
20 A = 7 1/2	140 A = 10
73 A = 32 1/2	490 A = 35

   Step 2: Selecting disconnect
   440.12(B)
   FLA = HP
   73 A = 32 1/2
   LRA = HP
   490 A = 35

   Solution: **The disconnecting means shall be rated at least 35 HP and be capable of disconnecting 490 amps of locked-rotor current.**

26. **440.12(A)(2)** and **Table 430.250**

   Step 1: Finding amperage
   Table 430.250
   10 HP = 29 A

   Step 2: Calculating OCPD
   440.12(A)(1)
   29 A x 115% = 33.35 A

   Step 3: Selecting OCPD
   Table 240.6(A)
   33.35 A requires 35 A

   Solution: **The size overcurrent protection device is 35 amps.**

27. **440.12(A)(2), Table 430.250,** and **Table 430.251(B)**

   Step 1: Calculating disconnect
   440.12(B)(1), Table 430.250, and **Table 430.251(B)**

FLA = HP	LRA = HP
38 A = 15	212 A = 15
28 A = 10	160 A = 10
24 A = 10	160 A = 10
90 A = 35	532 A = 35

   Step 2: Selecting disconnect
   440.12(B)(1)
   35 HP

   Solution: **The disconnecting means is required to be rated at 35 HP.**

28. **440.22(A) or Ex. 1, 240.4(G)**, and **Table 240.6(A)**

    Step 1: Calculating OCPD
        440.22(A) and **440.33**
        (20 A x 175%) + 2.5 A = 37.5 A

    Step 2: Selecting OCPD
        Table 240.4(G) and **Table 240.6(A)**
        37.5 A requires 35 or 40 A, Ex. 1

    Solution: **The minimum size OCPD is 35 amps.** (OCPD round down)

29. **440.22(A)**, **440.33**, **Table 240.4(G)**, and **Table 240.6(A)**

    Step 1: Calculating OCPD
        440.22(A) and **440.33**
        (20 A x 225%) + 2.5 = 47.5 A

    Step 2: Selecting OCPD
        Table 240.4(G), **440.22(A)**, and **Table 240.6(A)**
        47.5 A requires 45 A (Can's round up.)

    Solution: **The maximum size OCPD is 45 amps. per Ex. 2**

30. **440.22(B)(1)**, **440.22(A)**, **Table 240.4(G)**, and **Table 240.6(A)**

    Step 1: Calculating largest OCPD rating for compressor
        440.22(B)(1) and **440.22(A)**
        28 A x 175% + 2.5 A = 53.25 A

    Step 2: Calculating OCPD for feeder
        440.22(B)(1)
        53.25 A + 26 A + 2.5 A + 22 A + 2.5 A = 106.25 A

    Step 3: Selecting OCPD for feeder
        Table 240.4(G) and **Table 240.6(A)**
        106.25 A permits 100 A

    Solution: **The size overcurrent protection device for the feeder using a circuit breaker is 100 amps.**

31. **440.22(B)(1)**, **440.22(A)**, **Table 240.4(G)**, and **Table 240.6(A)**

    Step 1: Calculating largest OCPD rating for compressor
        440.22(B)(1) and **440.22(A)**
        29 A x 225% + 2.5 A = 67.75 A

    Step 2: Calculating OCPD for feeder
        440.22(B)(1)
        67.75 A + 26 A + 2.5 + 22 A + 2.5 A = 120.75 A

    Step 3: Selecting OCPD for feeder
        Table 240.4(G) and **Table 240.6(A)**
        120.75 A permits 110 A

    Solution: **The size overcurrent protection device for the feeder using a circuit breaker is 110 amps.**

32. **440.22(B)(1)**, **440.22(A)**, **Table 240.4(G)**, and **Table 240.6(A)**

    Step 1: Calculating largest OCPD rating for compressor
        440.22(B)(1) and **440.22(A)**
        28 A x 175% = 49 A

    Step 2: Calculating OCPD for feeder
        440.22(B)(1)
        49 A + 26 A + 2.5 + 24 A + 2.5 A = 104 A

    Step 3: Selecting OCPD for feeder
        Table 240.4(G) and **Table 240.6(A)**
        104 A permits 100 A

    Solution: **The size overcurrent protection device for the feeder using a circuit breaker is 100 amps.**

33. **440.32** and **Footnote to Table 310.15(B)(16)**

    Step 1: Calculating FLA
        440.32
        20 A x 125% + 2.5 A = 27.5 A

    Step 2: Selecting conductors
        Footnote to Table 310.16 and **240.4(D)**
        27.5 A requires 10 AWG cu.

    Solution: **The size conductors are 10 AWG THHN copper.**

34. **440.4(C)** and **440.32**

    Step 1: Selecting conductors
        440.4(C)
        30 A requires 10 AWG cu.

    Solution: **The branch-circuit selection current requires 10 AWG THHN copper conductors.**

35. **440.33** and **Table 310.16**

    Step 1: Finding FLA
        A/C unit #1 - 30 A + 3 A
        A/C unit #2 - 28 A + 2.5 A
        A/C unit #3 - 24 A + 2.5 A

    Step 2: Calculating FLA
        440.33

30 A x 125% + 3 A	= 40.5 A
28 A x 100% + 2.5 A	= 30.5 A
24 A x 100% + 2.5 A	= 26.5 A
Total load	= 97.5 A

    Step 3: Selecting conductors
        310.14(A)(3), IN (2) and **Table 310.16**
        97.5 A requires 3 AWG cu.

    Solution: **The size THWN conductors are 3 AWG copper.**

36. **440.34**, **215.2(A)(1)**, and **Table 310.16**

> **Step 1:** Finding FLA
> A/C unit #1 - 30 A + 3 A
> A/C unit #2 - 28 A + 2.5
> A/C unit #3 - 24 A + 2.5 A
> Other load - 80 A

> **Step 2:** Calculating FLA
> **440.33**
> 30 A x 125% + 3 A   = 40.5 A
> 28 A x 100% + 2.5   = 30.5 A
> 24 A x 100% + 2.5   = 26.5 A
> 80 A x 125%   = 100 A
> Total load   = 197.5 A

> **Step 3:** Selecting conductors
> **310.14(A)(3)**, **IN (2)** and **Table 310.16**
> 197.5 A requires 3/0 AWG cu.

Solution: **The size THWN conductors are 3/0 AWG copper.**

37. **440.41(A)**, **430.248**, and **430.251(A)**

> **Step 1:** Finding HP
> **Table 430.248**
> 22.5 A requires 5 HP

> **Step 2:** Finding LRC
> **Table 430.251(A)**
> 5 HP requires 168 A

> **Step 3:** Sizing HP
> **440.41(A)**
> Higher HP rating must be used

Solution: **The size controller required is 5 HP.**

38. **440.52(A)(1)** and **(A)(3)**

> **Step 1:** Sizing overloads at unit
> **440.52(A)(1)**
> 20 A x 140% = 28 A

> **Step 2:** Sizing overloads using fuses
> **440.52(A)(3)**
> 20 A x 125% = 25 A

Solution: **The size overload relay required is 28 amps and the size fuses are rated at 25 amps.**

39. **440.62**, **440.62(B)**, **240.4(D)**, and **Table 310.16**

> **Step 1:** Finding conductor amps
> **Table 310.16** and **240.4(D)**
> 10 AWG cu. requires 30 A

> **Step 2:** Calculating amps
> **440.62(B)**
> 30 A x 80% = 24 A

Solution: **The maximum size conductor ampacity permitted is 24 amps.**

40. **440.34**, **Table 210.24** and **210.23(B)**

> **Step 1:** Finding amps
> **440.34**, **Table 310.16**, and **240.4(D)**
> 10 AWG cu. requires 30 A

> **Step 2:** Calculating amps
> **440.34(C)** and **210.23(B)**
> 30 A x 100% = 30

Solution: **The maximum conductor ampacity permitted is 30 amps.**